RECEIVED

THE
GREATEST
FURY

THE
GREATEST
FURY

*The Battle of New Orleans and
the Rebirth of America*

William C. Davis

CALIBER

CALIBER

An imprint of Penguin Random House LLC
penguinrandomhouse.com

Copyright © 2019 by William C. Davis
Maps copyright © 2019 by National Park Service, Denver Service Center, Denver, CO
Penguin supports copyright. Copyright fuels creativity, encourages diverse voices, promotes free speech, and creates a vibrant culture. Thank you for buying an authorized edition of this book and for complying with copyright laws by not reproducing, scanning, or distributing any part of it in any form without permission. You are supporting writers and allowing Penguin to continue to publish books for every reader.

DUTTON CALIBER and the Caliber colophon are registered trademarks of
Penguin Random House LLC.

LIBRARY OF CONGRESS CATALOGING-IN-PUBLICATION DATA

Names: Davis, William C., 1946– author.
Title: The greatest fury : the battle of New Orleans and the rebirth of
America / William C. Davis.
Other titles: Battles for New Orleans and the rebirth of America
Description: First edition. | New York : Dutton Caliber, an imprint of
Penguin Random House, [2019].
Identifiers: LCCN 2019021231 | ISBN 9780399585227 (hardcover) |
ISBN 9780399585234 (ebook)
Subjects: LCSH: New Orleans, Battle of, New Orleans, La., 1815.
Classification: LCC E356.N5 D38 2019 | DDC 973.5/239—dc23
LC record available at https://lccn.loc.gov/2019021231

Printed in the United States of America
1   3   5   7   9   10   8   6   4   2

BOOK DESIGN BY TIFFANY ESTREICHER

For Chris, Dick, and Pam,
dear friends who left too soon.
May they go swiftly on their way.

And for my "Bird,"
Who is always with me.

CONTENTS

LIST OF MAPS

THE
GREATEST
FURY

Preface

I T WAS A time of omens. The greatest comet in memory stretched a million miles across the night skies. The most powerful earthquakes in recorded history twisted the great Mississippi at will, swallowing communities, spitting up islands, and ringing church bells from New Orleans to Boston. With the heavens and the firmament in conflict with each other, Shawnee mystics foretold a war between the living and the dead.

In an atmosphere redolent of Revelation's forecast of "woe for the earth," it was fitting that men make war among themselves, even a small war for little reasons. In 1783, when Great Britain bid grudging farewell to thirteen colonies in North America, it still had an empire in the vastness of Canada, the islands of the West Indies, and elsewhere. Nine years later, when Britain began two decades of war with France, success depended on sustaining her thriving mercantile economy to fund the contest, and that meant holding supremacy on the seas, both of which threatened the Americans, whose burgeoning carrying trade depended heavily on France. Heavily committed in Europe, Britain neither needed nor wanted a conflict with the infant United States. Still, if Yankee trade or alliances threatened its efforts on the Continent, John Bull would accept a war with America better than lose a war with France.

The new nation across the Atlantic sailed an uncertain course through waters peppered with political shoals and reefs, trying to safeguard its flowering commerce and growing national pride. It flirted with neutrality, an alliance with France, and an implicit alliance with Britain, but sitting on the fence in a world at war only makes a better target. For three years the

United States and France even fought a so-called naval Quasi-War that hard-pressed Napoleon soon enough halted. A brief peace in Europe in 1802 could not hold, and a year later they were fighting again, each striking at the other by acts to curtail its trade with America. That only aggravated other issues, chief among them the "impressment" policy of British naval captains who forcibly removed seamen from American vessels on the pretext that they were deserters from the Royal Navy. The number actually taken was small, but it was an emotional issue that outraged national pride exaggerated dramatically.

The United States responded to this and other provocations by barring all British imports, and then by a total embargo on all American foreign trade that fathered a thriving smuggling enterprise. In 1809, Congress allowed trade with all nations but Britain and France to resume, and two years later removed the ban on France. No matter how America tried to use its foreign trade as a weapon, it failed, harming Yankee merchants and exporters more than it did the European combatants.

Watching and condemning all of this was Thomas Jefferson's new Democratic Republican Party, and especially a wing of younger congressmen mostly from the southern and trans-Allegheny states called "War Hawks." They took office in November 1811. Their inflammatory rhetoric reflected the comet still blazing overhead, even as their incessant hammering on commerce and national honor echoed stresses just weeks away from fracturing the earth's crust. Backed by Jefferson's successor, James Madison, they ultimately persuaded Congress to take a more aggressive stand toward Britain. In June 1812, as the waning comet still fluttered faintly above continuing aftershocks of the great quakes, Madison and Congress declared war on Britain.[1]

The War Hawks' biggest—indeed only—weapon was posing a threat to Canada. The colonists had tried without success to take it into their embrace during the Revolution. Now, with a new war on their hands, Madison's generals seized the initiative by sending three "armies" north to try again, only to have two of them forced to surrender while the third retreated without a fight. The following year the Yankees tried again with more success with a naval victory on Lake Erie that secured their hold on most of future Michigan, Indiana, Illinois, territory west of Lake Michigan, and even a bit of Canada itself. Elsewhere, however, the British drove invading forces out of Ontario and Quebec and then followed them into New York.

Hundreds of miles to the south, a portion of the Creek tribe allied itself with the British in hopes of regaining tribal lands and pushing the Americans out of the Alabama country. That launched a war within a war, but a series of Yankee victories over mostly outnumbered Indian forces culminating at the Battle of Horseshoe Bend on March 27, 1814, effectively ended the Creek conflict. Elsewhere the Americans were not so successful. Two more invasions of Canada came to little or nothing, ending the Canadian dream and allowing the British to call the tune thereafter, especially as the fall of Napoleon in April allowed them to focus more attention and manpower across the Atlantic. An attempt to take upper New York failed, but they took possession of eastern Maine. Far worse, another army drove Madison's forces from Washington long enough to take it on August 24 and put the government to flight, burning the Capitol, the Executive Mansion, and many other buildings. The British were only prevented from taking Baltimore three weeks later by the death of their commander, Major General Robert Ross, and their naval auxiliary's failure to eliminate Fort McHenry.

A fortnight before Washington's fall, commissioners from the warring nations opened peace discussions on August 10 at Ghent, Belgium. The close of the war with France essentially removed Britain's reasons for fighting the United States. She needed now to concentrate on building a Europe suited to her interests. The Americans wearied of a war that had gained them nothing worth its cost in blood and treasure. Both nations wanted an end to fighting and the disruption of trade, yet their diplomats faced a third and common enemy as they commenced deliberations.

It took at least five weeks for news from the Atlantic coast to reach Ghent. Two consequences loomed, neither desirable. They might agree on terms only to learn later that the dynamic in America had changed, one party now having such advantage that it could have dictated more favorable terms had it but known. Indeed, had they settled before the end of September, the subsequent arrival of news of the victory at Washington might have done just that. Worse yet, fighting could continue for weeks after a treaty was agreed upon, and weeks more before ratification in London and Washington actually ended the conflict.

Therein lay opportunity, especially with Bonaparte out of the way. Treaty or no, the war would not be over until the fighting stopped. Even as Washington smoldered and peace commissioners argued in Ghent, British commanders in America and leaders in the Admiralty and War Office in London planned another campaign in a new theater. With no guarantee that Ghent would produce an agreement, they needed to maintain momentum. Should they be successful, the gain to Britain might be of epic proportion.

Their target was the Americans' soft underbelly, the Gulf coast of

Louisiana, and New Orleans, the key to an inland empire of more than 800,000 square miles fed by the Mississippi and its tributaries. The wealth flowing from that system was measured by the tens of millions. New Orleans itself was the emporium of the Gulf, with the West Indies and Caribbean islands largely dependent on its exports and its markets for their own goods, not least slaves. The nation commanding it held the back door to Canada and the Pacific and controlled the future westward expansion of the United States.

Moreover, even an agreement at Ghent might leave Louisiana in play. As the commissioners began their meetings, prevailing wisdom said they would settle on a basis recognizing the prewar status quo. Any territory changing hands through conquest by either side during the conflict would be returned to its prewar owner. In that diplomat's game, Louisiana could be a wild card, for its title was as muddy as the Mississippi. Spain held dominion there for almost forty years, until 1801, when a powerful France virtually dictated a treaty that traded the vast territory to it for several promises it never kept. Napoleon also engaged never to sell Louisiana to a third party, an undertaking he honored for two years and forty days before he sold it to the United States in 1803.

What did that mean if a British expedition should take New Orleans and much or all of Louisiana before, or even after, a Ghent conclusion on a status quo basis? It would not be unheard-of to keep such a conquest despite the treaty, although it would risk renewing a war Britain did not want, but otherwise to whom should she give it back? France all but took it from Spain, broke its own treaty by not paying for it in full, then violated another commitment in selling it to Jefferson. Meanwhile, even after 1803, the Yankees left Spanish officials in de facto control of substantial portions of the territory. So, just who was the lawful prewar owner, the Americans or Britain's ally Spain? It was a question fraught with baffling uncertainties and tantalizing possibilities. Whoever walked away with Louisiana would have an empire that reached to the Pacific, covered a third of the continent below Canada, and controlled the destiny of the adolescent United States.

It was a question that challenged even lowly mapmakers. That fall an Englishman stepped into the shop of a London cartographer to buy a map of the United States. The proprietor suggested that he wait a few weeks and then return. Events occurring across the Atlantic were about to change boundaries, he explained. Being prudent, he would not be completing any new maps of North America just now, for he expected that a considerable part of the Union would soon be returning to Britain.[2] Like so much in time of war, it would all depend on a battle.

One

A Spot on the Globe

N EW ORLEANS ASSAULTED the senses with friendly weapons. Bitter aromas from its coffeehouses mingled with smells from European, African, and Caribbean kitchens, spilling into streets redolent of rose and citrus gardens, warehouses of pungent sugar and tobacco, the acrid droppings of cart horses, and the fishy tang of the great river. Street mongers' cries hawked everything from bread to silks, vying with shouting auctioneers selling cattle and slaves, the rhythms of shod hooves and ironbound carriage wheels, the boasts of carousing riverboatmen, and the puffing stacks and belching boilers when a steamboat made landing.

Most of all, there were the sights of the city: the many-colored wooden buildings lining most of its seventy blocks, broadclothed and beaver-hatted gentlemen in their countinghouses, aproned merchants at shop doors, buckskinned upriver backwoodsmen on the streets, ladies in Parisian fashion strutting the *banquettes*, and Choctaw women in deerskin and gingham. Everywhere were the dusky faces of slaves and the formerly enslaved, and the coffeed complexions of mulattoes and quadroons inhabiting the city's almost unique terra incognita between white and black. A sightseer might roam the known world or simply come to the crescent bend of the Mississippi and see it all in New Orleans. No wonder a late war visitor declared, "I could scarcely imagine myself in an American place."[1]

Some 25,000 people inhabited the place by late 1814, forty percent of them slaves or freedmen, making it the infant nation's sixth largest city. Americans were but a quarter of the white population.[2] The rest bled French or Spanish blood, most of them *creoles* born there or in the Caribbean, and most resenting the American *arrivées* since the 1803 Purchase. The *creoles* clung to Catholicism, spurned English, and practiced an indolence that affronted the ambitious Yankees. Everything was an excuse for a party, even saints' days, when sexes and races mixed inappropriately, the men got drunk, and everyone feasted.[3]

Language defined politics and loyalties. Few Federalists or Republicans here; they were French or American. Even the Francophile Jefferson feared the *creoles* were so immured in French and Bourbon ideology that New Orleans might drift back to France or Spain.[4] Whoever governed it controlled the commerce and security of the entire American interior from the Alleghenies to the Pacific.[5] More than a third of the nation's produce now passed through its wharves and warehouses. Attorney Abraham Ellery was not overly hyperbolic in calling the city "the deposit and Key of the *Western World*."[6] Nor is it any wonder that, before he bought Louisiana, Jefferson foretold that "there is on the globe one single spot, the possessor of which is our natural and habitual enemy." It was New Orleans.[7]

English eyes had long looked in that direction. Leaders in London considered a plan to overwhelm the Spaniards there in 1770 to seize its trade in indigo and furs.[8] Two years later the British commander in North America proposed to anchor transports in Lake Borgne, northeast of the city, and send boats rowing eighteen miles from the lake up its sluggish tributary Bayou Bienvenue to land just seven miles from the city, and in 1781 another plan emerged that proposed to do the same.[9] Now, more than three decades later, a new war raged, yet the *creoles* outside the city took so little interest in it that the American deputy attorney general feared only a British invasion could rouse them.[10]

An invasion is exactly what they got. Shortly before dawn on December 13, 1814, an American commodore commanding a miniature squadron of seven sailing sloops and schooners, with just 25 cannon and 204 men, had his flotilla off Malheureaux Island, 75 miles northeast of New Orleans and 30 miles from the entrance to Lake Borgne. As the first glimmers of light penetrated mists blanketing the water, a nightmare emerged from the gloom to crawl toward him. The British had not forgotten those earlier plans. Forty-five boats mounting 42 guns were rowing 1,200 redcoats toward him to board his squadron. The commodore knew very well that at that moment he was all that stood between the enemy and New Orleans.

THE WAR OFFICE in London meant to change the dynamic in North America. In 1812–1813, Kentucky and Tennessee sent thousands of militia north to threaten Canada. Divert that supply of volunteers elsewhere, and His

Majesty's hold in Canada would be more secure. The raid on Washington and Maryland was one such diversion. A similar strike somewhere below Tennessee held promise of diverting even more. The ideal place was the Gulf Coast and particularly New Orleans.

Ironically, even Americans had mused on plots to take the city. In 1804 the embittered vice president Aaron Burr, his presidential ambitions dashed, proposed to seize newly purchased Louisiana and hand it to Britain in return for half a million dollars. London ignored Burr's offer, but by 1806 he planned to use Louisiana as his base for the conquest of Spain's Mexico and Texas provinces, implying that he would create a new southwest empire with himself as ruler.

Many in New Orleans supported him, not least the Irish-born lawyer Lewis Kerr.[11] An early champion of Jefferson's Republicans, he had a magnetic attraction for controversy. In 1802, on the advice of his friend Colonel Andrew Jackson of the Tennessee militia, Kerr moved to Natchez, where he made a fast friend in the governor of Mississippi Territory, William C. C. Claiborne, who appointed him attorney general.[12] Aged just twenty-seven, that precocious Virginian had already been a supreme court judge in Tennessee, the youngest congressman in history, governor of Mississippi, and then, in 1803, governor of the Orleans Territory of Louisiana, a position the jealous Jackson had coveted.[13] Claiborne actually sent Kerr to New Orleans ahead of himself to survey the local militia, and on taking office made the Irishman its chief of staff.[14]

The authoritarian Kerr was unpopular, thanks not least to his claims of kinship to Robert Dundas, soon to be Viscount Melville and Britain's First Lord of the Admiralty, and Lieutenant General John Hely-Hutchinson (Baron Hutchinson). Some suspected Kerr's loyalty, but Claiborne steadily advanced him and even had him codify the territory's criminal law.[15] Then Kerr fell under Burr's spell. He began recruiting men for an "army" that he would lead to conquer Spain's provinces in North and South America and promised British assistance, thanks to his influential "relations."[16]

Kerr courted officers of the United States Army and tried to enlist the already legendary Reuben Kemper. Six feet tall, powerfully built, hazel eyes glowing from a face deeply scarred by Spaniard foes, Kemper and his brothers had led resistance to Spanish rule in the West Florida parishes above New Orleans that both Spain and the United States claimed. The nation watched via newspaper coverage in 1805 when the Spaniards beat and kidnapped the Kempers from their Mississippi homes, only for them to be saved from prison or death by the United States military. Reuben later confronted his kidnappers one by one, exacting revenge with bullwhip and knife, and carved notches in the ears of one as a warning to all.[17]

This was the kind of man Kerr wanted. He met with Reuben and his brother Samuel, boasted of the important backing he enjoyed, asked them to raise men in Kentucky and Tennessee, and promised money in abundance, even if banks must be robbed. Then another Irishman stepped into the picture, Judge James Workman. He had earlier called on Britain to forcibly seize Louisiana. When he was ignored, he approached Jefferson, who showed no more interest than the British.[18] After the 1803 purchase, Workman moved to New Orleans and soon fell into Kerr's orbit.[19] In January 1805 they joined lawyer Edward Livingston, merchant Beverly Chew, *Orleans Gazette, for the Country* editor John Bradford, and several others to form the Mexican Association of New Orleans, with Workman as president and its goal to seize Mexico.[20] The connection with Burr was transparent. The Kempers wanted nothing to do with the scheme, and Reuben went to Washington to alert Jefferson, but the president was already aware of Burr's plans.[21]

Governor Claiborne also refused to cooperate and fell out with both Irishmen, Workman dismissing him thereafter as "a mauled bitch." By temperament affable, Claiborne quickly adapted to dealing with the prickly *creole* population, married the daughter of a prominent family, and confronted the daunting task of merging a population of Catholic Frenchmen and Spaniards with the predominantly Protestant American *émigrés* and their new democratic institutions. "There was a strange fascination in his manners," recalled one of those Americans, but there was also a crafty politician. "He never refused, but always promised."[22]

His diplomacy did not work with General James Wilkinson, sent by Jefferson in 1806 to secure the city against further plots. Greedy, autocratic, and treasonous, Wilkinson was a paid Spanish spy as well as an American general. He simply ignored the governor and began arresting anyone suspected of complicity with Burr, with whom he was himself in league until he betrayed Burr, too. Wilkinson censored mail and instituted virtual martial law, one observer declaring that "his visit to New-Orleans was like that of a pestilence."[23] Wilkinson arrested Kerr and Workman, accusing them of sedition, but juries twice failed to convict.[24] Both just disappeared in early 1809.[25] Workman settled in Havana for several years.[26] Kerr moved to the Bahamas to practice law.[27] "I was one of those every day kind of characters that, in absence, are seldom remembered long," he told a friend, but neither he nor Workman were forgotten. Neither were they forgiving.[28] Both nurtured grudges and they were not yet done with New Orleans.

The widely publicized plots of Workman, Kerr, and Burr, and the kinetic efforts of the Kempers and others, kept the Spanish constantly on the alert, and the Americans in Louisiana ever aroused. Wilkinson's departure in May 1807 brought relief, but there remained the specter of Spain and mistrust of the Spaniards in the city. They still believed that Louisiana rightfully owed allegiance to the Bourbon crown. The French remained interested as well, despite Bonaparte's sale. General Jean-Victor-Marie Moreau visited the city in January 1808. Once one of Napoleon's leading captains, he had been banished in 1804 for suspected disloyalty, becoming an exile in the United States. His visit may have had a motive other than sightseeing, and some suspected he was involved with Burr in yet another plot.[29]

Real hazards hovered on the southern and western horizon. In January 1809, Vice Admiral Sir Alexander F. I. Cochrane landed a 10,000-man army on Martinique to operate against French possessions in the Indies, but rumor said he already had a taste in his mouth for New Orleans and meant to enforce free navigation for British shipping on the Mississippi.[30] At the same time, Spanish border provocations west of the river fed speculation that the Diegos—a British nickname for Spaniards that soon eroded into the derogatory "dagoes"—meant to reclaim what Bonaparte sold. A month after succeeding Jefferson in the presidency, James Madison responded with a military and naval buildup at New Orleans that included the return of Wilkinson.[31]

A year later the Kempers' dream came to realization when a two-minute revolt pushed the Spaniards out of Baton Rouge and the West Florida parishes. The rebels proclaimed a new commonwealth and sent now-colonel Reuben Kemper to seize Mobile. He just got in sight of his goal when the infant republic winked out on December 10 as Claiborne, representing Madison, took possession of West Florida in fulfillment of Jefferson and Madison's claim that the Louisiana Purchase always included those parishes.[32] West Florida's "president," Fulwar Skipwith, was powerless to resist. Neither Spain nor England recognized the legitimacy of the momentary republic, nor of Madison's opportunistic occupation. A year later Jefferson advised the seizure of the rest of Spanish Florida before England did so.

Despite mounting provocations, Britons commonly agreed that there was little to gain from war with America, though little to fear, either, from a nation with scarcely a dozen warships, virtually no standing army, and a reliance on disorderly militia. Louisiana and New Orleans might make an easy harvest.[33] An army landing in, say, Spanish Pensacola or Mobile, could march westward on a decent road, live off the land with aid from Creek allies, and take the city virtually unopposed, a prospect not lost on Orleanians, who as early as 1810 heeded Jefferson's call to seize Pensacola before the British.[34]

There was even a threat from within. On the night of January 8, 1811, two dozen slaves on an upriver plantation attacked their sleeping masters with machetes and cane knives. Soon they numbered in the hundreds, killing and attracting more adherents as they moved south toward a city that soon fell into panic. Federal soldiers, local militia, and a posse of planters congealed the next day to attack and disperse the rebels, killing more than fifty on the spot and capturing and executing at least fifty more in the following days, displaying their heads and mangled bodies along the river as a reminder of the price of rebellion.[35] It was the largest slave rebellion in the nation's history, and after it Orleanians never again slept entirely at ease. Every new rumor awakened fear of a repeat or worse, and persuaded the British that with the right encouragement the slaves would rise in their thousands.[36]

Among the volunteers who brutally quelled that revolt were two companies of free black militia that had existed since before the Purchase. New Orleans's 7,500-strong free black community was the largest in the nation, and the rest of the population did not know quite how to deal with them. Led by white officers, they had helped put down an earlier slave rebellion as well, making Claiborne hope that they might be a bond between the races, but they also posed a challenge. Few were comfortable with black men being armed. The planter Major Pierre Lacoste commanded them, and some were property and slave owners themselves who had a stake in defending their city; but the governor feared that if Americans withheld their confidence from the black militia, the British might woo them to alliance.[37]

All New Orleans needed was yet another source of danger, but then the Creeks took advantage of the United States' distraction with its war to begin sporadic attacks on families as far north as Tennessee, a precursor of the Creek War to come. With slaves killing their masters and Indians killing whites, some laid the chaos to British agents stirring both to "carry fire and sword" across the frontier.[38] Then came the comet and the earthquakes. In a time of millennial fervor, it seemed that the world was coming to the end of days. A few panicked Orleanians even sought to hide from the cataclysm aboard the American gunboats on Lake Borgne.[39] Then, on June 18, 1812, Madison declared war.

WHITEHALL PAID LITTLE overt attention to the Gulf Coast at the outset, but Louisiana, and especially New Orleans, did not escape notice. Two months before the war began, Cochrane already had his eye on Louisiana. "The places where the Americans are most vulnerable is [sic] New Orleans and Virginia," he told Kerr's presumed cousin Viscount Melville. Take New

Orleans and Britain controlled the Mississippi Valley's trade. "Self interest being the ruling principle with the Americans," said Cochrane, the interior states, like Tennessee, Kentucky, even Ohio, would withdraw from the Union to "join the party that pays for their produce."[40]

By September 1812, speculation in London predicted the seizure of Louisiana, and one plan after another to accomplish that object came forth, all from the Navy.[41] In November, Admiral Sir John Borlase Warren proposed taking the city and stationing black West Indies units there as garrison, thinking fear of their fomenting slave revolt would induce the southern states to surrender first. He suggested much the same thing again the following February.[42] At the same time, Captain Sir James Lucas Yeo reported New Orleans unequipped to defend itself and suggested that a single frigate light enough to get over the sandbar at the river channel's mouth could sail up to take the city, where every faction was arrayed against the others, the local Indians hated them all, and a black regiment or two would spread panic and discontent with the war along the coast.[43] Another report from Captain James Stirling of the ship *Brazen* suggested that Britain should enlist the Creeks as allies while a small squadron took New Orleans to exact from it a ransom under penalty of being sacked, a measure that would surely add to the Americans calling for peace.[44]

With all these reports in hand, and those earlier proposals dating back to the 1770s in his office files, Melville ordered further study by Stirling. In March he submitted a comprehensive statement of Louisiana and New Orleans's vital strategic import to the Americans' economy and security and the ever-present threat it posed to the security of Spain's provinces while it remained in Yankee hands. Its population was divided, and he believed many would welcome being removed from the United States. "A small body of troops from this country might effectually wrest this invaluable Territory from the hands of the American Government," he added, "and place the interior states of Kentucky, Ohio, Tenesee and part of Virginia at the mercy of Great Britain." Noting that blacks outnumbered whites, he thought they could be employed to do "much mischief." As for General Wilkinson, he could be bought, and even then the London press reported that American troops at New Orleans refused to serve under him. The Creeks were now at war with the Americans, and the Spaniards at Pensacola hated the Yankees more than they distrusted the British.[45]

Despite all this, Melville concluded for the moment that New Orleans would require too many resources needed elsewhere to take and hold for the present, although he did not entirely dismiss it, either.[46] Public opinion showed rather more interest. Take New Orleans, and Britain would close the outlet for all industry and produce of the West and thereby divide the states, ran the argument. Take the city and it could provision Britain's islands in the West Indies at half the cost of goods from England. Take it, and Spain's possessions in America could be preserved from greedy adventuring.[47] Everyone knew it could be done so easily. That was one point of agreement, at least, with some Americans. Britain could take the city in sixty days, Senator Obadiah German of New York had warned on the floor of Congress. "Should she get possession of New Orleans," he cautioned, "it will cost much blood and treasure to dislodge her."[48] And yet Madison's administration seemed to be "under an infatuation," accused one critic, that kept it from providing for its defense.[49] Louisiana senators James Brown and Eligius Fromentin, and its sole congressman Thomas B. Robertson, struggled into the fall of 1814 to get the administration to take notice until the capture of Washington got Madison's attention at last.[50]

Preparations had come slowly. By the end of 1811, Captain John Shaw commanded just two brigs at New Orleans, with nineteen seaworthy gunboats and an unfinished blockship, so called for the immense weight of its broadside, that could be anchored to close passes into Lake Borgne with its massive armament. Wilkinson's reinstatement did not build confidence. "I hope to God, our country shall never have to blush for placing confidence in such a man," Fromentin told Livingston.[51] The general demanded supreme power, subject to no superior authority, and returned to his dictatorial ways. Still, he began surveys for new fortifications and commenced repairs to older defenses, even making the novel suggestion of mounting cannon on the decks of six of the new steamboats plying the Mississippi. Freed from dependence on fickle winds, they could go wherever needed.[52] He also ordered some waterways obstructed, giving careful consideration to avenues by which the enemy might approach on land and sea. One that he dismissed, however, was Lake Borgne.[53]

Meanwhile Claiborne struggled with a balky legislature to raise militia.[54] He had no doubt his city would be attacked, even complaining of Washington's lethargy to newly commissioned major general Andrew Jackson.[55] It did not help that some Federalists regarded New Orleans as already all but lost.[56] Finally, in January 1813, Washington haltingly began to address the danger. A study considered possible enemy lines of approach, including an admittedly unlikely landing on the southern shore of Lake Borgne, whence small boats could use Bayou Bienvenue to disembark troops on dry land a dozen miles below the city.[57] Meanwhile, Congress passed a secret act authorizing the seizure of Mobile, claiming that it was originally a part of the Louisiana Purchase. Wilkinson took Mobile on

April 15, giving the Americans control of the Gulf Coast east to the Perdido River, but by this time he had so alienated everyone that Madison relieved him and sent Brigadier General Thomas Flournoy in his place.[58]

Washington gave, and Washington took away. In June it ordered the 3rd United States Infantry elsewhere, leaving Louisiana seriously exposed, even as the legislature still resisted summoning militia. Flournoy arrived to find just 1,500 regulars and the same number of volunteers, undermanned, untrained, and short thousands of muskets.[59] "With this force," he frankly told the governor on June 14, "it is impossible that the District Can be defended."[60] Claiborne lamented to one of his militia commanders that "we are surrounded by dangers and we must unite our best efforts."[61]

Flournoy was scant improvement on Wilkinson, antagonizing almost everyone when he took command of the 7th Military District, but he faced tough questions. Could he stop the coastal trade between New Orleans and Pensacola, where supposedly neutral Spanish authorities allowed British warships to revictual on American provisions and enemy commanders gave arms to the hostile Creek Indians? Would Shaw's flotilla at New Orleans act under his orders? Since the Choctaw seemed friendly, could he pay them to follow his banner?[62] Could anyone get cooperation on manpower from the legislature?

For months Claiborne politicked, cajoled, and threatened in order to get the state government to approve his calls for militia. The French *creoles* controlled the senate and the Americans the house, and neither would cooperate. Brigadier General David Bannister Morgan sat in the house, grumbling that few of the French felt any love for the United States. Rather, some openly looked to the day when Napoleon would come to reclaim them and Louisiana. "Our Politics here, are not Federalist & Republican," Morgan explained on January 14, 1814. "They are clearly & distinctly understood to be French & Americans." He feared the two factions might declare war on each other.[63] None of this made command easier for Flournoy, who complained to the secretary of war that "I do believe that there is not one person in twenty throughout this State, that is friendly to the United States, or who would take up arms in its defence."[64]

Claiborne still had faith in the patriotism of the people, and knew there were many faithful citizens in the city, but confessed to Jackson in August that, if attacked suddenly, the city would fall. The only salvation might be regulars and Kentucky and Tennessee militia. He begged General Jackson, who replaced Flournoy in June, to march to New Orleans, even though it lay outside his own military district.[65] Meanwhile, Captain John Shaw now had only the eighteen-gun brig *Syren* and the twelve-gun *Viper,* the newly purchased *Louisiana* still being fitted out with sixteen big guns, half a dozen gunboats, and a few sloops and schooners. Washington sent him few resources, complaining of the expenditure and waste on the New Orleans station, but still he amassed an abundance of artillery and ammunition.[66] Should the British invade, he expected them to come overland via Mobile, although he saw the possibilities of Lake Borgne.[67]

By October 1813, Secretary of the Navy William Jones wearied of Shaw's protests of unreadiness and replaced him with Master Commandant Daniel Todd Patterson.[68] Patterson was fifteen years in the Navy now, most of them spent on the New Orleans station, which had special advantages in that Edward Livingston was his cousin, and that attached him to the *creole* families of Livingston's wife, Louise Davezac. Just the month before taking his new assignment at his new rank, he had enlisted Livingston's aide in politicking for promotion.[69] Even among the Americans at New Orleans, family entanglements were omnipresent.

As Shaw left, three British warships anchored off the mouth of the Mississippi, sending parties ashore, and on April 24 several small boats from them raided upriver to within twenty miles of the city.[70] They were minor but telling incursions. New Orleans had come into British view at last. Meanwhile, Patterson found wood rot on the *Louisiana* that made her temporarily unfit for service. Then Secretary Jones halted work on the blockship when it was nearly complete, ordered *Syren* and *Viper* off after British ships blockading the river mouth, and further weakened the station by sending the armed schooner *Carolina* in chase of smugglers.[71] When Patterson warned Jones in July that the British would surely strike that winter, Jones all but ignored him.[72] General Jackson, then occupied subduing the Creeks in the Alabama country, paid more attention, and that same month advised Claiborne and Governor David Holmes of Mississippi Territory that Mobile and New Orleans were so important strategically that the enemy must want them, "and I have no doubt these will be their objects."[73]

He was right. By that spring, outcry in Parliament and the London press called for "*vigorous war with America!*" Britain wanted to halt the Americans' territorial expansion in all directions, expel them from the fisheries north of Maine, and exclude them from all trade with the British East and West Indies. Some demanded the cession of New Orleans to secure British rights to Mississippi navigation, claiming that France had no right to sell it to the Yankees.[74] There was the added attraction of as much as $14 million in cotton trapped in New Orleans warehouses by the British blockade of the river, with 1814's crop still on the plantations. More than $1 million worth of sugar was there, too, as well as untold Kentucky whiskey, flour, pork, tobacco, and more. A fortune awaited the taking.[75]

It was an attractive prize, but Britain would have to seize virtually all of the Louisiana Territory to contain the Yankees. The Spaniards and Indians, though allies now, would be difficult neighbors, and how would Britain cope with the region's 100,000 slaves? On reflection, taking and keeping New Orleans or Louisiana presented too many problems. Few who presented plans for seizing New Orleans considered what would come afterward, and no one in government seems to have advocated permanent possession. Admirals and generals did not speak for Whitehall and had no decisive voice in its policy.[76]

In April the Admiralty gave command of the North American Station to the fifty-six-year-old son of the impoverished 8th earl of Dundonald, thirty-year veteran Cochrane. Financial straits dogged the family—his older brother once pawned his clothes to eat—and Cochrane himself, though comfortable, was never far from debt.[77] He had fought the French in 1795 and captained a line ship in 1799. Some accused him of inventing intelligence of Spain preparing a hostile expedition, which precipitated a British attack on a treasure fleet at Cape Santa Maria that yielded considerable prize money and led to war, but he realized not a ha'penny himself. He got in Admiral Nelson's bad books somehow and was sent away to the West Indies, where he performed creditably, winning knighthood in 1806 and promotion to rear admiral the following year. Now he was Vice Admiral of the Red.[78]

Thanks to political differences, the Duke of Wellington had no use for Cochrane. Early in the planning for New Orleans, he snidely sneered that "spoils lay somewhere at its root," and a year later felt even more convinced that Cochrane's aim was plunder.[79] Admirals and generals shared one-eighth of the realized proceeds of the sale of captured enemy ships and property, while the overall commander in chief received an eighth for himself.[80] The prospect of such prize money as a useful incentive was ever on naval officers' horizons and contemptuously exaggerated in army circles.[81] Cochrane could certainly use it, but restoring reputation after failures on the Atlantic coast was the currency he coveted, and taking New Orleans would make a fine close to his war.

Before assuming his new command, Cochrane had already sent Captain Hugh Pigot to the Gulf Coast to reconnoiter New Orleans's defenses and sound for interest among the Creeks in an alliance. The Indians, and runaway slaves from Georgia, could significantly reinforce an invasion force.

Cochrane had also heard rumors of disaffection and dissent among the white population of Louisiana and wanted to know if they might also act as auxiliaries. Then he ordered Pigot to look into "a set of Pirates or Free Booters" operating from "a place called Baritaria." Could they be lured or hired to support an expedition against New Orleans? Not unmindful of the city's riches, he instructed Pigot to assay the market value of the goods stored in the city.[82]

Pigot reached Apalachicola, 140 miles east of Pensacola, on May 10, and four weeks later reported to Cochrane in the Bahamas. In March Jackson had ended the Creek War in victory, but surviving chiefs promised 3,000 warriors to the British, boasting that with another 3,000 redcoats they could together expel the Yankees from Louisiana and the Floridas. Pigot thought they could be made ready to move in early August.[83]

Armed with Pigot's report, Cochrane drafted a proposal on June 20.[84] He would land 3,000 redcoats at Mobile to move overland with 1,000 Creeks to take Baton Rouge upriver from New Orleans. At the same time he would disembark more using light draft boats to convey them into Lakes Borgne and Pontchartrain to approach New Orleans while sending a flotilla of gunboats up the Mississippi. New Orleans would be cut off and forced to surrender without resistance.[85] By March 1815 he promised to see "the Keys of the Mississippi placed in the custody of Gt. Britain."[86]

The admiral got started without waiting for approval. He turned now to one of his favorites, marine major Edward Nicolls, to manage the Indian part of the equation. One of the most remarkable soldiers ever to serve Britain, the thirty-five-year-old Irishman had a fighting reputation second to none, and the scars to earn it. By 1814 he had suffered a broken left leg and a wounded right, bullets through his body and right arm, a saber cut on his head, and a bayonet thrust in his chest, which combined gave him what a fellow officer described as "a fantastical deportment."[87] He established a camp at Apalachicola in July to arm and train Creek warriors and runaway slaves and persuade them to join in an attack on New Orleans when the time came.[88] Nicolls issued Cochrane's July 1 proclamation promising to arm all the warriors who came and calling on slaves in Georgia and the Carolinas to rally to his standard.[89] Encouraged by Nicolls's initial reports, Cochrane revised his estimate of regular soldiers needed from 3,000 down to 2,000 and boasted to the secretary of state for war, Lord Henry Bathurst, that he would give the Americans "a complete drubbing before peace is made," adding that he would see "command of the Mississippi wrested from them."[90]

Thanks to communications taking fifty days or more to pass between

London and the fleet, Cochrane had no way of knowing that an army of 7,000 had already been designated to be sent to Point Negril at the western tip of Jamaica by November 20, where he was to meet them with Ross's army from the Chesapeake.[91] When Cochrane's reduced estimate of necessary manpower reached him, Lord Melville revised plans to put Cochrane in overall command of the expedition.[92] Even though Wellington was skeptical of the operation, he gave it his blessing, and on August 10, Melville informed Cochrane that his plan was adopted.[93] In addition to 2,900 of all ranks from the Chesapeake, London would send 2,130 more, including the black 5th West India Regiment from Jamaica, which numbered among its privates a soldier aptly known simply as "Affricanus."[94] At Jamaica, Cochrane would also take on small craft for transporting soldiers from their ships into the lakes and bayous, and more would be sent from England.[95]

Cochrane received Melville's July 29 authorization on September 17. He departed for Barbados about October 5, fully confident of success, leaving Admiral Sir Pulteney Malcolm in command of the Chesapeake fleet to bring that army to the rendezvous. Once he took New Orleans, he would move the army into Georgia and South Carolina to pound the enemy without respite as long as the war lasted.[96] He might have preferred Bermuda or Barbados as a rendezvous point rather than Point Negril, since it stood at the threshold of the Gulf. Any sighting of a major fleet there would suggest New Orleans as an objective.[97] Still, Cochrane felt assured that the Americans had no inkling of the invasion.[98] That was not to last for long.

Nicolls had gone to Nassau to collect more men and officers for his mission, and by July 26 was ready to return to the Gulf Coast. The night before he left, he wrote Cochrane of his complete confidence in success. "A most intelligent gentleman" there had convinced him that the *creoles* in New Orleans were anxious to be rid of the Americans, gave him a map of the area, a full account of its defenses, and a letter to another man somewhere on the coast who could help enlist men in the city to cooperate. His Nassau informant was Lewis Kerr, and the letter was to James Workman, who was not back in New Orleans but somewhere on the Gulf Coast.[99]

Nicolls reached Havana on August 4 aboard Captain William Percy's *Hermes*, accompanied by Captain Robert Spencer in *Carron*. Even before they landed in port, someone let slip that their ultimate goal was New Orleans.[100] When Nicolls learned there that their Spanish allies would not allow them to land at Pensacola, he angrily went to a tavern, where frustration or rum fueled declarations that he might land at Pensacola anyhow and that he could take the whole coast with little opposition from the Yankees once their slaves flocked to Nicolls's banner.[101] The day after he left, a man in

Havana wrote to London that Nicolls was headed for New Orleans. Attentive ears had heard Nicolls's boasts and passed them to others, a second breach of security.[102]

A pair of those ears belonged to Washington's commercial vice consul, diplomat and slave dealer Vincent Gray.[103] The day before Nicolls's arrival, a letter from Jamaica alerted Gray that an agent of Cochrane's had let slip that Britain would invade Louisiana. When *Hermes* and *Carron* anchored in Havana's harbor, Gray accompanied the port inspector aboard them and heard enough from Percy and Spencer to conclude that the British intended to strike New Orleans. He wrote to Jackson, Secretary of State James Monroe, Patterson, Claiborne, and others, and sent the letters through multiple portals, hoping one or more would get through. Calling Nicolls "an impatient blustering Irishman," he urged them to arouse the people, for there was not a moment to lose.[104] Gray kept writing through early October as he learned more, even passing on word that Cochrane expected to take New Orleans in time to winter there, but never knowing if any of his letters made it to their addressees. Several were intercepted, but those to Claiborne, Monroe, and Jackson got through.[105] Slow communications blunted the import of some of what he wrote, but his flurry of letters was a dramatic intelligence coup for the Americans, another of the security lapses that compromised Cochrane's hope for secrecy.

After landing at Apalachicola on August 10, Nicolls moved to Pensacola four days later to hear of Jackson massing men to march on the town.[106] Learning that the Spanish population and garrison did not intend to make a fight, he simply took over the town himself.[107] The Indians were slow in flocking to him, runaway slaves from Georgia even less forthcoming, but while he waited for General Jackson to appear at the gates of Pensacola, he set in motion a plan to enlist the third of his promised auxiliaries in the campaign to take New Orleans. He sent a mission to Barataria to see the man he called "Monsieur Lafette."

Two

"Bloody Noses There Will Be"

F OR YEARS, OCCASIONAL reports appeared in England of smugglers who infested the bayou country below New Orleans. From the northwest end of Grand Terre Island, commanding one of the passes into Barataria Bay, they used questionable commissions from revolutionary juntas in Cartagena, Colombia, Venezuela, and other Spanish provinces, to sail as "privateers" and prey on Spanish merchant vessels. A privateer was not necessarily a pirate. The latter was a man with no country, taking whatever vessels he could, regardless of their nationality, and keeping all the plunder he took. A privateer was theoretically licensed by a government to prey on its enemies' shipping in return for a share of the proceeds of the sale of goods captured. The problem with the Grand Terre privateers is that their commissions, or letters of marque, usually came from juntas that no other nation recognized. Every week the privateers sailed their pirogues, filled with the stolen bounty, up the bay and into the twisting bayous to an open market where they held sales, then smuggled any remaining goods into New Orleans itself.[1]

The United States wanted an end to the enterprise, which robbed the cash-strapped government of customs duties and drained hard cash from the city. Yet Louisianans almost gleefully encouraged the black-market business. Merchants openly placed the privateers' stolen goods on their shelves while customers shrugged.[2] Indeed, the smugglers were romanticized, and one had already become a national folk hero. Independent though they were, many of the privateersmen called him "the Governor."[3] He and his brother left most of the sailing to others, rather acting as middlemen to get goods to the markets, and in return the corsairs acknowledged their loose authority. They were the Laffites, Jean and Pierre, half brothers from Pauillac in the French Médoc. Pierre was the elder at forty-four, probably dominant in planning their enterprises, but poor eyesight and occasional seizures kept him from being very active. That left the more stylish and dynamic Jean, aged now about thirty-two, to manage affairs in the field. He was their public face, often seen on the city's *banquettes* walking arm in arm with merchants who bought their goods.[4] Stories of their smuggling empire had been circulating for some time when Lord Byron published his poem *The Corsair* in February 1814. Depicting a pirate in the Aegean, the work referred to an apocryphal story in the British press about the generosity of a "Monsieur LaFitte" of Barataria. Readers leapt to the false conclusion that Jean Laffite inspired Byron's hero. The poem proved so popular that in April the story debuted on the London stage.[5]

There were less benign views of the Baratarians, as they were commonly known. Rumors said they might aid the British in an invasion.[6] The New Orleans press accused them of outright piracy, melodramatically attributing 1,500 murders to them that no one could prove since "dead men tell no tales." In fact, they murdered no one, and routinely released captives after robbing them. Still, an editor warned that the brothers would soon take over New Orleans itself, and asked "whether we shall still constitute an integral part of the American union, or be compelled to swear allegiance to John Lafitte."[7]

That sounded good to Edward Nicolls, who thought the Laffites could command eighty hundred followers.[8] Their numbers might not be significant, but their knowledge of the approaches to New Orleans and its environs could make them of immense value as pilots and guides. As men without a country, they might be bought. On August 29, Nicolls and Percy sent Captain Nicholas Lockyer's *Sophie* to make contact with the smugglers.[9] At midmorning on September 3, *Sophie* sighted Grand Isle. Jean Laffite himself met Lockyer with a pirogue but did not reveal his identity, instead persuading him to come ashore, where he finally identified himself.

Lockyer handed him a proclamation by Nicolls calling on Louisianans to rise and rally to him, and letters from Nicolls and Percy promising Laffite a captaincy in the colonial militia and generous land grants in Britain's American colonies if he handed over his "fleet" to Percy, with a stern admonition to remain neutral otherwise and not aid the Americans or Percy would destroy the establishment at Grand Isle and every vessel there. Laffite responded at first that he would not fight against the Americans, but that did not entirely preclude being of some service. In fact, he stalled for time and finally sent Lockyer back to his ship, telling him that he needed fifteen days to reply to the offer, after which "I will be entirely at your service."

He had not explicitly accepted the British offer, but he forestalled any British act against Grand Isle by implying that he would agree. In fact, Percy had offered him nothing. Giving their ships to the British would put the privateers out of business, and land grants would not turn corsairs into farmers. Laffite cannily realized that, regardless of who won the war, his enterprise faced extinction. Either victorious nation could sweep his associates from the Gulf, while the peacetime end of embargoes would kill their virtual monopoly on foreign goods. From informants in New Orleans, Laffite also knew that at that very moment Patterson planned to raid Barataria to prevent it from aiding the British. Moreover, Pierre had been caught and jailed in the city, indicted in federal court for piracy. If Jean helped the Yankees, it might halt Patterson and open the cell door for his brother. Self-interest, and not romanticized patriotism, dictated that he stall Percy and inform the Americans. Jean immediately enlisted city banker—and privateer investor—Jean Blanque to act as go-between with Governor Claiborne, sending him Lockyer's documents.

Laffite played a deep game with the British.[10] Refusing their offer might help Pierre. Actually, aiding in New Orleans's defense might even yield pardons for Pierre and others. As it happened, Pierre broke out of jail before Jean's letter reached Blanque. Then within a few days Vincent Gray's August 8 letter to Claiborne came into Jean's hands and he sent it to Blanque as further evidence of his good faith. When Pierre reached Grand Terre on September 10, the brothers decided to offer to defend Barataria against their common enemy, perhaps hoping to forestall Patterson's strike and give them time to get their associates' vessels safely to the Mexican coast. "I am the stray sheep, wishing to return to the fold," Jean wrote Claiborne that day, asking in return for quashed indictments and a general pardon.[11] Their lightly armed schooners and feluccas could be nimble gadflies on the bays, closing a back door to New Orleans.[12] He never answered Nicolls and Percy.

Claiborne should have welcomed the Laffites' offer, for the security of New Orleans seemed threatened from within as well as from without. Rumors that summer spoke of a *creole* plot to disrupt the state government.[13] Other gossip warned that Spain would declare war on the United States unless it abandoned its claim to Louisiana.[14] By mid-August the divisions within the population had the governor complaining that if he must rely on local militia alone, he could not defend the city, begging Jackson to come assume command.[15] The general had heard from others of a "rottenness" among the city's people and how they would flee at sight of the enemy, but he tried to calm Claiborne, promising they had more to dread from internal enemies than from the British; but if they remained vigilant, all would be well.[16]

Then came a turn in sentiment, perhaps because Nicolls's presence at Pensacola made the threat suddenly more tangible, and his call for runaway slaves conjured new fears of servile insurrection. When Washington and Jackson ordered Claiborne to raise several new militia companies, the city press supported him and the chosen company captains promised their co-operation.[17] By late August the governor felt guardedly more optimistic, as did loyal men in the city. Sixteen-year-old Henry Palfrey enthusiastically volunteered, promising his family that if the enemy came, his company would be ready to meet them and "return their visits & their Shot with Interest."[18] At the same time another Orleanian wrote a friend in New York that "I presume we are as secure as you are."[19]

Certainly, people in New York and all across the nation felt concern for New Orleans as they looked on from the vantage of distance and time. An information revolution had taken place in the post-1776 generation. Newspaper circulation exploded to more than 22 million copies.[20] Thanks to editorial exchanges, pieces from one journal migrated to dozens of others, traveling on more than 36,000 miles of government post roads.[21] It was slow, to be sure, routinely taking just over a month for New Orleans papers to reach Washington, but they gradually spread information at destinations along the way, meaning readers in Tennessee or Ohio could learn of events in Louisiana weeks before the capital.

As a result, Americans were better informed than ever, and that summer they all knew of a planned invasion of Louisiana.[22] They also knew there was talk of making peace, but when or at what cost, none could say. Rumor said the enemy would demand yielding Louisiana as a condition, and indeed they did at the first meetings in Ghent, where the British agents denied the legitimacy of Jefferson's Purchase.[23] They wanted far more besides that, which America's diplomats flatly rejected, calling instead for a return to the prewar status quo. Unfortunately, they bargained from weakness, with no leverage except threats to halt the talks. The British could afford to stall and await favorable news from the Gulf to strengthen their hand.[24] Yankee delegate Albert Gallatin warned Secretary of State Monroe that the British very much wanted New Orleans, and if they got it, it might be impossible to get it back.[25]

Until he could come himself, Jackson asked Tennessee militia commander Brigadier General John Coffee to raise 1,000 mounted men, which Coffee soon tripled and had on their way. Meanwhile, Jackson ordered detachments of the 7th Infantry to the city to augment Colonel George

T. Ross's 44th Infantry, which unfortunately had but three hundred men, and half of its officers were questionable *creoles*.[26] Perhaps worse, Ross frequented the American Coffee House, drinking something stronger than coffee, and often had to be carried to his lodgings.[27] Jackson promised to visit the city soon but meant to go home to Nashville for a few weeks' rest first. He saw no need to hurry.[28] Then, on August 26, he received incontrovertible evidence that the British were coming with as many as 10,000 redcoats to invade and take New Orleans.[29]

Soon came news of the British offer to the privateers' leader, Laffite. Claiborne, Patterson, Ross, militia major general Jacques Villeré, and others met to examine the letters delivered by Blanque. Thinking them forgeries, all but Villeré recommended that they refuse to deal with the Laffites.[30] But Villeré countered that he knew the brothers and they were legitimate privateers, not pirates.[31] A wavering Claiborne thought the Laffites might be useful and proposed postponing Patterson's raid, which Patterson emphatically refused. His orders allowed him no latitude, and Washington had returned his armed schooner *Carolina* with its orders to clean out the nest. Ross seconded him, Patterson was ready, and that settled the matter. In the predawn hours of September 11, he launched the operation.

New Orleans was a city of few secrets. Word of Patterson's departure reached the Laffites before the raid's boats left the Mississippi. Privateers were not fighters. They preyed on unarmed vessels and most never fired a shot in action. When Jean called the captains together to discuss options, he told them that for his part he "never would fight against the Americans."[32] He left the rest to choose their own courses. They held a big sale on Grand Terre on September 15 and sold as much as they could, intending to hide the rest and then get their ships to sea and safety. In the end they managed to conceal only several thousand gunflints and some gunpowder before Patterson appeared the next morning.[33]

The smugglers made no resistance. The Laffites and some associates rowed pirogues up Barataria Bay to take refuge in the interior. Patterson's boats landed Ross's men, their commander once more drunk, and in several hours of burning and looting destroyed the privateer base.[34] They took ten vessels and $200,000 in booty, eliminating any possibility of the smugglers lending their fleet to the enemy, and showing that the British were not the only ones interested in prize money.[35] What would the Baratarians do now? Pierre was free, their fleet was gone, and little incentive remained for them to come to the city's aid. Would they seek vengeance for their losses by helping the enemy after all? Like most other questions outstanding that fall, the answer would depend on Andrew Jackson.

Wars make heroes, and this one made its share thus far, but no star in that constellation shone brighter at the moment than Jackson's. He was forty-seven now, a native of colonial South Carolina, where as a boy during the Revolution he had been captured by the British and given a sabre cut on his forehead that left a lifelong scar. After the war he studied law and moved to Nashville, where he prospered, married Rachel Donelson, daughter of one of the town's first families, and became territorial attorney general at age twenty-four. When statehood came in 1796, he was elected Tennessee's first member of the House of Representatives. As a Jeffersonian Republican, he won a Senate seat a year later, only to resign when he became disgusted with congressional politics.

What launched Jackson on the path to commanding the 7th Military District in this war was his 1802 election as major general of the state militia. Killing an opponent in a duel tarnished his reputation for a time, and then he ill-advisedly endorsed Aaron Burr's nebulous projects until he learned that they included taking New Orleans from the United States. When war came in 1812, the War Hawk Jackson first led his militia on a wasted march to Natchez and back whose only benefit was to give him the priceless sobriquet "Old Hickory" for his resilience. Another duel on his return to Nashville left him with a bullet in his shoulder for the rest of his life. No one could say he lacked courage. "When danger rears its head," he boasted, "I can never shrink from it."[36]

Jackson's career to date also revealed a character hotheaded, violent, vengeful, and ever ready to see plots and conspiracies against him in the motives of others. He displayed many of the salient traits of the Appalachian South's poor white population: resentment of the privileged, mistrust of the wealthy, and suspicion of the landed aristocracy. Unlike them, however, he was neither lazy nor shiftless but an energetic, driven, self-made man.[37] Imperious and disinclined to care about consensus, he preached democracy but showed the instincts of a dictator. When Jefferson gave the Louisiana governorship to Claiborne rather than himself, "Old Hickory" fell out with both, his contempt for their class suiting him to a role he already played for his army as a champion of the common man.[38] Now in wartime his position freed his petty side to tweak Claiborne with veiled insults and condescension that Jackson never lost an opportunity to inflict. He was also loyal to a fault, generous, unselfish, and absolutely devoted to his wife, a man of many friends and many feuds. He had the rare ability to inspire.

The Creek War made "Old Hickory" a national figure. In June 1814, Washington made him a brigadier general in the regular army, then days later elevated him to major general and assigned him command of the 7th Military Division that included Tennessee, the Mississippi Territory, and Louisiana. Antipathy to England was the bedrock of his Republican Party.[39] "I owe to Britain a debt of retaliatory, Vengeance," he told his wife that summer. "Should our forces meet I trust I shall pay the debt."[40] Settling that debt might take him to New Orleans.

After defeating the Creeks, he moved to Mobile on August 22, not expecting to go to New Orleans until late September or October. Clearly he felt no particular urgency.[41] Then, late in the afternoon of August 27, a caller handed him Vincent Gray's letter, while another letter from Gray arrived directly.[42] Undaunted by Gray's revelations, the general resolved to ensure that "bloody noses there will be" before the enemy took New Orleans.[43] He stayed up nearly to midnight drafting orders to muster friendly Indian volunteers and the militia from Tennessee, Kentucky, and Mississippi Territory. His eyes so sore from writing by candlelight that he could hardly see, he wrote that night to the secretary of war that "we must now trust to the Justice of our cause and the bravery of our citizens."[44] Warning Claiborne to be watchful for spies among the disaffected Spaniards and to guard all roads in and out of the city, Jackson told him that "our friends must be seperated from our enemies."[45]

The British were not long in coming. On September 13 a combined force under Percy and Nicolls attacked Fort Bowyer on the western tip of Mobile Point, which commanded the entrance to Mobile's bay. Confined to a sickbed with dysentery, the redoubtable Nicolls crawled out on a frigate's deck to help man her guns, only to add to his catalog of wounds when grapeshot from the fort hit his leg and put out an eye.[46] The attack repulsed, Nicolls suspected that traitors in Pensacola had warned the defenders, and he was right, one of them being an Irish priest who heard the Spanish governor's confession, including a mention of the pending attack, and broke confessional sanctity by sending word to the Americans.[47]

The failure to take Mobile was a setback, but hardly critical, for Cochrane had not yet left the Atlantic coast. At home the planning for an expedition was still evolving. The Admiralty settled on December 1 for a landing on the Louisiana coast, well after the hurricane season, then worked backward from that date to determine when the several components of the invasion must be on their way. Components from England would sail to Barbados or another British island, refit and resupply, and then rendezvous off Negril about November 15. Cochrane and Ross's Chesapeake army would meet them at the same time. A fortnight's sail from Negril would put them on the Louisiana coast by December 1.[48]

Orders headed "Most Secret" went out. Eventually Cochrane was to be sent about 3,000 soldiers and instructions that he should command overall but share strategic decisions with General Ross.[49] Sailing from Ireland would be the 93rd Sutherland Highlanders; the 95th Rifles; detachments from the 21st Royal North British Fusiliers; the 44th East Essex Regiment; the 4th King's Own and the 85th Bucks Volunteer Light Infantry, with a company of artillery; a detachment from the 14th Duchess of York's Own Light Dragoons; a company of "rocketeers" with Congreve rockets; and engineers and other ratings. At Jamaica they would take aboard the black 5th West India Regiment and at Guadeloupe the 1st West India. Adding his own command, Ross would have 6,000 men.[50] Meanwhile, logistics began assembling muskets, carbines, pistols, artillery, rockets, more than a million rounds of ammunition, and shoes, clothing and medical stores, and more than eight hundred tons of provisions.[51] By mid-September a dozen ships were to depart when weather allowed, including a "rocket ship" from which the rocketeers could practice on the voyage. Orders went to Admiral William Brown commanding at Jamaica to collect small craft for the landings. Every precaution was being taken, every detail attended to. It was a perfect specimen of British organized war.[52]

Whitehall also refined Cochrane and Ross's goals. It did not want permanent control of the Mississippi Valley, but the expedition ought to "occupy" an important place or places whose return in a treaty could be the condition of better terms for Britain, or of which they might even demand indefinite possession for themselves as a price of peace. Secretary of State for War Lord Bathurst did not specify New Orleans, leaving Cochrane and Ross wide latitude. Moreover, Bathurst did not believe it could not be held long without substantial reinforcement, which could take months. They were free to lend aid if the inhabitants opted for independence or return to Spain, but under no circumstances were they to encourage hope of Louisiana coming under permanent British rule, and they must not encourage slave revolt. When the admiral and general felt the time suitable, they could leave a small force of occupation and withdraw the army to Bermuda. The British public followed much of this with interest, and by late September common opinion said the expedition was bound for an easy conquest of New Orleans, where they would make the Yankees "little better than prisoners at large, in their own country."[53]

Meanwhile, on the American coast, Cochrane wanted more specific information to make the army's landing and march on New Orleans as smooth as possible. He turned to Captain James Alexander Gordon, a battle-seasoned Scot with twenty-one years in the Navy, who stood an imposing six feet, three inches tall. He had served with Admiral Nelson at the Battle of the Nile in 1798, then in the West Indies and the Caribbean, winning promotion to captain when just twenty-two. Gordon liked to amuse his men by standing in an empty water cask and then jumping from it into five more in quick succession. His jumping days abruptly ended on November 29, 1811, at the Battle of Palagruža in the Adriatic, where he commanded the frigate *Active*. A cannonball took the leg off a seaman standing in front of Gordon and then shattered his own left knee, leaving the lower leg dangling by tendons. With typical aplomb, Gordon insisted that the ship's surgeon tend the wounded sailor first. Then, as he was being carried to his cabin, he recognized one of the men holding him as an impressed Yankee sailor who earlier had protested that he had a useless arm and could not serve. "I am sorry you have lost your leg," the American told the captain. Having seen the man working one of the ship's guns with both hands earlier, Gordon quipped back, "I am happy to see you have found your arm."

In seven months he was back at sea, a "cork-leg" thanks to a wooden peg, and now commanded the thirty-eight-gun frigate *Seahorse* in Cochrane's fleet. He led a raid on Alexandria, Virginia, in August that resulted in considerable prize goods and some modest destruction in the city, for which he would be branded a vandal in the United States.[54] He served Cochrane well, adding luster to his reputation as a fighting captain.[55] The two clearly liked each other. "Sir Alexander is just the man for the Americans," Gordon told his wife, Lydia, and knew how to deal with them. When Cochrane resolved to match Yankee destruction in Canada by doing likewise in the States, Gordon concluded that "it is the only way to treat an American."[56]

In mid-September, Cochrane ordered Gordon to command a squadron cruising the Gulf, where the admiral would join him in November, and gave him a secret directive to find an anchorage for the fleet and a landing place near New Orleans for soldiers.[57] Beyond that, he should aid Nicolls and look for shallow-draft boats to move soldiers through the lakes and bayous to attack New Orleans. He should also scout enemy defenses at the water passes between Lakes Borgne and Pontchartrain and elsewhere, as well as roads redcoats might use. Gordon was even to sound sentiment among the *creole* militia to see if some might assist with the invasion. He could even try to take the city himself if he found it lightly defended and felt he could hold it. In addition to much more, Cochrane also charged Gordon to hire coastal pilots to conduct the fleet from the Atlantic past the Bahamas and Florida Keys into the Gulf.[58]

Gordon's most immediate concern was security. He would tell his officers nothing until some distance at sea, but Cochrane gave it away himself aboard his flagship *Tonnant* when, at dinner with Gordon's officers, he asked if *Seahorse* would chart a course through the Straits of Florida or sail farther south into the Caribbean to pass around Cuba. Any officer knew that passing the Florida Straits or around Cuba meant heading for the Gulf. Gordon tried to cover for the gaff, replying that "I am not to know where I am going, sir," but the damage was done. Hours later Gordon wrote Lydia that "he had let the secret out."[59]

Once at sea, the flotilla moved southward, Gordon entertaining hopes of considerable prize money to come, and looking forward to seeing Nicolls. "I have known him many years," he wrote Lydia. "He is as gallant a fellow as ever stepped, but I think he is rather too venturous." He even joked that Nicolls might wind up commanding an Indian/slave/*creole* army to take the city, and "*I* may be made Governor of New Orleans!"[60] In fact, many expected much of Nicolls, but the distinguished artilleryman Lieutenant Colonel Alexander Dickson disagreed, regarding him as an impractical fraud who served his own interest with Cochrane.[61] When Gordon anchored off Pensacola on October 31, he learned of the Fort Bowyer debacle, saw how few Creeks had actually been enlisted, and could have had doubts of his own.[62]

Worse, Jackson was coming. "*Victory or Death*" was their watchword, Old Hickory told Coffee, who organized his volunteers even as they force-marched south, sleeping in the open for want of tents, to meet Jackson just a few days' march from Pensacola in early November.[63][64] Gordon and Nicolls offered to help defend the town, but when the Spanish commander wavered, Gordon began an evacuation to Apalachicola on November 3. Nicolls stayed to make a brave but Quixotic defense, then joined Gordon and left the city to the Americans. Gordon meanwhile dropped Nicolls and his Creeks at Apalachicola but decided not to remain, joking to his wife that "the ground is too soft for my wooden leg." A few days later he headed for Negril.[65] "We are now going to strike a great blow," he believed, although he had no idea "what part of the play I shall act."[66]

Cochrane ordered Malcolm to move the Chesapeake army to Negril by November 20, and wrote ahead to Admiral Brown to have pilots, landing boats, and provisions ready.[67] The admiral himself expected to reach Guadeloupe by November 1 to meet the fleet from Plymouth and then proceed to Negril. They would take Mobile and make it their base of operations. Again secrecy was vital, lest the Yankees reinforce the Gulf. In private correspondence, however, Cochrane made it clear that the government wanted him to take New Orleans, while at home the prime minister informed Wellington that the city was Cochrane's goal.[68]

The admiral still expected his crony Nicolls to produce a small army of Indians, but a spy in the major's camp at Prospect Bluff above Apalachicola kept the Americans steadily informed of his efforts.[69] Nicolls remained optimistic of success. Before leaving Pensacola, one of his subordinates even sent a playful announcement to New Orleans that they expected to be dancing with its ladies on Christmas Eve, though, to date, their feet's only activity was the hasty flight to Apalachicola.[70] Then, in the first week of December, orders came from Cochrane. He was off Pensacola and summoned Nicolls and his Creeks to meet him for the push to New Orleans.[71]

By this time people in that city felt increasingly exposed, with little to defend them but "mud, musquitoes & Climate," according to a shopkeeper.[72] Claiborne fussed over fears of enemy infiltrators, asking for the arrest of anyone deemed suspicious, and ordered nightly patrols of town and suburbs, warning Major Nicholas Girod that they were "exposed to much danger from *without* and from *within*."[73] The disaffection among the ethnicities still worried him. Traitors might be on every street, and reinforcements too late to help. He was not sanguine that in such a state the city could be defended.[74] With Patterson and Ross still at Barataria, only militia guarded the city. Citizens formed mounted patrols to guard against any slave revolt seeking to take advantage of the moment, and on September 14 city authorities banned plays and dances for slaves, forestalling large gatherings that might attract enemy agents.[75]

Then, as September progressed, signs looked more hopeful. The governor's efforts with the militia began to yield better results. A detachment of the 7th Infantry arrived, and two mounted volunteer companies arrived from Feliciana Parish, the first new militia to rush to New Orleans.[76] Word also came of the meeting at Ghent, although peace was not to be taken for granted. Federalist merchant William Kenner thought it possible but not inevitable, and if the enemy came to New Orleans first, he believed that "we shall certainly have 'scissors to grind.'"[77]

With that in mind, on September 15 a group of merchants and leading citizens met at the call of Edward Livingston, whose older brother Robert had negotiated the Louisiana Purchase for Jefferson and shared credit with Robert Fulton for developing the first practical steamboat.[78] He offended some yet enjoyed almost unqualified respect as a lawyer from others. The ardent Republican was an authority on history and literature, spoke four languages, and could read more. He seemed to lack grace or dignity, but his talent showed in his face.[79] He would inspire perhaps the most famous political insult in American history when the brilliant John Randolph of Roanoke declared that "he is highly talented and utterly corrupt, and stinks and shines like rotten mackerel by moonlight."[80]

The meeting convened at Bernard Trémoulet's Exchange Commercial Coffee-House, which sat on Levee Street facing the Place d'Armes, the open square in front of the St. Louis Cathedral and next door to the state capitol known as Government House. It was a noisy and ill-kept venue, the resort of leading men and legislators.[81] Livingston called on them to unite in the crisis and presented resolutions repudiating division, supporting volunteers, and calling for a nine-man Committee of Defense to lubricate relations between civil and military authorities. After its unanimous approval, the meeting made Livingston president of the committee and then appointed members equally from the French and American communities, but not one Spaniard. Then it issued an address by Livingston that emphasized the threat to their property and called on them to unite and "form one body, one soul, and defend to the last extremity your sovereignty, your property."[82] Almost at once over $4,000 in pledges for defense came from their pockets—a modest sum, but a beginning.[83]

Livingston and Claiborne loathed each other, and the unofficial committee was a direct challenge to the governor, who was apparently unaware of the meeting. It began corresponding directly with Jackson rather than through Claiborne, who reacted by having the popular General Villeré propose creation of an official defense committee two days later, which secured commitments for up to $10,000 to mobilize militia, all but one of the pledges coming from *creoles*.[84] Villeré and Claiborne called for increased surveillance of strangers and slaves and any signs of enemy incitement to rebellion, especially where Spaniards lived in numbers.[85] In some districts men organized informal nightly patrols to discourage slaves from being about after dark, while militiamen kept watch on waterways.[86] Slave owners themselves applied constant pressure for protection, one suggesting that slaves should not be allowed to practice trades, especially blacksmithing, by which weapons could be made. "Until such a measure be taken," he told Livingston, "we shall never be perfectly secure from the Slaves."[87]

In New Orleans itself, the captains of eleven companies of the state militia pledged to forgo pay and even rations to defend the city in an emergency.[88] This was the spirit the governor had longed to see from his people. He wrote to Madison to inform him that they were "beginning to manifest the most patriotic disposition," although many of the *creoles* were still slow to come forward.[89] Now he reorganized the state militia into two divisions, one under Villeré and the other for Brigadier General Stephen Hopkins at

Donaldsonville, sixty miles upriver.[90] The governor also made Captain Bartholomew Shaumburg his aide-de-camp, unaware that he was inviting a crony of Wilkinson's into his administrative family.

Jackson tried to help solve the manpower problem on September 21 by sending Claiborne a proclamation calling on free blacks to volunteer for separate militia companies, promising the same pay and land bonuses offered to white men. Claiborne hesitated. For years whites had resisted the existing free black militia. Now his own defense committee said it could only support the measure if any such companies were banned from the city after the war, fearing that, having acquired skill with arms and a soldier's pride, "they would prove dangerous."[91]

Clearly the sudden and tangible British threat made the difference, as a new militia requisition filled quickly and people found confidence in signs of preparedness.[92] Unfortunately, when the legislature reassembled on October 5, the old factionalism erupted to threaten the veneer of unity. The Americans suspected the *creoles*, the *creoles* distrusted the Americans, elements of both championed or loathed Claiborne, and no one trusted the Irish or Spaniards or other foreign *émigrés*.[93] Preoccupied by petty disputes and quarrels, all sides at Government House lost their focus on defense.[94]

At least there was urgency in Washington. Vincent Gray's August 13 warning finally reached Monroe, and early in October Jackson received a copy. It told Old Hickory nothing he had not known since late August, but now the situation had Monroe's attention, and in late September he superseded the ineffectual John Armstrong as interim secretary of war. He told Old Hickory to go to New Orleans. It was a conditional order with no hint of urgency, but it was Washington's first instruction to elevate the city's defense in his priorities.[95]

Even as Monroe's letter arrived, the general was still telling his wife that he hoped to visit New Orleans once the Mobile district was secure, but he saw no need for haste despite multiple hints that the city might be at hazard.[96] He felt Louisiana best protected by a resolute defense of Mobile and Pensacola. In mid-October, even after receiving ten letters warning of British movements, his focus remained unchanged.[97] Part of that may have been perverse stubbornness, for he was sick of Claiborne's appeals for him to come to the city, and complained to Monroe that his entire force would not satisfy the panicked governor's demands.[98]

Happily, New Orleans's mercurial spirits revived somewhat when more companies of the 7th Infantry led by Major John Nicks arrived on October 17.[99] With them came Orderly Sergeant Isham Lewis, with three years' good service and a recent recommendation for promotion. He would have told few that he was Jefferson's nephew. Three years earlier, in Kentucky, he and his brother Lilburn got drunk on the evening of December 15, 1811. Enraged when a slave named George accidentally broke a pitcher, the brothers forced Lilburn's other slaves to watch as they nearly severed George's head with an axe, then made the blacks dismember and burn the body, their grisly work interrupted shortly after two a.m. by the first of the New Madrid earthquakes. Arrested pending trial in April 1812, Lilburn killed himself, while Isham escaped and fled to Natchez, where he enlisted in the 7th when war came.[100] His uncle had once recommended Louisiana to him as a land of opportunity. It might also be a place for redemption.[101]

By now the city's defenses tallied thirty-seven cannon with more than thirty tons of powder, several thousand muskets, and tens of thousands of rounds of ammunition.[102] It made for an impressive arsenal, but half of the cannon were mounted in forts and too heavy to be much use if the British bypassed them, and some of their wooden carriages were riddled with rot and might collapse when fired.[103] Still, optimism returned by mid-month. An afternoon banquet at the Conde Ballroom on Chartres Street on October 15 saw factional jealousies relaxed as merchants and civic leaders toasted Madison and recent victories at Niagara and Lake Champlain, sang patriotic songs in English and French, and drank to their state and to Jackson, who would surely come to protect it.[104]

Two days later Claiborne released a September 21 proclamation sent by Jackson, a masterpiece of inflammatory adjectives that had just reached him.[105] It raised the specter of Indian uprising and servile insurrection fomented by the enemy, and revealed the British approach to the "hellish banditti" of Barataria.[106] In a well-timed effort to strengthen popular resolve, Claiborne had the documents provided by Laffite published two days later.[107] Coincidentally, a week later Livingston would approach Madison over the "hellish banditti." They needed the Baratarians. In his committee's meetings he frequently advocated giving them pardon or immunity in return for their services, not mentioning that Jean Laffite had written to him to ask that Livingston broker a deal for the brothers and their followers.[108] Assuring Madison of the Laffites' powerful influence, Livingston suggested that an amnesty to all who enlisted would ease the public mind and could add at least five hundred experienced sailors and artillerymen to the city's defense.[109]

More and more men took heart.[110] "The horror has dissipated," Villeré wrote Senator Fromentin.[111] Overly optimistic, he even assured Congressman Robertson that "the actual crisis has passed," the greatest concern now being spies in their midst.[112] The number of men in Louisiana actually collaborating with the British can never be known, but there were a few, including Workman and other British natives, and some Spaniards, and the atmosphere of fear created an opportunity for some to settle old scores by creating rumors about innocent men.[113] It did not help that business was at a standstill, all the more reason for vigilance on the streets and *banquettes*.[114] Light being the enemy of clandestine mischief, the city bought half a dozen new ladders for the evening lantern lighters.[115]

Claiborne's confidence continued to grow, and by October 24 he believed the population was firm for defense and loyalty to the Union. He would soon have 2,000 militia under arms and advised Monroe the following day that unless attacked by overwhelming numbers, "you may fear nothing for our safety."[116] That moved him to take a chance by publishing Old Hickory's other September 21 proclamation calling for free black enlistments.[117] With no apparent sense of irony, Jackson addressed them as "sons of freedom," the republic's "adopted children," and promised them the same $124 bounty and 160-acre land grants given to white volunteers, with equal pay and rations. He even engaged to prevent their being hazed or taunted by white soldiers, and promised that any glory achieved would be their own.[118] It remained to be seen how many would step forward, but Old Hickory felt it had a good effect in winning support from that community.[119]

Meanwhile the white Battalion d'Orleans mustered its five companies, two hundred strong, mostly middle-class city men in their thirties, including artisans, bankers, merchants, and civil servants. Their officers came from the wealthy elite, and all but their commander, Major Jean Baptiste Plauché, were *émigrés* from France and Saint-Domingue. They had stood by the government during the Burr scare and they did not waver now.[120] Captain Joseph Dubuclet's mounted troop from the Attakapas country west of the Mississippi arrived now, distinguished by one-tenth of their forty-one-man complement being the four sons of Madame Félicité Louise Henriette Latil Devince Bienvenu.

Claiborne once more begged Jackson on October 28 to come, but by the time his letter reached Mobile, Old Hickory was not there.[121] Five days earlier he learned that Madison had ordered another 7,500 volunteers for his support, and received Monroe's letter in which he did not order the taking of Pensacola but did not forbid it, either, maintaining an official pose of neutrality toward Spain should Jackson decide on his own to do so. By now all of America knew Old Hickory well enough to know that he would not hesitate once he decided to act.[122]

Nor did he. The day he received Monroe's letter, Old Hickory left to meet Coffee. Acknowledging that he did so without orders or permission to attack a Spanish outpost, he sanctimoniously declared that even if it cost him his commission, "the salvation of my country will be a sufficient reward."[123] He had to expel the British from Pensacola before the reinforcements he had been warned of arrived.[124] A week after he left, another letter from Monroe came confirming that redcoats would be sailing from Ireland.[125]

A new urgency seized Old Hickory as he called out every resource, writing more letters on October 31 than on any other day of the campaign to come.[126] He ordered General William Carroll, who had succeeded him in command of West Tennessee militia, to get volunteers he was raising on the road even though not yet armed.[127] He wrote Governor Isaac Shelby in Kentucky to dispatch volunteers immediately and asked Governor David Holmes of the Mississippi Territory to mobilize. More orders went to friendly Choctaw and Creeks, and he notified Claiborne that thousands of volunteers would be on their way to the city.[128]

The governor needed that encouragement. Press coverage of affairs at Ghent disheartened him, and Britain's unacceptable demands for Louisiana meant the looming invasion would become reality.[129] On November 4, not yet aware that Jackson was moving on Pensacola, he told one of Old Hickory's officers in New Orleans that he saw no hope of peace and "every reason to believe that Louisiana will soon be attacked." His optimism for the growing unity of his people was still strong. There were still disaffected elements, and he worried what posture the legislature would take when it convened again in a few days, but several members gave him positive predictions.[130] A few days would tell him which way that breeze blew.

Happily, volunteers began appearing without waiting for a militia call. Captain John-Claude Hudry spent $9,705 from his own pocket to arm and equip sixty French veterans and native Louisianans, most of them from the poorer classes, to form the Compagnie des Francs, which attached itself to Plauché's battalion.[131] Three *creoles* offered to raise companies of free blacks in response to Jackson's call.[132] Exaggerated rumors of volunteers coming from Tennessee and Kentucky soon had New Orleans expecting an army of 15,000.[133] Patterson had *Carolina* back and *Louisiana* sufficiently repaired for service, and there were those six gunboats on Lake Borgne protecting communications with Mobile.[134]

The city council made its own preparations. Expecting that any enemy bombardment would set buildings ablaze, the mayor had eighty of the city fire brigade's water buckets repaired.[135] People felt comfortable that Fort St. Philip, some eighty miles downstream, should be able to stop enemy warships trying to come past it, while Claiborne personally browbeat local militia into erecting earthworks to defend the tightest turn in the river at Détour des Anglais, better known as English Turn, seventeen miles downstream from New Orleans, meanwhile ordering roads and bayous west of the river to be blocked.[136] The situation looked stable, even promising.

Then came November 10 and the legislature's gathering. For a week it did nothing, and Claiborne feared it would be too slow to act and would cripple his ability to defend the state.[137] One week turned into two, with no appropriations, no militia call, and no laws addressing the emergency. Not a dollar's appropriation was forthcoming.[138] Louis Louaillier of the ways and means committee accused his fellow delegates of culpable negligence whose reward would be surrender.[139] Adding to the problem was the fact that almost no money circulated in the city. The banks hoarded specie and people cut coins into fractional currency for small purchases.[140] Slave sales all but stopped, those sold at sheriff's sales going for as little as $350, and cotton plummeted to ten cents a pound if a buyer could be found, and half of that was on credit.[141]

Unaware of all that, Jackson expected Claiborne to have militia ready to move on command.[142] Once Coffee's mounted Tennesseans joined his force from Mobile, Jackson occupied Pensacola without a fight on November 7.[143] He remained only a couple of days and had no plans to go to New Orleans until late November, and no expectation of meeting the enemy there.[144] Discounting reports of enemy plans for Louisiana, or dismissing them as panicked rumors, especially when they came from Claiborne, he still thought Mobile would be Cochrane's objective.[145] Now, however, with Pensacola in hand and Mobile secure, he could comfortably leave them in subordinates' hands while he went to see to New Orleans's defenses, and along the way he could identify likely spots that the British might choose for a coastal landing.[146] Writing to his wife on November 21, he did grant the possibility of the British getting there before he did, but told her there was really "no danger."[147]

Jackson rode out of Mobile at five o'clock in the afternoon on November 22, his staff and Major Henry Peire of the 44th Infantry accompanying, and expected to arrive by December 1.[148] He left Brigadier General James Winchester in command behind him and sent Colonel Arthur P. Hayne ahead to survey the city's defenses. He also dispatched to Georgia his trusted scout Major Sam Dale, yet another of the living frontier legends of the campaign. Sometimes called "the Daniel Boone of Alabama," the raw-boned Virginian leapt into folklore the year before when he and three companions stood in canoes on the Alabama River using muskets as clubs to kill eight of nine attacking warriors. "The Canoe Fight" instantly entered frontier lore and was the first "victory" of the Creek War in months.[149] When he needed hard riding, Jackson turned to Dale, and now he carried an alert that volunteers from all parts of the district were converging on New Orleans, and Georgians would be needed, too.[150]

Indeed, the volunteers were coming. Jackson himself directed Coffee and a company of Mississippi dragoons toward New Orleans. Governor Shelby had raised three Kentucky regiments with 2,250 men brigaded under Major General John Thomas from Louisville. Accompanied by former senator John Adair, who had paced uncontrollably for almost two years after the murder of captured Kentuckians in the Michigan territory, they embarked on November 21 without blankets, tents, or pay, a motley assemblage in homemade jeans and buckskins.[151] Three days later General Carroll had 2,000 volunteers embarked on flatboats at Nashville for the trip down the Cumberland to the Ohio and thence for the Mississippi.[152] Jackson had assumed the volunteers would come armed, but most had no weapons. Thousands of muskets, bayonets, gunflints, and cartridges were en route from Pittsburgh aboard two keelboats, expected to reach Baton Rouge by December 15, but the captain of one was unwisely authorized to make stops along the way to take on other paying cargo. Special riders were bringing Old Hickory $25,000 in cash for expenses.[153]

Colonel Hayne's arrival a few days ahead of the general confirmed that Old Hickory was really coming, news that boosted confidence. Citizens felt themselves perfectly secure now and, though still expecting the enemy approach, regarded themselves united and beyond enemy reach.[154] Even the legislature took heart, enacting taxes to fund defensive works.[155] The only discouraging words came in the eastern newspapers arriving in late November, for they told of Federalist New England states refusing to answer militia calls and Massachusetts calling for a convention of the New England states to meet on December 15 in Hartford, Connecticut, to discuss their mutual concerns and remedies, including the possibility that the dissident states might secede from the Union. Republicans in New Orleans viewed it as a triumph of Federalist disloyalty, while Louisiana's developing unity was a victory for Republicanism, but underlying all was a concern that disunity anywhere weakened their capacity to resist threats on the Gulf.[156] Then, in mid-October, came a false report that the Ghent meeting had failed and the Americans were coming home.[157] A month passed before more reliable intelligence arrived, by which time an American victory on Lake Champlain had disrupted British strategy for the North and shifted any hope of progress southward.[158] However much a month's delay getting information frustrated the Americans, it was worse for the British now in the Caribbean, for whom the delay in communication with London was double. Moreover, they knew virtually nothing of Jackson's movements and thought him still at Mobile.

But Jackson was on the road, and on November 24 his mounted party fell in with Coffee. They reached the Pearl River by forced marches in three days, from there on carefully noting any geography that might host an enemy landing. Two more days brought them to Madisonville on the north shore of Lake Pontchartrain, just thirty miles from New Orleans.[159] On the last day of the month, a packet boat took them across the lake to Bayou St. John. They mounted and rode six miles down the bayou road, crossed a bridge, rode another two miles, and reached the city shortly after ten o'clock. Almost no one noticed.[160]

Three

"By the Gods I Think You Will Have Warm Work"

THE HMS *TONNANT* weighed anchor on October 13 with a fair wind behind her.[1] The ship's cabins and tween decks were a confusion of midshipmen, surgeons, and clerks, while artillery, horses, and munitions filled her holds, promising action ahead. Yet, as she plowed through Atlantic waves on a southward heading, Admiral Cochrane kept their destination to himself. Even *Tonnant*'s captain, Rear Admiral Edward Codrington, was in the dark, writing to his wife, Jane, that until Cochrane chose to reveal their destination, he was on "a cruise of curiosity." Speculation belowdecks said that they were bound for the Indies and New Orleans, and only after eight days at sea did Cochrane finally reveal Guadeloupe as his aim, but nothing more.[2] Aware of his commander's financial straits, Codrington suspected that the Guadeloupe stop was to collect prize money still due from his earlier tenure there as governor.[3]

In fact, Cochrane expected to find the fleet from Cork there awaiting him.[4] When he arrived on November 2, there was no fleet, but he remained over a week arranging water and provisions for the coming vessels, then once more breached his own security by telling the acting governor that Malcolm's flotilla was heading for Negril and thence to attack New Orleans.[5]

Then news came that Admiral Brown had died of yellow fever before receiving Cochrane's orders to have shallow-draft boats ready.[6] The next senior officer was then at sea and in his absence Captain Frederic Langford commanded at Jamaica. He was a well-regarded officer, and until Cochrane reached Jamaica himself, he could only hope that he was also energetic and discreet.[7] By November 11 the admiral could wait no longer for the Cork fleet and departed for Port Royal, Jamaica, to check on progress in gathering landing boats.[8] He could not know that Wellington had just advised Robert Jenkinson, Lord Liverpool, that Britain's commissioners at Ghent should insist upon the handover of Louisiana as a separate article to any treaty, regardless of any other terms.[9]

Cochrane anchored in Port Royal off Kingston a week later to find Malcolm there ahead of him, but that almost no progress had been made in acquiring the shallow-draft boats.[10] Worse, when his orders to the deceased Brown had arrived around October 8, Langford was absent, and they were delivered instead to Captain William Fothergill. Despite "Most Secret" being clearly market on the packet, Fothergill showed the contents to others, and even to non-naval eyes the sum of their import was a major operation aimed at either Mobile or New Orleans; the giveaway came in a reference to needing boats suited to operate in Lake Pontchartrain.[11] Fothergill made it worse by ordering the station's transportation officer to gather light-draft boats for the shallow waters "in the neighborhood of New Orleans."[12]

Within hours of the secret packet's arrival, the expedition to New Orleans was a common topic in Kingston's taverns and in the local press.[13] Cochrane also learned that the evening after the packet arrived, John Thomas Hudson, an Englishman running a ship chandlery on Levee Street in New Orleans, had cleared Port Royal in his schooner and made sail for the Gulf Coast to get the news to Jackson. Port officials made no attempt to stop him.[14]

Everyone knowing the source of the leak did not lessen the embarrassment. Cochrane and other officers roundly condemned Fothergill.[15] Nearly three months of leaks made further pretense of secrecy pointless, especially since weeks of preparations—fitting out transports, loading victualing boats, and more—told of something big in the offing.[16] An artilleryman attached to the expedition, Ensign Benson Hill, almost laughed at what he called "the farce of mystery" now.[17] Sensing that his best hope of surprise rested in reaching New Orleans before reports of his plans reached Jackson, Cochrane put Gordon to hiring or buying flat-bottomed boats and made $80,000 available for the expense.[18]

After four days taking on provisions, water, and troops, including printer William Tremayne and a printing press for printing proclamations, Cochrane detailed a ship to remain at Jamaica to receive any "treasure" he might send from New Orleans, and left Kingston on November 24 bound for Negril, missing by just hours a visitor who might have made up for the collapse of security.[19] Jasper McCalden Graham, a Scot claiming descent from royal Stewarts, had lived some years in the American South before settling on Jamaica's north coast.[20] He claimed to have vital intelligence on New Orleans's defenses and defenders, gained by bribes paid to friends in the United States. "The Golden Key, unlocks the door to many a secret," he hinted, making it clear that he would pass along what he knew, and much more to come, if the admiral put a Golden Key in his door.

Cochrane had just sailed when Graham arrived in Kingston, so he met with an army officer to whom he passed some useful information in good faith, including a copy of Barthélémy Lafon's superb 1806 map of the Orleans Territory, *Carte Général du Territoire d'Orléans*, which revealed enough detail to show all of the water approaches to the city.[21] In addition, he passed on a lengthy and rambling set of observations laden with details of Mississippi River depths, width, and current, and portraits of the defenses surrounding New Orleans, whose artillery he exaggerated by more than double.[22] He also claimed that he had seen Jackson's early October dispatches detailing what troops were coming from Kentucky, Tennessee, and elsewhere, although he could have inferred that from American newspapers received in Jamaica.[23] In sum, he was nearly right about much, and quite wrong about more, but it raised the possibility that someone close to Jackson's headquarters had copied or intercepted his correspondence.[24] Graham's letters eventually reached Cochrane, but the admiral regarded them as curiosities, not hard intelligence, and the War Ministry later concluded that Graham had furnished nothing of value. He never got a farthing.[25]

Cochrane had more urgent matters before him and reached Negril on November 25 to find Malcolm waiting.[26]

Rear Admiral Sir Pulteney Malcolm was a forty-six-year-old Scot who had seen wide service in the Mediterranean and Indies. He had sailed from the Chesapeake on October 14 with a fleet of ten warships counting among them 388 guns, and ten transports with some 2,900 redcoats aboard, a mixed bag of experience behind them.[27] Commanding was Lieutenant Colonel Arthur Brooke, whose own 4th King's Own numbered six hundred veterans, as did the 85th Light Infantry, and the 44th East Essex. The 4th had a fine record, although Ensign Arthur Gerard jauntily called their recent experience on Chesapeake shores a "Buccaneering expedition."[28] The largest regiment was also perhaps the toughest, the eight hundred men of Lieutenant Colonel William Paterson's 21st Fusiliers.

Yet another Irishman, William Thornton from Londonderry, was colonel of the 85th, still suffering from a Bladensburg wound that enhanced his dubious reputation as the most wounded officer in the army. Nevertheless, many regarded him as the best regimental commander of the lot, although his had been a troubled regiment whose officers virtually mutinied under a previous colonel. Re-officered and sent first to Wellington, the 85th got to America in time to participate in burning the United States Capitol.[29] The 44th answered to fifty-two-year-old Major Thomas Mullins, the son of a baron, recently brevetted to lieutenant colonel during the Chesapeake campaign when he assumed command of the regiment from Brooke. He won mention in dispatches from Ross for his performance at Bladensburg in temporary command of a brigade, and when Brooke succeeded the fallen Ross, he commended Mullins again for his conduct.[30]

Meanwhile the 21st Fusiliers prided itself for counting among its company commanders perhaps the most highly regarded younger officer in the army. Scottish-born Captain Robert Rennie was approaching his thirtieth birthday and had already won brevets to major and lieutenant colonel the past summer for gallantry in action.[31] He dwelled under good stars and bad. When generals wanted daring and indifference to danger, they turned to him, but bullets found him in every engagement. Mistakenly reported killed in action at Bladensburg, he was still recovering from a painful wound taken there and another received three weeks later at Godly Wood.[32] Being the soldier's soldier did not spare him frustration, however. No one got his name right. Renny, Reaney, Reddy, Rinnie, and a dozen more were the misspellings, and more to come.[33]

The rest of the complement included five hundred artillerymen and engineers for constructing field fortifications, suggesting at least a chance of laying siege rather than fighting an open field battle for New Orleans. Malcolm flew his flag as Admiral of the Blue aboard the seventy-four-gun *Royal Oak*. Two other "seventy-fours" accompanied her, including *Ramillies*, noted not least for its commander Captain Sir Thomas M. Hardy, in whose arms Lord Nelson died at Trafalgar.[34] Malcolm had spent twenty days at sea without incident, an interesting complement of officers finding much to pass their time. Brevet Lieutenant Colonel De Lacy Evans of the 5th West India led one hundred men who had stormed and taken the Capitol building in Washington.[35] Captain Charles Grey of the 85th was called "Old Grey" because years before he had lost much of his hair to a fever, though but thirty. He and his best friend, Ensign George R. Gleig, took up keeping diaries aboard *Volcano* during the voyage.[36] Eighteen-year-old Gleig was a Scot, son of the bishop of Brechin. Bound originally for divinity school, he enlisted instead in the 85th and saw service and a slight wound at Bladensburg.[37] He often stayed on deck in the moonlight, finding that "the ocean is so smooth, that scarcely a ripple is seen to break the moon-beams as they fall."[38] Some officers brought wives, and occasionally they danced with their husbands and others, Mullins's wife, Parnell, being a special favorite.[39] As usually happened on long voyages, tragedy also struck when the wife of Captain S. H. Douglas of the 21st took fever and died.[40]

Malcolm had dropped anchor off Port Royal on November 3 and remained for a fortnight, giving his soldiers and sailors something of a holiday in Kingston while awaiting Cochrane and the Cork contingent. They drank and whored and after dark marveled at the fireflies dancing like sparks from a smith's anvil.[41] Some lodged ashore to be entertained at balls and dinners as residents feted the conquerors of Washington, and Gleig for one almost dreaded having to leave such friendly climes to "return again to a country where every man is an enemy."[42] Over cool glasses of sangaree they indulged in the inevitable speculations, all assuming they were bound for Louisiana, only to learn that news of their arrival and numbers had sped to New Orleans.[43]

When the order to board ship came on November 16, it arrived so fast that some almost missed the departure.[44] Three days later they anchored in Negril Bay, the first to arrive.[45] A week later, at nine a.m. on November 26, they sighted *Tonnant* sailing into the bay and dropping anchor.[46] To make a suitable impression as *Tonnant* drew close, Cochrane donned full dress, including the star and ribbon of a Knight of the Bath, and stood on his quarterdeck to be seen. "I scarcely ever saw a finer old man than Sir Alexander," recalled Ensign Hill. Still, darker impressions momentarily overshadowed the reunion. A few days earlier Private Hugh Lister of the 21st received a tongue-lashing from his sergeant, and later attacked him from behind and killed him. As Cochrane stood in his finery aboard *Tonnant*, Lister's lifeless body swayed from a yardarm in Malcolm's fleet.[47]

Then, with almost incredible timing, the other half of the army arrived. The war machine in London, coordinated largely by Brigadier General Sir Henry Bunbury, undersecretary of state for war and the colonies, had been wonderfully efficient. He sent Lieutenant Colonel John Burgoyne to London to arrange the artillery, ordnance, and engineering supplies for the expedition.[48] They included the new Congreve rockets developed by William Congreve, which carried exploding anti-personnel projectiles 1,500 yards or more at a much faster rate of fire than conventional artillery, and requiring far fewer men and horses. They were erratic and inaccurate in flight, and their psychological impact probably outdid any damage they actually inflicted. The people of Baltimore still had fresh in their memory the frightening sight of "the rockets' red glare" during the September bombardment of Fort McHenry. Captain Henry Lane's 1st Rocket Troop had five hundred twelve-pounder rockets and forty "rocketeers" to accompany the expedition.

Since mixing rockets with other cargo could be dangerous, Bunbury ordered a vessel to carry them separately.[49]

In the following weeks, more detailed preparations assembled the materiel to go to Negril.[50] Six ships were to carry thousands of arms and tons of munitions, including almost 2 million rifle and musket cartridges, some of them what the Americans called "buck and ball," a single bullet and three or four buckshot, which increased every shot's chances of hitting a mark even if the main projectile missed.[51] Then the redcoats themselves began to arrive, the premier 93rd Sutherland Highlanders being first on the scene. Led by Lieutenant Colonel Robert Dale, and nearly one thousand strong, it won note for a morality hardly the norm in the army.[52] They built their own church at the Cape of Good Hope, maintained a missionary fund to educate regimental children, and maintained another fund for its widows.[53]

Five companies of the 95th Rifles wore their unusual green uniforms and carried rifles rather than muskets. Originally called the "Experimental Corps of Riflemen," now they were known as "the Prince Consort's Own." A squadron of 160 blue-clad troopers from the 14th Dragoons, only just returned in July from France, were aboard, led by Brevet Lieutenant Colonel Charles M. Baker. They were expected to capture or purchase mounts on reaching the Gulf Coast. The fleet also carried a company of 120 artillerymen and Lane's 1st Rocket Troop. Added to the nearly 3,000 from the Chesapeake being brought by Malcolm, they should total 5,300 in round numbers.[54]

On September 12, command went to Major General Sir John Keane, a tall, bearded Anglo-Irishman, formerly of the 44th Foot.[55] He had served in Egypt and Sicily, and won his knighthood under Wellington on the Peninsula, being promoted to major general just the previous summer. His rise came in part due to a daring that approached recklessness, a quality Wellington valued as highly as judgment, and which many of his younger officers emulated. Keane was to be Robert Ross's executive officer when they joined forces, but if Ross could not be there, Keane was to lead the army subject to Cochrane's command.[56] Of course, no one could know that Ross would be killed two days after Keane got his orders.

Escorted by the seventy-fours *Bedford* and *Norge*, and ten other ships, the transports weighed anchor and spent seven weeks at sea, sailing a longer-than-usual route for secrecy, but conjecture on the decks already predicted New Orleans as their destination.[57] They anchored off Barbados on November 4, the same day that Cochrane reached Kingston, nine hundred miles to the west.[58] Keane sailed on to meet Cochrane, leaving his command to spend a week getting their land legs and talking too much.

Within seventy-two hours of their arrival, it was open knowledge on Barbados that they were headed for New Orleans.[59] Within three days the word spread up the Antilles to the Leewards and Saint-Barthélemy.[60] Cochrane's efforts at security dissolved in every port.[61]

Two weeks later they met Malcolm and Cochrane at Point Negril with the news that Ross had been shot and killed in skirmishing near Baltimore, whereupon Keane assumed overall command of the army and organized it into two brigades.[62] The first included the 93rd, and the 1st and 5th West India, totaling 1,550, while the Second Brigade held the 4th, 44th, and 21st regiments, totaling 2,535. The 14th Dragoons and the artillery remained unbrigaded for the moment, and Colonel Thornton was assigned his 85th, the 95th, and the rocket troop as an "advance" force of 984.[63] All told, including artillery and engineers, Keane commanded just over 5,500.[64] The sight of Cochrane in his finery and Lister swinging on his rope reminded all that they stood on the verge of glory and death. "I think we shall have some promotion before our return to England," the 85th's Captain John Knox wrote a friend, "for if bullets do not give it the climate will."[65]

Now Cochrane's logistical plans began to break down. No flatboats met him at Negril, and those brought from Kingston were hardly adequate. He had scant news of Jackson's whereabouts, thought New Orleans was yet undefended and that he could salvage a surprise if he moved quickly. Without the flatboats he would have to make an unopposed coastal landing somewhere west of Mobile and march overland on New Orleans, or else approach via a navigable bayou close to the city. He did not yet have a reconnaissance report from Captain Gordon, but when he did the picture would be clearer. Until then, the admiral adjusted to the situation and determined to leave for Pensacola, where he might learn more.[66]

Cochrane and *Tonnant* set sail again on November 26 in company with *Ramillies* and the brigs *Anaconda*, *Dover*, and *Calliope*, carrying Keane's contingent.[67] Malcolm raised anchor the following morning with orders to rejoin Cochrane off Mobile, which would be their staging area for the expedition.[68] Fifty ships lifted anchor at the same moment and with all canvas set they left the anchorage, caught a fresh breeze off the headland, and left Jamaica astern before dark, everyone's spirits high.[69] Two days later Malcolm passed Grand Cayman with a good wind behind him and headed for the Yucatán Channel and the Gulf of Mexico.[70]

Just nine days after Keane sailed from Cork, news of Washington's fall reached London. Lord Bathurst, the secretary of state for war, quickly decided to send additional men and Major General John Lambert for what all orders referred to as "a particular service."[71] The frigate HMS *Vengeur* lay at anchor, ready for him and his staff, with a fleet of transports to convoy his men and stores.[72] Lambert would have 877 men of the 7th Royal Fusiliers, 991 in the 43rd Monmouthshire Light Infantry, and 159 in another unmounted squadron of the 14th Dragoons. With assorted trumpeters, drummers, and other ranks, there were 2,094 men in all.[73] Tragically, there were casualties even before they sailed. On October 10, when lighters took the 43rd Regiment to its transports, one drifted onto the rocks in Cork Sound and went to the bottom, drowning several soldiers. Captain John Henry Cooke of the 43rd took it as an ill omen.

Major Sir John Maxwell Tylden took over as chief of staff for Lambert, and soon thereafter as adjutant general. He found the forty-four-year-old general easy and "open of manner," and the two would work well together.[74] Just days later came the shocking news of Ross's death, meaning another overall commander for the expedition's army was needed. Lambert outranked Keane by date of commission, but an army soon to approach or exceed 10,000 required someone more senior. The new grand commander, whoever that might be, would have to follow Lambert.

The squadron got under way early on October 26 under a veil of secrecy that made Tylden uneasy, wondering how many in the convoy would never go home again. He could not concentrate, even to write to family. England was exhausted by war. The commissioners at Ghent might make a peace with the Americans that rendered this expedition pointless. One day out of Cork he confessed that "I never left England with so much regret."[75] Meanwhile the men made the best of the long voyage. Sailors danced and played games, while Captain Cooke and the surgeon of the 43rd played at least two chess matches every day.[76]

By November 1 everyone assumed New Orleans was their ultimate target.[77] Just over three weeks brought them to the Tropic of Cancer, when, in an old tradition, a seaman dressed as Neptune demanded grog from those who had it, while those who did not were shaved and baptized with seawater.[78] They made Port Royal on December 11, to learn that Cochrane had left weeks earlier. Tylden feared that "we shall come a day too late for the fair," but two days later they reached Negril Bay and soon saw the frigate *Statira* enter the anchorage, hailing them with the news that the new commanding general was aboard.

Speculation about Ross's successor had immediately turned to Major General Sir Edward Michael Pakenham.[79] Like so many others now, he was an Irishman, and actually six years younger than Lambert. Educated first at a grammar school, and then at the Royal Classic School, he entered the army at sixteen, his father, Lord Longford, buying him a commission. Two more purchased promotions made him a major of dragoons; then in 1803 he rose to the colonelcy of the 7th Royal Fusiliers, which he led to Ireland in 1806. There he saw his sister married to a dynamic officer of growing reputation, fellow Irishman Arthur Wellesley.

A year later Pakenham was off to fight Napoleon, then to Canada and the Caribbean and home again in 1809, where Wellesley was knighted for defeating the French at Talavera and later created Lord Wellington. After five years on Wellington's staff, Pakenham got his own infantry brigade in 1811. His rise continued until January 1812 when, aged just thirty-three, he was promoted to major general. He engineered British victory in the Battle of Salamanca and thereafter served as adjutant general, winning his own knighthood in September 1813. Having no interest in fighting the Yankees, when the war against Bonaparte ended in April 1814 he actually congratulated himself that "I have escaped America."[80]

Pakenham enjoyed wide respect and admiration as one of England's best and bravest soldiers. Being Wellington's brother-in-law also afforded him considerable protection, for none dared to impose on him.[81] Wellington himself believed that Pakenham might not be brilliant, but certainly he was "one of the best we have."[82] It is no wonder that Bathurst called him to London on learning of Ross's death. What was needed was an experienced officer who had served with Wellington and learned from his example.[83] Sir Edward was not best pleased, however, grumbling to his mother that "I confess to you there is Nothing that makes this employment desirable."[84]

He was to leave immediately to assume command of the forces where he found them, his instructions virtually the same as Cochrane's regarding the inhabitants of Louisiana, their property, and their slaves, though with the addition that if they wanted Britain to occupy and govern them while the war lasted, he could encourage them, and even act himself as an interim governor.[85] Bathurst made it clear that plunder was not the purpose of this campaign, although that did not extend to property of the United States government or of any who sought to obstruct his operations. But such seized property must be properly condemned before an admiralty court, and he and Cochrane were to determine on distribution of the proceeds.[86]

There was one more point. Pakenham might hear that a treaty had been agreed on at Ghent and sent to President Madison for ratification. Unless and until Pakenham received definitive news of that ratification, he was to continue hostilities. At the moment Bathurst thought Madison might not sign and the war would continue. He should not risk serious losses for a minor gain, but if the opportunity for a significant success like taking New Orleans presented itself, he should seize the moment. He should be cautious but not too cautious, and to that end half a dozen more regiments would be on their way to him in time. Whitehall intended to guarantee victory.[87]

Unfortunately, caution was not what was needed to take New Orleans.

On October 31 Pakenham reached Portsmouth to find the *Statira* waiting to take him to the Gulf.[88] Also waiting was Major General Sir Samuel Gibbs, a thirty-year veteran of service in Canada, Gibraltar, the Low Countries, the Mediterranean, India, and more, promoted to major general in June 1812. Another mountain of clothing, shoes, dragoon equipment, and rifles waited nearby on transports.[89] While their ship made final preparations for the voyage, Pakenham passed the time with Majors George Napier and Harry Smith and others who would travel with him. Smith found him unaccustomedly solemn and confessing private doubts of the wisdom of the expedition and the accuracy of Cochrane's information on Louisiana. Napier told the general not to expose himself in action as had been his wont. Many of Wellington's younger generals did so, and it got several of them killed or seriously injured, and Pakenham twice wounded. He promised to be careful but added that sometimes a commander had to put himself at the forefront of his troops under fire and that "I must not flinch, though certain death be my lot!"[90]

Pakenham carefully kept their destination to himself, speaking ashore about Charleston for the benefit of any unfriendly ears overhearing. Early on November 1, Pakenham, Gibbs, Burgoyne, artilleryman Lieutenant Colonel Alexander Dickson, their staffs, and some thirty other passengers, including some officers' wives and possibly a few civilian administrators, boarded *Statira*, and at 8:15 raised anchor.[91] The general remained quiet as to their destination, but Burgoyne took it for granted that they were going to Louisiana.[92] Six weeks' sailing brought them to Negril on the morning of December 13 to see *Vengeur* and Lambert's transports at anchor.[93] In a wonderful feat of seamanship, two separate flotillas leaving six days apart, from ports separated by 150 miles, had crossed more than 4,000 nautical miles at four knots an hour to reach the same destination within ninety minutes of each other.

As Cooke and the surgeon of the 43rd played the last of their ninety-five games of chess, Lambert informed Pakenham that they were sixteen days behind Cochrane, who left no orders for them at the rendezvous. At least they ended any remaining suspense among their officers by telling them their goal. Tylden, for one, thought they would take the city without resistance and that the internal dissent and disaffection from the United States was such that its people would surrender as soon as they heard of the British approach.[94]

Cochrane had entertained the same hope. About noon on December 3, people in Apalachicola saw *Tonnant* anchor just outside the bar covering the harbor mouth, and by the next morning she was joined by dozens of vessels of all description. That evening a gig dropped a man ashore, then rowed back to the fleet. He was a Yankee civilian, arrested back in July on suspicion of being a spy and finally released now when Cochrane believed he could learn nothing from him. The next day the man went to a doctor known to be acquainted with Old Hickory and told him what he had seen of Cochrane's fleet and the soldiers aboard, and the prevailing opinion that they were headed for New Orleans. The doctor immediately sent the news to General Winchester at Mobile, adding that he had heard officers boasting that they would eat their Christmas dinners in New Orleans. He warned Jackson to be on the alert, for "by the Gods I think you will have warm work."[95]

Cochrane had known for a few days of the loss of Pensacola but was not dismayed. He certainly did not fear Jackson's army, which Codrington believed would be ineffectual in the face of experienced redcoats.[96] Aboard *Tonnant*, Colonel Frederick Stovin, Keane's adjutant general, expected to attack New Orleans in less than a week, and with no doubt of success. They should outnumber Jackson and could pit discipline against inexperience. He thought Cochrane both amiable and talented, and paid rapt attention when some in the admiral's cabin declared that, if they succeeded, there would be "a good deal of Prize Money."[97]

The fall of Mobile did upset the admiral, for it lost his preferred staging area for an overland march on New Orleans. Now he sent Gordon and *Seahorse* ahead to look for likely landing places near Lake Pontchartrain.[98] First, Gordon stole into Pensacola by night in disguise to kidnap a coastal pilot in Pensacola familiar with the Mississippi and the lakes, and some of the Spanish fishermen inhabiting the shores of both. Gordon brought him back to *Seahorse*, where interrogation gleaned the names and whereabouts of men who could guide landing boats through the bayous to dry ground below New Orleans.[99]

Cochrane meanwhile moved on to the coast off Pensacola. On December 5, Tremayne's printing press birthed a proclamation written by Codrington and addressed "To the Great and Illustrious Chiefs of the Creek and Other Indian Nations." Cochrane came with irresistible power, it declared. The Americans were "The People of the Bad Spirit" who had robbed Indians of their lands. He came with fleets and armies to defeat their oppressors and called on them to rally to him. He would give them weapons and all they need do was help him to regain their lands.[100] Nicolls was to collect the Creeks and any runaway slaves enlisted thus far and be prepared to join the expedition west of Mobile.

Cochrane and Nicolls both departed the Pensacola area on the afternoon of December 7, leaving orders for arriving vessels to meet him at anchor 120 miles westward between Ship Island and the Chandeleur Islands off the Mississippi coast, just forty miles from the entrance to Lake Borgne. The next day the admiral left the ship with a small squadron of armed boats to reconnoiter the coast personally.[101] Behind him, Nicolls arrived with two Creek chieftains and some of their warriors, to spend the next three days dining and drinking.[102] Despite Nicolls's sunny expectations, this handful were the only Indians the British would see.[103] Disappointingly few blacks came with him, either. Most slaves wanted their freedom, of course, but many regarded the British with no more trust than they did their masters.

Cochrane was due for a stroke of good luck. All hope of surprise was gone, for he now believed—erroneously—that Jackson had left for New Orleans in mid-November.[104] He had already decided not to contend with shifting winds and the serpentine bends of the Mississippi to approach New Orleans. Mobile and Pensacola were lost to him as bases for an overland campaign. The manner of approaching the city had always been left to him, and his willingness to adapt his plans this far into the expedition revealed commendable flexibility.[105] Armed with a report from Gordon, he determined to land somewhere on the shore of Lake Pontchartrain if he could and find a direct route to strike the city itself.[106] Then he somehow came in possession of Lafon's 1806 *Carte Général du Territoire d'Orléans*, perhaps the copy sent by the accommodating Jasper Graham, and the very same map carried by Jackson.[107]

Two lakes dominated the map north and east of the city, but the big men-o'-war drew too much water to get nearer to them than the Chandeleur Islands more than forty miles eastward, although there was good, deep water for his lighter frigates near Malheureux Island thirty miles closer to the entrance to Lake Borgne. Four miles north of the city sat Lake Pontchartrain, an estuary of the Gulf forty miles long and twenty-four wide, but not much more than a dozen feet in depth. At its eastern extremity a navigable channel ten miles long and 350 yards wide called the Rigolets ran to Lake Borgne, sometimes called "Blind Lake." An earthwork named Fort Petites Coquilles—"Little Shells"—guarded the shallow channel's entrance. Seven miles southwest of the Rigolets flowed another pass locally known as Chef Menteur.

Lake Borgne was no lake at all but a 280-square-mile lagoon off the Gulf that controlled access to those channels to Pontchartrain. Its generally ten-foot depth further limited vessels reaching its larger neighbor. Any boat passing through the Rigolets or Chef Menteur could cross Lake Pontchartrain straight to the mouth of Bayou St. John on its southern shore, and up that four-foot stream almost to the Gentilly road for a short walk to the city. The road also ran to Chef Menteur, thus offering another avenue to New Orleans from Lake Borgne's shore.[108]

A cypress swamp stretched from Lake Borgne's southern shore toward the Mississippi, in some places to within a mile of the river. The dry plain between swamp and stream was the only firm ground on that side between New Orleans and the Gulf. Several sluggish bayous flowed from the swamp into the lake, the largest known to the French years before as the St. Francis River or Bayou des Pêcheurs—the Bayou of the Fishermen—but now most called it Bayou Bienvenue or Catalan.[109] Several tributaries fed it—Bayous Jumonville, Mazant, Laurier, among others—and the first two actually touched that plain of dry level land skirting the Mississippi. Anyone getting up those bayous had a mile or less to travel overland to the wagon and coach road running along the river levee nine miles northwest to New Orleans.

Cochrane also learned of sufficient dry ground beside the bayou's mouth on the lake to use it as a staging area for troops.[110] From such a point he could neutralize the enemy fort guarding Chef Menteur and send small boats to the west side of the big lake to land close to the river and the road above New Orleans, cutting it off. Cochrane preferred that option, but the bayou might be worth considering if he could reconnoiter it first.[111] Either way, Keane's soldiers would have to travel at least sixty miles in their light-draft boats from the Ship Island anchorage to reach the bayou or Chef Menteur. They would be vulnerable to larger vessels, and Gordon and *Seahorse* now reported seeing Yankee gunboats on Lake Borgne. They must be neutralized.

Soon the rest of the expedition began arriving. Malcolm's squadron hit rough seas out of Negril, but by the morning of December 11 they spied Cochrane's fleet at anchor and came into the anchorage throughout the day and into the evening.[112] By noon the next day they were all there, Midshipman Robert Aitchison musing that the fleet had "gathered size like a snow ball."[113] By that time the British had also spied the Americans, and been seen by them. *Seahorse*, *Armide*, and *Sophie* sailed west in advance of the main fleet, and three days earlier off Dauphin Island they sighted two armed sloops in the distance. Patterson was keeping two gunboats on lookout well to the east of Lake Borgne. The two small vessels boldly fired on the thirty-six-gun fast frigate *Armide* before withdrawing to the other three gunboats, and thereafter watched the enemy buildup off Ship Island until they saw an armada of warships, barges, and transports.

At the same time, standing in the rigging at their mastheads, Cochrane's captains watched the five Yankee gunboats in the distance.[114] He thought of sending a squadron of smaller boats to confront it, but the weather remained rough and the chance of failure too great. Codrington was convinced the gunboats could be taken, but kept his view to himself, as he did increasingly now. The two admirals agreed on one thing, however. Having been sighted where they were, all remaining hope of surprise evaporated. A British fleet on this scale sailing southwestward along the coast could only be bound for Lake Borgne. That told the Yankees the direction of Cochrane's attack.[115] Still, he might salvage some surprise, for he began considering Bayou Bienvenue as his objective. His plans were still evolving, of course.

But first he must do something about those gunboats.[116]

Four

"One of the Most Brilliant Things on Record"

T HE SUN HAD been down for hours by the time Jackson and his small entourage rode into town. The general was to stay that first night at the impressive home of Bernard de Marigny on the Champs-Élysées, the principal avenue of the virtually all-*creole* Faubourg Marigny neighborhood immediately below the older Spanish town. Marigny, who sat on the legislature's defense committee, eagerly anticipated the honor of hosting the general, but Jackson was ill, having suffered from dysentery for weeks, and at times found it difficult to stay astride his horse.[1] Needing a physician's care immediately, his staff took him instead to Dr. David Kerr's house on Conti Street in a mixed section of Americans and *creoles*.[2]

The next morning, rested but hardly well, Jackson emerged to join an escort of local officers and leading citizens to ride to Fort St. Charles at the foot of Champs-Élysées, where he would stay until permanent quarters were ready. It was within sight of Marigny's home, and the *creole* regarded Jackson's move as a rejection of his proffered hospitality, a resentment soon shared by the French citizens. Nevertheless, Jackson's arrival inspired calm.[3] Privately, he feared the enemy might seize Mobile behind him, march to the Mississippi's left bank above New Orleans, severing the city's upstream communications, and thus isolate and squeeze it into submission, but he kept that to himself, publicly presenting the face of confidence.[4] William Kenner was buoyed to hear him speak of beating back the British, although privately Jackson confessed that his expressions were "somewhat more than I felt."[5]

Once in his headquarters on Royal Street, Old Hickory almost immediately began filling out his staff.[6] He had brought a few along with him, including adjutant general Colonel Robert Butler and his confidential aide, young Major John Reid. Knowing little of the polyglot population, Jackson still had some grasp of the need for what Reid called "delicate attentions" to ethnic sensibilities, and met with leading men from all factions to assemble a cadre of local volunteer aides.[7] Leaning heavily on Livingston's advice, he made Captain Henry Chotard an assistant adjutant, and appointed Pierre Duplessis and Livingston's brother-in-law Auguste Davezac as aides. Recognizing Davezac's legal acumen, Jackson shortly made him judge advocate general and the two quickly became intimate friends.[8] Livingston also recommended the French engineer Arsène Lacarrière Latour, then working on Fort St. Leon below English Turn. Jackson immediately commissioned him major and chief engineer, making Livingston's son Lewis an assistant to Latour.[9]

There were a few complaints with those appointments, Claiborne's aide Shaumburg dismissing Davezac as an "ugly profligate fellow," but greater disappointment grew from all other staff assignments going to Americans.[10] The Laffites' friend lawyer John Grymes and planter Abner Duncan became aides, likely because they were Livingston's political and social allies.[11] Livingston himself long wanted a place on Jackson's staff. They had known each other in Congress but had not seen each other for sixteen years. Old Hickory had encouraged the lawyer to correspond with him as chairman of the defense committee, and Livingston sent him information and charts, including the 1806 Lafon map and perhaps a map of his own making that detailed the levees, roads, and plantations a few miles below the city.[12] To prepare himself, Livingston studied books on tactics and military history and read biographies of Napoleon, Nelson, and even Wellington. Jackson did not disappoint him.[13] He already leaned on him as translator, so it seemed logical to make Livingston his principal aide.[14] Unfortunately, many in the French community and some Americans like Claiborne loathed Livingston, suspicious of the man's connection to the Laffites. Before long a few even believed that Livingston manipulated and directed Old Hickory.[15]

Governor Claiborne, who daydreamed of glory, surely mindful of how it would play at the polls in future years, saw opportunity in Jackson's appointments.[16] The legislature had just asked him to lead local volunteers personally, and he intended to do so if invaders came. While he did not want to challenge Jackson, he resolved not to recognize the authority of any officer of any rank, regular army or militia, to command his militia. He soon asked Secretary of War James Monroe, who would succeed Jackson in the event of his incapacity or departure, blatantly hinting that Monroe should direct Old Hickory to acknowledge Claiborne as his successor.[17] The two seemed destined to compete, and it showed in Jackson's staff appointments. Most were Claiborne's political enemies, and he privately complained that Jackson had surrounded himself with men who would try to undermine him with the general. From the moment of those appointments, the governor felt his relations with Jackson start to deteriorate, beginning with Jackson's failure to give him an important position as he organized his forces.[18] Old Hickory was not about to make him a second-in-command.[19]

As he built his volunteer staff, the gaunt and jaundiced general began learning what he could of the city's defenses and was astonished to see scant preparation.[20] There was a good stock of big guns in the artillery yard on Levee Street, but Fort St. Charles was pitiful. It commanded the river with seventeen embrasures for cannon, but their rotting wooden platforms dated back to the late 1700s and many would likely collapse at the first firing. Manpower was almost as discouraging. The only regulars were Captain Alexander White's 528-man detachment of the 7th United States Infantry and 395 soldiers of the 44th Infantry, both trying to recruit more men with mixed success.[21] Although the 44th was still saddled with the inebriate Ross, it could at least boast of a captain who had done something unique in that garrison. In 1803, Nathaniel Pryor enlisted with Captains Meriwether Lewis and William Clark to explore and map the new Louisiana Purchase. He had been to the great Pacific and back.[22]

Before inspecting defenses downstream from the city, Jackson addressed the vulnerability of its land side via the lakes. The coastline he saw on his journey to New Orleans convinced him that the British could not land for an overland march anywhere west of Mobile. They would come via Lake Borgne, he believed, and most likely pass through the Rigolets channel to Pontchartrain, and thence to the Bayou St. John road, or else across the lake for the short march to the Mississippi.[23] However, just in case they should attempt the Chef Menteur pass seven miles southwest of the Rigolets instead, he sent Captain Pierre Jugeat and his small company of Choctaw volunteers with Major Pierre Lacoste's battalion of free men of color to guard it, and ordered Colonel Jacques Plauché's white militia to Fort St. John and Fort Petites Coquilles to watch the Pontchartrain approaches.[24] At the same time General Villeré took command of units near Lake Borgne.[25]

While his public activity boosted enthusiasm, Jackson's private demeanor won him favor.[26] On his second evening in town he dined at the home of Edward Livingston, whose wife, Louise, had been expecting a rude and rustic Tennessean, but Old Hickory surprised them and conducted himself as a perfect gentleman. "Is this your backwoodsman?" Louise asked her husband after the general escorted her to dinner on his arm. "He is a prince!"[27] In succeeding days the optimism spawned by his arrival continued. Seeing the regulars and militia on parade, few as they were, inspired confidence, and rumor helped by grossly exaggerating the numbers of Kentucky and Tennessee volunteers coming. After just three days the citizens were taking renewed heart in their security.[28]

If Jackson's first days in New Orleans were any measure, the legislature was going to be less cooperative, although relations commenced well enough. On December 3 it passed a unanimous joint resolution of thanks to Jackson for coming and sent a committee including General Morgan to present the honor.[29] In the ensuing week, however, Governor Claiborne's calls for more volunteers and other measures to aid Jackson and Patterson got lost in committees. Some wanted to suspend the privilege of the writ of habeas corpus, declare martial law, and embargo all vessel departures so Patterson could draft experienced seamen. Others disagreed, and hence they debated without passing any of Claiborne's defense proposals.[30]

By that time Old Hickory was already touring defenses downriver. He had been advised by Colonel Hayne that obstructing the multiple entrances from the Gulf into the Mississippi was impractical.[31] Instead, Hayne suggested Fort St. Philip was the spot to defend against a river approach, with English Turn as backup. Accompanied by Latour, Patterson, and a few aides, Jackson sailed downriver to Fort St. Philip on December 4. He found it in excellent condition and well manned under Major William Overton, a fellow Tennessean known to Jackson and regarded as an intelligent and courageous man by some of his officers, although others thought him cold and aloof. Perhaps less well regarded was Overton's executive officer, who commanded the fort's artillery, Englishman Captain Charles Wollstonecraft. He came from a nonconformist family that included his deceased sister Mary, who published in 1792 a pioneering tract on feminine equality titled *A Vindication of the Rights of Woman*.[32]

Still, Old Hickory felt confident in both Overton and Wollstonecraft. Their fort's guns commanded the river, and there was no place below it for an enemy to land and bypass it by marching overland. After ordering more guns mounted on its parapet, and its field of fire on an approaching foe enlarged by cutting timber some distance downstream, Jackson moved on to English Turn. There he found militia finally obeying Claiborne's order to build a defensive line from the river back to the swamp. Pleased with that, the general stayed barely five minutes before departing, which the major commanding took as an insult to a regiment already suffering poor morale, in part because a number of its men were Spaniards unwillingly drafted into the militia. Just days earlier one of them verbally abused the colonel commanding, who sentenced him to "ten slaps on the bear but [sic] with a paddle."[33]

Jackson returned to Fort St. Philip, where he ordered Latour to design a gun emplacement across the river to give Overton a cross fire on enemy vessels coming upstream, and another battery half a mile farther up. He also considered enhancing old Fort St. Leon, commanding English Turn, which could impede a fleet coming upriver or a land force marching along the west or "right" bank. Since Bayou Terre-aux-Boeufs entered the river at the upper end of the Turn, Fort St. Leon could protect that avenue as well. The New Orleans Navy Yard had a good inventory of artillery of all calibers, and Patterson offered to loan as much naval ordnance as he could spare for the defenses.[34] Chief engineer Major Howell Tatum was so encouraged by what he saw at English Turn that he concluded no invader could get past it even if it successfully sailed by Fort. St. Philip.[35]

Jackson agreed, or pretended to agree, although he still had private doubts about all the forts but St. Philip.[36] Returning to New Orleans on the evening of December 9, he told Claiborne the next day that he believed both banks of the river were defensible.[37] He asked the governor to requisition planters' slaves to dig earthworks at Fort St. Philip and English Turn, and to ask the legislature for appropriations to cover the expense. "Not a moment is to be lost," Old Hickory warned. "With energy and expedition, all is safe—delay, and all is lost."[38] The batteries at and above Fort St. Philip, English Turn, and Fort St. Leon would give him a defense in depth, each in succession battering any invader trying to come up the river.[39] That same day he got the good news that Coffee's mounted Tennesseans were nearing Baton Rouge, prompting him to send Coffee a rather flippant message that by Christmas they "may or may not have a fandango" with the British.[40]

The general returned on December 9 to a citizenry almost smug in their conviction of safety: "This country is more secure than any part of the United States"; "Every thing convinces me that the British will be glad enough to sheer off should they have the temerity to attack us"; "I don't believe we have any thing to fear from the enemy in this place."[41] One merchant had already sealed his letter but felt moved to write outside the packet that "all apprehensions of an attack have subsided."[42] Claiborne echoed those words, writing that night to Fromentin to say that "the apprehensions of Invasion seems to have subsided."[43]

Still, some men in the city felt sufficiently convinced that the British would come that they openly speculated on their avenue of approach.[44] Most expected Cochrane to land infantry on the Lake Pontchartrain shore to advance by Bayou St. John but believed Jackson could close that route with 1,000 men behind a breastwork of cotton bales. If the enemy got past that, there would still be four miles to march on a narrow built-up road surrounded by deep swamp on either side. The great fear was that the enemy would strike there and send his fleet up the Mississippi to pinch the city between two fires simultaneously.[45] Despite such musings and more, onlookers saw that New Orleans's people seemed bent on defending their home to the last.[46]

Having seen to defenses downriver, Old Hickory turned to the lakes. An anonymous letter from Pensacola reached Patterson on December 7 warning that Admiral Cochrane had been off Apalachicola the day before and was bound for New Orleans. In response, Patterson sent six gunboats and an armed sloop to watch the waters around Ship Island just east of the entrance to Lake Borgne.[47] That revelation made it all the more vital that Jackson visit the forts protecting the lakes. After just one night in the city he set off again with Tatum, Latour, Livingston, and others for Chef Menteur. A bayou no more than 150 yards wide flowed into the pass at a spot where the water ran just five feet deep. Jackson set Latour to work designing a small battery emplacement for the mouth of the bayou to stop small boats getting through to Lake Pontchartrain. The Gentilly road ran alongside that bayou to the eastern outskirt of New Orleans, but fortunately it was too narrow and marshy for British artillery should they attempt that approach.[48]

Moving five miles southwest along the coast of Lake Borgne, they found the mouth of the bayou of many names, Bienvenue. The ground was marshy there, too, but Tatum feared it might still support an invader's landing. Wherever Jackson went, he took the Lafon map with him; but it had its limitations, and no one on the ground seemed fully to understand the terrain between the lake and the Mississippi.[49] Rather, the inhabitants showed an infuriating want of curiosity about anything beyond the boundaries of their own plantations, and some pretended to know almost nothing even of their own property. Jackson was astonished at everyone's ignorance of the topography. "The numerous bayous & canals communicating with the lakes appear to be almost as little understood by the inhabitants as by the citizens of Tennessee," he complained. "Every man will undertake to give an exact description of the whole of them; & every man gives an erroneous one."[50] Major Tatum suspected that their feigned ignorance was really to protect private smuggling passages from discovery.[51]

Having seen and learned what he could, Old Hickory returned to the city on December 11 and ordered the obstruction of all the bayous, canals, and creeks that small boats might use to approach New Orleans by felling trees into or across them. Large earth-filled wooden frames were to be sunk in the channels of the wider streams.[52] Particularly concerned about the complex of bayous between Lake Borgne and the river, including Mazant and Bienvenue, he gave three successive orders for their blockage—first to Captain White and the 7th, then to militia colonel Denis de La Ronde, and finally to Villeré.[53] Villeré's own plantation canal connected with Bayou Bienvenue, hence it seemed logical that he would be most familiar with the stream and where best to block it.[54] In response to his call, planters offered thousands of enslaved men to perform the labor, moved by patriotism and the fear of an enemy-inspired slave uprising.[55] At the same time Jackson ordered guards and picket parties out on all routes to provide early warning of enemy sighting, and sent reinforcements to Fort St. Philip, while Claiborne put General Morgan in command of the militia at Fort St. Leon.[56] He did not intend to be surprised.[57]

There was much more to do, and none could guess how much time they would have. In fact, it would be just hours. The same day he returned to the city, word arrived that Cochrane's ships had been seen near the Chandeleur Islands. The British were coming.

THAT SAME DAY Admiral Cochrane decided that the weather had eased enough to go after the enemy gunboats. Codrington ordered the fleet's launches, barges, and pinnaces to assemble around *Tonnant* by one o'clock the following afternoon with water and provisions for three days aboard and up to four marines per boat. Cochrane gave Nicholas Lockyer command and instructed him to board crews, oars, sails, and guns and leave the anchorage to clear the enemy gunboats from the path to Lake Borgne.[58] Expecting casualties, Codrington detailed *Gorgon* to act as a hospital ship once it unloaded its complement of soldiers.[59]

Lockyer organized the boats into three divisions, himself commanding the first, Captain Henry Montressor from *Manly* the second, and Captain Samuel Roberts of *Meteor* the third. The thirty-two-year-old Lockyer had been in the navy since the age of eight, rose to commander's rank in 1806, and took over the new brig *Sophie* in the fall of 1809. Since the outbreak of war, she had taken seventeen Yankee privateers and merchantmen, not to mention his mission to Laffite and his part in the attempt to take Fort Bowyer. Everything about Lockyer suggested energy and determination. That same evening he took his flotilla out of the anchorage and rowed west to find the Americans while behind him soldiers and sailors alike cheered from the decks of the towering frigates and ships of the line.[60]

The fleet itself sailed west the next day into the shallower waters of Cat Island Passage, which offered smaller vessels safe inland and coastal navigation behind a chain of islands paralleling the coast. Arriving at Cat Island itself, about thirty miles from the Rigolets, Cochrane had the fleet run aground on the soft bottom to await Lockyer's return.[61] Île au Chat, as the *creoles* called it, puzzled some as to the origin of its name, for there seemed not to be a cat on it.[62] In fact, there was one nearby stalking its mouse: Nicholas Lockyer.

That mouse was every bit Lockyer's match. Thomas ap Catesby Jones was a precocious young Virginian who retained the Welsh usage "ap," meaning "son of." He had been on the New Orleans station as a midshipman since 1808, already commanded several gunboats before the war, and in the late summer of 1812 cruised west of the Mississippi along the Mexican coast. In January 1813 the navy promoted him to lieutenant at the age of twenty-two, after which he patrolled the Gulf through that summer and participated in Wilkinson's expedition against Mobile. There were four other lieutenants senior to him, but since they chose shore duty, he had the only sea command under Patterson. He took part in the Barataria raid, and thereafter his five gunboats had to combat privateering as well as keep lookout for a British approach. He had been under a cloud this past year after he disciplined a midshipman, and the junior officer retaliated by accusing Jones of homosexuality, although a couple of witnesses seemed to support the accusation. An inquiry loomed over his head even now.[63]

When he learned of *Armide*'s sighting on December 8, he warned Patterson that New Orleans must be the enemy's object, and that Cochrane would approach via the lakes. Too weak to offer effective resistance in open water where he was, Jones concluded to withdraw to the Malheureux Islands, the narrowest point of the entrance to Lake Borgne. There he could make a stand, although it could only be a delaying action, considering the odds against him. He probably did not know that *malheureux* meant unfortunate.[64]

The next day Jones pulled back toward Bay St. Louis just north of the Malheureuxs to be better posted to meet the enemy, and at the same time better placed to withdraw to Petites Coquilles if necessary.[65] Having only five gun vessels did not help. The gunboat fleet on the New Orleans Station was intended to number five times that, but lax funding, inattention, and other delays meant only these five were operational, far too few for the job at hand.[66] They varied in design and size, most being single-masted sloops with a couple of twin-masted schooners. Anywhere up to seventy feet long and eighteen feet wide, they carried so much weight in armament and crew that they moved sluggishly and answered their helms slowly. Still, their light draft made them good in shallow waters.[67] For maneuverability in unfavorable winds, some were equipped with oars.

Apparently not deemed important enough to warrant names, they bore only numbers on their bows. *Gunboat #5*, commanded by Lieutenant John D. Ferris, had thirty-six men and five guns; *Gunboat #23* carried thirty-nine men and the same complement of artillery answering to Lieutenant Isaac McKeever; *Gunboat #162* had five guns and thirty-five men led by Lieutenant Robert Spedden; and *Gunboat #163* was in the hands of Master George Ulrich with three cannon and thirty-one men. Jones himself commanded them all from *#156* with five guns and the largest crew at forty-one. Sailing Master William Johnson's schooner *Seahorse*, with one six-pounder and fourteen men, and Sailing Master Richard Shepperd's sloop *Alligator*, mounting one four-pounder with eight men, completed the squadron.[68] All of the gunboats had one long-range twenty-four-pounder and McKeever's mounted a long thirty-two, while the rest of their guns were an assortment of twelve-pounders, six-pounders, five-inch howitzers, and smaller deck-mounted swivel guns for raking an enemy's decks.[69]

Jones was still heading for Malheureaux when he saw Lockyer's flotilla approach out of the morning gloom on December 13. There were forty launches armed with a single carronade, one with a nine-pounder, another with a twelve-pounder, and three gigs with only small arms in the hands of its men—forty-five boats, forty-two cannon, and 1,200 men and officers.[70] Jones sent word to New Orleans at once. At ten o'clock they appeared to head for the shore at Pass Christian northwest of Cat Island. By early afternoon, however, they had passed that point and were still coming, convincing Jones that he was the mouse. As he tried to retreat westward toward Malheureaux, the island lived up to its name and the wind turned against him. The water depth was unusually low there, and three of his gunboats had to jettison everything nonessential to keep from grounding. Finally, at 3:30 that afternoon, a flood tide gave them enough water to get under way and tack into the wind.

After only a quarter of an hour Jones saw three enemy boats break away and make for shore at Bay St. Louis, where his *Seahorse* was busily removing vital stores. Seeing the British barges approach, Master Johnson sent gunners to a bluff overlooking the bay where two old six-pounders protected the storehouse below. As a crowd gathered to watch, the brace of cannon opened fire on the barges. Onlookers soon got something more when they saw Isabella Hutchins Claiborne, the wife of Dr. Thomas A. Claiborne of Natchez, approach the guns. She was just thirty-five, but after four years of declining health looked older; a friend who knew her from Natchez thought she looked as if "the slightest breath would annihilate her very existence." Ignoring the danger of fire from the guns on the British boats, she helped others carry cartridge bags of powder and shot from the magazine to the gunners.[71] After twenty minutes the cannon fire drove the barges back to their fleet, giving Isabella a taste of victory, but Johnson had no route of escape for his ship or the stores he hoped to save. At 7:30 that evening he torched stores, storehouse, and *Seahorse*, setting off an explosion heard for miles across the water.[72]

Jones struggled to make headway past midnight, but his wind failed entirely at one a.m., leaving the boats unmanageable, so he anchored the squadron at the west end of St. Joseph's Island just off the Mississippi coast and directly north of the Malheureuxs. Unless the wind returned, and from the right direction, he would be stuck there in the morning with no option but to fight or yield.[73] That night he considered the virtual impossibility of resisting with any reasonable chance of success. His only advantage was the larger caliber and longer range of most of his cannon, but with now six boats against forty-five, and 190 men against 1,200, he had no hope of victory. Prudence suggested he should destroy his boats rather than risk their capture, then take his men overland to join Jackson's army. He had sent warning to Patterson, which was all he could reasonably be expected to do now, but he believed he might barter bravery and blood here to delay the enemy for precious hours to allow Jackson to be ready. He could not do much against Lockyer, but he could buy time.[74]

At dawn on December 14, Jones looked in vain for wind, and an ebbing tide told him he had gone as far as he could. *Alligator*, returning from taking Jones's first report of his enemy sighting to Patterson, had already run aground to the south, and Master Shepperd frantically tried to break her free to join the squadron. Summoning his commanders, Jones ordered them to anchor their boats abreast, parallel to each other in a line across the St. Joseph Pass between the mainland and Malheureaux Island, their bigger bow guns pointing forward toward the foe. Ferris's #5 stood nearest to Malheureaux, then McKeever, Jones in the center to take the brunt of the attack, Spedden above him, and finally Ulrich closest to St. Joseph's. The men ran rope netting from the decks into the rigging to entangle boarders, loaded their guns, and then waited for the enemy to come at them.[75] Jones's lieutenant's pay was $80 a month. He intended to earn it.[76]

Lockyer's flotilla had rowed and sailed into the night before anchoring. Dawn's light gave him a glimpse of Jones's squadron some nine miles distant, and more sun revealed it prepared for action.[77] Shortly after nine a.m., Captain Roberts saw *Alligator* aground and volunteered to take her. With four barges, he soon showed Shepperd that resistance was futile, and at about 9:20 she struck her colors while Jones watched helplessly from the deck of #156.[78] Now Lockyer rowed straight for the American line until about ten o'clock, when he came in range of those twenty-four-pounder bow guns and McKeever's long thirty-two-pounder. He ordered his boats to anchor while soldiers, sailors, and marines prepared muskets and pistols for action and readied grapnel hooks to throw into enemy rigging to draw boats in for boarding. His crews exhausted from rowing, Lockyer gave them half an hour to eat a breakfast despite being almost under enemy fire.

About eleven o'clock they began rowing again.[79] Jones saw them start forward in a single line abreast. With the tidal flow running against them at three miles an hour, it was slow going, but by noon, firing their own bow guns as they came, the British approached the Americans. Jones's bow guns began firing grapeshot to bring down men and rigging, and solid round shot to smash decking and bulwarks. Lockyer's lead barge, along with another from Gordon's *Seahorse* and two from *Tonnant*, made straight for Jones in #156.

The fight for #156 opened the contest and was the fiercest of the engagement. The Yankees first repelled *Tonnant*'s barges, mortally wounding Lieutenant

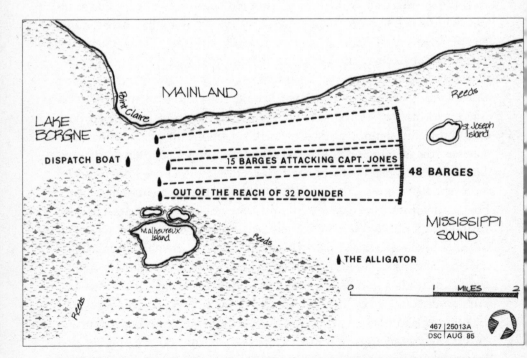

The Battle of Lake Borgne, December 14, 1814. Captain Lockyer's barges approach from the right while Lieutenant Jones's squadron sits drawn up in a line between the mainland and Malheureux Island. Note that in the action, Jones's gunboats were not drawn up presenting their broadsides to the attacking barges, but were anchored parallel to one another with their bows facing Lockyer.

James Uniacke by shooting off one of his legs, and costing Midshipman John O'Reilly an eye that he lived to tell of.[80] Then Lockyer's boat ran in but failed to board, suffering several killed and more wounded, including almost all its officers, and Lockyer received the first of three wounds.[81] One of *Tonnant*'s launches sank under fire beside *#156*, but then Lieutenant George Pratt from *Seahorse* got a boarding party aboard Jones's gunboat.

It had been Pratt who had set a torch to the United States Capitol building under Admiral Sir George Cockburn's orders that past summer. Now he tried repeatedly to climb aboard *#156*, only to be knocked back by bullet after bullet from American guns. Jones himself aimed a pistol at the Englishman to deliver what he believed to be a death wound, yet, despite being hit fully a dozen times, Pratt would live another three weeks before he died in his friend Captain Gordon's cabin. Two of *Seahorse*'s midshipmen made a try to board the gunboat, but Thomas Moore fell dead while boarding, and a cannon discharge shot away both of John Mills's legs, while a boarding pike thrust down from Jones's deck punctured an ensign's lungs and wounded him mortally.[82]

As Pratt was falling after Jones shot him, several bullets perforated Jones's uniform, and a marine on the barge fired at him. The bullet hit his left shoulder, shattering the joint, then coursed downward to lodge between the shoulder blade and ribs. He carried the bullet for the rest of his life as it gradually cost him the use of the arm.[83] Even after he went down, Jones may have taken a sword wound in the same shoulder.[84] Meanwhile the wounded Lockyer rowed his barge up again and this time got aboard, taking another wound in the offing. After what he called several minutes of "obstinate resistance," they took the gunboat and began pivoting her bow gun to fire on the gunboats on either side of them. The other divisions of British barges came up against the Yankee line, Captain Roberts arrived after taking *Alligator*, and within five minutes the other four gunboats yielded, with little loss on either side.[85] Watching through a spyglass from the bluff at Bay St. Louis, Master Johnson thought the fight lasted an hour and believed Yankee fire sank half of the enemy barges, which meant his view was not very clear.[86] Cochrane watched from a small boat closer to the scene.[87] Back at Ship Island, soldiers and sailors perched atop the mastheads of *Tonnant* and the other vessels saw little but flashes and smoke as they viewed the battle almost twenty miles away.[88] Aboard *Seahorse* off Cat Island, Captain Gordon confessed feeling "the greatest suspense" as he watched and awaited the names and number of casualties.[89] That evening he saw at a distance the procession of trophies as Lockyer's battered flotilla rowed and sailed back toward the anchorage with five gunboats and the *Alligator* as prizes, their crews all killed, wounded, or prisoners. The victors were so exhausted from the physical and mental stress of the battle that Lockyer had to drop anchor at eight o'clock at nightfall and wait for dawn to get to their ships.[90]

When Codrington got confirmation of the success, he granted that the Americans must have made "a very gallant resistance."[91] The list of casualties soon confirmed that. Lockyer lost five officers killed or mortally injured and at least fourteen more wounded. Among the seamen, eight were killed and about fifty wounded, no fewer than seventy-seven in all.[92] Returning men told of Yankees who climbed their rigging carrying cannonballs to throw down on boarders, the intensity of the combat showing in their own losses.[93] The Americans lost six killed and thirty-five wounded, at least one mortally, and half of them all from the fight for #156. Their wounded were on barges to Ship Island for transfer to the hospital ship *Gorgon*, while 141 captured officers and crew went to *Bedford* for later transfer to the ersatz prison ship *Plantagenet*.[94]

There was also a little plunder, more in the way of souvenirs. From #5 they took Lieutenant Ferris's sextant.[95] Then there were silver cups and spoons, some mathematical instruments, a fine writing desk, a pair of dueling pistols and rather an elegant fowling piece, not to mention the more everyday articles of housekeeping aboard ship.[96] Another find of a different kind was William Little or Lyddle, a deserter from the British Navy, taken on one of the gun vessels. He would be sent back to England to face court-martial.[97]

Hearing the details from participants, an officer on the *Nymph* declared that Lockyer had "performed one of the most brilliant things on record."[98] When Lockyer was back aboard ship, Cochrane personally congratulated him, gave him command of the squadron of captured vessels, and promised that he should have his own thirty-six-gun frigate soon.[99] Codrington saw great potential in the captured gunboats. They could be used to take Fort Petites Coquilles, guarding the Rigolets pass, whose loss should demonstrate to the enemy the folly of resistance, and the gunboats promised to give them command of Lake Pontchartrain prior to the landing he still expected to make on its shore.[100] The admirals already had a meticulously diagrammed plan for that landing, involving eighty-nine flatboats, barges, cutters, and launches, in multiple waves across a broad front. In less than a week, unexpected circumstances would render it unnecessary.[101] That, however, did not dampen the British elation over their complete victory in the first engagement for possession of New Orleans. "It is a most brilliant affair," Codrington wrote his wife immediately afterward, "and brilliant consequences may attach to this success."[102]

Indeed, they might.

Five

"The American States Are Doomed"

IN A CITY already on edge at news of an enemy sighting, the distant thunder of heavy cannon fire that echoed from the direction of Rigolets only added to the anxiety.[1] The morning after the battle, an eyewitness reached town to confirm their fears that the gunboats had indeed been lost.[2] Now all the navy that the Americans had left was the schooner *Carolina* and the sloop *Louisiana* at New Orleans, plus a single gunboat at Fort St. Philip.

With Cochrane having full command of Lake Borgne, the city could come under attack at any time; and if the volunteers from Kentucky and Tennessee did not arrive soon, it could be lost.[3] Under such strain, Jackson sent Coffee a renewed entreaty to hurry and to bring with him a company of Mississippi dragoons he might find waiting at Natchez. Old Hickory reasoned that if the British landed at Chef Menteur or on Pontchartrain's shore to march on the Gentilly road, Coffee's volunteers could harass and delay the redcoats, who would be easy targets.[4] Now Jackson lamented even more the unfinished blockship. Had it been completed and stationed to protect the Rigolets and Chef Menteur, its forty-four guns might have repulsed Lockyer and kept the enemy out of Lake Borgne.[5]

Jackson did not conceal the news of the loss of the gunboats from the New Orleans public.[6] Details were scant, but exaggeration and imagination quickly made up for any deficit in details.[7] There was some panic in the city, and so much conjecture that it was all but impossible to glean the truth, which was bad enough.[8] Fearing pillage or worse, many families packed hastily to leave for Natchez or the interior.[9] Still, the dominant attitude was a tempered determination to fight.[10]

To calm a restless public, Jackson told people there was no cause for excitement, and issued a proclamation in both English and French, chiding the people for their alarm and reminding them that they need only remain united and they would prevail. "Look to your liberties, your property, to the chastity of your wives and daughters," he said. They must know their friends from their enemies, and deal with the latter accordingly. He promised to execute anyone caught passing information to the enemy or undermining morale, and discouraged any hope of Louisiana ultimately going back to Spain.[11]

With news of Cochrane's arrival on Lake Borgne, the legislature passed a resolution appropriating $20,000 for defense, allowing Claiborne to use state money to encourage enlistments, but still refused to adjourn so he could act on his own authority, leading him to insinuate angrily to Jackson that the legislature was just "rotten."[12] Old Hickory agreed. Ever since his arrival, he had heard reports of information going to the enemy via traitorous Spaniards in the city and agents like Lewis Kerr in the surrounding area.[13] Others, like James Workman, he did not yet know of, nor of intelligence of Cochrane's movements coming into the city from Pensacola, while word of his strength and expectations was going out to Cochrane on the lips of travelers leaving for Havana.[14] Old Hickory knew if he acted too high-handedly to deal with such disloyalty, he risked offending the libertarianism common to recent immigrants.[15] Nevertheless, obsessed with security, preoccupied with managing a population of discordant ingredients, and working with fractured and indecisive civil authorities, he had been considering a declaration of martial law. Leading citizens recommended it, and he had discussed it more than once with Judge Dominic Hall of the Federal District Court, who tacitly acknowledged the necessity of the moment.[16] Now the news of Jones's defeat brought Old Hickory to a decision on December 15.[17]

The problem was an absence of precedent. No general had ever declared martial law in the United States before. Jackson consulted lawyers Livingston and Duncan and got mixed opinions. Suspending civil governmental functions would put all citizens under Jackson's authority, but the two attorneys differed on its legality. Livingston believed Jackson would be acting on his own authority and at his own risk; Duncan argued that the Constitution's provision for suspension of habeas corpus in extraordinary times implicitly acknowledged a potential need for martial law, else there would be no process for justice at all. General Wilkinson's authoritarian excesses were fresh in the local mind, meaning Jackson might risk alienating the people. Washington's reaction was also an issue, but it would take at least two months for any response to come back from the capital, and by that time the fate of New Orleans would be decided.

Meanwhile, the city was a powder keg with multiple sputtering fuses: a divided population, want of confidence in the civil authorities, a potential threat from the Creeks, geographic isolation, a slave population with a history of revolts, and more.[18] Under such conditions, Jackson concluded that "laws must sometimes be silent when necessity speaks."[19] The next morning, December 16, he published a general order declaring martial law in the city and environs. Anyone entering New Orleans must apply for a pass, and no one could leave without written permission. No boats were to leave the city or exit Bayou St. John without a passport from Jackson, Patterson, or their staff. A nine o'clock curfew was declared, when streetlamps were to be extinguished. Anyone found on the streets thereafter, or away from their homes without permission, would be arrested on suspicion of spying and held for interrogation.[20]

Perhaps to his surprise, the declaration was met with overwhelming approval. Judge Hall met with Jackson that morning and was heard to tell him, "Now, the country may be saved."[21] Even Governor Claiborne, despite his own jealousy of the general, told Jackson that "enemies to the country, may blame your prompt and energetic measures, but in the person of every patriot you will find a supporter."[22] In another time and under different circumstances, Jackson's declaration might not have been appropriate, but there and then he made the right decision.[23] Outnumbered and ill-equipped in everything but artillery, he inherited a divided citizenry and confronted the crisis with determination and without fear of responsibility. He could generate the moral force to defeat division if people saw the necessity for a single controlling hand. Martial law was the answer, and with it the imperative of a simple choice to be with him or against him.[24]

Resolution grew in the wake of the decree. The strict discipline imposed on the city streets gave even civilians a feeling of being soldiers.[25] Within hours an outpost just east of the Rigolets sent in a schoolteacher suspected of dealing with the enemy and arrested for treason.[26]

Jackson followed the proclamation with a flurry of activity. He sent Patterson's remaining gunboat to observe enemy ships off the river mouth and created an express line of boats and mounted scouts to rush information to him quickly from Fort St. Philip. Major Lacoste and his 382-man Colored Battalion of Louisiana left with two brass field pieces for Chef Menteur, treating the city to the sight of black volunteers marching to its defense.[27] A day later Latour and the younger Livingston followed them to lay out a fort and battery.[28] Jackson ordered Captain Francis Newman, commanding the fort at Petites Coquilles, to defend his post until forced to withdraw, and then fall back to reinforce Chef Menteur.[29] More men went to Petites Co-quilles as well, which would still have just eighty to one hundred men to garrison its unfinished walls and the incomplete works protecting men and guns against bombardment. The fort guarding Bayou St. John was in no better condition.[30] Guards appeared on every road into town and he re-peated his order to obstruct waterways, especially Bayou Bienvenue, which he unwisely sent Colonel Ross to handle, although surely Jackson knew of his bouts with the bottle by this time.[31] Yet more messengers went off to Baton Rouge, three days distant, to find Coffee and Carroll and rush them on.[32]

Perhaps reluctantly, Old Hickory put General Morgan in command of all Louisiana militia in the city. Claiborne had been drilling the assembled militia twice daily, but Jackson preferred Morgan, even though he was him-self one of the governor's appointments and a member of the "rotten" legis-lature as well.[33] Old Hickory's instructions fairly dripped want of confidence in the man, who that very day had failed to go through proper channels in ordering supplies. He warned Morgan that if there was any laxness or inat-tention, "you [will be] held responsible."[34] With his new authority under martial law, he decreed that he would impress for labor any slaves or free blacks found on the city streets, as well as wagons and all other means of haulage.[35]

Jackson's declaration stiffened the legislature a bit. Hours after the order came out, it passed an act to enroll seamen in the city for Patterson, em-powering Claiborne to arrest any who did not step forward without a valid excuse. It also ordered militia captains to furnish lists of able-bodied men not yet enrolled in a company and set aside an additional $25,000 as an emergency reserve. With stores closed and volunteers unable to earn money while in service, it decreed a thirty-day suspension of payments on debts. In all but name, the legislature had issued its own declaration of martial law.[36]

In the streets, citizens took their own actions. Hundreds from all walks of life volunteered for a battalion commanded by Major Jean Baptiste Plau-ché. Pierre Roche, a printer and bookseller at number 6 Royal Street, had been an officer with Napoleon. Now he became captain of Plauché's first company of "carabineers." Charles De St. Romes, editor of *Le Courrier de la Louisiane*, took the lieutenancy of a mounted company. Henri de St. Gême once served the British at Jamaica but now would lead the 3rd Company of Dragoons, and Irishman Captain Maunsel White formed a 4th Company of fellow Emerald Islanders. Notary Michel De Armas closed his book to enlist with Plauché, his last act recording the purchase of a slave by a free woman of color.[37] The half-breed Captain Jugeat already had about fifty Choctaw. Excepting his and White's companies, the men under Plauché were almost all French.

Then there were the Negro and mulatto companies, all commanded by planter-merchant Colonel Michael Fortier, Sr. He paid from his own pocket to arm and equip the 353 men who volunteered for six companies of the First Battalion of Free Men of Color, to be led by Major Lacoste. Their company officers were all black, with Vincent Populous as Lacoste's executive officer, and most were from Saint-Domingue.[38] Lacoste was no sooner off to Chef Menteur than Fortier called for volunteers for a second battalion, and by December 19 some 256 free black volunteers appeared at his home to enlist. They elected Major Louis Daquin, a white baker, to command them, but Jackson himself appointed mulatto Major Joseph Savary to serve on Daquin's staff. Fortier soon had several hundred damaged or defective muskets adapted and repaired to arm them.[39] A few other smaller companies formed, including a home guard of seventy-nine blacks for duty in the city.

No company in American history could match the New Orleans Riflemen. Thomas Beale, the forty-four-year-old register of wills in the Orleans probate court, had a reputation as a marksman. That same day he began raising a volunteer company. The querulous city merchant Vincent Nolte, who disapproved of almost everyone, thought him "a great braggart," but dozens joined him, men with a stake in Louisiana, educated merchants and professionals, many there since 1811 or earlier, but still "new" compared to the *creoles*, who looked on them as *arrivistes*. Almost all were Americans from the Northeast.[40] They locked their shops to volunteer for ninety days to defend their city. Men of office and trust stepped forward, like Judge Joshua Lewis of the first district court, who became Beale's second lieutenant. Former mayor Denis Prieur volunteered. Notary John Lynd joined, as did lawyers William de Peyster and Kenneth Laverty, and both partners in the law firm of B. P. Porter and Hiram Brown. Joseph Saul left the city branch of the Bank of the United States, as did fellow banker Benjamin Story, and editor Thomas Anderson of the *Louisiana Gazette* shut down his press to volunteer.[41]

Not all of them were from the North. Thirty-one-year-old George Commyns, who served as a city constable, had been born in Spanish Pensacola. Married and divorced, he owned three slaves, whom he probably hired out, since he had no other property and lived in a boardinghouse. It did not occur to him to compose a will when he enlisted in what could be a dangerous service.[42] Oliver Parmlee Jr. was not three weeks past his twenty-ninth birthday.[43] Originally in business in Boston selling general wares like wine, paper, hats, coffee, mackerel, apples, and more, he came to New Orleans in the fall of 1811 to engage in mercantile trade until the embargo cut him off.[44] On December 16 he joined Beale's company. More prudent than Commyns, he had the good sense to make out his will the night before.[45]

Merchants came forward in numbers. Bostonian Judah Touro of Chartres Street enlisted, as did William Flower of Flower & Faulkner on Magazine, both partners of Kenner and Henderson, cotton balers and shippers, Nathaniel Cox of Bartlett and Cox on Conti Street, and William Montgomery, who had establishments on Levee and Magazine.[46] Tobacconist John Randolph became first lieutenant, second-in-command to Beale himself. A cabinetmaker and a cooper and three grocers took off their aprons. The bachelor merchant B. Laborde of Conti Street joined their number.[47]

Then there was William Carr Withers, a Virginian who came just two or three years after the Purchase. Thirty years old, married the year the war began, he erected a steam-operated sawmill on the bank of the river where steamboats often made landing. He could claim a distant connection to General Jackson, for his cousin had married Lewis Robards, Rachel Donelson Jackson's first husband. His mill provided cypress lumber to the military in New Orleans, but he left it now to enlist with Beale.[48] Apropos to a company of riflemen, Withers brought a special attribute to the company. According to a friend, Withers's rifle "never missed his mark."[49]

When completed, Beale's company numbered sixty-six. Probably the last to join was Beverly Chew. He was in Natchez when news arrived of the British fleet's sighting off the Chandeleurs sent a wave of panicked refugees fleeing to the town. Hearing that volunteer companies were forming, he rode to New Orleans to enlist as a sergeant with Beale, proud to boast that his company was "the leading men of the City, and formed of the most respectable material."[50] Beale expected the men to provide their own provisions, and in at least one mess every man had a black servant attending him. One young man failed to bring an attendant and faced some disapproval from his messmates. He considered moving to another mess but concluded that since "I have joined their tent I cannot well back out."[51]

The militia companies marched and drilled almost all day, and by evening the military bustle and parade showed everywhere.[52] It was assumed that an attack might come any day, but with the citizens at last under arms, a nervous confidence prevailed. A visitor in town thought they would fight if well managed, but worried about the volunteers being "a mixed multitude."[53] The divisions that worried everyone were still there—an "internal broil," one man called it. If they could set that aside, they had a chance, but some feared that their unity was too frail to hold long.[54]

By the end of the day, December 16, Jackson fully realized the magnitude of the problem before him. He had lost his advance sentinels. His waterborne line of communication between New Orleans and Mobile was gone, making both cities vulnerable, and the foe could use the gunboats to help take Mobile. If it fell, that isolated the settlements up the Alabama and Mobile Rivers, leaving New Orleans further at risk.[55] That very day an express from Mobile reported forty enemy ships offshore, with more arriving, although the news really related to the passage of Cochrane's fleet and transports on their way to Ship Island.[56] The enemy held Lake Borgne now, and rumor had it that they had taken the fort at Petites Coquilles (which they had not).[57] They could already be on Lake Pontchartrain. One of Patterson's officers even heard that another expedition was coming from the West Indies.[58]

Knowing that Coffee was getting close leavened any gloom, and that same day Colonel Andrew Hynes, Carroll's aide, arrived with the welcome news that Carroll was rushing to get there. Captain Henry Shreve's steamboat *Enterprise* had tied up at the riverbank the day before, bringing ordnance and military stores from Pittsburgh. Now Old Hickory commandeered the vessel and ordered Shreve back upstream to meet Carroll and bring down as many of his men as possible.[59] The Kentuckians might arrive in a fortnight as well, and Major Overton returned from furlough to resume command of Fort St. Philip. And the men of Louisiana still stepped forward lively. Jackson had embargoed all boats from leaving the port to keep experienced seamen available for Patterson, but now crewmen from the keelboats and flatboats organized a company under Captains Robert Sprigg and David Wallace, and Captain Peter Ogden, merchant and president of the Livingstons' Mississippi Steam Boat Navigation Company, formed another cavalry company.[60]

Jackson typically refused to act like a man facing disaster. By nightfall that first day he believed he would have defense of the Mississippi complete in a few days, and he would be ready to meet and defeat Cochrane wherever he tried to land. Should the enemy try to come up the river itself, he would never get out of it again except as a prisoner.[61] Given the opportunity, Old Hickory would seize the initiative and attack at the first opportunity. It might throw the foe off balance long enough for his reinforcements to arrive.[62] "Heaven knows our fate here," a captain wrote late that night, but the men in the ranks knew that their fate was in the hands of Old Hickory. "Under him," wrote a volunteer, "they will go through fire and water."[63] That trial would come soon. It might well all be over by New Year's Day.[64]

With the militia off to their points to guard, the city was bare of all but the aged and invalid, what one woman called the "old white headed men."[65] Claiborne summoned them, too, for a "Corps of Exempts" that included fathers of families, city firemen, and others excused from militia service, making Gaspard M. Debuys its captain.[66] Fifty-two-year-old Fulwar Skipwith, cousin of Jefferson, once consul general to France, governor of the momentary Republic of West Florida, and now president of the Louisiana senate in the legislature, enlisted as a private to do nightly watch duty with the city guard despite his poor health.[67] Free men of color too old to serve formed an auxiliary home guard. Ironically, in addition to duty arresting curfew violators and putting out the streetlamps at night, they served with a militia guard detailed by Claiborne to keep watch on slaves with so many white males absent.[68] Jackson commandeered black males to work on his fortifications without regard for their free or slave status, and *creole* militia summarily impressed its seven slave deckhands and sent them to Bayou St. John to fell timber.[69]

Jackson scheduled a militia review in the Place d'Armes on December 18 to capitalize on the shift in public mood. His address to the militia and people, written and read in English and French by Livingston, complimented them for setting aside their differences of class, color, customs, and language and coming forward to risk their lives and fortunes to protect their families and property. In a special aside to the black volunteers, he said he expected much from them, knowing their capacity to endure hardship. "I knew that you loved the land of your nativity," Old Hickory told them, "but you surpass my hopes."[70] For a man generally alien to subtlety, Jackson—or Livingston—set exactly the right tone.

No sooner was the review concluded than the general sent Plauché to guard the bridge on Bayou St. John, but before they left, Plauché's officers handed him a petition backed by resolutions passed in both houses of the legislature the evening before.[71] They wanted Jackson to open the Cabildo cells holding the Baratarians captured in September. It was time to bring the stray sheep into the fold.[72]

The Laffites and many of their associates were still in hiding west of the Mississippi. Knowing nothing of the brothers' offer of help, people at first assumed that the smugglers had joined the enemy, whereas Patterson's breakup of the Barataria operation nullified most of their usefulness to the British. On October 4, Jean approached Livingston "to pull me out of the trouble where I am," and the lawyer obliged with approaches to Claiborne and even the president.[73] Coincidentally, within days Byron's *Corsair* hit the eastern press along with news of Jean's rebuff of Percy's offer, and before the end of November a melodrama titled *Lafitte, and the Pirates of*

Barataria debuted, presenting the Laffites as patriots.[74] With public opinion favoring the Laffites, Madison authorized Claiborne to initiate pardons for Baratarians who volunteered to defend New Orleans.[75] Relentless local pressure from the Committee of Safety, the legislature, and his own staff softened Old Hickory toward them, but it took Judge Hall to get around their federal indictments in his court. "I am the general in this matter," he declared, and he essentially halted further prosecution.[76] The legislature quickly followed suit, which left everything in Jackson's hands.

The loss of the gunboats won him to their side.[77] Jackson was short of gunflints, without which the locks on pistols and muskets could not fire.[78] A gunflint could work twenty-five times, or shatter at first fire. One hard-fought battle might exhaust his supply, but the Laffites had 7,500 or more, and now Jean got word to Old Hickory that they were his for the asking.[79] With a safe conduct from Hall, he himself came into the city to confer with Jackson, and that settled the matter.[80] The general ordered cells opened and the release of all Baratarians who took a pledge of allegiance and enlisted in the militia. At the same time, word went west of the river that those in hiding could come in on the same terms. A day later they were in the city, lining up to enlist.[81] Almost everyone approved of a stroke both practical and politic. Not only were the corsairs and smugglers determined men and handy with artillery, but they were also mostly from the ranks and popular with their ethnic brethren.[82]

The move was more politic yet when news reached town late December 17 from agents sent by Patterson to seek parole and return of the gunboat fight's wounded.[83] The enemy had one frigate, several brigs and schooners, and what looked like at least fifty transports, clearly heading for the Rigolets. Catesby Jones, despite his severe injuries, had tried to feed the British exaggerated reports of American strength, hoping to deter them from approaching that pass by inflating the one-hundred-man garrison at Fort Petites Coquilles to five hundred, but it did not work. The evening of December 16, Patterson's agents saw ten British schooners scarcely six miles from the passage, and the five captured gunboats were actually at the Rigolets' entrance and heading toward Petites Coquilles. They warned Patterson that in ten days the enemy could have as many as forty vessels across on Lake Pontchartrain.[84]

The next day, December 18, Plauché received and forwarded from Bayou St. John a two-day-old letter.[85] Jean Baptiste Labatut, whose resort or "seahouse" sat atop the bluff at Bay St. Louis, reported the approach of sixty barges filled with soldiers. As he watched them burn his own house and warehouse, he feared they meant to destroy all in their path and estimated they could be in New Orleans in four days. "They hold no parleys, but proceed steadily forward to their object," he warned. "It is the city they are aiming for."[86]

Yet ironically, a day after Labatut's warning arrived, some local conversation actually carried hints of disappointment that the British were moving too slowly. Some Orleanians' confidence in their ability to hold almost pushed them to hubris, and a ridiculous rumor even fluttered that Old Hickory had already fought the enemy somewhere to the east, as if he and his small army could have left the vicinity without being noticed.[87] The sensible knew that the foe was approaching in considerable force.[88] One of Beale's riflemen, Francis Coxe, told his father that he saw "determined spirit" all around him that day and that even if the enemy took the city, it would not impede the future greatness of the United States. Years of European wars had so disrupted the world order that Britain could no longer lead other nations.[89]

Men and women in that Britain rather disagreed. Everyone knew Cochrane was headed for New Orleans, where he would certainly wage a brilliant campaign in the coming months. He would take Louisiana before the war closed, predicted a Cambridge editor. That done, "the American states are doomed."[90]

Six

Treachery Opens a Way

OBSTACLES NEVER TOOK Admiral Cochrane's eyes from his prize. The loss of Mobile had forced him to shift to Lake Borgne, but the shallow water kept his warships and transports back at the Cat Island anchorage instead of running in close to the lakeshore for a conventional landing. Worse, the want of sufficient shallow-draft boats to land the whole army at once haunted him. There were only enough barges and other small craft to move a third of the army at a time. Undaunted by these and other challenges, he was determined to find a staging area midway between the deep anchorage and the mouth of Bayou Bienvenue. He would have to get the men to it in multiple waves over a long distance by sailing and paddling light-draft transports and boats, exhausting both soldiers and crewmen, and then do it again to get them from the staging area to the lakeshore.

Cochrane had Quartermaster Charles Forrest draft the landing plan. Colonel William Thornton and 1,300 men of the 85th, the 95th, and the Rocket Brigade would go first, then 850 of the 4th, followed by 650 of the 44th, and last the 21st, the 93rd, and 5th West India.[1] With the captured gunboats in hand after December 15, Cochrane used them to board Thornton's advance early the next day and sent them in company with Gordon's *Seahorse* the thirty miles to a long swampy island formed by the eastern and western branches of the Pearl River near the lake's north shore.[2] It went by many names. Locals called it Manequin Island, while Spaniards called it Isla de Guisantes, or Pea Island. Others knew it as the Isle of Pines, Pigeon Island, Mosquito Island, even Blind Island, but mostly it was called Pine Island. It had just enough dry land to accommodate the whole army, and its western tip virtually constituted the north shore of the entrance to Rigolets. Upon landing, Thornton found a cluster of thatched reed huts called *le village du manaquinos*, thanks to the island's thousands of pigeons.[3] Half a dozen fishermen met him, social outcasts who supplemented their income by petty smuggling. To these men, most of them Spaniards, the war with the British represented a fresh source of potential revenue. This was the island and these the men recommended by Gordon's kidnapped Pensacola pilot.[4]

Though considering a landing at Bayou Bienvenue, Cochrane still looked to Lake Pontchartrain as his probable line of advance.[5] He went ashore on December 17 in a pirogue with Keane and Codrington to learn more and within the next few hours got from those fishermen information to change his thinking. The mouth of Bienvenue was entirely unprotected, possibly the only unguarded spot on the lake coast where a landing might be made. Having used it themselves to get fish and contraband to market, the fishermen could add that small boats could travel the bayou almost to the bank of the Mississippi.[6]

Hearing that, Keane decided on a reconnaissance, and two officers took the mission.[7] Captain Robert Cavendish Spencer, though just twenty-three, had risen fast and was one of Cochrane's favorites. Descended from the Duke of Marlborough, and the younger brother of the Earl of Spencer, he had commanded the HMS *Carron* in the effort to take Fort Bowyer back in September, and spoke both French and Spanish. Just as daring was army lieutenant John Peddie. Losing his right arm at the Battle of Salamanca in 1812 had taken him out of field service, and now he was on half pay as Forrest's assistant quartermaster.

Spencer and Peddie were to disguise themselves as locals and journey the route up the bayou, secure more guides and pilots if they could, and report as quickly as possible. Most of all, the two were to determine if the ground along the bayou could support an army landing and how far toward the river their small boats could pass.[8]

For Cochrane, the opportunity to sneak his troops to within striking distance of New Orleans was tantalizing. If that bayou could get Keane's men to dry land near the Mississippi a few miles below New Orleans before Jackson discovered their coming, Cochrane might still manage a surprise attack, despite the security leaks. None of them knew anything of that coast, of course, but gold from the admiral's locker hired one of the island's fishermen who sometimes used Bienvenue to get his catch and contraband to market.[9] Once he got them to the stream's mouth, they should find a new guide at another fishermen's village a little inland.[10]

Spencer and Peddie sailed roughly twenty miles along the coast of Lake

Borgne on December 18, reaching the bayou mouth before dark.[11] Their guide took them up it a mile or two to a scattering of crude huts clinging to the muddy bank, where they found a motley assemblage of Spaniards and Portuguese fishermen and smugglers, some of whom had already supplied information to Cochrane on their return from selling fish in New Orleans.[12] Now three of them took the king's gold and agreed to get the captains up the sluggish stream in a pirogue that same night.[13]

A waxing crescent moon lit their way as the tall reeds lining the banks waved and danced above their heads in the fresh offshore breezes. The bayou flowed at first through an immense marshland between Lake Borgne and the dry ground along the Mississippi. Wider at its mouth, it steadily narrowed as they passed the confluences of smaller bayous that fed it. After three miles Bienvenue turned off to the north, but the main channel, here known as Bayou Mazant, continued southwesterly. Tangled mats of floating reeds lined its banks, some so dense they reached the bottom and could be walked on with care. The guides told Peddie and Spencer they were called *prairies tremblantes*, "shaking marshes."[14] They could hardly support artillery or horses, but soldiers might march along those banks in places until traffic beat the mats down into the swamp.

Another four miles, the bayou ever narrowing, brought them to the opening of a man-made ditch or canal that ran to their left toward the river, the first of several canals that connected river plantations to Lake Borgne via Mazant and Bienvenue. This one was General Villeré's.[15] Another mile brought them to Pierre Lacoste's, and just beyond it the bayou ended at the canal serving the plantation of Denis De La Ronde. There the swamp gave way to firmer ground in a densely wooded cypress swamp the locals called *cyprières*.[16] The captains stepped onto nearly dry land to find that just three-quarters of a mile along that canal the woods ended in favor of the flat, dry ground of De La Ronde's sugar plantation. From there the main river road along the Mississippi levee lay just one and one-half miles ahead of them. In the predawn half-light, they stole through De La Ronde's cane fields to the road, crossed it unseen, climbed over the levee, and dipped their hands into the Mississippi.

They had not seen one American—no sentinels, no guards, no defensive preparations anywhere along their trip. They had found hard ground between the edge of the cypress swamp and the river, and looking from the top of the levee they saw similar ground almost a mile wide running back at least to the Lacoste's and Villeré's. Even Cochrane's lightest craft could not go as far as De La Ronde's, but his boats could pass as far as the Villeré canal, and dry ground there would make a good place to disembark troops.

1 Jumonville	18 Montreuil
2 Villeré	19 Bronier
3 Lacoste	20 Daunois
4 De La Ronde	21 Suburb Marigny
5 Bienvenu	22 New Orleans
6 Chalmette	23 R. Avart
7 Rodriguez	24 Caselard
8 McCarty	25 Flood
9 Languille	26 Jouran
10 Sigur	27 Castañada
11 Delery	28 Le Fevre
12 Piernas	29 Mayhew
13 Solomon	30 Duverge
14 Dupre	31 Dupuy
15 Butler	32 Morin
16 Dupleais	33 Andry
17 McCarty	34 Woods Ville

The bayous leading from Lake Borgne to plantations along the east bank of the Mississippi. General Keane followed Bayou Bienvenue past the Fishermen's Village, then onto Bayou Mazant. At the point where the British later built a defensive redoubt after the battles, Keane turned onto Bayou Villeré to reach Villeré's plantation and the river.

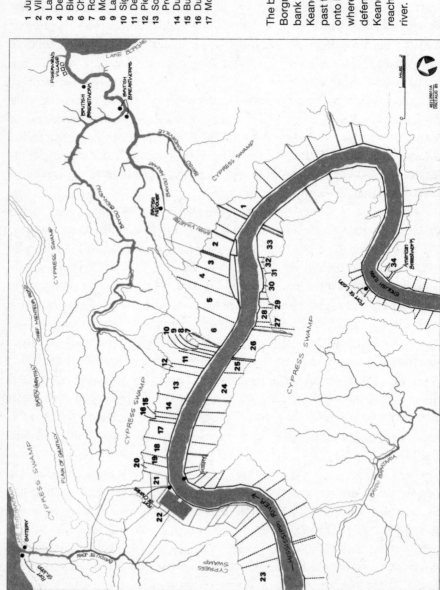

Their guides told them that from there the main road led just seven miles northwest to Faubourg Marigny and New Orleans.[17]

When Peddie and Spencer reported to Cochrane and Keane late on December 19, the bayou route ceased to be just an idea, their decision reinforced by the fear that even their lightest-draft transports might be too deep to cross Pontchartrain. Moreover, in a curious coincidence, some of the British thought the Americans did not know of Bienvenue.[18] Jackson did, of course, but in reverse the Yankees assumed it to be unknown to their enemy. Now Cochrane ordered Pigot to take *Nymph* to a spot known locally as the Balise, which commanded multiple channels from the river to the Gulf. There it could blockade the Mississippi, a diversion to make Jackson think the invasion would come via the river.[19]

While Peddie and Spencer had been scouting Bienvenue, the flotilla of small boats rowed thirty miles back to the fleet to board another wave of redcoats. During the return trip, exposed to heavy rain and cold wind, the boats were so cramped that the men could scarcely move, and some almost overturned repeatedly in the choppy waves. Some boats even ran aground in the shallows. Finally reaching shore, soldiers found that Pine Island itself seemed to be a wretched desert populated only by birds and alligators.[20] No trees afforded firewood, and there had been no room in the boats to bring tents. Night temperatures sank below freezing, a foretaste of hardship to come. Officers tried to sleep in the boats, but rest proved elusive.[21] Codrington spent the wettest night of his life beneath a leaking marquee with Cochrane as a bitterly cold gale raged outside, his valet and a few midshipmen sharing the admiral's gig covering themselves with a sail against frost and wind. The ice that night formed nearly an inch thick.[22] The next day the soldiers scavenged to make rude shelters before another night of misery. There was nothing to eat but salt meat and ship's biscuit, and nothing to drink but rum. Hunger made some men eat two days' rations at once, but the salty food only made them thirsty, and hungrier. Some shot pigeons to roast.[23] Cochrane had sent parties to catch loose cattle back on Ship Island and to buy more from locals, but Jackson had already ordered most of the beeves near the shore to be driven inland, so there would be little fresh beef to augment moldy ship's pork.[24] Captain Gordon did his best to entertain the midshipmen with jokes and stories of his adventures to keep their spirits up, but even he complained of the cold.

Throughout the night and day, the boats kept coming from the fleet anchorage, until all but the 1st West India were finally ashore.[25] That regiment had left Negril with five hundred strong, but now it was down to four hundred thanks to sickness. No one had anticipated that men who had spent their lives in the tropics might need warm clothing to protect them from the cold, and when they arrived on December 19 to spend their first night on Pine Island, they suffered even more losses, as some men froze to death.[26]

Keane ordered a review of the assembled troops for the morning of December 20, but when he arose before dawn, the discovery that a few of his men had succumbed to the cold put him in a foul mood.[27] After the review he reorganized the army into an "advance guard" and two brigades. Thornton had the Advance, almost 1,250 men from the 95th, the 85th, assorted artillerymen and field engineers, and two ineffectual three-pounder cannon.[28] The First Brigade had the 21st, the 44th, the 1st West India, and more artillerymen, totaling almost 2,050 under Colonel Brooke, while Lieutenant Colonel A. M. K. Hamilton's Second Brigade would be the 4th, the 93rd, and the 5th West India Infantries, plus more artillerymen. Keane kept the unmounted 14th Dragoons as a headquarters escort.

Despite milder weather that day, Keane felt uneasy. The available boats limited him to landing only a third of his troops at the bayou at a time. Spencer and Peddie had spotted no Americans on their reconnaissance, but if a strong enemy force should take Thornton's advance guard by surprise once landed, it would be many hours before more of the army could reach him. With that risk uppermost in their minds, Cochrane, Malcolm, Keane, and Forrest augmented the advance guard with the 4th Foot and a brace of four-pounders. They would embark aboard the transports at nine a.m. on December 22, to anchor just below Chef Menteur, where at seven p.m. the men would transfer to the small boats and row to the mouth of the bayou.

About dusk, with Peddie as guide, Thornton was to start up the stream, expecting to reach the Villeré canal an hour before dawn on December 23.[29] Sappers and engineers with him could widen the channel if it pinched the boats, reinforce the banks if they had to get out and tow, and bridge ditches once they landed.[30] Peddie would oversee disembarkation at Villeré's, and once Thornton established a secure position, the boats were to return to the fishermen's hut village, which Gordon and Malcolm would use as a base for forwarding men and matériel as they arrived. The second wave ought to reach Villeré's the evening of December 23, so Thornton would only be on his own perhaps a dozen or more hours before reinforcements arrived, and the balance of the army should be up an hour before the next dawn. Three of the captured gunboats, now renamed *Eagle*, *Harlequin*, and *Firebrand*, would land six three- and six-pounders, two 5.5-inch howitzers, and five bigger guns—two nine-pounders and three mortars, along with a full complement of ammunition and three hundred gunners. Carrying a sting to match her name, the schooner *Hornet* would offload 80,000 musket cartridges and 10,000 for rifles.[31] Only the 1st West India regiment was to remain on Pine Island.[32]

Shortly after the review, men came to the island and volunteered that Keane's bayou path was clear, Jackson was as yet unprepared, and taking the city would be "an easy business."[33] They may have been disaffected *creole* planters or more Spanish fishermen or both, and later that same day Spanish fishermen hired by Peddie arrived to guide the succeeding waves of the landing up the bayou.[34] Regardless of who told the British what, Jackson's aide Reid later grumbled that "treachery opened a way."[35]

Amid rain, frost, and freezing gale winds, the expedition spent the intervening hours packing ammunition to keep it dry and loading stores aboard the transports, while Cochrane sent *Sophie* to join *Nymph* at the Balise, perhaps the germ of an idea of actually sending light warships up the Mississippi.[36] The advance guard was ready in their transports on time, along with Keane and his staff, two of Nicolls's Choctaw chiefs, and two fishermen as guides. Aboard one of Jones's gunboats alongside, Admiral Cochrane gave the signal for them to shove off.[37] By noon they were out of sight.[38]

Thornton's most immediate enemy was the lakebed. Some transports made no more than two miles before grounding, and all of them did occasionally.[39] The men were so crowded in the boats that they could scarcely move during the crews' hours of laborious rowing. Hard rain all morning mocked their discomfort, but just after noon it cleared with enough wind to raise sail, rest the oarsmen, and make up time. The advance guard reached position on schedule that evening and transferred into the small boats by seven p.m. to wait for their guide to the bayou.[40] Before long a boat approached from that direction, and their guide gave them the unwelcome news that in the last day or two an American guard post had been established at the hut village they intended to be their base, known to locals as Des Pêcheurs—"the Fishermen."[41]

Still they pressed on. When their wind died, they rowed on into the darkness until they reached the mouth of the bayou about midnight. A scout soon confirmed the Yankee picket guard at the huts half a mile up the bayou. Thornton sent ahead two boats with Captain James Travers and thirty men of the 95th Rifles, and they silently rowed upstream until they saw through the reeds and cypresses a fire ahead off their right bow, where the cluster of huts clung to a mound of earth surrounded by swamp.[42] If the redcoats did not bypass or capture the Americans before they sent an alarm back to Jackson, Cochrane's great surprise would die aborning.

The coast was not as unguarded as Peddie and Spencer had reported.

The two officers had failed to see a small militia outpost at Proctor Point, a few miles beyond the mouth of the bayou, and since their reconnaissance Villeré had obeyed Jackson's orders by stationing a squad of *creole* militia at the hut village. They monitored fishermen going to and returning from the lake, and otherwise passed the boring hours of isolation in their hut playing cards. Occasionally one looked down the bayou for fishermen coming in with the day's catch, but otherwise they stayed inside where it was warm and dry.

There was a game on again this evening, with no sentinel posted. One of the players went out as usual and he heard something. Crouching down in the brush on the bank to watch and listen, he heard coming from the foggy darkness a faint rhythmic noise. He ran back into the hut yelling, "The British are coming!" but his companions convinced him he had been spooked by water and wind beating the reeds.[43] What he heard were the oars of a boat Travers sent gliding past the outpost to land men above it while he banked his other boat just downstream. A few hours later Ensign Gleig would tell his diary that "no persons could be less on their guard than the party here stationed." They had posted not a single sentinel.

Once on land, the soldiers from above and below the village moved inland to form a semicircular line with both ends on the bayou. Then they slowly advanced, the line contracting as they approached.[44] The first hint of danger the Yankees got was the sound of musket butts being grounded outside the hut. A few stepped outside to be confronted by bayonets, while others inside still slept.[45] Some ran for the reeds and two got to a pirogue before being caught. Four ran into the swamp but soon enough chose surrender over the darkness and mud. Only one man escaped to a nearby bayou, where he found a canoe and paddled northward toward the Gentilly road.[46] Not a shot had been fired.[47]

Soon the rest of the boats arrived at Des Pêcheurs and continued on their way, the redcoats struck by the shabbiness of the huts.[48] Gordon set men cutting the tall reeds at the landing to make room for the next wave of troops to come ashore while waiting for Thornton's boats to return for them, and then Cochrane and Codrington arrived to make quarters in a reed hut whose thatch stopped neither wind nor rain.[49] Soon another boat rowed past carrying Keane on his way to join Thornton, and as he passed the general jauntily yelled to Gordon that "no living creature was ever here before but ducks and alligators!"[50]

At times reeds on the banks entirely obscured the bayou, which soon began to narrow, making the oarsmen's work all the more difficult. After a few miles the banks closed in so that there was no space to get their oars in the water, so they used them as poles to push against the banks to keep moving.[51] The captain of the three-pounders had to tie his boats one behind another, and everyone bundled against the sleet and frost.[52] Thanks to the ebbing tide on the lake, the bayou was shallower than normal and the boats rarely kept going even half an hour without grounding, forcing their occupants to get into the freezing water to push and lift them free.[53] Already an officer from *Ramillies* marveled at their achievement. A mere fifty well-placed men on the bayou could have frustrated the whole operation, he thought. Now a gaping doorway to complete surprise lay before them and it seemed evident that the enemy had not the least idea where their landing might come.[54] A fellow naval officer in the boats soon gloated that the Yankees had fortifications and batteries everywhere "but where we really came."[55]

Peddie in the lead boat approached the Villeré canal just before daybreak. The night and the shallow bayou had dispersed the boats somewhat, and Keane decided that he could better concentrate his force by leaving the boats at that point.[56] The lead boat emptied first onto a marshy bank to confront a seemingly impenetrable sea of cane seven feet tall with a thick cypress forest beyond. Peddie had planned for this, and immediately behind him Captain Robert Blanchard's party of Royal Engineers stepped ashore to begin clearing a path through the cane to the wood.[57] It took two hours, for most of which Thornton's soldiers remained in their boats, some mistaking the sound of the engineers at work for Americans felling trees to block their route.[58] When finally they disembarked, the narrow bayou kept the boats lined up one behind another in the swamp with only the lead boat touching dry ground. Soldiers in the rearmost craft had to step forward in single file from one boat to another, and then another, to reach the bank, making it more than an hour after dawn before all were ashore.[59] Immediately the boat crews began the grueling business of returning to the hut village, now dubbed "the landing."

With Travers in the lead, Thornton trekked the last yards along the bayou to the canal, stepping on or over the reed mats that an Irish soldier dubbed "shaking bogs."[60] Mats laid over planks and ladders bridged several small ditches, and Ensign Benson Hill manhandled the pair of three-pounders over the same crude pathway.[61] At times the dense forest of reeds was taller than the men, lending an eerie feeling of being surrounded.[62] The engineers were still working ahead of them and by nine a.m. finished the road through the cane and Thornton had the 95th and 85th moving through the cypresses. Once through the wood, they saw ahead of them level, dry sugarcane fields stretching westward to the levee a scant half mile away.

Closer to them stood Villeré's plantation house, outbuildings, and slave cabins. A number of unsuspecting militiamen lounged after their breakfast in the yard.[63] Just beyond lay the road to New Orleans.[64]

A FEW MILES up that road, the flurry of the city had come to a halt. The coffeehouses had ceased their bustle, and the shops were shuttered. Those who sought spiritual solace could not even find a Bible for sale.[65] The city government barely functioned. Mayor Girod worked without salary, and city treasurer Charles Louis Blache turned to the Cabildo jailor for emergency funds.[66] The stagnation told in the books of the notaries who handled the transactions elsewhere conducted by clerks of court, from the sale of slaves to debt collection. By December 17 slave sales ground to a halt, people hoarding their hard cash refused to pay debts, and the notaries just closed their books and joined Beale's riflemen or Plauché's militia.[67]

All over the city, men were leaving their shops and countinghouses and official duties, heeding patriotism's call to take arms in defense of their homes and property, even at the risk of their lives. Claiborne felt so good about the spirit of the city now that he wrote Fromentin, Brown, and Robertson that "old and Young are a like prepared to meet & Repel the Foe."[68] Sadly, that unity did not extend to relations between the governor and the general. Claiborne and Jackson still continually sparred with each other.[69] By his own admission, Old Hickory never let a slight or challenge go unnoticed, and Claiborne, generally the more mature of the two, on December 22 asked for a private interview with him, stressing the need that they work to maintain "a co-operation zealous and cordial."[70]

The general's testiness stemmed from more than just his personality. Most activity had shifted to preparing the forts and closing the bayous, and there were still vulnerable points as well as subordinates in whom he had only limited confidence.[71] The river Chenes ran parallel to the Mississippi through several small lakes to Bayou Terre-aux-Boeufs, which came within four miles of the Mississippi below General Morgan's position at English Turn. The enemy might conceivably use that route to land below and behind him, forcing Morgan to withdraw and leaving the great river open all the way to the city.[72] Jackson scolded Morgan for leaving that route open despite his instructions, and gave him peremptory orders to close and guard all such passages. Like Villeré, Morgan was showing himself to be tardy about obeying orders.[73] While Claiborne had confidence in Morgan, Jackson's was eroding, and the militia general's subordinates felt a growing resentment and discontent with him that approached hatred.[74] Some of his acts certainly raised questions about his judgment. On December 20 he warned Villeré of men at the Turn whom he thought disloyal, then appointed one of the suspects to his own staff.[75]

That evening Plauché reported enemy transports off Chef Menteur, apparently moving toward Bayou Bienvenue.[76] Old Hickory intuited a critical moment at hand and renewed efforts to close all doors and guard all avenues. A flatboat was armed to protect northwestern approaches in case the enemy landed on the river above the city.[77] He sent Ogden's mounted men scouting the east bank of the Mississippi below the city just hours before they might have spotted Thornton's approach.[78] Old Hickory also took time that same day to chide General Philemon Thomas, onetime commander of the West Florida republic's tiny army, for not enforcing the call for militia to turn out around Baton Rouge. They must emulate the patriotism of Orleanians, he warned, for their only safety lay in resistance and vigilance.[79]

Jackson now ordered Villeré to obstruct the bayous directly south of New Orleans, principally Barataria, and had just the man in mind to help with the job.[80] Only a day or two earlier the Laffite brothers came into New Orleans.[81] The general met them and sent Jean to join militiamen on Bayou St. Denis commanded by Major Michael Reynolds.[82] Laffite took fifty men and artillery to Reynolds and conducted them to a place known as the Temple, the most defensible spot on a route that could bring enemy boats from the Gulf into Barataria Bay, through Little Lake Barataria, past the narrows at the Temple, and eventually up Barataria Bayou to the Mississippi just a few miles upstream from New Orleans. The smuggler and the major worked with commendable energy, and two days later Reynolds sent him back to the general to report the job completed, after which the smuggler returned to the Temple.[83] Seeing the Laffites taking arms with the defenders excited the citizens, and Jackson's engineer Tatum believed that the Baratarians would make gallant defenders.[84]

Jackson's confidence grew with each day that passed with no report of British sightings. Everyone expected an attack now. They knew the enemy was on Lake Borgne, but more than a week had passed since the gunboat battle, with no further hard news.[85] Some began to relax, and there was little to do but patrol the streets and wait. A few civilians even began to discount the threat, concluding there was little danger after all.[86] Had it succeeded, a mission Patterson initiated the day after the loss of the gunboats might have illuminated enemy movements. He sent Ensign Thomas Shields and Dr. Robert Morrell under a white flag to seek permission to tend the American wounded and bring them back.[87]

The next day they reached Pine Island, where Captain Gordon took them aboard *Seahorse*, and the next morning they met Cochrane, who read

Patterson's request without comment and then sent them to the island. They had seen too much of his buildup for the invasion, and he suspected that spying was their true mission all along.[88] He would not allow them to leave until the coming battle was fought and New Orleans's fate decided. They went to the hospital ship *Gorgon* but did not see Jones's wounded at first for fear of their learning what the Yankee sailors had seen and heard. As a further precaution against them getting intelligence back to Jackson, the boat they came in was sunk. For days they bounced from *Sophie* to *Gorgon* until December 24, when at last they got to see their wounded.[89] Meanwhile, well through December 22, the American guard boats patrolling Lake Borgne clearly overlooked the buildup of small craft just above Bayou Bienvenue.[90] In less than forty-eight hours Cochrane would have nothing more to hide.

Old Hickory's anxiety abated considerably on December 19 with the arrival of General Coffee.[91] Jackson trusted no one more than John Coffee, whose wife was Rachel Jackson's niece. Coffee had repeatedly proved himself a solid and dependable subordinate who was every bit as combative as Jackson himself. Coffee had pushed his men on an exhausting march, much of it through continual rain.[92] Old Hickory repeatedly sent expresses to urge him on with all speed.[93] Coffee left Baton Rouge at dawn December 17 for a forced march with eight hundred men healthy enough to ride, leaving the rest to catch up.[94] He hoped to reach the city by December 20, and on December 18 was within fifteen miles of New Orleans, to be met by an urgent, almost panicked, dispatch from Jackson written the day before that the enemy might even then be within six hours of the city.[95]

Jackson was not above hyperbole when nervous. In fact, even if a perfect wind put enemy boats on Lake Pontchartrain on December 17, they would still be at least eighty miles and a dozen hours from Bayou St. John. The point to his exaggeration was that he desperately needed Coffee, and quickly.[96] By the morning of December 19, Coffee camped just four miles above the city, having covered 120 miles in thirty-six hours of actual riding.[97] The rest of his command arrived the next day, inspiriting civilians hourly expecting to see the enemy on their streets.[98]

Jackson needed more troops and now anxiously waited to hear from his old friend General William Carroll, whose volunteers had an eventful voyage from Nashville down the Cumberland River to the Ohio and thence to the Mississippi, sometimes practicing maneuvers on the decks of their flatboats.[99] On the way they met one of the pair of boats that left Pittsburgh with arms for Jackson.[100] Hours later came the boats with now General Adair's Kentuckians. Carroll told him to take the arms rather than wait for muskets to catch up to him at New Orleans, but Adair inexplicably left them and continued on his way unarmed.[101] Carroll reached Natchez late December 13, just ahead of the keelboat, and finally took about 1,100 muskets from her.[102] His trip had been uncommonly fast thus far, but the last leg proved slower than expected and he reached Coffee's bivouac only on December 21, just five hours after the balance of Coffee's men arrived.[103] Carroll had covered almost 1,300 miles in twenty-one days on the water, averaging over 60 miles a day.[104]

Carroll's arrival on Coffee's heels boosted morale, especially after Major Thomas Hinds's company of Mississippi dragoons also came in that same evening. Some joked that Jackson soon would have more men than he could use.[105] Adair's Kentuckians were expected any hour now, and their arrival would inflate the army to 10,000 or more. To some that seemed to guarantee little chance of being overrun by a surprise attack. Certainly, people were still alarmed, but as more time passed with no sight of the enemy, familiarity would get them accustomed to the danger, perhaps even complaisant.[106] Soon rumor did its part by claiming—erroneously—that the British were actually withdrawing toward Mobile.[107]

Despite the impending arrival of heavy reinforcements, Jackson still needed that second keelboat load of muskets from Pittsburgh.[108] A steamboat would have put them in his hands long before now, whereas the missing keelboat was almost nine weeks out of Pittsburgh and still nowhere in sight.[109] As it was, as soon as Coffee's men got a night's sleep, Jackson put them to work repairing their old muskets and being issued fresh ammunition by his quartermasters.[110]

Fortunately, Jackson did find about 1,600 muskets in the city armory on his arrival, some with an interesting history.[111] Back in 1810, a man named Henri de la França sold three hundred muskets to West Florida's Colonel Reuben Kemper, who gave his personal note for $11,850. When the United States took over, he relinquished the weapons. Most went to New Orleans and were now in the hands of Claiborne's militia and Jackson's regulars, but Washington never assumed Kemper's debt to de la França.[112] Some of those muskets now went to the unarmed men among Carroll's regiments.

The army would not be short of gunpowder for those weapons. It had twenty-eight tons of powder on hand, as well as almost 22,000 musket cartridges, several thousand for cannon, and more than 28,000 shot for thirty-seven guns ranging from small six-pounders up to hefty twenty-fours.[113] More was on the way from Pittsburgh. On December 12 and 13, boats had left with seven more big guns, over 5,000 assorted shot, 1,500 muskets, and half a million musket cartridges, as well as another fifteen tons of gunpowder, and two and one-half tons of musket balls and buckshot. Depending on weather and river conditions, some of this might reach Jackson in time as well.[114] Until then, Lieutenant Patterson readily shared his naval stores.

By December 22, Old Hickory had about 3,200 at hand—600 men in the detachments of the 7th and 44th Regulars dispersed among forts and batteries, 2,150 under Coffee and Carroll, Major Hinds's 230 Mississippi Dragoons, Captain Smith's 40 Louisiana Dragoons, and 208 assorted army, navy, and marines crewing the *Carolina* and *Louisiana*.[115] That did not include several local militia units that, on paper at least, added another 5,500. In just the past week three troops of volunteer horsemen reached the city, one from the Attakapas country west of the river, another from Feliciana under Captain Jedediah Smith, and a troop from Bayou Sara, led by Captain Llewellyn Griffith. Two more companies of dragoons had been raised in New Orleans, and when all of Coffee's and Carroll's stragglers came in, and Adair's Kentuckians arrived, Jackson's total force—on paper at least—might top 12,000.[116]

The small outposts at Fort Petites Coquilles and Fort St. John were intended chiefly to provide early warning of enemy movement, and other than New Orleans itself and English Turn, the only position Jackson had to hold was Fort St. Philip, where Major Overton had nearly five hundred men, including a free black "Mulatto Corps," and ample heavy artillery. Month-old letters arriving from Washington brought Senator Brown's promise to keep pressing to get him more arms and men, and Congressman Robertson, unaware that both officers were out of the war with wounds, sent news that experienced regular army brigadier generals Winfield Scott and Edmund P. Gaines would soon be on their way to him.[117]

Thousands of miles away, in the city of Ghent, British and American delegates had given up trying to keep their wartime territorial conquests. The last obstacles were Britain's desire for free trade on the Mississippi and its lucrative business with the Indians. The Americans flatly refused the former, and the British did not press the latter. They agreed to return Indian property and rights to prewar status, which the Americans secretly had no intention of honoring.[118] Louisianans could not know it, but by December 23, as Jackson prepared an army to defend America's most valuable port from British invasion, the nations were within hours of a treaty to end the war.

At that moment in the city, Americans celebrated the gallant Tennesseans' arrival. Several miles below them, hundreds of redcoats moved unseen over the footpath beside the Villeré canal. Five hours of daylight lay ahead. The river road to New Orleans was in sight.[119]

Seven

"By the Eternal! I'll Fight Them Tonight"

Twenty-nine-year-old Major René Gabriel Villeré breakfasted that morning at his family home, where Captain Jacques Toutant's company of the 3rd Louisiana Militia maintained a guard post. He was writing a letter in the general's dining room during the meal.[1] His brother Caliste, just fifteen, sat with him. A sergeant just put the finishing touches on a muster roll while others relaxed outside or smoked cigars by the fireplace. A mirror over the mantel showed the smokers a reflection of the cane field behind the house and the cypress swamp in the distance.[2]

A minor surge of excitement had stirred them the evening before when a fisherman named Jesus came from Des Pêcheurs with a story of seeing the enemy landing at the bayou's mouth. Major Villeré refused to believe him and physically threatened him for "creating false alarms," finally releasing him on his promise not to spread his tale. Enough rumors excited the people already. There was no need to notify Jackson, nor did the major feel it necessary to investigate.[3]

Jesus was likely forgotten the next morning when one of the smokers glanced at the mirror and saw a battalion of the 95th Rifles noiselessly moving double-quick through the cane toward the front of the house. Before the Americans could scramble to the door, the house was surrounded and Villeré's twenty-seven-man detachment disarmed. Colonel William Thornton and a guard entered the dining room and put the Villeré brothers under guard by themselves in another room. Seeing the lieutenant watching them being none too attentive, Gabriel whispered to Caliste to stay there and offer no resistance, then dashed for a window and leapt out onto the gallery.[4]

He ran past surprised sentries, jumped a picket fence, and disappeared into the tall cane as scattered shots whizzed past him. His favorite hunting setter ran after him, and a squad of soldiers followed.

Once Villeré reached the cypresses he made to climb a tree to hide, when his dog began barking, which would surely lead pursuers to him. Taking a fallen branch, he clubbed the dog senseless, covered it with leaves, and went up the tree. Unable to find him, the redcoats soon gave up, whereupon Gabriel climbed down and crept along the edge of the swamp to a plantation below. There he met Colonel De La Ronde and a few others, informing them of the emergency, and the two rowed a skiff across the river to the plantation of Dusuau de la Croix. While De La Ronde remained behind to gather militia, de la Croix provided mounts for himself and Villeré to gallop up the river road to raise the alarm.

Behind them, it was perhaps ten o'clock when the rest of Colonel Thornton's advance guard emerged from the cypresses and formed in line to make a show of numbers if spotted. Once clear of the wood, they swarmed over the plantation. The Villeré home was a fine single-story house with wide galleries all around, set amid oaks and pecans, with a formal garden in front and a fragrant orange and lemon grove nearby. An avenue of shade trees ran from the front gallery to the levee, and Thornton's prime objective, the river road.[5] Immediately after capturing the militia, the redcoats pushed on cautiously. It was about 1,000 yards to the levee, mostly over level ground broken up here and there by rail fences and water-filled ditches and irrigation drains.[6]

Thornton took the road before noon and immediately thereafter the levee. He wheeled his men into a line with its left flank on the river and the right extending to the road, and then advanced. The main road was just a track on the soil but good and dry, running beside and sometimes atop the levee. They moved perhaps half a mile, crossing the canal separating Villeré's plantation from Major Pierre Lacoste's, and there Major General John Keane halted them. As they marched, the redcoats thoroughly searched houses, outbuildings, even slave cabins, finding that the white inhabitants had fled but many slaves remained.[7]

Keane's spirits were buoyed by the absence of any Americans, but his men were exhausted from their all-night travel. They needed rest, especially as they were likely to see combat in the next twenty-four hours. Besides, Keane did not want to risk being cut off or overrun before reinforcements came. He prudently halted to await the arrival of the rest of the army.[8] Lacoste's field to his right offered a good bivouac, so he sent a company of pickets under Travers down the road another half mile to watch against surprise, and one hundred men from the 4th back the way they had come to guard the road in their rear at the woods.[9] With Villeré presumably wandering the swamp, Keane was convinced that Jackson knew nothing of their presence.

WHEN VILLERÉ AND de la Croix reined their horses opposite New Orleans, they found a boat to cross the river, then raced to Jackson's headquarters to deliver the alarm even as others were not far behind with similar news.[10] They found Old Hickory in the parlor with Livingston, Davezac, and others.[11] It was just after noon.[12] What Villeré and de la Croix said now was startling. Gabriel had not lingered to determine the redcoats' numbers, but he surely glimpsed scores if not hundreds.[13]

The news should not have been entirely a surprise. The evening before, De La Ronde had sent him word of sails seen off Lake Borgne's lower shores. This very morning Old Hickory had sent a troop of mounted militia riding down Bayou Terre-aux-Boeufs to watch for any approach by one of the bayous connecting it with the lake.[14] He had also sent Latour and Tatum down the river road at eleven o'clock to reconnoiter. As they approached De La Ronde's plantation, they encountered fugitives running toward New Orleans and quickly learned that the British were at Villeré's and coming on. Major Tatum immediately rode back to warn Jackson, while Latour continued on carefully to learn more. By 1:30 he reached Lacoste's property to see just a few hundred yards below him a redcoat line stretching from the levee to the woods and swamp, and reckoned they numbered 1,800.[15]

According to de la Croix, when he and Villeré finished speaking, Jackson pounded his fist on a table and declared, *"By the Eternal! The British shall not sleep upon our territory!"*[16] Villeré recalled Old Hickory telling his aides, "Gentlemen the British have landed: By G—, we must drive them back to their boats," and concluding, "By the Eternal! I'll fight them tonight."[17] Whatever he said, it included an oath. Shortly before two o'clock he ordered an alarm gun at Fort St. Charles to be fired at intervals for an hour or more to summon his militia. He intended to take the enemy by surprise and attack.[18] If the sound of the gun carried downriver to the British, they made nothing of it.

From distant antiquity to the latest generation, a timeless measure of leadership has been a commander's response to the unexpected. Those who see opportunity through the gloom often achieve greatness. It is more than reactionary daring. Anyone can be brave. Recklessness worth the hazard is something else. It demands insight, the acceptance of responsibility as well as risk, and a cool grasp of the balance of probable loss versus potential gain. Often it is a matter of instinct rather than calculation. Half a century in the future, generals named Grant and Lee would demonstrate precisely these attributes, as would another Jackson of their time.

As did Andrew Jackson now. Confronted by one of the worst surprises in American military history to date, he resolved to do what he could with what he had rather than take refuge in a rationale for inaction. That afternoon he showed that he, too, had the capacity for greatness. He knew the opportunity was fleeting. A night attack posed many hazards, but should the fight go against him, he could withdraw with little fear of enemy pursuit over unknown ground and be in no worse position than he was now. Besides, he sensed greater danger in delay. If he waited for dawn, he could lose surprise, and a daylight battle on the open field favored the experienced British professionals.[19] Moreover, he recognized the advantages on his side: a peculiar geography favoring defense, and an army, if untrained and inexperienced, that had the powerful incentive of being on home ground with hearths to protect. His greatest advantage of all was indomitable will and enthusiasm tempered by sufficient maturity not to reach too far.[20]

Just that morning Jackson had concluded that the British had made no important movements since capturing the gunboats, remaining convinced that they would try the Rigolets–Fort Petits Coquilles route, thence to Bayou St. John, or else westward across the lake to land upriver and isolate the city from reinforcement. Wherever they landed, he expected to stop them.[21] At that instant his forces were best positioned to meet an enemy advance on the Gentilly road from Chef Menteur. The Kentucky volunteers were still in transit and only the portion of Coffee's command in good health and well mounted was camped a few miles above the city. Major Thomas Hinds, a good friend of Jackson's who had served several terms in the territorial legislature, had his dragoons camped near Coffee, but they were worn down from a 160-mile ride, and Jackson attached them to Coffee's command as a rearguard.[22] Major Thomas Beale's riflemen, bivouacked near Hinds's and Carroll's Tennesseans, were a few miles farther upstream. Plauché's volunteers were at Bayou St. John, three miles distant, and only the 7th and 44th Infantries were in the city's immediate environs, along with a few volunteer companies. Jackson could reasonably expect to consolidate all but Carroll at Fort St. Charles by late afternoon and determined to have him remain behind to augment the militia watching the Gentilly road.[23]

No one had expected the enemy to appear at Villeré's, but Tatum's confirmation of the enemy landing reached Jackson soon afterward.[24] The Americans puzzled for some time over the enemy's sudden and unexpected appearance, and what might have happened had not Jackson been warned.[25] Almost everyone assumed treason to be behind it, especially since the enemy came by almost the only unguarded route.[26] At first Jackson suspected someone in Villeré's command, but before long attention almost universally focused on the fishermen and oyster gatherers.[27] Others attracted suspicion, most notably Joseph D. Bellechase, a militia commander who had flirted with Burr in 1806 and was believed to be an associate of James Workman and Lewis Kerr. Should the culprits be identified to a surety, Edward Palfrey of Plauché's Battalion promised a few days later that "there will be some hanging work after it is all over."[28]

At Jackson's order, the alarm gun began firing at two p.m. It astonished many and stopped most from what they were doing.[29] "All at once we were drawn out of the uncertainty in which we were by the news which spread with lightning speed," one *creole* confessed.[30] Attorney Ellery thought that "a report of the descent of the English from a fleet of balloons, could scarcely have excited greater astonishment."[31] Old mulatto vendors ran aimlessly on the streets with their baskets of oranges and apples on their heads, fear contorting their faces and "yelling as if the whole circle of infernal gods was at their heels."[32] North of town, General William Carroll's recently arrived men were just then standing in line drawing rations and ammunition.[33]

The few stores still open shuttered their doors. The editor and pressmen of *L'Ami des Lois* closed down and went to their muster.[34] Several women at merchant Pierre Cenas's home on Royal Street had been sewing clothing for newly arrived volunteers and rushed to the balconies at the alarm, to stand there weeping and wringing their hands as the volunteers ran down the street below them toward the Place d'Armes.[35] Amid all the apprehension and excitement, some still felt relieved that finally something was about to happen.[36]

Jackson sent Edward Livingston to calm them with his assurance that the enemy would never reach the city.[37] Already rumors flew, and one report spread that up to 5,000 redcoats had come through the swamps and were within a dozen miles of town.[38] The last thing he needed now was public tears dampening the volunteers' willingness to leave their wives and daughters in the city while they marched to meet the foe, especially after another rumor quickly arose that the enemy was bent on plunder and perhaps worse.[39] Livingston quietly asked Pierre Laffite to get his wife, Louise, to safety in case of defeat.[40]

His course determined, Old Hickory sent Griffith's dragoons to see if the enemy had advanced since that morning, and summoned the 7th and 44th to the Place d'Armes to form ranks in front of the cathedral as scores of women waved their handkerchiefs from surrounding balconies.⁴¹ Jackson fired off verbal orders rather than take time to pen them, calling Coffee, Carroll, and Plauché in from their camps.⁴² Soon afterward Griffith ran into Travers's pickets, who opened fire, killing one or two horses and hitting Private Thomas Scott, the first American wounded in the defense of New Orleans. Griffith's report brought Jackson a guess at enemy numbers and the critically important information that Keane had not moved beyond Lacoste's.⁴³

Coffee was just finishing a letter to his wife, Mary, when a rider brought Jackson's order to march at once.⁴⁴ In moments Coffee was in the saddle, leaving Carroll to follow.⁴⁵ An hour later, from a balcony at the corner of Royal and Bienville, women watched the mounted Tennesseans jockeying through the city streets, many of them without a vestige of uniform but dressed as farmers and hunters and in long coats that reminded onlookers of Quakers.⁴⁶ Mud still clung to their clothing after a night on the ground without tents or blankets, and they drew cartridges from their commissaries as they marched.⁴⁷ The men knocked the necks from bottles of spirits and beer handed them by citizens along the way, and passed them through the ranks.⁴⁸

Jackson had ordered Claiborne to mobilize what militia he could, and the governor assembled and assumed command of about four hundred by three p.m.⁴⁹ Finding some with no muskets, he issued them pikes instead, and marched the cheering men to Fort Charles.⁵⁰ As soon as Coffee reported, Jackson gave him his orders. He and 695 Tennesseans along with 62 of Beale's Rifles, 50 of Griffith's dragoons, and 200 of Hinds's dragoons—just over 1,000 mounted men in all—would compose a left-wing brigade and reserve. Davezac soon had them on their way to Fort Charles to draw ammunition.⁵¹ Meanwhile, Plauché's Uniformed Battalion of Orleans Volunteers, numbering some three hundred men and composed of the combined companies of Pierre Roche, St. Gême, White, Hudry, Augustus Guibert, and Jugeat's Choctaws, was sprinting in from Bayou St. John at a pace one witness compared to lightning.⁵² Joseph Savary's 1st Battalion of Free Men of Color, led by Daquin, were also expected but not yet in sight.⁵³

When Old Hickory finished issuing orders for units to assemble at the Place d'Armes, he ate four tablespoons of boiled rice and half a cup of coffee—all he could keep down—then stretched out on a sofa at his headquarters for a nap.⁵⁴ He still suffered chronic dysentery, recurring pain from his dueling wounds, and now habitual lack of sleep, but he was up again in half an hour as the companies began arriving, and left with his staff for the Place d'Armes.⁵⁵ They rode past Beale's home, where Eliza Chotard, her two sisters, and their mother watched from a balcony in apprehension. Old Hickory stopped momentarily and assured them they had nothing to fear, that he would drive the enemy back to his fleet. Eliza never forgot the scene. "They were the most splendid horsemen I ever saw," she remembered, "being dressed in full uniform, well mounted and caparisoned, and as bright, and gay, as if going to a bridal ceremony." The women moved into a parlor to comfort each other but, despite intermittent rain, repeatedly returned to the balcony hoping to hear news.[56] It was going to be a long night.

At the Place d'Armes the general found five companies of the 7th and three companies of the 44th waiting, eight hundred or more strong.[57] There were also two six-pounders of Colonel William McRae's artillery and eighty-six men commanded by Lieutenant Samuel Spotts, as well as about sixty of Patterson's marines. In all Jackson had about 1,400 present, and he constituted them another brigade and assigned it to Colonel Ross. With Coffee's brigade, the army numbered about 2,300 all told.[58] Given that the mounted units could not operate at full strength after dark, and some units, like Savary's, might not reach him in time, he might have no more than 1,700 to 1,800 in action.

Shortly after five o'clock, Jackson put the column in motion. Before leaving, he sent Livingston to see Commodore Patterson. The general had seen enough to know that the Mississippi made an impassable barrier on Keane's left flank at Lacoste's, while the swamp and woods on the enemy right were as good as impassable. That left Keane nowhere to go but forward or backward. If the *Carolina* and *Louisiana* dropped downriver to a position in line with the British camps, and if they opened fire simultaneously with Jackson's attack when it came, the result could be devastating. Keane could hardly get at the ships to silence their fire on his flank and rear.[59] To frost the cake, Old Hickory sent General Morgan orders to move down his side of the river to a point below the enemy position across the river, then seize whatever boats he could find and cross his men to march up the road to hit the British rear. With Yankees coming at them from their front, the river, and their rear, even a modest demonstration could put the enemy into a panic.[60]

It was a plan emblematic of Old Hickory: quick, daring, on its face impetuous, but founded on solid reasoning. It was a strategy that included him among the great captains of history. Confronted by unexpected and seeming disaster, his instinct was to turn it to his advantage. Within two hours of confirmation of Keane's position and strength, virtually all the volunteers were on the move except a company of "ancients" left to guard Government House. Just after the army marched, one of those guards wrote a friend that they expected a fight but no one despaired of the outcome.[61] More exempts stood under arms guarding New Orleans while, mindful of the possibility of enemy infiltrators, Old Hickory had constables and other exempts posted to arrest anyone suspicious or lacking a passport to be in the city.[62]

Jackson wanted Coffee's mounted men in the van since they could move faster, to be followed by the 44th and 7th, then Plauché followed by Daquin.[63] A volunteer company of boatmen and traders had just been raised, and he gave them orders to move with the advance as well.[64] At virtually the same time, Carroll's Tennesseans began coming into town from the other side. On receiving his instructions from Jackson, he had ordered his men to break open the boxes of muskets sent ahead from Baton Rouge and march the four miles to the city. Meanwhile, Jackson had some anxiety that Keane's landing might be a feint, and similar misgivings about leaving Louisiana militia to defend the city. He directed part of Carroll's command to remain in town while sending the 2nd Tennessee forward on the Gentilly road in case the enemy's main thrust came via Chef Menteur.[65] Should Keane prove to be the only threat, he could summon the rest of Carroll's command quickly enough.

Each successive piece of information refined Old Hickory's planning. By late afternoon he had enough information to determine what he hoped to accomplish and make conditional plans accordingly. He could have only one objective when he met the enemy: he must drive them back to their boats or into the swamps. He could not give them time to consolidate their position or bring up more troops, especially artillery. He must seize the initiative now, or else the enemy would take it on the morrow and march on the city.

Jackson might not have had military training, and only modest battlefield experience, but he intuitively understood elemental tactics. He had commanded in a few skirmishes against outnumbered foes in the Creek War, but only at Horseshoe Bend had he conducted what could be called a real battle. Although he outnumbered the Creeks, still they held some advantage in a lightly fortified defensive position. He engaged them frontally with a part of his command and sent Coffee on a sweeping movement out of sight, to appear suddenly on the Creek flank and rear, virtually surrounding them. Only a fragment escaped.

Horseshoe Bend was not exactly comparable to the situation facing him now, but it came close. The foe at last report was stationary. The bend in the Tallapoosa River had constrained the Creeks at Horseshoe Bend much as the Mississippi and the swamp confined the British. With *Carolina* and

Louisiana acting as floating batteries midstream to rake the enemy camps, Jackson could hit them in their front with Ross's brigade while Coffee swept unseen around the enemy right to deliver a deadly flanking blow. He still needed three vital pieces of information before he could settle on more than that, however: Were the British still stationary or were they marching toward him? What were their real numbers? And did they occupy a line all across the land between the levee and the swamps, or was there room to get around their right flank?

Colonel Ross's brigade took fully an hour to pass onto the main road in files of two after Coffee rode out. Several men simply attached themselves to the column, among them Major Villeré, no doubt anxious to redeem himself.[66] Claiborne and the militia brought up the rear, but when the column was about three miles out of the city, Jackson halted it and told Claiborne to move to watch the Gentilly road to Chef Menteur.[67] The governor had hoped to lead his militia in the coming battle, and was severely disappointed to be shunted away, but it was a prudent move. The Gentilly road worried Jackson, suggesting that was the route he would have tried had he been in Keane's boots. Claiborne might at least stop or delay an enemy column there long enough for help to arrive. Old Hickory's orders made it clear that he expected Claiborne to protect the city or "bury his men nobly" in the effort.[68]

Jackson was also getting Claiborne out of the way. With dreams of military glory common to politicians of the era, the governor regarded the order as a deliberate effort to deny him his chance. Upon reading it, he complained to one of his regimental commanders that the general deliberately sought to keep him off the path to glory.[69] Some of the militia felt the same, and the order caused some murmuring in the ranks. Claiborne repeated his plaint to Shaumburg, but the captain pointed out the vital status of the Chef Menteur pass to their defense.[70]

Down the road from the advancing Americans, Keane held firm to his decision to remain in place, seconded by others who concurred in the prudence of awaiting the remainder of the infantry and more artillery.[71] He put his two little six-pounders together with Lane's rockets in a single line beside the road, with the 85th and 95th behind them in close order, and the 4th in a third line at the rear, followed by the companies of the 93rd.[72] It was about three o'clock, and some of the men were cooking their rations, when he heard shots several hundred yards up the road. It was Griffith's Feliciana cavalry running into Captain Travers' pickets.[73] Thornton sent Captain Halen's company of the 95th and a company from the 85th to support Travers, and after they fired a few rounds the Americans withdrew.[74] For the men in the camps it was a minor alarm soon forgotten as they spread out in a green field between the road and the levee to bivouac and began what many thought would be a peaceful day devoted to dinner and rest.[75]

Once allowed to break formation, those who did not collapse to sleep had a chance to look at the ground around them. Villeré's and Lacoste's fields were like almost all of the river road cane plantations. The main houses sat close to the road, their painted white walls raised several feet aboveground on brick piers for ventilation and to remain above the water when the flooding river broke the levee. Groves and avenues of orange and lemon trees, sometimes mixed with figs and even pomegranate, dotted the grounds and formal gardens. Behind the houses sat slave cabins that were little more than huts, and back from those the cane fields stretched as much as a mile to the swamp, with sometimes a patch of corn or rice, even tobacco, but little cotton, which did not grow well there.[76] Thornton's men soon helped themselves to fruit from the trees, sugar from the sugar houses, and cured hams and more, and sent some of it back to the landing place, where Captain James Gordon and others delightedly accepted the bounty.[77]

Ditches segmented the cane fields into two-acre parcels, providing irrigation when needed and drainage to keep the cane from spoiling in rainy seasons. Close to the slave cabins sat the sugar "factory" where farmers ground or "rolled" syrup from the cane with animal power and a few steam engines. The juice ran into iron kettles for boiling until the sugar crystallized. Cane had already been cut and the "rolling season" had just ended, so finished sugar sat in the plantations' barns and warehouses awaiting shipment. Cane cuttings to plant the next crop lay in the fields in so-called mattresses covered with fodder and earth to protect against frost.[78]

No one yet anticipated that the cane stubble, ditches, mattresses, and even the barrels of sugar and sorghum might become aids and obstacles in the days ahead. Ensign Arthur Gerard of the 4th thought everyone involved in planning their operation was sadly ignorant of the country's topography. Cochrane's copy of the Lafon map told nothing of the nature of the bayous and swamp or the irrigation and drainage ditches. Information from the fishermen and friendly creoles helped, but not overmuch. To Gerard's mind, that only compounded the problem of landing Keane's army in halves.

As a mere ensign, he was hardly privy to what happened in admirals' cabins and generals' tents, but he feared that his leaders' faculties had been somehow paralyzed by want of information. Every army has its croakers and ex–post facto strategists, but he outdid himself. Cochrane and Keane ought to have anticipated everything that Jackson was about to do, he later claimed. If the American commander had been "enterprising or courageous," he concluded, Keane ought to have been utterly defeated. As it was, having landed with an insufficient force, their greatest error was stopping that afternoon when they reached the road. Had Keane advanced instead, concluded Gerard from his lofty vantage of hindsight, they would have taken New Orleans.[79]

Perhaps so, but now someone else was moving on the river road. A mile or two after sending Claiborne to the Gentilly road, and as the twilight started to fade, the Americans arrested a black man on the levee. Tremayne's printing press had been busy, and he carried copies of Cochrane's proclamation promising that *creoles* would be unmolested if they stayed home. Jackson relieved the hapless man of his burden, but from that point onward, as they passed down the road, they saw copies of the proclamation pinned to fence posts, a reminder that the British believed much of the local population could be persuaded not to assist the Yankees.[80]

Coffee's advance had not yet torn the last of the proclamations from its post when the twilight faded out about 6:30. Yet his men still saw dim light ahead, the flickering glow of hundreds of campfires scarcely a mile away.

Eight

"Fury and Confusion"

WHILE STILL FORMING his regiments, Old Hickory sent another reconnaissance to assess Keane's numbers. At the same time he dispatched De La Ronde to his plantation immediately above Lacoste's to be ready to guide Coffee if Jackson sent him on a flank movement.[1] Pierre Laffite rode with Coffee at the head of his column and remained at his side through the rest of the evening as another guide and interpreter.[2] The march pressed on rapidly. Plauché's men had already double-quicked almost twelve miles, and some were plainly worn-out.[3] He notified Ross that he could not keep up and that Daquin's battalion, which was trying to catch up behind him, was equally exhausted.[4] Getting no reply, Plauché went to him in person, only to be ignored. Ross was drinking again.[5] If the Americans spread out too much on their march, Jackson would be vulnerable to a British surprise if he suddenly ran into redcoats concentrated to attack.

Then the latest reconnaissance came in to report seeing about 2,000 redcoats, with more arriving, and they were all preparing to camp for the night in the open ground between the Villeré house and the levee.[6] That was all Jackson needed to know. He might have fewer than 1,800 men immediately on hand, but the guns of *Carolina* and *Louisiana* would give him parity with the enemy, and if lucky he could catch the foe at rest in their bivouac. Better yet, his scouts also reported that the ground on De La Ronde's and Lacoste's plantations was clear of redcoats all the way back to the cypress swamp. Coffee could make a flank march to the left along the woods to appear unexpectedly on the enemy's right flank at the same time that Jackson launched Ross on a frontal attack. It was an opportunity he would only have tonight, and only if he moved quickly. That was a decision made for Old Hickory.

The sun was two hours gone when the general and his staff approached De La Ronde's at about seven o'clock. Jackson, Hayne, and Coffee rode forward across De La Ronde's fields and a few hundred yards onto Lacoste's until perhaps half a mile from the enemy camp. From what they could see by twilight and the glow from British campfires, Keane's men were at ease and cooking their suppers. Old Hickory ordered Coffee to move his men close to the woods on the boundary between De La Ronde's and Lacoste's, dismount them, then continue forward afoot until abreast of the enemy's right flank. Then he was to wheel right and swoop down on Keane's exposed right and rear. Patterson's ships opening fire from the river would be Coffee's signal to move, and the same for Ross, and should Patterson be delayed, they were to advance at the sound of each other's musketry. That would also signal Morgan to strike the enemy rear. Ross was to advance in a line and push forward until engaged, and then wheel the line to its right to push the enemy toward the levee.[7]

His orders given, there was nothing for Jackson to do in the next few minutes but wait. Seven hours earlier he had been taken by surprise. Now he planned not just to disrupt Keane but to erase him. Of course, there were intangibles. The unexpected, the weather, the terrain, human emotions, and more all impacted a battle, and none could be anticipated entirely. A military operation was like a machine: a commander might have everything in place, every contingency anticipated, but once movement commenced, friction inevitably set in, and components began to fail. Here and now, Jackson's "machine" was ready. Out in the gathering darkness the unexpected awaited.

A nearly full moon gave the Yankees some ambient light, but clouds and wisps of fog along the riverbank kept their movements unseen.[8] De La Ronde and Laffite were excellent guides, but several ditches in his path made Coffee take longer than anticipated to get in position, even with Hinds's dismounted dragoons going ahead of him to take down fences in their path.[9] If Coffee was late, a good river current had Patterson's ships approaching their assigned position in line with the enemy camps earlier than expected. That compromised Jackson's intended coordination before the first gun was fired, but planning a simultaneous action at night between two elements roughly 1,500 yards apart was always liable to upset.

Carolina had left her mooring about dusk, sails furled, for the two-hour float downstream, with *Louisiana* behind her.[10] Commanding *Carolina* was a nephew of George Washington's, thirty-three-year-old John Dandridge

Henley of Virginia, who had completed her crew only that afternoon.[11] The moon gave *Carolina*'s helmsman enough light to keep midstream, and once past the tight bend in front of the city the river ran nearly straight for four miles until it took a slight left turn.[12] It straightened again just as the ships came abreast of De La Ronde's. Had he known where to look, Henley might have climbed his rigging to see Jackson's army drawn up in the darkness beyond the levee. Knowing what to look for, Old Hickory saw *Carolina*'s mastheads as she silently glided past on the current.[13] Henley fixed his eyes elsewhere. Just 1,000 yards ahead, he saw scores of campfires that silhouetted hundreds of redcoats with their flames. It was about 7:30.[14] They were just minutes from action.

Beside those fires, most of Keane's men had not eaten since the day before, hunger adding to their weariness after the night cramped in boats.[15] The appearance of the Yankee mounted patrol interrupted them at preparing their camp, but after driving it off Keane allowed them to return to scavenging fence rails to make fires and waiting for their dinners to cook. Their arms were stacked. As the rations of salted pork and beef bubbled in pots, some men bought chickens and turkeys from a slave, while others just took them from the pens on Lacoste's plantation and started to roast them on bayonets as spits. The aroma of roasting fowl spread through the camp and out over the river as the first to finish cooking began to eat.[16] Ensign Gleig enjoyed an excellent dinner accompanied by a glass of claret, and prepared to lie down for the night.[17] Ensign William Graves of the 93rd was just roasting a goose brought in by his servant.[18] None seemed concerned that their bright fires might alert anyone. They had no doubt of complete success ahead.[19] Some Americans stealthily approaching thought they had "more the air of invited guests, than hostile enemies."[20]

Carolina did not go entirely unseen. Captain William Halen and eighty men of the 95th Rifles relieved Travers to establish a picket line between the levee and the road some nine hundred yards in advance of the camps, and behind a canal that separated the Lacoste and De La Ronde plantations.[21] He saw the ship's masts floating past perhaps a quarter mile distant, and sent word to Thornton, but *Carolina* moved faster than the messenger.[22] Others saw her as well but had no idea of her true mission. Some thought her a merchantman trying to leave port before the British took over.[23] A few believed she was bringing them supplies sent by welcoming citizens of New Orleans.[24] At about eight o'clock Gleig saw her drop a bow anchor directly opposite their camps, and men nearest the levee heard the splash as it hit the water. Some watched as she pivoted on her anchor cable and turned her head into the current, bringing her starboard broadside directly to bear on

Keane's camps.[25] Artillery officer George Chesterton, stationed near the road with the three-pounders, had his back to a fire for warmth while he and a comrade talked of the Christmas festivities friends and family at home would be having in a few hours.[26]

Barely a hundred yards from the bank directly opposite the British camp, *Carolina* dropped anchor with a splash echoing across the water's surface. Some of the redcoats mistook her for a trading vessel and ran to the shore, calling, "Schooner ahoy, what have you got to sell?" Henley answered by shouting, "Now, d—n their eyes, give it 'em" to his gun crews. The broadside lit up the river, casting the ship's reflection across the water.[27] Even then, a few redcoats thought it must be one of Cochrane's ships firing a salute, mistaking the yells of *Carolina*'s crew for cheering British sailors.[28]

Henley kept his fire as brisk as possible, hurling a shower of cannonballs, grapeshot, and even lengths of iron chain over the levee into the British camps to send stacked muskets flying, upset kettles, scatter fires, and bring down startled soldiers. Redcoats scrambled in all directions.[29] Several hundred yards in the distance, men with Jackson felt the rumbling concussion of the cannonade, and in the guns' flashes saw illuminated redcoats running to extinguish campfires as trumpets sounded and officers called them to their ranks, yelling, "Steady men, steady!" and "Remember, you are Britons!" Ensign Graves heard projectiles whizzing through the branches of the tree holding his cap and canteen, and looked to his side just as a length of chain shot separated Lieutenant John Sutherland of the 4th Foot from his head.[30]

Confusion approached panic in the darkness as officers struggled to buckle on their swords while privates dropped spoons and plates and ran for their muskets. Some took cover behind the Villeré house and outbuildings. Others, like Gleig, scrambled to the levee, which protected them from the hail of iron.[31] As they huddled there, some could hear *Carolina*'s crewmen talking with each other as they loaded and fired.[32]

The British were too seasoned to remain confused for long. The three-pounders near the levee being too close to fire over it, Thornton ordered rockets brought forward, but the ground was too uneven to aim them effectively, although they made a dramatic sight as they fizzed and sputtered sparks through the air.[33] The 4th being already to the rear of the camp, Thornton ordered them to form as a reserve under cover of the Villeré house and outbuildings.[34] The 85th was mostly under the levee now, and the 95th either with them or out exposed with Halen's picket.[35] Thornton rallied the men behind the levee and began moving them under its cover when, even as *Carolina*'s guns raked the shattered bivouac, he heard musketry up the

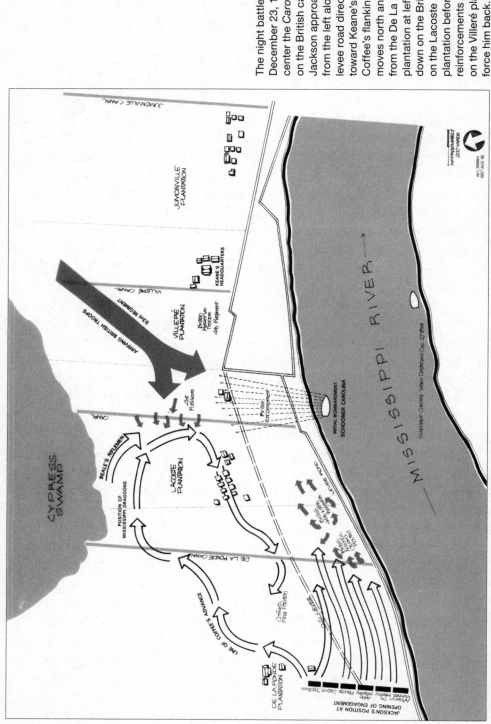

The night battle on December 23, 1814. At center the *Carolina* fires on the British camps. Jackson approaches from the left along the levee road directly toward Keane's advance. Coffee's flanking march moves north and east from the De La Ronde plantation at left to come down on the British rear on the Lacoste plantation before British reinforcements arriving on the Villeré plantation force him back.

road ahead of him and off to his right. The Americans were coming, and the flash from Ross's first volley revealed Halen's pickets to be almost surrounded by Americans.[36]

On hearing *Carolina's* fire, Jackson had put Ross's men in motion down the road to deploy into a line as they entered the De La Ronde plantation, with adjutants Chotard and Colonel Robert Butler to help Ross position the units.[37] It began well enough. They set Spotts's guns on the road and Jackson's quartermaster general Colonel William Piatt led Lieutenant Michael McClelland's company of the 7th down the road as a picket, accompanied by a few of Patterson's marines. The rest of the 7th formed line left of the cannon and then the 44th went into position to the left of the 7th. Thereafter, as each unit arrived, Ross was supposed to put it in a line extending to the left from the 44th; first Plauché's battalion, then Daquin when he appeared, followed by Jugeat's tiny company of Choctaw.[38] Last of all was the company of boatmen, who were to complete Jackson's line to the swamp and then pass through it if possible to the head of Bayou Bienvenue at the Villeré canal to close it to enemy boats and their landing more redcoats.[39]

Jackson put his regular regiments together beside the artillery, hoping the enemy would conclude he had concentrated his main strength there and decide to advance instead against Plauché and Daquin. When they did, they would be exposed to Coffee's attack on their right flank and rear if and when he got in position. Old Hickory formed his line at an acute angle to the road and the river and roughly parallel to the canal forming De La Ronde's upper property line. Spotts's guns had to move on the road, but it gradually bore away from the river, which would further contract that acute angle. Hence, as the line advanced, troops between the river and the road would be spread more thinly, while those left of the road would be increasingly compressed between it and the De La Ronde house and grounds. Anticipating that, Jackson instructed Ross to have each unit deploy in columns of two or more abreast as it left the road. When Daquin's left reached the De La Ronde grounds the line would be complete. Then they were to halt and face forward in an unbroken line two or more ranks deep.

He ought to have supervised such a critical movement in person, but he was more concerned with Coffee's flank march. Unfortunately, Ross forgot or ignored his orders and let units leave the road in a single line. The 7th and 44th fit between the road and De La Ronde's, but as they moved forward their line compressed and bent back in an arc that left no room for following units.[40] They also found the ground riddled with picket fences and ditches four or five feet wide and just as deep beside each fence, while more ditches out in the cane fields extended from the levee to the swamp.

Each ran directly across Jackson's line of advance. When his units left the road, they would have to scale or dismantle fences and jump or wade ditches, certain to disrupt organization, especially with a ground fog gathering in the cool evening.

Shortly after *Carolina* opened fire, Plauché's and Daquin's columns approached the front. Ross told Plauché to move to the left of the 44th, but in the darkness, fog, and now smoke from the schooner's cannon, they could not see the 44th. Plauché asked for a guide to lead him to the spot, but Ross seemed not to know where it was. Instead, he led the battalion back and forth aimlessly until a volley out of the darkness told them where the enemy was.[41] Plauché soon saw the cause of the confusion: Colonel Ross was drunk. Plauché ignored him and tried to find his own way.[42] He finally saw the 44th and the 7th but only after he had passed them, and now only spotted them as they were falling back from enemy fire on his right. He followed and they all stopped and deployed in a new line. Plauché went to ask Jackson for instructions and found him shifting the 7th and 44th to the right of the road and levee to ease the congestion on the line on the other side. Now he told Plauché to form on Spotts's left, and when Daquin finally arrived, Jackson sent him to extend Plauché's left.[43]

By the time *Carolina* opened fire, Coffee's brigade had reached a canal on De La Ronde's property and moved left along it to the edge of the swamp and wood, Beale continuing toward the front to engage any British pickets and mask Coffee's movement. In the distance several hundred yards ahead they saw the enemy campfires.[44] While the men themselves remained silent, Coffee challenged some of them that "you have said you could fight, now prove it."[45] In the flash of *Carolina*'s first broadside, Beale's men saw her illuminated; and as the firing commenced by the river, they heard a voice ahead of them call, "Who comes there?" Getting no answer, the redcoat pickets fired a volley that went over the Yankees' heads and then began yelling to put out their fires as general musketry opened over to the right on Jackson's front.[46]

With his units in place, Old Hickory ordered Spotts's six-pounders to open fire on Halen's picket, who immediately returned fire. The first British volley wounded Piatt and killed McClelland, probably the first American fatality of the engagement.[47] Plauché was in position now and opened fire, though not before officer brothers Pierre and Charles Roche gave each other what might be their last embrace.[48] The men fired vigorously, although targets were dimly seen, and Plauché found it difficult to calm his men's enthusiasm.[49] Soon he began to take casualties, including a feather in Henry Palfrey's hat broken by a bullet.[50] The left companies of the 7th, somewhat disorganized by the ditches and fences, finally got up to help force Halen back, and other than Ross himself, the regulars performed well, as professionals should have. Still, the best news for Jackson was that, despite fog and confusion, his militia and volunteers were standing fire well in their first action.[51]

Once recovered from surprise, the redcoats huddled behind the levee, formed ranks, cheered, and began returning fire with muskets and Congreve rockets.[52] Most of them were armed with the New Land Pattern musket, better known as the Brown Bess. It weighed almost ten pounds, measured four feet seven inches long from the muzzle at the tip of its .75-caliber smoothbore to its butt, and fired a patched or wrapped .69-caliber round ball with some accuracy up to fifty yards. A triangular bladed bayonet extended its total length by eighteen inches. Using paper cartridges, the Brown Bess could be fired three times a minute until the bore became so fouled with powder residue that it had to be cleaned out. The 95th, true to its name, carried the .62-caliber Baker rifle, which took better than three times as long to load but was considerably more accurate.[53]

When Thornton heard firing in the direction of Halen's picket, he sent a reinforcement from the Rifles.[54] Halen soon retired, bringing with him a bewildered American regular who had walked right up to his picket line in the fog. Unable to see or recognize the Rifles' uniform, the man innocently asked to be directed to Jackson's 44th Infantry and was taken prisoner.[55] That told Thornton that enemy regulars were in his front. He sent the 95th's quartermaster, William Surtees, with twenty years in uniform, forward to the right to bring over a company of the 85th posted beside one of the Lacoste houses to bolster Halen's skirmishers. Somehow Surtees passed Halen in the darkness and wound up in the garden of the De La Ronde house, within a few feet of Americans he could hear but not see. He hid until he thought the Yankees had passed, and then ran back to warn Thornton of the advancing enemy.[56]

Thornton soon sent the rest of the 85th forward to cover the 95th's right flank and hold his advance line. Led by Brevet Lieutenant Colonel Richard Gubbins, the 85th ran through cane stubble beside the road under heavy fire from *Carolina*, Captain Charles "Old Man" Grey's company in the lead. At the upper edge of the field they saw a group of men ahead of them, but with the fog and battle smoke it was too dark to distinguish friend from foe. When the group opened fire on them, Grey held fire, at first thinking they might be fellow redcoats. Gleig suggested that he halt the company and take cover, while Gleig went forward to see who was there. He crept unseen to within ten yards of the mystery group when he made out the uniforms of United States regulars.

He raced back to his company and Grey led them forward to within twenty yards of the Americans, halting behind piles of reeds and a fence. Still unsure the men ahead of them were the enemy, Grey stayed in position while Gleig took a dozen men around to the right of the strangers to strike their flank if they indeed proved to be the enemy. On the way he ran into men of the 95th separated from their regiment. They joined his party and moved forward over a picket fence to head for the flank of what Gleig was sure were American regulars.[57]

Meanwhile, Grey moved and halted behind that same fence a hundred yards to the left of Gleig. The Americans now knew from prisoners who faced them and shouted, "Come on, my brave 85th!" to lure them over.[58] Other voices in the darkness yelled, "Don't fire, we are your friends," and offered to help them over the fence. Unsuspecting, Grey and others of Gubbins's regiment stepped up to take the proffered helping hands and found themselves almost surrounded by Americans demanding surrender. Instead, Gubbins ordered his men to attack. "I never saw or heard of such fighting," he said a few weeks later. At one point he and a score of his men found themselves in a ditch surrounded by a hundred Yankees, with a dozen enemy muskets pointing at them. In close quarters, the redcoats found they could not fire their own muskets. Somehow they fought their way out of the ditch with swords, bayonets, and Brown Bess butts, as Gubbins put it, "dipping our hands deeply in blood."[59] Keane seconded him, hours later averring that "a more extraordinary conflict has perhaps never occurred." The combat was hand-to-hand, first with bayonets until the standing cane knocked them from their muskets, and then the men used their guns as clubs.[60] To Keane's surprise, they heard orders shouted in French as well as English, then muzzle flashes illuminated the red and green pom-poms atop the hats of Plauché's men.[61] Many had believed the French would not fight for the Americans, but the Uniformed Battalion proved that wrong.[62] It was probably one of their muskets that sent a ball drilling into Old Grey's head, killing him instantly.[63]

The 7th and 44th regiments fell back, leaving a handful of prisoners, while other Yankees tried to finesse the Rifles to Gubbins's right. "Come on, my brave 95th," yelled some, and a few of the Rifles were fooled and came forward to be captured.[64] Some in the 95th heard American officers shouting the commands "Ready—present—fire." Seasoned professionals fell prone at "present" and the coming volleys passed over them harmlessly. Then the British rose to fire their own in return.[65] Captain Robert Rogers and some of his officers of the frigate *Dover* were on that firing line, and after each enemy volley he shouted, "Now, my lads, up and give them another broadside!"[66]

Meanwhile, Gleig's small company pushed back some of the enemy in their front until they reached a group of slave huts, where they freed some recently captured comrades. Looking over the cane field to his left, Gleig saw a long line of men and walked over to identify them. From the now-foggy darkness a voice called on him not to fire, the speaker saying they were Yankees cut off from their unit. Gleig pretended that he knew who they were and replied that their regiment was over to his right, telling them to stay put and his company would take them to their friends. Returning to his men, the ensign had them fix bayonets and led them to the Americans, who recognized them too late. Gleig himself grabbed their commander's sword in his hand, declaring that they were surrounded and his prisoners.

The Yankees laid down their muskets, but then glimmers of moonlight or gun flashes revealed how few men Gleig had. The Yankees began picking up their muskets to make a fight. Gleig boldly demanded another officer's sword, and when he refused and turned to run, Gleig swung his sword at him and just nicked the back of his head. The redcoats rushed the group and soon put them to flight, though not before one nearly killed Gleig with a bayonet thrust that caught in his collar. As the Yankee reached for his trigger, Gleig slashed his head with his saber and the man dropped his gun and ran to the rear, after which Gleig returned his men to the slave huts.[67]

The confusion was soon epidemic. Men on both sides complained that the smoke and fog obscured almost everything, making maneuvering nearly impossible.[68] The fiery muzzle flashes darting through the gloom seemed to one redcoat like "the tails of so many comets," leading Surtees to assert that "as strange a description of fighting took place as is perhaps on record."[69] Adding to the fog was the acrid white smoke from small arms on both sides. Jackson's regulars carried the Model 1795 Springfield musket, a .69-caliber smoothbore that, in the best of conditions, fired three rounds a minute before powder residue fouled the barrel, and in action it was more like two rounds. It claimed some accuracy up to one hundred yards, and a fifteen-inch bayonet extended the bearer's reach in hand-to-hand fighting. The volunteers and militia carried a confusion of other models in calibers ranging from .50 to .64 and larger, a few virtual antiques, and many officers carried the .54 Model 1806 Harpers Ferry pistol. As a rule, British gunpowder was superior and more reliable than American.[70]

Following up his initial success, Gubbins headed toward Spotts's guns. Jackson saw his center getting disorganized and sent Hayne to straighten it out, but his line was starting to arc and the darkness made it impossible to correct entirely. Then the marines, commanded by Major Daniel Carmick, fell back, endangering Spotts's pieces, so Old Hickory sent Butler, Chotard, and the wounded Piatt to rally them and the 7th, while the 44th, temporarily out of position in the smoke, came back in line. Jackson sent Major Reid to address his now crescent-shaped line and then also dispatched Ross, whose intoxication must not have been apparent in the darkness.

Among them, they shifted the marines and parts of Plauché and Daquin to the right of the road to protect that flank and allow the line left of the road room to straighten itself.[71] Almost all of Ross's brigade were engaged now, and after a short struggle they stopped the enemy charge and Gubbins withdrew one hundred yards to a ditch and fence, from which he began laying a heavy fire on the Americans.[72] Spotts directed his attention to them and then Jackson ordered a charge that drove them out, only to have the redcoats halt in the cover of another ditch in their rear. Once more Jackson advanced and expelled them. The British tried a countercharge on the exposed left flank of the 44th, but Daquin and others quickly came to its support and repelled the assault. In the renewed confusion Americans accidentally fired on Americans in the fog.[73]

Although he held his own, Jackson saw his command on this front taking a battering. Spotts was about to exhaust the ammunition for his six-pounders.[74] The initial effectiveness of his fire and *Carolina*'s dwindled after doused campfires all but eliminated targets in the darkness. Old Hickory also knew nothing of Coffee's progress, although he should have been able to deduce from the sparkles of gunfire around the Lacoste house and grounds that Coffee had gotten that far. Sending a rider to confirm Coffee's status, Jackson kept Spotts firing at the flashes from British muskets, but now it was hard to tell which were American and which redcoat.[75] Had Spotts been able to do so, he might have detected other muzzle flashes. Enemy reinforcements were arriving and heading for Coffee's rear.

Before *Carolina* opened the battle, Coffee, Beale, and Hinds rushed forward in line of battle to climb fences and jump ditches in the darkness, the air on that part of the field still sufficiently clear that Coffee could see his way.[76] Tennesseans made up the bulk of the line, with Hinds and Griffith on his left, and Beale not far from the cypress swamp.[77] When they came to the fence on the Lacoste plantation, Hinds stayed behind in reserve while Coffee went ahead to Lacoste's canal. There, following his orders, he wheeled his line to its right until perpendicular to the ditch and drove straight toward the river, where the flashes of *Carolina*'s guns now acted as a beacon to guide his advance.[78]

As De La Ronde and Laffite guided him onward, Coffee put Beale's Rifles and two companies of Tennesseans led by Colonels Robert Dyer and John Gibson, about two hundred men in all, under command of Colonel

James Lauderdale.[79] They pushed through below and behind an enemy outpost of 150 men on the Lacoste canal and were soon approaching the main road. Opening fire on the foe, Beale and the Tennesseans soon pressed the redcoats back to the buildings and groves around the lower of two Lacoste houses, where they made a stand. Unlike the rest of the army, Beale's Riflemen provided their own guns, most privately made long weapons generally from Pennsylvania, though erroneously called Kentucky rifles. Intended for hunting rather than military use, they came in smaller calibers, like .36 and .40, effective at ranges up to three hundred yards or more, though the gloom now negated any advantage of range.

The main body of Keane's command at hand were just on the other side of the road behind the cover of an old levee. As Coffee's main line approached an orange grove surrounding the upper Lacoste house, the enemy opened a brisk fire but fell back as Coffee pushed them through the grove and past the house.[80] Passing through the redcoats' abandoned camps, the 1st Tennessee Mounted Gunmen found turkeys, chickens, ducks, and quarters of mutton still sizzling over the embers of abandoned campfires. Without stopping, they picked up the juicy morsels and dined as they advanced.[81]

In their positions among the lower Lacoste slave cabins, the redcoats stayed hidden until the Tennesseans were virtually among them, then rushed out to engage them hand-to-hand. Having no bayonets, the Americans used their muskets and rifles as clubs. Some of Coffee's men carried tomahawks and long knives and used them effectively as they pushed the enemy back to the old levee.[82] From that position the British put up a heavy infantry fire and then began coming over the levee again as the musketry from both sides grew in intensity.[83] Tennesseans took cover where they found it as the combat broke down into isolated skirmishes in the darkness with little or no control by Coffee.[84] One private, William B. Fort, soon afterward remembered that "balls were whistling about my ears in every direction."[85]

Patterson's orders were to cease firing as soon as he heard or saw Coffee's flank attack opening fire, to avoid firing on the Tennesseans by mistake.[86] Unfortunately, he could not isolate the sound of Coffee's guns from other musketry, and as a result the Tennesseans came under friendly fire from *Carolina*, then after eight o'clock obscured visibility enhanced the confusion.[87] One of Coffee's officers found individual companies of regiments getting separated from each other, while units from both sides became jumbled in the blind melee.[88] Both American and English voices called hoarsely in the fug, trying to find friends, and instances of individuals and groups mistakenly bumping into an enemy multiplied.[89]

Friends fired on friends.[90] No one knew where they were or what

happened. Unable to discern Yankee from redcoat, it became a matter of
"pull Dick pull Devil" as one Tennessean put it.[91] Colonel Dyer got turned
around and rode the wrong way until he encountered a force in the darkness that demanded his identity. Lieutenant Colonel John Gibson of his
regiment was with him on foot and they answered that they were with Coffee. As they approached, they heard men expressing curiosity as to who
Coffee might be, and they turned to run back. Gibson stumbled and fell,
and before he could rise a redcoat appeared over him and thrust down with
his bayonet. The blade missed Gibson's body, went through his clothes, and
pinned him to the ground before he pulled free, kicked the foeman aside,
and ran to safety. Dyer, still mounted despite the darkness, only got fifty
yards before a bullet killed his horse. As it fell, his legs tangled with the animal's and he was trapped against the ground when a bullet struck his leg.
Happily, his men were close enough to hear him order them to fire a volley
over his head, stalling the British long enough for him to get free and lead
his men back to Coffee.[92]

While Dyer was lost, Lieutenant Colonel James Lauderdale succeeded
him in command and, recognizing familiar accents around him, rushed
between some Tennesseans accidentally fighting each other in the confusion; he was beating down their raised muskets with his sword when fire
from others hit him squarely in the head.[93] Behind the firing line, Major
Charles Kavanaugh called for volunteers to pass among the milling groups
of men to alert them that they were firing at their own people. Lieutenant
Andrew Jackson Edmondson undertook the dangerous mission and got to
within twenty yards of the firing when he yelled out that Tennesseans were
shooting at Tennesseans. A dimly seen man demanded to know his unit.
Edmondson replied that it was the 1st Tennessee and asked if the voice was
from the 2nd Tennessee. It said it was but just then the lieutenant glimpsed
a British uniform. Its wearer called for him to surrender, but he ran just in
time as the redcoat and others with him opened fire.[94]

In crossing a fence on the Lacoste plantation, a battalion of the 1st
Mounted Gunmen accidentally got separated from the regiment and wandered to its left past the house. When it got about one hundred yards from
the enemy behind the levee, someone opened fire on its rear. The battalion
halted immediately, concluding that it was taking friendly fire from its own
regiment. Although men and officers yelled that they were Tennesseans, the
fire kept coming, fortunately without much injury, and the unseen troops
approached to within thirty or forty yards. Still the gunmen held fire and
kept yelling that they were friends until some in the mystery command were
dimly seen waving their swords and calling on the group to lay down its

arms. Captain Thomas Jones and Lieutenant John Walker had their men pretend to put down their arms as the other party approached until their British uniforms were unmistakable. Walker and Jones lunged at their officers with drawn sabers, while behind them their men could only hear the clashing of the swords. Jones escaped unhurt, but Walker's sword was badly battered, two bullets hit his shoulder and back, and another punctured his hat.

Four of their men took wounds, one was killed, and four more captured, one of them Cornet Daniel Treadwell. His captors neglected to search him and sent him to the rear with a pistol concealed under his coat. Diverting his guard's attention, Treadwell pulled the pistol and shot him, seized the man's musket, and ran to get away, only to bump into more British soldiers, who made him prisoner a second time. As another guard took him to the rear, sudden firing broke near them and distracted the guard's attention. Treadwell knocked him down and ran in the direction he thought his comrades might be. Suddenly he came across Captain James McMahon of his regiment, mortally wounded. The dying man asked Treadwell to stay with him, and he could hardly refuse. Soon both were captured by the enemy, and this time, as a fellow Tennessean put it, Treadwell "stayed taken."[95]

Captain John Donelson had halted his company close to the Lacoste garden, when he, too, heard and saw someone firing on his rear. Thinking them friends, he hailed them and they yelled back that they were Tennesseans, but when they got within ten paces of him, their officer demanded that Donelson's "damned yankee rebels" surrender. Donelson yelled back to them to "be damned" and ordered his men to fire. That halted the enemy momentarily, giving him time to join Colonel Thomas Williamson's 2nd Mounted Gunmen. Then the British advanced again and fired a volley unlike any Donelson ever experienced, killing three of his men and forcing Williamson to withdraw leaving three of his men prisoners, including Major Kavanaugh.[96] The British were somewhat astonished at their captives. In their long coats, the Tennesseans might look like Quakers, but they hardly behaved like them, and one redcoat concluded that "the Louisiana quakers were the d——t fighting fellows" he had ever seen.[97]

The redcoats continued to push hard, sending the Tennesseans sidling off to their right around the Lacoste orchard and gardens and separating Beale's command, which was still on the other side of the canal. The British counterattack cut the Riflemen in two, Beale with the larger portion on the right, and Judge Lewis on the left with just fifteen men, three of them wounded, and eleven British prisoners in tow.[98]

Beale got the worst of a galling fire and paid for his bravery as the British all but surrounded him. Beverly Chew led one fragment and took at least one prisoner himself, and killed or wounded more than one redcoat as he knocked them down with his clubbed rifle.[99] Banker Benjamin Story fell wounded. A ball went through both of William Flower's thighs. A bullet broke Nathaniel Cox's arm and then comrades lost sight of him.[100] Constable George Commyns was struck a mortal wound.[101] Amid the chaos, a musket ball that might have been British or American struck Oliver Parmlee squarely in the forehead, killing him instantly.[102]

The rest of them fought their way out, still taking prisoners as they did so. At the same time, more of the Rifles became prisoners themselves— Cox, notaries John Lynd and George Pollock, the fun-loving Irishman Kenny Laverty, and more.[103] At one point about twenty-five of Beale's contingent saw a body of men ahead of them. Thinking them some of Coffee's, they moved toward them and one of the Rifles called out, "Huzza for Tennessee." A British voice ordered them to drop their arms. Several did, while the rest changed direction, including Henry Clement, brother of Captain Samuel Clement of the steamboat *Vesuvius*, who joined Beale because he found the militia "disagreeable."[104] A bullet in the leg brought him down, but Clement still captured a British soldier and made him carry him from the field.[105]

Judge Lewis had to think fast. At that moment his isolated contingent was the extreme left flank of Jackson's army, with nothing to protect his own left except the Villeré orange grove. He probably saw or heard the sounds of freshly arriving enemy reinforcements coming in from the second boat contingent now reaching the landing place. Unable to see or contact Beale or Coffee, he decided to get out before being overwhelmed. Pulling his men back toward the swamp a thousand yards to his rear, he marched them across the back of the Lacoste and De La Ronde plantations toward town.[106] Both he and Beale had no choice but to leave behind their wounded, whom they could not find in the darkness.

At about 10:30 Keane saw what appeared to be a large column of the enemy approach his center near the upper Lacoste house. His own line had been pushed back so that it now formed across the main road. He ordered his adjutant, Colonel Frederick Stovin, to send the 93rd forward, supported by part of the 4th Foot from his reserve. Lieutenant Colonel Robert Dale led the charge, Stovin himself being wounded in the action, but the Tennesseans in their front pulled back rather than engage.[107] Just then Keane saw Captain David Price of the bomb vessel *Volcano* limp onto the Villeré veranda on a wounded leg, bringing with him a captured American soldier and the heartening news that fresh men were coming.

Admiral Malcolm sent Price from the landing place where he oversaw the disembarkation of the second wave of the army. Hearing the firing in the distance, Malcolm wanted Keane to know that reinforcements were coming. Making his way through the darkness, Price ran into a group of Yankees who fired at him, one hitting his thigh, but he escaped and then happened to take a prisoner while finding his way to Keane.[108] Malcolm also sent artilleryman Benson Hill to say that he would have two three-pounders up in an hour as crews dragged them by ropes toward the river road.[109]

Within minutes of Price's arrival, Lieutenant Colonel Brooke came out of the swamp with two battalions of the 21st Royal Scots Fusiliers with their distinctive short muskets slung over their shoulders to keep their hands free.[110] Several carried casks of musket cartridges sent by Captain Gordon.[111] They ran straight to Dale to stabilize his line against further threat. Behind them came the 1st West India, who had heard *Carolina*'s guns for hours as they approached Villeré's. They found the path along the canal a puddle of slime from the tramp of Thornton's advance. They ran to the melee right behind the 21st to keep Coffee from collapsing the British flank around the Lacoste plantation and were soon in hand-to-hand combat.[112] It was the first time that a black West Indies regiment went into action outside the Caribbean.[113] In the confusion Colonel Thornton and a party were for a time cut off and surrounded but cut their way out.[114]

Soon enough the Americans tried again. They drove in Thornton's forward elements but he held his ground and countercharged, driving the Yankees back. Midnight approached.[115] Virtually the whole British command on the field was united now, the remnants of the 85th and 95th astride the main road, the 21st and the 1st West India in a strong post to their right in the Lacoste yard, and the 4th on its right extending to the woods.[116] Soon the three-pounders arrived but they could not fire at the enemy without hitting their own men facing Ross and Plauché.[117]

In fact, the British fired their few cannons little if at all that night, and only a handful of Captain Lane's twelve-pounder rockets fizzed pointlessly toward the *Carolina*.[118] One of them flew past Jackson and instinctively he ducked his head. Embarrassed, he told Livingston at his side that he did not ordinarily "salute" an enemy's fire, but since the one just passed was the first he had seen, "he could not do less than pay his respects to it."[119] A little bravado in a general might be good for morale, but Livingston thought that being Jackson's aide was dangerous work.[120]

With Beale's disintegration, Hinds's Mississippians held Coffee's extreme left flank now. A handful of them, including Reuben Kemper, were cut off from the rest, like Beale before them. Kemper still mourned his brother Samuel's death from camp disease just a few weeks earlier, but his mind was fixed on the fight now. He sensed rather than saw three redcoats nearby, when a break in the fog and musket flashes revealed them running to a tree. "G-d. D—m your souls!" he shouted. "What do you do there?" One yelled back that they were seeking their regiment. "What regt. Do you belong to?" he demanded. When they yelled it back to him, he covered them with his musket, pointed to Coffee's rear, and shouted, "There it is G-d D—, you," and marched them in as prisoners.[121]

For the next half hour desultory firing continued as Coffee rallied his men. Command had broken down almost completely in his brigade. No one got orders. Fragments tried to fire in the right direction, join other detachments, or avoid being caught behind enemy lines, which happened more than once.[122] Since both combatants used the same language, and a distinctive American accent had not yet fully diverged from its British roots, knowing one from the other was even more difficult.[123] Finally Coffee disengaged his scattered units and re-formed to the left of the De La Ronde house to await Jackson's orders.[124] He had taken several prisoners, but many of his own men lay on the field dead, dying, or captured. Fire from *Carolina* was still a hazard, initial British confusion had settled into a calmer resolve, and Beale was back in line but severely battered. The fog and darkness remained relentless.

It was midnight. As Coffee steadied his men and Jackson tried to control his part of the line, Keane thought the Yankees were re-forming for a final assault, a good reading of Old Hickory's mind. He faced a choice fraught with risk. He had disrupted the British camps, driven the enemy in his front, and hoped Coffee had forced them back to the river below him. He had achieved much already, and if he kept pushing, he might end the invasion there and then. He could not know that Keane did not mean to move on New Orleans until the morrow, of course. Still, trying for too much could risk all, and Jackson prudently determined to hold his position for the night and renew the attack in the morning. He called Carroll and Claiborne to join him now, as it seemed evident that he was meeting the enemy's main, if not only, thrust.[125]

Hardly had he sent off the orders, however, before he had second thoughts. Would he risk losing all his gains by continuing the engagement at dawn? Reflection urged caution. The British were rallying and giving him heavy fire on his left flank. The fog and darkness worked against him as much as the enemy. The temperature had dropped to freezing or below.[126] His army had performed well in its first action together, and for the militia their first ever, but the 44th and 7th were badly jumbled, the former now led by a captain.[127] Griffith's Feliciana dragoons had advanced so far that they were in front of the 44th and taking friendly fire. He had no sure idea how Coffee had fared, but if Coffee had pushed the British in his front to the river, a renewed attack before daylight could bring the two wings of the American army into collision with each other. British deserters and prisoners told him that Keane would have thousands more men by morning, and more coming. They might be exaggerating, but they might not.[128] Perhaps most bothersome, he had no word from Morgan. The only way he could gather what happened outside his limited range of vision was from the sound of musketry, but the noise from his own guns and the enemy's made hearing firing elsewhere almost impossible. When there was a lull, however, one thing he did not hear was firing downriver from Morgan.

The men at English Turn chafed to get into the fight when Jackson's instructions arrived, and Morgan soon had 320 men of Colonel Alexander Declouet's 6th Louisiana Militia ready to march. Then he just kept them there. Either Morgan did not receive Old Hickory's order to cross the river or he pretended not to understand his instructions. When Declouet's officers protested that they must get moving, Morgan refused to budge until he got specific instructions. The officers continued to beg to march, and it was with difficulty that they kept their men from leaving on their own initiative. Only when Morgan heard *Carolina*'s guns did he relent at last.

When the main fighting stopped, they were at Bayou Terre-aux-Boeufs, still six miles from the enemy as they marched through mud on the river road. Declouet begged Morgan to hasten to pitch into the enemy rear, but the general remained in the grip of crippling indecision, if not obtuseness. It was well after midnight when his advance finally ran into British pickets, who fired on them. The column also encountered a British artilleryman, apparently drunk and lost, who mistook them for fellow redcoats and exhorted them to "come on, my lads, for the Yankees never got such a licking in their lives!"[129]

After a half-hearted effort to push through the enemy picket, Morgan told his advance to run back to the main column, sparking a silly panic that had men jumping over fences and piling on top of each other in confusion before they finally redeployed in a line.[130] Then he kept them standing in formation until two a.m. or later, when his officers suggested they might as well go back to English Turn. Morgan refused to do that, too, until a council of officers agreed on retreat, not knowing how Jackson had fared. Back they marched through the mud to their barracks, disgusted with a general whom a sergeant of the 6th Regiment dismissed as "an old woman."[131]

Declouet's adjutant soon determined there had been no more than five hundred redcoats in Morgan's front.[132] Had he moved as Jackson intended, his appearance might have sent the British reeling toward their landing and into the swamp, and attorney Abraham Ellery suggested that a single gun, fired in the British rear, might have decided the battle.[133] Some of the British felt obliged to agree.[134] Morgan was the broken gear of Jackson's machine.

Jackson did not know Morgan had taken himself out of the fight, but he had no reason now to expect an attack on the enemy rear. But for fog and smoke hampering his movements, he believed there had been a chance to take Keane's entire command.[135] Now he decided not to press his fortune on what was already a lucky day. The safety of the city depended on his army, and he must not risk it incautiously.[136] The rider sent to Coffee brought news that bolstered his decision. Enemy camps extended half a mile along the river, which suggested substantial numbers. Coffee had taken many prisoners but also suffered many accidental casualties. Even then Coffee heard firing, indicating that more of his cut-off men were fighting their way back to him.[137] And now Coffee knew enemy reinforcements were arriving on the field on his battered and exposed left rear. That settled Old Hickory. He ordered Coffee to hold while Jackson withdrew to his original position above De La Ronde's to re-form and reorganize his men, then Coffee could come into line on his left, with Hinds on Coffee's left to watch the army's flank.[138]

Jackson pulled Ross's brigade back and the British did not pursue. The musketry died away, then Jackson distinctly heard the Tennesseans' guns for some time until Coffee got his new orders.[139] Coffee fell back half a mile over open ground, bringing off such wounded as he could while Hinds sent out videttes to watch through the night.[140] There still might be another battle on the morrow, whether Jackson wanted it or not. The initiative was Keane's now for the taking. Some of his officers that night asked a captured Tennessean how far it was to the city. He answered that it was six miles, and they boasted that "we will be there to-morrow." The defiant Yankee replied that "it is not *far*, but it is a *very rough road*." Asked what stood in the way of their triumphal advance, he responded simply, *"Old Hickory."*[141]

Nine

"The *Best* Fought Action in the Annals of Military Warfare"

I T HAD BEEN a day of the unexpected. Each army in turn had been taken unawares, and their fighting hallmarked by fury and confusion.[1] Men on both sides freely confessed astonishment at their foemen's actions, and officers of the King's Navy, rarely reluctant to fault the army, almost gloated. Admiral Codrington added his voice to others when he wrote to tell Jane that "the truth is our army was taken by surprise."[2]

Cochrane's shifting the landing to Lake Borgne, the help from the fishermen and a few disaffected *creoles*, Peddie and Spencer's daring reconnaissance, and careful planning overall led to Keane's stunning achievement in fielding half his army undetected a scant eight miles from New Orleans's almost undefended southeastern suburb. No American army to date had suffered such a surprise.[3] That did not necessarily mean Keane could have taken New Orleans. Stiff and tired, Thornton had to eat to continue. Keane could not move without feeding them, establishing a base at Villeré's, and a secure line of communications back to Gordon and Malcolm. Nor could he count on an unimpeded march to the city, and only a miracle would likely see him reach the city still undetected. With everything in his favor, he might reach Fort St. Charles by twilight to face whatever opposition he encountered as darkness came on. Under the circumstances, his decision to await the next contingent was prudent. Hindsight showed that it was also smart. The 7th and 44th Infantries were in the city, as were Beale and other volunteer companies. He would outnumber them, but his brace of little three-pounders was overwhelmingly outmatched by the bigger guns in the city. In any attack on New Orleans that evening, and coming from that direction, odds favored the Americans.

A five a.m. reveille in the British camp ended a fitful sleep disturbed by false alarms that twice sent Keane's exhausted men into line of battle.[4] Dead of both sides lay tangled in frost-covered clumps, and although there was no sign of the American army, *Carolina* still lay anchored midstream and resumed fire at dawn, harassing men collecting the dead and wounded. Keane sent Ensign Hill back to Malcolm to hurry forward a pair of nine-pounders to answer her fire.[5] Redcoats rifling the pockets of the American dead found Jackson's note on Lauderdale's body, inviting him to "stick his spoon in the platter of glory." It seemed a cruel jest now.[6] From *Carolina*'s masts, her officers watched carts gather enemy dead and wounded throughout the day. One or two deserters came to Jackson to report high losses in their ranks.[7]

Jackson might have left the field to him, but Keane could hardly crow victory. He had been badly surprised and badly battered, losing 46 killed, 167 wounded, and 64 missing or taken prisoner. The 95th suffered half of the 23 killed, forty percent of the wounded, and two-thirds of the missing, as well as its commander. The 85th sustained over a third of the loss, and the 1st West India much of the rest. In all, eleven percent of Keane's 2,500 engaged were out of action.[8] Codrington had to lament at least fifteen officers he had known among the killed and wounded.[9] Before long, redcoats exaggerated their loss to four hundred, and Jackson's army to 10,000.[10]

Gleig found "Old Grey's" body during the battle and wept over it before being ordered away. "Had he been my brother it would not have shocked me more," he told his diary. Now he ventured out to retrieve the body. On finding it, he marveled at the tiny red spot on his friend's forehead, so small it scarcely left a hole. He and a few companions bore Grey to the Lacoste garden and dug a grave. The rest of the day Gleig could scarcely remember what he did.[11]

Ambulatory captives numbered about seventy. Keane ordered Gerard and a dozen guards to escort them back to embark for Cochrane's ersatz prison ship. On the way, some Yankees naïvely said that Jackson had no defenses on this side of New Orleans. Keane could still expect Jackson's army to be somewhere between his own and the city, however, and held to his determination to await reinforcement before moving.[12] He sent wounded prisoners to the Lacoste and Villeré outbuildings, where they languished without food or medical care until that afternoon, when they got bandages and some beef broth. Even then they shivered without fires.[13]

Naturally, British surgeons tended their own first, and *Carolina*'s shells unintentionally disrupted parties removing wounded of both armies from the field. One exploded amid a group of the 85th, a fragment striking a corporal in the lower back and emerging from his chest. He shivered a moment, then fell dead. *Louisiana* soon joined the desultory bombardment, and before long, shells and solid shot hit the Lacoste and Villeré houses, where lay some of the wounded. One ball knocked a knapsack from beneath the head of a wounded redcoat using it as a pillow, while others killed soldiers taking cover behind the hospitals and in Lacoste's orange grove.[14]

The British saw no sign of Americans in their front that morning, but in the afternoon a squad of four of the Rifles on outpost duty near the swamp saw sunlight glittering on steel in the distance ahead of them. It was a Yankee reconnaissance with four of Hinds's dragoons in front as pickets. The Rifles fired a single volley that brought down at least three of them, their panicked horses running into British lines.[15] That evening Keane shifted his line back to the Villeré house and canal, placing pickets above and below after getting an exaggerated report that Morgan had 1,500 at English Turn.[16] Although Morgan had done nothing the night before, word of his appearance persuaded Keane to keep patrols in constant motion on watch.[17] Ensign Gerard commanded one patrol, jesting that, during a stop at the Jumonville plantation house, his men augmented their armament of pistols and swords with silver spoons from the pantry.[18]

Back at the fishermen's village, Cochrane and Codrington concluded from the distant cannonade the night before that Keane had advanced and attacked an enemy fort. As more boats arrived from Lake Borgne, the admirals forwarded them to Villeré's, and this morning sent the nine-pounders Keane requested plus more cannon, including a heavy howitzer to lob shells over the levee at *Carolina*.[19] Codrington moved their headquarters from the miserable hut where he had spent the night into a tent within a tent for warmer accommodation.[20] For the comfort of the boat crews, he had canvas covers made to protect them from rain, and put ships' carpenters to felling trees to make poles and paddles to replace those broken or lost moving the boats through the shallows.[21] He also ordered a bonfire to burn nightly at the mouth of the bayou as a beacon to guide boats bringing troops and matériel. The men tasked with feeding the blaze felt none too easy for fear that alligators "might make a meal of us."[22]

Keane had nearly made a meal of Jackson, which Old Hickory never admitted. He had seriously considered the Villeré approach but focused more on Chef Menteur and the Gentilly road. If Villeré ignored orders to close Bayou Bienvenue, the avenue remained important enough to merit more of Jackson's personal attention.[23] Still, he reacted with a brilliant surprise of his own, cobbling a concentration of forces at least equal to Keane's. His greatest weapons were *Carolina*'s big guns and his own iron resolve. Keane surprised Old Hickory with his appearance at Villeré's. *Carolina*'s blazing twelve-pounders and the demoralizing attack out of the darkness stunned Keane. Although the engagement became almost unmanageable, Jackson controlled it to the extent he could by making good use of his staff, especially Butler, Piatt, Chotard, and Livingston.

Scarcely was the sun above the horizon before the city began lionizing the volunteers for "prodigies of valor" in their first engagement. Surely they acted like seasoned veterans and the city owed to them its salvation.[24] As for Jackson, his night attack certainly forestalled disaster.[25] No one denied the confusion in the darkness, nor several tragic instances of friendly fire, but still it was a victory.[26] The redcoats fought well, but the Americans fought like demons.[27] Adjutant Robert Butler believed that only the smoke and fog saved Keane's army from being captured.[28] Jackson gave much credit to Plauché's steadfast battalion, Beale's daring riflemen, and the "great bravery" of Savary's black company.[29] By all accounts, Old Hickory himself was fearless in the biggest open field battle of his life.[30] Rarely encumbered by undue modesty, he called it "the *best* fought action in the annals of military warfare."[31]

Jackson had remained just above the De La Ronde plantation until shortly before dawn weighing alternatives. Carroll had arrived ninety minutes after the battle ended, but Spotts's resupply of ammunition was not up from the city yet. Colonel Lacoste sent word from Fort St. John that the rest of the British transports anchored off Chef Menteur had been seen earlier sending the small boats off for Bayou Bienvenue, which meant that by morning Jackson could face several times his own numbers. Meanwhile, Coffee's outposts were seeing enemy reinforcements coming in from the bayou.[32] Jackson's total effective numbers were no more than 3,000 now, and probably less, with only five hundred regulars, many new recruits in their first action.

He had achieved much, but the sunrise called for caution. Prisoners said that Keane would withdraw or surrender if attacked again, but they knew nothing of their commander's intentions.[33] Old Hickory's big risk in the night assault had paid off, but he knew Keane would not be surprised again, and surely now had his men placed well defensively. Attacking him again under entirely different circumstances would be, thought Jackson, "so deep a game of hazard" that he dared not take the risk. He would leave the field to Keane and himself withdraw to a stronger position. Consulting with his engineers, he settled on an old, nearly dry millrace about two miles in their rear on Edmund McCarty's plantation. At five o'clock he sent Hinds's Mississippians forward as videttes to cover the withdrawal.[34] Then he withdrew Coffee first, then Carroll, followed by Plauché, the Regulars, and Spotts's guns.[35] Movable wounded went back to the city, but some had to be left where they fell along with most of the dead.[36]

By dawn Old Hickory was placing his units on a new line just five miles from the boundary between the city and Faubourg Marigny, a position noted or pointed out to him on his earlier inspection trips. There the river on his right and the swamp on his left protected his flanks, and numerous ditches and canals crossed the ground in his front. The old millrace—still known locally as the Rodriguez Canal, thanks to an earlier owner—lay just below McCarty's house.[37] Notary John Lynd once owned the property and its small, one-room-wide two-story house.[38] Jackson explored the length of the canal personally and concluded that he could make it an effective defense.[39] The distance from the river and levee on the right to the trees and swamp on the left was perhaps eight hundred yards. He envisioned an entrenched line behind the canal's upper bank stretching from the river to the woods and another two hundred yards into the swamp. Level ground extended below McCarty's property to the plantation of Ignace Martin de Lino de Chalmette and offered a clear field of fire on the entire area between river and swamp over which the enemy would have to advance to attack.[40]

At one p.m. he set his men to digging out the canal to a depth of several feet, piling the mud and earth behind it to form an embankment, and then ordered the levee sliced open at the west end to flood the canal and make it a moat several feet deep in places.[41] Jackson pushed the work rapidly and established his headquarters in the McCarty house near the road, where he could monitor progress constantly. Edmund McCarty certainly did not object. He had died not quite six weeks earlier and may never have lived in the house. A galleried wooden upper story sat atop a raised brick ground floor with pillars and porticos on all four sides. Ornamental box beds faced the river road, while a thick perimeter of orange trees on the other sides surrounded four acres of garden walks and flower beds bordered by myrtles and live oaks. From the upper story Jackson had a clear view of the Chalmette ground several hundred yards below between river and swamp.[42] Thirty yards above the canal and about five hundred feet back from the river sat the old Rodriguez house, a typical galleried two-story planter's home with slave cabins nearby. It sat nearer the rampart than McCarty's, and Old Hickory could use it, too, and its well offered fresh water. Its well-stocked wine cellar dangled greater temptations.[43]

It had been an anxious night in the city during and after the engagement. The "exempts" posted at Government House saw distant veiled flashes of *Carolina*'s opening fire make the fog glow, and moments later the guns' report aroused fear and alarm on the streets.[44] At midnight, after the firing ceased, most people expected the fight to resume in the morning. Then they heard Carroll's beating drums as his command marched through town, making them expect renewed fighting with the dawn.[45] All that night people took comfort from the sound of the old veterans patrolling the streets, calling the hours and the "All's well."[46]

With the dawn, people sensed that the next few hours might be decisive and rushed to write letters and get them to the weekly post rider before he left. "The day is breaking," read one, "and we are in anxious expectation of hearing it ushered in by the sound of our artillery."[47] At six a.m. they expected to hear the guns in half an hour, an expectation that frightened some.[48] Anxiety seemed written on every face. Surely the fighting, when it came, would be furious.[49] Almost in unison, multiple pens wrote that "this day must decide the fate of our city."[50]

Resolution was everywhere. For all the doubts about the *creoles*, all sides complimented their fidelity.[51] Now they turned out admirably to assist in the aftermath of battle. Women gathered anew to sew clothing for the volunteers.[52] So many more volunteers arrived from Feliciana that only forty white men remained to guard the parish's slaves and property, and from St. Martinville in the Attakapas country west of New Orleans came the fifty-two-year-old widow Félicité Bienvenu, known as "Grandmère Devince," granddaughter of a French general. She had six sons in the volunteer companies and a seventh yet too young to volunteer. In his stead she offered herself as a nurse and quickly became a fixture with the wounded.[53]

Anxiety made some hope for the crisis to end quickly, whichever way it should go.[54] It was a worry fed by uncertainty over their men at the front.[55] Contradictory stories and rumors about casualties swarmed the city streets.[56] When Beale and Judge Lewis reached town at about one a.m., they brought thirty prisoners with them, then went home to sleep before returning to the field. With them came more rumors of what they had seen—or, more to the point, not seen in the darkness—of American casualties.[57] More definitive word arrived about eleven a.m. when a rider appeared on the streets at full gallop waving his sword and shouting the news of victory down Royal Street as ladies emerged on their balconies crying and wringing their hands in anxiety over loved ones at the front.[58]

The final cost of December 23 would not be known for days yet, but one of Coffee's officers declared that "there has been great havoc among our troops," and Jackson frankly admitted that "we have lost some fine fellows."[59] Initially he believed his losses totaled one hundred killed, wounded, and missing.[60] Coffee was closer to the mark when he thought they lost twenty-five killed and forty wounded, with up to seventy men captured.[61] American casualties actually tallied roughly ten percent of the forces present. The killed included one of Spotts's artillerymen, an officer and six men from the 7th, seven privates of the 44th, Colonel Lauderdale, and two officers and six men of Coffee's, a total of twenty-four. The wounded tallied 115, including ten of Beale's men and one of Daquin's. Coffee was the heaviest hit with forty-three. The aggregate missing and presumed captured came to seventy-four, all from Coffee's brigade, making total casualties 213.[62] Among those captured was Major Gabriel Villeré, who had attached himself to Plauché's command that afternoon, only to be made a prisoner twice on the same day.[63]

Beale's company was seemingly shattered. Only twenty-two of the sixty-three who went into action remained.[64] Some reappeared late on December 24 after hours wandering lost in the swamp.[65] Lynd, Pollock, Laverty, Montgomery, and more were in British hands.[66] The banker Benjamin Story was wounded and captured.[67] Unaccounted for was Nathaniel Cox. Comrades saw him hit in the arm and perhaps in his body as well, but no one knew whether he was living or dead.[68] William Montgomery and New Orleans merchant and importer John Brandegee both had brothers missing.[69] Almost miraculously, only two were killed or mortally wounded. George Commyns would die from his wound in a few days, leaving his estate to pay his outstanding December boardinghouse bill.[70] Everyone commented on Oliver Parmlee. "Poor Parmlee is killed," mourned Brandegee, and another lamented him as "a most amiable young man, universally regretted."[71]

First encounters between captives and captors took many forms. Lynd endured redcoat boasting of their presumed victory, then rolled his eyes, shook his head, and replied, "Oh, the end has not come yet! The end has not come yet!"[72] Later that night, when Captain Gordon met prisoners sent down the bayou, he assured one that the invaders would respect private property after taking the city. The plucky captive replied that such a promise came as "ill grace" from Gordon, given his reputation for sacking Alexandria. "My dear Sir," Gordon playfully replied. "Do you not perceive the infinite difference in these two cases? The citizens of Alexandria *offered* us their property, and we should have been d——d fools to refuse so good an offer."[73]

Yankee prisoners taunted, too, but at some little risk. Both sides gave the best medical attention they could to enemy wounded. A British surgeon about to amputate an American prisoner's mutilated limb asked if anyone could distract the sufferer by playing the physician's violin. Sergeant David Hubbard of the 2nd Tennessee Mounted Gunmen, himself with a wounded hip awaiting care, volunteered and played throughout the surgery. As the surgeon finished, Hubbard bowed into "Yankee Doodle," which set off cheering among the other prisoners. The annoyed surgeon seized the fiddle and broke it over Hubbard's head.[74] On the other side, one of Coffee's captives was Major Samuel Mitchell, commanding the 95th Rifles. He it was who set the torch to the public buildings in Washington, or so many believed, and that might well have earned him rough treatment now.[75] Instead, the wounded Colonel William Piatt visited him and offered clean linen to him, since his own was soiled in the action. Mitchell haughtily but politely declined, saying that his own baggage would be up in a few days when Keane took the city.[76]

Neither side got much useful information from captives, as each exaggerated to mislead the other. Prisoners told Coffee that Keane had more than double Jackson's numbers and at least 2,000 more coming during the night.[77] An American ensign concluded that the best information established Keane's numbers at 5,000 to 6,000.[78] Redcoats taken by Beale said Cochrane had double that number with him, and that 3,000 were already with Keane, while others claimed that Keane had as many as 15,000.[79] They repeated the same exaggerations to guards at the Cabildo cells, saying they had expected to take the city that morning without resistance."[80] Others pretended that Thornton's advance numbered no more than three hundred redcoats, an apparent attempt to lull the Yankees.[81] No one downplayed the ferocity of the action in the fog, however. Seasoned veterans in the 85th and 95th freely admitted that never in their European campaigns had they encountered such firing.[82]

Some prisoner encounters turned tragic. When the 21st arrived late in the fight, they captured several of Coffee's men. "You are my prisoner," one Fusilier shouted to a young Tennessean taken by surprise. "I suppose I am," the man replied. "Can I see your Com[mandin]g Officer?" His captor conducted him to the rear to Captain William Conran, who had himself been a prisoner of war in France two years before.[83] "You are the comdg. Officer I presume," said the American. When Conran said he was, the prisoner pulled a hidden knife his guard had missed and stabbed Conran in the chest, killing him instantly. Shocked redcoats immediately perforated the Tennessean with such ferocity that their bayonets lifted him from the ground.[84]

Jackson was at pains to learn as much as possible about the foe before him, but news came scanty and contradictory. An early report during the night said Keane had left Villeré's and was heading for Terre-aux-Boeufs, abandoning his boats in the Villeré canal. It was false, but Old Hickory ordered a reconnaissance out on the Terre-aux-Boeufs road nevertheless.[85] Before dawn he also sent six hundred of Coffee's Tennesseans forward toward Keane's right to recover horses lost during the night's fighting and determine what they could of enemy movements in their front. When the redcoats fired on their advance party, Coffee learned enough to report back to Jackson about four p.m. that the foe was digging in and showed no sign of advancing. Hinds also reported sighting more enemy reinforcements arriving at Villeré's. Jackson would later claim that the night attack panicked Keane, which was hardly the case, but he rightly concluded now that Keane did not intend to advance until his forces united, and feared that Jackson might attack again. Old Hickory had hoped to stop the enemy long enough to buy time to prepare a strong defensive line, and it had worked.[86]

Mayor Girod sent spades and mattocks to use in digging the earthwork, and soon the general had half of his command working on the canal and the other half on guard in rotating shifts. He sent Arsène Lacarrièr Latour with fatigue parties to try digging notches or crevices in the levee to flood the fields between his new line and Villerés, and especially the swampy ground on his left. The river was falling at the moment, but even if the openings let in only a few feet of water for a few days, it could still delay an enemy advance long enough to complete his line.[87] At the same time he got a rider to Morgan with instructions to cut the levee below the British encampment, a task Morgan undertook with sufficient vigor for a change in that he did more than $19,000 in damage to Charles Jumonville Coulon de Villiers's cane crop.[88]

Old Hickory already had Major Michael Reynolds establishing batteries guarding the pass into Bayou Barataria, with orders to stretch a "chain" of iron cannonballs across it to stop enemy boats trying to use it as a back door to the right bank of the river above Jackson's new line.[89] Jean Laffite was helping Reynolds, and this morning they clearly heard *Carolina*'s guns even though they were thirty miles away. That made the smuggler anxious to return to the city, probably concerned for his brother, and he arrived this afternoon bearing a report from Reynolds on their progress. He was soon on his way back to Barataria with equipment Reynolds needed for his iron chain.[90] While in town, Lafitte may also have arranged for Jackson's militia to collect the 7,500 concealed gunflints that Patterson's raid missed. Although the city arsenal had more than 12,000 on hand in October, by December 10 Jackson had almost none that were usable. They would be vital if the armies engaged again.[91]

Jackson called in every available man and sent an express rider to Governor Holmes in Mississippi with orders for General Thomas to rush his Kentuckians to New Orleans as soon as he reached Natchez.[92] Even as the men began working on the earthwork they quickly dubbed "Line Jackson," he directed inspections of arms and ammunition to make ready for immediate service.[93] Security became a greater concern than ever, now that the enemy was actually before them. All was well so far, but he exhorted his officers to "maintain your post, nor ever think of retreating."[94] Daily signs and countersigns were promulgated. On December 24 sentries challenged anyone seeking to enter or leave the lines by saying "Jackson." None could pass without the countersign "Holmes."[95] Guards arrested anyone without a written pass, and within a few days Mayor Girod complained that the city guardhouse was almost full. Jackson released those agreeing to enlist in the militia, but others remained behind bars for weeks.[96]

Old Hickory placed Coffee on the left of his line extending to and into the swamp, then Carroll on his right, then Plauché, the regulars, and Beale on the far right at the levee.[97] Where the line met the swamp, engineers made an oblique work bending backward for two hundred yards to avoid standing water and make it more difficult to turn that flank.[98] By two p.m. on Christmas Eve he had two twelve-pounders and a 9.5-inch howitzer on the line, and embrasures ready by nightfall to take Spotts's two six-pounders on the road, and two heavy twenty-fours from the naval arsenal. Meanwhile, *Carolina* had annoyed the enemy considerably that morning and continued to do so. Claiborne reported false alarms of redcoats in his vicinity, bolstering Old Hickory's opinion that he was not a fit commander. Although the general claimed that he took no other notice of them, he still sent scouts to confirm that the Gentilly road was free of the enemy.[99]

A cold night passed as Hinds constantly reconnoitered between the lines and disrupted the enemy's sleep by sniping at his pickets silhouetted in their campfires.[100] Keane was not moving, but Hinds did confirm reinforcements arriving at Villeré's and men working on defensive works near the swamp to protect Keane's supply line.[101] The Christmas dawn brought no holiday rest. One of Coffee's men joked about their "Christmas phandangoes," but there was nothing festive in either camp.[102] Hinds sent Corporal Michael Trimble and Private Levi C. Harris to retrieve horses that had wandered between the lines in the night, sardonically promising to retrieve their bodies if they should be killed. Dashing to the horses, the men ran around them shouting as the enemy opened scattered fire that wounded a few animals and spooked others, but they got most of them back safely.[103]

The shifts worked ceaselessly on the earthwork, deepening and widening the canal and piling the mud on the growing breastwork. When Hinds notified Livingston that Keane appeared to be sending more soldiers back to the landing place for ammunition and provisions, Livingston feared the enemy had discovered a route to other canals that could take them to the rear of Jackson's camps. Pierre Laffite thought that unlikely but suggested that they extend Line Jackson's left flank through the woods and into the nearly impenetrable swamp, which protected their left as effectively as the river did their right.[104] Jackson acted on the suggestion, assigning the work and the position to Carroll. It was the most uncomfortable part of the line. Carroll's men would work by relays day and night in mud, rain, and freezing temperatures, with no shelter. He put men with rifles on the oblique arm, and those with muskets facing the open field in front.[105]

By end of day Jackson felt he had a position well designed to repel any enemy attack, and men in good spirits to hold the line. Artillery would be the key. Jackson had worked all day bringing big guns from the city into the embrasures as they were completed, and even inexperienced enlisted men saw how formidable their big guns would be against an infantry assault. Jackson ordered the magazine across the river from the city to send him ample powder and ammunition, keeping a further supply aboard a boat to anchor midstream upriver, ready for him should he be forced to retreat. Then the magazine would be blown up.[106] It was Jackson's first reference to the possibility of abandoning the city, but that was farthest from the minds of his army at that moment. "Glory fills our bosoms," Adjutant Butler told Morgan, and they gloated that, despite his boast, the enemy would not dine in New Orleans this Christmas.[107]

Old Hickory also ordered Morgan to draft slaves near English Turn to dig more cuts in the levee. Flooding the ground both in front of and behind Keane might contain the British where they were and keep them from crossing the river to the west bank.[108] Jackson ordered him to watch for any enemy movement in his direction and, if attacked, to return to the right bank. Only in the last extremity was he to disable or abandon his artillery.[109] A holiday present came with the arrival of more volunteers, including more rivermen who joined Captain Robert Sprigg's Company of Boatmen. Some went to guard the city customhouse and others to Chef Menteur, where, for want of accommodation, they slept in their boats.[110] Jackson also wrote to Governor Holmes imploring him to ensure that supply boats headed for New Orleans not be allowed to stop even momentarily in Natchez at this "critical moment."[111]

It was critical to the British as well. Hubris over their landing taking Jackson by surprise turned to relief for some who concluded from the severity of the fighting that if Old Hickory had anticipated their coming, the result might have been disastrous. As it was, they felt confident that British bravery had completely defeated the Yankees in an unequal contest in which Jackson surely had 5,000 to Keane's mere 1,500.[112] A naval officer from *Ramillies* wrote home to declare that "I do not profess to hold the Americans too cheap, but on this occasion they did not fight as they ought to have done." Had any troops other than those with Jackson attacked them, he believed, "all would have been made prisoners or destroyed."[113]

Unbeknownst to Keane's confident, if sobered, army that Christmas Eve, the *Statira* reached Cochrane's deep anchorage that morning with Pakenham, Gibbs, Lieutenant Colonels Dickson and Burgoyne, and Pakenham's aide Captain Alexander Wylly aboard.[114] Anxious to see Cochrane, Pakenham took *Statira*'s gig to the inner anchorage, arriving about two o'clock that afternoon to learn that Keane had landed the morning before. Pakenham reached Pine Island late that evening to find that Cochrane had gone to Bayou Bienvenue. After ninety minutes and a hasty meal, Pakenham's suite rowed and sailed twenty-five miles across Lake Borgne into a cold, freezing wind. A red flag flying from a pole marked Bienvenue's mouth, and from there they saw Cochrane's ensign half a mile inland flying atop the lone tree at Des Pêcheurs. A mile of rowing up the winding stream brought them there about eight o'clock on Christmas morning.[115] Cochrane was just breakfasting when the party joined him in a hearty if uncomfortable meal in the cold with neither chairs, stools, nor table. The admiral was all cheer and hospitality, and as they dined, Pakenham told the admiral that the 7th, 40th, and 43rd Regiments and additional artillery were on their way with Lambert. Then Cochrane gave him a fuller account of the recent engagement.[116] They were still eating when they heard *Carolina* open fire again, making Pakenham the more anxious to reach the front. In two small gigs with him, Gibbs, and Burgoyne in one and Wylly and Dickson in the other, they reached the landing place about eleven a.m.[117]

After a brief conference with Malcolm, Hill led Pakenham and the others to the Villeré house as Burgoyne and Dickson plied him with questions.[118] On reaching Keane, Pakenham got a briefing that did not please him. Now, with virtually all units present, the army totaled 7,189 of all arms.[119] That was inadequate for the job, and even with Lambert would not be enough. He distrusted his naval support after the failure to provide enough landing boats and the refusal of the senior captain at the Ship Island anchorage to send a vessel looking for the overdue Lambert. The general did not like having a single line of supply on the bayou and canal, and he did not care for provisions and even munitions coming from the canal on soldiers' backs. Captain Gordon actually had redcoats carrying cannonballs and shells in their arms. He was unhappy that Cochrane had started ground operations before Lambert could arrive.

Pakenham found little comfort in the forces present, either.[120] The 4th and 93rd regiments were excellent, but the 85th was battered down to just three hundred effectives and the 95th even fewer. He thought the 21st had bravery but no discipline, and could find nothing good to say of the 44th. Only a dozen of the 14th Dragoons were mounted, making them inadequate for reconnaissance, and thanks to the weather the West India regiments were of no use whatsoever.[121] At least Pakenham had an outstanding staff, distinguished by Dickson and chief engineer Burgoyne. With Stovin wounded on December 23, Colonel Harry Smith took over as military secretary and adjutant and was always at Pakenham's side, sharing the same room at night.[122]

What army he had was confined in a cul-de-sac between the river, the swamp, and Line Jackson, and he saw no way to retire the army to a better position.[123] If Pakenham found that frustrating, he may have spoken of it, for subordinates not present at the time later spoke of him implying that the best he hoped to do was get them out of where he found them.[124] Codrington shared his misgivings. The wholesale collapse of Cochrane's security had given the enemy too much time and opportunity to assemble a strong defense. "I believe there never was a more arduous service undertaken under these circumstances," he wrote Jane. He marveled that Cochrane could stand the frustration.[125]

Pakenham first addressed the reorganization of the army, dividing it into three brigades. The First Brigade would be Lambert's two regiments when they arrived. Gibbs would lead the Second Brigade, including the 4th, the 44th, the 21st, and the 1st West India regiments, while the 85th, the 93rd, the 95th, and the 5th West India constituted Keane's Third Brigade.[126] It was not an ideal arrangement. Keane got only one full-strength regiment, the 93rd, the rest of his brigade being badly mauled in the recent fight. Gibbs got the excellent 4th, but also two other regiments whose discipline Pakenham questioned. No one had confidence in the West India units. The manpower was spread evenly among the brigades, with Gibbs somewhat the stronger, but only Lambert would have experienced, full-strength regiments. If he arrived in time.

Pakenham's greatest want was artillery, which made him fortunate to have Dickson, arguably the army's ablest artillerist. He was known to be temperamental and irascible, but withal even-handed and open-minded. Associates and subordinates would put up with much from him thanks to his acknowledged ability. "Although I would resent to the utmost another's temper," declared a fellow officer, "if Dickson were to spit in my face and kick me, I would pull off my hat and thank him for it."[127]

The two nine-pounders that arrived on the boat ahead of Pakenham were followed by a heavy 5.5-inch howitzer, all rushed to Villeré's to deal with *Carolina*.[128] That gave Dickson a dozen guns, with more coming: two nine-pounders, four six-pounders, two 5.5-inch howitzers, and four light three-pounders. There was also Lane's rocket company armed with 150

Congreves, and three 5.5-inch brass mortars commanded by a marine captain. The guns were all too small to counter fire from the Americans' ships. Worse, while up to ninety percent of the army's musket and rifle ammunition had reached Villeré's by now, there were only 60 to 120 rounds per cannon on hand. He ordered 800 to 1,000 rounds each for the six- and nine-pounders and the howitzers, to be sent from the fleet at Ship Island, but it would take days to arrive.

Meanwhile, Dickson decided to silence the *Carolina* and *Louisiana* by cutting embrasures into the levee at night to mount the nine- and six-pounders and the howitzers to bear on the *Carolina* at her anchorage on the opposite bank. For the work, Codrington provided hundreds of pickaxes, shovels, spades, felling axes, machetes, saws, and almost six miles of yarn to make rope.[129] Dickson needed it all to make embrasures, and even more to create field defenses, as well as to build an improvised furnace to heat cannonballs until red-hot to fire at ships to set them ablaze.[130] Work parties started the embrasures at nightfall and had their guns in place and concealed, ready to open fire by the next dawn.[131]

Elsewhere the redcoats were largely inactive thanks to occasional fire from the American ships.[132] Now and then an exploding shell injured an unprotected soldier, although only one man was killed.[133] Gerard and others picketing the army's rear ate a spare Christmas meal while under arms, their only gift being relief from lonely duty that evening by the 21st.[134] Sadly, Lieutenant W. Hickson of the 85th died of a battle wound that day, adding to the gloom felt by Gleig and others as they pooled rations into what he dubbed "a melancholy Christmas dinner."[135]

Elsewhere there had been such expectations. People in London the day before read in their press a statement from Monroe that the United States would never relinquish its rights, and certainly it would never give up New Orleans, the "great inlet and key to the commerce of all that portion of the United States lying westward of the Alleghany mountains."[136] That amused many, for they expected that by Christmas Day Pakenham had taken the city.[137] As Gleig and Gerard and thousands of others made what they could of a holiday meal in the cold and damp and mud of Louisiana, signatures were already a day old at Ghent on a treaty ending the war. The question now was: Could the Crown in London and the president and Senate in Washington ratify the document in time to prevent another battle in America?

Ten

"Cannon and Batteries Are Its Proper Defence"

W HAT WAS OLD Hickory to do next? A Frenchman in New Orleans heard "several braggadocios" panting to renew the attack at once.[1] Jackson was wiser. Keane and Pakenham's prudent shyness about taking the offensive gave him time to press the work, and he kept men augmenting the earthwork at a pace so furious, some thought it miraculous.[2] He ordered Mayor Girod to furnish horses, and carts and drivers—most of them slaves—to work with the volunteers leveling ditches and digging out others, often knee-deep in standing water. The men spent their nights on or beside their growing mound of mud, Plauché's, Coffee's, and Carroll's men sleeping on wet ground without cover.[3] At the oblique arm on the left they laid parallel rows of stacked logs about two feet apart and filled the interval with mud, the men contending with mire a foot deep. The few with tents pitched them on small mounds surrounded by pools of mud.[4] The engineers also dug down behind the breastwork as much as a foot and up to forty feet back, so men moving there would be better protected.

Steamboatman Clement thought the thick mud could stand head-high and perpendicular without support, but Jackson took no chances of that and seized nine acres of picket fencing worth $10,000 from surrounding plantations to shore the work so he could raise it higher.[5] He dismantled slave cabins, stables, even chicken coops, and when those sources ran out, he contracted with William Withers of Beale's Rifles for his sawmill to produce thick cypress boards at four and a half cents a running foot. Dr. William Flood's mill across the river provided another 100,000 board feet of planking and 6,000 cypress pickets at a cost of $4,480. Old Hickory also commandeered 250 two-by-nine-foot bags of cotton to make "epaulments," or shoulders flanking the sides of the gun embrasures, to prevent erosion from the rains. Some of it was Nolte's. When he objected, Livingston chided that if his cotton was so valuable, it ought to give him an incentive to defend it. In all, the seizures tallied over $160,000.[6]

After three days the breastwork was strong and getting stronger.[7] As the work went on, Jackson's gunners and the *Carolina* shelled the distant enemy from their six-, twelve-, twenty-four-, and thirty-two-pounders.[8] Advice from locals as well as his own observation convinced Jackson that the narrowness of the river road approach to New Orleans made artillery the most effective defense. Patterson was a godsend for sharing artillery from the naval stores, as well as a few gunners and expendable officers from the *Carolina*, and the Baratarians brought equally welcome experience with big guns.[9] Major John Nicks, whose wound on December 23 forced him to hand the 7th Infantry to Major Henry Peire, took over Fort Charles and forwarded artillery and ammunition from the arsenal and powder magazine there as quickly as he could.[10] As Jackson brought more guns into the embrasures in his line, he maintained picket skirmishing day and night to keep the men active and alert and feeling they were accomplishing something as work continued.[11]

When completed, Line Jackson would offer an excellent field of fire covering the entire area between the river and the swamp and cypress wood. Chalmette, immediately in front of his position, was the largest of the properties between Jackson's line and Villeré's, stretching three-quarters of a mile along the river. Like all of these plantations, thousands of years earlier it was the seabed of the Gulf of Mexico until an adolescent Mississippi created the lower delta. Uninhabited prior to 500 BC, it was populated by Chitimacha and Muskhogean-speaking peoples when Hernando de Soto and the first Europeans arrived, but they had disappeared by the time the French settled in 1714.[12]

Immediately below Chalmette was Pierre Antoine Bienvenu's plantation. Below it sat De La Ronde's, and below that Lacoste's. Cypress picket fences with ditches or canals on either side separated all of them, and every one was an obstacle to a British advance. Obstacles faced Old Hickory as well. The Chalmette house was large, with at least seven other plantation outbuildings and nine slave cabins. Bienvenu's house was a large two-story brick edifice, galleried all around, and his property had as well a brick sugar house, a steam engine building for his cane-crushing mill, a curing house big enough to store almost two hundred hogsheads of sugar, and thirty-three slave cabins. De La Ronde's was also large, perhaps the biggest in the area, with at least five milling and storage buildings and fifteen or more slave cabins.[13] At least seventy-five or more buildings of greater or lesser size stood to afford shelter to the foe, as could the ditches and canals, not to mention the avenues of trees extending from the main houses. If Pakenham launched an assault, the challenge getting through or past all these would pose to maintaining organization in his lines could be offset by the conceal-ment they offered his line.[14]

Thus they sat the day after Christmas when Old Hickory wrote a friend that "we are now in sight of each other."[15] He and Patterson concluded to move *Carolina* upstream, closer to the new defensive line, where her guns could support Jackson's against an enemy advance. Patterson left Lieuten-ant Henley in command and moved his flag to *Louisiana*, but Henley found the wind too light to make headway upriver.[16] He sent men out to try "warping"—rowing a small boat with an anchor ahead of the schooner and dropping it, whereby the ship could pull herself forward by hauling in the anchor cable—but the current ran too fast. That left *Carolina* stuck across the river from Villeré's, unaware that Dickson was stoking his makeshift hot shot furnace for the morrow.[17]

General Villeré sent the good news that Chef Menteur still showed no signs of enemy activity, nor did the bayous connecting with Bienvenue that some feared might be used to get between Jackson and the city.[18] General Morgan finished cutting breaches in the levee and then moved his com-mand back to the west bank and Fort St. Leon. Within a few hours he would put his men and most of his artillery on the march up that side to a position opposite the British camps.[19] Once again Old Hickory was planning to catch the enemy in a cross fire if chance afforded. That same evening he wrote to Secretary of War Monroe that both armies were making preparations for action, and forecast that as significant as the December 23 action had been, "something far more important will take place."[20]

In the city, townspeople and authorities spared little effort to support soldiers in the field. Committees formed to establish hospitals in homes, while others began subscriptions to provide Coffee's and Carroll's men with blankets and shirts. The legislature appointed Louis Louaillier to monitor the committees and coordinate multiple donation drives.[21] Older men formed more companies to police the streets and transport the cloth-ing and provision donations to the army.[22] The city guards continued to challenge strangers, and one poor veteran from Maryland who had come with his musket from Baltimore to volunteer found himself in the parish prison when he could not produce a pass.[23] During the day Louaillier sat on the legislature's military council with Skipwith, and spent his nights with militia commandant Gaspard Debuys walking city rounds.[24] The drafted militia answered reports of fires and other threats on the plantations to protect inhabitants in case of slave insurrection.[25] No one seemed to entertain serious fears for the city's safety after the December 23 fight. "We are entrenched and perfectly safe," a citizen wrote the day after Christmas, "even if there were 10,000."[26]

They might have been still more confident had they seen Pakenham's temper that morning. His pickets in the army's rear were embarrassingly lax, distracted, or terrified by the alligators crawling from the swamp to approach the road before returning to the water.[27] Pakenham discovered that Morgan had cut the levee 150 to 200 yards below his pickets and found water rushing through. He ordered work parties to stopper the opening and went to upbraid Captain Archibald Maclean of the 21st Regiment, who had charge of hourly patrolling the levee. The general was less happy still to learn that Major Edward Nicolls, now arrived with a few Creek and Choctaw chiefs, had sent half a dozen of them down that road to collect horses and cattle and they had passed the same pickets unchallenged. Maclean only discovered the Indians when they came racing back up the road with stolen horses, chased by outraged citizens whose firing at them prompted the picket to return fire. Pakenham gave the pickets a severe tongue-lashing and placed Maclean under arrest, with the threat of a court-martial to come.[28]

Having done with Maclean, Pakenham took Dickson to an outpost at the Lacoste house half a mile above Villeré's, where Thornton had the 85th, 95th, and some three-pounders in hasty earthworks. Another three hundred yards beyond that was their most advanced position in and around a wooden barn and a small house from whose upper story they could look over the plantations in front of them. The officers arrived just in time to see a company of Coffee's horsemen ride along the edge of the wood to their right and then across the open ground in front of them to within about four hundred yards of the outpost, where they began setting fire to sedge grass and cane stubble that ignited in spite of recent rain. Jackson hoped to screen his defensive preparations behind a wall of smoke, but from Dickson's point of view the burning simply cleared the field for British advance. Minutes later *Carolina* opened fire for the first time that day, targeting headquarters at Villeré's, which, unknown to Henley, was where the British kept their ammunition.

Seeing activity at a nearby building, *Carolina* shifted her fire toward it, unaware that it was being used as a redcoat hospital. An enraged Pakenham at first wanted Dickson to open fire on *Carolina* from his new levee battery, but the artilleryman persuaded him that it would ruin the surprise he planned and his hot shot furnace was not yet completed. Other problems added to Pakenham's discomfiture. The artillery had almost no horses, Cochrane having counted on buying or taking them from locals. Nicolls's Indians had rustled perhaps thirty, and some of the regimental officers brought their horses aboard ship, so Pakenham ordered them all sent to Dickson to select the ones best suited to pull cannon. Some officers sent only the worst animals, a violation of the order that hinted of a crack in the army's respect for its new commander.[29]

December 26 was little more active for the soldiers than Christmas as they awaited completion of Dickson's furnace.[30] Officers enjoyed using the elegant and well-furnished planters' homes, Major John Michell finding them superior to country houses he had seen in France during the European war. Moreover, at first they found provisions abundant and inexpensive until the storehouses were emptied.[31] With some trees still bearing oranges and Villeré's storehouse full of hogsheads of sugar, officers put servants to boiling the fruit in sugar to make marmalade that ornamented their rations.[32] More troops and matériel kept arriving, the focus now on bringing up heavier artillery. Several score sailors and marines from the fleet arrived to volunteer for the land operation, and even three ship's captains came hoping to see action.[33]

The oarsmen on those long trips back and forth had to sleep in their boats in the bitter-cold nights, and more of the hapless West Indian soldiers died from exposure.[34] Even senior officers enjoyed few comforts. Villeré's "Consiel" could not accommodate all of the generals and their retinues, forcing staff officers like Dickson into empty slave cabins.[35] In quarters shared with Cochrane, Codrington stayed cold all day and night, and could find neither a table, a chair, nor even a stool to sit upon.[36] There was less comfort still for the British and American wounded being tended. The Yankees were confined to plantation buildings and allowed outside only in small groups under guard two or three times a day for necessity. Many had no blankets, and the Tennesseans who had had blanket rolls on their backs in action were relieved of them for the benefit of British casualties. The ice that morning was thick in places, and their captors finally allowed the American wounded to have fires, and the next day gave them blankets as more came in on the boats. Thereafter the prisoners received good treatment, Pakenham himself calling on them to ask what they needed.[37]

Louisiana and *Carolina* remained his chief concern. He could not move so long as they were free to bombard his left flank. Before daylight that day Colonel Dickson had his artillery hidden behind the levee, ready to go into newly cut embrasures spread over about 250 yards of the embankment.

Cane stalks hid them to prevent detection, and Dickson withdrew all of the workers and artillerymen from the scene to avoid arousing suspicion. Pakenham doubted the nine-pounders were sufficient to the task and suggested waiting for eighteens to arrive, but Dickson was confident that he could set the enemy vessels ablaze with what he had.

After sundown, the hot shot furnace complete and cannonballs ready for the oven, Pakenham ordered Dickson to open fire on the *Carolina* in the morning. Dickson returned to the cluster of slave cabins the officers called "Villere" to await the dawn. In one of several oversights, the quartermasters had issued enlisted ranks blankets and overcoats but provided officers none but what they had brought themselves.[38] They took what comfort they could that night from a crude fireplace and some oranges miraculously still edible.[39] Around the hearth they ate and talked of what would come once the Yankee ships were out of the way and the army could march forward. Ensign Benson Hill volunteered a forecast that New Orleans's fall would be inevitable from the moment Pakenham told them to advance.[40]

At two a.m. on December 27, Dickson kindled the fire in his furnace. Six hours later his shore battery's nine-pounders fired their first glowing shot at *Carolina*. Soldiers saw commotion on her deck and believed the crew were thunderstruck with surprise, as indeed they were.[41] Captain Henley's light twelve-pounders could not throw shot or shells from her west bank anchorage with any accuracy, even if he could see the concealed guns firing on him. Only his single long twelve-pounder could make the range, and he returned fire intermittently while trying to raise sail to get upriver to safety. Unfortunately, the only wind was light and out of the north, denying him headway against the current. Just the second discharge of Dickson's guns lodged a red-hot ball in *Carolina*'s main hold under her steering cables in a place that could not be reached to douse it with water. A fire started quickly and spread rapidly.[42]

Now Henley was as much a helpless target as the redcoats under his guns four days before. Dickson immediately knew he had the upper hand. *Carolina*'s long twelve fired fewer than half a dozen times.[43] Dickson's two nine-pounders had the right range at eight hundred yards, and his four six-pounders added solid shot while his two howitzers and a 5.5-inch mortar began to lob exploding shells onto *Carolina*'s deck. Soon, answering fire from the schooner ceased entirely.[44]

Within minutes of the first gun, Henley was in a desperate position. A hot shot passed through the main cabin and into the "filling room" where sailors prepared bags of powder to take to the gun deck. He quenched that threat but then other shot began breaking down bulwarks, and at least one plunging shot from a howitzer that came down on *Carolina*'s deck plowed its way through her bottom. She began to sink slowly, and meanwhile other fires spread toward her magazine, putting her at risk of explosion. No matter how Henley considered his condition, his schooner was doomed to sink or blow apart within minutes. Shortly after dawn he gave the order to abandon ship.[45]

Dickson was firing at leisure now, when he saw flames flickering through a shot hole in her side. He watched the fire spread to the outer bulwarks and saw a large column of smoke arise from her midships. His gunners poured more hot shot into her, and soon smoke billowed from her stern and bow. Through the spreading cloud he made out one lone Yankee on the burning deck before going ashore, then a mass of black smoke obscured the whole hull.[46]

That lone man was probably Henley, looking for any remaining men aboard before being the last to leave. "We all had to jump overboard, to save our lives," local volunteer William Murphy told his mother later that day. They evacuated so quickly, they had no time to take hats or jackets to protect them from the cold once they swam to shore.[47] A quick head count revealed six wounded and one man killed. With nothing else to do, they began walking along the bank to the *Louisiana*.[48] That ship, through good luck, had been three hundred yards upstream and better positioned to catch a slight increase in wind that came up while *Carolina* was under fire. Patterson got her moving and out of range with only one or two casualties, as most shots aimed at her passed harmlessly overhead. When she anchored again, Henley and his crew caught up to her and Patterson joined them to walk into New Orleans.[49]

For two hours Pakenham and his redcoats stood on the levee and watched the smoke and flames consume the dying schooner.[50] Finally, between nine and ten o'clock, the fire found her stern magazine and it exploded while her masts and the rest of the burning hull collapsed. Dickson's barrage had thrown 173 iron balls at her, many straight from the furnace, and another 24 exploding shells. They did their work well, but he only had 719 rounds of all description available that morning, which meant he expended more than one-fourth of his ammunition on this one target, and *Louisiana* had escaped.[51] Remembering what the schooner's guns had done to them a few days earlier, the British erupted in cheers when she "*exploded beautifully.*"[52]

Seeing *Carolina* go down now, everyone expected Pakenham to advance soon, and so he planned.[53] He ordered the army to cook two days' rations and be ready to advance at one p.m. that afternoon. Dickson pulled the six- and nine-pounders out of his levee embrasures and got them ready to move with all but seventy-seven rounds of his remaining ammunition.[54] If that gave his general pause, it should have. If Dickson ran through that without victory in the initial engagement, he would have little to fall back on in case of a counterattack. Of course, more arrived daily from the fleet, but the flow was slow, and the more Pakenham advanced, the farther it would have to come. Then he learned his commissary officers could not get meat rations to the men in time. His artillery could fire on slim supply, but soldiers had to eat to perform. The general reluctantly deferred the attack until the next morning, although many of his officers did not know why.[55]

Pakenham used the extra hours to hone his plan. Gibbs's Second Brigade would cross the cleared fields midway between the levee and the swamp, taking three three-pounders and half of Captain Lane's rocket brigade. They were to clear enemy pickets posted in and around buildings and then cover the advance of Keane's main column on the river road with the rest of the rockets and some small mortars to lob shells behind Jackson's line. Major John Michell's two nine-pounders and a heavy howitzer would follow Keane in reserve with two other sixes. Dickson would post two other six-pounders and the 5.5-inch howitzer together as a battery on the riverbank to occupy the *Louisiana*.[56]

The postponement gave Dickson time to organize his artillery and equip it as properly as he could. All told, now he had a dozen eighteens, two nines, three sixes, four twenty-four-pounder carronades, five 5.5-inch howitzers, and a supply of twelve- and thirty-two-pounder Congreve rockets—twenty-six cannon in all and more coming from the fleet. He could use only the lighter guns in an advance, however, especially as he was still short both horses and harness. He made Villeré's plantation his artillery depot and set men to digging defensive earthworks to protect men and guns. Pakenham reiterated the order to send horses to Dickson to pull the guns and this time got a better response. Animals not strong enough to work the artillery he doled to staff and orderlies, who would need to move quickly on the field during the coming action.

Dickson also got seventy marines led by Cochrane's son-in-law, Captain Sir Edward Thomas Troubridge of *Armide*, and two score soldiers from the 1st West India. With their help he moved the nine-pounders and howitzers on the main road for the planned advance. Dickson felt uneasy about the blacks. The cold simply wore them down, made worse by the failure to clothe them adequately. Everyone had counted on Cochrane's assurance that Louisiana in December would be temperate. Now Dickson found the West Indians lethargic and weakened, and the poor men were still dying.[57]

After directing that every man carry twenty rounds of ammunition, Pakenham sent special instructions to Major Robert Rennie of the 21st Foot. He commanded its "light company," a group specially equipped to move faster than the rest of a regiment. Such companies often got the most dangerous assignments, and Rennie had shown himself the man for that in earlier actions. The general wanted him to be ready to move through the cypress woods at the edge of the swamp to get around Jackson's left flank, the very eventuality Pierre Laffite warned Jackson to anticipate.[58]

The navy's role for the advance was to keep the small boats in good repair for continuing their supply runs, every boat equipped with paddles and oars as well as sails, and their crews rested whenever possible. Codrington ordered that every craft be fitted with an awning to provide some minimal cover from the elements, and for every oarsman to have a blanket against the night chill.[59] That night, in "as miserable a hovel as you ever saw," Codrington struggled to warm himself while surrounded in smoke from a green-wood fire.[60] Out on the field, Jackson's pickets maintained their occasional firing at British sentries, which added to the apprehension of the assault on the morrow. Writing in his diary with the sound of Yankee sniping in his ears, Ensign George Gleig confessed that it "kept us in a state of constant alarm all night."[61]

Alarm was Old Hickory's goal, to keep the British off balance. American confidence remained high, especially as rumors said the Kentuckians might arrive the next day, which would swell Jackson's numbers to over 10,000 or more. Few now feared that Pakenham could overrun the city by surprise or from sheer force of numbers, and some feeling even spread that the enemy feared to test Line Jackson.[62] With the Yankees seemingly getting stronger every day, one wrote that evening to predict that "we shall have something decisive in a few days."[63]

That morning the first definitive news of the December 23 fight reached anxious eyes at St. Francisville and Natchez beyond, putting the countryside on the alert.[64] Better yet, letters written shortly after the fight stopped began to arrive. A correspondent at Natchez passed their content on toward Louisville, Kentucky, assuring that every man was under arms in the city and Orleanians felt confident of being able to defend themselves.[65] That scarcely began to sate the outside appetite for information. Letters coming from New York begged Livingston for more mail, and Senator Brown frantically appealed, "For Gods sake give me more of your letters."[66] That morning's mail left New Orleans carrying the good news that the city still held.[67] As news gradually spread up the Mississippi and Ohio, then across the Appalachians community by community, it brought the first assurance that the enemy was not going to take New Orleans easily. Unfortunately, as reports passed from one person to another, error and exaggeration infected the news. Newspaper readers in Kentucky in mid-January read that Jackson had decisively defeated Keane on December 23.[68] A week later, on January 20, 1815, people in the village of Warrenton, North Carolina, a few miles short of the Virginia line, heard cheering from the home of William Ruffin after a passing postrider told him that Jackson had won a great victory and killed or captured 4,000 redcoats.[69] Confusions further contaminated early reports. In St. Francisville an impression took hold that the British commander on December 23 was actually an American, Richard Reynold Keene, former United States attorney for the Orleans Territory and a minor player in the Burr mysteries. In time, a report in England balanced that by claiming that Keene actually commanded the American forces, and elsewhere even odder claims appeared. In Bermuda the word spread that Pakenham's headquarters was actually a country house belonging to Old Hickory.[70]

Through the morning of December 27, Major Hinds made sorties that confirmed the British at Villeré's were growing in strength, and evidently preparing to advance.[71] The loss of *Carolina* did not seem to dampen American spirits, and her destruction actually did the Americans a good turn when the explosion propelled two of her deck guns onto the riverbank, where they were easily recovered.[72] Old Hickory observed the schooner's bombardment through his telescope from a dormer window of the McCarty house.[73] The prevailing mood after the ship's destruction seemed to be more resolution than dismay, and young William Murphy told his mother after reaching the city that he, Captain Henley, and the rest of the crew intended to go to *Louisiana* in the morning to renew their own bombardment.[74]

As work on Line Jackson continued, every fresh spadeful of mud seemed to add weight to their feeling of security in their growing defenses.[75] Work continued on into the night, with three batteries completed and guns mounted, and the work of placing others in progress.[76] Rain fell again about eight p.m. as the men hauled the first twenty-four-pounder through the mud and frost to the earthwork. It came with wooden beams and boards to build a platform to mount it in its embrasure, but no gunners to supervise the work until volunteers—*creoles*, Baratarians, or both—appeared to work through the night to have it ready.[77]

Late that night the quartermaster at Fort Charles walked to Clement's *Vesuvius* mooring and asked him to find a boat and go upriver to a sawmill—probably Withers's—to fetch more milled planks and scantling for shoring the defensive works. Clement and his crew did as asked, and were floating back downstream with the lumber when he steered into shore when he thought he had reached McCarty's plantation. It was well after midnight, and as he floated past several groups of men standing and talking, he could almost make out their conversation, but no sentry hailed him. No sooner did he land the boat and unload its cargo than he went to Jackson to complain of careless security along the river.[78]

It was not a convenient time for relations between Old Hickory and Claiborne to deteriorate further. The governor had remained with his militia on the Gentilly road since December 23, augmented by one of Coffee's regiments, a company of boatmen, and one of Carroll's regiments sent on Christmas.[79] Jackson had ordered Claiborne to find a canal or other defile closer to Chef Menteur to fortify to defend the road should any enemy appear. General José Álvarez de Toledo y Dubois, recently defeated in an attempted revolutionary takeover of Spain's Coahuila y Tejas Province immediately west of Louisiana, was in New Orleans at the time and assisted Claiborne in selecting and fortifying the position. Old Hickory was much satisfied and complimented Toledo, but in the same breath criticized Claiborne.[80] The general was too threatened by their conflicting ambitions to see that the governor was his greatest ally. In the face of repeated snubs and humiliations, Claiborne maintained a patience and self-effacement entirely foreign to the general's character. Meanwhile, Jackson's staff was composed largely of the governor's political enemies, men losing no opportunity to play on his manipulable suspicions and spiteful nature to drive general and governor farther apart.

By December 27, Jackson directed Claiborne to fall back to Bayou St. John and send his artillery to Fort St. John. He also ordered Coffee's and Carroll's men to rejoin their commands to help with building backup lines of defense. During the rest of the day Jackson shifted, readjusted, and consolidated some of Claiborne's militia companies, chiefly to watch canals behind his lines that extended to Bayou Bienvenue.[81] No longer concerned about an enemy approach through Barataria, Jackson ordered Major Reynolds to sink his artillery in shallow water where it could be raised quickly if needed and then move immediately to the magazine opposite the city, presumably bringing Jean Lafitte with him.[82] Finally, Jackson ordered virtually all militia outside the city to march to New Orleans.[83] It was all prudent and sensible, but it steadily diminished Claiborne's command. On paper, as governor he commanded five brigades composing two divisions of the state militia, totaling that day more than 8,800 men.[84] In reality Jackson left him with a remnant that scarcely required a colonel, let alone a governor. He could hardly fail to see it as yet another snub.

Claiborne returned to the city to make a personal check of guard posts, still expecting Jackson to redeem a promise to place him in command of some piece of the defense line.[85] He probably met a few members of the legislature like Skipwith making their patrols in the city after nightfall. If so, he heard disquieting whispers, and he was not alone. For some days now a muffled rumor spread that the well-to-do *creole* legislators planned to make a separate peace with Pakenham to spare themselves and their city the fate of Alexandria. Never a concerted plot, it was probably just disgruntled grumbling that Jackson might ruin them all by fighting a battle there and then, but it was unsettling all the same.

That evening Colonel Declouet rode through the city to his brother's plantation for the night and thought he saw alarm on faces he passed in the streets. After he reached his brother's, speaker of the house Magloire Guichard arrived to use a bed as well. He seemed in a panicked mood and retired to his chamber after less than an hour. Declouet followed him into his bedroom to talk and sat down beside the fire, but Guichard apparently ignored him, undressed and got into bed, and went to sleep. Declouet then retired himself, fearing something ominous pended with the legislature. He had apprehended that Louisiana might be divided since the outbreak of the war, and that fear, added to recent rumors, made him overreact. He concluded that some, perhaps a majority, would give the city to the enemy to save it, which to him seemed the course to ruin.[86]

Jackson apparently knew nothing of that unrest. He remained seemingly tireless despite his declining health. He kept half of his troops under arms all night in case the enemy should try a night attack of its own, and kept his staff on the line constantly monitoring progress and communicating with him. Three times during the day he personally inspected Line Jackson before returning to his headquarters for the night.[87] Finally this evening, his line approaching completion, he allowed himself some rest. No one had seen him lie down since that brief nap on December 23. Like everyone else, he had good cause to expect an enemy advance in the morning, and he needed his wits fresh to meet the occasion.[88] He little suspected that he might have to deal with an enemy in his rear as well.

Nearly 4,800 miles northeast of Pakenham's bustling camp, Henry Carroll, secretary to the American legation, left Ghent the day after Christmas with copies of the treaty in his keeping to begin a seven-week journey to Washington.[89] The following day, as the *Carolina* disintegrated in flames, the London press speculated that a permanent British occupation of New Orleans would deal a fatal blow to American expansionist hopes in the vast Louisiana territory. President Madison could avert that by signing the treaty, but none could say what he would do if the city fell before he received the document, or if Pakenham stalled in the effort. Would Madison hesitate? Might he even refuse to sign?[90]

That same day Bathurst dispatched a copy of the treaty to Pakenham, adding that Prince Regent George would sign it on behalf of his ailing father King George III, which in fact he did later that same day, most likely because the prime minister, Lord Liverpool, told him to do so. Bathurst promised to notify Pakenham as soon as he had definitive word that President Madison had ratified the document. Hostilities should cease immediately and the general was to counsel Britain's Indian allies to make peace with the United States. Bathurst said nothing about what the general should do if by that time he had taken New Orleans.[91]

Eleven

"I Am Now on the Move"

PAKENHAM FOUND HIMSELF in a difficult position, and rumors in his bivouac made it worse. Campfire gossip rumbled that he did not expect to succeed—that, inheriting command thanks to General Ross's death, he felt forced to make only a token effort, since the expedition had already consumed so much time and money.[1] Whispers even said he would abandon his position, re-embarking the army to try the route via Chef Menteur and the Gentilly road.[2]

Cochrane's false expectations of local disaffection, fed by Kerr, Workman, and others, continued to let the general down. A few *creoles* did affirm French and Spanish neutrality, and a report to Havana even said that they were anxious for British protection.[3] Yet *Ramillies*'s officers and at least one of Pakenham's complained that neither Frenchman nor Spaniard afforded the least assistance. Instead, the British found plantations abandoned, livestock driven off, and none but slaves to inform them, and they knew little of worth.[4] Of course, Bellechase, the Spanish fishermen, Workman, and others provided geographical information, at least, and some believed Kerr actually accompanied the redcoats.[5] Some on Jackson's staff even thought traitors constantly passed the swamps and bayous on his left to take information to the enemy.[6] While later claims that no inhabitants helped the British were mistaken, the few who did came by droplet rather than torrent.[7]

Pakenham might lack detailed intelligence, but he knew Jackson had spent four days building a defensive line, another good reason to postpone his December 27 advance by a day. He might not know Old Hickory's strength, but he did know that large numbers of Tennesseans and Kentuckians were daily expected. Most critically, he did not know the number and size of Yankee artillery except for what he had seen of *Louisiana*'s big guns in action. He knew his enemy was a daring risk taker, a foe not to be taken for granted, good cause for him to be prudent. Hence, committing his whole army now would be premature.

Pakenham took Burgoyne, Adjutant Smith, and others to his advance pickets at dawn on December 28 to survey the American position. Viewed through a spyglass, the mud-banked American earthwork gave no clue of the manpower behind it. Intervening buildings obscured much of the right half of Jackson's line, and a projection of the cypress woods blocked all of his left from view. Just then they saw Tennessee riflemen one hundred yards distant and creeping toward them. Smith admonished Pakenham to take cover, but he only laughed, the bravado for which several of Wellington's generals were known.

Instead, Pakenham asked if the enemy earthwork could be stormed successfully. Burgoyne thought not, and feared that in case of a repulse, their retreat on the levee road would be under *Louisiana*'s guns. Here was the folly of Cochrane's enterprise. The army had come all this way to find itself in a position where its only option was a risky costly frontal assault with no safe line of retreat. Burgoyne argued that the army should return to the fleet to seek another line of approach. Smith seconded him, though less pessimistically. Neutralize *Louisiana* as they had *Carolina*, and take the batteries sprouting on the opposite bank to eliminate their fire on Pakenham's left, and they could launch an assault with some hope of success.[8]

Pakenham knew something they did not. He had to act quickly. Every day allowed Jackson to strengthen his works and welcome reinforcements. With all of Keane's and Gibbs's regiments on the scene, delay worked against morale, although Lambert would soon arrive. Pakenham had just faced an embarrassing example of the divided feelings within his command. Ensign A. J. Hamilton of the 5th West India was in fact a native of Massachusetts, to date untroubled in British service, since his regiment never left the Caribbean or faced Americans in action. Today would change that. A deeply conflicted Hamilton went to his colonel and handed over his sword, saying that his conscience would not let him fight his countrymen. Pakenham arrested him until he decided what to do with him. Eventually he would be allowed to resign.[9]

Pakenham simply could not have officers refusing to serve. If there was a chance of taking the American works, the moment would soon pass. He had to act, but that depended on what Old Hickory had on and behind his parapet. He decided on a reconnaissance in force, a strong but conditional advance to lure Jackson into revealing his strength, in particular his artillery. If the enemy response suggested that Pakenham could punch through the breastwork, he could on the spot convert his probe into a full-scale attack or fall back to plan a later assault according to what he had learned.

Keane and Gibbs had been in position since before dawn. Pakenham called in his pickets and put them in motion, Keane on the main road and Gibbs to his right on a lesser track. On the far right, Rennie and his light company moved along the edge of the woods. As Keane advanced across the Lacoste plantation and onto De La Ronde's, a curve in the road kept him from getting anything but fleeting glimpses of the American earthwork well over a mile distant. Gibbs's view was no better, and none could see the Tennesseans behind the cypresses. The redcoats moved with no opposition and no idea what lay ahead.

Immediately in their front, Hinds and his dragoons had completed five consecutive nights of picket duty within four hundred yards of the enemy bivouac, sleeping beside their saddled horses, their weapons always in reach, with no fires against the cold.[10] Occasionally one or more crept close enough to the British outposts to fire at them, scattering men in all directions and occasionally getting closer to kill specific targets.[11] It had kept the redcoats off guard, but now the early light revealed enemy columns in the distance. The redcoats were some minutes on the march before Jackson received Hinds's warning, and Old Hickory had just finished reading it when he saw the flash of rockets rising in the distance. In their concealment amid uncut cane, Hinds's men heard but did not see the Congreves until the British fired some directly through the stalks. The Mississippians withdrew at once, and Jackson sent them to the rear to await orders.

It was about 7:30. Across the river at *Louisiana*'s mooring opposite Line Jackson, Patterson saw Hinds hurrying back, then heard opening rounds from enemy six-pounders on the road and saw the first of Lane's sparkling rockets rising into the air. *Louisiana* could not immediately bring a single gun to bear on the advancing British, so while gunners on Jackson's line prepared to return fire, Patterson dropped an anchor several yards to his portside rear and hauled in its cable to pull, or "spring," her stern to port, which turned its starboard broadside to bear on the ground immediately below the American line.[12] It was nearly 8:30 when enemy artillery and rockets began to address *Louisiana*, and Patterson mistakenly believed that they fired hot shot at her.[13]

Jackson stood at a second-floor dormer of the McCarty house, straining to get a view through an old telescope given him by one of the *creoles*, but the distance was too great for him to see his pickets fall back before the 85th and 95th as they advanced onto the Bienvenu plantation while Gibbs drove others from the De La Ronde buildings, one of which the pickets left in flames.[14] Jackson had ordered the demolition of those buildings to clear his field of fire, but the work was incomplete—a benefit for the moment, since the structures obscured the redcoats' view of his line. Then, just as Keane reached the Bienvenu house and outbuildings, American pickets fired on the Chalmette house a quarter mile ahead of him, its smoke further obstructing his view of Jackson's line.[15] Looking on the fiery trails of the rockets, Major Reid thought it "a scene of terror and alarm" calculated to panic the raw troops in Jackson's army.[16]

Pakenham's columns made a slight turn to the right as they passed across the Bienvenu plantation, and then for the first time faced directly toward the Yankee earthwork a mile and a half ahead of them. Jackson's batteries immediately opened fire. A cannon directly in front of Gibbs's column drew first blood with a shot that took down four men in the center of the 4th Foot.[17] Just then *Louisiana* opened on the British left, her first shot dividing the 85th's Ensign Sir Frederick Eden from his leg.[18] Four guns in front of Keane—two served by the Baratarians—opened simultaneously with a salvo that felled eleven men and two officers in Gleig's company. The din of cannon and musketry, cries of the wounded, and the sight of comrades mangled before their eyes spread disorder in the ranks until Keane formed the men in line in a field to the right of the road and advanced them once more. Some of the Chalmette buildings to their right promised cover at first, but within a few minutes Yankee shells set many of them on fire and others were already ablaze thanks to withdrawing American pickets.[19]

For the first time, but hardly the last, Yankee onlookers likened the cannons' effect to a scythe mowing grain. Confusion broke out again in the redcoat ranks.[20] Keane and Gibbs halted near the Bienvenu house to return fire with their six-pounders, and more rockets went fizzing harmlessly above Jackson's line as the Yankees fired another salvo.[21] Seeing the enemy stop, some Yankees believed the redcoats refused to go farther, and mistook officers brandishing sabers as desperate attempts to prod their men forward.[22] The Americans began taunting the enemy with huzzas and shouts of "Hail Columbia," but then the redcoats came forward again.[23]

The strength of Jackson's line took Dickson and others by surprise, and it was almost immediately evident that they could advance no farther without heavy fighting.[24] Caught between fire in their front and from *Louisiana*, the columns tried to keep going. Keane sent the 85th and 95th forward another one hundred yards into a heavy fire of grape- and round shot until they reached musket range, when the fire became so hot he ordered the men to take cover in a ditch.[25] There they found themselves in water to their knees and there they remained for an hour under the heaviest artillery fire many could remember.[26] To Keane's right, Gibbs dispersed his men in a ditch as well.[27] Keane brought up the rocketeers to fire more Congreves, while Dickson sent forward a brace each of nine-pounders and sixes, with a howitzer, to divide their fire between the *Louisiana* and the intimidating weight of enemy guns in their front.[28]

Considering where he started five days before, Jackson had come a long way. His line extended from Coffee's 1st and 2nd Mounted Gunmen in reserve to the left, virtually in the cypress swamp itself, then on their right Carroll's three regiments from the edge of the swamp, to the 44th Infantry, then Daquin's 2nd Free Colored Battalion, then Lacoste's 1st Free Colored Battalion, then Plauché, the 7th Infantry, and finally Beale between the road and the levee.[29] Including Major Carmick's fifty-four marines, the Baratarian gunners, Hinds's pickets, Jugeat's Choctaw, and Smith's forty Feliciana dragoons, and other small volunteer companies, Jackson had over 3,300 on or near the line, double his strength on December 23, and the Kentuckians were expected to arrive almost momentarily.[30] The United States would not field such a force as this again for decades. It was an army of multiple nationalities, white, black, and red, regulars, volunteers, drafted men, soldiers, sailors and marines, even stateless smugglers and privateers. That diversity came of necessity, not design, but in it Old Hickory had created the first truly *American* army.

The earthwork they raised grew steadily over the past days, essentially doubling their strength against attack. It ran just under a mile from levee to swamp, where it bent back two hundred yards into the marshy ground on its left flank. The ground below the line sloped slightly downward from the river toward the swamp, leaving some of it sodden at the best of times, which worked in Jackson's favor. Recent rains and opening the levee between the American and British positions left standing water covering much of it by several inches, and from places on Line Jackson it appeared to be a single sheet of water.[31] Ditches and post and rail fences starting five hundred yards in front of the breastwork ran roughly parallel to it and offered the enemy some cover. Thick tufts of sedge grass covered much of the ground below the first ditch, and bushes dotted the ground.[32] Otherwise, but for buildings, it was open to view some distance from the breastwork.

The real power of the line was its guns. Jackson started with Lieutenant Samuel Spotts's pieces pulled back from the December 23 fight. The next day Patterson sent him three cannon from the naval depot, and thereafter

Jackson brought up more to create a wall of iron.[33] On the right of the line he established Battery No. 1 with two twelve-pounders and a six-inch howitzer just two hundred feet from the levee.[34] Late on December 27 a big twenty-four-pounder arrived in the rainy darkness and he put it in a new Battery No. 2 embrasure ninety yards from the first battery, after Captain Jean-Claude Hudry, a forty-year-old native of Savoy and wealthy cotton broker, aroused the men of his Compagnie des Francs and put them to manhandling the gun tube out of the mud and onto a carriage. They finished just before dawn that morning.[35] Plauché's battalion backed both Batteries No. 1 and 2.

Another 150 feet along the line, Battery No. 3 held two more twenty-four-pounders, capable of firing twenty balls or shells an hour over a distance of a mile and a half. The Baratarians manned those pieces, commanded by Renato Beluche and Dominique You, both captains of their own privateering vessels.[36] Nearly seven hundred feet northeast sat Battery No. 4 with the biggest gun on the field, an intimidating naval thirty-two-pounder managed by Lieutenant Charles Crawley and men from the *Carolina*, with Lacoste's and Daquin's companies on either side. One hundred and ninety yards from it were two six-pounders in Battery No. 5 on the right flank of the 44th Regulars, Lieutenant Henry Perry in command. Jackson designated everything to that point as his right wing under Colonel Ross of the 44th. His left wing began with Carroll's command, and one hundred feet from Battery No. 5 sat Battery No. 6, with a brass twelve-pounder tended by Lieutenant Étienne Bertel. Battery No. 7 lay another 190 yards along in the middle of Carroll's line, where General Antoine Garrigues de Flaujac commanded an eighteen-pounder and a smaller gun. Spotts commanded Battery No. 8, a single gun on a carriage so faulty that it might not be safe to fire, which sat sixty yards beyond at the edge of the swamp where Coffee was in reserve.[37]

That did not include the cannon across the river.[38] Patterson had suggested erecting batteries on the right bank levee and volunteered to locate and construct them. That would add more guns to *Louisiana*'s to disrupt the enemy left flank if it advanced against the main line. Jackson ordered Morgan to bring up the bulk of his command to help Patterson and to establish a defensive line to protect the batteries. He ultimately planned a chain of emplacements stretching almost a mile along the levee, mounting everything from twelve-pounders to twenty-fours, complete with hot shot furnaces to fire buildings on the opposite side that sheltered the enemy.[39]

One thing Old Hickory did not need was distraction, but it was coming. Shortly before the sound of the opening guns reached them, Guichard and

Declouet arose and the colonel renewed the conversation about the temper of the legislature. To escape his prying, Guichard went to his room, but the relentless Declouet followed and grabbed his arm. They spoke of several things, which included agreeing that the British had shown more consideration for *creole* planters' property than Jackson, especially when it came to seizing cattle. They also concurred that if New Orleans and its environs fell to the enemy and the Americans retook it by force, the country and everyone's property would be lost or destroyed.

His irritation mounting, Guichard tried to deflect the conversation to General Morgan's failure on the night of December 23, but bulldog Declouet would not be decoyed, demanding to know why the legislature had been meeting in the evenings. Guichard shrugged his shoulders in the Gallic fashion, and then Declouet challenged him to explain the legislature's refusal to adjourn at Claiborne's request. Guichard had no use for the American governor and said so, and refused to be questioned further. Declouet would not let go and, *creole* that he was, declared that "there is in that d . . d legislature, so many intriguers who would either seize all the authority or see the country overturned, that I place no reliance upon them." Guichard accused him of unreasonable suspicion and left the room, saying that in a crisis like the present, the legislature must be ready to take any measures necessary.[40] That was equivocal at best, making Declouet fear the legislature stayed in session so it could take measures to save the city from itself from becoming a battlefield if the enemy pushed Jackson back from Chalmette.

Declouet left at once to report his fears to Claiborne: that there was a plan "to save private property, by a timely surrender," and that the conspirators included Guichard, Marigny, and the Laffites' friend Jean Blanque, who feared Old Hickory would wage a scorched-earth campaign like that which defeated Napoleon at Moscow.[41] Whispers even alleged that they intended to debate surrender two nights hence.[42] Soon rumors reached Jackson that Guichard had made a clandestine visit one foggy night to Pakenham's camp.[43]

Claiborne already mistrusted some of the named conspirators, and asked Declouet to present his concern to Jackson. The colonel raced at full gallop for the front and met Jackson's aide Abner Duncan on the way, unfolding his story to him.[44] Duncan was not surprised. He knew that a couple of legislators served at the front, that the body often sat until late hours, and had himself heard rumblings of a plan to cede the old West Florida parishes to Britain to save the city from being sacked if captured. Declouet asked Duncan to go directly to the general.

Jackson had just left the McCarty house to ride to Coffee and check his readiness should the enemy try their earthwork, when an agitated Duncan reined up.[45] Shouting over the artillery and rockets, he gave the general Declouet's verbal message from Claiborne. Unfortunately, a number of soldiers were within hearing, and Jackson's first thought was the morale effect of such news on their ears. Shouting back to be certain everyone heard, he dismissed Duncan's news and declared with typical Jacksonian hyperbole that if the story was true, Declouet should be arrested for spreading it openly; and if it was false, he should be shot.

As Jackson made to ride on, Duncan said Claiborne awaited orders on what to do. Repeating his skepticism, and again for the benefit of troops within hearing, the general shouted that if the governor found the legislature's threat real, he ought to "blow them up if they attempt it." After that outburst, he followed up with a marginally more temperate written order. Claiborne should investigate, and if he found the rumor true, he was to shut down the body to prevent it taking action.[46] Jackson later claimed that he meant the governor should put a guard around the building to isolate members if anything was said on the floor of capitulation, but the body might otherwise continue its ordinary business.[47] If the people heard that the legislature considered making terms with the enemy, it could demoralize the militia and divide the army between them and the regulars.[48]

Duncan wheeled his horse to return to the city, and on the way encountered Colonel Michael Fortier, who knew nothing of the business. In relating Jackson's order to close the legislature, Duncan apparently added on his own an injunction to use force if necessary, and asked Fortier to deliver the order to Claiborne.[49] Fortier got only a mile on the road back to town, when he met the governor on his way to see Jackson on the same business. Suddenly it had become a parlor game. News went from Declouet to Duncan to Jackson. The response went from Jackson to Duncan to Fortier and now passed on yet again to Claiborne, who was astonished at Old Hickory's orders.[50] Saying nothing of blowing up the legislature, Fortier said Jackson wanted the body's doors closed and guarded, and anyone trying to force his way into the chamber to be shot.[51] Claiborne rode back to Government House at once, arriving about ten a.m. to find standing outside several legislators whom he informed of his instructions. He ordered General Labatut to close it to all and fire on any who tried forcible entry, and had his secretary issue the order in both French and English so that none could mistake its import.[52]

By that time Jackson reached Coffee and took heart as he saw along the way that he had the British hopelessly outgunned, while Dickson's small guns had no impact and Lane's rockets were all but useless. Congreves fired at the *Louisiana* flew wildly over the river and beyond into the swamp on the other side, while those aimed at Jackson's line for the most part fizzled over it harmlessly.[53] Pakenham's columns were stopped and under cover within four hundred yards or less, and under American musketry at long range, as their staff officers observed the Yankee fire, trying to deduce the placement and strength of Old Hickory's artillery.[54]

Pakenham was with Gibbs thus far and now rode to tell Dickson that the enemy line seemed strong enough that for the moment he would withhold his decision on converting the reconnaissance into an attack until he knew more, meanwhile ordering his own artillery to keep firing and probing the enemy line. At the same time he ordered Keane and Gibbs to hold on. Accompanied by Dickson, he returned to Gibbs's front to find the brigade sheltered in a ditch and standing cane.[55] At least they were covered from enemy fire, and the cypress outcropping on the far right gave them even better protection. The ditches occupied by Keane's men were not deep enough to conceal them entirely, so they stooped in cold water up to their knees, their exposed torsos somewhat hidden by rushes and brush. At that, many hid as best they could behind plantation buildings under constant fire.[56] While the generals sent out skirmishers from time to time thereafter to engage the Yankees in musketry, these ditches were as far as the British would get this day. Under a hail of iron from Line Jackson and *Louisiana*, they had nowhere to go.[57]

Pakenham concluded that Old Hickory had between four and ten pieces of artillery, including at least one twelve-pounder and a long thirty-two, with as many as five or six guns facing Keane's five cannon on the road. His observations were quite inaccurate, hardly worth the cost of hours of his infantrymen hugging the ground and ditches for cover.[58] A daring engineer climbed a tree for a better view and reported that he saw a water-filled ditch—the Rodriguez Canal—running in front of the entire enemy fortification. That meant a frontal assault must rush through the cane and sedge, then cross multiple ditches before wading that canal's unknown depths, to climb out of it and clamber up the slick muddy slope of a steep earthwork already more than head high. All of that would have to be accomplished without ladders or other means, and all fully exposed to American artillery and musket fire. Even men who had taken French strongholds in the recent war in Europe blanched at the likely cost of such an assault. Cognizant of that, Pakenham told the engineer to pay special attention to what he could see of the ground to the right of the American earthwork. The report was no more encouraging. The cypress wood and swamp appeared too impenetrable to allow a serious movement to outflank Jackson.[59]

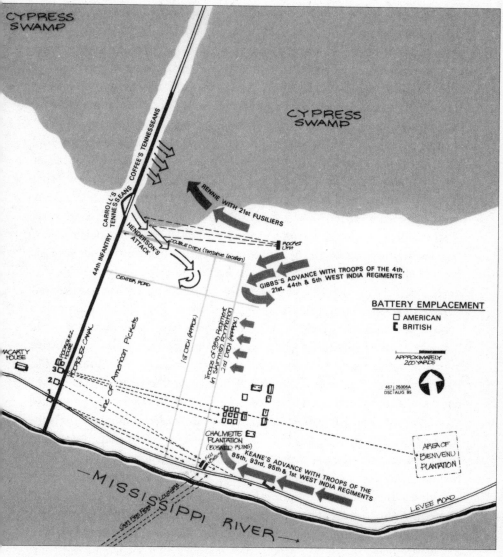

The skirmishing on December 28, 1814. Pakenham advanced his infantry to the Chalmette plantation in case fire from his rocket battery and other guns silenced American artillery or made a breach in Line Jackson. Fire from Jackson's batteries effectively stymied British guns and prevented any infantry advance. Rennie's effort to find a way around Jackson's left and rear is shown at top, as well as Colonel Henderson's ill-fated flank movement against General Gibbs.

Staff members watching Pakenham in those minutes fairly burst with pride. He seemed animated, sensitive to the lay of the ground, his own resources, and Jackson's strength, although he certainly misread the last. He reminded them of his brother-in-law Wellington.[60] Few appreciated his position, however. Time, season, morale, and expectations, both of his superiors and subordinates, weighed on him. Virtually all of the army then present took part in the reconnaissance, yet he knew Jackson expected daily reinforcement. To fall back now would disappoint men and officers, making it the more difficult to rouse their spirit to move again when he felt ready. He was not yet prepared to entirely abandon the idea of a general assault, and in the circumstances at that moment it was a prudent judgment.

He ordered Dickson to erect a work in Gibbs's rear about seven hundred yards from the American line. It would mask a battery of half a dozen or more cannon to silence Jackson's guns and cover an infantry assault. That expectation seemed inexplicable. His own observations, inaccurate as they were, reported up to ten Yankee guns, and several of them much more powerful than the six- and nine-pounders and a howitzer that he now ordered Dickson to move across the field to the battery from Keane.[61] Prudence fading, Pakenham was yielding to pressure and wishful thinking.

Meanwhile, he did not give up on turning Jackson's left. He had ordered Rennie to scour the cypress wood ahead of the general advance to protect Gibbs's right as it advanced.[62] Having done that, the resourceful major made his own reconnaissance to see if troops could get around Jackson's flank and concluded it could be done. He reported to Gibbs, who took him to Pakenham with the welcome news. Rennie volunteered to take his light company through the tangle of trees and undergrowth, and if they got around the end of the American earthwork, they would open fire on Jackson's exposed flank and rear. That might incite confusion and panic among the Yankees and create a diversion, allowing Gibbs to make a successful frontal assault on Carroll. Should Gibbs get over Line Jackson, the rest of the enemy line would be compromised and probably withdraw to save itself, allowing Keane to advance, and the whole army could march to New Orleans and victory. It might be a house of cards, but Pakenham was thinking like Wellington. In the face of multiple obstacles, he conceived a devastating triumph. Sir Edward immediately assented, and Rennie left to take his men into the cypresses.[63]

Looking out over their parapet and through its embrasures, Yankees gleefully watched the effect of their fire.[64] Some thought the redcoats advanced three or four times, but in fact it was one single, if halting, forward movement.[65] There was equal disagreement on enemy intent, their dispersing into the ditches striking one American as evidence of a plan to attack the earthwork, while others saw in it an effort to lure Jackson out of his works to attack them.[66]

British rockets, cannonballs, and shells passing overhead did slight damage behind the earthwork, but it protected Jackson's men from enemy musketry. The Congreves fascinated the Americans, who took foolish risks with them even after Old Hickory ordered them to keep their distance.[67] Carroll's men dodged and danced around the sputtering curiosities, and the general feeling was that they caused more alarm than injury.[68] Despite the number of rockets fired, they had little effect, wounding only two men and killing one, Private William Banks Anthony of Coffee's 2nd Tennessee Mounted Gunmen.[69] Major Daniel Carmick, commanding the detachment of marines, came dangerously close to being a second victim.

This army was a family affair for Carmick, Major Reynolds, and Colonel Ross of the 7th Infantry, who married three sisters. Carmick, a veteran of service on the USS *Constitution* and the Marine Corps' first landing on foreign soil, commanded the three hundred marines attached to Patterson's station. As the second-ranking officer of the corps, he stood in line to be its commandant one day, if he lived.[70] Today, as he sat on his horse behind the line, he bid fair to be the most wounded soldier in Jackson's army when a Congreve went off above him. Flying case shot tore into his right arm in three places, another ball cut away his right thumb, a fifth wounded his head, and a sixth may have killed his horse. He suffered badly from his wounds but was expected to recover.[71] A few days later an Orleanian told a friend that "our gallant friend Major Cormick, [sic] has immortalized himself."[72]

While the Americans stood in the open behind their mud wall, Pakenham's men spent miserable hours huddled in their soggy ditches and hiding places as the bombardment continued. Some veterans of the European campaigning thought it the heaviest cannonade they had experienced since the siege of Badajoz, Spain, in 1812.[73] Dickson found a route for moving Keane's guns to the new battery but discovered that *Louisiana's* fire had blasted the six-pounders' axles and wheels, knocked the gun tubes from the carriages, and forced the nine-pounders to withdraw to the cover of a burning house. Only one lone officer remained with the howitzer. Dickson sent to Villeré's for two more sixes, waiting an hour for them to arrive, then marked time until he received the order to take them to the new site. Meanwhile casualties mounted, including Captain Francis Collins of the 1st West India, who lost his head to a cannonball.[74]

Rennie got his company unseen close to the left end of the American line before two musket shots in his front wounded one of his advance skirmishers and killed another. He ordered the company forward, expecting to hit the enemy's unprotected flank or rear, only to be surprised when he hit Laffite's oblique line running into the swamp. Shifting left to a rail fence and ditch about two hundred yards from the earthwork, he confronted the left end of Carroll's Tennesseans. In an instant they exchanged a hot musket fire.[75] If Rennie sent any word back to Pakenham, it was that the enemy would not be vulnerable here.

Jackson reacted promptly to Rennie's unexpected probe, ordering Coffee to send Lieutenant Bayless Prince of the 2nd West Tennessee and a company of riflemen toward the fence to fire several volleys. That had no effect, so Carroll turned to Lieutenant Colonel James Henderson commanding the 1st West Tennessee and sent him with two hundred riflemen over the earthwork to the cover of another old fence immediately in its front. Henderson was to halt there while the two sixes under Colonel Henry Perry and the batteries of Spotts and Crawley hit Rennie's left flank with a barrage of grape- and canister shot, at the same time pummeling Gibbs's right flank to keep him from supporting Rennie. With the British position rattled, Henderson could advance to the swamp's edge to pass Rennie's right, hit his flank, and drive him out.

Henderson completely misunderstood his orders. Instead of stopping at the fence while Jackson's guns opened, he moved beyond the fence into open ground in front of the earthwork where Perry's guns dared not fire for fear of hitting Tennesseans. When Jackson's adjutant Butler yelled to Henderson to come back, he compounded his error. Instead of moving left toward the swamp as ordered, Henderson moved to his right through ground still marshy from the opening of the levee, directly across Rennie's front. His men's shoes splashing in the water kept Henderson from hearing Butler's pleas, so Carroll sent an officer to remedy the situation; but before he arrived, Henderson stopped to form his men on a low dry knoll in a line directly facing Rennie's, exposing his own right flank to fire from Gibbs.

Volleys erupted from both directions.[76] Henderson and two others immediately paid for his blunder with their lives. The rest stood the fire and returned two volleys before retreating to their line, leaving one of their wounded out on the field. He stood and tried to run back twice but fell each time. He rose again and started running under fire from Rennie, when Major John Simpson and Captain Barbe Collins and two privates from the 1st Tennessee jumped over their works and across the ditch to help him to safety. Tatum called it "as great an act of bravery as was witnessed on the lines during the siege." At last Crawley and Spotts opened on Rennie as Coffee's men with Lieutenant Prince renewed fire, forcing Rennie to break off.[77] That brief engagement was the only close small-arms fighting of the day.[78]

Across the field, Patterson and *Louisiana* continued to pitch iron at Keane. Almost all the ship's crew were *creoles* enlisted in New Orleans during the fortnight past, two-thirds of them scarcely able to understand English, yet they fired some three hundred rounds from her starboard battery, filling Patterson with admiration. Despite Dickson's best efforts with his own six-pounders and rockets, most of his fire passed over the ship or burst overhead, littering its deck with shell fragments but wounding only one man.[79]

By about three p.m. Jackson's artillery all but silenced the British guns, and grape and canister kept the enemy pinned to the ground until dark.[80] Patterson even tried leveling Louisiana's guns to skip shells across the water like flat stones to ricochet over the levee and explode in British lines.[81] His shelling continued another hour until the enemy began to retire, making some believe that Louisiana was almost alone responsible for the retreat.[82] Redcoats later told Yankee prisoners that they believed they could have taken Line Jackson but for Louisiana's fire.[83]

The more Pakenham tested Jackson's line, the stronger he found it to be. There was no way through or around it this day except by total commitment, and no realistic expectation of that without more preparation and equipment. He needed Lambert's regiments and bigger guns from the fleet for a classic infantry assault. Pakenham signaled Rennie to quit the swamp and sent Dickson, Keane, and Gibbs orders to break off and begin a gradual withdrawal.

Rennie pulled back first and formed line on the right to cover Gibbs's retreat regiment by regiment.[84] Keane extracted his men a unit at a time and in some disorder, starting with the 93rd, then the 85th, as they continued taking fire from Louisiana on their flank and Jackson's line in front.[85] They made a new camp on the lower part of De La Ronde's plantation almost two miles below the American line, just out of range of the Yankee batteries but still in almost full view. The 95th withdrew last to take post in advance in and around the Bienvenu buildings and sugar house, from which they sniped at the Yankees through the evening. Keane also left pickets digging defensive works near the river and main road about three-quarters of a mile below the Americans, out of sight thanks to Bienvenu's orange groves and some tall trees in the plantation gardens.[86] The Louisiana still threw the occasional shell their way, and that evening a ball from one of Jackson's guns newly placed across the river unkindly knocked the 95th's bubbling dinner pots from their fire.[87] Troubridge and some of his sailors volunteered to retrieve the dismounted six-pounders from the road and dragged them to the rear under fire without casualty.[88]

Jackson's big guns continued firing through the evening and night, although their shot buried itself harmlessly in the marshy ground.[89] Still, they annoyed the foe, Ensign Gleig writing his sister that evening to complain that "I am disturbed every minute by a shot or shell falling near me."[90]

Ensign Graves and others occupied the Bienvenu house, but American artillery soon drove them outside to the seeming protection of a ground-floor archway. Graves had half a biscuit, and there he met a major who had a cold roasted chicken. Pooling their resources to make a meal, they had just sat down, when a ball from an eighteen-pounder passed above their heads, peppering them with shattered brick and mortar. They sat down again, cut the bird and biscuit in halves, and spread it on Graves's haversack while they drank water to clear the dust from their throats. At that moment another enemy ball hit directly above them, covering their ill-fated meal in half a foot of mortar dust and rubble. It was the second time Graves was nearly killed trying to have a meal on the battlefield.[91]

Ensign Gerard took thirty-one men of the 4th to an advance post to guard against surprise, and spent a nervous night expecting to be attacked.[92] Pakenham brought his headquarters forward to a Bienvenu house in the rear of Gibbs's bivouac near the woods, and put his staff and the day's wounded in a nearby sugar house.[93] Considering the length of time the redcoats lay under heavy fire, casualties were few though brutal—sixteen killed and thirty-eight wounded, and two men missing, either deserted or left on the field. Ensign Eden would die on the morrow.[94] Dickson observed that most of the wounded had lost limbs to cannonballs.[95]

From the other side of the American guns, Carroll's adjutant Colonel Hynes thought the British lost 100 dead and 230 wounded, but agreed that the artillery accounted for most of them.[96] Jackson's losses were almost paltry—seven killed in all and five wounded—with no one unaccounted for.[97] Parties that night retrieved the bodies of Henderson and the other Tennessee dead.[98] Though all grieved Henderson's death, Jackson could not withhold his judgment that he had "died *bravely*, but very imprudently."[99] Others agreed, and Colonel Butler almost flippantly wrote a friend that Lauderdale and Henderson had "bit the dust and are no more." When that appeared in the eastern press, an offended editor grumbled that "the use of this disgusting expression seem[s] like sporting with the agonies of death."[100]

That evening, as the British withdrew, a few men decided they had had enough and crawled to the American line to desert. Most provided some information, none of it very informed or useful. At least three came in that night with exaggerated accounts of Pakenham's losses, one maintaining that just one regiment suffered almost triple the whole army's real loss. In succeeding days more deserters inflated the figure even further.[101] The deserters were better informed on the want of provisions in their army, and the discomforts of camping on swampy ground.[102] Some also told of the hazard they faced in deserting. The route least likely to get them caught and returned to their own camps was through the woods and swamp, which brought them to the Tennesseans' line. Carroll's and Coffee's men sometimes fired on them before the redcoats could yell out "friend," which changed the minds of some about deserting. Those who reached American lines safely testified that these Louisiana Yankees did not fight like the men they put to flight at Washington, calling them "*those fellows with dirty shirts,*" or "Jackson's Indians," thanks to their swarthy faces and their yells and whoops in action.[103]

Pakenham had hopes of a victory to end the campaign, but his own evaluation of available intelligence let him down. Captain Peddie would boast several weeks hence that Pakenham had half a dozen informants in New Orleans sending him information daily on Jackson's forces and positions, but it was all bluster. The fact that the British consistently overestimated American numbers, and their admittedly complete surprise at the strength of Line Jackson, argue instead that whatever information they did receive from collaborators was of scant worth.[104]

Putting the best face he could on the day, Pakenham sent Cochrane a report that evening to inform him that "I am now on the move." So he was, but only to the extent that his camps tonight were two plantations above where he bivouacked the night before. He would never take New Orleans advancing cane field by cane field.[105]

Twelve

"Giving Us the Whole Campaign"

T HE YANKEES TOOK justifiable pride in their mud line. Unaware that Pakenham's movement was only a reconnaissance, they read the withdrawal as an attack repulsed, proof that Line Jackson could counter anything the enemy could throw at it, and their own cannon could bombard the foe at will until the Kentuckians arrived, when Jackson would lead them in an attack.[1] Moreover, all classes and colors had behaved well.[2] Men on the works felt cocky. They stood fire in what in their inexperience seemed like a conventional daylight battle, and felt superior in numbers and confident of driving the enemy back into the Gulf.[3]

Jackson wisely refused to effuse, within hours writing Secretary Monroe that he could not assume the offensive without the Kentuckians, more regulars, and those damned muskets from Pittsburgh. Downplaying his own numbers, he cited deserters' estimates of more than double his number of redcoats, and it is clear he did not yet fully realize the full advantage of his position. Moreover, his health was increasingly uncertain, and when he begged for more officers, he asked for one to take his place should he be incapacitated.[4] It was a futile gesture, since this campaign would be long over by the time Washington saw his report.

With nightfall Jackson returned to McCarty's, where Duncan soon appeared with Declouet, who unfolded the story of his conversations with Guichard and his opinion that the *creole* majority of the legislature was suspect.[5] Meanwhile, the guard posted at Government House had stopped members at bayonet point from entering their chambers for the evening session. Speaker Guichard and Skipwith angrily confronted Claiborne, who

explained Jackson's order and added that the general had positive information of an embryonic scheme to surrender to the British.[6] Other members
met at city hall to confer, and it appeared that a fissure in their hard-won
unanimity might be opening between *creoles* and Americans.[7]

As twilight turned to evening darkness, exaggerated rumors emerged
that Old Hickory intended to blow up the ammunition magazine and torch
the city rather than see it fall. Citizens hearing the rumor approached Skipwith and Labatut, but they could neither confirm nor deny.[8] As the evening
wore on, apprehensions subsided, and soon after midnight Claiborne recalled the guard at Government House.[9] At that moment Jackson knew
only what he heard from Duncan and Declouet. What if these *creoles* really
tried a separate peace with Pakenham? He could not hang half a legislature,
and his deteriorating relations with Claiborne hardly balmed the situation.
Ironically, at that very moment Whitehall was not sure it even wanted the
city, and no one yet knew that four days earlier the treaty was concluded at
Ghent.[10]

Although Jackson had much to dampen elation over the day's outcome,
and the promise of more uncertainty on the morrow, there was cause for
relief as well. Unaware of multiple reasons for delay behind British lines,
Old Hickory could congratulate himself that his night attack on December 23 appeared to have halted the British in place for four days and bought
him vital time to prepare. "Giving us, at this critical moment, these four days,"
Attorney Ellery believed, "was virtually giving us the whole campaign."[11]
Many believed that now, twice drubbed, the enemy would not attack again.[12]

British actions now seemed to reinforce that hope. Though they saw
movement in the enemy camps that morning, none of it looked menacing
and none approached within artillery range.[13] About noon, redcoats advanced to start work on the redoubt that Pakenham had ordered for his
right flank battery, but Patterson had brought *Louisiana* downstream the
evening before, and her fire, along with some long-range musketry, drove
them back. A party assembling a levee emplacement for guns Pakenham
hoped would challenge *Louisiana* were driven off by Yankee fire, and another emplacement that helped destroy *Carolina* threw hot shot at her before her guns and cannon from Line Jackson forced them to fly and abandon
one of their guns. When a party of seamen went to retrieve it, *Louisiana* put
a shot right in their midst.[14]

In the following days Jackson maintained constant watch on the enemy.
A reconnaissance through the swamp toward Bayou Bienvenue that afternoon reported soldiers bringing supplies from the landing place, including
beef cattle and what horses Pakenham's agents could purchase or confiscate

at Terre-aux-Boeufs.[15] To cover that mission, and to scout the enemy right flank and any progress on Pakenham's new redoubt, Hinds's dragoons made a daring dash almost to the British camp before racing back to safety, and without suffering a single casualty.[16] The exploit kept the redcoats off guard and a bit intimidated by Yankee boldness. More enemy deserters told of West Indian soldiers dying in the cold and the rest rendered ineffective.[17]

Security remained ever atop Old Hickory's priorities. He posted more guards along the swamp and on both sides of the river to intercept anyone seeking to reach the enemy, and put watch boats on the river to stop any traffic moving up or down past his works. He tested his sentinels on the night of December 29 by setting two flatboats adrift and was rewarded by their being spotted and the alarm raised as *Louisiana*'s guns sank the decoys.[18] His spies confirmed that Pakenham had about 7,000 in all now, a number he believed he could match if another fight came.[19] Brigadier General Stephen Hopkins was due with 800 to 1,000 Louisiana militia from west of the river, and surely the Kentuckians would arrive at any moment.[20]

To boost his forces at Line Jackson further, he ordered Morgan to send militia to Chef Menteur to relieve Lacoste's four-hundred-strong free black battalion, which he ordered to come, complete with its band, to join his main line on Beale's left.[21] There was some protest from the battalion at being removed from what it considered an important posting, and Jackson was not accustomed to his orders being questioned. He summoned Lacoste's officers and lectured them that "mutiny & disobedience at this crisis would be fatal" and exacted their pledge to be accountable for their men's obedience, which quelled the discontent without it becoming known on the streets.[22]

He pushed work on the defenses relentlessly, borrowing or commandeering more slaves to relieve the volunteers at the spades and picks, raising the parapet higher and thickening the wall of mud and earth. Jackson also ordered Latrobe and a separate party of slaves to throw up another defensive line a mile behind Line Jackson, and believed that enthusiasm following the enemy's repulse had whites and blacks cheerfully working well together.[23] Forced by instinct and circumstances to be opportunistic, Jackson learned that evening of a flatboat loaded with cotton that broke free of its city mooring and began to float downstream. He ordered it brought to the bank about thirty yards behind his line and off-loaded twenty-nine bags of cotton that he kept behind the rampart to use as needed.[24]

Latour suggested this day that they build a redoubt—Tatum called it a "demi-bastion"—on the far right of their line at the levee, but in advance of the main line. Guns placed there could rake the entire plain in front of the main defenses, adding their fire to that of the other batteries, shells from *Louisiana*, and the batteries on the right bank, and also firing directly into the left flank of any of the enemy who reached the ditch below the earth- works and tried to scale them. The general doubted that the bastion could be completed before the enemy launched the inevitable main attack, but when Hayne supported the suggestion, Jackson gave in and the work com- menced.[25] They also began another battery near the swamp and one farther along the line, pleased that the water level in the ditch seemed steady at five to six feet, more than enough to impede efforts to wade across.[26]

A different mood prevailed in the army on the other side of that ditch. Cochrane took December 28's outcome less philosophically than Paken- ham, perhaps because he was already in a bad mood. Persistent whispers of his supposed preoccupation with prize money irked him, and just now he learned that someone in England had published a pamphlet accusing him of taking refugee slaves seeking British protection and sending them in- stead to his plantation in Trinidad. In fact, he had sent some to Halifax and Bermuda, but regretted even owning his Trinidad property, where he had not increased slave holdings for years and, as he told Bathurst, had no inten- tion of "ever dipping deeper into that species of property."[27]

That rumor was damaging enough to his reputation. Pakenham's deci- sion not to attack on December 28 risked adding to that. Cochrane sent an account to Cockburn that made the reconnaissance in force sound more like an attack, and gave an unenthusiastic impression of the campaign's prospects as well as his own for prize money.[28] In a day or two Cochrane wrote to Bathurst to try to confirm just how and where to adjudicate shares of "Booty or Prize Money."[29]

If the rank and file did not share Cochrane's funk, morale remained a concern. Letters home spoke of a small but mounting number of deserters.[30] Work details seemed incessant, what with picketing, making roads, and hauling heavy guns and ammunition, all while suffering from want of food, rest, good water, and warm clothing.[31] Thanks to wind patterns and ocean temperatures in the Pacific, the tropics including the Gulf Coast United States experienced an "El Niño" winter of colder-than-normal temperatures and precipitation. Daytime highs probably were not rising above the forties, and at night temperatures dipped well below freezing into the twenties.[32] Unaware of the climatic anomaly, Cochrane had not anticipated hard rain and freezes, and most soldiers and sailors had no cold-weather gear. Fortu- nately, the rain had stopped now for a few days, but officers still retreated to their tents in groups to lay close together in "spoon" fashion for warmth, or else exercised vigorously outside to keep their blood circulating. Captain Sir

Thomas Hardy and his crew were two years now on the American coast and had suitable winter clothing for most circumstances, but even they could hardly bear this Louisiana December. Hardy blamed the cold for many seamen losing use of their limbs.[33]

The cold and frost continued taking a heavy toll on the West India regiments. It put over eighty of them on the sick list at one time, and killed fifty, compared to only one lost to enemy fire.[34] The blacks inherited much of the labor of bringing heavy guns from the fleet, work arduous enough that two white officers of the 1st West India died of exposure.[35] When not knee-deep in freezing water, the men huddled at the artillerymen's fires, and some were simply unable to function, attracting the sympathy of white officers, who stood the temperature better. Never having encountered frost, the poor soldiers were mystified by an invisible enemy attacking their skin. "No can fight here Massa," some answered when urged to work or action. "Something bite him no can see him."[36] Stories circulated in the bivouac that some of the West Indians escaped the ground ice by climbing up trees to sleep, only to be found frozen to death in the morning.[37]

Another morale dampener was seeing Nicolls's vaunted thousands of Creek and Choctaw allies number to date just half a dozen chiefs in gaudy uniforms.[38] The Yankees did their part to dampen spirits as well. Dickson and the others, while hauling up their guns that day, clearly saw Americans working on new batteries across the river, intended to add fire on Pakenham's camps and left flank when he advanced.[39] When completed late that day, the new batteries opened fire and continued it thereafter.[40] Although it was an annoyance at best, now and then a ball or shell tumbled down among the redcoats or into their quarters, bringing confusion and death.[41]

As soon as his army established its new bivouac, Pakenham turned his attention to countering Jackson's artillery and defenses to allow him to make a general assault, and soon.[42] He needed horses for his artillery, more and bigger guns to dent those earthworks, and a number of eighteen-pounders to place on the river to deal with *Louisiana*. Since his line of advance was obvious to the enemy, who could take defensive measures accordingly, he also proposed that Cochrane distract Jackson's attention elsewhere by threatening a landing at the Rigolets or sending ships to the mouth of the Mississippi.[43]

Pakenham hoped to launch a general attack as soon as January 3, if not before.[44] He had engineers improve the road connecting the landing place to Bayou Bienvenue to handle the heavy ordnance expected from Cochrane. He instructed flatboats built to haul men and guns across the Mississippi to deal with American batteries on the west bank that were adding their mote to his discomfiture.[45] Most important, he planned to counter Jackson's artillery advantage. As with provisions and other supplies, logistical planning for the artillery had fallen victim to the difficulty of getting everything from the fleet to the scene of action. Dickson found barely enough ammunition for a few hours' firing just for the guns then on hand when he first arrived, and nowhere near enough for a real battle or a campaign to batter through Jackson's earthworks. Given that an average artillery piece could fire one hundred rounds in a full day and a twenty-four-pounder could fire twenty rounds an hour if ably served, supplies needed to be based on that. In his campaigns Wellington tried to have 350 rounds per gun on hand before an action.[46] Fortunately, a fresh supply came up from the fleet that very afternoon, but Dickson would need much more.[47]

Meanwhile, he sent the disabled six-pounders back to Villeré's for repair and repositioned the withdrawn guns about 2,200 yards below the Yankee line, placing half of Lane's rockets and a three-pounder with Gibbs, and the rest of the rockets, the two nine-pounders, two newly arrived sixes, as well as the howitzer with Keane near Bienvenu's. Better yet, Pakenham's first two eighteen-pounders arrived, as well as a 5.5-inch howitzer, and the general sent them to the battery haltingly being built near the levee to deal with *Louisiana*. At the same time, he directed staff to lay out an artillery redoubt to be built near the woods to protect his right flank.[48] He intended for these batteries immediately on completion to pummel breaches in the enemy line before he sent his regiments forward again. Until then, he ordered the rest of his cannon to open fire and continue firing all night to disrupt American efforts to enhance their defenses.[49]

Pakenham sent urgent orders for eight more eighteen-pounders that he believed could punch a hole in Old Hickory's earthwork, or at least dismount his guns. The two naval eighteen-pounders that had just arrived had been dragged up to Villeré's on their deck carriages, but Dickson commandeered two oxcarts to move them to Bienvenu's house near the levee road to continue forward. Going to the site himself, Dickson left to find a shorter route to get more guns across the De La Ronde property to the Bienvenu site. He put a party to work strengthening the plantation roads for the heavy guns, anticipating that he would bring the first eighteen-pounders to their posts that night.[50]

Meanwhile, Dickson sent a repaired six-pounder and a howitzer to join the guns emplaced next to the levee.[51] Pakenham decided to enhance that position by using the plentiful hogsheads of sugar from planters' warehouses to build a redoubt to protect the guns, expecting to place more eighteens there when they arrived to deal with *Louisiana*.[52] The memory of the havoc wreaked by *Carolina* guided much of his planning for this part of the field, and a false alarm that night spread more concern when Jackson's guns opened on the decoy flatboats, and at first the redcoats thought it was *Louisiana* coming to bombard them.[53]

That added urgency to getting the first two eighteen-pounders up the main road to deal with *Louisiana*. They were laboriously dragged to their assigned location, only to arrive to find the platforms to mount them incomplete. At three a.m. that night a working party came to complete the platforms. That left the backbreaking job of getting the gun tubes from the oxcarts onto their wooden carriages. With no hoist to lift them, they had to take the wheels off the carriages, turn the carriages on their sides, drop the gun tubes from the carts to the ground and roll the tubes into position, secure them, and then by brute force with ropes and levers pull the carriages upright and lift them as one wheel at a time was replaced. By dawn on December 30 the two eighteens were in place and concealed from enemy view, along with a small furnace for hot shot, with Lieutenant R. A. Speer in command.[54]

Pakenham consulted his staff on their next move and encountered varying opinions. Some officers wanted to hold any assault until Lambert arrived. Adjutant Smith argued that they should only dare attack once they had destroyed *Louisiana* and driven the Americans from their batteries on the opposite bank. The general agreed and produced a sketch of Jackson's works he had made based on observations the day before and information received from scouts and perhaps people from New Orleans itself. While work continued on the battery in front of Gibbs, he proposed to concentrate guns at other concealed positions just below the Bienvenu-Chalmette boundary about 650 yards from Jackson's line. During the night of December 31, they would be mounted on platforms behind protective walls of earth-filled sugar hogsheads. In conjunction with Speer's eighteens by the levee, these new batteries should destroy *Louisiana* and silence Jackson's artillery. He did not know when Lambert might arrive, and if a propitious opportunity arose for an attack before then, he might not wait.[55] Meanwhile, he still wanted Cochrane to create a diversion against Chef Menteur or on the Mississippi itself, to coincide with his assault.[56]

Confidence in victory still ran high in much of the bivouac and beyond. Agents buying beef cattle from drovers near the mouth of the Pearl River told sellers they would be able to collect their payment soon in New Orleans.[57] Certainty of success showed itself in the courtesy Pakenham's officers showed their prisoners. Ensign Hill befriended Beale's Nathaniel Cox and furnished him with pen and paper to send a letter through the lines to his wife to tell her he still lived, and promised to see it delivered if a flag of truce allowed.[58] When customs collector Denis Prieur from Beale's company was brought before him, Keane insisted that the British came not to make war on the *creoles* and sent him home the next day, hoping he would spread word of his treatment and thereby soften support for Jackson.[59]

Greater fraternization occurred sixty miles away aboard the fleet at anchor, and again the captors particularly befriended Beale's men, probably because of their social and economic station. Cochrane offered the *creoles* among them immediate release if they took with them his proclamation to the people of Louisiana. When they refused, he released several of them anyhow, including Major Villeré.[60] That cordiality did not extend to Shields and Morrell, prisoners for two weeks now, for they had seen too much. From their confinement aboard ship they asked for thirty minutes with Captain Hardy to try for their release, but their confinement had not yet run its course.[61]

Apparently recovered from his dispiritedness, Cochrane even entertained some of the prisoners at dinner. Over wine he assured them he felt no doubt of the complete success of his expedition, exaggerated his numbers to 15,000 to impress on them its invincibility, and declared a determination to take, fortify, and hold New Orleans and lower Louisiana. Sensing that they were not unlike himself, he confessed astonishment that such "men of property and standing" took arms against Britain.[62] How could merchants fight the very nation that brought them commerce? Believing the exaggerated reports of divisions within the community, Cochrane told them that he had expected when he came to Louisiana to find the people giving "balls and suppers" for his officers. Irishman Laverty responded that "we have given you the *balls*: you must now look out for the suppers." Cochrane took the pun in good humor, turning to one of his officers to say, "Take that out of your wig."[63]

December 30 brought little change in the routine. The pickets stayed out all day, changing every few hours, finding the cold disagreeable, and the constant artillery fire from their front and across the river more so. Gleig and some of the 85th did picket duty behind one of the houses on the Bienvenu property, dodging as Yankee balls sent shutters and bits of framing flying about them.[64] Still hopeful of finding a way to turn Jackson's left, Pakenham sent one of his most trusted engineers, Lieutenant Peter Wright, and five men on a reconnaissance through the area. Wright it was who had climbed up a tree for Pakenham on December 28 to study Jackson's line. They got perhaps as far as Rennie had two days before until a volley from Tennesseans hit them. Wright ordered his men to disperse and get back to their lines. Four did return, one of them wounded, but two musket balls left Wright dead in the woods.[65]

Dickson found more oxcarts to haul guns, and four more eighteens arrived that day, now making eight in all. That Pakenham had these big guns was due not just to the navy's cooperation in furnishing them but to its personnel as well. The whole operation to date owed much to the webfoot service. For almost three weeks officers and seamen had been moving provisions and matériel and men from the ships to Villeré's, all the while suffering in the weather night and day.[66] Dickson concealed four of the big guns at a depot he established on De La Ronde's plantation, two more at Bienvenu's, and the first two in the emplacement near the levee. Meanwhile parties brought forward ammunition for all the guns to a depot near Pakenham's headquarters, where Dickson established a "laboratory" at the head of the Villeré canal. There he put 220 men to work folding, filling, and sealing paper "cartridges" of powder for the big guns. By the end of the day he had 463 rounds ready for the eighteen-pounders and enough powder waiting to make 770 more. That would be more than 1,200 rounds for the eight big guns, but still it was only 150 rounds each, just a day and a half's supply in a heavy bombardment. When Dickson's men found the paper too bad to use, his men raided surrounding houses for wall hangings, curtains, and linens, and went to work with needles and thread sewing more bags.[67]

In New Orleans, the larger-than-usual outgoing mail teemed with enthusiasm as virtually all agreed with Claiborne that "we are united as one man."[68] When the Kentuckians arrived, Jackson would surely seize the offensive and drive Pakenham into the Gulf, and Old Hickory was actually at some pains to curb his soldiers' ardor.[69] That confidence quickly escalated to a belief that Pakenham was already considering retreat, that in a short time he must either surrender or evacuate. By sunset the rumor spread that his officers wanted to withdraw, and that, like Cortés and Alexander the Great, Cochrane and Pakenham had burned their ships to make retreat impossible. They would have to take the city or themselves be taken.[70] Those questioning such rumors still felt sure of victory. As one of Hinds's dragoons wrote that evening, "Something decisive will be done in a short time."[71] Trust in their generals soared, Hynes concluding that "Gens. Jackson, Carroll and Coffee are worth more than their weight in gold."[72] With that confidence came resolve. "Our men fight like Tygers," a volunteer at Fort St. John wrote that night. "If I should be killed, I will die at my post."[73]

Some wisely remembered that Wellington's veterans were strangers to defeat. This army was mostly militia who could hardly expect to best experienced regulars in open-field maneuvers, but Old Hickory prudently intended not to fight them on their own terms. He would stay behind his defenses and await their attack, for if he met them out in the open, a defeat could result in a precipitate retreat that could lead to loss of the city itself, which at that moment was guarded by the aged and infirm.

The city itself showed scant life now, with virtually all business at a standstill.[74] Edward Palfrey opened the family store's doors, but with no customers he passed the day answering letters for that day's mail.[75] Twenty-two-year-old French-born Laura Florian found the streets so quiet, she felt as if its only inhabitants were ghosts and specters, reminding her of the cities destroyed by Vesuvius. "You would take it for a second Herculaneum," she wrote a friend.[76] Cigar maker L. C. Hardy of Burgundy Street, viewing stores and houses shuttered, with not a person on the streets, found that there was nothing to be seen but the exempts' sentinels pacing their solitary rounds.[77]

Whole neighborhoods were abandoned as families collected at friends' homes. City treasurer George W. Morgan's house on Royal Street hosted several, and he sent provisions from his plantation upriver to feed them. It was a rare meal that passed without an alarm or a rush to the balconies for fresh news. Officers from Line Jackson allowed to return to their homes in the evening regularly stopped to repeat rumor and gossip. Women sewed gold coins into the hems of their clothing should they have to evacuate, although few knew where they might go, since they also feared slave insurrections upriver. Many American women seldom left their houses, while their *creole* counterparts occasionally looked out their front doors or stepped into the street to talk with neighbors. If the volume of the constant cannonade grew louder, or someone imagined they heard enemy boots on the cobbled streets, they ran back inside yelling "*fermez les portes*"—"close the doors."[78]

Many women spent their time sewing. Louaillier's subscription lists began to produce results with money to buy or make clothing for the Tennesseans who arrived with insufficient blankets and coats.[79] The men in Carroll's command rejoiced at the promise of a suit of clothes, especially after nights out on duty sleeping on the ground in weather cold enough to layer them with ice.[80] The day before, benefactors pledged over $500 for the fund, as well as providing more than two dozen barrels of hulled rice to feed the volunteers.[81]

The legislature's closure at bayonet point two days earlier did create resentment. Some members nursed outrage at Jackson, although many citizens concurred in its necessity.[82] The body had reconvened on December 29 and again that day, and sent a committee to the general to seek an explanation.

He made time for them this evening. It could hardly be lost on him that the callers—Marigny, Blanque, and Louis Rouffignac—were all from the anti-Claiborne *creole* faction that he most suspected, and Declouet had specifically named the first two as suspected conspirators.[83] If the composition of this deputation was a message, it was that their faction was in control and intended to yield nothing more than absolutely necessary.

In an apparently cordial meeting, Old Hickory kept his temper and the *creoles* convinced him that he had been misinformed. They had no intention of trading surrender for safety.[84] But they did ask him what he intended to do if forced to abandon the city. Ever mindful of security and that one or more of them with him might not be trustworthy, he replied that if he thought a hair on his head knew what he would do, he would cut it off. If he did have to fall back, however, they could tell the legislature that "they may expect to have a very warm session." Marigny later claimed he thought Jackson meant he would burn the city before abandoning it. That made no sense, however, since whether he burned the city or the British took it, there would be no legislative session, warm or otherwise.

Nearly a decade later Jackson claimed that "I would have destroyed New Orleans, leaving nothing for the enemy, and then tried to cut off Pakenham's supply line to compel him to leave the country."[85] It was a typical example of Jacksonian hyperbole, but when Villeré later asked Old Hickory what he would have done, Jackson replied through an interpreter that he would never give up the earthwork. If the enemy got across Line Jackson, it would have been over his corpse.[86] More hyperbole, perhaps, but it has more the ring of authenticity.

Americans on the line awoke on December 30 to see Pakenham's details continuing to work on the battery in front of Gibbs's position. By ten a.m. Jackson's artillery opened on them and kept firing for hours.[87] Other redcoats worked on the smaller battery near the levee, and Ensign Graves bravely attempted yet again to eat under fire. A servant brought him a tin cup of maggoty salt pork and weevil-infested ship's biscuit, mashed together and boiled into a glutinous pulp. He had just raised it to his mouth when a Yankee shot hit the sugar hogsheads beside him, glanced slightly off his hip, and threw him against another officer as it knocked his "meal" to the ground.[88] After three near-death efforts at combat dining, he ceased trying.

The British answered fire as they could, and the cannonade continued through the rest of the day and into the evening, by now a commonplace if unnerving background to daily life.[89] "The report of Cannon is now as familiar to me as eating," Edward Palfrey wrote a brother that day.[90] It accompanied their meals, broke their sleep, and rattled their windowpanes. Innumerable soldiers and civilians commented on it as they wrote their letters.[91] A new brace of thirty-two-pounders emplaced across the river added to the omnipresent concussions from the guns on the line and aboard *Louisiana*, and even forty miles away, on the lower Bayou Lafourche, men heard the distant rumble.[92]

Old Hickory had to stretch his inductive reasoning to compass what might be happening at distant places like Bayou Lafourche, or what ought to be happening. A general knew little more than what he saw through his telescope. He had to take observations and information that could be five minutes old, or five days, and use it to project who ought to be where and when. It was perhaps the most difficult task facing a nineteenth-century commander. Sometime that day he got the good news that a reconnaissance down Bayou Lafourche to the seacoast had seen no enemy vessels, suggesting that avenue of advance on New Orleans was still secure.[93] From downriver on the west bank Major James Gordon reported that redcoats with axes and tools were at work on the other side building flatboats, presumably to cross the river. He also saw enemy cannon moving along that bank to the levee batteries confronting *Louisiana*. Meanwhile, Morgan was creating a battery with four twenty-four-pounders raised from the *Carolina*, with one more still to mount. At Fort St. Leon above English Turn, Gordon began impressing slaves to strengthen its works.[94]

In his immediate front, Jackson sent men into the swamp from the outpost at Madame Piernas's plantation along the same route used by enemy deserters, to see what they might behind Gibbs's pickets. They observed enemy soldiers digging out and deepening the Villeré canal, which meant heavier enemy ordnance would be coming. Out between the lines, sporadic picket firing rang throughout the daylight hours, the Tennesseans taunting their British counterparts to march up to them rather than lie down in the cover of weeds and "lay there like snipes!"[95] Carroll's men went out nightly in parties of twenty or thirty to shoot at enemy pickets.[96] Other pickets on daytime reconnaissance found dead redcoats in heaps of two or three as evidence that the midnight sniping took a toll, and retrieved their muskets.[97]

Jackson still kept Hinds's dragoons in his front with ardent eyes. They were mostly young men, easily the wealthiest company in the army, some twenty or more being worth above $20,000. Their affluence did not dampen their daring. That afternoon they spotted a party of redcoats trying to move unseen through a wide ditch across their front and Jackson ordered them to learn more. Hinds formed the battalion and announced that *"I'm going over it*," meaning he intended to ride directly toward the ditch and jump it, and the men understood. They set out at full gallop and actually vaulted the ditch. Looking down into it as they passed over, they saw the startled enemy crouching down to avoid flying hooves. That done, Hinds's men made a circle in front of Gibbs's line and then rode back to fly over the ditch again, firing their pistols into it as they did. The stunned British only recovered their wits sufficiently to fire a ragged volley at them, wounding three men and two horses, one of which carried Joseph Emory Davis of Woodville, Mississippi— who had a six-year-old brother at home named Jefferson Davis.[98]

Private Trimble thought the whole affair "phenomenal and almost supernatural, nor was that an end to it.[99] Jackson kept Hinds within two hundred yards of the enemy for fully ninety minutes, hoping to lure the foe into the open for his artillery. Hinds actually ran his men through drill evolutions to taunt the British in full view of both armies, but the redcoats would not play. When the Mississippi dragoons at last rode back to Line Jackson, the men lining the parapet gave them three cheers and Jackson sent Colonel Hayne to them with the compliment that "your undaunted courage this day has excited the admiration of our whole army."[100]

More information came of discontent in the enemy camp, and of men wanting to desert if possible, ever more disillusioned by the failure of the local Spaniards and French to come to their assistance.[101] By this time almost everyone but Cochrane was realizing that local Spaniards might be happy at Britain taking over Louisiana, but their joy fell short of impelling them to actively assist or to risk their lives taking arms.[102] A staff officer grumbled that none of the "Dons and Blacks" seemed anxious to be their allies, leading him to complain that, except for the Mississippi itself, "there is nothing else in this quarter worth coming 6000 miles to see."[103]

Certainly, the *creoles* continued putting the lie to questions of their fealty. Many complimented their rush to arms, and all but a few had resisted efforts to buy their neutrality.[104] Ultimately Cochrane's policy realized only the tangential benefit of some Americans interpreting the special treatment offered *creoles* as proof that the British did receive aid and assistance from some of them.[105] Still, some enemy deserters who came through the swamp to the Piernas picket post more than a mile behind Jackson's line brought papers allegedly showing them the route.[106] The question of where they got that information kept Americans' suspicions alive. The exempts watched for men trying to get information covertly out of town.[107] In the countryside men looked for strangers instigating slave unrest, and false alarms continued. So did false arrests, including that of a legitimate government party surveying navigable waterways for the United States customs collector to gather information on smugglers' routes. The false arrest at least brought the collector to Jackson's headquarters, where he was able to provide details on bayou approaches in the Lafourche country.[108] Jackson could not afford to ignore intelligence from any source. With 1814 waning, the New Year would surely not escape its infancy before the enemy made a move somewhere. Preparation was survival.

Thirteen

"Thunder, and Smoke, and Slaughter"

Y EAR'S END FOUND the two armies within point-blank artillery range of each other. All day New Year's Eve the Americans watched the enemy building his big battery.[1] To discomfit that work, they maintained their own bombardment from *Louisiana* and Line Jackson and at least stunted its progress.[2] In response, it appeared that the British had nothing bigger than twelve-pounders to fire at them, which gave the Yankee twenty-fours and thirty-two-pounder the advantage. Everyone on Line Jackson saw the battering their guns gave Pakenham's battery as its walls went up, one thirty-two-pounder shell landing with great effect in the middle of a party of mounted redcoat officers.[3]

Old Hickory already had more men now than he could accommodate in his Chalmette line, but Fort St. John remained a concern, as well as General Morgan across the river and Forts St. Leon and St. Philip downstream. When militia in the Lafourche country failed to report for duty, General Philemon Thomas had them arrested and brought to Baton Rouge.[4] Calls for more volunteers to enlist went out elsewhere, even as far away as Rapides, Natchitoches, and St. Landry Parishes, where officers summoned men for the new 17th, 18th, and 19th Consolidated Louisiana regiment at Opelousas, more than 120 miles west of New Orleans. They were to muster on January 8, 1815, but it would take days for them to reach New Orleans. No wonder Clement's sister-in-law Elizabeth quipped that "every creature, within 300 miles, that can be spared from guarding the country, has arrived in town."[5] Meanwhile, everyone looked for the Kentuckians, who at that moment were riding the river current past St. Francisville, yelling to people ashore that they should reach New Orleans by January 2.[6]

The last day of the year saw no dent in the defenders' optimism.[7] Trust in Old Hickory soared, and more and more some wished the general would bring on the battle and "finish this business."[8] Major Gordon at Fort St. Leon promised Morgan that if the enemy appeared in his front, "I'll give them hell!"[9] In a city noted for frolic, some already looked past the current threat to February 14 and Mardi Gras, predicting that "the *Carnival* will be gay and brilliant this winter."[10]

To better his civic relations, Jackson sent the legislature a clarification that he did not order Claiborne to close its doors, but only to investigate allegations and then, and only then, to act if they appeared subversive.[11] That mollified the body, which had already acted to dispel suspicion by adjourning for several days. Some Orleanians misread that to mean that the members went to the front to shoulder firelocks, but only four of them actually did so, not one of them from the delegation sent to Jackson.[12] As for Old Hickory, he had not explicitly dismissed Declouet's allegations. He was ever a suspicious man when there was a whiff of conspiracy.

Now worrying tidings came from Fort St. Philip. Its commander, Major Walter Overton of the 3rd United States Infantry, had word that lookouts at the mouth of the river had sighted Cochrane's flotilla of two bomb ships with mortars, a rocket ship with Congreves, a frigate, two sloops, two brigs, and a schooner. Their crewmen were seen lightening the ships to float over the sandbar outside the main channel. That news was a day old when Overton got it, and he reckoned that the enemy fleet could reach him as early as January 2. Jackson would know if and when they attacked St. Philip, said Overton: "Listen and you will hear."[13] Major Gordon sent a similar report from Fort St. Leon.[14] Clearly the danger was far from past. Bluster aside, most in the army realized that 1815 would grow no whiskers before they faced their greatest peril. With just hours of the old year left, one citizen reflected that at any moment he expected a battle "which will decide the fate of this country."[15]

As Jackson looked for General Adair, so Pakenham watched for General Lambert. Near the mouth of Bayou Bienvenue, Admiral Malcolm had a soldier climbing a tree every few hours to scan Lake Borgne for any sign of the reinforcement, but he looked in the wrong place. Thanks to dense haze, Lambert actually passed within a dozen miles of Cochrane's main fleet at anchor without seeing it. It was December 30 before they discovered their error and changed course to the northeast. Not knowing any better, some aboard wondered if that meant New Orleans had fallen already and they were headed now for Charleston. The next day they met one of Cochrane's ships heading for the Balise, which told them of Keane's landing, the taking of the gunboats, Pakenham's arrival, and that Jackson still held the city with 15,000, a third of them regulars, false information probably furnished by a prisoner.[16]

Lambert was days away yet. Pakenham could not wait for him. With Keane's and Gibbs's full forces on hand and as much artillery as he could get present or coming, Pakenham was as strong as he could be for now. He knew as much as he was likely to glean of enemy strength, and the trigonometry of time and resources told him further gains from waiting for his army to grow larger would be offset by Jackson doing the same. On or just before December 31 he concluded it was time to make an all-out effort.

Pakenham and his staff spent that day planning an attack for New Year's. Before dawn the redoubtable Robert Rennie would repeat his December 28 exploit, taking eighty men of the 21st and one hundred of the 5th West India on a circuit through the cypresses and swamp around Jackson's left flank and conceal themselves until the general attack commenced. Dickson's new batteries would go up during the night and open at sunrise to silence Jackson's artillery and batter breaches in the American works. Once there was a breach, a line of one hundred skirmishers from the 4th Foot would advance on Carroll's Tennesseans, followed by three hundred more in a line three-deep with their muskets slung on their shoulders. Each of the three hundred would carry a fascine—a tied bundle of reeds and sugarcane—and rush forward while the skirmishers' fire tried to keep heads down on the earthwork. Dropping the fascines in the canal or ditch immediately in front of the breach in the enemy works, they were then to extend in line on either side to open the way for several battalions from Gibbs's brigade to rush forward in a column, cross the ditch on the fascines, and storm the breach.[17] They would take the works with the bayonet.

With the Yankees stunned by successive battalions of bayonets, another column was to advance to the breach to continue the assault while Rennie distracted Coffee's attention as much as possible by firing their rifles, blowing bugles, and threatening the enemy rear if he could. As an overall diversion to support Gibbs, Keane was to make a demonstration or "false attack" on the regulars and Plauché on Jackson's right while other elements of Gibbs's brigade were to advance along the edge of the woods on the enemy left. Keane would command these feints with strict instructions not to allow them to become a full commitment of troops unless a favorable opportunity presented itself. Meanwhile, three companies of the 4th Foot would stand ready in Rennie's rear as a reserve should he need it, as well as to stop any effort by Coffee or Carroll to mount a sortie against the right flank of Gibbs's assault column.[18]

That chain of events dangled from a single link, its weakest. Pakenham's artillery had to silence Jackson's batteries and blow a sufficient breach in the Yankee earthwork to allow his redcoats to walk or clamber through without ladders. Even after the bruising December 28 reconnaissance, Pakenham still did not appreciate how outmatched his six-, twelve-, and even eighteen-pounders would be by the Yankees' eighteens, twenty-fours, and thirty-twos. Equally important, he and his staff failed to consider a fundamental difference between earthworks and the masonry fortifications British artillery had pulverized on the Continent. An iron ball hitting a wall of stone or brick inevitably cracked or crushed some bit of it, and successive impacts at the same spot could wear away more until the wall was breached. Cannonballs hitting a moist mud earthwork of this size and depth just buried themselves in it harmlessly. Even exploding shells did little good unless their fuses could be timed perfectly to go off immediately on impact. Pakenham also counted on mortars and howitzers to arch shells over the earthwork and cause havoc behind it, but elevating the guns enough for shells to clear the parapet meant that most would land far to the rear and well behind the defenders.

Speed was essential if the plan was to have any chance of success. Parties of sailors brought up more guns from the landing place, and by the time Dickson finished, he had six eighteen-pounders ready to move into the new large battery. These were to pound the breach in the Yankee defense. That afternoon, the twenty-four-pounder carronades reached the depot at De La Ronde's. Seamen and soldiers dragged them there on their naval deck carriages, whose wooden wheels absorbed so much friction that they smoldered. Only smearing them with grease prevented their taking flame. Then smaller guns and the howitzers came up, their mission to silence musketry.[19]

Dickson's ammunition depot had 680 rounds for the eighteens and 160 for the twenty-fours. It was not enough for the job. He begged another day to bring up more, but Pakenham could not give him more time. The ammunition at hand only gave their guns three or four hours to disrupt enemy earthworks and artillery, and on top of that, the carronades' carriages were so unmanageable that those guns would have to be manhandled into position and re-aimed after every discharge.[20]

Colonels Burgoyne and Dickson were to supervise the working parties putting up the batteries during the night. After pushing enemy pickets back far enough to be unable to see or hear the work going on, Burgoyne would lay out the perimeters of the batteries before the working parties came forward to get started. There would be four in all. On the levee road just beyond the main Bienvenu house, two eighteens commanded by Captain William Lempriere would fire directly on the right of Jackson's line. To its right, three 5.5-inch mortars under Captain William Lawrence would lob shells behind Jackson's right to catch men on the works between Keane's fire in their front and exploding shells in their rear. To further demoralize the foe there, Lane was to set up his rocket battery in advance of the mortars and hopefully send his sputtering messengers in that direction. To Lane's right, two nine-pounders and five heavy howitzers in the hands of Major John Michell would batter the Yankee center, hoping to drive the gunners from their batteries.

Four hundred yards to the right of the howitzers, on a plantation road that crossed from Bienvenu's into Chalmette's parallel to the levee main road, Pakenham wanted his powerhouse battery. Burgoyne should build it to hold six eighteen-pounders overseen by Captain Peter Crawford and the four twenty-four-pounder carronades commanded by Captain James Money. Crawford was to knock out Jackson's Battery No. 6 and break a hole in the center of the earthwork where Carroll's Tennesseans met the 44th Infantry, while Captain Money bombarded Coffee on the American left. To the right of the big battery, another battery of rockets under Lieutenant John Crawley would take station to assist. Should the *Louisiana* or other enemy boats come downstream, Lieutenant Speer and his pair of eighteens already in place by the levee must deal with them.[21]

Every man was needed for the ambitious night effort. Gibbs even released from arrest the inattentive Captain Archibald Maclean of the 21st, though not without another lecture.[22] Colonel Thornton's advance moved up to the Bienvenu house to cover the battery builders on the left while the 4th Foot took position to cover men working on the huge battery in front of Gibbs. Dickson spent much of the day preparing to move ammunition to the batteries after their completion that night. Carrying the shot and shell to the batteries would require hundreds of men, among whom Dickson included the men who would be operating those guns, so they would know where everything was and lose no time hunting for cartridges or shot. They might be severely fatigued on the morrow after working through the night, but that was a risk he had to take.[23]

At dark the skirmishers drove in the American pickets in Gibbs's front with little difficulty.[24] By seven p.m. he sent forward the working parties gathered at his headquarters, but those detailed to erect the massive ten-gun battery took two hours blindly meandering to reach their site. Then the officer bringing up its first gun completely missed the growing battery and passed it in the dark, coming dangerously close to exposing himself and the plan to the Yankees before an engineer found him and brought him back. Dickson supervised filling scores of empty sugar casks with earth and mud and used them to build walls one cask thick and one cask high on three sides of each battery, leaving gaps as embrasures for the guns. Men with picks and shovels hurriedly dug out the earth inside to pile and pack it against the casks inside and out, then laid uneven planking within for gun platforms.[25] Over to their left the 85th and 95th advanced to cover the same work erecting the batteries in Keane's front. When those guns were in place, the infantry pulled back one hundred yards to cover in some rushes. With not even a cloak for warmth, Ensign Gleig sarcastically told his diary that it was "a pretty way to spend the last night of the year."[26]

Dickson kept the first parties at it until two a.m. and then brought up relief crews of sailors, engineers, and artillerymen to complete the job. The last gun went into place on its platform at 5:45 a.m. He knew the batteries were flimsy and inadequate, but they could do no better with the time and resources at hand. Men working the guns would be exposed to Jackson's rifles and muskets from their lower breasts upward, and no one knew if the earth- and sugar-filled casks would stop balls from big guns. There was just over an hour before sunrise.[27]

At year's end a rumor swept British camps that Jackson sent Pakenham a message by flag of truce that day. Expressing sympathy for the redcoats' "awkward predicament," Old Hickory supposedly offered them ten days to re-embark and leave Louisiana. Should Pakenham decline, Jackson refused to be held to account for the consequences. Pakenham sent a laconic but defiant reply that in ten days he would "give him an answer."[28] It was nonsense, of course, but as the sun set on the year, many rumors floated. One now on its way to Jamaica claimed that Cochrane and Pakenham had cleared the enemy from the banks of the Mississippi, taken his forts, destroyed or captured his shipping, and stood before New Orleans in such strength that it must fall in a few days.[29] Even better than that was the report reaching Havana that Jackson had burned New Orleans and Pakenham even now governed as conqueror.[30]

That evening, as the working parties assembled to go forward, men on Lambert's convoy saw an unsettling sunset phenomenon. A mysterious red spot appeared on the southwestern horizon. It was probably a low cloud, backlit and illuminated by the setting sun, but to Adjutant Tylden it had "all the appearance of Fire."[31] No one had an explanation, but sailors were wont to see signs in such things.

At that moment in England the New Year had begun, and with as much difference of opinion as ever on the American war but universal anxiety about the expedition to the Mississippi. Londoners might know that the treaty had been signed, but it would be a month before Washington did, and another month for the news to reach Cochrane and Pakenham. The fate of the expedition would likely be decided before then, and some dreaded that the troops were already landed and might have met the enemy in battle. With the northeastern war closed for the winter, legions of western militia would be free to concentrate on Pakenham, exposing him to great hazard. Whitehall should have anticipated such a potentiality, and one editor feared that "ministers have not had sufficiently large ideas to execute such a plan."[32]

Now that execution depended solely on generals 6,000 miles away. The British had also built two covered redoubts on the Bienvenu plantation as stations for pickets and for storing weapons and material for an assault. The more advanced went up just below the boundary of Chalmette's and a mile below the place where Jackson's line met the cypresses. The other stood just over a quarter mile to its right rear, both of them in front of Gibbs's command. Pakenham stored the fascines in that advance redoubt, along with his few scaling ladders, and assigned Lieutenant Colonel Thomas Mullins's 44th Infantry to carry them to Jackson's line in the assault. He had been to the redoubt as officer of the day on occasion and knew it well enough, or should have known it.[33]

A heavy ground fog met the British when they rose at four a.m. It shielded them from enemy sight but slowed their movement. Intermittent showers added to the gloom, yet dawn found the columns in position.[34] A few days later a rumor claimed that Pakenham addressed the men, pointed to Jackson's line, and said if they passed those works, they could plunder the city for four days.[35] It was nonsense, but the fog threatened to defeat it at the outset by delaying the opening artillery barrage. The 85th and other troops who spent the night in front of the batteries withdrew two hundred yards to take cover in dense rushes along a ditch and waited for the fog to lift.[36] Finally, at about nine o'clock, the redcoats could see Jackson's line a few hundred yards ahead.[37] From an informant, they knew his headquarters was in McCarty's. Lawrence's and Michell's batteries aimed for its upper story.[38] With everyone ready, Pakenham ordered his batteries to fire.[39]

Old Hickory and staff were eating a hurried breakfast when they heard the guns, then felt cannonballs hit the house. Pakenham firing at his headquarters was not lost on Jackson, who soon concluded that someone in the city had told the foe where to aim.[40] He got everyone out, their uniforms peppered with plaster dust from shattered walls, and walked forward to the line. He identified three of the batteries erected in the night, and Lieutenant

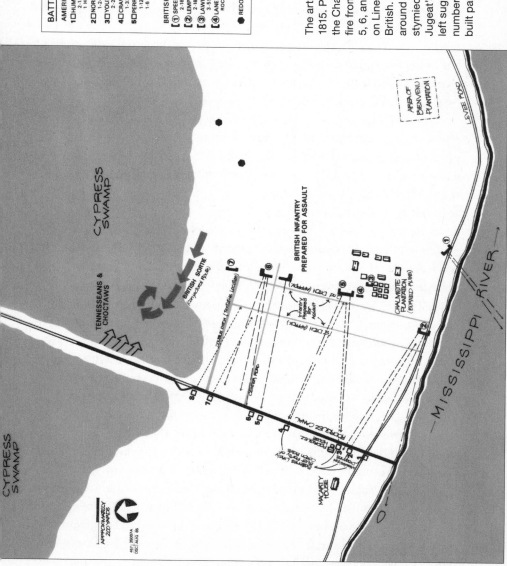

BATTERY EMPLACEMENT

AMERICAN

1 ☐ HUMPHREY
2-12 PDRS
1 HOWITZER

2 ☐ NORRIS
1-24 PDRS

3 ☐ YOUX/BELUCHE
2-24 PDRS

4 ☐ CRAWLEY
1-32 PDRS

5 ☐ PERRY
1-12 PDRS
1-6 PDRS

6 ☐ GARRIGUES
1-18 PDRS
1-6 PDRS

7 ☐ SPOTTS
1-18 PDRS
1-6 PDRS

8 ☐ HARRISON
1 HOWITZER

BRITISH

[1] SPEER
2-18 PDRS

[2] LEMPRIÈRE
2-18 PDRS

[3] LAWRENCE
3-5½" MORTARS

[4] LANE
ROCKETS

[5] MITCHELL/CARMICHAEL
2-9 PDRS
3-6 PDRS
2-5½" HOWITZERS

[6] CRAWFORD/MONEY
4-24 PDRS
6-18 PDRS

[7] CRAWLEY
ROCKETS

● REDOUBT (APPROXIMATE LOCATION)

The artillery engagement on January 1, 1815, Pakenham again had his infantry on the Chalmette plantation when he opened fire from his newly erected Batteries 2, 4, 5, 6, and 7. Once more, American batteries on Line Jackson easily outgunned the British. Rennie's renewed effort to get around Jackson's left flank appears at top, stymied by Coffee's Tennesseans and Jugeat's Choctaws. The note at bottom left suggesting that American batteries numbers 1 through 4 might have been built partially of cotton bales is incorrect.

Speer's two eighteens by the levee. Farthest from his vantage was Pakenham's big battery, apparently behind a ditch. Well to its left, facing the center of the American line, he saw Michell and Lawrence firing at him from
behind the same ditch. Keane's column stood plainly in view on the main
road near the Bienvenu house, with more redcoats taking cover in a ditch
there and another sixty yards to its rear. Clearly, Pakenham meant to attack
once his guns had softened Line Jackson.[41]

REMEMBERING RENNIE'S ABORTED earlier flank movement, Old Hickory
anticipated something against his left. He left one of Coffee's regiments in
place and ordered the other and Captain Dejean's company back three hundred paces to new works on its left rear.[42] Then he ordered Captain Enoch
Humphreys to open fire from Battery No. 1, and one by one the other batteries followed while he began walking to his left flank, stopping at each
battery to check on guns and crews as they went into action.[43]

Through a glass, the British saw bits of McCarty's porticos flying off,
although they did not know if Jackson was still there.[44] When American
guns made no immediate response, some believed they had surprised the
enemy, and through telescopes both Dickson and Forrest thought they saw
confusion behind the enemy works. In fact, of course, they could only have
seen heads bobbing above the parapet and at the gun embrasures.[45] For a
few minutes or more the Americans were quiet before their guns barked.[46]

Some officers thought this the moment for the assault—that they could
reach the enemy line before it recovered, rush the ditch, and climb the earthwork on scaling ladders to overpower the defenders.[47] It was an improbable
hope. The British had a third of a mile of soggy ground to cover to reach the
canal with their fascines and ladders, and then men who had run carrying
heavy muskets must start climbing. That could hardly be done in less than
four or five minutes. Even if Jackson's gunners remained inactive, Plauché,
Lacoste, Daquin, the 44th Infantry, and others stood behind the line with
muskets at hand. American cannon returning fire made the question immaterial now. For two hours or more the firing from both sides did not cease.

As showers of rockets flew over Jackson's line, they made the fog above
the earthwork glow as they passed, while cannonballs landing short furrowed the ground in front of it and plowed their way onward. Shot or shell
hit every house and building immediately behind the line, and balls pulverized the walls and pillars supporting McCarty's upper gallery, which soon
tumbled.[48] No one on Line Jackson failed to be impressed by a cannonade
greater than even the experienced among them had seen.[49] Dudley Avery of
Baton Rouge thought that "the shott seemed to come in showers," and

Coffee's Adjutant Hynes described "one continued blaze of fire." Yet he and others soon found that there was little to fear, telling a friend that "I believe there is more alarm in the sound & blaze of fire than real danger."[50]

On the extreme left of Jackson's picket line, Hinds had men patrolling a fifty-yard front in the fog. When it lifted, they saw the new enemy battery about two hundred yards before them, and fifteen minutes later Dickson's guns opened. The first ball came so close to one of Major Hinds's men that he felt the "commotion of the air" as it passed his face. Pickets also thought they saw Rennie's column moving along the swamp toward their left flank. Before long Hinds's men withdrew as the shot, shells, and rockets began falling all around them.[51] At the same time, redcoats melted into ditches and fences as a storm of Yankee iron began flying at them.[52] A few days later Gleig wrote a sister that "my Newyears-day amusement was listening to shot passing over my head."[53]

The Yankees recovered quickly, Dickson counting fire from a dozen well-managed cannons. It was soon painfully evident that Jackson still outgunned him and that his own batteries were making no impression on the enemy works.[54] The hastily built platforms in his batteries were uneven, threw off the gunners' aim, barely supported the weight of the guns, and so cramped operations inside the walls that loading and running the guns up to their embrasures was difficult, especially the bigger eighteens and twenty-fours from which Pakenham expected so much. The unwieldy twenty-fours recoiled completely off their platforms into the mud at every discharge. The scant protection afforded by the hogshead walls slowed their fire even more as gunners often had to duck and dodge as enemy balls flew through the barrels.[55] Crews on the few guns operating efficiently inadvertently elevated them too high and fired over the American works, which none noticed until their ammunition was almost gone.[56]

It was Michell's misfortune to duel directly with Crawley's Battery No. 4, the only thirty-two-pounder on the field, served excellently by crewmen from *Carolina*. Its every shot seemed to perforate the flimsy hogshead walls. Watching through field glasses from outside the battery, Surtees saw the big gun's balls as black spots surrounded by white smoke when it fired, then watched the spots grow steadily larger as they approached. If one looked about to hit the battery, he yelled inside for the men to take cover. Observing from the interior, Keane himself narrowly missed being hit.[57] When the battery ran low on fuses, subaltern George Chesterton sprinted four hundred yards in the open to the ten-gun battery to get more. He passed Gibbs and staff on the way, the general warning him, "You'll be shot, to a certainty, if you continue in that direction." Gibbs obligingly pointed to a hedge Chesterton could run behind as he moved.[58] When Chesterton returned to Michell, he found Dickson perched in the branches of a tree inside the hogshead walls, calmly looking through a telescope while conversing with officers below.[59]

The flimsiness of all the batteries' walls was everywhere apparent. Enemy shot pierced them at will as casualties inside mounted.[60] As a result, Chesterton saw "thunder, and smoke, and slaughter" all around.[61] Before long Dickson lost thirteen artillerymen wounded, and an even dozen killed. Lieutenant Alexander Ramsay of Edinburgh, son of the captain of the warship *Regulus*, held a commission in the Royal Artillery, although Chesterton thought him a frightened youth unsuited for war. To overcome that, Ramsay had asked to be with one of the forward batteries, but he ran to the rear when American guns began battering the barrel defenses. The battery's captain shamed him into returning, but when he did, a Yankee ball shattered his body.[62]

Still, Pakenham's batteries kept their working guns firing. From the opposite bank, Patterson heard shells from Lempriere's eighteen-pounders soar overhead and saw a few plunge through his earthworks without injuring anyone. He did not engage *Louisiana*, having heard from a deserter that Pakenham had hot shot furnaces ready. She had to be preserved to cover the army from the river in case it retreated.[63] He got her guns in the fight from her upriver mooring, aiming at Speer's and Lempriere's eighteens near the levee and road.[64] His batteries on the bank delivered ample flank fire on the enemy, those guns firing nearly seven hundred shots that day.[65]

Patterson himself was with one of the thirty-two-pounders and watched one of its shells land amid the 93rd regiment, and believed he saw it kill fifteen of the Sutherland Highlanders.[66] Other shots from his guns may have damaged carriages in the enemy's big battery.[67] Thanks to thickening smoke between the lines and the barrel walls around enemy batteries, the Americans could not tell definitively what damage they were doing and tended to exaggerate their effect. At Battery No. 6 the brass twelve-pounder under the immediate direction of Lieutenant Étienne Bertel had only been in position a matter of some hours, manned by nine volunteers with no experience. Bertel, however, had spent fifteen years as a gunner in France and knew his way around cannon. Concentrating his fire on Michell's battery to his front left, he believed he silenced it after an hour, which he certainly did not.[68]

Line Jackson offered excellent protection. The longer the Americans saw enemy shot plunge harmlessly into the mud embankment, the more confident they felt. They continued to regard the rockets with derision, some dubbing them "Kentucky boats with a long steering oar," thanks to the long poles on which they were mounted. Adding fancy to contempt, one declared that the pole was actually a handle for throwing the rockets by hand, and that the enemy fired nearly 1,000 of them during the bombardment.[69] Nevertheless, the Congreves did begin to inflict casualties, most of them behind the line.[70]

None could say how many the rockets injured, but at the end of the day some Americans believed they had killed four or five and wounded between five and twenty-five more, although most of their victims were a few dozen of Coffee's horses killed in the rear.[71] In peacetime Louis Desforges was a violinist and music teacher who composed and conducted for a small orchestra. Now he was a private in Plauché's Battalion. A Congreve that cleared the earthwork exploded in the air directly above him and shrapnel struck his head, tore away a piece of his skull, and knocked him senseless, tragically leaving the musician deaf for life.[72]

Another probable rocket victim was thirty-nine-year-old Jewish merchant Judah Touro, who with partner Rezin Shepherd ran a store near the levee that imported soaps, candles, and dried cod from New England. Despite poor health, he enlisted in Dejean's 1st Militia but was too unwell to be on the front line that day. Still, he was carrying ammunition forward to Humphreys's battery until a fragment of shell struck his thigh and brutally tore away a mass of flesh. Friends took him to a field hospital behind the wall of a ruined building, where Dr. Kerr bound the gaping wound but despaired of Touro's life, telling Reuben Kemper the merchant must surely die. When Shepherd crossed the river on an errand for Patterson, he encountered Kemper, who told him his partner's fate. Forgetting the errand, Shepherd took his friend to the house they shared to nurse him, and within a few days Touro would be on the way to full recovery.[73]

At Battery No. 3, Dominique You, Pierre Laffite, and the Baratarians maintained fire from their twenty-four-pounders.[74] Lempriere's and Michell's gunners for some time concentrated on them and batteries immediately to their left, and when Dominique exposed himself at an embrasure to look through a spyglass, a shell fragment, probably from one of Lempriere's howitzers, hit his arm. A cannonball from one of the enemy nine- or eighteen-pounders broke the carriage of one of You's guns.[75] Notary Pedesclaux happened to be beside You's battery with hatmaker Baptiste La Borde standing behind him. As Pedesclaux bent to his side to light a cheroot from another volunteer's cigar, a ball flew past the notary's chest and instantly killed the hatter.[76]

It was dangerous behind the lines as well. Jackson kept Hinds's and Ogden's dragoons near McCarty's, since there was no immediate need for them elsewhere. They watched with curiosity as Congreves came over the earth-work, and dodged cannonballs and rockets that wounded four or five of the Mississippians and killed several horses.[77] With Ogden was Columbus Law-son, clerk of Judge Hall's court, and one of the city's best-read men, with a library of more than seventy volumes of political and legal writings from Adam Smith and John Locke to Rousseau and Montesquieu. Now a shell or rocket wounded him fatally.[78] Despite that, one of Hinds's men declared that "danger has become so familiar, as to leave no impression on me."[79]

Other British shells passed far above the works to injure people on the river road and levee a mile beyond, and did not discriminate. Among those Jackson impressed to work on the earthworks was an enslaved man named Antoine, known as "a good cart-man," who belonged to a free black named Francis Larche. Antoine carried wounded in his cart to a hospital near the levee, which brought him in range of enemy guns. He had just approached the hospital when a cannonball hit him, and soon afterward an officer found him dead on the road by the levee.[80]

Two hours into the cannonade an exploding Congreve damaged the thirty-two-pounder in Crawley's Battery No. 4 and set off one hundred pounds of powder in its nearby caisson. Not long afterward enemy fire blew up the magazine of another battery on the line.[81] Yankee fire slackened for some minutes as crews moved other caissons to better protection, and Dickson, noting slackening American fire, thought his guns had put some enemy guns out of action. His own ammunition ran so low now that he had to reduce his own rate of fire, but when American guns resumed their earlier tempo, Dickson could no longer answer round for round.[82]

"Why don't we go on?" waiting redcoats asked one another when no or-der came for an assault.[83] They could not see what Pakenham saw. His bat-teries had failed.[84] More than three hours of firing the eighteens and twenty-fours in the big battery had almost exhausted their ammunition, Michell's seven-gun battery was being beaten to pieces, several of its gun carriages were broken, and a howitzer was disabled. Pakenham and Dick-son agreed that their guns had no hope of silencing Jackson's and gave the order to cease fire at about three p.m.[85]

The Americans detected the enemy's slowing rate of fire, and that the two batteries on the levee and road went almost silent. When Lawrence's and Michell's guns did the same, the Yankees thought they had knocked them out of action. When the enemy's big battery ceased firing on Dickson's order, once again the Americans thought they must have damaged or de-stroyed the redcoats' heavy guns. Soon Jackson's gunners debated among themselves whether Pakenham was reduced to just two working guns or none at all, begetting a rumor in the city that Jackson had actually captured all British artillery.[86]

For a change, numbers were oddly immaterial. Jackson had 3,961 with him that day, but virtually all of the action engaged just 150-odd gunners operating his thirteen cannons and the men bringing forward ammunition from their caissons and magazines.[87] Only on his left flank did enemy infantry attempt a threat, and Old Hickory had allowed for that after Rennie's effort on December 28. In addition to the slight breastwork of felled trees and mud that ran obliquely two hundred yards back from the end of the main earthwork, Coffee cleared brush for thirty or forty yards in front of it to forestall surprise and clear a field of fire. Men on that line had scarcely a foot of dry land to stand upon and had to lie on logs and piles of brush to sleep above the water.[88]

From Jackson's vantage, it appeared that much of Money's and Crawley's fire aimed for Coffee's log breastwork, which he read as an attempt to soften it for an attack where his defenses were not as high and there was no ditch to cross. He warned Coffee to look out for an approach in his front, and thus they were ready. Rennie and two hundred of the 21st Fusiliers had successfully struggled through the thick undergrowth and boggy swamp to a position facing Coffee's Tennesseans. On the way they came upon the body of the missing Lieutenant Wright. It lay undisturbed, and Rennie retrieved his sword, spyglass, and half a dozen gold doubloons for his family. Once in position, Rennie waited for the sound of the general attack that never came.

At one point either the Fusiliers or Coffee fired a volley. They exchanged fire for some minutes before Rennie pulled back, expecting the foe to advance, which led the Tennesseans to think they had repulsed an enemy charge.[89] Rennie then waited on circumstances to determine his next move. When he heard British artillery cease, he sent a subaltern to report his position and ask for orders.[90] Obviously the Americans knew Rennie was there now, and when Dickson and others heard the musketry die away, some feared the silence meant Rennie had been captured. Then his messenger reached headquarters, and Pakenham ordered him to return to the bivouac.[91]

Once more Pakenham made the prudent decision, although today he had no choice. His bombardment had failed completely. There could be no moving the guns under fire, so he ordered his gunners to abandon them and retire to the rear, while the advance regiments remained in their ditches to protect the guns should Jackson sortie from his works. When night fell, Keane and Gibbs were to bring the cannon back and retire themselves to the positions they held on December 30.[92] No sooner did Pakenham call a cease-fire than the rain recommenced and lasted all afternoon, making the infantrymen even more miserable. Adding to their discomfiture, they heard a triumphal shout from thousands of throats behind Jackson's lines. Some believed they heard fiddlers and trumpeters on the enemy earthworks, and bands on both sides of the river taunting them by striking up "Yankee Doodle."[93] Jackson soon sent a sortie over the works to disable the enemy eighteens and twenty-fours by driving soft spikes into their firing vents.[94] As they approached the big battery, a company of the 4th Foot jumped up to fire a volley that drove the Americans back and closed the engagement.[95]

The American cannonade lasted into the night. When it was dark enough to move onto the field unseen, redcoats began manhandling Captain Lewis Carmichael's brace of six-pounders, and Michell's and Lawrence's guns to the main road and then to the rear. Thanks to the persistent rain, their shoes sank into the mud at every step, and even the road was a mess. Pulling and dragging the heavy ordnance without horses exhausted the men nearly to the point of insubordination, and the big battery was hardest to empty. The 4th Foot began the work, hours later relieved by the 21st, and both balked as they struggled in the mire. Men who had spent the whole day lying in wet ditches under fire were not in high spirits for work best suited for animals. Some simply walked away.[96] The seamen were no more enthusiastic. After spending the night before bringing troops up the bayou, they had just settled into their boats for the night, rigging sails as awnings against the rain. In Codrington's gig, Midshipman Robert Aitchison half filled a wooden tub with earth as an ersatz hearth and was drying his clothing before the fire when the order to help retrieve the cannon arrived. He was so tired that he forgot his greatcoat and had to slog three miles in the mud to reach the big battery.[97]

The work took all night.[98] Pakenham's adjutant Smith oversaw it and after a few hours awoke Pakenham at the De La Ronde house to tell him he might not get the guns to safety before dawn. The general and Dickson went to the field to find a deplorable scene. Cart axles broke under the weight of the guns, and only one or two had been removed. Much of the working party just disappeared, and the area around the big battery had been churned into a knee-deep loblolly of mud. Now Pakenham showed why he was a general. "Exertion and determination will effect anything," he told Harry Smith. First he tried persuasion, then threats, and when none of that worked, he ordered forward fresh detachments of hundreds at a time, working through one regiment after another. He kept his good humor throughout, even sending Dickson a note joking that what they needed were canoes that would glide over the soft mud.[99]

The approaching dawn lit two eighteens and two carronades returned to Gibbs's headquarters, and the other big guns withdrawn some four hundred yards and at least inside the British picket line. There men removed the gun tubes and covered them with rushes, then concealed the carriages in a nearby ditch.[100] They had also dismantled the platforms in the batteries, leaving only the remainder of their walls to shelter pickets in days ahead.[101] Colonel Forrest proudly declared that the whole army had become a working party, but Admiral Codrington worried that they had worn down the army in the effort.[102] An exhausted Aitchison briefly slept in the mud once they finished, then rejoiced to return to Codrington's gig and his tub of fire.[103]

There would be little other rejoicing. Where the December 28 reconnaissance provided some inaccurate information of the strength of the enemy line, Pakenham had only casualties to show for today's effort. Besides the killed and wounded among the artillerymen, enemy shelling found the infantry in their ditches. Ensign Hill tallied the casualties and found the 93rd hardest hit, with nine dead and eleven wounded. The 5th West India lost four killed and two injured, the 85th and 44th two dead each and nine wounded between them, and the 4th and 21st both with one man killed and five injured. Army casualties totaled thirty-two dead, forty-four wounded, and two men missing from the 95th Rifles.[104]

Late that night a deserter from the 44th United States Infantry brought Pakenham the welcome news that one of Jackson's cannons had been dismounted and one or two others damaged, but that was nothing compared to damage done to British guns. The deserter also reported a camp rumor that Old Hickory meant to use hot shot himself to destroy the houses on the field being used by Dickson as ammunition depots. That, at least, was useful intelligence, and Pakenham directed that powder and shot still in those houses be concealed out in the fields.[105] That same night a rifleman from the 95th deserted, and another from the 21st, its second or third now.[106] Codrington's concern over morale in this worn-down army was not idle.

Morale soared upriver. Postmaster Thomas Johnston thought the result glorious and speculated that Pakenham's retirement to his bivouac was the first stage of a full evacuation.[107] Jackson had suffered just eleven dead and twenty-two wounded, and the deserter from the 44th.[108] One of his wounded, probably Columbus Lawson, reader of Virgil and Homer, had written a poem just the night before. Comrades found it on his body:

To-morrow's rising sun shall see
Opposing ranks in combat close—

His parting beams may light the free
Triumphant o'er their fallen foes.

But if our homes must be the prey
Of ruffian bands, by ruffians led;
If freedom's sons, less skill'd than they,
Are doom'd in vain their blood to shed;

I'd rather this poor body fling
To bar one bayonet's hostile way,
Than be the talking, coward thing,
With patriot name, and statesman's sway![109]

Looking through his telescope that evening, Jackson saw apparent con-fusion in Pakenham's bivouac.[110] The deserters said their army had suffered at least 140 casualties, and perhaps over 200.[111] Hinting at discord in its ranks, they implied that Pakenham had made today's effort to boost lagging morale in an army discouraged at waiting over a week since the Decem-ber 23 action to do something. They also added that redcoats had a particu-lar dread of Coffee's Tennesseans, whom they called "devils & not men."[112]

Once again Old Hickory proved himself. For a third time they had foiled enemy plans. That evening one of Beale's merchant-soldiers paid tribute to Old Hickory's bravery and ability. "The people here both love and fear him," he wrote. "He does not stick at trifles in these times of peril."[113] Some found good omen in the engagement's occurrence on a holiday symbolizing re-birth, while others saw irony in the armies exchanging fiery iron on a day usually marked by trading tokens of friendship.[114] No certain news reached the city until Butler rode through town announcing the enemy withdrawal. Even then, Laura Florian called it "a most awful day."[115] At headquarters, however, Jackson issued an order wishing his army a happy New Year.[116]

At midday during the engagement, an officer from *Ramillies* left to re-turn to his ship. It took him two days, and on his way a false report reached him that the American earthwork had fallen and the *Louisiana* was de-stroyed. In a letter home he wrote a jubilant prediction that Pakenham must surely be in New Orleans by then.[117] When his letter reached the English press in late February, its import electrified.[118] While some pointed to the treaty ending the war, others riposted that until the Senate ratified and Madison signed, they were still at war.

New Orleans could yet be a fair prize and fairly won.

Fourteen

"The Necessity of Doing Something"

COCHRANE AND PAKENHAM had cooperated amicably thus far, but nothing had gone right in this campaign, and now they seemed to have had a conflict. If the general chafed at being subordinate to an admiral, he kept it to himself. For his part, the admiral had let the general plan a land campaign that left the navy out of the action when he might have preferred another approach. Waves of discord overlapped their banks now, most tellingly from Codrington. He blamed Dickson's artillery for the day's failure and feared that Jackson would only gain spirit by his success.[1] That was only for his wife's eyes, of course, for he told her he "could never presume to offer any opinion to an officer of such character as Sir E. Pakenham."

Still, when the general asked for Codrington's views on January 2, he spoke candidly. These planned frontal assaults against a fortified position may have worked in Europe, but they were a needless sacrifice of life in what he dismissed as "an exhibition of bravery." Pakenham should approach the problem in "the most regular scientific manner" by making a night crossing of the Mississippi to take Patterson's batteries, and then turn them on Line Jackson's right flank and rear, which would force Old Hickory to pull back. Chastened by two setbacks now, Pakenham seemed to agree.[2]

Rumor soon had the commanders arguing heatedly, Cochrane charging Pakenham with unnecessary delay that jeopardized the expedition, and the general retorting that in the span of five days he had made two attempts, meanwhile accusing the admiral of grossly misleading the war ministry about the local population. Cochrane supposedly insisted that they would do it his way now, sending a flotilla up the river past the forts to blast

Jackson out of his line.[3] Whether or not such a confrontation really occurred, rumor alone could hurt morale. Cochrane usually stayed in his covered gig at the mouth of the bayou, but he was at Villeré's on January 1, and
tactical thinking did change rather abruptly after the day's failure.[4] Learning that Lambert had reached the fleet anchorage, and that additional reinforcements were expected, he sent *Sophie* and other vessels to cruise between
Mobile, Pensacola, and Negril, to intercept new arrivals and direct them to
him.[5] Codrington resolved that so long as Cochrane played a role in the
campaign, "I shall be ever at his elbow."[6] Nestled therein may have been a
hint that others were losing confidence.

Pakenham honestly characterized January 1 as "a severe and unexpected
blow to our hopes." Further operations must wait for Lambert now, and for
the moment he concentrated on extending the bayou road to the fishermen's
huts to move men and matériel more speedily.[7] The general and admiral compromised on a combined operation promising both services a measure of
glory. Cochrane's ships would pass the forts to appear off the city behind
Jackson's line, a chancy approach entirely hostage to river bends and winds.
Meanwhile, Cochrane also proposed widening the canal from Bayou Bienvenue and extending it to the levee, which workers would cut through to flood
it from the river. A score of small boats would then pass through the cut to
the river, ferrying soldiers across in the night to take Patterson's batteries and
turn them on Line Jackson. Should Cochrane's flotilla not get past the lower
forts, the same boats would then convey troops upstream and land them behind Jackson's line to attack his rear. With Old Hickory thus preoccupied,
Pakenham would launch an assault with a real prospect of success.[8]

The plan agreed upon, Cochrane left for the fleet to set his part in motion, his final act before leaving being an order to Nicolls to place himself
and his handful of chiefs under Pakenham's command, handing an annoy-
ing detail to a commander who already had enough distractions.[9] As the
senior major of all services present, Nicolls asked Cochrane to let him lead
the marine contingent in an attack, but the admiral reasoned that if he lost
Nicolls, no one else could handle their Chickasaw and Choctaw allies. By
this time there were perhaps two hundred more Indian men, women, and
even children in camp. The admiral wanted Nicolls to take the warriors and
marines to Cockburn, where his knowledge of the tribes would be more
useful than in Louisiana, and as a sop promised the major that he would
lose nothing if not engaged with Pakenham, and to recommend him for the
permanent rank and pay of a lieutenant colonel.[10] For the sake of diplomacy,
Pakenham dined with Nicolls and the chiefs a few days later but thereafter
all but ignored him.[11]

January 2 was quiet but for occasional firing.[12] American pickets occupied the remains of the abandoned batteries during the day while they harassed their British counterparts, and after nightfall Pakenham decided to deal with them, starting with the battery nearest the cypress wood. He sent a company of the 4th to capture them, and Ensign Gerard, who knew that ground somewhat, volunteered to go in advance with a sergeant and six men on what he archly called "a forlorn hope" to get behind and storm the position. They reached it undetected and rushed the battery. The Yankees killed one of them and wounded two others, but then ran out and got away to the woods. Left with only four men, Gerard returned them to their own lines, wet, gloomy, and disappointed.[13]

There was no gloom in the American line. The volunteers were in great spirits, their faith in Old Hickory soaring. No one doubted that they were ready for whatever Pakenham tried next, although there was little resting on laurels.[14] Seeing movement in the British camps, Jackson sent Hinds's dragoons on another dash near their line that discovered the enemy had successfully retrieved all of their cannon safely.[15] An examination of his own line was encouraging. He saw that British shot had done no material damage to the earthwork. Having withstood one bombardment, it should stand more, but still he had work parties continue making it higher and thicker.[16] Men also went over the parapet and ventured as far as the dismantled enemy batteries, where they found abandoned tools and equipment, a few barrels of gunpowder, and more than two hundred shells and cannonballs, all of which they could use.[17]

The general had earlier decided on a backup line of defense two miles to the rear of Line Jackson. If forced from the front works, his dragoons could delay the British while his infantry withdrew to the new line. Villeré virtually completed an earthwork called Line Dupré by December 31 and manned it now with 175 men of the 6th Louisiana Militia, to whom Jackson soon added almost 400 more, giving each man five precious flints and two dozen musket rounds.[18] Even with the Laffites' gift of flints, the army still had too few, and its powder was inferior to the enemy's.[19] Happily, Fort Petites Coquilles was in good shape with nine eighteens and twenty-fours and three hundred rounds of ammunition, as well as marines, two companies of artillerymen, and one hundred Baratarians, including Pierre Laffite.[20] Fort St. John mounted another four nine-pounders with ample ammunition.[21]

The best comfort of all, however, was the final appearance of the Kentuckians. They had been seven weeks coming since leaving Louisville on November 21.[22] Some boats were too small and there were not enough, and provisions ran low from the outset.[23] Major General John Thomas took command on November 26, but within two days crowding forced some men to walk along the shore.[24] Every morning a trumpet signaled to prepare to board their boats, another at 7:30 told them to push off, while two horn blasts in the evening pulled them in to shore.[25] Adair and Thomas refined organization and established a strict code of behavior that forbade profane language or entering a property without permission. "We are called upon & have come into the field to save our Country," Thomas told the men. "Let us not then give occasion to our Countrymen to brand us a band of marauding robbers."[26] Officers even convened courts-martial while floating downriver.[27]

When they reached the mouth of the Cumberland River on December 2 and were halted while awaiting provisions, discontent over slow progress and inadequate equipment erupted in a minor mutiny.[28] Anonymous declarations appeared on trees in the camps vowing that "wee the Soldiers do refuse to go on board to leave this until we are furnished with tents kettles, &c." Men defiantly said they would not move until paid, and it galled further when Carroll's men passed through well furnished by Tennessee with rations, arms, and equipment, while Adair's had little but slim rations and had to purchase even those privately. Officers quelled the incipient mutiny, but when they departed again on December 9, there were still too few boats. The cold and rain made the open boats miserable, and when they reached the Mississippi the next day, they had to dodge collision with huge chunks of floating ice.[29]

Their rations ran low, and shore stops yielded little.[30] Adair had to cut the meat ration by a quarter, with little prospect of getting more until they reached Natchez.[31] Some men wandered from camp at night to forage and got lost, while others deserted.[32] After three weeks Captain Thomas Joyes's company alone lost twenty percent of its men.[33] Accidents added to mounting frustration, and on December 15 came their first two deaths from disease, probably the first army deaths of the campaign.[34] Frustration erupted anew when heavier boats outpaced the lighter ones, and on December 21, General Thomas high-handedly arrested the captain of a lesser officer's boat that floated in front of his own.[35]

Tragedy struck on Christmas Day when Ensign John Fig of the 15th Kentucky rowed to shore and accidentally passed directly under a "sawyer," a drifting tree lodged upright in the muddy bottom. It suddenly crashed back into the water, knocking Fig from his skiff, and when he swam for shore, the current swallowed him as his comrades looked on helplessly.[36] Deaths from disease continued, and more fell ill, including General Thomas.[37] Fig's replacement, Ensign David Weller, tallied all told twenty-five men "dead and drownded" on their voyage.[38] When they reached Natchez in midafternoon of December 28, they learned of the loss of the gunboats, the British landing, and the December 23 night engagement.[39] Excited by the news, they cast off at 3:30 a.m. the next day with a renewed sense of urgency.[40]

By the morning of January 2, they were close enough for Adair to ride ahead and reach Jackson's headquarters that evening. The man striding into the McCarty house reminded some of Reuben Kemper with his simple dress and rough-and-tumble look.[41] With Thomas still unwell, Old Hickory put Adair in command of the Kentuckians and took him on a tour of the defenses.[42] Asked what he thought of their ability to hold, Adair thought the highly disciplined redcoats could only be stopped by bringing them down in their columns as they advanced before they spread out to assail the works. Jackson must also have a powerful reserve ready to hurl at the main thrust wherever it came—Adair's hint that his men should be that reserve. Jackson agreed, and when intelligence from deserters suggested that Pakenham's main strike might be at Carroll in the center of the earthwork, he ordered Adair to place his armed men behind the Tennesseans when they arrived, and added a company of Orleans militia between Carroll and the 44th Infantry.[43]

When the first several hundred Kentuckians approached later that day, Jackson had them camp on the Piernas plantation a mile behind the main line.[44] The remainder joined them there over January 3 and 4, and Adair moved some of them to their assigned position behind Carroll.[45] Those with tents put them up and tore apart their boats to make more shelters.[46] The question of arms was paramount. Only about a third of them had muskets, and many of those needed repairs. Arming earlier arrivals had left the city arsenal bare, so Jackson appealed to Claiborne for any weapons the city could spare, and the governor turned to Gaspard Debuys, commanding the "Corps of Exempts," who offered 250 to 300 guns as a loan to Old Hickory and issued shotguns and pikes to his men in their place.[47] Then Claiborne asked General Labatut to go door-to-door collecting all the arms he could find.[48] It yielded a multiplicity of weapons of every description, caliber, and antiquity, and one man handed over six.[49] Finally, Jackson discharged visitors to the city whom he earlier pressed into volunteering, and their arms went to Colonel Gabriel Slaughter's 13th and 14th Kentucky regiments.[50] Everyone in New Orleans knew Adair was desperately short of muskets, which meant that before long the British would know it, too, and meanwhile Jackson still looked for the keelboat from Pittsburgh.[51]

These Kentuckians immediately became objects of considerable interest and curiosity. Off duty, they wandered into New Orleans occasionally, but most remained at the front, keen not to miss anything that might happen.[52] In recent years a new American paradigm had come to maturity, the distinctive product of the second American frontier extending from the Appalachians to the Mississippi, and the Ohio to the Gulf. He was a rough backwoodsman, a welding of Daniel Boone, Sam Dale, Reuben Kemper, and other frontier characters, unintimidated by anything or anyone, crude though a gentleman, scrupulously honest, with a distinctive regional patois, an unerringly true aim with his rifle, and a flair for exaggeration and boast, to the point of declaring himself to be *Half Horse, half Alligator.*[53] He epitomized what some in the East aspired to be, what some in the West already were, and stood poised to step into mythic folklore.

Something about Kentuckians particularly captured the American imagination by the time war came. In a short span of years, the fame of "sharp-shooting Kentuckians," as one officer put it in 1810, assumed mythic proportion.[54] The fabled marksmanship of Tennesseans already intimidated the British facing New Orleans, and one of Adair's volunteers now found that some in the city thought the very word "Kentuckian" instilled terror in the enemy ranks.[55] The reality for the moment was that the unarmed men were little threat to anyone, and Old Hickory stationed them on Line Dupré to make it appear fully manned, forbidding communication between his two lines to keep their lack of arms from arousing anxiety.[56]

Claiborne believed Jackson would take the offensive now, a fair indication of how little Old Hickory shared his planning with the governor.[57] Jackson might not have used the term, but he instinctively understood that his greatest strength was the geopolitical situation facing Pakenham. He had to do something soon, but his only options were a costly frontal assault on Line Jackson or withdrawing to Lake Borgne to seek another approach. He had no room to maneuver. Both sides knew that American artillery was dominant on the field. Any battle must be fought largely on Jackson's terms, and he would be a fool not to stay firm in his resolve to make the enemy come to him.[58]

American manpower kept getting better. On January 4, more than fifty Mississippians of the Natchez Volunteer Rifle Corps led by Captain James C. Wilkins appeared, and rumor put nine hundred men of the 3rd United States Infantry en route from Mobile.[59] Jackson had boats waiting on the Tchefuncte to bring them across the lake the moment they arrived, unaware that General Winchester had not yet put them on the road.[60] Also unknown to Jackson, a steamboat loaded with twenty-four-pounders, shells, and muskets passed Louisville on December 28, and a keelboat loaded with 3,000 muskets, nearly half a ton of gunpowder, and three tons of balls and shells followed on January 2. Added to the 1,300 muskets sent in late December, that put more than 8,000 guns on the rivers heading for New Orleans.[61]

But they were not there, and his always limited store of patience was exhausted. Hearing that the Pittsburgh boat was making private commercial stops on the way, he fumed on January 3 at "this supineness, this negligence, this *criminality*." He had held out for ten days by indefatigable exertion and unexpected good fortune, but he could not depend on that indefinitely.[62] An equally exasperated soldier virtually echoed Jackson's frustration at the overdue arms, fuming "God knows when they may arrive."[63]

Jackson would have taken encouragement at the state of feeling in the army facing him. Dickson's damaged guns mirrored morale among officers and men from whom so much had been expected. Hampered at the outset from want of sufficient ammunition, he blamed Pakenham for refusing to allow time for more to arrive. The hard fact remained that their guns had achieved nothing with the firepower they had, and more ammunition was hardly likely to improve on that. He well judged the imperative that drove Pakenham to act on January 1 by acknowledging that "the necessity of doing something had become every hour more urgent."[64]

Equal chagrin among officers and men in the ranks fed a slowly mounting unrest. Twice now the enemy had outgunned them. Pinned down by Yankee artillery the rest of New Year's, they went hungry, and finally retired to their lines cold and famished. Since then the continual bombardment stole their sleep, their provisions dwindled, and the prohibition of fires at night that might silhouette them for enemy snipers left them freezing.[65] On January 2 they had only dry Indian corn cakes and a small chunk of dried beef per man for breakfast, washed down by bottled "essence of coffee."[66] They foraged to supplement their rations, but farmers' storehouses and pens were empty now. One day Gleig found nothing but four geese, and that was a bonanza.[67] Word of a fleet of transports bringing bread and rum from Jamaica cheered them, but they could not eat rumors.[68] Their uniforms were worn and torn, some of them constantly soaked for days, and it took days for replacement trousers, stockings, waistcoats, and underwear to reach them from the fleet.[69]

Yankee guns peppered and annoyed them around the clock.[70] Enemy pickets harassed them day and night, and men still died. The 44th and 93rd both lost lieutenants on January 3.[71] Gleig heard for the first time a "murmuring" in the camp, but the unease did not surprise him. The army was entitled to grumble. Setbacks in the field against an enemy they could not reach had them muttering like "a chained dog."[72] Rumor said Pakenham admitted he had never seen stronger defenses anywhere. True or not, the story unsettled men expecting to attack those defenses.[73] More unnerving still, someone recalled General Moreau's 1808 visit to New Orleans and attached to it a story that Jackson's earthwork was on the very spot Moreau thought the best defensive position of all. "Give me five thousand men," he supposedly declared of Chalmette, "and I will defend it against any ten thousand."[74]

The story was a fiction that probably originated with an American. A deserter did come into British lines late on January 1, and Jackson might have used him to feed the foe false information.[75] Yankee pickets, often close enough to converse with redcoat counterparts, could have planted the Moreau story. More likely still, one or more of the several people Captain Peddie claimed regularly brought information from the city might have come primed with the story in anticipation of the harm it could do.

Cracks appeared in the spirit of the officer corps, too. Some obeyed orders sluggishly, and Keane arrested an ensign of the 95th for negligence.[76] Discontent festered in the 44th, with haughty Mullins the principal catalyst. He had invited Captain J. Debbeigg of his regiment to share his hut, but a long-standing misunderstanding blotted their relations.[77] A few days later Mullins fell out with Lieutenant William Knight and arrested him temporarily.[78] The year was not a week old before one of his grenadiers deserted.[79]

Mullins was bored, or at least less punctilious about his duty, perhaps from missing his wife, who remained aboard ship with the fleet. Starting January 2, he alternated with others in the role of field officer of Gibbs's brigade, his duty being to command from midnight until dawn in the advance battery at the upper property line of the Bienvenu plantation, now converted into a redoubt. British pickets used it as a field headquarters. The cramped interior did not allow him to parade and inspect his picket details inside, so he did it outside instead. The reason for the close quarters was that the army's fascines and scaling ladders had been hastily jumbled within after the canceled January 1 assault. Even in the dark, no one could step in without seeing—or stumbling—over them. Mullins consequently spent most of his time there outside the redoubt, but a few officers swore they saw him go in occasionally.[80]

Dickson set armorers repairing their recovered artillery pieces, some actually damaged while being dragged back to the depot. An artificer from *Tonnant* selected trees to make better carriages for the eighteen-pounders, and Admiral Malcolm came forward to coordinate naval assistance to the army, bringing with him the good news that Lambert's flotilla had arrived at last and was anchored with the fleet. In two days, perhaps even one, fresh regiments would join them, a cause, at last, for optimism.[81]

Lambert's had been a difficult passage. *Vengeur* and its transports approached Cat Island in a thick fog that obscured all view. When the wind died, the convoy laid to, firing a cannon at intervals to warn other vessels of their presence and avoid collision. When the fog lifted, they were amazed to see that they had drifted right amid Cochrane's fleet.[82] Lambert embarked the 43rd regiment for Lake Borgne that afternoon, with the 7th to follow. His adjutant, Major John Tylden, was immediately perturbed to find no depot established to forward men from the anchorage to the army, reinforcing his belief that the navy could not do anything efficiently.[83]

On January 2, Lambert, Tylden, and others cast off from *Vengeur* and spent all day sailing for Lake Borgne. The following dawn they found the entrance to Bayou Bienvenue and rowed up it to the fishermen's huts to find Captain Gordon performing vital logistical work moving men and matériel to the army.[84] Although Gordon would not know it for some time, that same day Prince Regent George made him a Knight of the Order of the Bath for his prior services.[85] From there, Lambert rowed another three hours to the landing place, arriving in the afternoon ahead of his troops to find the improvement of the road beside the canal well under way.[86]

His men did not enjoy such an easy passage. The scows and barges carrying them entered Lake Borgne next day at low tide, often running aground on oyster beds in the shallows. Ahead were another two days of pulling, hauling, and towing to reach the mouth of the bayou, where they transferred to the smaller launches awaiting them.[87] Some never got that far. A boat carrying seventeen men of the 7th and four seamen, with a midshipman in charge, capsized on the lake and all but one drowned.[88]

After hours of rowing in the darkness, the last of Lambert's men saw a fire ahead at the landing place and found a tent surrounded by boxes of provisions, cannonballs, casks of fresh water and more, piled in a circle around sailors warming themselves by the blaze. After a bracing tot of grog, they began marching on the soggy reeds beside the bayou, each man carrying in his pack a cannonball or shell for Dickson, and by midnight reached Villeré's to find most of their regiments already asleep in cane stalk huts.[89]

Fresh units were a tonic.[90] Codrington saw the high spirits and confidence of Lambert's men revive the army.[91] Gleig thought the reinforcements increased their numbers such that they would be irresistible anywhere else in America, and the news of Lambert's coming infused everyone with a belief that the grand attack would be soon.[92] They were right, for, from his vantage, Codrington saw Lambert's appearance decide Pakenham on making a committed assault. "I believe there never was a more arduous task undertaken," he wrote to Jane the day after Lambert arrived, "but we shall perform it yet, & the greater glory will be our due."[93]

The new general himself felt less effusive after a few hours surveying the army's situation. Pakenham told him that he believed Line Jackson was a straight earthwork behind a ditch about four feet deep that narrowed as it approached the swamp. He thought about eight heavy guns defended the works, with another dozen in the batteries across the river.[94] Estimates of Jackson's strength varied wildly, especially after the arrival of the Kentuckians, of which Pakenham was fully aware now. Lambert felt uneasy that they did not know more. "Want of information has been very prejudicial to us," he lamented, and the fact that no one could—or would—tell him what efforts had been made to gather accurate intelligence suggested that Pakenham depended overmuch on what came voluntarily from friends inside the city.[95]

Adjutant Tylden was even more candid. "The more I get acquainted with the situation of the army the more do I see the strange way in which things have been carried on," he wrote in his journal on January 5, "and the more do I perceive the uncommon difficulties which exist." Once again the fault was with the webfoot service. Cochrane should have seized command of the Mississippi. It was deep enough for most of his warships, and Tylden believed they could pass Fort St. Philip easily. If they had control of the river, New Orleans would be theirs in a day. The line of approach chosen by Cochrane meant men and supplies had to travel sixty miles from the fleet, a journey whose hazard was tragically demonstrated by the recently drowned soldiers and sailors. Jackson's position was such that Pakenham needed a greater force than he had, even with Lambert's addition, and Tylden felt scant optimism of success.[96]

Lambert's men also expected to find more progress when they arrived. Subaltern John Cooke of the 43rd met his friend Captain Thomas Wilkinson of the 85th, then brigade major for Gibbs, and teased him: "Wilky, how is it that you have not provided us with good quarters in New Orleans, as we expected?" Wilkinson told him to say no more, grumbling that the army had been hesitating there for a fortnight. "Bullets stopped us," he groused. "Bullets—that's all."[97]

While the British fretted for want of intelligence, Old Hickory sought every scrap of information, and sent spies out the day after the engagement.[98] Half a dozen British deserters came over by January 4, and the next day an enemy subaltern arrived bringing a register that listed eight regiments with Pakenham as of about January 3, as well as the rocketeers, marines, and artillerymen—in all about 8,000, which was remarkably accurate, with more expected shortly. The deserters also brought the puzzling word that General Sir Thomas Picton had arrived, when of course it was Lambert, and that Cochrane had left on New Year's Day to take his fleet up the

Mississippi.[99] More useful yet, if true, was the report on January 5 that Cochrane now planned a combined attack, and that he and Pakenham were not getting along.[100] If true, dissension in the enemy headquarters could only be good for the Americans.

Jackson had to be concerned about his own desertions, though few, and any information they took to the enemy. The man from the 44th Infantry was perhaps the first, although little of value went with him to the foe. On New Year's Day itself, two men came to Fort St. Leon claiming to be from Declouet's regiment, just escaped from the British and bringing important information. Convinced they were spies, Major Gordon sent them under guard to Morgan to be confined.[101] One or two nights later a picket deserted armed with the watchword by which sentries challenged newcomers, and the countersign they needed to identify themselves as friends. Thereafter officers selected new watchwords and countersigns, sometimes daily.[102]

The possibility of Cochrane coming up the river never left Jackson's thoughts, making speedy intelligence vital. Major Gordon at Fort St. Leon established an express courier line connecting the lower end of the New Orleans levee to Fort St. Philip with four stations for riders to change mounts on the seventy-eight-mile ride.[103] Morgan set almost 200 drafted slaves to work enhancing its works and emplacing guns for the 154 men from Declouet's regiment composing the garrison.[104] Soon he sent an officer to round up more blacks, fearing the fort was still more than a week from being in a condition to defend against enemy vessels. He also sent parties to destroy any boats in the vicinity that the British might use if they got that far, and to drive all local cattle out of enemy reach.[105]

Then on January 3 a report reached Gordon that the enemy had been spotted across the river, probably foragers collecting beeves.[106] Though short on bread, the enemy was getting plenty of beef cows from Terre-aux-Boeufs.[107] Morgan ordered Gordon to be vigilant for such detachments, and to capture them if possible. Warning that the sentinels placed a dozen miles above and below Fort St. Leon were inadequate to cover such a distance, the general feared the enemy might cross the river and effect a landing unobserved, reminding Gordon that Jackson "makes great calculations on our diligence and Patriotism."[108]

Downriver at Fort St. Philip, Major Overton heard on New Year's Day that a British fleet was coming to bombard him, news that created serious alarm in New Orleans.[109] He set men to building magazines about the fort and distributing ammunition among them so that if an enemy shell set off one, the others would remain to feed his guns. He also commenced erecting shelters to protect the garrison and removing anything combustible from within and outside the walls.[110] To support Overton, on January 3, Jackson summoned Captain Shreve, who had been using his *Enterprise* to transport supplies and matériel from the city down to the front line. When Old Hickory asked if the steamboatman thought he could get past the British battery at the levee, Shreve accepted the challenge. After taking on munitions for Overton, Shreve muffled the boat's paddlewheel and then used hooks to secure bags of cotton to its port side to absorb British fire. Aided by the nightly fog, *Enterprise* paddled unseen past the British to reach Fort St. Philip the next day and returned safely that night after coming under minor musket fire, perhaps the first time an "armor"-clad steamboat went to war.[111]

Overton sent repeated assurances that he could hold his fort against whatever came, but Jackson worried. Patterson still had gunboat *No. 65* and ordered Lieutenant Thomas Cunningham to take her down to the fort, where her guns and crew were ready to help with its defense. Overton also had a huge fifteen-inch mortar to pitch shells onto enemy decks, although its fuses were unreliable and its crew inexperienced. In the event that Cochrane's ships got past St. Philip, Jackson had Latour start another battery on the river just below Fort St. Charles to support Overton, as well as a defensive line extending from that fort to the swamp parallel to and a mile above the Line Dupré, calling it Line Montreuil.[112]

On the right bank, General Morgan advised on January 2 that he was ill-prepared to defend his new position and needed 150 more slaves to put up defensive works.[113] Jackson also sent him Dejean's 1st Louisiana Militia, Colonel Zenon Cavelier's 2nd Louisiana, and several companies of De La Ronde's 3rd Louisiana, with the firm admonition to keep vigilant watch on enemy movements, particularly any effort to cross the river at night to take him by surprise.[114] Morgan did not begin his breastwork until January 4, emplacing three three-pounders that Gordon sent from Fort St. Leon.[115]

Patterson landed four more twelves from *Louisiana* on the west bank and prepared "fire ships" to send downriver to set ablaze any of Cochrane's vessels that passed Fort St. Philip and approached the city. He also built furnaces for the hot shot that Jackson began firing at the plantation buildings in his front.[116] It was a hard policy, for not a few men then serving in his army watched as Patterson set ablaze homes and storehouses filled with harvest.[117] Ignace de Chalmette's house burned to the ground.[118] Hot shot set the Bienvenu house ablaze (although the fire died out) and started fires in several slave cabins at Bienvenu's, most of the occupants having fled into New Orleans. The guns continued throwing hot shot until they were all in flames.[119] Parties of men from Line Jackson went out to fire other buildings. Corporal William O. Butler of Kentucky commanded a small guard in advance of the line and set out to drive enemy pickets from a house in front of his position. On his approach, all but one of the redcoats withdrew, and Butler and two others captured him when they went to torch the house. Just as he was about to kindle the fire, the redcoats returned, rushed inside to grab him, then threw him against an outer wall so hard that he broke through the siding and landed outside, to race back to his lines under fire before leading men back to finish the job of destroying the house.[120]

What damage Americans did not do, British occupation did. The Villeré, De La Ronde, Lacoste, and Bienvenue plantations were essentially laid waste.[121] Major Lacoste's cane crop was entirely ruined, and Villeré lost all of his fencing and one hundred slaves, with the rest of his movable property plundered or destroyed. De La Ronde lost twenty tons of sugar, a cane field ravaged as a battleground, his slaves, his library, and more, all valued at over $40,000. Bienvenu's and Lacoste's slaves ran away to the British. Jumonville de Villiers saw $19,250 worth of cane soaked and ruined when Morgan cut the levee, and there were more losses on the opposite bank.[122] Every plantation between the lines lost fences converted to campfires and redoubts, and when Carroll made the home of Francis B. Longville his headquarters, it became a target for British eighteens that did $2,250 in damage and destroyed its outbuildings.[123] Even if they had no choice in the face of Pakenham's and Jackson's military presence, no one could accuse these *creole* planters of not suffering to save their city and country.

And there would be more to come.

Fifteen

"Strike Our Foes with Fear"

CONDITIONS WERE HARD for the enslaved men building earthworks. By January 6 an estimated—and exaggerated—7,000 of them worked night and day.[1] Some whites drove them almost mercilessly, one officer's excuse being that "the greatest severity" was necessary to keep them working and from running away. Jacob Purkill's eighteen-year-old slave Arche toiled for weeks cutting timber around Fort St. John, working up to his hips in the swamp, until someone saw him spitting up blood as he lay on a pile of boards in the mud. He lingered another eight weeks before he died on the day he was taken home.[2] For all of Jackson's earlier promises to free blacks and slaves, little succor was forthcoming to them other than for the enrolled black militia.

Conditions were not much better for some of the white volunteers. Lacking tents or baggage, the Kentuckians slept on the rain-soaked ground by their arms, occasionally relieving the Tennesseans on the line. In places, especially in Coffee's sector, men lived in standing water, to which many attributed a growing incidence of camp disease. Dark rumors whispered of men dying every day in the dozens, but reality was bad enough, and already sickness had killed more men than enemy fire.[3] Thanks largely to Louaillier's efforts, the legislature appropriated $6,000 to purchase clothing for the Tennesseans and Kentuckians in particular, as well as those militia in need. Starting in late December, he had taken charge of raising public subscriptions for multiple purposes so that, by the first week of January, he had more than $16,000 committed for food and clothing, treatment of the wounded, and the care of families uprooted by the invasion.[4] The city council assisted with funds, and city women gave money to buy mattresses, blankets, four hundred pairs of shoes from local merchants, and cloth for cloaks, waistcoats, trousers, and shirts, some of which began reaching the Kentuckians now.[5]

Society in the city continued in its peculiar way. Livingston was ever at Jackson's side, and his influence with him grew steadily, making the Livingston town home a destination for those seeking informed news.[6] Louise Livingston flaunted her husband's influence before social rivals, making herself something of an object of ridicule when she visited Line Jackson and extended her hand as she walked through the Tennessee and Kentucky ranks, thanking them on behalf of all the city's women.[7] Nevertheless, she also opened her home's doors to offer women and children refuge from the shelling.[8]

On January 3 the redcoats' glasses showed the Americans erecting a half-moon-shaped redoubt extending in front of Jackson's right by the levee, and two days later they saw crews mounting cannon.[9] Old Hickory had been doubtful about the bastion but allowed it to proceed nevertheless. They placed it in the lower riverside corner of McCarty's garden and extended it over the canal and across the main river road to the levee, leaving some orange trees standing within.[10] Meanwhile Jackson continued strengthening the main line, and on January 5 brought a mortar weighing six and a half tons from the naval arsenal, most likely intending it to hurl shells onto the decks of any of Cochrane's vessels that passed the forts.[11]

Pakenham and Dickson did not idle as Jackson's redoubt grew. On January 4, Dickson began a new battery on the main road for six of their eighteens to take on *Louisiana* or any other Yankee vessels, as well as to support the redcoats when they crossed the river. He finished it the next day and started rolling sugar hogsheads out of a Bienvenu warehouse to begin the work of another battery for the other four eighteen and the four twenty-fours, which would support the soldiers sent across the river as well as playing on Jackson's line during the main attack.[12] He took stock of equipment on hand for maintaining the guns, and was shocked to discover that the fleet provided all manner of things he did not need, while essential tools and equipment were not sent.[13] At the same time he tried to ensure that his guns would have enough ammunition for their next trial when it came. On January 4 he received more than 6,500 iron balls and exploding shells, more rounds for their threes, sixes, and nines, and over a ton of gunpowder, meanwhile asking for four hundred more Congreves as well as 200,000 musket rounds. By January 6 he had his batteries in place and enough ammunition for a real bombardment.[14] He did not intend to be caught unprepared again.

To facilitate supplies from the fleet, engineers improved the road to the canal, while others pushed it down the right bank of the bayou. The work went briskly without letup for several days, the men working six-hour shifts around the clock. Other parties dug out the space between the end of the Villeré canal and the river, and Dickson's workers installed a makeshift lock a short distance from the levee to raise the canal level enough to float their boats as close to the river as possible. When they cut out the last bit through to the river, the water flowing in should allow them to push their boats into the Mississippi. They thought it would be ready the night of January 6.[15]

Pakenham also began a defensive work called Fort Villeré at the landing place where Bayou Mazant flowed into Bienvenue, intending it as a last defense should he be forced to withdraw to the fleet.[16] Still, he hoped to dislodge Jackson by getting around his left flank. Twice Rennie had come close before being detected. If there was a path that would allow a few hundred to come out of the swamp on Jackson's left rear, it could decide the campaign. On January 4, Pakenham sent a company of the 4th Foot to seek that passage, but they got lost in the wilderness and gave up.[17] Had they but known, there was a route, if not a good one, and not just to Jackson's immediate left rear, for Bayou Bienvenue went all the way back to Madame Piernas's plantation a mile behind the main earthwork, putting both his own line and Claiborne's position on the Gentilly road in jeopardy.

Old Hickory did know of it now, for on the night of January 3 one of his scouts had reported the enemy approaching that way, a false alarm that nevertheless punctuated concern for his left. That called for Reuben Kemper. A visitor in New Orleans found him to be a "plain rough looking" fellow. Thanks to his war against the Spaniards, he was known throughout the Mississippi and Ohio river valleys as an enterprising and daring spirit.[18] On January 4, Jackson turned to him to take volunteers up the Piernas canal to Bayou Bienvenue, then up Bienvenue to Bayou Mazant to reconnoiter the enemy's growing Fort Villeré and keep that route clear of the enemy. Kemper took a dozen men in two canoes and left immediately. The next morning they were rowing down Bienvenue, stopping frequently to climb trees to look ahead, and as they neared Bayou Mazant they saw the fort from a treetop. Kemper went across the prairie to get a closer look but then saw boats coming up Bienvenue with sailor lookouts at their mastheads. He had been spotted, and Captain Daniel Lawrence of the troopship *Alceste* was coming to investigate. They scattered all the guards at Kemper's canoes except a lone *creole*, who explained that he was the Americans' interpreter, identifying their commander as "Major Camper." Lawrence's men set fires in the prairie grass, hoping to flush Kemper and the rest from the reeds, but they were back in Jackson's lines by January 7.[19]

Both sides gained something useful from the episode. Lawrence learned that the bayou was too shallow and its bottom too soft to allow Yankees to use it to threaten British communications with Lake Borgne, but Jackson also knew now that this avenue to his own rear was too difficult to present a concern. Reuben confirmed the strong guard at a redoubt protecting enemy stores and magazines where Bienvenue met Bayou Mazant, and the captured *creole* interpreter informed Lawrence that Adair's command had arrived at last.[20]

Smoke from the burning grass obscured a third of the eastern horizon. Americans thought Kemper had set it himself, while Dickson believed it meant Reuben was trapped in the swamp, which ought to deter others from snooping in the bayous.[21] The cynical Adjutant Tylden wanted to see much more of Louisiana ablaze, snapping that "I wish the whole country, fort, & all could be thus cleared."[22] They would both be disappointed.

There was more letdown ahead. At midnight on January 5, sailing master William Johnson took four boats and thirty-five sailors and soldiers through Chef Menteur to reconnoiter the British transport anchorage on Lake Borgne. In a rising gale, they got close enough to see the last of Lambert's reinforcements disembarking a transport to row to Bayou Bienvenue. Waiting a quarter hour for them to pass out of sight, Johnson boarded the vessel at four a.m. and took it and its small crew. With dawn approaching, he loaded his captives aboard his own boats and set fire to the transport, which exploded just as dawn approached on January 6. Soon an armed British barge approached the American boats but quickly turned aside when Johnson's men fired on it, and as more enemy boats appeared, he sailed safely back through Chef Menteur to Fort St. John.

Johnson's prisoners told him that loss of the transport's cargo of rum and bread would be a serious blow, which tallied with what deserters said of their army being nearly out of bread.[23] They confirmed that Lambert had arrived with up to 2,000 men. They also said the redcoats were making fascines and scaling ladders as fast as possible, planning "a desperate effort" on Line Jackson that might come as soon as January 7.[24]

The news spread quickly through the city and camps. Eyes and ears went on renewed alert for danger, and Postmaster Johnston found all around him expecting the enemy to attack.[25] Hundreds of Kentuckians remained unarmed. Some doubted the forts could stop Cochrane's warships on the river. Despite the stories of shortages in redcoat camps, Pakenham seemed to have steady communication with the fleet to keep supplied. Even Governor Claiborne's perpetual optimism faltered momentarily.[26]

Having dispatched warships to ascend the Mississippi and sent transports back to Jamaica for more provisions and matériel, Cochrane stayed busy awaiting the grand assault. Well aware of the dissidents meeting at Hartford, he issued an order to curtail "every species of warfare" in New England and authorized lifting the blockade of its ports.[27] Still in the grip of his delusion of the goodwill of the Spaniards and *creoles* in Louisiana, he ordered Nicolls to respect the property of all but those actively supporting the Americans.[28]

January 6 was another cold day as Pakenham's outposts huddled in the remaining buildings on the field. American hot shot had burned another house the previous night, and all day that day they fired at the Bienvenu home, where Ensigns Gerard and William Crowe of the 4th took cover in spite of Patterson's cannonballs passing through the house.[29] That evening workers finally completed the canal and the engineers cut through the levee to let the river in.[30] With Lambert barely arrived and work yet to do on Dickson's batteries, Pakenham decided to postpone sending troops across the river until the following night.[31]

He had not fully formulated his scheme of attack. The general made Tylden his adjutant, and as senior member of the staff, Tylden ought to have known Pakenham's plans. That afternoon he supposed the general intended to take Patterson's batteries and use them to rake Jackson's defenses while the army made a frontal assault, but he was troubled that he did not know Pakenham's precise intent. Meanwhile, although the men were generally healthy, Tylden fretted that the army had lost almost five hundred to sickness since Keane's landing.[32] Then came news of the transport's explosion that morning and the loss of her much-needed cargo.[33]

Still, optimistic predictions prevailed. On January 4, Cochrane sent *Diomede* to Kingston for supplies even as the sound of American guns boomed in the distance. Aboard her, someone interpreted the sound to mean Pakenham had launched his attack and expected New Orleans to fall by the eighth of January.[34] By the time she reached Kingston, that misconception evolved into Pakenham's guns breaching and storming Line Jackson on January 5, making the fall of the city inevitable.[35] Another report had *Louisiana* exploding the day before and Pakenham taking fifty cannon.[36]

Back on the field, American telescopes showed redcoats making fascines and scaling ladders and working on the Villeré canal, all of which shouted imminent assault.[37] Captain Isaac Baker of the 44th thought Jackson's defenses dependable but feared they were not strong enough to fight in an open field.[38] Across the river an officer issued a general order to inspirit his men against the enemy, declaring that no one was safe from Albion's rapacious grasp, beginning with "the chaste Matron."[39] In Washington, Secretary Monroe wrote to Jackson, counting on him to close every avenue to the city and "obtain a complete victory."[40]

British artillery fire phased no one. Carroll's Tennesseans looked indifferently on the rockets flying overhead like sputtering lightning.[41] Enemy shot, shell, rockets, and hot shot sent earth flying over their heads and plowed the ground at their feet, but men in the ranks seemed to look forward eagerly to Pakenham's assault. Farmers and shopkeepers had become warriors, and thus far Yankee casualties were so few, it seemed providential.[42] Behind Carroll, the "music of cannon" filled Kentuckians' ears all that day. They saw the enemy building his new battery or redoubt, knowing that, when it was done, the redcoats would come again, and deserters said they intended one more effort. A Bluegrass volunteer promised that if the British ever reached the city, "they will have to drench the plains of the Mississippi with their blood."[43]

Beyond the sound of the bombardment, anxiety for the city's fate prevailed. On January 3 an express from New Orleans reached Natchez after three days with an account of the December 23 and 28 actions. A mounted volunteer just leaving for the city feared he would arrive to find it in enemy hands but left resolved "to meet victory or death."[44] He would not have been cheered to know that this same day Old Hickory wrote to Monroe asking him to send an officer to New Orleans to relieve him—not immediately, perhaps, but "when my want of health, which I find to be greatly impaired, shall oblige me to retire from it."[45] He ate but little, battled chronic diarrhea, hardly slept, and suffered constant pain. Only iron will kept him going.

Far to the east, in Washington this January 6, Louisiana's delegates endured the frustration of detachment from home in distance and time. A few days earlier, when he learned that Jackson had arrived in the city, Senator Brown felt their spirits revived.[46] Today, however, Fromentin, Brown, and Robertson discussed four-week-old correspondence from New Orleans just arrived and concluded that there seemed scant hope of saving the city.[47]

Even farther eastward and across an ocean, that same day Henry Carroll, one of the secretaries to the American legation at Ghent, boarded a sloop at Plymouth to take copies of the treaty to New York. With him went a secretary for the British legation to receive Madison's signed copy and return it to London. Before leaving, Carroll told a journalist the terms were such that Madison and the Senate would surely ratify. London's anti-administration *Morning Chronicle* praised it as being to Britain's advantage, but the *Times* denounced it.[48] That same day London and the *Times* learned of Keane's landing, which both misinterpreted to mean he was at the city's gates. Confident of speedy victory, the newspaper looked skeptically at a treaty returning all conquered territory.[49]

The optimism at New Orleans seemed unaccountable elsewhere. With its press temporarily shuttered, no newspapers left the city, though Hilaire Leclerc of *L'Ami des Lois* kept a daily diary of events in type to be ready when he resumed publishing.[50] Regular mails left on Fridays, and every rider departing December 23 and 30 and January 6 carried bags bulging with letters. They took four weeks to reach the East Coast, where the press complained of frequent delays and unreliable information, and Federalist editors accused Madison of deliberately delaying bad news.[51] Jackson sent communications by faster express riders, and sometimes their news leaked along the way, but press and public mainly waited for the government to release authoritative reports.[52] Still, Americans were better informed than Britons. Washington learned of the gunboat defeat on January 8, twenty-five days later.[53] First news of the December 23 fight arrived on January 20.[54] By contrast, as of January 6, people in England knew only that Cochrane had arrived at Guadeloupe two months earlier.[55]

Thus, as of January 6 the East knew the British were close to Louisiana, and Jackson was not expected to arrive before New Year's Day. "We are induced to fear that New Orleans will fall," wrote a New Bedford editor. Whoever held it controlled the country west of the Appalachians, and all but the blind saw the nation's future inextricably bound with the settlement and development of the territory from those mountains to the Mississippi and beyond. The western states would not, and could not, long remain in the Union if it did not "*at all times*, and *in all circumstances*, possess New Orleans."[56] The British agreed.[57]

While month-old press reports fed fear in the East, men on the scene saw something else and tried to share it with the outside world. Jackson's earthworks daily rose higher and broader. Every day without an attack made their position stronger while the elements, the length of their supply line, and even greater distance from reinforcements, worked against the foe. Adair's arrival boosted morale, Livingston saw a glorious spirit all around him, and even Major Reid, despite his dark forebodings, felt his spirits soar when Kentucky came.[58] Little wonder that an artilleryman now concluded that "Orleans, I believe, is pretty safe."[59] Rumor even had British warships retiring downriver.[60] "We may have another *tug* with them," Beverly Chew told his brother, but the prospect did not disquiet him. "We have nothing to fear."[61] Heartening that confidence was the performance of the *creole* population, and some had praise even for the black men bearing arms.[62] They would make the redcoats walk over the bodies of the city's finest men before they took New Orleans.[63] "Nationalities no longer count," French consul Louis Tousard this day told a friend. "We are all Americans."[64]

They expected something decisive and knew it would come soon.[65] Confident or not, all looked to higher power for deliverance. "O! Lord wilt thou, protect us now, from threats & evils near," one wrote in prayer. "Stretch Mercy's hand, ore [sic] freedom's land and Strike our foes with fear."[66] For some the greatest concern was Old Hickory. He could only be the city's savior if he continued to command.[67] An army of volunteers keeps few secrets, and his severe dysentery was common knowledge. Many in his army feared he might not be able to continue, while others worried over his nonchalance under fire. It set an admirable example, but at high risk. A score of enemy eighteen-pounder balls perforated McCarty's house that day alone, and any could have killed him. "He exposes himself to[o] much," complained one of Patterson's officers. "Should a chance shot take *him* off, I know not what might be the consequence."[68]

Other than Jackson, their greatest advantage was time. For a fortnight now the antagonists glared at one another. The only open-field close contact since December 23 had been the small unit skirmishes in front of Carroll on December 28 and January 1. All the rest had been long-distance musketry and artillery fire, and as for that, Major Hynes found that "there is more *terror* in the sound of cannon than *danger*." Like everyone else, he understood that the longer the enemy delayed launching a major assault, the better the Yankees would be prepared to withstand it when it came.[69] Before sundown on January 6, an unknown writer finished his letter to a New York merchant by concluding that "the British have given us too much time."[70]

There would never be enough of that commodity to improve relations between Jackson and Claiborne, unfortunately. The two barely spoke now, and communicated almost entirely by messenger. Claiborne sent at least four notes this day, the first a complaint that Old Hickory had virtually usurped authority over his militia, and the last a renewed plea for Jackson to make good his promise to give the governor a line command.[71] When the general replied with a gossamer excuse, Claiborne rode to the line with Shaumburg to protest.

Jackson possessed great character offset by great weakness. A committed Democrat, his instincts were autocratic. He was generous, loyal, and courageous to a fault, but the bully within was never far from the surface. He enjoyed having power to torment those like Claiborne who challenged him. From his arrival in New Orleans he seemed determined to humiliate the governor and his supporters, whom Jackson dubbed a "little malicious *knot*."[72] He had no time for the man, especially not now. When Claiborne arrived, they openly quarreled in the hearing of a number of the volunteers. Old Hickory ended it with typical hyperbole he may not have meant but which played well before the men. "Governor if you are not more cautious in future," he said, "I shall have to shoot you." Rumors soon said that Jackson banned him from camp, and Shaumburg declared that "Jackson is at war with Claiborne."[73]

Others beside Old Hickory and the governor saw future political capital for themselves in a successful defense. Jackson never had much confidence in Morgan, especially after his tardiness on December 23. Adair's arrival so uplifted spirits that speculation arose that Jackson offered him Morgan's command. The Kentuckian had about him the look of a tough, unassuming westerner.[74] He had served in his legislature and briefly in the United States Senate, but connections with Aaron Burr doomed his reelection in 1806. Now another election approached in 1818 and a gallant performance here could erase his liabilities, but the right bank looked like a sideshow, and he needed to lead in major action. Better that he stay in reserve behind Line Jackson, where he might have a chance to save the day should that line be breached. If Old Hickory really did offer him the west bank command, Adair turned it down.[75]

Yet that front could prove a critical sector, as reports from deserters spoke of a British move across the river.[76] On January 6, Jackson sent his aide John Randolph Grymes to the right bank opposite the Villeré plantation to observe movements around enemy headquarters. Seeing evidence of much digging, Grymes advised Morgan to move his force to be in position to repel any attempt to cross, but, slow as ever to act, Morgan only sent a small advance under Major Paul Arnaud and Major Charles Tessier with 120 of Declouet's militia, many armed only with fowling pieces.

On the east bank, Old Hickory still believed he did not have the manpower to make a first strike or retard enemy preparations. He felt he did not dare risk an army overwhelmingly composed of inexperienced militia in the open field against well-disciplined regulars. They must await Pakenham's pleasure and use the benison of time given him by the enemy to vigorously press his own defenses.[77] Hence his soldiers watched and waited as their eighteens and twenty-fours and *Louisiana*'s big guns maintained the bombardment of enemy camps.[78] The British returned fire from their advance battery near the main road, and the skirmishing continued without letup.[79] Some of Coffee's men constantly moved ahead to confront redcoat pickets or probed around Pakenham's right flank to reconnoiter the British bivouac to look for any more artillery coming in from the fleet.[80] One of Coffee's privates went out as a sniper, his bullet pouch and powder horn slung around his neck as he crept through the swamp to the right of the enemy line. He waited for darkness. When he saw a sentinel, he shot him and crawled to the body to retrieve his musket. He did it twice more, bringing Coffee three guns as trophies.[81]

After Lambert arrived, Jackson prohibited anyone from entering or leaving the line or camps without a pass, and ordered the arrest of anyone arousing suspicion.[82] He posted American, Spanish, and French soldiers at multiple guard posts on the road from Line Jackson to the city, some of whom spoke no English, and most civilians stopped visiting the men at the earthwork for fear of being suspected as spies.[83] For fear mail might fall into enemy hands, officers censored their own letters, suppressing details about the army.[84] Consul Tousard would joke to a friend that the security concern was such that "I do not even allow myself to talk."[85]

Jackson also increased sentinels to keep deserters from reaching the enemy, but this night one got through to reveal the day's countersign and watchwords and confirm that the American line was weak at its center.[86] John Farmer of the 15th Kentucky was on picket that evening. On his own responsibility he ventured close enough to the British pickets to hear them discuss the deserter's revelations. Farmer ran back to his lines with the news, and the watchwords were changed at once to prevent enemy infiltration.[87] That same night a British deserter reported that his army now planned to eat their postponed Christmas dinner in New Orleans on January 8.[88]

Rushed work on the new levee bastion was just two days in progress, and when Old Hickory found it unfinished, he lectured engineer Latrobe for positioning its left wall where it blocked one of Humphreys's Battery No. 1 cannon. He ordered the wall dismantled and moved to the right to give Humphreys a full field of fire, but even then the Line Jackson parapet behind the bastion was so low that if Humphreys fired grapeshot, the men in the bastion would have to duck their heads to avoid friendly fire.[89] Jackson kept inspecting the work as it neared completion, with two embrasures facing left from which it could deliver flanking fire on any foemen crossing the canal or trying to scale the face of the earthworks, and two others commanding the levee and main road. A fosse, or moat, encircled the bastion from the canal through the levee to the river, which was expected to rise shortly and fill the moat. The only communication between the bastion and Line Jackson was a plank set across the canal between them.[90] Jackson may have doubted the wisdom of thus placing men and guns in advance of his main line, and reportedly grumbled that it would likely give them trouble.[91]

The constant barrage of the previous week brought little comfort to civilians, keeping them anxious during the day and awake at night.[92] People abandoned homes near the arsenal for fear of explosion and to get away from neighboring wooden houses set ablaze by hot shot. Most people busied themselves somehow in supporting volunteers, tending wounded, or burying the dead. Abbé Louis Debourg at the Ursuline convent on Chartres Street opened its doors and converted houses on the grounds into hospitals, where nuns tended the growing sick list as well as the wounded.[93] Among the latter now were two of the city's better-known figures, Private Pierre Monier of the 2nd Battalion of Louisiana Volunteers, a favorite actor at the Orleans' Theatre, and the jeweler John Delarue of Royal Street, now with Plauché, who cast the silver buttons adorning many militia uniforms.[94] Sometime that day his friends raised $130 to buy a coffin and tomb for the poet-clerk Columbus Lawson.[95]

After a fitful night, January 7 dawned cloudy with a fresh breeze.[96] Commander Lawrence sent his small launches back to Kemper's last known location but found no Yankee threat developing on that flank.[97] A convoy of victuallers had finally arrived, and fresh provisions reached headquarters that evening, giving the men a fair supper at last, although they still foraged to supplement rations, including horsemeat.[98]

Pakenham awoke resolved that he must make a grand assault the next day. He knew at his cost that Jackson's line was too strong to breach with artillery. There was no room to maneuver around the Americans' right against the river, and multiple efforts showed he could not get through the swamp to their left. His commissaries pointed to dwindling rations despite the victuallers' arrival. The men were losing patience. Desertions, though few, remained steady. The much-vaunted *creole* assistance was illusory, and he believed Jackson's force now matched or exceeded his own, even if mostly militia. Every day Pakenham and Burgoyne had surveyed Line Jackson through telescopes, and guessed enemy numbers as high as 16,000 or more.[99]

Finally, this was Pakenham's first independent army command. Many expected much from him, particularly Wellington. Aware that negotiators had met at Ghent and that major operations had concluded on the Atlantic coast, Pakenham knew the war was winding down. His assault on New Orleans, if he made one, might be the final battle. It ought to be glorious.

It had to be a victory.

Sixteen

"We Await Our Fate"

A S A BAND played, officers reviewed and inspected their troops that morning. Spirits rose when the men learned they would attack on the morrow.[1] Pakenham spent some time perched in a tree seeking faults in Jackson's line through his glass.[2] At Villeré's, men and officers had impressed themselves by their achievement in deepening and widening the canal. Under Admiral Malcolm's direction, days of six-hour shifts around the clock finally completed the work to the Villeré house during the past night.

Soldiers erected crude screens to keep the workmen out of sight, but once again allowed uninformed assumptions about local sentiment to cross their purposes, this time with the Villeré slaves. Taking it as granted that the enslaved would naturally be opposed to their masters' cause, Admiral Malcolm allowed them free movement through the plantation. It seemed beyond comprehension that some of the blacks might feel themselves Americans first and slaves second. Whether or not they actually took information of the work to Jackson, the Britons' complaisant approach to local sentiment worked against them.[3]

This morning the flotilla of small craft was pulled up the widened canal to within 250 yards of the river, to be kept out of sight until sunset. Then they would pass the levee cut to load their human cargo and row to the other side within a couple of hours.[4] Men detailed for the trip lounged nearby watching the work.[5] Meanwhile, Dickson's shop repaired a damaged howitzer and readied other pieces to send along.[6] Everything hinged on getting through the levee to launch the amphibious force into the Mississippi.

They began the levee cut that afternoon, and by evening Malcolm concluded the opening was wide and deep enough.[7] So it was, but the river did not cooperate. Its level had receded enough that when the final barrier of earth came out, the water only rose a foot or less in the canal. Any water beyond that just flowed back through the canal and emptied into the bayou.[8]

No one could anticipate this. Carl von Clausewitz's classic study on war would appear in 1832, but Captain Robert Simpson of the 43rd Monmouthshire Regiment looked back now on what he saw in the almost empty canal, and anticipated the Prussian's conclusions. "It almost invariably occurs," he observed, "that in such operations there are delays which the most skilful combinations cannot at times guard against."[9] Engineers had no solution, nor was there time for another approach. At sunset they just began the exhausting task of manhandling the boats through the canal to the levee cut, half lifting, half dragging them over the clinging mud. It took fifty to one hundred men to handle each boat.[10] Barely fifty yards from the Villeré house, the boats just got stuck. The "machine" was breaking down.[11]

Old Hickory's barrage was renewed at seven a.m. that morning. One volunteer passed the time counting fifty-four discharges in an hour. As the men waited at Line Jackson, the cannonade provided their only entertainment. Indeed, after a fortnight of it, they were so inured to the constant din that they paid it no heed, and noted that even women who visited camp showed no fear of the roar. Major John Reid and many others wrote letters for the next mail with that deafening sound in their ears, one volunteer musing with his pen that "all that I have read of wars and battles is mere stuff" and "practice makes every thing familiar to the human mind."[12]

Sensing approaching crisis, civilians appeared asking to help with the guns. Captain Shreve joined Humphreys's crew.[13] General Flaujac in other times commanded a brigade of militia and held a seat in the state senate. Now he volunteered and took charge of Battery No. 7.[14] Jackson's batteries continued to be a work in progress, but by that afternoon they assumed their final form.[15] Humphreys' Battery No. 1 was thirty yards from the levee and behind the new bastion. It mounted two bronze twelve-pounders and a six-inch howitzer. Navy lieutenant Otto Norris's No. 2 stood ninety yards to its left with a hefty twenty-four-pounder. Fifty yards on Captains Dominique and Beluche commanded No. 3 with two more big twenty-fours. Two hundred and twenty yards farther on Lieutenant Crawley's No. 4 mounted a single thirty-two-pounder, the biggest monster on the field, and another 190 yards from it sat No. 5's two six-pounders under Lieutenants Perry and Kerr. Just over 100 feet to their left, Lieutenant Spotts had a twelve-pounder in No. 6, and 190 yards east of it lay No. 7's eighteen-pounder and six-pounder served by Flaujac and Captain Louis A. Chauveau. The last battery, No. 8, with an unreliable brass carronade, lay another sixty yards away, where the earthwork made a short concave arc before extending behind the cypress trees into the swamp.[16]

Still they added mud and earth to Line Jackson, some of Villeré's militia working now alongside the borrowed and impressed slaves.[17] It ran almost 2,000 feet from the levee to Battery No. 8. Lieutenant Andrew Ross took a company of the 7th Infantry into the new bastion, where Lieutenant Louis de Marans and men from the 44th would man two brass six-pounders. The remainder of Beale's riflemen held the main breastwork immediately behind the bastion. A company of 430 men from the 7th led by Major Henry Peire held the line between Batteries No. 1 and No. 3. Plauché's battalion of 189 and Lacoste's battalion of 280 free men of color occupied the works from there to Battery No. 4. Daquin's 150 Saint-Domingue free blacks and 250 of the 44th Infantry under Captain Baker defended the works between Battery Nos. 4 and 5. From that point onward, 1,200 of Carroll's Tennesseans filled the remaining eight hundred yards of the works to the edge of the cypress swamp, with those Kentuckians who had muskets in a four-hundred-yard line behind them as reserve. Five hundred of Coffee's men held the remainder of the line behind the woods and into the swamp.[18] Meanwhile, across the front of the whole line, the Rodriguez Canal had been widened and dug out to hold water in places five and six feet deep.[19]

The problem of arms continued to nag, and despite slow communications, people in the East certainly knew of the problem.[20] Federalists used it to step up their attacks on Madison, blaming him for not stockpiling munitions at New Orleans long before the enemy's appearance, and carping that it would have been a better use of funds than the planned purchase of Jefferson's books to replace the Library of Congress burned by the enemy the past August.[21] One of the letters leaving in that day's mail from New Orleans spat that "a horrible neglect exists some where, and New Orleans may fall for the want of arms."[22] The daily sight of hundreds of unarmed Kentuckians made it seem a reasonable fear.

One of those Kentuckians, Ensign David Weller, wrote home to warn that "you will hear of a great fight." Everyone around him agreed and looked forward to it.[23] Jackson spent most of the day at that upper-story window of McCarty's looking through his telescope. He saw the work on the Villeré canal. He saw redcoat infantry gathering near the levee. He saw soldiers creating stacks of fascines and moving ladders.[24] That evening Hinds's reconnaissance saw slave cabins set ablaze by Jackson's fire, illuminating redcoats dragging boats through the canal. That convinced some of the dragoons that the attack would come in the morning.[25]

Across the river, Patterson and his volunteer aide, Judah Touro's partner Shepherd, rode down the right bank that afternoon to follow up on Grymes's report of digging at Villeré's. It appeared to them that 1,000 of the enemy were working on the canal and notching the levee. They saw a few armed barges manhandled through, to be moored on the riverbank, and spotted artillery moving to the canal, with perhaps 1,500 redcoats nearby apparently awaiting orders to move. Patterson realized that Pakenham intended to cross to attack Morgan, surely to support an assault on Line Jackson.[26] He considered bringing *Louisiana* downstream to destroy enemy boats as they crossed, but realized that would expose her to British hot shot.[27] Meanwhile he sent Shepherd back to Morgan, who in turn dispatched him with the news to Jackson.[28]

True to form, General Morgan was ill-prepared. He only commenced an earthwork on January 4, and at the moment it ended 350 yards short of the woods, leaving his right flank badly exposed.[29] He had only two brass sixes and a twelve-pounder mounted on the line; most of the guns on that side of the river—a dozen twelves and twenty-fours—were in Patterson's shore batteries supporting Jackson's line.[30] Old Hickory was not pleased with Morgan's dilatory progress and sent another engineer with peremptory orders to see the defenses completed. He also admonished Morgan in writing that there was no more time for niceties and protocol, and he had better obey all orders thoroughly and at once. It was the last letter he would write until the following afternoon.[31]

Jackson did what he could to bolster Morgan, even summoning more militia for just four days' service, which revealed his own conviction that the crisis could be just hours off.[32] He sent 766 of Villeré's men and officers across the river, despite fifty or more yet to be armed. The rest went with two dozen musket cartridges per man and sufficient flints for one engagement. Almost a dozen of those militia companies, though pledged to defend the city even without pay or rations, were stipulating that they would serve no more than one full day without relief.[33] Jackson did not have time to address that now. Besides, from multiple indications that day, he might not need them more than twenty-four hours.

When the reinforcements arrived, Morgan had Captain Shaumburg, who was now his aide, order all to be ready to march immediately.[34] Yet he did not move. Instead he posted them behind his incomplete defenses facing downstream, Dejean's regiment on his left by the river, Cavalier's in the center, and Declouet's on the right. But rather than putting them in the works, he kept them in their bivouacs, with orders to practice marching up to the works. Too late now, Morgan finally gave orders to extend his defenses toward the swamp on his right.[35]

Early that evening Jackson directed Adair to send four hundred of his unarmed men to reinforce Morgan and have them take muskets from any of the other armed Kentuckians not then on the front line. Any remaining shortage should be filled by arms found in the city when they passed through.[36] At seven p.m. Adair sent Lieutenant Colonel John Davis of the 13th Kentucky to detail the men and leave immediately along with a company from the 14th Kentucky under Major Reuben Harrison.[37] Captain Thomas Joyes helped navigate the detachment through the multilingual guard points on the road, and reported to Quartermaster Thomas Butler, who directed him to boats at the river landing, where they found waiting an assortment of muskets, most in need of repair.[38] With only enough sound guns to arm 170 men, the rest returned to their camps.[39]

That evening half of the detachment crossed over, their boats returning to ferry the remainder. As they marched downriver, they passed more guard posts until within a mile of Morgan's line, where a sentinel refused to let them pass without countersign and passwords that no one gave Davis. He was still arguing with the guard when Patterson appeared and gave the password for them. Joyes hurried on to Morgan's camp to secure clearance for the rest of the Kentuckians to come on, all at the loss of valuable time.[40]

Across the river, redcoat pickets drove Hinds's dragoons from their position in front of the Yankee army to re-form behind the earthwork, but too late to prevent the horsemen seeing and hearing their preparations.[41] Other advance pickets also brought back similar advice that started a rumor of redcoats crossing the river and an impending attack in the morning.[42] Just before sundown Adair's armed units moved to a position two hundred yards behind the main line, and almost immediately the enemy sent three Congreve rockets their way. The first struck the ground just behind the earthwork. The second passed harmlessly overhead, but a third flew directly over the breastwork and sputtered straight at a Nelson County company of the 15th Kentucky. The men scattered in either direction and watched the missile pass directly between two men close enough to throw sparks on both of them.[43] Somewhat shaken, they passed the night sitting, standing, or lying down as opportunity afforded, tired and hungry and strangely silent. Not a sliver of moon illuminated the night sky, and a considerable fog further dampened their spirits.[44]

No such gloom troubled Pakenham, who spent much of that day with his staff completing plans for the attack. To avoid confusion, he prudently

drafted memoranda for his commanders. Samuel Gibbs, as senior brigade
commander, would command the main assault with his 4th, the 21st, the
44th, and three companies of the 95th, about 2,500 men. Keane's brigade
was to support him with the 43rd, the 85th, the 93rd, and two companies of
the 95th, totaling roughly 2,300. Lambert's reserve, the unmounted dragoons, and the balance of the West India regiments totaled perhaps 3,600.[45]
With marines, artillery, and other ranks, the entire army numbered perhaps 10,000.[46]

Keane and Gibbs were to fall in at four a.m. and move forward shortly
before dawn to the line currently held by the army's pickets. An advance
guard of 500 men from the 95th and 250 of the 44th, led by Mullins, were to
go forward to occupy the battery works abandoned on January 1. Gibbs
would then advance in a column of companies, starting with the one on his
far left, followed by each in succession as the former passed, while the advance guard at the batteries provided covering fire. As the lead company
approached the batteries, Mullins's advance was to rush to the enemy line
carrying fascines to fill the ditch, long ladders with planks over their rungs
to bridge the canal, and smaller ladders for scaling the earthwork. Pakenham further directed that Mullins determine the fascines' and ladders' lo-
cations that evening so there should be no delay in getting them the next
morning. Once they had been placed, Mullins's men were to join in opening
fire. Meanwhile, a battalion of the light companies of Gibbs's brigade with
one hundred men from the 5th West India regiment was to advance along
the edge of the cypress wood to protect his right flank. Assuming that they
would reach Jackson's line, the battalion was then to proceed over the works
to participate in pursuing the Yankees, whom Gibbs would put to flight.[47]

Keane's part of the attack hinged largely upon operations on the right
bank. If Morgan's artillery was taken and used to silence Jackson's advance
bastion, Keane should direct his attack to that point with the 95th in the
lead. He would begin by sending Rennie and a flanking column ahead to
take the new bastion and spike its guns, to divert attention from the main
attack by Gibbs. Major Rennie would have the light companies from the
7th, the 43rd, and the 93rd, with one hundred men from the 1st West India.[48] From his position Keane could support both Rennie and Gibbs and
take advantage of circumstances.[49] Pakenham believed that when his men
closed on the enemy works, Jackson would not be able to turn his cannon
obliquely right or left sufficiently to deliver a serious flanking fire. Once
they carried the American works, Rennie would drive through half a mile
toward the enemy rear. Sappers with the columns would bridge ditches and
the Rodriguez Canal. Pakenham added what he called an "after memo"

directing Rennie to leave one company in reserve while another drove back Yankee pickets on the main road and a third advanced at a slight angle to the right where he thought they would encounter less fire.[50]

Pakenham scarcely mentioned the right-bank part of the plan, but all Keane and Gibbs needed to know was that it ought to capture or neutralize Jackson's batteries across the river before they advanced, to spare them flank fire. There was much discussion among the planners about that mission to cross the river. Pakenham wanted men in position to take Morgan by surprise at first light, capture his guns, then fire a signal rocket announcing their success, whereupon he would launch his attack on Jackson.[51] At the same time, the men on the right bank would turn Morgan's artillery on Jackson's line while the infantry pushed on to a point opposite New Orleans, where their appearance ought to throw the city into panic.[52]

Codrington doubted that Pakenham really counted on this working.[53] Yet Admiral Malcolm and the engineers believed—wrongly, as it turned out—that the canal would work once they cut through to the levee. Someone suggested that they ignore Line Jackson entirely and just attack Morgan, since taking his guns and turning them on Jackson should force him out of his earthworks or else risk the British moving up the right bank to take New Orleans behind him.[54] The majority favored Pakenham's plan. He probably had Colonel William Thornton in mind for the west bank operation from the outset, but Thornton characteristically volunteered. Much could go wrong, and he would be isolated on the other bank for hours, with reinforcement virtually in sight.[55]

The plan was well conceived, a mirror image of Pakenham's scheme for the canceled January 1 assault, but it was not well expressed. Indeed, Rennie's part appeared to have been added almost as afterthought. Pakenham left much to Keane's and Gibbs's discretion, as he should have, and Lambert thought the proposal was the best they could attempt under the circumstances, but it depended entirely on separated segments of the army acting in concert: the "machine" had to run perfectly.[56] Some details were puzzling. His most experienced regiments, with extensive service on the Peninsula, were Lambert's 7th and 43rd, yet Pakenham kept them in reserve. The 44th and 21st spearheading his attack had not served with Wellington, and the 85th with Thornton was a troubled regiment with little battle experience until it came to America. Pakenham's aide Wylly thought the 4th and 93rd were fine regiments, but the 21st lacked discipline, and he had nothing complimentary to say about the 44th.[57]

Pakenham seemed too certain of success, or perhaps it was a pose for effect. He even told Lambert that carrying Line Jackson would be easy and "not be the least arduous."[58] His experience on January 1 ought to have taught him not to hope for a walkover. He actually divined better than Old Hickory that the right bank was the Yankees' Achilles' heel, yet he seemed to feel he must have a grand assault in his front. Not everyone saw his attack order that evening: Adjutant John Tylden, for one, took it for granted that Pakenham would secure the right bank first and be bombarding Jackson's flank across the river before Keane and Gibbs advanced against it.[59] There was an inescapable feeling of overconfidence about the whole business.

Pakenham had officers copy their particular instructions and take them to their brigade majors and regimental commanders to copy pertinent details for themselves. There must be no mistaking what he expected from them. Several, like Majors Wilkinson and Rennie, kept their copies in their pockets for instant reference.[60] Gibbs met with Colonel Mullins early that afternoon to give him orders for the 44th's role, which Mullins copied from Gibbs's draft of the plan.[61] As Pakenham emphasized, Gibbs also instructed him to confirm where the fascines and ladders were stored.[62]

Returning to his bivouac, Mullins sent Lieutenant Colonel A. Johnston and an orderly sergeant to determine where he would find the fascines and ladders in the morning.[63] Johnston rode to Gibbs's headquarters at the De La Ronde house to see senior engineer Captain Anthony Emmett, who confirmed that the fascines were in the advance redoubt and that Lieutenant Hammond A. Tapp of the engineers would be there in the morning to distribute them to the 44th. Further, Tapp would conduct Mullins's advance forward to the canal to oversee the depositing of the bundles and the setting of the ladders. That satisfied Johnston, but Emmett insisted on drawing a map for Mullins, with the fascines' and ladders' location clearly marked in the "advance redoubt."[64]

Johnston almost immediately encountered Gibbs and told him his mission at headquarters, which troubled Gibbs on two counts. First, the location of the fascines and ladders was almost common knowledge in the army, yet Mullins appeared not to know; second, Mullins sent a subordinate rather than coming himself. As a safeguard, the general wrote a positive order to be taken to Mullins: "The Commanding Officer, of the 44th will ascertain where the Fascines and Ladders are deposited this evening."[65] He meant for Mullins to do it himself.

Johnston reported all this when he returned at about three p.m., and whatever he told Mullins verbally, he handed him Emmett's map pinpointing the spot and Gibbs's specific directive to confirm the location.[66] Mullins summoned his hut mate Debbeigg, showed him their orders, and added rather glibly that "the 44th Regt. will have the forlorn hope to-morrow," and were likely to "*catch it.*"[67] Debbeigg copied the orders for Johnston, who reiterated that Tapp would be at the redoubt in the morning to turn over the fascines and ladders.[68] Johnston made to show the map to Mullins and Debbeigg, but Mullins waved it away and told him just to tell him where to find the ladders and fascines. Johnston said he believed they would be in the advance battery, but Emmett's note removed all doubt. Mullins just took the map and put it in his waistcoat without looking at it or showing it to Debbeigg.[69]

Sometime between five and six p.m., Mullins summoned the officers of the 44th to his hut. With all but Debbeigg present, he gave them their orders. They would move forward to the left of Gibbs's attacking column, picking up some three hundred fascines and ladders on the way. Lieutenant William Knight's grenadier company would carry the ladders, and when Knight responded that he thought the ladders were in the advance redoubt, Mullins did not correct him and tartly replied that "we all know where they are Sir." He went on to explain how their men would drop the fascines into the canal first and then Knight's company would pass to the front to plant the ladders across the ditch and against the breastworks. Then the grenadiers would storm up the ladders to be the first over the enemy breastworks and use their bayonets on the other side.[70]

When Mullins dismissed them, he was optimistic of success. At about eight p.m., when Debbeigg diplomatically suggested they make final arrangements for the operation—which would include obeying Gibbs's order to personally see where the fascines and ladders were stored—Mullins waved him away, saying there would be time enough in the morning.[71] Besides, Gibbs's directive only said that he was to "ascertain" the location, but it did not *specifically* state that Mullins must do it himself. He believed his place was with the regiment, not running errands that a lieutenant colonel was certainly qualified to perform for him.[72] Mullins remained in a good mood all that evening and perhaps just did not feel like bothering with details.[73] For a man facing a desperate assault in a few hours, Knight felt lighthearted, too, but he had doubts about Mullins. He remarked to Johnston and Debbeigg that "I hope there will be no mistake." Johnston reassured him. Had he not given Mullins the map with the location of the ladders and fascines?[74] Of course Knight already knew where they were, as did others of the regiment, for they were among the officers who placed them there after the aborted January 1 assault.[75]

That evening Pakenham sent artilleryman Benson Hill to Tapp with an order to communicate with Mullins regarding the placement of the fascines and ladders in the redoubt. Coincidentally, Mullins approached as Hill spoke with Tapp, and Hill read Pakenham's directions to him, asking if he had questions. Mullins said it was all quite clear, whereupon Hill returned to headquarters to assure the commander that the colonel knew what he was to do.[76] In all the discussion that day, no one noticed that some officers were referring to the "advance redoubt" and the "advance battery" as if they were the same. There were two differences. One was semantic. The other was a matter approaching half a mile.

After supper that evening. Pakenham gave Dickson the artillery's role. At the first sound of musketry, he wanted all British artillery to open at once, focusing on the enemy works where they joined the bastion Rennie was to take.[77] He also wanted artillerymen to rush forward with Rennie to drive soft iron spikes into the firing vents of the cannon in the bastion as soon as it was taken, to keep the Yankees from using them again should they have to be abandoned. Dickson actually got five volunteers for that dangerous assignment.[78] After he left, Pakenham continued refining his orders. He wanted Thornton to take the west bank batteries with the bayonet as quietly as possible, upon which he was to fire a signal rocket. Should he fail, he was to show a blue light on the riverbank. British sentinels seeing that would immediately alert Dickson, who would turn his cannons to bombard the west bank batteries to support Thornton.[79]

Unmentioned was what they would do with New Orleans once captured, although the question occurred to everyone in the army. Its cotton alone represented potentially the richest prize of the war, and there was much more in the personal wealth of leading citizens and the contents of stores and warehouses, even if the banks managed to secrete their deposits. Cochrane's appetite for prize money was beyond question, and he had no aversion to plunder or destruction of private property as a retaliatory measure. Yet there were sound reasons for restraint here. Should they conquer and hold the city for any period of time after the inevitable peace, the crown must govern its people. Taking their property would hardly make them placid subjects. Moreover, he and Pakenham knew how quickly plundering could become indiscriminate, and the impossibility of making soldiers understand that gold was gold, whether friend's or foe's. They would immediately take all public property belonging to the United States, but otherwise, to whatever extent the admiral and general considered a policy toward the conquered city, it must be marked by politic restraint.

Hence, neither issued a statement authorizing plunder. Yet neither peremptorily forbade it, either. Soldiers knew the riches of New Orleans, and some felt entitled to a share in return for their hardships, especially after

January 1 gave them hints of the blood it would cost to take Line Jackson. Some company and regimental officers felt the same, especially with peace not far away, and with it the prospect of going on peacetime half pay or worse. On this day, if not before, some officers and men at least informally discussed the potential for spoils and resolved to have it.[80] A few of the more brutish even fantasized of dalliances with city women, whether willing or not. Someone had already coined an alliteration for their hopes of "beauty and booty." Anticipating that possibility, Pakenham intended to give Lambert the job of keeping order in New Orleans once it was taken. But they must take it first.[81]

By nine o'clock Jackson definitely knew an attack was coming in the morning and looked to see his army ready.[82] He walked the length of the line with Major Henry Chotard, talking with the men at their fires as they drank coffee to stay warm. He told them he had done his best to put them in a good position to defend the city, trusting they would acquit themselves well in the moment of trial. He spoke with them at ease, familiarly as with friends and comrades, yet there was no forgetting that he was their commander.[83] He allowed companies on the breastwork to alternate with others in the rear to give the men some rest before morning.[84]

Later that night he got a few precious minutes of sleep on a sofa in his headquarters while several of his staff dozed on the floor. An hour after midnight Rezin Shepherd arrived with Patterson's latest message about the stirrings observed in the British camps and the enemy barges on the riverbank.[85] By that time, with Colonel John Davis on his way, Old Hickory had done all he could do to bolster Morgan, who must do the best he could with what he had.[86] A nervous Major Reid still nurtured doubt, fearful even that the redcoats might actually knock down their "slender mud wall," a disaster they might not survive. Desperate battle seemed certain. He anticipated "many deaths," he wrote that night, praying that it would not be a slaughter.[87]

There was a deathly stillness in town that evening, broken only by the distant boom of artillery. On the line, some men in their letters admitted it, and that the fighting might be desperate, but they believed they could hold the city. "In this manner," one volunteer wrote home, "we await our fate."[88] In the city the legislature seemed confident. It summoned Declouet to appear on Monday, January 9, in the matter of Claiborne's closure of the chamber, which implicitly assumed the city would still be in American hands then.[89]

The spirit of determination spread beyond the city. In Natchez, whose

riches could make it the next target should New Orleans fall, more volunteers went to arms, resolving to give any redcoats who came a reception that
would dissuade them from calling again.[90] On roads throughout the Louisiana countryside, more men were coming to Jackson. As far west as Opelousas, 150 miles distant, men gathered to enlist in the morning and march to
New Orleans. Among them were two brothers named Bowie, Rezin and his
eighteen-year-old brother James.[91]

In faraway Maine, some feared that New Orleans had probably been attacked already.[92] In New York, General James Wilkinson, at that moment
facing the third court-martial of his career, pompously declared that the
city was doomed because former secretary of war Eustis had ignored his
plan for its defense. Eustis shot back that the best hope for the city being
safe was that Wilkinson no longer commanded there.[93]

In Washington, Federalist congressman James Geddes of New York
spoke with Senators Fromentin and Brown, and Congressman Robertson,
who expressed their fears that New Orleans had already fallen. With control of the Mississippi lost, Kentucky and the Ohio Valley would probably
leave the Union for their own economic survival, and the United States, if it
survived at all, would be once more a strip of states confined to the Atlantic
coast. "The prospect of peace I cannot see," Geddes lamented, "and the
means of carrying on the war is, I believe, out of sight of every one."[94]

Among his last orders before going to bed that evening, at eleven p.m.
Pakenham directed that two hundred men go to the front in darkness to repair the battered redoubt on the river road about seven hundred yards from
Jackson's advance bastion so that it could aid in supporting Rennie's assault.
Unfortunately, every spade of earth they lifted to pile on the crude walls left a
hole that filled with seeping water, forcing them to skim the ground with
their tools to carry dripping mud to plaster on the works. They dragged some
cannon into the position, which would be in point-blank range of Jackson's
cannon in his bastion, but had no time to set wooden platforms for all of
them. That done, they simply lay down in the mud to sleep.[95]

That evening, as before all battles, each redcoat made peace with his
fears. Officers wrote what might be their last letters home. They had seen
enough to know what they were about to face. There would be heavy casualties, but they felt confident of success.[96] Fellow officers called Brigade Major
"Wilky" Wilkinson "the little corporal," thanks to his Napoleonic height.
He began writing a letter that discussed the differences of opinion regarding the operation, adding his own preference for the plan as it stood. He put
it unfinished in his uniform pocket along with his copy of the attack order,
expecting to finish it after the battle.[97]

In the 43rd Regiment, Cooke and his fellow soldiers finally traded their spades for their muskets with work on the canal done. They lay on the dew-dampened sod and reflected on what lay ahead. "All was silent," Cooke recalled. "I do not remember ever looking for the first signs of day-break with more intense anxiety."[98] Upon learning of the attack planned for the morning, several men in the light company of the 7th Fusiliers went to Lieutenant Colonel Edward Blakeney's hut and reminded him that their seven-year terms of service had expired weeks before and they should have been discharged before leaving Portsmouth. It could not be helped now, he told them, so they went to Pakenham's tent to petition being excused from the assault, but he was unavailable. They left with no choice but to take part in the attack and risk injury or death despite the fact that they were no longer lawfully soldiers. One of them just got drunk.[99]

Poor Ensign Graves writhed in pain most of the night from the dysentery he had suffered for several days, made worse by all those meals interrupted by Yankee artillery.[100] Lieutenant Colonel Robert Dale of the 93rd expected to be killed in the attack. There were always such premonitions before a battle. He gave a watch and a letter for his wife to the surgeon of his regiment, asking him to see that she got them.[101] Rennie and his friend Lieutenant Norman Pringle discussed their prospects. "I am always hit," said Rennie, which was virtually true, thanks to his reckless audacity. He showed Pringle his few treasures. "In case I should fall to-morrow," he told him, "I beg you will use every endeavour to recover this ring, this brooch with some hair in it, and my watch, and if you survive, deliver them to my sister." Pringle gave his word.[102]

In the darkness, Surtees and his commander inspected the ground they must cover the next day and located the wooden bridges over the ditches they needed to cross, but that shocked him. Other regimental officers should have been doing the same as he, but they were not. On the Peninsula at Badajoz and Nivelle, every company officer did that. Here, however, he felt either apathy or a "fatal security, arising from our too much despising the enemy."[103]

After nightfall, the scene around headquarters at Villeré's was chaotic, yet no one took notice. The 85th, camped nearby, prepared to board the boats, disappointed at being given the west bank sideshow, having hoped to show the "peninsula fire-eaters" that they could perform just as well as men who fought under Wellington's eye.[104] Slave huts still burned, casting too much light not to be noticed by the enemy, and the noise of moving men and boats seemed unduly loud, with workmen yelling, groups of others laughing around their fires to relieve tension, and a few who had rum reveling in it. It was a relief at last to be doing something, but the noise and light all but broadcast their intentions to the enemy. When some went to the river to look for signs of enemy fires on the other side, they found no sentinels posted on their own. Recalling a current slang expression for drunken revelry, Cooke and other subalterns concluded that "there was a screw loose somewhere."[105]

Asleep in the Villeré house, Pakenham might have agreed, but he retired early, his last comments to Harry Smith being about what they would do "when we are in New Orleans."[106] He had wanted the boats in the river and loaded by nine p.m., but midnight passed with most of them still stuck in the canal. At two p.m., Malcolm came to Tylden to say he could get no more through unless they made a dam back near the woods to trap enough river water in the canal to raise its level a foot or more. Tylden drafted some infantry, scoured the plantation for planks and old carts, and in ninety minutes sank the carts in the canal, then fixed the planks to them to make a wall that held back water.[107] The canal level rose to about two feet and the boats began moving, but then the river fell and only what Codrington called "exertion which is beyond belief" could push the boats the last 250 yards.[108] Members of the 85th watched from the banks, pitying the men wading knee-deep through the wet clay and slush.[109]

Almost miraculously, by four a.m., forty-seven boats floated in the Mississippi, but only four of the barges that mounted carronades that were intended to move upriver abreast of Thornton's advance.[110] The 85th began boarding, meeting more delay because the boats had been tethered bow to stern into the river. That forced them to board the tied boat first, walk to its stern, step into the bow of the next, and so on. It was five o'clock before the first nine were ready to go, carrying just three hundred of the 85th and nearly as many more sailors and marines. They would have no cannons but the carronades on the four barges.[111] The officer commanding one of those barges soon confessed that he dreaded the approach of daylight.[112]

The west bank operation was eight hours behind schedule, time they could never hope to regain to carry out the full plan.[113] Codrington thought they should delay another day, although he understood Pakenham's reluctance to postpone again.[114] Looking back a few days later, Tylden agreed, but generously granted that hindsight always allowed a man to judge better "after a business than before."[115] Cochrane had placed Captain Samuel Roberts of *Meteor* in charge overall.[116] He was young and daring, ideal for the assignment.[117] He and Thornton could have waited for more boats to load, but dawn rushed at them. Their oars muffled to dampen the sound of their rowing, the boats pulled into the current shortly before daylight.[118]

Back at Kingston, a Jamaican newspaper had forecast that Pakenham would take New Orleans today, January 8, 1815.[119]

In Washington, Congressman Brown could not sleep that night, dreading the next mail that might relieve his fear or confirm his gloomy anticipation.[120]

A few miles below New Orleans the first glimmers of light broke slowly in the east. Mist rose from the ground between the armies.

It was going to be another chilly morning.[121]

Seventeen

"We Shall Have a Warm Day"

The British were up at four a.m. in darkness. Since midnight Dickson had tried to get carronades and eighteen-pounders to what some called the "mud battery" on the left beside the levee, but no road and too many ditches made worrisome delays. He got the carronades placed by 4:30 but doubted the eighteens would make it, while Lieutenant Cooke and others had worked through the night readying the battery for them to fire on the McCarty buildings and support Rennie's advance.[1]

Well before dawn Cooke sensed shadowy forms passing silently, a detachment of the 95th moving up to watch the enemy and support Rennie. Soon the light companies of the 7th, the 43rd, and the 93rd Highlanders in their round Scots bonnets passed, about 240 in all. He saw his friend Lieutenant Duncan Campbell of the 43rd and asked their mission. "Be hanged if I know," said Campbell. When Cooke suggested that he leave behind his ornate blue short jacket, Campbell joked that "I will never peal [*sic*] for any American." They embraced as friends and the light companies disappeared into the gloom.[2]

Across the field, it was a short night's sleep for Mullins's 44th. They had to be up before the rest of the army to collect the fascines and ladders, so sergeants roused them before three a.m., and by 3:30 they were ready. Officers dressed in darkness and went to their places. Mullins took his place at the head of the column in a blue greatcoat over his red uniform waistcoat to keep out the cold, a quaint round cap on his head. By four a.m. he was ready to start.[3]

Engineer Tapp awaited inside the redoubt to distribute the ladders and fascines, but he did not hear the 44th's boots approach some minutes later on the soft wet clover. Mullins gave no indication that he knew what he came for was within. Both Johnston and Debbeigg knew the fascines and ladders were there, but neither said a word to him.[4] There could not have been a worse time for his personality to ripen its deadly fruit.

Now Mullins confused the redoubt with the advance battery some distance in his front, even though the map in his pocket would have erased any confusion had he looked at it. He sent a sergeant inside the redoubt to get a guide, and both men soon emerged, but, incredibly, neither said anything about the fascines and ladders scattered in the dark interior, even though Lieutenant A. M'Auley believed it impossible for anyone to go in without seeing them. Mullins himself had been there on January 2, and the matérials were there then.[5]

Now confusion dined on his subordinates' reluctance to speak to him. He sent Adjutant R. Barry ahead with one hundred men to help the 95th Rifles provide cover fire when the rest rushed the enemy works, then moved the 44th forward again as the guide took them to a ditch on the Chalmette plantation and the now-dismantled advance battery. That convinced some officers that the fascines and ladders must be there, yet when Knight and Debbeigg left the redoubt, they knew better.[6]

"Col. Mullins is forgetting the Ladders and Fascines," Knight told Debbeigg.

"They are here," he replied. "It is his own affair, he is such a man that no man dares speak to him."

Arguing that both the success of the attack and the honor of the regiment were at risk, Knight said he would speak with Mullins regardless of his personality, but when he sent a sergeant forward with a message, the colonel told the man not to bother him and to tell Knight to mind his own business. Knight could do no more.[7] It was not a good start to the day.

Worse yet, no one awakened Pakenham to tell him that Thornton was hours behind schedule in crossing the river. Harry Smith and others knew from experience that disturbing the general while he slept could be "as bad as the loss of a leg," so once again an officer's personality kept subordinates from bringing him vital information. Only when the general arose at five a.m. did he learn of Thornton's delay. Pakenham believed that Gibbs and Keane were in position now and would be in enemy artillery range when daylight revealed them. There was no time to change plans in response to the unexpected, although half an hour later at breakfast he did briefly consider canceling Thornton's movement entirely, since he could not possibly take Morgan's guns in time to turn them on Jackson's line simultaneously with Gibbs and Keane's attack. On reflection he concluded that even a late Thornton could make a diversion aiding his main assault.

"I have twice deferred the attack," he fretted to his staff. It was too late to do it again. Soon the Americans would see his columns and open fire before they could be withdrawn. A lone frontal assault might be costly, but it had to be made.[8] Dickson told him there was no time for the artillery intended for Thornton to cross the river now, so those guns and others could be gathered into a twelve-gun battery at De La Ronde's to go forward in support of Gibbs.[9] Just then Tylden arrived to report that Mullins ought now to be in position—which he certainly was not. Full daylight was less than ninety minutes away. The general could wait no longer. He sent Smith to Crawley's battery near De La Ronde's with an order to fire the signal rocket.[10]

During the next few minutes Pakenham seemed impatient for it all to commence. Then he mounted and set out, accompanied by Tylden and his aide Captain Duncan MacDougall. Riding beside the general, Tylden thought he seemed apprehensive, as if he dreaded what was coming as he rode toward the front.[11] When they passed Lambert's position, Pakenham spoke to no one but went to the main road by the levee.[12] By this time Thornton was supposed to have Patterson's batteries in hand and aimed at the right of Jackson's line, ready to open fire when Keane launched Rennie and followed up with the bulk of the 93rd and a company each from the 7th and the 43rd.[13] Now Pakenham told Keane in person to move diagonally to his right across the field to hit the enemy works just to the left of Gibbs while Rennie continued forward to take the bastion. That meant that if Rennie should gain a foothold, he would have no backup to push over the main defenses. He would be on his own, but neither general told him.[14]

Mullins and his lead company reached the advance battery expecting to find Tapp waiting for him. While his men lay down on the clover and some fell asleep, the colonel looked first for Tapp and then spent half an hour searching in and around the ruined works without finding a single fascine. He angrily accused Johnston of misleading him about their location, and Johnston no doubt tried to remind Mullins of what he had told him the day before. Their heated words escalated as Debbeigg came forward and risked telling their commander that he was surprised Mullins did not know the location of the ladders and fascines, since he had Emmett's note and map. Still Mullins refused to listen and belligerently shot back, "Sir, I have the command." Debbeigg simply turned around and walked back to the rear.

At last Mullins cooled and tacitly admitted his confusion and asked Johnston where the things were to be found, and Johnston told him. At the back of the column, Wilkinson rode up and encountered Lieutenant Knight.

"Good God, did no one tell Col. Mullins of his mistake?" the major exclaimed. Knight detailed Mullins's rebuffs and then Wilkinson went forward to ask Mullins just where he thought the fascines and ladders were to be found. The colonel stubbornly insisted that he had expected to find them at the advance battery.[15]

Later that day Dickson characterized Mullins's mistake as "the most extraordinary blunder," as indeed it was, an almost inexplicable series of errors attributable more than anything else to his conceit and irascibility.[16] Pakenham arrived at De La Ronde's just as Wilkinson returned to inform Gibbs of the problem. When Gibbs told him that Mullins would have to return to the redoubt to collect the fascines and ladders, Tylden saw "astonishment & utter disappointment" in Pakenham's face. He immediately sent Tylden to see if the 44th had picked up the materials yet, while privately the adjutant was already thinking to himself "God knows why" Pakenham had chosen Mullins to spearhead the assault in the first place.[17] It was not the last of his commander's orders that he would question that day.

It was nearly six a.m. now, with the attack signal imminent. Lieutenant Colonel William Paterson's 21st Fusiliers came up with the rear of the 44th at the advance battery. Since they stood rearmost of the column, Mullins asked him to send his men to collect the fascines and ladders, which would save a few minutes' time. Paterson declined, unwilling to be responsible for any delay in the attack plan. Mullins then had no choice but to order Debbeigg to take three hundred from the 44th on the errand while his remaining men stayed at the advance battery position.[18] As he began to realize the consequences of his own folly, Mullins in a near-panic told a sergeant "for God's sake" to go find Captain Wilkinson and ask him if there was a chance of their being on time after all with the fascines and ladders. The sergeant soon met Wilkinson and Gibbs on their way to the scene, while Mullins himself ran back to the redoubt.[19]

"Move on Grenadiers," Debbiegg shouted as his men turned and double-quicked to the rear past the 21st.[20] On the way he encountered Gibbs and explained as best he could what had happened. Gibbs ordered him to get to the redoubt as fast as possible, then rode on to find Mullins.[21] Accompanied by Wilkinson and Tapp, Debbeigg reached the redoubt in ten minutes. Tapp took another twenty to distribute fascines to one party of men, then joined Debbeigg as they ran toward the front while others handed ladders to Knight's company, which had a lot of distance to cover with the fascine party well ahead.[22]

Then the Congreve went up. Everyone remembered that rocket. At the mud battery, Cooke's men stood in a circle watching it whiz backward and

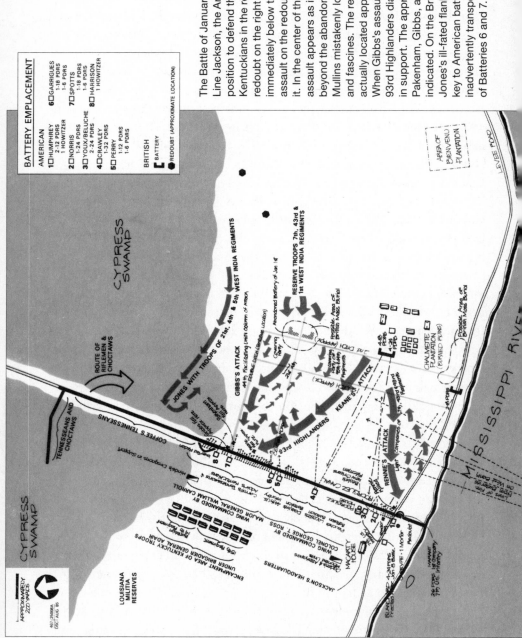

The Battle of January 8, 1815. On the left of Line Jackson, the American units are in position to defend the line, with Adair's Kentuckians in the rear in reserve. The new redoubt on the right of the line appears immediately below the levee road. Rennie's assault on the redoubt points directly toward it. In the center of the map General Gibbs's assault appears as it passed through and beyond the abandoned battery where Mullins mistakenly looked for the ladders and fascines. The redoubt where they were actually located appears well to the rear. When Gibbs's assault faltered, Keane led the 93rd Highlanders diagonally across the field in support. The approximate positions where Pakenham, Gibbs, and Keane fell are indicated. On the British right, Captain Jones's ill-fated flanking effort appears. The key to American batteries far right inadvertently transposes the commanders of Batteries 6 and 7.

BATTERY EMPLACEMENT

AMERICAN

1 □ HUMPHREY
2-12 PDRS
1 HOWITZER

2 □ NORRIS
1-24 PDRS

3 □ YOUX/BELUCHE
2-24 PDRS

4 □ CRAWLEY
1-32 PDRS

5 □ PERRY
1-6 PDRS

6 □ GARRIGUES
1-18 PDRS
1-6 PDRS

7 □ SPOTTS
1-18 PDRS

8 □ HARRISON
1 HOWITZER

BRITISH

▐ BATTERY

● REDOUBT (APPROXIMATE LOCATION)

forward so erratically that they feared it might land on them before it finally flew overhead and into the Mississippi.[23] Dickson, Burgoyne, and Hill were on their way to find Pakenham when they saw the rocket arch up at a high angle and fly over their heads toward the river. They turned immediately for De La Ronde's to see if the attack had truly started. When he arrived, Dickson expected his artillery to have opened fire, but the field was oddly quiet. He climbed to the second-floor gallery at De La Ronde's for a good view of the coming assault, but Gibbs was gone and no one could explain the delay. Dickson left for the redoubt to find Gibbs and was halfway there when he heard his guns open at last. He just made out Gibbs's column advancing as he closed on it, but all he saw of the enemy were muzzle flashes through the fog. Seeing that troubled him. There was too much light, he thought, and from that moment it would only grow brighter. More light meant more casualties.[24]

Before Knight and the ladders reached the fascine bearers, enemy artillery opened on them, and by the time they reached their comrades, Debbeigg found it already becoming seriously destructive. Knight saw men going down all around him as the growing light allowed the Americans to make every shot tell. Four grenadiers carrying a ladder fell to a single shell. On reaching the fascine party, Knight pressed forward one hundred paces to find order already eroding. Some men dropped their ladders and ran into other regiments, while others unslung their muskets and fired pointlessly at invisible enemies behind the breastwork. Some even fired on redcoats in front of them as officers struggled with indifferent success to get them to cease firing.[25] Mullins went back to the rear to urge the men forward as the American artillery fire intensified.

The 21st had kept moving, followed by the 4th, and now they were ahead of the stalled 44th. They saw Mullins, Debbeigg, and confused parties of four and five rushing up from behind with fascines.[26] Suddenly individuals and ragged groups of the 44th rushed past the 21st on its left in an informal column four abreast, but in their hurry to return to the front the 44th's officers never got them properly formed again.[27] Tylden saw Debbeigg's disorderly party moving forward, then reported to Pakenham that the 44th should soon launch the assault. In fact, its discipline had dissolved in dim light, on unfamiliar ground, with the 21st blocking its road.[28]

Then the grenadiers with the ladders passed the fascine bearers. Mullins led them through a gap between the abandoned January 1 batteries and into a field of cane stubble and clover broken by drains that defeated maintaining organization, especially for men carrying burdens.[29] Some ditches they vaulted, but others were four or five feet wide and had to be waded.[30] They stumbled over cannonballs and shells and a few unretrieved bodies from the January 1 bombardment.[31] The 95th covering party went ahead of them, ordered to halt at a ditch and spread left and right along its lip, then advance when the 21st passed the gap behind them.[32] When they reached the ditch, however, they moved obliquely to the right and kept going almost to the cypress wood before catching their error.[33] Unfortunately, Mullins and his part of the 44th followed them. Seeing that, Gibbs sent his naval aide Lieutenant Philip George Haymes to have him halt and face left to return to the road. At that moment, Debbeigg's fascine party came up and collided with the ladder bearers, then both stumbled into the remnant of the 44th at the advance battery.

Everything was out of order now with the ladders on their way to reach the ditch before the fascines. Chaos broke out in both detachments. Mullins ran to a fascine party and ordered it to rush ahead of the ladders. A sergeant at his side saw men with ladders badly spread out by the length of their burdens. Some parties maintained order, but overall most was confusion.[34] One fascine group never formed ranks. Another just kept marching in the wrong direction.[35] Gibbs rode to see Mullins as he struggled to re-form the 44th and began passionately reproaching him for his conduct. An aide sent by Pakenham arrived just then, and Gibbs angrily sent him back to their commander to inform him that Mullins had compromised their attack. Then he sent Mullins to the front of his regiment.[36] At the same time he ordered Major John Whittaker and two companies of the 21st forward at double time to try to get over the canal and up the parapet any way they could until the fascines and ladders came forward.[37] "I could just observe the day begin," Lieutenant R. Phelan of the 44th recalled, but a thick fog still spread over the river and rose from the plain. Even with the fresh breeze, it would be a while before wind and sun cleared the air.[38]

When British artillery began firing on the left center of the American line, Jackson's batteries and Patterson's across the river answered, both sides at first firing blindly in the fog.[39] Still, Cooke and comrades of the 43rd's light company, waiting to follow Rennie, saw occasional cannonballs from across the river fly through the cocoon of fog around them to land short and bounce or roll over the ground "like so many cricket-balls."[40] Across the field in front of Gibbs's column, cannonballs struck sparks as they hit the ground and the fog softened the flashes into eerie blue lights in front of the 44th.[41]

As he approached the scene, Pakenham saw the rear of Gibbs's column moving as planned. At first he assumed all was well, and spoke glowingly to his aide Major Duncan MacDougall of his confidence in the 44th in particular.[42] Then they heard musketry in Gibbs's column, and as they came closer saw men of that regiment running to the rear. Some were still carrying their fascines, while others dropped them. "For shame," Pakenham yelled at them. He pointed toward Line Jackson and shouted for them to "recollect you are British soldiers, this is the road you ought to take." In their panic, they ignored him.[43] Racing on, he found the column stalled in confusion. Along the length of it he saw men dropping fascines and ladders to fire their muskets. After Jackson's artillery brought down some of them, the rest dropped everything. The sight disgusted Tylden, and in a few moments he was more chagrined to see them break and run for the rear. Ahead of the 44th, the 95th also began a confused firing despite having no sure targets.[44]

Pakenham instantly realized his predicament. Everything had depended on simultaneous surprises on both sides of the river. All hope of that was shattered now, and perhaps he began to realize the impracticability of such a strategy in such a situation. He had expected Gibbs to take the enemy works before Jackson could react, but that idea evaporated immediately. If the column did not get going now, it would become a fat target for enemy artillery. Pakenham's mood transformed to anger in an instant, and as he spurred his horse to a gallop to find Gibbs, Dickson heard the general exclaim as if speaking to himself: "Lost from want of courage."[45]

A waning sliver of moon was out now, largely unseen for the low morning fog. The night had been unusually cold, and sounds carried far, but the Americans heard nothing of the enemy's earlier confusion other than occasional muffled murmurs on the night breeze.[46] At the McCarty house, Jackson's horse had waited saddled and ready since four a.m. After a bad day and night with his dysentery, he was up and had already walked the length of his line again. Well before dawn, pickets reported enemy movement in their front, and captured a few. One Kentucky picket mistook a redcoat counterpart nearby for a fellow Yankee in the gloom and chided him that he was out of position. When the redcoat lifted his musket to shoot, the picket snatched it from his hands and clubbed him with it before running back to safety.[47]

Jackson's drums assembled the men and then they marched to the breastwork, barely taking their places before the action commenced. Many were at their posts to see the signal rocket fly toward the river.[48] Old Hickory was at headquarters when it went up at about 6:20.[49] After a minute of what one soldier called "frightful silence," enemy artillery opened on the McCarty house. One of the first balls passed through the room where Old Hickory was sharing a cup of coffee with his staff. It struck a masonry wall and a flying brick knocked Chotard to the floor with a severe contusion, although he was soon up. Jackson grabbed his sword from a chair. "Come on," he told them. "We shall have a warm day."[50] In moments he was on the parapet to order his batteries to open fire.

A light breeze thinned the fog, and through it he caught the first shadowy images of ranks of the enemy approaching in deep columns. It was a sight not to forget: the redcoats of the 21st Fusiliers; the dark blue facings and waistcoats of the 4th King's Own; the black shakos of the 44th East Essex above their yellow-trimmed red jackets; the 95th Rifles in dramatic deep-green tunics. At their heads came the drummers in yellow and white, and flag bearers with a rainbow of regimental colors fluttering atop their staffs. It was at once thrilling and terrifying, the ghosts of a thousand times a thousand long-dead heroes gazing with Jackson at a scene eternal since the time men first mixed their war with ceremony. As if in response, Jackson's band played "Hail Columbia" and the "Marseillaise" and thereafter "Yankee Doodle" throughout the rest of the morning.[51] Cheering erupted from both sides. Two chaplains asked Old Hickory what they could do. He told them to "pray every minute."[52]

That morning his forces totaled on paper just over 4,800 of all arms: 154 at the eight batteries; 1,562 with Carroll holding the center; and 813 with Coffee spread along the left, with 526 Kentuckians under Slaughter behind them in reserve. Jackson's right under Colonel Ross anchored on the 7th and 44th Infantry detachments, 735 strong, along with 365 under Plauché, about 40 of Beale's men, 175 in the colored battalion, perhaps 85 marines, and several dragoon companies. They had to defend a line 5,100 feet from end to end. Carroll occupied 350 yards of the center, Coffee 616 yards on the left, and Ross the 573-yard right. Slaughter extended in a line behind Carroll.[53] The woods and swamp protected Jackson's left from major threat, but he put Louisiana militia at intervals along the edge of the cypresses as far back as the Piernas canal to watch for enemy flanking movements, posting a guard a quarter mile back from the earthwork and sentinels at the woods to prevent anyone leaving the field.[54]

There was no place for mounted men on the breastwork, of course, so Jackson ordered Hinds's dragoons to a position on the Delery plantation just a pistol shot from the works. There they would be ready with their mounts to move as directed, which made some grumble at being "merely silent spectators."[55] Old Hickory put Ogden's fifty Louisiana dragoons immediately behind McCarty's and moved the fifty-man Attakapas dragoons and Captain Chauveau's thirty Orleans cavalry to grounds immediately adjacent to McCarty's.[56] He had placed these reserves exactly where he might just need them.

Out on Jackson's line, soldiers watched the enemy signal traverse much of the length of their works before it fell into the river.[57] Hearing the rocket, Carroll grabbed his sword and ran out of his headquarters to mount his horse in such a hurry that he forgot to put on his boots.[58] At the breastwork he found his men already in place, as were Coffee's at their log defenses on his left. General Thomas had been so ill the night before that he could hardly mount his horse now. He and his staff would reach the line sometime after the action opened, but Adair would command the Kentuckians that day.[59] He formed them in two lines and marched them to within fifty yards of the breastworks. The fog still gathered thickly there, and he could only judge what happened in front of him by sound.[60] Then came the first enemy artillery. Men heard a sound they likened to a high wind rushing through a field of ripe corn as British shot and shell flew past them overhead, and then came the sound of enemy drums beating the cadence of their advance. Finally, emerging from the fog in the distance, they saw and heard a confused mass of redcoats "yelling like devils."[61]

Wearing his gray overcoat against the morning chill, Rennie started up the river road at a run on seeing the signal rocket, and moved so rapidly that he overran and captured a few advance Yankee pickets.[62] Simpson's light company of the 21st led, followed by men from the 7th and 93rd.[63] The rest of the 93rd and the 1st West India remained to their rear, originally intended to follow up but suddenly redirected by Pakenham to cross the field to support Gibbs.[64] Running from chimneys to plantation buildings for cover, Rennie raced forward, drawing fire from Humphreys and the bastion as well as rifle and musketry from Beale and others. Men fell almost immediately. A soldier who had protested the night before at being held past his expired enlistment was hit in the forehead and fell dead at an officer's feet.[65] Rennie's wounds from Washington and Baltimore were not yet entirely healed, and within moments he earned anew his reputation for being hit in every action as shrapnel tore away part of the calf of one of his legs.[66]

Somehow he continued onward, then turned left and ran to the riverbank, putting the levee between his men and the fire from Jackson's line. That exposed him to *Louisiana*'s guns and Patterson's batteries, but the light companies sped over a mud bank wide enough to let them run several abreast, and enemy gunners could not take good aim.[67] Bayonets fixed, the light companies fired not a shot.[68] There was just enough light now for one of Jackson's staff to see Rennie emerge from the mist one hundred yards in front of the bastion, racing at the head of what appeared to be two hundred or more redcoats still partially concealed by the levee.[69] Jackson saw them. So did Davezac at his side. He feared that Lieutenant Ross, with a mere fifty men of the 7th and a brace of brass cannon, could not possibly hold the bastion.[70]

Rennie's headlong rush impressed even the defenders for its "undaunted bravery."[71] Four days later Gabriel Winter declared that "never did more brave men make an attack."[72] From Beale's position above and behind the bastion, one of his men marveled at the "impetuous fury" of Rennie's charge, and another spoke of "intrepidity which has never been surpassed."[73] A Mississippian witness gave full credit that "it is impossible for any men to have acted braver" and that "such bravery could not but excite the admiration, even of an enemy."[74]

Captain Humphreys opened on the approaching column with steamboatman Shreve stepping up to help working a gun.[75] Their fire quickly discouraged the 5th West India, coming along behind Rennie carrying scaling ladders. Cold still hampered them, and this was their first action. Putting inexperienced men in the forefront of an assault was at best a cynical decision to save more experienced—and less expendable—white troops for the main effort. It was also self-defeating. It took elite units to make targets of themselves carrying ladders rather than muskets. Cooke believed that men who would carry and place ladders under a heavy fire were capable of anything, but the West Indians had neither training nor experience. Now it cost Pakenham as they dropped their ladders and fell flat on the mud to avoid Humphreys's shelling. They never picked them up again.[76]

When Rennie disappeared briefly behind the levee, Humphreys held fire.[77] By that time Rennie's command moved at a full trot. Lieutenant Ross barely had time to fire two rounds from his guns before the British swarmed up to their embrasures.[78] With Captain Simpson's company, Rennie reached the moat first. Hesitation now meant lives. Rennie pressed on, waded the ditch, then clambered up the muddy sloping face of the bastion toward a gun embrasure. No wonder his friend Lieutenant Norman Pringle of the 21st thought him "one of the bravest soldiers that ever drew a sword."[79] Simpson regarded it as a formidable position, as strong as any defender could desire.[80] The outer slope of its parapet briefly shielded the attackers at the forefront from defenders' fire, but the companies behind them took hits, and officers went down.

With pistols in both hands, Rennie pushed through the embrasure, firing into the crowd of defenders as his men followed or swarmed through another embrasure and over the wall itself. What followed was "a short but very severe contest," in Simpson's words, while a subaltern of the 43rd described his comrades as "seized with a frenzy."[81] Major Tatum at first thought Lieutenant Ross's defenders fell back in disgraceful confusion, but

Tylden later heard from Rennie's survivors that the Americans never wavered.[82] Yankees on Line Jackson saw Ross's men resist and take casualties.[83] Both of Lieutenant de Marans's ears were bleeding from the concussion of his guns and Humphreys's battery, his hearing permanently shattered.[84] A private of the 7th fell dead, and Rennie's pistols killed both a corporal and an orderly sergeant.[85] The sergeant was Isham Lewis, Jefferson's nephew who fled to Louisiana after the brutal murder of his brother's slave. In the muddy bastion by the levee he found atonement.

Stunned by the force of Rennie's assault, most of the defenders crossed the plank over the canal in good order to join Beale on the main works above and behind the bastion, to begin firing on the redcoats below.[86] With dazzling swiftness, Rennie had taken a foothold in the Yankee works, the first time the British took anything from the Americans on land. It happened so quickly that the men rearmost in his column were not yet engaged. Now Simpson's men turned the six-pounder on the left of the bastion to fire at the main earthwork to support Gibbs.[87] All was according to plan, here at least, and Simpson believed that at that instant the battle was going in Pakenham's favor.[88]

With the enemy off balance, this was no moment for pause. If another push got the light companies over the main defense, and if Keane gave them support, they might exploit this breach into a decisive movement giving them the main road and a chance to isolate Jackson from the city. Of course, Hinds, Ogden, and others waited in reserve beyond the earthworks, as well as Villeré on Line Dupré, but bursting through here just as Gibbs struck Carroll could force Jackson to withdraw. The resulting retreat under front and flank fire could turn to confusion and then panic. If Pakenham sent Lambert forward as well, the Yankees might not stop retreating at Line Dupré, or even New Orleans itself. After three weeks of disappointments, Rennie's success at the bastion might be the open door to a victory of staggering consequence.

A brief lull followed, which some believed to be a Yankee ruse to lure the British into coming over the parapet into a trap.[89] In fact, when news of the bastion's fall reached Jackson, he immediately ordered reinforcements to his right and had his mounted units close at hand if he needed more. They were uneasy behind the lines thus far. A cornet in Hinds's company thought theirs a more dangerous spot than the front line, for it seemed to him that hundreds of enemy cannonballs and rockets flew above their heads.[90] Events moved so swiftly, however, that the fight for the bastion would be decided before any reinforcements could arrive.[91]

More than tactical advantage impelled Rennie to push on. His men made easy targets for musketry from the main works above and behind them, and more of the redcoats began falling. The bastion was also open on its river side, so Patterson's batteries could fire directly at them.[92] Thanks to the fog, his gunners could see neither Rennie nor Mullins some 1,600 yards distant, so their aim was off and their balls and shells fell a hundred yards or more behind the British advance columns.[93] Rennie could not know that from his vantage, however, and it appeared that he must move on or risk annihilation. He had no time to reload his pistols. Drawing his sword, he called to his men to follow him.[94] With what Simpson called "singular intrepidity," Rennie led them across the plank over the canal and climbed the steep, slippery slope of the main defense, clawing his way toward Humphreys's embrasures.[95] One more push promised victory.

It would be his last push. With Captain George Henry of the 7th and another officer, Rennie reached an embrasure, then shouted to those behind him that "the enemy's works are ours." He yelled something else that to the defenders sounded like "surrender, you d——d Yankee Rascals, or you shall all be put to death."[96] The lumber miller William Carr Withers was waiting for him. A friend claimed of Withers's marksmanship that he never missed his target. He had watched Rennie come through the lower bastion and resolved to bring him down if he got an opportunity. Ramming two balls down the barrel of his rifle, he stood just behind one of Humphreys's guns. As fortune decreed, that was the embrasure Rennie chose to enter. Withers stood barely a dozen feet before him when Rennie's head appeared in the embrasure as he climbed above its sill to demand surrender and yell back to his comrades that "the day is ours."

"Not yet," shouted Withers. He pulled his trigger, and at that range he needed no marksman's skill.[97] One or both balls liquefied Rennie's left eye as they plowed into his brain, rendering superfluous another defender's body thrust with a pike.[98] Even enemies credited Rennie's singular courage. "He was certainly a man of uncommon bravery," Tatum said a few hours later.[99] Coincidentally, Captain Henry fell on the earthwork at the same time, killed by a bullet through an eye.[100] Lieutenant Pringle now had a promise to honor.

Few got as far as Rennie before Yankee fire pinned them down as helpless targets. Beale's riflemen simply held their rifles above their heads and pointed them downward into the bastion to hit the occasional redcoat, and then *Louisiana* opened on them again.[101] Simpson and others crouching in the moat looked in vain for support from Keane. Even then he thought events might have seen a different outcome if they had been strongly reinforced. Taking the bastion gave them a route around Jackson's flank via a

Vice Admiral Sir Alexander F. I. Cochrane, originator of
the expedition. *National Portrait Gallery, London*

New Orleans in 1803, looking down Levee Street, by John L. Boqueta de Woiseri.
A flag flies over Fort St. Charles at right. *Historic New Orleans Collection*

Major General Sir John Keane achieved a stunning surprise on December 23, leading to a tantalizing "what if" that remains unsettled. Portrait painted circa 1839, when he was Baron Keane of Ghuznee.

British Library, London

Hot-tempered Major General Samuel Gibbs (right), senior British brigade commander, stands beside Major General Edward Pakenham in their monument at St. Paul's Cathedral. He suffered a horrible death.

St. Paul's Cathedral, Londc

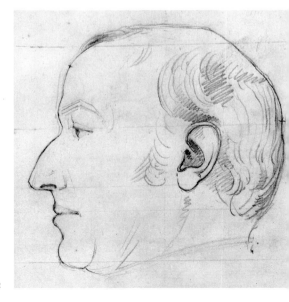

Rear Admiral Edward Codrington, Cochrane's capable flag captain, worked ably keeping the army supplied from the fleet but fell out with his difficult commander.

National Portrait Gallery, London

Colonel William Thornton commanded the British advance despite wounds old and new. Perhaps only careless delays by others kept him from routing Jackson's army.

National Portrait Gallery, London

Major Edward Nicolls was a veteran of one hundred fights and more than one hundred wounds, almost too unbelievable to be real, yet he was, and daring to a fault. Portrait painted circa 1855 after his honorary promotion to general.

Royal Marines Barracks, Stonehouse, Plymouth, UK

Major General Sir John Lambert led the British reserve and was left to command the army after Pakenham and Gibbs fell. He oversaw the withdrawal, and refused to join Cochrane in another campaign for New Orleans.

National Portrait Gallery, London

Major General Sir Edward Pakenham inherited command of the land operations and found himself forced to make the best of a bad situation. His own misjudgments helped lead to defeat and his own death.

Major General Andrew Jackson used luck and great judgment to forge America's most stunning victory. The above is a miniature painted in New Orleans by Jean Francois de la Vallee in 1815 and presented to Edward Livingston on April 1, 1815.

Bard College, Montgomery Place Collection,
Annandale-on-Hudson, New York

Governor William C. C. Claiborne had to combat a discordant population, a combative legislature, and a spiteful Jackson but managed to forge enough unity and resolve to rally New Orleanians to their own defense.

Historic New Orleans Collection

Edward Livingston became Jackson's chief volunteer aide, earning the praise of many and the loathing of others. He played a crucial role in bringing the Baratarian smugglers into the army.

Historic New Orleans Collection

French-born mayor Nicholas Girod barely spoke English yet worked effectively with Claiborne and Jackson in raising local militia to defend his city and arming volunteers who arrived without muskets.

Historic New Orleans Collection

Brigadier General John Coffee was Jackson's most trusted commander. His Tennessee volunteers arrived just in time to help possibly save the city from falling to General Keane on December 23.

Historic New Orleans Collection

Major General William Carroll brought more Tennesseans in time for the battle, tired, hungry, and barely clothed, but they held the left of Jackson's line and helped repulse Gibbs's assaults.

Historic New Orleans Collection

Brigadier General John Adair had fought in the Revolution and commanded Kentucky's militia, which he led to New Orleans ill-equipped and unarmed. Their performance there would embroil him in an argument with Jackson.

Kentucky Historical Society, Frankfort

Rear Admiral Pulteney Malcolm brought Keane's brigade to Louisiana and performed hands-on service in the landing at Bayou Bienvenue, thereafter organizing funneling men and material to the army on the field.

National Portrait Gallery, London

Admiral Malcolm's own sketch showing the line of small boats conveying Keane's soldiers from Lake Borgne up the bayou to the Villeré plantation.

Malcolm Papers, Clements Library, University of Michigan

Commodore Daniel T. Patterson began preparing New Orleans for defense before Jackson arrived, and his gunboats on Lake Borgne sacrificed themselves to buy vital time.

Naval History and Heritage Command, Washington, DC

Major General Jacques Villeré commanded the first division of Louisiana militia and failed to block the Bienvenue bayou, which brought Keane to his plantation and home. He later served well in command of Line Dupré.

Historic New Orleans Collection

Secretary of War James Monroe strove tirelessly in the capital to get men and weaponry to New Orleans in time to aid Jackson, but obstacles and ineptitude saw thousands of muskets arrive too late. Portrait by Samuel F. B. Morse, circa 1819.

White House Historical Association, Washington, DC

President James Madison agreed to offer pardons for all crimes to Baratarian smugglers and privateers who enlisted with Jackson's forces, giving Old Hickory scores of irreplaceable artillerists. Portrait by John Vanderlyn in 1816.

White House Historical Association, Washington, DC

ABOVE LEFT: The only known portrait of Jean Laffite, executed by someone who claimed to have known him, this sketch was made sometime prior to 1874. It may bear no resemblance to Laffite and could be pure invention.

Galveston, Daily News, *September 19, 1926*

ABOVE RIGHT: This ghostly miniature purporting to be Pierre Laffite was reputedly found in 1925 among items surfaced belonging to General David B. Morgan and supposed to have been painted in France in the late 1790s.

New Orleans, Times-Picayune, *August 23, 1925*

Brigadier General David Bannister Morgan, earnest but inept commander of Louisiana militia defending the west bank of the Mississippi, repeatedly failed to obey Jackson's orders promptly and put the army at peril.

Louisiana State Museum, New Orleans

Lieutenant William Hole of the *Trave* commanded one of the boats that attacked the American gunboats on Lake Borgne, and painted this watercolor of the affair. He later commanded a boat accompanying Thornton's attack on the west bank.

Historic New Orleans Collection

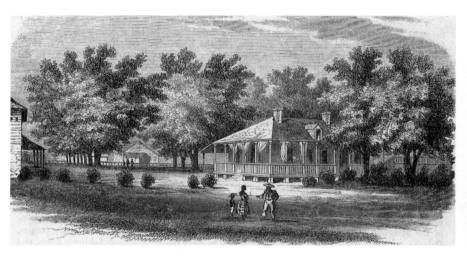

An 1868 woodcut of Conseil, the home of General Jacques Villeré, which became headquarters of the British army. Major René Gabriel Villeré jumped over the veranda rail to escape and bring news of the British landing to Jackson.

Historic New Orleans Collection

Major Jean Baptiste Plauché commanded the Battalion d'Orleans, which was made up of a number of independent companies, including the free black volunteers.

Louisiana Digital Library

An 1861 sketch of the McCarty house that bears some resemblance to its 1814–1815 appearance, when it was Jackson's headquarters on the field behind Line Jackson. A damaged upper floor and gallery have been removed.

Historic New Orleans Collection

An April 1861 sketch of the remains of the Rodriguez Canal, which by that time was much leveled and eroded. In the background stands the unfinished battle monument that remained incomplete until 1908.

Historic New Orleans Collection

An 1868 woodcut of Major Pierre Lacoste's house, which was severely damaged during the British occupation but later rebuilt much to its original appearance.

Historic New Orleans Collection

Ensign George R. Gleig, best known as the Subaltern, wrote probably the two most influential and quoted British memoirs from the War of 1812. This postwar sketch shows him around 1832 as chaplain of the Chelsea Hospital. *National Portrait Gallery, London*

Lieutenant Colonel Alexander Dickson commanded Pakenham's artillery and served him well, despite his own doubts about his commander's decisions. He appears in an engraving made late in 1815 following his knighthood.

National Portrait Gallery, London

Captain James Alexander Gordon, the daring and capable commander of the *Seahorse*, who kept up the spirits of seamen and soldiers and climbed trees with a wooden leg. This Andrew Morton portrait shows him late in life as an admiral.

National Portrait Gallery, London

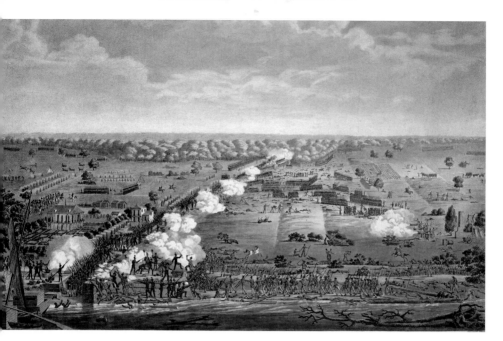

Jean-Hyacinthe Laclotte's 1818 bird's-eye view "Defeat of the British Army" shows the morning battle on the east bank on January 8, 1815, with Rennie's storming of the American redoubt in the foreground.   *Historic New Orleans Collection*

A woodcut engraving dating from 1882 or earlier inaccurately depicts the death of Major Rennie at left as he surmounts the American redoubt. To his right, Majors Henry and King fall as well.

Historic New Orleans Collection

n an early example of use of the battle to narket consumer goods, this snuff box top epicts General Pakenham's death at center s he falls from his horse, presumably ictim to the American cannon at right.

Historic New Orleans Collection

The song that helped create the enduring American myth of the Kentucky rifleman. One of several early broadside versions of "The Hunters of Kentucky," circa 1821.

Filson Historical Society, Louisville, Kentucky

Engraver William Charles of Philadelphia probably made this satirical print, "John Bull's Naval Heroes," immediately after the war. It lampoons British defeats including New Orleans, and shows Pakenham (4) standing at center and Keane (5) mounted next to him.

Historic New Orleans Collection

narrow opening between the levee and the riverbank. Troops might have used it in the moments after Ross's retreat from the bastion, but confusion had already set in on Pakenham's right, and the generals' attention was focused there. There would be no support.

Fearful of a counterattack, British officers tried a ruse for time, shouting at the Yankees to stay put or they would shoot men captured when they first took the bastion.[102] The redcoats held the bastion and its six-pounders for only five minutes, or so it seemed.[103] Beale's and Ross's rifles and muskets blazed at them from the parapet with fire so heavy that the redcoats had no time to spike the guns before they retreated."[104] They also found they could not load and fire the six-pounder they had turned to bear on Jackson's line without becoming targets themselves.[105] A Natchez dragoon behind the earthwork described Simpson's predicament a day later as "a slaughter pen."[106] With most officers dead or seriously wounded, and the Yankees preparing to counterattack in force, the few able soldiers remaining in the bastion got out of it as best they could, leaving behind their dead and wounded, including Simpson, now too badly injured to get away.[107]

As the British backed through the embrasures or over the forward wall of the killing pen, Ross raised his sword and led a charge down the main section of the earthwork and across the ditch, supported by Beale's fire, to the admiration of Davezac and others watching from the other works. They took the bastion and wounded several redcoats, while the remnant took cover in the moat and against the forward face of the outer wall to escape Yankee fire.[108] Behind them lay thirty-one dead and an equal number of wounded.[109]

Within hours, most of the army and soon the nation believed that Rennie's column had been annihilated. The next day a *creole* wrote that "not one of those who attempted to cross the entrenchments escaped," and others spoke of them being "exterminated."[110] They all died as the price of their courage, every man with wounds too many to number.[111] That evening Tatum believed that none escaped being casualties.[112] Exaggeration to the contrary, the reality of Rennie's losses was grim enough. Simpson was not being hyperbolic when he called their mission "a forlorn hope."[113]

Within a few hours Simpson, now a prisoner of war, told a Natchez dragoon that he feared only five of the sixty grenadiers he led into the fight had escaped and that, for the time the action lasted, it was the hottest he had ever witnessed.[114] Beverly Chew watched it all through an embrasure and believed Rennie's penetration might have been decisive had not Beale made every man who entered the bastion "bite the dust."[115] Lieutenant John Fort of Ogden's dragoons was effusive in praise. Beale's little company had saved

Jackson's right from being turned, he believed, and attorney Ellery concluded that if the enemy had focused his main attack there rather than on the center, Jackson's line might have been pierced, with disastrous results.[116]

Of course, Plauché's battalion on Beale's left had contributed scattered musketry to the defense and stood well.[117] Farther to the left were the bulk of the 44th and Captain Nathaniel Pryor, who had crossed a continent and seen the great western sea. Nearby was his recently arrived brother, Lieutenant Robert Lewis Pryor, in the 5th Kentucky, and they, too, sent a few loads of buck and ball toward Rennie.[118] But Beale's men had no doubt that they themselves deserved the real credit. When they repulsed Rennie, declared one Orleanian, they "saved New Orleans."[119]

Yet the battle was only begun.

Eighteen

"A Spectacle of Carnage"

S ALVATION WAS NOT yet at hand. At Battery No. 2, Lieutenant Otto Nor-ris, late of *Carolina*, looked seven hundred yards to his left to see Gibbs's much-delayed column approaching the ditch in front of the American works. He admired their courage as Yankee grapeshot blasted holes in the 44th and their fascines and ladders, but they kept coming, and it dismayed him to see in his own lines that some men who had never before faced an approaching enemy became distinctly uneasy.[1]

Seeing Gibbs's column marching toward the center of Carroll's line seemed to confirm that spies or deserters had warned the enemy where Jackson's line was most vulnerable. Gibbs was coming straight toward Flau-jac's eighteen-pounder and six-pounder, taking flank fire on his right from Battery No. 8 and on his left from Spotts's twelve-pounder and Battery No. 5's two six-pounders. Even Crawley's thirty-two-pounder in Battery No. 4 fired on the head of Gibbs's column.[2] The sheer weight of the grape and canister flying at him with each salvo was staggering, and deadly. An onlooker ob-served that the American projectiles and shells cut lanes through the ad-vancing column, while Carroll purposely held fire from his men until the leading ranks of the enemy column came within sure range. Then the rifles and muskets opened on them with "buck and ball."[3]

Carroll's first volley caught the 44th ninety yards from the ditch. An onlooking visitor from St. Francisville found the din of musketry almost deafening, and as the redcoats came closer, the volume of Yankee fire grew greater.[4] Men on the line generously paid tribute to the bravery and disci-pline of the men coming toward them. Coffee believed he saw redcoats filling gaps in their columns just as quickly as American fire created them. But then he also believed that while grape and canister from Jackson's cannons mowed down scores of foemen, that was overshadowed by "the carnage of our Rifles and muskets."[5] Already some Americans were erroneously crediting damage done by artillery to shoulder arms instead.

A friend of Congressman Robertson described an atmosphere "filled with sheets of fire, and volumes of smoke."[6] Old Hickory's artillery fire became a deafening roar heard as far away as Donaldsonville, nearly eighty miles to the west.[7] "It is impossible to describe to you the cannonading," a Natchez volunteer wrote within hours. "It can only be compared to a continued roaring of thunder."[8] At its height during one thirty-minute period, the sustained roar all along the line without letup was such that men could not distinguish individual cannon discharges.[9] It was not yet full daylight, and amid the clouds of smoke and the remaining fog, flashes from the guns created eerie images. To Major Reid, "the whole atmosphere seemed to be enveloped in flame."[10] It was a vision of hell.

The redcoats got within a few paces of the ditch before falling back, then came again when reinforced. Carroll believed perhaps four hundred got close to the ditch, to be killed or captured. He could hardly credit it himself, sharing Coffee's misconception of the effectiveness of his riflemen when he added that only a few score of the enemy reached the ditch before being brought down by "the deadly aim of our Tennessee mountain boys." It was a proud moment for him, and he feared those not there might not believe the Americans' stand. "No you will not," he wrote a friend, "but it is no less true."[11]

"Big Sam" Dale arrived at the height of the action. He had landed at Fort St. John that morning on a boat from Madisonville across Lake Pontchartrain, after seven days riding from Georgia to bring dispatches. Quickly remounted, he rode to Royal Street to learn Old Hickory was with the army at the front. As he galloped through the streets of town to the river road, Dale heard the reports of the big guns ahead.[12] When he reached Line Jackson, he beheld "a magnificent vision" of Yankee artillery sweeping away swaths of the enemy out on the field. He, too, could not withhold his admiration for the officers he saw rushing to the fronts of their columns, waving their swords and cheering to rally their men before being cut down themselves.[13] One of Coffee's privates marveled that the British kept coming even "up to the mouth of our cannon."[14] Some assumed that Pakenham must have assigned his best men for the attack and that the leading officers were all surely volunteers.[15] Coffee admired the order in Gibbs's column, and Adair accorded them his respect for their dash and courage.[16] The noun that most Americans settled on to characterize the redcoats' advance was "intrepidity," and Major Reid called it "obstinate bravery."[17] Carroll felt enough sympathy for them to aver that "their determined perseverance and steady valor, were worthy a better cause."[18]

After passing Knight at double time, Whittaker's companies hit the canal in front of Carroll at the concave indent in the works, where they found a few fascines arriving but only one ladder. The ditch before them was ten feet wide and beyond it the breastwork appeared to rise eight feet at least.[19] Men pushing forward from the rear compressed the lead companies of the 4th, the 21st, and remnants of the 44th, causing a confusion in front that Pringle found indescribable.[20] The Yankee fire now was unbearable. "Our column was absolutely mowed down," Pringle said later, and the smoke was so thick as he approached the front that he could not see Whittaker's companies ahead of him until he reached the ditch himself.[21]

Mullins was there. However much he had blundered earlier, none could fault him now as he took part of the 44th toward the canal. With men falling all around, he got within a dozen yards of it and sent Johnston back for remaining fragments of the fascine and ladder parties. As he left, Johnston looked back to see Mullins leading the men with him to the ditch.[22] Soon Mullins sent another man back to rush stragglers to the front with their fascines and ladders. Advancing toward the enemy, Mullins was hit in the shoulder. Ignoring it, he sent a sergeant with another plea to forward every man in the rear, but three grapeshot or bullets brought him down, so Mullins sent two more grenadiers with his plea and kept going. No more than one hundred of the 44th made it to the ditch with him, and they fell fast to Yankee fire.[23] Hat in one hand and sword in the other, he stood his ground, cheering his men on and threatening to shoot any man who dropped his fascine or ladder to run.[24]

Knight collected four score steady men and kept going. The fascine and ladder parties bumped into the rear of the rest of their regiment, now hemmed in by the advancing 21st on its right. Mullins or Johnston ordered the companies in front to shift left to make a gap between the regiments, and Knight led his grenadiers through it even as he saw increasing confusion on either side of him and men falling back without orders. He had just reached the head of the column when someone shouted to retreat. Then Knight saw the commander of the 4th King's Own, Lieutenant Colonel Francis Brooke in his cocked hat, yelling to him that no one had given such an order and to press on. By then many of the 44th were moving to the rear as Debbeigg tried to stop as many as he could to face them forward again.

When the grenadiers reached the front, Knight saw engineer Tapp with a small party carrying fascines and ladders, and moved toward them.

Behind him he saw men dropping ladders to open fire with their muskets, and Debbeigg running to order them forward again, when a shell fragment hit his head and stunned him. Knight sent back sergeants with drawn swords and orders to use them on anyone who dropped their ladders, and finally reached Tapp just thirty yards from the canal.[25]

Tapp had led about 150 men through the chaos to reach the head of the column, but only half of them arrived with their fascines. As they came under heavier fire, he looked back to see organization crumbling, and by the time Knight reached him, Tapp had only a few fascine bearers left and just three or four ladders. Still he pushed on. By the time he reached the canal, most of the other advance parties were down and fewer than half a dozen men remained with him. They threw their fascines into the canal and quickly fell back on Knight, who pushed forward with the few ladders remaining.[26] Lieutenant Phelan was leading grenadiers toward them with a few more ladders and perhaps one hundred fascines when he went down.[27]

Johnston had collected a few men with fascines but on approaching the front saw only Knight and a few others near the ditch, trying to set their ladders in place. The fire was so heavy, and the muddle of wounded and fleeing men so thick, that Johnston could not reach them.[28] Mullins got close to the ditch, his last few yards measured in blood. In the first section of his grenadiers, only half a dozen made it, soon joined by four others with one ladder. A sergeant of the 44th took a fascine from a man killed in front of him and reached the ditch, to find only a few fascines in the canal and a single ladder in place.[29] Absent the fascines to fill the ditch, they laid what ladders they had across it from one bank to the other, then laid planks on the rungs to use it as a bridge. A quartet of Irishmen of the 44th—O'Neal, Cooney, Sullivan, and Callaghan—just placed their ladder across the ditch near Mullins when, within seconds, all four fell dead.[30]

Tapp ran back to report the failure of the fascine party to Gibbs and ran into confusion everywhere on his way. The balance of the 44th had been supposed to cross the ditch first, but when they got there and could go no farther, they became disorganized, and their confusion spread quickly.[31] It was about seven a.m., solid daylight now, as fascines were finally reaching the ditch, but they were far too few.[32] Adjutant Barry got to within a dozen yards of the canal to find not a single ladder in place in that sector. He helped Knight set up the first.[33]

Gibbs's brigade major Captain Wilkinson was just twenty-one, the "little corporal" much loved and respected by fellow officers.[34] He was mounted at the beginning of the assault, but his horse went down and he rushed forward on foot, urging fragments of the 21st, 93rd, and 44th to follow.[35]

Pushing his way to the ditch, he leapt across at a narrow spot while a Yankee officer looked on from above. He may actually have been the first to plant a ladder against the American parapet, which he began climbing immediately.[36] He was near the top when a bullet sent him tumbling back into the ditch.[37] Gasping for breath, he asked another officer, "*Now*, why do not the troops come on? *The day is our own.*"[38]

Where the advance of the 21st reached the ditch, they found it ten to twelve feet across and three or four feet deep. Lieutenant John Fonblanque thought they could have crossed easily had the fascines and ladders been in place. As it was, the first men there just jumped into the waist-deep water to wade, when they stumbled on some heavy planks and timbers the Americans had stuck in the bottom as obstacles. The redcoats dislodged some of them from the mud and made a makeshift bridge instead. The earthwork before them ran eight to ten feet high, which put men in the ditch in a blind spot where Tennesseans on the other side could not see them directly or fire at them without climbing atop their works and exposing themselves.[39]

Pringle and about two hundred of the 21st crossed, then, having no ladders, used bayonets to dig steps and handholds into the muddy face of the breastwork. Whittaker went up with the first, to be shot dead as he reached the top. Colonel Paterson went down badly wounded. Still more came on behind them, and some reached the top to fire into the Yankees on the other side.[40] Major J. Alexander Ross and others actually went over the top to confront Carroll's muskets and rifles.[41] Ross yelled back for the 44th to come on, but a Tennessean stepped up to him with pointed musket and said "the 44th was in Hell" and if Ross did not "surrender d——quick," he would join them. Ross was wounded and all but alone. He had no choice but to yield, but as he handed over his sword, he asked that his captors remember and mention in their reports of the battle that he was taken on their rampart.[42]

Above the milling redcoats, Carroll's men, with two ranks of Adair's Kentuckians behind them, had steadied themselves to meet the enemy.[43] They were confident of the strength of their works, which were twelve feet thick there and more in places, and nearly as high.[44] David Urquhart in Dejean's company felt secure that they were "entrenched up to their chins."[45] Yet there was a vulnerability. Nowhere along the line was the ditch as shallow as here. The British could slide down one side and scramble up the other, needing neither fascines nor ladders. The rampart was a little lower in places, too.[46] The wounded twenty-five-year-old Lieutenant John Leavach of the 21st scaled the earthwork there and dropped down inside. At first he saw only two American officers in his immediate vicinity, and with commendable bravado demanded their swords. He was himself taken prisoner instead, but ever after believed that at that moment Carroll's Tennesseans were giving way, and that if other British regiments had only followed him, they would have been victorious.[47]

Yankee losses on the front line were few, meaning the men in reserve did not have to fill their places.[48] Instead, with the best marksmen on the line firing, the Kentuckians stood in ranks three- and four-deep behind them, reloading muskets and passing them forward so that the front maintained virtually a continual volley. Men in front clawed holes in the thinner parts of the rampart to make firing portals, and an officer at the McCarty house observing this front believed that "such a Blaze of fire was perhaps never seen."[49] Behind the firing line, Adair's men were ready, one of them soon declaring that "all the legions of Hell" could not get over the parapet in the face of that fire, and if they did, "a hedge of bayonets" awaited them below.[50]

Unarmed Kentuckians in reserve actually envied and even cursed the Tennesseans in front for having all the action, and shouted for them to "give way and let the *horses* come." A few hurled brickbats and billets of wood over the works, and during occasional lulls, as enemy officers re-formed their men at the ditch, a Kentuckian or Tennessean went over the top and jumped down to retrieve Brown Besses dropped by fallen foes.[51]

Many of the Kentucky volunteers never forgot the murder of wounded Kentuckians by the redcoats' native allies after the Battle of the River Raisin. Lieutenant Willoughby Ashby of the 15th Kentucky ran back and forth along the line now, exhorting the men and shouting over the parapet, "We'll pay you now for the River Raison, d——n you!" He had no gun himself, but when the 44th and 21st reached the ditch below, he threw a barrel over the parapet at them and followed that with a heavy iron bar.[52]

While the British advance looked resolute and disciplined to the Americans, it was largely illusory. By the time they reached the ditch and earthwork, the attackers were falling in heaps.[53] Amid the cacophony of belching cannons and screaming men, Tennesseans could hear enemy officers on the other side of the mud wall exhorting their men forward to the ditch, shouting, "Well done my brave fellows, mount the works! take the city!—and you shall have money and women in plenty!!!" Pakenham had made no promise of plunder, but officers now resorted to any expedient to keep their men going.[54]

After the first repulse, they came at least twice more, only to stop, close ranks, and come on again.[55] Once in the canal, many realized the hopelessness of trying to go farther without ladders but refused to fall back, instead milling about, trying to find a way up.[56] Adair saw Tennessee and Kentucky volunteers leap atop the breastwork to fire down into the men in the ditch, and Alexander Henderson of Natchez watched in amazement as some redcoats took off their shoes for their toes to get a better grip on the breast-work's muddy slope.[57] One American believed that every officer who tried to come up the rampart was shot down.[58]

The sight of the carnage they were wreaking struck the Yankees force-fully.[59] An astonished Tatum believed that "such destruction of men, for the time it lasted, was never before witnessed."[60] Macabre allusions to a bloody harvest aptly abounded. Men were "mowed down" and felled "like oats by a cradle."[61] The slaughter to his right shocked Coffee, who had witnessed bat-tle before.[62] To men who looked out embrasures or over the parapet, full daylight revealed a plain strewn with dead and wounded in heaps where they fell.[63] The ditch immediately below them squirmed with writhing wounded among the dead, and a few of the uninjured hiding among them to escape the hail of lead.[64]

Joseph Winter wrote of the redcoats that Yankee fire "tore them literally To pieces," and when Captain Alney McLean of the 14th Kentucky peered over the parapet, he found "the whole face of the earth was strewed with them."[65] Adjutant Hynes believed they had shattered the flower of the Brit-ish army, men who deserved a nobler and better fate. The world would ad-mire their courage, but they had been "led forward to slaughter."[66] Ten days later Postmaster Johnston described the scene to First Lady Dolley Madi-son. It was, he said, "a spectacle of carnage."[67]

For Jackson, it was confirmation that even the strongest adversary could not best what he called "a rampart of high minded men."[68] It did not come entirely without loss. Ensign Weller was on or near the line to the right of Carroll when a Kentuckian was hit. "He had his Brains Shot out on me and I was as Bloody as a Butcher," Weller recalled a few days later. It was the only fatality in his regiment, and thus far one of very few in the army that morning.[69]

The disorganized withdrawal of the 44th stalled and disrupted the 21st behind it. With all but one of its field officers and almost half of the com-pany captains out of action, command of the 21st fell to a captain who called on survivors to advance again. With the color bearers down, a ser-geant stripped the regimental colors from their staffs and wrapped them around his body inside his tunic before he went forward, only to be cap-tured before the 21st retreated for the last time.[70] It fell back on the 4th, which tried to force its way through the milling mass but could not until Gibbs ordered the 4th to split into two to make a gap for the retreating 21st to pass through. It worked, but the 4th took heavy fire in the process, and then when it rushed on to the ditch, it met the same obstacle to crossing as the others. Every officer with that part of the 4th was killed or wounded.

Along with another ensign, Gerard carried the 4th's colors in the advance. A ball shattered the other's flagstaff in his hand and killed him, while another broke Gerard's staff.[71] Another ball knocked Lieutenant Peter Bowlby unconscious when it struck his forehead above his right eye and buried itself in his scalp.[72]

Finally, General Keane came in sight. The 93rd's regimental pipers played the reel "Monymusk" during their grueling march across nearly 1,000 yards of the field, subjected to fire from battery after battery on the American works.[73] They even risked friendly fire for a few minutes when their diagonal course put them in front of Dickson's batteries fixed on the McCarty house and Crawley's thirty-two-pounder until they briefly ceased firing.[74] Then, as Keane approached within eighty yards of the enemy line, he, too, saw no fascines or ladders at the ditches for him.

Lieutenant Colonel Dale ordered the 93rd to halt. There they stood in position, taking casualties from Spotts's and Flaujac's grape and Carroll's musketry as they awaited orders. Dale went down killed. More followed, so many officers falling that some confusion briefly ensued with no one to give orders. Still they stood. Captain Charles Head carried the regimental colors to the front and tried to rally the men. Beside him stood Ensign Graves, who had begun the day rolling on the ground in pain from dysentery. He had just caught up to the regiment to take his proper place, when he felt the concussion of a shell exploding nearby. Suddenly Head was there no more.[75]

All the Highlanders could see through the smoke were the muzzles of enemy muskets atop the parapet and the hats on the heads of the Yankees firing them. An officer rode up to their line to yell, "Ninety-third, have a little patience, and you shall soon have your revenge." Still no orders came, so still they stood, and died, in a leaden rain.[76] Someone on Jackson's staff actually thought he saw the 93rd's drummer boy cheering them on from a tree, although the field was mostly treeless.[77] Orders that morning told the Highlanders to move light and take nothing with them, but they were not called "the psalm-singing regiment" for nothing. Many carried small Bibles in their pockets, and they needed their comfort now.[78] Even the navy paid them tribute, Admiral Codrington crediting the 93rd with "the best of the very Wellington stuff" for standing their ground under such fire.[79] While the 93rd held its ground, retreating men of the 21st ran back through them, further stalling momentum; and when Lieutenant Colonel Andrew Creagh took over and tried to advance, they were turned back.[80]

Keane soon discovered that the ditch on Gibbs's left was probably too deep to wade. He was encouraging his men to try it, when two balls hit him. One caused a severe contusion, but the other punched into his thigh, carrying with it part of the worsted webbing of his pantaloons.[81] Assisted by aides, he walked to the rear, reassuring officers along the way that they could still carry the day if Rennie succeeded.[82] None of them yet knew the outcome at the American bastion, but here the Highlanders never reached the ditch.

At nearly the same moment, Pakenham and MacDougall appeared nearby and Gibbs rode to them.[83] "Sir Ed, I am not able to make these men move on," he shouted. "They will not follow me."[84] Pakenham turned his horse toward the head of Gibbs's disrupted brigade as a hail of American grapeshot and shells from Flaujac's sixes and eighteens exploded all around them, enhanced by musketry from Carroll's Tennesseans. More officers went down.[85] Then Tylden approached to find great confusion throughout what remained of Gibbs's column. At the same time he plainly distinguished American heads and faces gathering on the breastwork ahead of them.[86] Fearing that Jackson might take advantage of the confusion with a sortie against his right flank, Pakenham sent Wylly to the right to stiffen the men.[87]

Then he rode toward the milling mass, took off his hat, and began cheering the men. In the past, Wylly had taken him to task for unnecessarily exposing himself to enemy fire, but in this emergency a daring gesture was needed to rally the troops. With so many of the officers killed or wounded, only Pakenham could breathe new life into the soldiers.[88] He first encountered the 93rd as MacDougall led his horse past them, just brushing Ensign Graves's shoulder moments after his friend Captain Head was killed. Seeing the men fuming at the needless waste during their halt, some of them in tears, Pakenham yelled, "Come on, brave 93d," waving his hat above his head, then turned toward the enemy. Then a ball struck Graves's leg, he became faint, and he fell.[89]

Pakenham's gesture worked momentarily. Men followed him for about five yards, but then wavered again and started to fall back. At that moment a bullet or grapeshot killed his horse under him, partially pinning him to the ground, and at nearly the same instant a shell fragment ripped away most of the flesh from Gibbs's thigh and knocked him from his saddle.[90] MacDougall helped disentangle Pakenham from his fallen animal and found another, but as he helped the general remount, two projectiles struck Pakenham almost simultaneously. One hit his thigh close to the knee. The other passed through his lower abdomen and crashed into his spine. He fell into MacDougall's arms.[91] Clearly dying, he tried to say something. All he got out before he lost consciousness was "Tell General . . ."[92]

Carroll's men and the gunners at Batteries No. 7 and 8 saw couriers riding to and from a mounted officer just over two hundred yards in front of them. Then he was shot from his horse and a number of redcoats turned aside from the attack to carry him to the rear, half of them falling themselves as they ran.[93] Captain Hudry thought he saw a mounted general and his staff out on the field and watched as Lieutenant Étienne Bertel aimed his brass twelve-pounder from Battery No. 6 and sent a canister load at them that brought several to the ground. No American knew who either of these generals was or if they were one and the same, but in time Hudry claimed it must have been Pakenham.[94] More likely it was Gibbs. Regardless, the fallen man's horse panicked and ran straight for the rampart, miraculously remaining on the field without being hit.[95]

As MacDougall took his dying general to the field hospital at Gibbs's headquarters, Tylden rode to report Pakenham's and Gibbs's wounding to Lambert. On his way he passed through a field littered with abandoned fascines and ladders and saw crowds from the 44th and 21st running to the rear, firing wildly in all directions in their panic.[96] The heavy fire that all the redcoats came under slowed their own rate of return fire. Unable to stop in the storm to reload, they tried to do it on the run, often dropping the lead balls before they could ram them down their musket barrels.[97] It only got worse when soldiers saw Keane stumbling to the rear, Gibbs being carried to his headquarters, and near-lifeless Pakenham borne away.[98]

MacDougall got his general to the De La Ronde house to see him die just as they arrived. He rushed to the redoubt that had figured so tragically in the day's confusion to inform Dickson, on the way encountering a group carrying the body of Major George King of the 7th. Dickson learned a few minutes earlier of the near collapse of Gibbs's column, convincing him that the attack had failed, but then he saw the column appear to go forward again as Pakenham led them. He was just forming some field artillery behind the redoubt to support the move, when MacDougall's news stunned him. Dickson refused to believe it at first, but the shambles at the front came before his eyes as numbers of soldiers ran past in panic. To his left he saw Carmichael's battery pulling back. It had fired barely five times before the head of Gibbs's column broke. The fleeing men ran back right in front of its guns so that they dared not fire, although the enemy was still firing at Carmichael. Rather than remain a helpless target, he withdrew, and had already lost a three-pounder. Dickson left at once to find Lambert.[99] Back at Villeré's, Codrington heard the growing ferocity of the Yankee artillery, and as sketchy reports of the fallen filtered back, he feared the worst.[100]

Rennie's remnants were still clinging to the shelter of the bastion's moat. Their bold engagement lasted perhaps forty minutes, but it would be some time before survivors escaped their perch outside the bastion wall.[101] None dared to show his head above the parapet without risking Yankee bullets from Beale. Balls riddled the hat of a carelessly tall lieutenant of the 7th. Finally, they made a Yankee prisoner embrace a redcoat so closely that the Americans dared not fire for hitting him, and with him as cover stood to look to the right to see the course of the action in that direction. They saw Pakenham's battered columns retreating and hundreds of bodies in red strewn over the plain. At the same time they saw Lieutenant Ross preparing to come over their works at them.[102]

It was time to break for safety. Rennie had been unsupported from the outset. By the time the 7th's light company came up, the assault had already failed, and it joined the rest in the moat.[103] The 93rd was supposed to support the assault here, but then Pakenham ordered them to the right to support Gibbs.[104] Ultimately, many blamed Mullins, even—and wrongly—suspecting him of cowardice, and Chesterton would bitterly charge that Rennie and his party were "victims of a pusillanimity unheard of in the British army."[105]

One frustrated officer in the moat threw rocks at the top of the main earthwork behind them. Then, in a desperate ruse, they placed their caps on their bayonets and raised them just above the bastion top, shouting to make the Yankees think they were about to attack. That provoked a volley, and before the smoke cleared and the Americans could reload, the redcoats broke and ran toward their rear, once more exposed to artillery from across the river. It was a death gauntlet, and they stooped as they ran. A bullet hit Henry Axhorn of the 7th in the hip, then ran up through his body to stop behind his right eye. A cannonball exploded the head of a man beside John Cooper of the 7th, scattering his brains onto Cooper's cap, and farther along they passed one of the West India soldiers sitting on the ground, the lower half of his face gone and his eyes missing. Not far from him, a soldier of the 43rd was holding his entrails in his hands.

Crossing the levee, they dropped into a ditch before another volley came.[106] Of the officers who went forward with Rennie that morning, only three remained uninjured.[107] The light companies had been crushed and nearly annihilated, and not a man of them set foot in the Americans' main line.[108] Even now, looking backward, Simpson believed the battle might still be won. Properly supported, they could have retaken the bastion and used its guns to rake Jackson's line while Lambert's reserve reinvigorated Gibbs's remnants. But Pakenham had fallen. With that, he believed, "the seal of our misfortune was irrevocably fixed."[109]

Five miles behind the chaos in front of Line Jackson sat a city in silence. Charles Gayarré was a day short of his tenth birthday that morning. He remembered the city's deathly quiet as if it were holding its breath in suspense. Then he heard the first guns and with others of his family spent the next few hours on the upper-floor balcony of Madame Helene Porée's house at Dumaine and Royal listening to the cannonade. Everyone was "petrified into absolute silence by the apprehensions of the moment."[110] Over in the Faubourg Marigny, the steamboat captain Clement's house sat barely two miles from the battlefield, where his wife, Elizabeth, heard what seemed like "one continued peal of tremendous thunder" that morning. The sound filled her with indescribable horror as she and her family prepared to flee the town, thinking its destruction inevitable.[111] Merchants and civilians alike feared that the morning's events would determine their fate.[112] At the office of L'Ami des Lois, editor Leclerc arose before dawn to print his diary of events through January 1, when he and his pressman heard the gunfire and dropped their work to rush to Chalmette.[113]

In the city guardhouse the distant booming did not surprise one of the exempts on duty, as there had been such firing every day; but when it gained intensity, he left his post to head to the front.[114] Soon the big guns' concussions shook houses. Louise Livingston tried to describe the sensation, concluding that the sound was more terrifying than the reality, which was little comfort at the moment.[115] Every house in the city was shaken, enough so that residents feared friends elsewhere would not believe them.[116] Laura Florian told Mrs. Roosevelt in New York to "imagine claps of thunder, while the echo prolongs the sound undyingly till another clap overpowers the roar of that and continues increasingly till a third and so on." Even then she found herself challenged to describe the sound assailing her ears, or its emotional effect.[117] Eliza Chotard saw first suspense and then despair in faces around her as the morning wore on and minutes seemed interminable. In their heightened anticipation, they more than once thought they heard British boots on the streets. "We wept, we wailed, and we wrung our hands in terror," she recalled.[118] Within a few hours Laura Florian simply exclaimed, "What a moment is this."[119]

The same sentiment was felt down on the line. From the time he first saw the approaching foe, Old Hickory passed from company to company, battery to battery, calmly speaking with the men to cheer them. After the firing commenced, he ran along the line, shouting, "Give it to them my Boys lets finish the business today," further cementing his grip on their loyalty. "He is a noble fellow," Winter declared the next day, "& the men adore him."[120] To at least one, he seemed almost godlike: "He thinks, speaks and acts like no other human being."[121] Standing on the defensive meant that Old Hickory mostly needed only to react to circumstances, as when he had

Adair send companies of the 15th Kentucky to reinforce the bastion against Rennie, and then back again to the left as Gibbs's column approached.[122] Meanwhile, Jackson was pleased to see his men stand enemy fire, and it pleased them, too. "After the first few rounds [I] felt composed & regardless of danger," Virginian Hector Organ soon recalled. "The sound & Buzzing of balls & Rockets was truly sublime, & its inchantment was heightened by occasionally seeing some poor victim snatched off to eternity by my side."[123]

Not everyone stood fire with the same equanimity. Most of the slave laborers ran away, some back to Line Dupré and others farther.[124] Natchez lawyer George Poindexter had joined Carroll's staff days before. He was not a popular fellow. "There was nothing romantic, picturesque or imaginative about Poindexter," said one who knew him.[125] Adair thought him loud and abusive, a man designed by nature to be a town bully.[126] He was also ambitious, obsequious, untrustworthy, and a bit of a coward. When the artillery opened fire and Carroll left his quarters, Poindexter and others at first stayed behind, and almost at once a British cannonball passed through their room, sending brick fragments flying. One hit his arm and he lay on a mattress for a few minutes but dismissed the wound as slight. Then the group moved behind some chimneys, where so many took shelter that Poindexter was left to perch preposterously on the lap of Carroll's black valet, Henry. When Henry complained of his weight, Poindexter just told him to sit still.[127]

Others chafed to get to the fight. When they heard the artillery open, Claiborne and Shaumburg checked with Labatut to see that he was ready to defend the city, then left for the front. They arrived just as the British assault was crumbling, but shells still passed overhead when the governor went to the parapet and saw the "astonishing slaughter" wreaked by Jackson's guns.[128] Then Shaumburg and others thought they heard a bugle blowing across the Mississippi. The river fog denied them a sure view, but they concluded that Morgan must be under attack.

Jackson watched, too. He knew the enemy had crossed soldiers to threaten his flank and rear. Finally he and others on the parapet in front of McCarty's could see Thornton's men advancing along the opposite riverbank accompanied by their gun barges. Adair was observing beside him as Old Hickory yelled to the men and officers around him to wave their hats and cheer as loudly as possible to encourage Morgan. Adair smiled and was just telling Jackson he doubted Morgan's men could hear or see them through the fog and smoke, when a sudden clearing revealed the distant American line dissolving before Thornton's advance.[129]

Jackson immediately ordered the guns in the bastion to turn on Thornton's column, and soon they temporarily drove the redcoats away from the levee road.[130] Then he sent his adjutant Butler to arrange reinforcements for Morgan. Butler met Claiborne and Schaumburg and told the latter to go back and muster every man possible to send over the river, and to order Villeré at Line Dupré to join them. Claiborne and Shaumburg left at once. At Line Dupré, Villeré protested to Shaumburg that he had but one hundred armed men and they were guarding five hundred slaves as well as the few British prisoners taken so far that morning. Claiborne continued on to town to have Labatut prepare boats, but before he arrived a message from Jackson caught up with him.[131] The general was sending all the men he could spare. Claiborne must take command and deal with the case. The British numbered no more than five hundred, he believed, and he was certain Morgan had more men than that.[132] Stop Thornton, Old Hickory told him bluntly. "They must be destroyed."[133]

Suddenly there was another battle to fight.

Nineteen

"The Greatest Fury"

JANUARY 7 HAD been an agonizing night at Villeré's. By 3:15 a.m., as General Gibbs's sergeants were about to rouse their men, only nine boats were through the levee and floating in the Mississippi. At four o'clock Thornton dared wait no longer and began loading the 85th, although he could embark only a third of his force. The boats would have to return for the rest, leaving him isolated for a time on the other side of the river.[1] Another hour passed before the boats shoved off.[2] Behind them General Lambert, Colonel Tylden, and others who knew of the delay thought they should not have gone at all.[3]

Captains Roberts and Money, Midshipman Aitchison, and Lieutenant William Hole from the *Trave* commanded the gun barges.[4] The strong current and overloaded boats made for slow going, and they had difficulty keeping together. They reached the right bank just as glimmers of dawn tinted the southeastern sky.[5] Roberts disembarked the men unopposed on the Manuel Andry plantation and Thornton immediately started them up the levee road while Roberts and three of the accompanying gun barges moved along the shore in step with his advance to cover his right flank. Within minutes they saw the moving glow of the signal rocket as it went up across the river, then the fog-softened muzzle flashes of artillery, and three and a half seconds later they heard the boom of the guns.[6] The battle on the other side had begun.

Late the night before, Morgan had sent Major Charles Tessier and a company from Declouet's regiment down that bank to resist a landing and delay enemy advance. Shortly after five a.m. someone sighted boats loaded with redcoats on the river, heading to land perhaps two miles below Morgan's line.[7] The river current took Thornton some distance below Tessier, but that hardly mattered, since Tessier immediately disobeyed his orders when he saw the foe and took his men into the swamp, giving the enemy the river road with not even a pretense of resistance. Had he contested the landing, even his small command could have slowed Thornton, if it could not stop him. The timid major later offered the gossamer the excuse that he thought the British intended to go downriver toward English Turn rather than upstream against Morgan.[8]

Within minutes Colonel Davis and his Kentuckians reached Morgan's camp, hungry and exhausted from want of sleep. They carried the weapons they had picked up in the city, which one dismissed as little more than "refuse," scarcely a quarter of them with bayonets.[9] Patterson met them during their night march and noted their poor arms and fatigue.[10] Yet Davis said nothing to Morgan now about his men being ill-equipped, and the general ordered them to drop their knapsacks and rush down to confront the enemy wherever they met him.[11] Should Davis be repulsed, he should retire along the levee, maintaining a constant fire on the British until he reached Morgan's still-unfinished defensive line.

To reinforce Davis, Morgan sent along Major Paul Arnaud and 120 militia from General Stephen Hopkins's brigade.[12] It was close to six o'clock when they approached the Thaddeus Mayhew plantation just over three-quarters of a mile below Morgan's line. In the dim light they saw no immediate sign of Thornton ahead, but across the river they saw Pakenham's signal rocket and heard the opening artillery. Davis halted them and ordered them to form ranks in an open field and dig in if they could, his Kentuckians on the left and Arnaud on the right. Within minutes there was movement on the road ahead.

As sounds of the gathering cannonade rumbled across the water, the 85th pushed ahead quickly for a mile or more from the landing place. They passed over the Paul Duvergne plantation to a deep canal bordering Mayhew's, crossed by a bridge Morgan obligingly had not thought to dismantle.[13] On the other side Davis and Arnaud clustered in the cover of Mayhew's buildings and their own hastily thrown-together works. Thornton did not see them at first, but Roberts did, and his barges fired a few rounds of grapeshot, provoking return fire from Davis that revealed his position.[14]

Thornton sent Captain C. Shaw and twenty men from the 85th to deal with them. They fired a volley and the Kentuckians replied with three or four, but Arnaud's militia almost immediately broke ranks and started running back.[15] Davis tried to stem the route, but Arnaud protested that he

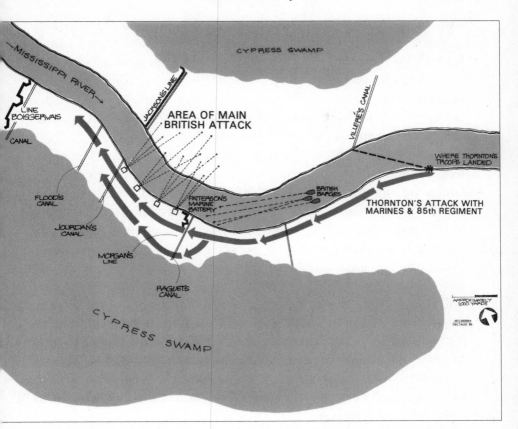

The British attack on the west bank, January 8, 1815. Colonel Thornton's crossing of the river appears at right, and then he progressed along the river from right to left and divided into two prongs to strike Morgan's line at center left, forcing Patterson to abandon his batteries supporting Jackson's fight across the river. Morgan only stopped retreating at Line Bois Gervais at far left. The danger Thornton posed to Jackson's right and rear over the river is evident. Note, four armed barges supported Thornton's attack, not three as shown.

could not stop them, giving Davis no choice but to withdraw his own command up the levee road under fire, taunted as they ran by cheering from the 85th.[16] Over on one of the gun barges, Lieutenant Hole boasted that "we at first rather headed them."[17]

Morgan's main line a mile above Mayhew's crossed the Juan Castañeda plantation with a fair earthwork extending three hundred yards south from the levee toward a cypress swamp. He had 640 men behind that line: John Dejean's 1st Louisiana on the left, Colonel Zenon Cavelier's 2nd Louisiana in the center, and Declouet's regiment of drafted militia on the right. Over one hundred of them were unarmed, however, and more than a dozen of those with arms only had shotguns, which would be of no use at any distance. Nearby, Morgan had another 220 of all ranks, several of them unarmed as well.[18] About four a.m. that morning a brace of brass sixes arrived, which Morgan turned over to John Nixon, adjutant of the 1st Louisiana. He placed them on the levee road at the left end of the line.[19] Otherwise, Morgan ineptly disposed his men to man just two hundred yards of the earthwork, leaving the last hundred yards on the right unoccupied. Beyond that, an expanse of open ground led to the swamp, with only a shallow dry canal extending from the earthwork to offer any cover for defense.[20]

Nixon had only a dozen rounds per gun. Earlier that morning, on hearing that Thornton had been spotted, Dejan ordered Nixon to unfurl the 1st Louisiana's colors. Unfortunately they could not find the lieutenant who had the flag, since he had fallen ill the evening before and given the banner to a private without telling anyone else. Nixon was still searching for the flag, when the British approached.[21] He first saw Arnaud's and Davis's men running back in some disorder toward Morgan's line, with redcoats in pursuit. The fleeing men passed by Nixon and over the earthwork before Colonel Davis managed to stop and re-form most of them in the rear. Morgan then led them to the right to take cover in the canal, somewhat filling the gap he had left between the end of his earthworks and the cypress swamp. In a move that probably looked comical even to men who had just fled from an advancing enemy, the general dismounted and stepped down into the canal, then went down on one knee to show them how he wanted them to stoop to load and then stand to fire.[22]

Thus, as the enemy approached, Morgan had six hundred or more Louisiana militia behind just six hundred feet of works on his left, meaning that with only one foot of works per man, they could present barely a third of their number on the line at a time, while Davis and fewer than two hundred had to hold the remaining breastwork and another three hundred yards of open canal. No artillery or other defense protected his right flank, which lay ripe for being turned.[23] Even worse, there was a bridge over this canal to the right of Davis's position and another near Davis's center, and it never occurred to Morgan to take them down.[24] A Natchez newspaper editor later characterized Morgan by saying that "as a man and a citizen, no man was more respected" but had to add that "as a General, he was destitute of every qualification except courage."[25] He was right.

Following the fleeing militia, Thornton reached an orange grove around a house neighboring Castañeda's. From there he saw what appeared to be a formidable redoubt seven hundred yards ahead, although at nearly half a mile he could make out few details. Behind it he estimated several hundred Yankee defenders. He had barely 450 men at hand, but he was already fully eight hours behind Pakenham's timetable and needed to regain time. Daring as ever, he decided to risk trading lives for minutes. Davis's right flank on the canal looked vulnerable, so Thornton ordered two companies of the 85th under Lieutenant Colonel Richard Gubbins to strike there. Shaw's company of the 85th and one hundred seamen, with Captain Money in charge, would threaten the enemy left and Nixon on the riverbank. Major Peter Deshon with the rest of the 85th and one hundred marines would hit Morgan's center.[26]

Setting up stands for the Congreves he brought with him, Thornton fired rockets to soften the Yankee position, then he advanced again.[27] Patterson was still firing his shore batteries at Rennie at the moment, when word reached him that Thornton was coming.[28] Seeing the enemy form for an assault, Patterson turned one of his twelve-pounder batteries to fire on Money's contingent on the levee road. Nixon opened on them as well, and when the redcoats came within about sixty yards, they seemed for a moment to waver.[29] At that moment both Americans and redcoats might have heard amid their gunfire the cheers from across the river as Jackson's men stood on their parapet waving their hats in encouragement as Thornton's line staggered.[30]

In fact, Gubbins was only halting momentarily to make an oblique turn to his left to drive for the open ground beyond Davis's right flank.[31] Just then Roberts's gun barges came up and opened with more rockets and their deck carronades. A bugle sounded. Money's men shouted a loud "Huzzah!" and the British surged forward. Nixon gave them a few of his precious rounds of grape as the militia fired eight or nine volleys of musketry, and the enemy column staggered and fell back, with the Americans shouting "Victory!" after them. They were premature, for part of the 85th quickly came up to support Money, and the redcoats surged forward once more. Looking over to his right at that moment, Nixon saw Davis's Kentuckians flying back in confusion from their canal and running across the plain in their rear before Gubbins's charge. They had scarcely fired a shot.[32]

The Kentuckians were already skittish as Gubbins approached. Congreves had set ablaze some acres of corn and cane stubble in their rear, making them feel trapped between two fires as Gubbins rushed their line with bayonets.[33] Americans with working muskets got off a round or two but could do nothing to prevent the foe from passing around their right flank and across the open bridge to commence firing on their flank and rear.[34] Then Money's column on the road rallied and advanced as Nixon and the Louisiana militia renewed their fire. For a few moments smoke obscured the field, but then a breeze blew it behind the American line to reveal that Gubbins had pushed through the Kentuckians and was marching across Morgan's rear toward the levee road.

With men in complete disorder flying in all directions, Morgan's staff tried to re-form them in a line, but they were not to be stopped.[35] It happened so quickly that when Davis's adjutant briefly fell wounded as the rout commenced, the redcoats had already passed him in their pursuit by the time he stood again.[36] Captain Joyes and thirty men of his company ran into the swamp on their right when Davis's line collapsed, hoping to make their way under cover to friendly lines, but got lost and did not find the rest of their comrades until long after the fight was over.[37] Other Kentuckians in the swamp wandered six miles upstream before they emerged to find themselves directly opposite New Orleans.[38] Next the Louisiana militia fell back, and suddenly Lieutenant Nixon found himself on his own and out of ammunition. He scarcely had time to spike his guns and run up the river road, the last to abandon the line, and with the British hard on his heels.[39]

General Morgan was near the center when Davis gave way. Buying into the lore of their fabled marksmanship, he had placed great confidence in the Kentuckians.[40] Now he and Dejean rode along the fleeing mass, haranguing their officers to stop the rout, but Davis could only protest that they were out of control. Morgan accused him of not trying hard enough, but had to confess that he did not himself know how to stop the rout.[41] One fleeing Louisiana militiaman briefly stopped running to turn about and make a defiant face at the enemy, but it cost him the worldly goods he was carrying when he dropped them in the rush to continue his flight.[42] A portly militia officer had tied his horse to a tree. When the rout began, he ran to his mount, jumped into the saddle, and gave it spur. The animal did not move. He spurred again, swearing at his steed, but it remained immobile. Only then did he notice its reins still tied to the tree.[43]

A cornet in Chauveau's company thought the militia refused to take further orders out of disgust with their general, and some would soon blame the disaster on his "incompetence and cowardice." Patterson saw Morgan trying to restore order with little aid from his officers, however, and credited him with bravery if nothing else.[44] The naval officer believed the Kentuckians could have fallen back a short distance to their rear to use his shore batteries as an anchor, but Morgan gave no such orders, and now the collapse of his line put those batteries in jeopardy as well.[45]

Seeing the Kentucky militia flee, Patterson ordered his riverbank batteries to turn their fire on Gubbins. Even though he was at the moment under fire from Pakenham's levee battery on the opposite bank, Captain Henley and his crews were about to open on Gubbins, when the fleeing Kentuckians ran right into his line of fire, and he could not discharge his guns without hitting Americans. Had the infantry stood firm long enough to send a few musket volleys at the foe, Patterson believed his artillery could have done the rest and driven Thornton back. Now, abandoned and with only thirty men himself, Patterson had no alternative but to dump his ammunition in the river, spike his guns, and pull out.[46]

Taking Morgan's line cost Thornton just three killed and perhaps two score wounded. Casualties among officers were disproportionate.[47] Captain Money went down, both major bones in one of his legs broken.[48] Lieutenant Beauchamp C. Urquhart of the 85th took a serious but not life-threatening wound.[49] William Thornton, "cool as he was brave, and adored by his men," shared every risk, making it no surprise that a bullet found him.[50] It hit the very spot where he was still healing from his wound at Bladensburg.[51] Still ambulatory but too sore and stiff to lead the men, he handed command to Gubbins.[52]

With Nixon's guns, captured provisions and ammunition, and the colors of the 1st Louisiana as trophies, Thornton's men cheered so loudly that Captain Simpson, now a wounded prisoner on the other bank, took pleasure in the looks of consternation on the faces of his captors.[53] Still hoping to influence the fight on the other side, Thornton's last command was to launch Gubbins on a pursuit that quickly overran Patterson's abandoned guns and drove the Yankees back to Dr. William Flood's plantation, immediately opposite Line Jackson across the river.[54] The sailors not aboard the gunboats charged one American battery with pikes, its defenders quailing before the terrifying weapons.[55] Lieutenant Hole commanding one of the gun barges exulted that the west bank objective that many had thought dauntingly difficult had turned out to be "an easy prey."[56]

Morgan had stopped enough men to try to lead a counatercharge, but more Congreves disrupted them and they ran back three hundred yards past Patterson's abandoned guns to see their crews running to *Louisiana's* levee mooring farther upstream. With no wind to make sail, Patterson, Nixon, and others broke out a hawser and began towing the ship to safety.[57] Morgan, meanwhile, rode a mile to the rear to unfinished works on the Jourdan plantation, hoping to make a stand there, but he could not stop the militia in their flight.[58] He tried and failed again at the next canal back, and kept riding until he passed all of the fleeing men and got word that Captain James C. Wilkins's company from Natchez awaited him ahead.

A brusque, decisive businessman who controlled much of Natchez's river commerce and most of its cotton, Wilkins had arrived in New Orleans only that morning, when he commandeered two ferryboats to cross to Morgan. Once over, he marched down the levee road to the Bois Gervais line, a set of unfinished earthworks laid out by Latour that afforded the best backup defenses above Morgan's original position. Wilkins sent notice of his arrival to Morgan and minutes later saw the panicked militia, many unarmed, coming toward him as their officers vainly tried to stop them. When they saw Wilkins's company standing steady, Nixon and the Louisiana militia halted as well, and Wilkins and Morgan began stabilizing a line.[59] Davis soon appeared to report that he had only about thirty men left after falling back a mile and a half.[60] Morgan began the day with roughly 1,000 men, and even though fewer than fifty had been killed or wounded, he now had no more than four hundred effectively under control.[61] The rest just evaporated.

About then Pierre Laffite arrived with an order from Jackson for them to hold their ground. Morgan sent the smuggler back to report that he had been forced to retreat. "The men have ran [sic] away," he moaned, and blamed it on Davis's Kentuckians. He had many wounded, his men had not eaten, and the fog at times limited visibility to no more than 150 yards. He wanted to counterattack, he protested, but feared that his men "are not good pluck," and he had lost almost all of his artillery. Paralyzed by indecision, Morgan asked Jackson to send Laffite back with instructions.[62]

A lull of about ninety minutes followed, and Thornton made good use of it. He wrote a hasty report to Pakenham, unaware that the general was dead.[63] The gun barges continued some distance upstream and reached a position above Jackson's headquarters before American guns threw shots their way.[64] Gubbins had captured three big twenty-fours, three twelves, six nine-pounders, two brass fours, and an unmounted twelve-pounder carronade. Roberts's seamen also captured a brass ten-inch howitzer on which they found engraved words that now seemed ironic: "Taken at the surrender of York Town 1781."[65] Altogether those guns could throw enough weight of iron to put Jackson's right flank at serious risk, and not all of their powder had been thrown into the river. Major Michell quickly set men to clearing the spiked vents, and they were just about to train the repaired guns on Old Hickory's line, when Colonel Burgoyne arrived with staggering news.[66] They were ordered to withdraw.

Across the river the British shambles had continued as the army's command bled and died on the clover. Pakenham, one colonel, two majors, five captains, two lieutenants, and two ensigns had been killed and a score of others wounded, some, like Gibbs, mortally. The 44th began the day with sixteen officers; four were still standing.[67] As the 4th Foot approached the ditch, a sergeant yelled that "it's of no use going any further" and pointed to the rear. A staff officer came to the front of the remnant of the 21st and ordered it to move over to the cypress wood.[68] Lieutenant William Knight looked back to see the whole attack column dissolving, some running to the rear and others to the closer cover of the cypresses. He told his men to throw their ladders into the canal and run for the woods, where he could see portions of the 4th and 44th lying down. On the way he asked a sergeant how many remained of the seventy or more Knight had collected shortly before. The sergeant counted himself and eleven others, three badly wounded.[69] Major Pringle's remnant heard a bedlam of orders by men he could not see, some shouting to advance, others to retreat. Finally, Major John Kipping of the 4th told him to collect what he could and get out. With about 260 of the 21st, Pringle dashed for the cypresses and reported to Colonel Brooke, now commanding Gibbs's brigade.[70]

That morning Pakenham had detailed Captain Timothy Jones of the 4th to take four hundred men from his regiment, the 21st, the 95th, and 5th West India to retrace Rennie's January 1 route through the woods and swamp to occupy Coffee's men at their log works, and to cover Gibbs's right flank should Jackson attempt a sortie against him.[71] They got in position all right, but when Jones launched an assault, it met unbearable musketry. He fell with a mortal wound as he cheered his men on, and four from the 5th West India went down, the only black redcoats killed in action that day.[72] Further efforts proved equally costly until a staff officer from Gibbs or Lambert arrived with orders to fall back. As they retreated, Tennesseans came over their works to pursue. Redcoat fire stopped them, and then Captain Lawrence of the *Alceste* set some dry grass on fire to hinder pursuit. As Jones's men emerged from the cypresses, they looked to their right at the main line to see Gibbs's column now shattered into small groups fleeing before American artillery and musketry that appeared to be a solid sheet of flame.[73]

Once the 21st and 4th withdrew toward the wood, other scattered elements of the 44th followed. Knight covered the five hundred yards or more to a concave bend in the woods that put trees between him and fire from Battery Nos. 6, 7, and 8, and from Carroll.[74] He arrived with only three of his grenadiers, to be met by a staff officer whom Lambert had sent to organize a defense should Jackson counterattack.[75] Mullins was still on the field ten yards from the ditch with a few others when the remainder of the 44th retired. He and one private were last of the 44th to leave the field. No one remained behind but the wounded and the dead.[76] Minutes earlier he sent a sergeant back to try to collect and bring up stragglers. The sergeant encountered Adjutant Barry, heading forward with a small party. At that moment they saw the attack stopped and men falling back toward the cypresses. Barry turned his party to meet them and in moments ran into a disoriented

Mullins, who wondered how Barry had managed to escape from the front, when he had never been there.[77]

Seeing them approach, a grenadier sergeant recently suspended for striking a soldier ran to show them where the others lay concealed. Once there, Mullins found Knight and they compared experiences, Mullins asking if the lieutenant thought they might have gotten over the enemy works if the ladders and fascines had been in place. Knight thought they could have, which was no comfort to Mullins now.[78] Nearby, the living of the 21st looked out on the field to see fallen comrades whom they could not help. A sergeant wrote in his diary that "there was nothing but horror to be seen."[79]

Perhaps the last to leave for the wood were those companies of the 93rd that crossed the field with Keane. A bugle sounded their recall, but officers had to grab men and forcibly turn them around to get them to obey.[80] Too faint to rise and join them, Ensign Graves lay on the clover, still holding the regimental banner's staff. He saw a fleeing soldier stopping to plunder the pockets of the fallen as he passed, and when the man approached him, Graves rose on one knee and brandished the staff, warning the man to move on. Moments later a 93rd sergeant passed, and Graves handed him the colors before fainting again.[81] That left only the original covering companies of the 95th in position in front of the abandoned advance battery. Spread out as they were, they offered less of a target for enemy artillery and took few losses as they ran for the woods.[82]

When Tylden gave Lambert word of Pakenham's death and conditions on the battle line, he added that, in his view, any chance of victory on this side of the river was gone, and they must withdraw. The musketry across the river told him that Thornton was attacking at last, but too late to retrieve the disaster here. The battle had been decided before Thornton even reached Morgan's line.[83] On taking command, Lambert took his reserves forward.[84] When he got within 250 yards of the enemy line, he saw the confusion ahead, and put the 7th, the 43rd, the 1st West India, and the dismounted 14th Dragoons in line with orders to hold there while he ascertained the situation in front.

Men from the shattered assaults soon began rallying to Lambert's reserve line. Cooke and his party from the far left came across the field to join the 7th and the 43rd. Before them was a scene from *The Inferno*. Clouds of acrid smoke billowed overhead. The concussion from enemy artillery made the soil beneath their feet vibrate "as if the earth was cracking and tumbling to pieces," while muzzle flashes from the embrasures looked like fire belching from the ground.[85] "All order was at an end," Cooke realized, although thanks to the smoke and remaining fog he still could not tell the full state of affairs. A fleeing redcoat passed him without stopping, yelling only that "we attacked, Sir."[86]

Looking back toward Rennie's route of advance, Cooke saw his friend Duncan Campbell staggering in a circle, still holding his broken sword in his hand as he fell and rose repeatedly, then finally stayed down, blinded by a ball that had torn open his forehead. Ahead of him lay several days of delirium until death's release. Moments later Colonel Frederick Stovin appeared, bleeding down the left side of his face from a ball that had entered behind his right ear and passed out behind the left one, miraculously missing his skull and just grazing his spine. The concussion of the hit knocked his hat from his head but he could still walk, although he soon quipped that he would in future make fewer bows. "Did you ever see such a scene?" Harry Smith yelled as he passed at full gallop. It was the most murderous fire he had ever experienced, and now only Lambert's men maintained discipline. He told Cooke's party to join them and prepare for a counterattack should it come.[87]

Cooke obeyed but then realized that, with Rennie repulsed, the Yankees on Jackson's right could rush down the river road as much as a mile almost without opposition and get behind the reserve with only a company of the 93rd still at the mud battery in the way. Fortunately, the 7th and 43rd held their ground, Benson Hill likening them to a pair of seventy-four-gun ships of the line stubbornly holding their position. The companies of the 95th also held, though catching a cross fire of artillery from their front and enemy batteries over the river.[88] Amid the confusion, Hill noticed an acoustic anomaly. The sound of enemy fire appeared to come from the cypresses to his right, while the muzzle flashes on Line Jackson seemed silent. Regardless of the firing's source, the ground before him was plowed by shot like a furrowed field.[89]

Lambert soon confirmed that the situation was irreparable. He could renew the attack with his reserve, but they were the only reliable troops now, and the cost would be high.[90] Some fugitives from the storming parties rallied when they reached the reserve, but the sight of groaning wounded and dead on the ground all around risked demoralizing them as well as his own men.[91] He rode to Villeré's to find Cochrane and informed him that he would not continue the attack. That done, he returned to his reserve and had them take cover in the reeds and mud.[92] It was about ten a.m. when he learned of Thornton's success and sent Dickson after Burgoyne to see if captured enemy artillery was usable. His order found Dickson at the De La Ronde house amid a horrifying scene. The wounded and dying crowded every room. Pakenham lay dead beside a doomed Gibbs, who writhed in agony. Amputations progressed all around. The surgeons did not stop even to remove soldiers' hose before severing legs and tossing them in a basket. Hill knew he could never forget the sight. At least Keane seemed likely to survive.

Apparently, when he reached Thornton, Colonel Burgoyne withheld details of Pakenham's death and defeat, but the fact that the order came from the army's fourth-ranking general clearly meant something had happened to the three ranking above him. Rumor swept through the ranks, and Major Michell immediately began spiking the captured artillery save for two brass four- and six-pounders they would take with them, along with the "York Town" howitzer. They were not about to lose that gun to the Yankees two wars in a row.[93] An outraged Captain Roberts believed that with a few guns he could drive Jackson from his line if only Thornton held his ground, but then he was young, and daring, and by his later accounts of the affair regarded the engagement on the right bank as rather a "frolic."[94]

Then Dickson arrived. In the confusion attendant to preparations to retire, he found some of the sailors and marines scattered and immune to orders, while others plundered Morgan's tents. He got them in order and then he, Michell, and Peddie went forward to where the 85th was about to burn Flood's mill and a bridge over the canal they were using as a defensive line. Looking to his right, Dickson could actually see behind Jackson's main line. If they could just use the captured artillery, they might still force Old Hickory out of his works. However beaten they were on the left bank, they could still salvage a piece of a victory on this side, and that might be enough to enlarge upon to retrieve the battle, and honor.

With the bulk of the army under Lambert bloodied and disorganized now, it hardly mattered. Thornton had only 650 to 700 men at hand, some disorganized, and the battered 85th the best of what remained. He could not afford much risk. He reported his situation to Lambert and then found the left of his new line vulnerable to being turned by several paths and canals, so he ordered it back some distance until he heard from the general. Ensign Gleig's picket acted as rear guard while Gleig himself, having gone nearly a month without a change of clothes, picked up an abandoned American tent that promised some small comfort.[95] When some of the enemy appeared to rally for a counterassault, he formed his guard in line and gave every indication that he meant to advance. At that, the Yankees retired once more, and Gleig about-faced his men, set fire to the rest of the Flood buildings, and behind the cover of their smoke destroyed the canal bridge to cut off pursuit.[96]

Dickson pulled the line back yet again as the 85th completed spiking the captured guns. That done, Dickson returned to Lambert in person to report that the position there was still a good one, but it needed 2,000 men at least to make it secure. Hearing that, Lambert met again with Cochrane for some time before he finally and definitively decided to pull Thornton over from the right bank.[97] Burgoyne soon returned to argue that having Patterson's guns meant they could still renew the main attack with hope of success, but Lambert was done with that and sent him over the river once more to recall Thornton.[98]

The British were just withdrawing when Captain Shaumburg arrived. He found everything scattered and demoralized, with the men blaming their leaders. "Give us officers and we will fight better," some told him. He showed Morgan Jackson's order that Thornton must be destroyed, but Morgan candidly said he could not do it. Then the colorful General Jean Joseph Amable Humbert arrived unexpectedly saying that Old Hickory had sent him to take four hundred of Morgan's men and eliminate Thornton. Morgan demanded to see a written order, but the career adventurer Humbert answered that his instructions were verbal, whereupon Morgan retorted that even if he had four hundred men he could depend upon, he would not let Humbert have them without written direction from Old Hickory. At that, Humbert just left in a huff.[99] With the enemy clearly withdrawing, Morgan and Humbert gave Thornton a gift of vital time to get to his boats while they disputed which of them ought to command.[100]

Now Governor Claiborne appeared. Labatut had commandeered every craft and crew he could find, even small market boats, to get the last reinforcements across. Once over, Claiborne rode ahead and arrived shortly after the rebuffed Humbert left.[101] When Labatut's reinforcements marched up to Bois Gervais, the commanders discussed a counterattack; but when they weighed the condition of Morgan's command, and the deteriorating weather, Claiborne determined against it, a decision with which the others agreed. Instead, he decided to consolidate the line at Bois Gervais and send Jackson a frank statement of conditions there.[102]

To many it seemed the narrowest of escapes. Gabriel Winter believed Thornton could have marched all the way up the levee to Baton Rouge had Lambert not recalled him.[103] In reality, of course, Thornton had spread himself thin to get this far, fully five miles from his landing, and New Orleans lay another five miles beyond. Advancing beyond Flood's would take him even farther from either support or escape. The close of the attack on the other side left Jackson free to reinforce this side, and he already had four hundred more of Adair's Kentuckians running to the city to cross over. Pitiful as Morgan's resistance had been thus far, it still cost British casualties.

Even if the Yankee rout were renewed, it would cost still more. Most of Patterson's captured artillery was too cumbersome to help in an advance, and almost all of its gunpowder lay soaked in the river. The critical predawn hours of delay could not be charged to Thornton's account, and when he arrived, he achieved everything asked of him, but Pakenham's expectations of a precisely coordinated attack and an easy seizure of Patterson's artillery to use against Jackson were somewhat unrealistic. Judging from what Patterson actually did, he would have destroyed his ammunition as soon as his guns were threatened, rendering them as good as useless.

Thornton's was a victory barren of fruit. The next day Admiral Codrington told his wife, Jane, that "this whole operation succeeded beautifully," but the men involved felt rather differently. By the time they could make an impression on the fight on the other side, it was already over, and the lieutenants commanding one of the gun barges complained that "they seemed altogether to have forgot us on the left side." After setting fire to a sugar house and other outbuildings as a distraction, Thornton marched unopposed back to the boats, Major Michell grumbling angrily that "our triumph has been useless."[104]

Across the Mississippi, Lambert withdrew the soldiers in the cypresses to safety. To cover the movement as well as check the enemy left for any sign of counterattack, he sent Knight and a detachment of the 44th along the path taken by Jones. With them went a marine ensign still carrying a prized sword the wounded Keane gave him for safekeeping as he headed for the hospital. Knight, ensign, sword, and fifty others did not return.[105]

Lambert's reserve covered the withdrawal of the rest to their old camps, and Tylden admired the steadiness of the 7th and 43rd, wondering anew why Pakenham chose Gibbs's command to be the attacking column when Lambert's men were more experienced and reliable. "Had they led the attack," he believed, "the place would have been carried if it had been possible."[106]

They could not know that, six hours before the signal rocket went up, a London editor, considering the circumstances of the expedition last known to be at Jamaica, forecast gloomily "our fear that its results will not be prosperous."[107] Prosperity seemed indeed to forsake His Majesty's forces that morning. Tylden reflected on an army mostly broken and dispersed, with only two regiments really capable of stiff resistance should Jackson counterattack. Sensitive to Lambert's sudden and unexpected thrust into top command, Tylden admired his aplomb. "I never saw anything more cool than Genl Lambert's conduct," he concluded, "& his arrangements were as able as it was possible to expect under such extraordinary circumstances." With their left along the main road vulnerable, Lambert quickly had Tylden collect scattered squads of the 95th and the 5th West India and sent them over to the mud battery to bolster its defense.

Jackson's line cheered at seeing the enemy's shattered columns breaking for the woods.[108] Yankee artillery still pounded them as Old Hickory remained alert for a renewed assault, but this battle was done. No one agreed on how long it had lasted, because no one agreed on when it had begun or when it had ended. Tatum thought it raged for forty-five minutes. Major Reid believed it was almost an hour. Others timed it at seventy-five minutes, and one officer suggested one hundred. Four days later a witness said it raged as long as two hours and forty-five minutes, but most agreed with Carroll that about two hours was right.[109] Hence it was about ten a.m. The morning was yet young, but hundreds now lying on that field would never grow another hour older.

"This has been a proud day for our country," declared one of the victors that afternoon.[110] The next day Alex Henderson of Hinds's battalion called it "a most brilliant event," and an Orleanian said with marked even-handedness that "there was never more determined bravery on both sides."[111] Their success frankly surprised many Americans. "I dont [sic] suppose there ever was men fought more Bravely," David Weller wrote home.[112] With pardonable pride, they boasted of standing "like a rock."[113] It was "the warmest day," said another, with no thought of weather in his mind.[114] On both sides the living congratulated themselves for surviving what a *creole* officer within hours looked back upon as "the greatest fury."[115]

Twenty

"All Fear Is at an End"

L AMBERT KEPT HIS 7th and 43rd Regiments lying in the mud and reeds until dark.[1] After nightfall Dickson spiked the guns they could not bring in from the field, threw their powder and shot into the canal, and pulled the tubes from their carriages. At ten p.m. the general moved the rest of the battered army back to its camps and soon afterward Cochrane, Malcolm, and Codrington joined him on the picket line. Codrington, in charge of feeding the army, knew that they had just ten days' provisions on hand and within a few days must go on half rations. Ill-equipped for a siege, exhausted from moving the heavy guns, and dogged by one organizational miscarriage after another, the army must either attack again in the morning, he argued, or retire.

Almost all of the officers counseled returning to their ships while not necessarily giving up the campaign.[2] Tylden thought a night assault might carry Jackson's defenses, but the army was badly battered. Even if they took New Orleans, he doubted they could hold it, and they dared not risk being shut up there and besieged.[3] Lambert made no immediate decision, but Dickson was sure he would withdraw the army.[4] In fact, the general decided the next day to pull out, advising Cochrane they should instead pursue a softer target, like Mobile.[5]

Shortly after the fighting stopped, Lambert sent Major Harry Smith under a white flag to seek a cease-fire to collect the wounded and bury the dead. Jackson agreed to a suspension of hostilities until noon the next day, but only on his side of the river, since at that moment Thornton was still on the right bank facing Morgan. He further stipulated that neither army was to send reinforcements to the other side before midnight, January 9. Jackson had already sent four hundred to Morgan, so he felt comfortable that he could hold his ground there. Lambert also finessed a bit. Instead of immediately accepting the terms, he waited until ten o'clock the next morning, by which time he had pulled Thornton over to the main army.

Wary of allowing enemy officers a closer look at his defenses, Jackson set the truce line at a ditch three hundred yards in front of his works.[6] The British gathered the dead and wounded on their side of the line, while the Americans bore enemy dead on their side to the truce line and took enemy wounded back to their hospitals for care. It was grisly work. The ground in front of Line Jackson appeared to many to be completely covered with the redcoats' dead.[7] In the area where Gibbs's attack had failed, Jackson's men gathered more than three hundred bodies and laid them in rows by the ditch.[8] At the same time they brought five hundred or more wounded back as prisoners, most badly injured, and many mortally.[9] On the field Captain Maunsel White heard a wounded officer calling for help. Fearing the man might bleed to death, White carried him into camp on his own back. Livingston happened to be escorting other wounded redcoats to the city hospital when he saw White's burden. Jackson allowed Livingston to take the man to his home, where his wife could minister to him, and there they learned that he was Ensign William Graves.[10]

It was worse for the British details. A staff officer of the 7th lamented that "nothing could be seen before them but the dead and dying."[11] Captain Gordon had seen many battles, but this was the worst of all, and he confessed that the list of killed and wounded made his blood run cold.[12] A false rumor spread within hours that forty men in Lambert's burial parties were so demoralized by what they saw that they deserted on the spot.[13] They did not, but deserters did begin to filter in to the American lines day after day. The British buried some dead in their abandoned batteries, most of their officers in the Villeré garden, and the rest on the Bienvenu plantation, though not before shivering soldiers stripped the dead of their bloody shirts to wear themselves.[14]

Americans took things, too. Withers removed Rennie's watch, snuff box, a ring, and a brooch from his body after killing him. Jackson had his 7th Regiment give Rennie an honorable burial, and when Pringle sent via flag a request for Rennie's effects, Old Hickory had Withers hand the souvenirs to Captain Simpson for safekeeping and delivery to Rennie's widow, a considerate act that Pringle called "a green spot in the wilderness of American campaigning."[15]

A few Americans gloated when they handed over the dead. "Well, what do you think of we Yankees?" one asked on officer of the 95th. "Don't you think we could lick any of the troops of the continent?" When the irritated Englishman expressed doubt, the other pressed the point. "Didn't the French beat the troops of every other continental nation?" he asked. "Didn't you beat the French in the Peninsula?" he said further. "And haven't we beat you just now?"[16] One Yankee officer, strutting with sword in hand, declared, "I never saw the like of that!" as he looked at the rows of bodies. Unimpressed, a Yorkshireman in red shot back, "That's nout, man; if you'd been wi' us in Spain, you would ha' seen summat far war!"[17]

Benson Hill saw gloomy faces everywhere in Lambert's camps as the mangled wounded came back to the surgeons. All the doctors could do was make men with head or internal wounds as comfortable as possible and leave them to live or die while they hacked the ruined limbs from the rest. Cooke's friend Duncan Campbell never emerged from his delirium. Friends buried him and read a service at the grave until an American shell burst sent them flying.[18] The next day four more officers died, one of them General Gibbs, who expired after forty-eight hours of agony. Purportedly his last words were excoriations of Mullins.[19]

Deserters told the Americans their army suffered 3,000 killed, wounded, and missing in the battle, and 4,500 since they set foot in Louisiana. It was a gross exaggeration, but the real number was horrible enough.[20] Despite his wound, adjutant Stovin collected reports showing 291 killed, 1,262 wounded, and 484 missing. The 4th Regiment was almost annihilated, losing 400 at least.[21] The 93rd Highlanders' loss of 506 killed and wounded was more than half the regiment.[22] At least 100 officers were dead or wounded, not counting many like Mullins with slight injuries. In the fortnight since December 23 the army had suffered 371 killed, 1,511 wounded, and 552 missing, including 129 officers. That came to at least 2,434 out of nearly 10,000 composing the army.[23] Three days after the battle Gleig wrote his sister that "it has been a bloody business."[24]

Many expected Jackson to launch an immediate counterattack on January 8.[25] If ever there was a moment to strike a decisive blow, this should be it as the foe reeled from its loss of officers and men, badly disorganized, with its back to the swamp. Old Hickory did not yet know that three enemy generals were out of action, but Lambert's signature on truce messages suggested a disruption in their high command.[26] Jackson met with his officers to discuss a counterblow. Coffee and Adair were frank. In the open field against trained veterans, both feared their men might not stand.[27]

They only confirmed Old Hickory's decision. Trying for too much risked turning a near miracle into a disaster. Unaccustomed to singing paeans to

Old Hickory, even Shaumburg complimented his coolness and caution in not venturing out from his line.[28] In the following days the general husbanded his men carefully, limiting sorties to reconnaissance and a night raid on January 13 through the cypresses to Villeré's canal to test the defenses of Lambert's escape route.[29] When a Louisiana company begged permission to make a sortie, Jackson refused, telling them, "I prefer to keep for Louisiana four or five fathers, rather than making four or five prisoners."[30] As an aide of the general's put it when asked why Jackson did not attack, Old Hickory was "protecting his victory."[31]

In the city, huddled citizens heard the artillery start to taper off at about 9:30 as the battle began to close. Ninety minutes later a horseman galloped through the streets shouting "Victory! Victory!" until his voice went hoarse.[32] Soon more news filtered into town. Eliza Chotard could not believe that her uncle and brother were safe after the ferocity of the cannonade.[33] When the Kentuckians Jackson sent to reinforce Morgan jogged through the streets, crowds ran to them singing and dancing in joy and relief. "People held out baskets of biscuits and cakes to the men as they passed. Few stopped to eat, but many stuffed the edibles in their shirts and nibbled as they ran."[34]

The Americans reportedly suffered fewer than a dozen deaths and perhaps thirty wounded. It seemed incredible at first, but the more thoughtful recognized the advantages Jackson had in his powerful batteries.[35] A disquieting silence settled over the town.[36] Laura Florian thought it almost ghostly, as if the only inhabitants were shades and specters of a dead city.[37] Almost every literate home began releasing its anxiety on paper, some like Florian writing letters until her aching hand made her stop. "I can give you but a poor idea of things as they really are," she closed one letter, mildly complaining that women were "generally left in the dark as to the true state of affairs."[38]

The price of victory was stern. At least forty carts brought wounded from the field, all but a few of them redcoats. Ten pirogues brought more up the river to the waterfront, and the parade of the suffering continued well into the next day.[39] When the main hospital and the arsenal filled with sufferers, Jackson sent British prisoners from the city jail and parish prison upriver to Natchez to free more room for their wounded.[40] Viewing the shattered bodies, one merchant thought the sight "enough to make the bravest sick of war."[41] Many had been hit eight or ten times by grapeshot.[42] Laura Florian's slave woman returned from a hospital visit sobbing at the condition of the injured.[43] Free black women hired out at $10 a month as nurses, and many white women sent servants or turned out themselves, among them "Grandmere Devince" Bienvenue, who despite her age helped care for the men.[44]

"I have nothing to give but the labor of my hands," Florian said the day after the fight. *"If the bravery of our men is to be commended, the humanity of the ladies deserves no less praise."*[45] Still, the British wounded died constantly. The much-loved "Wilky" Wilkinson breathed his last just hours after the fighting closed, to be buried with honors by foemen who admired his courage.[46] They continued expiring regularly, as did a few of the American wounded, and there was little nurses could do for most.[47] With not a Bible to be had in the city's closed stores, the Louisiana Bible Society, less than two years old, distributed several score testaments to Americans and Englishmen alike.[48]

Private homes opened for the more fortunate wounded officers. For days Louise Livingston looked after Graves, admitting some satisfaction that one who had come to conquer was not a prisoner. He was one of the lucky ones, for in time he recovered, taking with him a permanent limp as his only prize from New Orleans.[49] Maria Laveau Trudeau nursed enemy wounded and captured the eye of British surgeon Josias Kerr from County Tyrone in Ireland. Three years later he returned to New Orleans to marry her.[50] A few days after the battle one of Beale's men believed that everyone in the city not under arms was tending wounded redcoats.[51] There were even family concerns for a few of them. Lieutenant Alexander Geddes of the 21st and his father, Captain William Geddes of the 43rd, were cousins of French consul Tousard's wife. Everyone knew the 21st was part of Rennie's struggle, and Tousard worried that young Geddes might be "among the killed of a regt. which was almost entirely destroyed."[52] In fact he survived, though severely wounded.

Having been brutally treated by redcoats as a boy in the Revolution, and despite his later denunciations of the British, Old Hickory respected enemy soldiers. His major motive was to repel invaders, and he passed up repeated opportunities to exact revenge on British soldiers and officers, showing instead kindnesses to prisoners, the wounded, and the dead's bereaved.[53] The day after the fight he assured Cochrane that he would release all the wounded he could to their own surgeons and promised every comfort to those too badly injured to be moved.[54] Captain Simpson never forgot the "courteous civility" shown him, and Jackson even sent a bottle of claret to ease his discomfort.[55] The Yankees showed universal respect for Rennie, one calling the major a "great and most brave man."[56] Word of Yankee treatment of British wounded reached Lambert's camps, where Tylden granted that "the Americans have behaved with some degree of kindness to our wounded."[57] One of Beale's men predicted that Louisiana would earn high rank among the states both for its conduct in battle, and the humanity shown to the vanquished.[58]

The first two hundred prisoners came to town shortly after the firing stopped, impressing onlookers with their dignity and fine appearance.[59] Within days their number rose to 250, while hundreds more filled the ersatz hospitals.[60] They confessed surprise at their treatment, having been told to expect the Yankees to be "semi-barbarian."[61] The redcoats were particularly curious about the Tennesseans and how they had laughed at the rockets and met the assault so steadfastly.[62] Prisoners also endeared themselves with exaggerated statements that even with 50,000 they could never have taken the city. Speaking of the battle, Simpson told some that the fight at the bastion had been hotter than any he had witnessed in Spain or France.[63]

For the American wounded, Louaillier immediately raised $2,000 for the Charity Hospital, and women sent cotton lint for bandages, blankets, pillows—even mattresses—for the comfort of the sufferers.[64] By the end of the month donors subscribed more than $7,000. Women made trousers, shirts, and coats for the Kentucky and Tennessee men, and contributors provided 440 mattresses. Claiborne and the legislature acted to provide pensions to families of men in the colored companies who lost their lives.[65]

In a few days civilians began to relax. "Louisiana is still American," a relieved Mrs. Livingston wrote on January 12.[66] As shops reopened after nearly a month's closure and smiles returned to faces, a *creole* rejoiced, "*Vive les Etats Unis.*"[67] *Banquettes* resumed their former vitality, and gloom gave place to joyfulness.[68] One young man delightedly exclaimed that once more there were "beautiful girls to be seen," and young love was renewed when Isaac Longteau of New Orleans and Anne Eleonore Joubert of Sant-Domingue registered their January 9 marriage with Pedesclaux in the year's first notarial act.[69]

Commerce began anew and commodity prices rebounded. Within a week cotton sold at ten cents a pound, and soon doubled.[70] The steamboat *Enterprise*, proud of its small part in the defense, had fifty paying passengers ready to leave for Natchez on its first voyage since the battle.[71] Expecting peace in a few weeks, merchantmen crowded the wharves preparing to return to sea, streets filled with merchants' carts, and everywhere was bustle and commotion, Claiborne soon reporting that "our harbor is again whitened with canvass."[72]

That meant renewed vitality in slave sales.[73] Several notaries' first transactions were slave purchases, in one case just eight days after the battle. De Armas recorded the sale of a young woman to one of Coffee's mounted gunmen, and free black men and women bought and sold as before.[74] On the obverse of the "peculiar institution's" Janus mask, three masters applied to emancipate their slaves when the parish court reopened.[75]

On January 25 both the *Louisiana Courier* and the *Louisiana Gazette* printed special editions, then a week later the *Gazette* resumed publication. Manager Alexis Daudat reopened his theater at 64 St. Philippe on January 28 with a one-act play written for the occasion, titled *Le Camp de Jackson* and dedicated to the general.[76] Soon a visitor reported that "every thing in New Orleans begins to wear a pleasing aspect."[77] Validating the city's return to commerce as usual, the parole, countersign, and watchwords on January 26 were "Business," and "plenty."[78]

Rumor became social currency, and conversations with the wounded and prisoners seemed to confirm enemy plans for conquest and occupation.[79] Within three days of the fight, the story spread that Pakenham intended to be governor-general of conquered New Orleans and had brought with him a mayor, a collector of customs, and other officers for civil government with their families and even their household goods to move into the fine homes they expected to appropriate, and letters from wives found on the bodies of officers supposedly asked husbands to get them the best houses. Cochrane's printing press seemed sure proof of an intent to govern, and within a fortnight Orleanians heard that Pakenham's wife was with the fleet, waiting to reign as "governess" of Louisiana, a fable untroubled by awareness that he died a bachelor.[80] Even Jackson came to accept that the British intended to establish a colonial government.[81] Skeptics dismissed all this as mere rumor, which it was, but it primed the gullible for a more inflammatory story to come.[82]

Old Hickory's losses in the battle were almost minuscule. Adair lost one man killed, eleven wounded, and two missing as prisoners. Coffee lost a sergeant dead and three privates wounded. The artillery and navy suffered three killed. In the army as a whole, and including Morgan's combat, he lost just thirteen dead, thirty-nine wounded, and nineteen missing, although later skirmishing would add to the figure.[83] In the main battle on the east bank it was just six killed and seven wounded. For the campaign as a whole since December 23, his losses were 55 dead, 185 wounded, and 93 missing, the greatest losses being from sickness in Coffee's command and the 44th.[84]

Jackson wisely acted as if the enemy would make another attempt, although he did not expect one.[85] Patterson seemed certain of it at first but felt confident their defenses would easily withstand another assault, while some in the ranks actually hoped the redcoats would come again and give them another victory.[86] The arrival of the delayed muskets from Pittsburgh on January 11, and a schooner from Tchefuncte delivering reinforcements two days later, spurred their ardor. Now they had an excess of men and plenty of arms, and the spiked guns lost by Morgan had been repaired.[87] Meanwhile, Old Hickory meant to give the British no rest. He kept half the army ready to march at all times, banished liquor from the camps, and imposed tight restrictions.[88] Men intoxicated with victory welcomed the discipline. Bands at the breastwork played "Yankee Doodle" and other patriotic airs, and taunted the enemy with "Rule, Britannia." Men displayed banners on the works with fighting mottoes, and some stood atop the parapet hurling rude gestures at the foe.[89]

Jackson had matters elsewhere to consider. Cochrane had sent *Nymph*, *Aetna*, *Herald*, *Meteor*, *Thistle*, and *Pigmy* to test the Mississippi as a back door to New Orleans. They sighted Fort St. Philip just as Pakenham's shattered legions huddled in the swamps and cypresses on January 8.[90] Overton learned of their approach earlier that day, and the next morning saw three vessels anchor downstream beyond range of his guns. He immediately sent Davezac to Jackson with a warning that the enemy might try to pass the fort that night.[91] When he passed Fort St. Leon, Davezac shared the news with

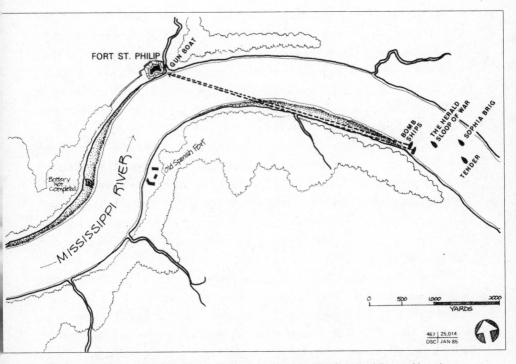

The bombardment of Fort St. Philip, January 9–17, 1815. The British ships and bomb vessels coming up the Mississippi appear at right. From that point they sent more than 1,000 shot and shells at Fort St. Philip without doing significant damage as the fort effectively stopped their effort to reach New Orleans.

Major Gordon, who had five eighteens and twenty-fours and a garrison of just over four hundred men, but no experienced gunners and no shot furnace.[92] The resourceful major immediately began wrapping a concoction of resin, turpentine, saltpeter, and sulfur in shoe leather to make "fire balls" he hoped to fire onto the enemy's decks if they came.[93]

At 3:30 the ships below Fort St. Philip opened fire, lobbing mortar shells in a high arc over the fort's walls.

Overton sat out the bombardment into the evening, and late that night sent an express to Jackson with the news that so far enemy shells did no damage. When the shelling continued next day, some in the city feared the British might pass the fort. If that happened, their victory at Chalmette might be for nothing, one officer fretting that if the enemy got by Overton, "we shall be in a bad way."[94] As backup just in case, Jackson sent a 13.5-inch mortar, a battery of twenty-four-pounders, and a portable hot shot furnace from Fort St. John to support Morgan's earthworks. By the next day Patterson had the guns in place and ready, and Old Hickory admonished Morgan to hold his post, for "the safety of the Country and my army in a great measure depends on it."[95]

On his own front, Jackson resumed his bombardment when the January 9 truce expired, bringing *Louisiana* downstream to add her broadside. A Yankee joked that the guns fired at the enemy occasionally just "to keep their eyes open," but the cannonade was almost ceaseless.[96] On January 10, Alney McLean counted fifty discharges during the time it took him to write a 180-word letter, better than one shot every four words.[97] The following week of shelling did little damage but kept the enemy on guard and apprehensive.[98] Jackson destroyed remaining buildings and fences between the lines, offering the plantation owners the cold comfort that "the imperious dictates of public duty require the sacrifice."[99] For Lambert's benefit, he ordered drums to beat assembly some mornings as if he meant to attack, then sent his men to breakfast, and on January 13 began firing the mortar every two hours in the night as a signal for other batteries to send salvos to disrupt enemy sleep.[100]

There was precious little rest for the redcoats. Few could sleep on the soggy ground amid frequent rain. Some bedded on tree branches to get above the muck, but a Yankee shell could send them diving. A tremendous storm on January 10 further soaked the bivouac, capping their misery.[101] The shelling itself caused only five wounded in the 43rd and 85th. Then, after more than a week of it, early on January 17 Lieutenant Edward D'Arcy of the 43rd lay asleep in a slave cabin, when a shell exploded outside. Shrapnel killed a nearby private and flew in to amputate both of D'Arcy's legs, driving one of his feet deep into the mud, where friends found it later. Kentuckians on Jackson's line could hear D'Arcy's screams. Somehow he clawed his way out of the cabin, and miraculously survived.[102]

Inactivity fostered discontent, even anger, that the Americans did not attack.[103] Succor for their bodies came on January 9 when a supply fleet reached Lake Borgne with quantities of provisions, and two days later fresh supplies began reaching the army.[104] Men and officers hunted wildfowl to supplement their diet, and commissaries bought beef and bullocks from local Spaniards. With abundant sugar and oranges at hand, they boiled them to make candied orange peel for what an officer called "sweets without cost."[105] Three dozen cannon arrived as well, and reinforcements were coming, the 40th "Second Somersetshire" regiment having come up the river in transports and landed some distance below Fort St. Philip late on January 9. They were on their way upstream now.[106] For the soul, the Presbyterian 95th held services on January 15, one from Proverbs: "My son, give me thine heart, and let thine eyes observe my ways."[107]

Truce flags passed back and forth almost daily, and with them arose rumors of an armistice or even peace.[108] When an express mail rider arrived the day after the battle, just sixteen days out of Washington, a rumor flew through the camps that he brought word of a treaty, news that quickly reached British ears. Codrington doubted it was true but prayed it might be, at the same time shocked to think they would have suffered a bloody defeat *after* the war's end.[109] Days passed without confirmation, and the wishful thinking winked out, then during a truce on January 12 the rumor rekindled yet again.[110]

The bombardment continued on into January 12, with men anxiously expecting hourly to hear from Overton. Then two explosions shook the atmosphere. Major Reid took it to mean that several enemy vessels had blown up, but others feared it was Fort St. Philip itself.[111] A false report of its fall soon reached Cochrane, who sent a dragoon through the lower bayous to ascertain the facts.[112] Tylden doubted that the flotilla had passed the fort, and even if they had, "it is now too late." Then an express reached Jackson with the happy news that it was enemy ships blowing up.[113]

As the bombardment of the fort continued, an American lieutenant listening from a distance counted one discharge every twenty seconds.[114] At Fort St. Leon, Gordon's anxiety was such that on January 14 he begged Morgan, "For god sake write me a little news."[115] There was actually less anxiety in the fort itself. Most British shells either sank into the beach outside its walls or bounced off its thick masonry. With twenty-eight twenty-four-pounders, a pair of howitzers, more than 700 cannon cartridges, five tons of powder, and 3,800 balls and shells, the fort could bite back.[116] Those twenty-fours accounted for the two exploded vessels and would be deadly if others came in range. Wollstonecraft had a thirteen-inch mortar, but it was mute thanks to improper fuses.[117] At night British barges rowed close enough to fire grapeshot to disrupt the Yankees' sleep as the garrison endured the shelling in whatever protection they could erect.[118] The strain told on one officer who stayed drunk enough during the shelling to be insolent to Wollstonecraft.[119]

Back at Villeré's, apprehension afflicted the British. Cynically dismissing their campaign as Cochrane's "Quixotical Expedition," Tylden expected it to take a week to reembark the army if Lambert so decided.[120] While engineers laid out defensive lines in case the Americans advanced, Lambert put the remnant of the 44th to making a better road along the canal to the landing place, and from there along the bayou to the fishermen's huts. Thornton and the walking wounded left on January 11 in a cold wind for the nine-mile journey to the village. Learning that the 40th Foot was arriving downriver, Lambert ordered it to return to its transports.[121] On January 12, Dickson got the mobile artillery and ammunition on the way back.[122]

The next day the remaining movable wounded were on their way, as well as some local slaves who had run away to the army. Codrington sent an advance alert to *Alceste*, *Bucephalus*, and *Fox* to act as hospital ships, then he and Cochrane left on January 14, leaving Malcolm to organize the naval part of the withdrawal.[123] Two days later, coming as no surprise to any, Lambert announced that the infantry would commence departing at nightfall January 18.[124] Retreat on top of defeat only made hard labor now more onerous, and officers heard constant murmurs and complaints in the ranks.[125]

Jackson had a good idea of what was happening. On January 12 a scouting party found eight spiked enemy guns in one of their abandoned batteries.[126] The next day he got sightings of the men and stores leaving for the bayou. Lookouts on Lake Borgne reported enemy vessels with flags at half-mast in mourning for Pakenham.[127] Expectation swept the army that the foe would retreat.[128] By January 17, Old Hickory was convinced of it, and enemy movements and one or two deserters confirmed suspicions.[129] He sent Kemper to reconnoiter again and ordered Morgan to send six hundred men by keelboat downriver. Should Kemper confirm enemy withdrawal, Morgan would cross the river below the abandoned British camps to attack Lambert's rear and flank on the Villeré canal while Jackson struck him in front. They might just catch Lambert's army strung out along the bayou, cut off part of it, and force the rest to surrender.[130]

Jackson put his frontline units on alert with full cartridge boxes.[131] It was a Jacksonian plan, founded on sound intelligence, insightful projection of enemy movements, good judgment of the achievable, and the instinct to stretch fortune a bit beyond those limits. Unfortunately, Morgan's performance was typically Morganian. Acting with neither celerity nor daring, he barely got moving before it was too late, reinforcing yet again Jackson's crying need for just one regular general he could depend on in place of planters and politicians turned soldiers.

Captain Gordon and Admiral Malcolm labored hard at the fishermen's huts organizing the embarkation. The captain worked with uncommon activity for a man with "timber toes," even when high tide made the ground so marshy, his wooden stump sank into the mud as he walked.[132] Malcolm strove with equal energy, and Gordon thought him the most active man he had ever served under.[133] Cochrane and Codrington joined them briefly at the huts on their way to the Lake Borgne anchorage to prepare to take aboard the army.[134]

The day after the battle Cochrane proposed a prisoner exchange, and Jackson agreed. With Harry Smith acting for the British and Livingston for the Americans, meetings produced lists of captives' names, but Cochrane omitted some prisoners he had already dispatched to England.[135] Knowing the Americans had more prisoners to trade than he did, he tried to pad his list with the names of civilians to increase his leverage, but Livingston and Jackson saw through him.[136] Smith and Livingston got along amicably and exchanged many courtesies for others, as when the commander of the 43rd managed to send Captain Simpson his baggage.[137] Smith tried to give no hint of the impending withdrawal, but abundant signs of it worked against him.[138]

They concluded their agreement on January 17. American prisoners in the British camps were to be turned over the next day, and any elsewhere would be delivered to the Rigolets, whereupon Jackson would deliver an equal number of redcoats to waiting ships at the mouth of the Mississippi. The agreement also included a trade of ambulatory wounded.[139] Lambert had his captives brought forward to the De La Ronde grounds that same day, purposely concentrating some of Dickson's artillery there for them to see to discourage suspicions that he planned to withdraw.[140] With departure at hand, some redcoats became skittish. That evening some fired on grazing horses after mistaking them for enemy cavalry. Three men from the 7th deserted into that same darkness.[141]

January 18 came cloudy and cold, threatening rain. As the prisoners of both sides returned to their comrades, Jackson's bands played solemn tunes as the flags of both armies waved, the soldiers at attention watching in silence.[142] Major Craven Luckett of Kentucky was moved by what he saw, confessing that "never in my life had I such feelings."[143] A few last acts of cordiality occurred. Everything movable had been taken from Villeré's house except an armoire with his daughter's clothes, and a pilferer had pocketed the key even for that. Now he gave the key to one of the American prisoners to return to her.[144] At the same time, Benson Hill asked Nathaniel Cox to look after a wounded friend Lambert had to leave behind with other unmovable wounded. Cox agreed, neither apparently realizing that the request gave away the withdrawal.[145] In a final ruse, Smith bid farewell to Livingston, saying, "We shall soon meet in New Orleans."[146]

When darkness fell, the dragoons and movable artillery began the evacuation.[147] At about 6:30, the rest followed with the rearmost first, the 21st, the 1st and 5th West India, and the 4th Foot. At 7:30 the 93rd, the 85th, and the 95th followed, then the 4th at 10:30, the 7th an hour later, and finally the 43rd.[148] Torrential rain fell as the second contingent departed, turning violent for half an hour and making some fear it might delay or even halt their retreat, but it soon broke to leave a fine night.[149] Back on the field, the gunner Speer and others fed blazing fires to deceive the enemy that all was normal.[150] Dickson left Lane and one hundred rockets behind as a rear guard, while he spiked remaining guns he could not remove and threw their ammunition in the river.[151]

There was a brief alarm at about one a.m. when American batteries opened again, but it was only the Yankees firing at a loose raft floating past. Lambert, Dickson, and Burgoyne left on an armed barge that overtook the marching column halfway to the fishermen's huts, which they reached at about ten o'clock the next morning. Gubbins commanded the pickets left behind to cover the departure. At three a.m. he walked into the woods, the last man to turn his back on the scene of their defeats.[152] All that remained of them now were Pakenham's and Gibbs's entrails, buried beneath a pecan tree at Villeré's. It was the only American soil they occupied successfully.[153]

It would not be an easy march. Engineers used the ill-fated fascines to make what some called "a kind of basket road" over marshy spots on the path, and laid sturdy bridges, but traffic wore down the road and men often slid into the swamp. Cooke saw some sink to their knees, others hip-deep, and a few splayed out flat. An officer coming to keep them moving sank to his neck, and another went in up to his armpits. A bugler of the 95th sank out of sight completely for a time.[154] At about one a.m. high tide on Lake Borgne backed up the bayou, thoroughly soaking the path, and some of the 7th and 43rd went in up to their waists. One wide boggy spot almost swallowed several men until Malcolm brought shovels and boats to get them out. Peddie and the engineers came last to break up the bridges.[155] By daylight the files extended for miles, all of them studies in mud.[156]

At the village, Gordon welcomed arriving officers into a large smoke-filled hut with a blazing fire. Some were covered with mud to their knees and Colonel Paterson of the 21st to his shoulders.[157] Perhaps two-thirds of the army spread along the bayou, washing and drying their uniforms. In the ensuing hours they repeatedly watched the indefatigable Gordon, wooden leg and all, as he climbed a lone tree to look out for pursuing Yankees.[158] At least the sound of Yankee cannonades through the night suggested that Jackson did not yet know of their departure. Just in case, two launches with bow carronades remained behind to slow any pursuit.[159]

Cochrane and Codrington had reached one of the captured gunboats four evenings earlier, to spend two days in what the latter called "a stinking cabin" before being rowed to the *Armide*. The weather, the country, and their defeat told on them. "I wish that I may never again see this accursed country," Codrington wrote to Jane, calling it "a very Hell on earth." Repeated challenges to his authority from Nicolls made it worse. Codrington thought him a lying braggart, yet Cochrane repeatedly sided with his favorite, refusing to listen when told Nicolls had criticized the conduct of the campaign. Instead, Cochrane lectured Codrington, who offered his resignation. Nicolls fed the breach between the admirals such that Codrington refused even to write his name in letters. As for Cochrane, "he has something of a cloven foot," Codrington told Jane. Thereafter he felt he must regard his commander with suspicion, and for a time he even communicated with Cochrane by letter despite their being on the same ship. The damage was done, their relationship another casualty of the expedition.[160]

Cochrane certainly was testy. First he tried to pass responsibility for the disaster to Pakenham, writing Melville on January 20 that Jackson had outnumbered them substantially and that the general had waited too long to launch his attack, which Cochrane said should have come three hours before Thornton attacked Morgan. He implied that he had suggested this, but Pakenham disagreed, and now the result was 2,000 or more casualties and nothing to show for them.[161] "There is now no help for it and we must make the best we can," he told Melville. They were still strong, and he could yet take Louisiana. He proposed to return to his original plan: blockade the Mississippi, and land Lambert at Mobile to march overland to Baton Rouge. That would isolate New Orleans, force its fall, and allow him to give Melville "more cheering news." To do that, he must have younger senior officers to replace the dead and relieve the inept, adding that some of the regiments "are but badly commanded," surely a reference to Mullins. Supplies, muskets, and sabers were coming for Nicolls, and a ship to convey him and his Indians to Apalachicola to invade above the Alabama River and perhaps into Georgia to support Cockburn. That should free the Creeks to push the Yankees into Tennessee and occupy them there, relieving Canada from threat. He still counted on New England to secede, go to war with the United States, and send militia to cooperate with the British in the Carolinas—unaware that the Hartford Convention had concluded on January 5 having shown no interest in secession.[162] He was building castles in the sky.

Cochrane ordered ships at the main anchorage to load six to eight weeks' provisions and then waited for the army to board, unaware that another withdrawal had commenced sixty miles away.[163] Overton's morning express on January 17 vented frustration. Sometimes he got so angry at the enemy that he fired back with his batteries despite knowing they did not have the range. "I would agree to lose my right arm if I did not sink the whole in thirty minutes if they would come up and fight fairly," he wrote Morgan.[164] That evening proper fuses for the big mortar arrived, and Overton gladly ordered Wollstonecraft to open fire. The first discharge so unsettled the British that the next morning they weighed anchor and dropped out of sight.[165] At that very moment Cochrane's order to withdraw was on its way to the squadron.[166]

Overton found on inspection that the foe had fired almost 1,000 shells and solid shots at him. Hearing that, Colonel Butler in New Orleans amused himself by estimating that if every enemy shell fired cost $25, the British had spent roughly $25,000 for nothing.[167] The fort's casualties were slight, with eight wounded in Wollstonecraft's battery, two killed and one injured in another, and three infantrymen hit.[168]

When the news reached New Orleans, it quieted all concern of a naval attack on the city. Added to the knowledge that Lambert had withdrawn, it virtually erased all remaining apprehensions. Writing to a friend in Kentucky on January 20, one of Patterson's officers declared that "all fear is at an end."[169]

Twenty-One

"The Finger of Heaven Was in This Thing"

O NCE AGAIN TO cover a failure, Cochrane dismissed the bombardment of Fort St. Philip as a mere diversion to mask Lambert's withdrawal, but the mission's origin days before the January 8 battle made a liar of him. He simply could not acknowledge a second defeat, this one exclusively the navy's.[1] It was never likely to succeed. Winds, a falling river—even rising tides—were likely to defeat him without the Yankees firing a gun.

Old Hickory got Overton's good news late that night or early on January 19, and when just a few hours later the fog cleared at about eight a.m., he learned that Lambert was gone. Men on the line still saw redcoats behind their camp defenses, but on their works scouts found only fifty or sixty "paddys": uniforms stuffed with cane and straw as decoys.[2] Jackson immediately rode over to the abandoned camps and met a British surgeon with a message from Lambert asking for humane treatment for the eighty immovable wounded. Jackson so ordered. All but one missed arms or legs blasted off by artillery or amputated.[3] More shocking were the ditches turned mass graves, some almost uncovered by the rain.[4] A fortnight later legs, arms, and heads still protruded from the ground amid an effluvium of decaying flesh that was sickening.[5] Lambert also left fourteen heavy cannons and a few stragglers quickly made prisoner.[6]

Jackson sent the welcome news to Monroe that same day, predicting that the enemy would not come again. With typical Jacksonian bluster, he claimed that, but for the delay of arms from Pittsburgh, he would have captured or destroyed the entire British land force.[7] As it was, he had defeated "the choice of Wellington's army" and crowed likewise to Winchester at

Mobile that "I have defeated this Boasted army of Lord Wellingtons."[8] He can be forgiven for being unaware that more than half of Pakenham's units never served under the duke.

The mail departing New Orleans the next day, January 20, carried exultations in its pouches. The turnout of volunteers and the courage they showed under fire were universally applauded.[9] Victory put modesty in short supply. "Allow us to boast a little," a friend wrote Congressman Robertson.[10] The British had never taken such a beating anywhere in the world before, they said, and "those monsters" would never pollute Louisiana's soil again.[11] But that was too self-effacing. Major Reid, General Coffee, and others declared that no army anywhere in the world had ever achieved such a triumph.[12] Tennessean Duke Sumner bested them all at hyperbole. Their victory was the greatest "since the invention of gunpowder."[13]

Beyond their hubris, some took a longer view. They had saved New Orleans, "the great key and outlet" to all the immense and rich produce of half the infant nation, and the future commerce of a continent.[14] One soldier calculated that a line of earthworks less than one mile long had saved a territory equal to the island of Great Britain—surely a victory that would force Europe to open its eyes to America's growing strength.[15] It also opened some Americans' eyes to an identity until then ill-defined in their minds. Noel Baron, the *creole* cornet of Chauveau's mounted company, told a fellow *creole* that now "I have a flag to defend that I would abandon only by losing my life."[16]

Many like Coffee credited a higher power and wrote of Providence taking a hand.[17] Jeremiah Lambert, of Plauché's battalion, told his father, Senator John Lambert of New Jersey, that "providence has been with our army from the commencement."[18] Jackson himself affirmed that their victory was "the signal interposition of Heaven."[19] A storm had broken over them, one *creole* told his mother, "but thank Heavens the bolt fell on the head of the enemy."[20] An anonymous soldier concluded simply that "the finger of Heaven was in this thing."[21]

Everyone granted that Old Hickory had had a hand in it, too. Tousard, not long to be the general's admirer, compared him to George Washington.[22] On every street, paeans to him came from soldiers and civilians alike for inspiring their confidence in unity, and calling forth their dormant strength. Surely he had saved the country, and even Captain Shaumburg, no friend to Old Hickory, conceded that the general had "done better than any other man could."[23] No one effused like Livingston, who could not say enough about the general's "energy, firmness, courage and moderation" during hours of danger and difficulty, or for his indifference to the personal consequences of his decisions.[24] In some places he had been so little known that some thought him born in England, while a man who claimed long and intimate acquaintance with him called him "Alexander" Jackson.[25] New Orleans changed that. In weeks he was the most celebrated man in America, a fact not lost on the man himself.

Shrove Tuesday was already a celebration in New Orleans, and now in their gladness city and soldiers expected the coming carnival to be splendid.[26] Joy appeared on virtually every face, and everyone felt the enemy would not call again.[27] In the ranks from Kentucky and Tennessee, thoughts immediately turned to returning to their firesides. "The moment is pleasant," Coffee wrote Mary on January 20, "and turned to that domestic enjoyment that awaits me at home."[28]

Jackson gave Adair's men a chance at redemption by sending them with Hinds and Carroll to take a redoubt on the bayou blocking any potential pursuit, but it proved a fiasco when the Tennesseans failed to appear, and the Kentuckians fled at the first fire.[29] He regretted the lost opportunity, but it reinforced his wisdom in not risking a counterattack with an army of militia. Still, he had much to celebrate. Prisoners exaggerated their losses as high as 6,500, which Old Hickory was happy to believe, telling Tennessee governor Willie Blount that "the flower of their army" was destroyed, a fact that he thought would have greater impact on the Ghent negotiations than anything else. That, he concluded, was "the harbinger of peace."[30]

Jackson dispersed most of the army to dryer ground for the men's health, and to cover other potential approaches to the city. Before they departed, they assembled at six a.m. on January 21 to hear a congratulatory address Livingston had penned in prose of deepest purple, portions of which the aide's antagonist Shaumburg thought bombastic and some just farcical.[31] Old Hickory had already written some personal notes of thanks, in particular to Beale's company for their courage and sacrifice on December 23.[32] Notes and address pointedly ignored Morgan and his humiliation on the right bank.

By that time several thousand redcoats crammed the soggy ground around the fishermen's village. The retreat had been remarkably quiet and efficient, even if they did lose at least six men who just disappeared in the muddy swamp. Despite defeat, the men had been cheerful on the march, delighted to leave a scene of hardship and embarrassment behind. At the village, Malcolm and Peddie took charge of embarking the army, and Lambert found a problem awaiting: a score of runaway slave families wanting to go with them. Some officers like Tylden thought they ought to be taken along. "Who would not wish for liberty?" he asked.[33] Lambert forbade his officers from taking any as servants, although several had already done so, and notified Jackson that he would allow planters to come try to persuade their slaves to return, and he would send back any willing to go.[34] He would force no one to return, however. Codrington arranged for some runaways to join others aboard the *Cydness* and allowed commanders of the captured gunboats to enlist up to ten slaves each, while taking aboard others wishing to leave.[35]

With their recently arrived stores packed for reshipment, the men subsisted on short rations and what they could catch or shoot, cooking over burning piles of the inescapable reeds. Patrolling alligators made sleep uneasy, but the shy monsters left them alone.[36] The artillery embarked for the fleet on January 19 and 20, along with Dickson and the rocketeers, followed by the 44th and part of the 21st the next day. It went slowly. "The Navy are the worst arrangers in the world," Tylden complained,[37] but it was high southwest winds blowing water out of the lake that dropped its level and delayed the boats' return, trapping the rest of the army ashore with few provisions, little drinkable water, and scant fuel for fires.[38] After two days the lake rose and the boats returned, but Tylden still blamed the admirals because "the Navy are strange beings."[39]

The 4th embarked next, the 93rd and some of the 95th on January 24, and the following day the balance of Lambert's brigade.[40] Unrelenting rain threatened them with flooding and, ever the slave to interservice prejudice, Tylden blamed that, too, on the navy. "Lord help us," he moaned. Granting Malcolm credit for his effort, he had to add that "he makes the most erroneous calculations in the world."[41] Meanwhile, Captain Gordon endeared himself by doing all he could to make an inhospitable spot hospitable, at least for the officers.[42] It was January 26 before the last prepared to embark. With them went some Spaniards from the village who had given them information and could expect no thanks from the Americans.[43]

They must sail and row seventy-five miles to see the masts of their transports.[44] The last redcoat left the village at about four a.m. on January 27, and they were all aboard the fleet anchored late that night after more than a dozen hours of hard rowing.[45] With the last of them went the slaves. Tylden was glad of that, at least. "The poor devils would have been infamously treated had they been left," he believed. "There must be some truth in it, or they would hardly trust themselves to the chance of what we may do with them."[46] They were the only people to gain anything from the invasion, and even that remained to be determined.

Lambert had good reason to get away, for Jackson was not idle. His congratulatory address done, the units marched off to their new posts with bands playing a salute to their general as they passed in review.[47] Old Hickory and staff, with Hinds's dragoons as escort, rode to his old headquarters near Fort St. Charles.[48] Over the next few days he monitored enemy movements, and there was a light skirmish with the British rear guard on Bayou Bienvenue, but nothing more.[49]

The irrepressible Thomas Shields was much more active. Cochrane had released him and Morrell on January 12 as a separate condition of the prisoner exchange agreement, and they reached Petites Coquilles the next day. Instead of going on to New Orleans, Shields set out first for revenge.[50] While a prisoner, he had overheard that Cochrane expected to return to the fleet on or about January 16, and now proposed that he could capture him.[51] Patterson gave him five boats at Fort St. John, and on January 17 Shields set out.[52] "I am just starting on a secret business to avenge myself," he wrote in a farewell message before leaving. "If I succeed, the affair will be creditable to me—if I fail, the world, at least, shall say, 'there lived a man.'"[53]

He left Chef Menteur at seven p.m. two nights later with fifty-three men. Three miles out they came on a transport close to shore with forty men and officers of the 14th Light Dragoons and fourteen seamen. Shields took the boat without resistance, the 14th's commanding officer throwing his sword into the lake before it became a trophy, and only one man escaped. The next night Ensign Bowlby pulled into the same spot in rough weather with another boatload of soldiers, and the escapee hailed him. Learning what had happened, Bowlby raised anchor and risked high seas to row to their ships. These men of the 14th were one-fourth of the regiment's complement with the army, and the only casualties it suffered in the campaign. For days Lambert only knew their boat was missing and feared that it sank with all aboard.[54]

Shields deposited his prisoners at Chef Menteur on January 20, sortied again without success, then again at five a.m. on January 21.[55] He steered for the Rigolets and began taking isolated boats, ending with a schooner, six transports, and seventy-eight prisoners. Adverse winds forced him to burn the schooner, and the rest of the flotilla spent hours trying to get into the pass, which they finally reached at about two p.m. Then seven armed boats approached bent on attack. Sending most of the prisoners ashore, Shields opened fire for perhaps twenty minutes before the enemy sheered off. But then the prisoners aboard two of his captive boats overwhelmed their guards and escaped, after which Shields stepped ashore to parole and release his prisoners, excepting a few civilians he thought might be intended for an occupation government. He rowed to shore at the Rigolets by eleven p.m., moved on to Fort St. John, and on the morning of January 24 returned to New Orleans having netted 112 prisoners in one of the most daring operations of the campaign.[56]

The process of exchanging such captives continued after Shields bagged the boatload of dragoons. Negotiations became niggling and testy when Cochrane took offense at Patterson's tone in a letter and refused to communicate with him further. Patterson responded in similar pique through a secretary, but soon they wrote directly to each other again. The last American prisoners were on their way on the schooner *Speedwell* on January 29, and four weeks later the *Enterprise* finally took the last of the British captives to the Balise for release.[57] Meanwhile, *Tonnant* discharged fifty-seven Americans, including Jones's gunboat crews and several of the men captured on December 23.[58] An order also headed to Havana to catch Hardy's *Ramillies* and have him release prisoners aboard.[59] When Jackson released the remainder of the ambulatory wounded prisoners, Wollstonecraft coordinated their delivery to the Balise.[60]

Jackson and the British observed other niceties. Codrington returned personal property taken on the gunboats, an act of chivalry that may have prompted a reciprocal request.[61] After Keane was taken from the battlefield, a surgeon tugged gently on the worsted band of his underwear, driven deep into a leg by a bullet. Surprisingly, the ball just popped out of the wound, and the general was healing rapidly.[62] Having entrusted his sword to an ensign captured with Knight's company just after the battle, Keane wrote to Jackson to request its return, and Old Hickory sent it with his compliments.[63]

Returned Yankee wounded brought British camp gossip that soon spread through the city. Lambert had suffered a breakdown under the stress. Jackson heard it on January 19, and the next day men in the ranks believed that the general had gone mad with grief.[64] The rumor prowled the city streets for two weeks, and Jackson seemed still to believe it when he speculated that the British general might try one last desperate effort somewhere on the coast "in a fit of madness."[65] Cochrane did not doubt Lambert's sanity, but on January 20 he did write Lord Melville, hinting that he thought the general unsuited to army command.[66] Still the madness rumor persisted. In time it had Lambert hearing voices in the darkness calling, "Surrender! Surrender!" "You'll be to[o] Late," and "Shoot! Shoot! Shoot!" during the retreat, and him yelling back in panic that he would surrender in the morning, only to discover with the dawn that what he had heard were croaking marsh frogs. Overcome with shame, he supposedly lost his senses and had to be confined to his cabin on reaching the fleet.[67] In fact a quite sane Lambert boarded *Tonnant* on January 28.[68]

The soldiers were simply stuffed on the transports at random without concern for organization, glad enough just to quit that cursed coast. They sent letters to go home aboard *Plantagenet* when she sailed on January 31 with Keane and Thornton and other wounded officers, and the bodies of Pakenham and Gibbs in their spirit casks.[69] Few hid their relief at being back aboard ship. Some simply could not face describing the battle, which was still too fresh in their minds.[70] Gubbins boarded Captain Gordon's *Seahorse* with conflicting emotions, glad to be there but mindful that thousands could not say the same that day. He tried to limn the hardships and horrors but gave up, saying "it is altogether too shocking to describe."[71] *Plantagenet* also carried William Little or Lyddle, a deserter from the Royal Navy who was captured serving on one of Jones's gunboats. Seizing such men from American ships helped bring on the war. Now he was on his way to trial aboard a ship carrying the wreckage of the war's last major battle.[72]

Malcolm returned to *Royal Oak* and Tylden to *Bucephalus*, comfortable for the first time in weeks.[73] Gordon returned to his *Seahorse* to write his wife that, despite the exertions and failure of the campaign now past, he looked forward to the next.[74] Aboard *Belle Poule*, Benson Hill dined on china and drank wine from cut glass, which struck him as "some fairy feast," then slept on a soft cot between white sheets, making the weeks of mud and sour oranges seem a bad dream.[75] Gerard boarded *Weser* in time for his first good breakfast in weeks.[76] Gleig returned to happy memories of his friend Charles Grey on *Golden Fleece*, and there learned that his friend had willed him his pistols, his books, his spyglass, and a dog.[77] Major Michell wrote from *Royal Oak* that he was glad just to escape and all he wanted was to see home again. "Would to god that we had leave," he wrote his wife.[78] Several vessels had wives watching in suspense for husbands who did not return.[79] Perhaps not everyone who embarked reached the ships, either. One boat carrying a sergeant and sixteen men of the 7th Foot reportedly sank in the lake. A redcoat deserter soon exaggerated that forty boats sunk and 1,000 men drowned.[80]

No such gloom infected New Orleans. Chotard's daughter Eliza described the city in those first days after the enemy departure: "A carnival of pleasure ensued."[81] The city's women planned a grand celebration for January 24, and in honor of the event attorney Ellery wrote a long poem titled "The Retreat of the English. A Yankee Song."[82] At nine a.m. that day church bells pealed and a crowd estimated at 10,000 assembled in brightest finery.[83] On the Place d'Armes a triumphal floral arch spread over two platforms, while on either side of the path to the platforms eighteen virgins stood in white representing the states, holding flags blazoned with mottoes. Some pitied the youngsters stuck representing the New England states that attended the Hartford Convention. Onlookers climbed to overlooking eaves and even the cathedral roof to get a view.

At ten o'clock the volunteer companies formed on either side of an avenue leading to the arch and cathedral. Jackson and his staff arrived at noon, young women strewing roses before them as the watching crowd fell silent. Only the bands still played. As Old Hickory passed mounted between the platforms, the girls held their wreaths over his head—omitting the caution to Roman conquerors that he was only a mortal—and the rest waved banners and dropped more rose petals in his path. A *creole* officer greeted him with kisses to his cheeks, a city woman presented an ornamented address from the state that he tucked into his uniform blouse, and then they led him on foot into the cathedral, followed by a crowd shouting huzzahs. There a women's chorus sang songs composed for the occasion and a harpist played. A lady sitting behind Old Hickory became so enrapt in the scene that she still held in her lap the flowers she should have strewn before him when he entered. At last the priest took Jackson's hand and led him to the door, where he remounted and returned to his headquarters.[84]

That evening almost every building in the city illuminated its interior, virtually stunning visitors, as the whole city seemed a blaze of light.[85] Livingston's son Lewis marveled, "Was there ever a finer sight."[86] Several balls closed the day of celebration in dancing, drinking, and frolic.[87] A very few sneered at the near deification of Old Hickory. Shaumburg cynically said the women of New Orleans had made him "their King & Emperor."[88] Laura Florian agreed. She had been in at the beginning of the Old Hickory worship. Barely twenty-four hours after the battle, she credited him with being "the Saviour of Louisiana."[89]

Old Hickory returned the favor on January 27 with a letter to the mayor, probably written by Livingston, complimenting the city council and its people for their patriotism and courage, their humanity in caring for the wounded of both sides, and their liberality in providing for the families of men at the front and helping to clothe the volunteers. Having bravely faced war's hazards, they had earned peace. Shrewdly forecasting the New Orleans of the future, he said that in the hands of a foreign power the city would be a mere colony. As part of the United States, however, it "must become the greatest emporium of commerce that the world has known."[90]

At 11:30 p.m. the evening before, a message from Chef Menteur had reached Jackson. Lookouts climbing a tree that morning saw the sails of the last enemy ship drop out of sight below Lake Borgne's eastern horizon.[91] He could not guess whether Lambert might regroup and return, but he resolved vigilance notwithstanding his message that day to Senator Brown that "Louisiana is again free."[92] In the city a grocer crowed that "we are safe from all future attacks," and as more reinforcements arrived, one wag joked that the new arrivals would "glut the market." Confidence spread so that the city's quadroon population declared they could whip the British.[93]

There was near unison in fearing the foe might still try to come again via Baton Rouge or up bayous and across the Attakapas country west of the Mississippi. Consequently, out in that western country, there continued to be pressure to enlist every man who could shoulder a musket.[94] Despite his confident public face, Jackson took no chances. He asked Washington for 5,000 regulars, began new batteries near the river bastion, had Morgan and Patterson do the same across the river, sent Tatum and Latour to inspect every bayou connecting Borgne and other lakes with the ocean to establish forts and obstructions, and pushed Major Reynolds to finish a fort at the Temple to close the Baratarian route.[95]

Furthermore he restricted everyone to camp and required general inspections to keep weapons in good order, clothing clean, beards close-cropped, and even hands and faces washed. They must be ready with thirty rounds per man at all times, and no absences allowed.[96] He intended to be prepared on every possible avenue of approach, especially since returned prisoners from the December 23 fight reported the common assumption on enemy ships that the British would come again to strike above the city, the very route Cochrane had proposed. They also reported seeing boats being built for bayou passage, and some redcoat tars had told them that reinforcements were coming to "try for Orleans again."[97]

By early February, Jackson believed that failure had so upset Cochrane that he did not know now what to do, and Lambert was so battered that he posed little threat.[98] Nevertheless he drilled the army daily to keep them strong and ready to repel an invasion.[99] Happily, after weeks of exhaustion and ill health, Jackson himself felt better and stronger now, an improvement that may have been hastened by anticipation of Rachel's arrival on February 19.[100] She had wanted for some time to come to New Orleans, but he worried for her safety on the long and sometimes hazardous river journey.[101] She joined Colonel Butler's and Colonel Overton's wives in Nashville on January 13 to await Jackson's call but changed her mind and left the next day, before news of her husband's victory reached town.[102] Her party reached Natchez on Valentine's Day and landed at New Orleans five days later.[103]

The general's wife found local society hospitable as she and Old Hickory enjoyed almost nightly entertainments. Doyennes loaned jewelry that she be suitably adorned, but behind her back they sniped at her dark complexion and what one called "enormous corpulence." The pair made quite a contrast, virtually the Jack Sprat and his wife of folk rhyme, he long and haggard and she a short, fat dumpling. In her Baptist zeal she called the town "Babylon-on-the-Mississippi," yet she made a few good friends, especially slender Louise Livingston, who by contrast made Rachel appear even more fleshy. At parties she also befriended Major Wollstonecraft, then in the city trying to settle problems at Fort St. Philip.[104] "What is to be done with me I know not," he lamented to Livingston. His officers were insubordinate, and when Overton left him in command in February, they reveled through the night on whiskey, breaking crockery and firing pistols in the officers' mess. Wollstonecraft was already resolved to leave the army and America after the war.[105]

Amid the city's relief a rumor resurfaced. "Let us drive the plundering banditti from our shores," a writer there declared the day after the battle.[106] On January 17, Shields illuminated that when he claimed that Pakenham promised his men "FORTY-EIGHT HOURS PILLAGE & RAPINE."[107] Within two days the rumor swept the city. Postmaster Johnston wrote to tell Mrs. Madison that day that Pakenham's goal had been rape and pillage.[108] A day later Tousard heard that British prisoners claimed to have been promised the plunder of the city for up to a week, their reward for victory again being "Beauty and Booty."[109] That same day a civilian or soldier said that on January 7 the redcoats were promised three days of "indiscriminate rapine and excesses of every kind," and a regular officer wrote that the British watchword the night before the battle was "Beauty and Booty."[110] Yet another letter left that day suggesting that the city's women were greatly relieved now due to "it *being notorious* that the watch word and countersign on the morning of the 8th inst. were 'BEAUTY AND BOOTY.'"[111]

Carroll's volunteer aide, the timorous Poindexter, said the same that day, claiming that he, too, was told by prisoners that the alliterative "beauty and booty" was the enemy watchword and countersign on the morning of January 8.[112] A day later common rumor on the street said British officers had promised their men three days of pillage and worse, but then for the first time a hint of skepticism emerged. One writer raised a doubt about its veracity but suggested that Jackson's men had heard the rumor prior to the battle and that it had "nerved every arm" on January 8.[113] Within a week the story was a street commonplace.[114] Later that year London publisher William Cobbett, who had no sympathy for Louisianans, whom he dismissed as "base and cowardly French and Spanish merchants, and paper money makers," made veiled hints of it in London when he wrote of "the city and all its spoils," and added that before the battle Pakenham's soldiers had been "stimulated, and steeled against relaxation, by assurances the most gratifying to their tastes and wishes."[115]

Jackson credited the rumor, or else it suited his purpose to appear to do so at the moment. Certainly he had read and approved Livingston's statement in the January 21 address to the army that they had saved "your wives and daughters from insult and violation."[116] Coming within hours of multiple letters written the day before repeating stories of "beauty and booty," it could hardly be coincidental. Claiborne hinted at the subject a week later when he wrote Jackson that Lambert had "disapproved the system of *rapine* of other British commanders," although he feared that he might yet give in to plunder.[117] Some months later Livingston called Cochrane's "a predatory incursion" aimed at plundering "the cottons and sugars of New Orleans."[118]

Pakenham made no such promise to British soldiers. A few weeks hence, several British officers boarding in Havana awaiting passage home pronounced it a lie.[119] An American writer that March pointed out that the British army had already stopped using watchwords and countersigns and hardly needed them anyway in a daylight battle.[120] Lambert, Keane, Thornton, Dickson, and others later swore jointly that no one gave such an order. As late as 1840 a subaltern in the 4th Foot fancifully claimed that "beauty and booty" really came from a standing toast among the Baratarians to *"Butin et Beauté"* and to them was due credit for that "classical, elegant, and apt alliteration."[121] Regardless of fact or logic, Louisiana preferred to believe the story. Three months after the battle, someone sarcastically suggested that New Orleans erect a monument to Pakenham and that its plinth declare: "To inflame the Lust and Avarice of his brutal followers, he proclaimed Three Days of Plunder & Licentiousness, and Gave as watch-word for those days BEAUTY and BOOTY!!!"[122]

Cochrane certainly had hopes for the "booty" part of the alliteration. On January 17 he prohibited any officer but himself from sending "treasure" out of the command without a regular convoy.[123] Letters from more fortunate friends taunted him. The prize money from taking St. Mary's, Georgia, in February, promised to be up to £50,000.[124] Officers on other stations wrote of plenty of plunder, even referring cynically to making "a *good harvest* before peace takes place."[125] Cockburn even teased that "*an ugly account of peace*" threatened a halt to all prizes.[126]

Perhaps it would, but Cochrane was already determined on his next move.[127] They would go to Dauphin Island, a sandy spit twelve miles long commanding the approach to Mobile Bay; land part of the army on the western end, where Lambert could reorganize and reassemble his regiments; then land the rest close to the Yankees' earthwork fort at its eastern end and take it. They would then have command of the bay, and he could move on Mobile itself if he thought there was anything to gain, or march to Baton Rouge and close the Mississippi to Yankee traffic while Cochrane's frigates stoppered the mouth of the river.[128] Between army and navy, they could starve New Orleans to submission, or Lambert could move down-river at leisure to strike the enemy on ground of his choosing and more to his advantage.

Yet Lambert was not going to bite off too much. In fact, he and Co-chrane fell somewhat at odds on what to do next. New Orleans shook him. "From what has occurred I shall be disinclined to undertake any operations that I may not think very practicable," he warned Bathurst on January 29, and he was not accepting any more sunny expectations of British sentiment ashore.[129]

Lambert and Malcolm had reached the fleet and *Tonnant* at anchor off Ship Island the day before, and the army were all aboard their transports two days later. The weather turned so foul, however, that the ships at the in-ner anchorage could not get out until February 5. Happily, many of the wounded were fast recovering, especially those hit by the "buck" part of the Yankee buck and ball loads. Lambert estimated that by February 10 he would have the army in good condition again save for the West India regiments so disrupted by the cold weather.[130] Less healthy, however, were some high com-mand relations. Cochrane, Lambert, and others conferred aboard *Tonnant* the morning of February 3 and found their unity strained. The admiral wanted to send Nicolls with 3,500 Creeks and blacks into Georgia, half to cooperate with Cockburn and the rest to join Lambert. He believed Jackson expected him to move against Mobile, and—without any intelligence to that effect—he concluded that Yankee troops were already marching to reinforce the town. In fact, Old Hickory had diverted reinforcements away from Mo-bile to New Orleans, believing it was of no interest to Cochrane, one of Jack-son's few strategic miscalculations.[131]

The admiral argued that the British ought to take Mobile and had already sent Burgoyne ahead to reconnoiter the approaches to Dauphin Is-land.[132] In cloaked criticism of Pakenham's delays attacking Jackson, Coch-rane sagely told Lambert the obvious: that "I have now found that prompt measures are the best."[133] To ensure that, he now intended to command the expedition in person, but then logician Malcolm pointed out that Cochrane had failed to prepare for any such overland campaign and had neither big ships, transports, provisions, nor troops ready to go.[134]

The rift with Codrington also worsened. "How little I expected this break up betwixt Sir A. & myself," he wrote Jane. Cochrane now treated him as a glorified secretary, while his blatant favoritism toward a few syco-phants rankled even more.[135] The discord between them mirrored the feel-ings of others after the Chalmette disaster. Their targets on Dauphin and Mobile were well known among the officers, and not everyone approved. When they made sail finally on February 5, a discouraged Tylden feared another bloody defeat in the offing, and that "neither the Town or Fort are worth the lives it will probably cost to take them."[136] Four days earlier, on February 1, a British prisoner exchange vessel had inadvertently crossed the cease-fire line off the Rigolets, and Fort Petites Coquilles's batteries fired on her. They were the last shots of the campaign for Louisiana.[137]

Twenty-Two

"Rescued Is *Orleans* from the English Wolves"

F AR FROM LOUISIANA, rumors and speculation heated anxiety for weeks before and after the battle, and the farther from New Orleans, the greater the want of news. By early February, New York and Boston knew only of the December 23 battle.[1] Worse, on January 16 a report reached Philadelphia that the city had actually fallen on December 22, and even into early February correspondence reaching southwest Virginia told of New Orleans's loss to the enemy.[2] Nowhere was the anxiety greater than in Washington. People expected news of the city's fate in every arriving mail, and no news quickly became bad news.[3]

Relief was coming, and it flew eastward with a pace and breadth of coverage never before seen on the globe. News of the victory left New Orleans primarily by two routes. One was through Natchez to Nashville and Cincinnati and then eastward to Washington and Baltimore. The other route diverged at Nashville for Knoxville, Charleston, and then up the coast to the Chesapeake. Either way, the first news came in letters sent to Natchez by Kempe and Henderson of Hinds's company, which appeared in the *Mississippi Republican* on January 16 and sparked the nation's first victory celebration with a parade to a tavern for songs and toasts.[4]

Thereafter in town after town heading eastward, those letters borrowed from copies of the *Republican* joined others to frame the nucleus of Americans' first confirmation of victory. All of that was informal, of course. Jackson sent his official report on the faster and more secure new Federal Road linking New Orleans to Fort Stoddert above Mobile, then across the Mississippi Territory to Fort Decatur on the Tallapoosa, and on to the Georgia capital at Milledgeville.[5] Jackson held his full report pending the outcome at Fort St. Philip. Just after midnight on January 18, Major Reid was copying Jackson's report, when Sam Dale reached headquarters with fresh dispatches and Old Hickory asked him to rest an hour and leave with the report. Dale said he would ride fast from dawn and midnight with "light weights." When Jackson asked what he meant, impish Big Sam replied, "An empty belly and no saddle-bags."[6]

The boom of Jackson's guns firing on Lambert's empty camps was in Dale's ears as he left.[7] Ten days later, on January 28, he rode into Milledgeville after covering 525 miles and handed his dispatches to another rider. The local *Georgia Journal* issued an extra, the first newspaper of the original thirteen states to announce the victory.[8] Jackson's express packet spent another seven days on the post road out of Milledgeville, passing Augusta, Columbia, Raleigh, and Richmond, and reaching Washington just seventeen days out of New Orleans, a trip that took regular mail almost four weeks. On its way, the packet actually passed slower-moving word of the January 1 fight.[9]

The War Department released the news immediately. "History records no example, of so glorious a victory, obtained, with so little bloodshed," Monroe wrote Jackson.[10] A grand illumination lit the city that evening, and Congress quickly passed a resolution of thanks to Jackson and his army.[11] In Baltimore later that day, an artillery salute boomed from Hampstead Hill, and United States troops paraded to "Hail Columbia" as townspeople prepared for their own evening illumination.[12] Later, in Philadelphia, the new frigate *Guerriere* fired salutes to honor the victory, while a city editor displayed a huge "transparency"—a tissue-thin painted fabric illuminated from behind by oil lamps—with Jackson's portrait over a paraphrase from Shakespeare's *Henry V*: "This day shall ne'er go by, from this day to the ending of the world, but He, in it, shall be remembered."[13]

Editors repeatedly turned to the Avon's bard. "Advance our waving colors on the walls," another borrowed from *Henry VI, Part 1*. "Rescued is Orleans from the English wolves."[14] Letters postmarked at New Orleans after January 8 were opened and read first by anxious postmasters even before addressees got them, the one at Shrewsbury, New Jersey, penning on the envelope the apology, "I was overpowered by curiosity for which I ask your pardon."[15]

Old Hickory had won immortal laurels, of course. Monroe told him he deserved universal gratitude, and speculation arose over how he might be rewarded.[16] Before the victory was known, some felt that saving the city would place Jackson "on very high ground" for future advancement.[17] Now a Virginia assemblyman told him the victory entitled the western country to sire the next president, that he was the man of the hour now, and that he should look to 1816.[18]

Americans would have been more than amused to see the reports heading toward Britain at that moment. New Orleans's fall was certain, said some. Others actually announced its fall on January 15, a Liverpool editor crowing that "it closes our military operations against the United States with some ECLAT."[19] British Canadians actually got first confirmation of sobering reality. "When shall the measure of our humiliation be filled?" moaned the Montreal press. Britain, which had struck all Europe with terror, "has succumbed to the pitiful republic of America; a people yet in the cradle."[20]

Mainland Britain got irrefutable confirmation of disaster on March 5, and Lambert's report arrived two days later to appear in the press on March 8.[21] Politicians sought cover as a public outcry and backlash questioned the wisdom of the expedition in the first place, and calls were made for an official inquiry.[22] Some officials tried to make the failure Cochrane's and Pakenham's alone, but gossamer rationalizations were too thin to cover ministerial backsides.[23] Accusations of "a mere adventure of spoil" emerged and implied Cochrane was the culprit.[24] Furious over the death of his kinsman Pakenham, Wellington himself joined that chorus.[25] The release of casualty lists was even more shocking.[26]

Anti-war gadfly William Cobbett was merciless. "Gracious God! It is too shocking for animadversion," he wrote Lord Liverpool. Half a dozen such bloodbaths, he charged, and Britain would scarcely have men left to parade at St. James's Palace. They must face reality and acknowledge the Americans as an independent people and seek their friendship, for in a few years, he predicted, the United States would assume "the highest rank in the estimation of the world."[27] Keeping New Orleans would help accomplish that, for it was "the key and connecting link" to vast strength and boundless resources.[28]

Some of that strength would come through means of information that the campaign revolutionized. Distance from its army kept British readers ill-informed by months-old official statements and reports. The voices of soldiers and subalterns were virtually mute. But the weekly mails from New Orleans carried hundreds of personal letters to a hungry readership and brought to life dimensions of events never before presented to Americans. Recipients from Maine to Georgia gave those letters to local editors to print, and the mails then took their issues to other towns and other editors. At least four hundred letters by Americans and *creoles*, soldiers and civilians, appeared in print wherever press, ink, and paper made their miracle.

Nothing like it had yet been seen in the world, and it helped make a new nation of readers.[29] When the war began, something over four hundred newspapers were published in the country. The first years after Jackson's victory saw that number more than double.[30]

In an information-hungry world, confidences were hard to keep. Cochrane's decision to move on Mobile was not secret for long. With memory of New Orleans fresh, a Bermuda editor predicted he would need a miracle to succeed, and advised his readers to prepare themselves "to hear of fresh disasters."[31] There was no need, for almost everything that went wrong before New Orleans went right off Mobile Bay. The expedition anchored on the night of February 5 and next day approached Dauphin Island. Cochrane and the deepwater vessels landed on the ocean side of the island, while the lighter-draft ships under Malcolm stood off until ordered to disembark on the landward side.[32] Lambert landed Gibbs's brigade unopposed at dawn on February 8 and pushed forward until they drove back American skirmishers half a mile from the small fort with twenty-two guns on the island's eastern end. Lambert was not risking another infantry assault.[33] By daylight on February 11, he had sixteen guns ready for a two-day bombardment.

Dickson wanted his cannons to reduce the fort to redeem their performance at New Orleans, but Lambert gave the Yankees a chance to capitulate first. Isolated and heavily outnumbered, there was no question what Major William Lawrence must do. At three p.m. he agreed to yield, much to the disappointment of redcoats anxious to erase their own humiliation before Line Jackson. The next day the fort's garrison marched out under arms, drums beating and colors flying.[34] Old Hickory had not anticipated Cochrane's Mobile move, at first thinking the enemy would head for Bermuda.[35] It was his only major miscalculation, evidence that even he believed his victory had ended the campaign.

"We certainly finished the war with more éclat by the capture of this fort," felt Gerard.[36] Lambert told Bathurst that taking the fort meant their campaign yielded some fruit after all by closing Mobile Bay to enemy shipping, but it was a transparent effort to gloss over the greater failure. When Cochrane proposed another overland campaign on New Orleans via the Baton Rouge approach, Lambert flatly refused, especially since the admiral had not come prepared with more than eight days' provisions, and those were running out.[37]

Food for their spirits came on Monday, February 13, when HMS *Brazen* brought word of the Ghent treaty. Cochrane took it hard, Codrington crediting the admiral's funk to disappointment over the lost prospect of prize money. Now Cochrane could not wait to quit the Gulf.[38] He proposed to leave Lambert and about 5,000 troops, along with Nicolls and his Indians, to invade western Georgia and cooperate with Cockburn. That should keep Kentucky and Tennessee militia from threatening Canada and pin Jackson to New Orleans. If Madison refused to ratify and the war went on, Cochrane would meet Lambert on the Georgia coast, which had yielded good prize money the year before. He said nothing more of New Orleans.[39]

Dauphin Island welcomed the news, and Keane, Lambert, Dickson, and Gordon learned of their knighthoods at the same time.[40] Codrington could hardly describe his sensations at the news. He had hoped for another chance at the Americans, but at least peace would free him from Cochrane and his cronies.[41] On February 18, *Tonnant* made sail, leaving Malcolm and Lambert in place until notified otherwise. Cochrane was so anxious to leave that he failed to give Lambert further orders, which the general was determined not to heed in any case.[42] That still left Lambert with the problem of runaway slaves with his army. On February 7, Livingston, Shepherd, and Maunsel White arrived to negotiate return of the enslaved to their owners. Cochrane detained them at first, but it was not an entirely unpleasant "captivity" for the Americans or their hosts.[43] Livingston amused British officers with a fund of stories and became especially cordial with Lambert. He also brought Keane's sword and other personal items for the families of dead officers like Rennie.[44]

After the news of the treaty, Cochrane released them, but confusion resulted in the delegation leaving empty-handed on February 16.[45] Still, Lambert promised to release runaways to owners who came in person and persuaded their people to return, although he would not compel any to go.[46] Those who stayed could enlist in one of the West India regiments or be transported to Trinidad.[47] Perhaps not coincidentally, Cochrane's own plantations were there, and his nephew Cochrane Johnstone had a farm at Demerara on the South American coast not far distant.[48] In the end, few slaves returned to Louisiana but hundreds were taken to Bermuda and Trinidad, where some served in the colonial marines.[49] Rumor said some wound up slaves again on Cochrane Johnstone's plantation.[50]

Late on February 18, Livingston reached New Orleans and electrified the city with news of the treaty on its way to Washington.[51] Jackson distributed a handbill cautioning that they must wait for official confirmation, but editor Godwin Cotten would not sit on the story and printed a *Louisiana Gazette* extra mistakenly claiming that Cochrane had asked for an armistice in light of the treaty. Jackson responded with another handbill accusing the press of being ignorant and dishonest, and prohibited further such publications without his approval.[52]

For a fortnight people watched for verification.[53] Finally, an express arrived on March 6 to give Jackson a packet from the War Department. On the outside Monroe had written that it contained a copy of the fully ratified Ghent treaty, but Adair saw Jackson's elation dissolve when he opened the packet to find no treaty inside. "Where's the peace?" Old Hickory exclaimed. Somehow it had fallen out on the trip or failed to be enclosed.[54] Everyone believed the end had come, but without that treaty Jackson would not regard it as official.[55] A week passed before another rider brought final notification on March 13.

The treaty had reached Washington a month earlier on St. Valentine's Day. Congressman Philip Barton Key, whose nephew wrote a popular poem soon known as "The Star-Spangled Banner," saw the capital "drunk with joy" at the news.[56] At Monticello, Jefferson was ecstatic. American militia were unbeatable when heroes led them, he gloated, and peace came all the more welcome when "we closed the war with the whorra! of New Orleans."[57] Even Jackson's critics credited him with showing this generation worthy of its sires of Bunker Hill and Yorktown.[58] Few cared that the battle came after the treaty.[59] The war was quite definitely over.[60] Jackson printed announcement handbills that evening, and the celebrations began the next day with illuminations on the streets and flags flying from *Louisiana*'s rigging.[61]

During the weeks since Lambert's departure, Jackson's men finally got tents, kettles and pans, buckets for water, and paper, goose quills, and sealing wax for their letters. Keelboats with holds full of corn tied up on the shore, and gradually muskets and bayonets came into the hands of those still unarmed.[62] The day after the battle, whiskey was in high demand at seventy-three cents a gallon.[63] Other than that, their only comfort came from the Bibles given them by the Bible Society as three and four men tried to read at once, or gathered around one who read aloud.[64]

They needed spiritual comfort, for now they faced enemies deadlier than Pakenham's legions. Weather, poor nutrition, inadequate sanitation, and exposure to germs and viruses, made sick lists burgeon.[65] Illness depleted General Hopkins's militia at Donaldsonville. By early February, Carroll's Tennesseans were increasingly sickly from exposure, and perhaps two hundred had already perished.[66] Hynes blamed swampy conditions at the main breastwork, and most of the men relocated to dryer camps, but the damage was done. Surgeon Robert Cobb diagnosed typhus, pleurisy, measles, perhaps even malaria, and every one of them a killer.[67] Measles and mumps surged through men whose rural lives had denied them exposure to otherwise common childhood viruses. General Thomas's brigade had seven hundred on its sick list, a third of his command, on February 10.[68] One barracks became a virtual hospital where little could be done but spread hay to absorb the over-flow from their chamber pots.[69] Kentuckians died there every day.[70] Men were sent to Natchez to recuperate, yet more died there as well.[71] By the end of February, Carroll and Coffee had nearly four hundred dead, and as a whole Jackson lost perhaps five hundred to wounds, exposure, and camp disease, to be buried in a mass trench grave behind Line Dupré.[72]

Despite peace and sickness, Old Hickory knew not to relax discipline. There was a flurry of courts-martial for every infraction from disloyalty to desertion. A court acquitted Major Villeré of carelessness, but some still believed Jackson's mind had been poisoned against the *creoles*.[73] Expecting Morgan to be charged, Lieutenant Nixon wrote a deposition just hours after the fight.[74] A tribunal scrutinized the right-bank action, as Morgan and Davis demanded inquiries to clear their names, and concluded that Major Arnaud had disrupted Davis's command, whose flight was deemed "excusable."[75] Another court relieved Colonel Ross of command of the 44th Infantry for drunkenness, while an inquiry fully exonerated Lieutenant Andrew Ross for temporary loss of the bastion to Rennie.[76]

More than one officer faced suspension or arrest for disobedience and insubordination, and even General Villeré was not immune to reprimand.[77] Old Hickory also went after vandals preying on planters, Morgan's men being the worst offenders, and *Louisiana* became a prison ship for men caught looting.[78] Absenteeism and desertion escalated as Daquin's company almost dissolved and militia at the Villeré canal left ranks, and Jackson arrested a Louisiana major for inciting mutiny in his command.[79] Two deserters from the 4th Louisiana were caught, convicted, and sentenced to be executed within hours.[80] When finally his agents found the contractors who delayed the flatboat of arms from Pittsburgh, he charged them with aiding the enemy. When a court acquitted them, he docketed its verdict with his disapproval.[81] Meanwhile he harped about preparedness. "We have been always too backward with our preparations," he complained to Monroe. "When the enemy comes we begin to think of driving him away, & scarcely before."[82] He little knew then that another battle was coming with an enemy quite unexpected.

Enemies real and imaginary surrounded Andrew Jackson. The term "poor white" was yet uncoined, but he closely fit the die. Lacking the archetype's indolence and irresponsibility, he had raised himself from nothing through will, application, and hard work, but he never shed the other hallmarks, like mistrust of landed wealth, old money, and blue blood. He saw unseen foes ever arrayed, plots and cabals aplenty, and enemies scheming against him and his friends. Men like Coffee who accepted his authority became close friends. Those challenging him faced an implacable foe. Given Louisiana's people and culture, and Jackson's personality, it was inevitable that they would clash. Just two days after the British evacuation, his battle with the city began.

Nothing equipped him to deal with the old *creole* population, or the more recent French *émigrés*. He did not trust what he did not understand, and their language, habits, work ethics, and morals were foreign to him. He made necessary allowances, like embracing the Baratarians. Guided by Livingston, he showed good judgment and some sensitivity in embracing men like Chotard, and remained lifelong friends with Plauché and Davezac. Still, and with exceptions like Claiborne, he most trusted men with no Gallic syllables in their names: Coffee, Carroll, Hinds, even the hopelessly inadequate Morgan. A dozen years later he brilliantly summed up his view of Louisiana's dominant population during his time there. "I went on my way to duty," he supposedly said; "they went off to dance."[83]

With the restraint imposed by external threat gone, New Orleans soon rose to white heat in the crucible of martial law. Two Louisiana militia regiments that fled on the west bank threatened mutiny if they were punished, and a spirit of insubordination spread.[84] On February 1 the legislature voted thanks to Daquin and Savary's free black companies, but now they refused to perform heavy labor previously done by slaves. Then a new rumor reignited the terror of a servile rebellion, making suspect all blacks in the city, free or slave, and their movements were curtailed.[85] Although Jackson entrusted the defense of Chef Menteur to Major Lacoste's black militia, he shared the apprehension; and when Savary's officers appealed to him to uphold their rights, he did nothing, nor did he exert much effort to redeem pledges of freedom for slaves who enlisted, an indifference shown Captain Jugeat's Choctaw as well.[86]

Claiborne played bellows to the embers. He still hoped to command troops away from Jackson's oversight, preferably on the right bank, for if the British passed Fort St. Philip, they would appear in his front and give him a chance for glory.[87] The last thing Jackson wanted was Claiborne where something might happen, both from fear of his ineptitude and a petty desire to thwart his ambitions. Claiborne went over on his own to supersede Morgan, but Jackson frustrated him by sending Morgan an order making his men independent of the governor's militia. Left with a command scarcely befitting a major, Claiborne returned to the city and demanded Old Hickory's apology for the insult.[88] Andrew Jackson did not apologize.[89] Instead, he scolded Claiborne for a host of shortcomings and warned him that in the future "an Explanation will be demanded for every failure."[90]

Claiborne's dream of military glory blasted, his battle with Old Hickory was anything but done, but he had few allies now with the emergency over and old fractures reopening. One leading *creole* dismissed him as "good for nothing, a third class lawyer," saying that if Claiborne had commanded on January 8, the British would be dining in the city.[91] Jackson called him "a perfect old woman" and mendaciously accused Claiborne of hiding at a hospital during the battle.[92] The governor's futile efforts to quell restlessness in the militia only worsened the situation.[93] By early February, Jackson communicated with only Claiborne in writing.[94] The governor struck back at "the violence of his character" and on March 2 protested directly to Monroe that Old Hickory's arbitrary acts had destroyed their hard-won unity.[95]

Then someone conceived the idea that foreign nationals were not liable to military service, and a flurry of applications for certificates of citizenship went to Tousard and Spanish consul Diego Morphy. Tousard alone quickly issued 158.[96] Having no choice but to release some on their certificates, Jackson reacted typically by banishing them from the city until peace was confirmed.[97] That put him at odds with the local federal justice system. When Louaillier protested the banishment, Old Hickory arrested him. When Judge Hall's reopened court issued a writ of habeas corpus for Louaillier's release, Jackson arrested him, and then arrested Louisiana's attorney general when he issued a writ.[98] Tried before a military court for inciting mutiny, Louaillier was acquitted, but Jackson rejected the verdict and kept him behind bars until martial law ended.[99] Meanwhile, Old Hickory grew increasingly arbitrary.[100] Over five weeks beginning on February 1, he jailed more than thirty citizens, some without charge or explanation, and merchant Edward Hollander just for speaking critically of him.[101] A Terre-aux-Boeufs planter accused of feeding enemy officers in his home was condemned to be hanged, fulfilling one citizen's prediction that "there is some probability of a demand for Hemp."[102]

Predictably, Jackson cracked down on the press, declaring that freedom of speech eroded military discipline, risked giving information to the enemy, and incited mutiny in the militia.[103] He forbade all mention of strengths, reinforcements, defenses, and guns, and decreed that editors have his permission before printing them.[104] An outraged editor Cotten protested that "every man may read for himself, and *think* for himself," and stopped publishing in protest, which suited Jackson.[105] He clamped down on what soldiers wrote in their letters and kept men closely confined in camp and largely ignorant of events.[106] Perhaps symbolically, the watchword in mid-February was changed to "Secure."[107] Still, news sifted out, in part because the editor who printed Jackson's orders shared their content before they hit the streets.[108] No wonder a visitor said that "every thing here becomes *publick*: and no secrets are thought worth the keeping."[109]

By early March letters left the city complaining of the general's "despotic sway" and "reign of terror."[110] They had made him their "deity of Orleans," and now they must bend the knee to him. At the Exchange Coffee House, a man tore down a transparency proclaiming, "Jackson and Victory." Officers arrested him, made the proprietor hang another, and set a guard to prevent any effort to remove it. One Orleanian accused Jackson of inexcusable violations of the Constitution, and others called him a usurper for imposing "a complete military despotism."[111]

Jackson's answer was that until he had definitive word of peace, martial law must prevail, and he would recognize no authority but his own.[112] The consequent outcry was confirmation of a conspiracy against him, Claiborne at its head. He considered arresting the governor himself after hearing that he had accused Jackson of alienating the legislature, infecting army morale, and brewing the worst civil unrest the nation had seen.[113] When Claiborne sent thanks to Adair, Carroll, Coffee, Hinds, Thomas, and others in late February, he sent none to Jackson. The legislature voted thanks to several officers, but none to their general. When the American majority in the house voted to give him a presentation sword, the French majority in the senate refused.[114] Louisiana seemed bent on expunging its proclaimed savior from its history.

New Orleans was the first American community to endure martial law, and no polity in the nation could have been more difficult. No precedent guided Jackson. The Constitution was mute beyond authorizing suspension of habeas corpus in time of invasion or insurrection, but then failed to say who could do so, Congress or the president. Washington might as well be in another solar system for all its ability to react to events 1,000 miles away. The decision had to be made on the spot, and Jackson was justified in making it, as the support of governor, legislature, mayor, federal court, and others attested. Open to question is how long he should have maintained it. There circumstances colluded with his personality to make him twist its cords tighter with each affront to his authority. Challenges from disgruntled militia, governor, legislature, court, and press gave him cause to fear that if he ended martial law too soon, New Orleans might not accept resumption of it should occasion demand. Hindsight suggests he maintained it too long, but what he saw in the moment told him to keep tight rein on the city until confirmation of peace. He could have been gentler, but that was not Old Hickory's way.

By contrast, leagues to the east, near tranquility reigned on Dauphin

Island. The British had little to do but entertain themselves, and Tylden joked that "no nation understands the art of being & making themselves comfortable, more than the English."[115] They decorated their tent bivouac and fought mock battles with pinecones, and Burgoyne's engineers built a log theater with a sail for a roof and an alligator skin for a door.[116] Lambert himself attended its twice-weekly performances.[117] Meanwhile, the remaining prisoners were returned, and on the last day of February, Malcolm sent Lawrence's garrison to the exchange point.[118] Among the last released was the irrepressible Thomas Shields, who had become a prisoner yet again after his capture while observing British positions on Dauphin.[119] It was the last hostile act of the campaign and an anticlimactic close to a war, which Shields and his captors learned had been over for weeks when a boat carrying emissaries from Jackson arrived on March 16 with news of Madison's signing.

Anchoring abreast of "Oatlands," they fired a salute, and hundreds of cheering soldiers rushed to the shore as a band aboard played "Hail Columbia" and "Yankee Doodle." Somehow the redcoats understood that the boat brought news of peace.[120] "Thanks God all our toils are nearly at an end," Gleig wrote in his diary. Admiral Malcolm sent a messenger after Cochrane to inform him of the ratification, and Lambert declared an immediate end to hostilities.[121] The Americans shared provisions with the famished English, who had barely a week's rations left.[122]

Lambert left soon afterward, though not before asking Livingston to visit him if ever he went to England.[123] Much of his army remained a bit longer until word came that, on February 26, Napoleon had fled the island of Elba and once more Britain marshaled her legions to confront him. The veterans of New Orleans were needed. As soon as arrangements could be made, Malcolm embarked the troops on their transports and set sail for Havana. Before going, Captain Gordon affixed their theater's alligator hide to the bow of *Seahorse* as a memento.[124] When New Orleans learned of Bonaparte's escape, the *creole* and French population staged a torchlight parade with illuminations declaring "Vive Napoleon, vive Jackson."[125] It was perhaps a last exhalation of the unity that Old Hickory and Claiborne had forged to save their city.

When Jackson had received Monroe's letter on March 13 confirming ratification, he immediately rescinded martial law and pardoned all convicted or arrested under that authority, including those awaiting execution.[126] A few days later, with no attempt at irony, he told Plauché that martial law had been necessary to preserve civil liberties.[127] After discharging the militia on March 16, he held a farewell review.[128] Coffee's brigade set their loping stride for Baton Rouge early next morning, to reach home in mid-April.[129] Thomas's Kentuckians left the following day.[130] Those who had them took their New Orleans Bibles home, even if it meant discarding something from their packs to make room.[131]

Freed from their cells, Hall, Dick, Louaillier, and others counter-attacked, charging Jackson with contempt of court. He calmly appeared in court on March 24 as ordered, with Livingston and Duncan as counsel, when Judge Hall ruled that he had failed to show cause for his action and ordered him to pay a $1,000 fine for contempt.[132] Jackson paid it immediately and then, with martial law at an end, called on all to obey the authorities.[133] He would respect the court's authority now, but not the judge, for Old Hickory saw Hall as the head of "a few Traitors" backing Claiborne, who was "the moving machine behind the curtain."[134]

A metamorphosis unfolded. Jackson became again the darling of the moment, if not of all Orleanians.[135] When he left the courthouse, a crowd put him in a horseless carriage and pulled him through the streets in triumph.[136] Public dinners honored him, and men spoke of the great things he had done for Louisiana: He had united a divided people; he had made peace with the Baratarians; and he had saved the country in battle.[137] At one dinner Old Hickory thanked Pierre Laffite for his efforts as "one of those to whom the country is most indebted."[138]

After handing command to newly arrived major general Edmund Gaines and saying farewell to the remaining regulars and city volunteers in a brief but affecting ceremony, Andrew and Rachel Jackson left New Orleans on April 6. Beale's company presented him with a sword and a moving address crediting him for saving themselves and their city.[139] They would miss him. Some would miss Rachel as well, especially her friend Wollstonecraft, who soon told her that "your departure was the death of Parties."[140] Superlatives flowed for months after the victory, some declaring Jackson the greatest general in the young nation's history.[141] Behind him, he left New Orleans more divided than ever, and he had done much of the division.[142]

Back home by May 15, Jackson heard from Livingston that New Orleans was tranquil despite what Old Hickory called "the little malicious knot" of those in confederacy against him.[143] Still, he never stopped lashing at Claiborne and others.[144] A Jackson needed enemies, and he soon had another in Adair over his rebuke to the Kentuckians who panicked with Morgan and Hinds.[145] For two years they exchanged an increasingly acrimonious correspondence that exposed Adair's occasional foolishness and Jackson's pettiness, doing credit to neither.[146] Only as his presidential aspirations crystalized and he once more needed Kentuckians did Old Hickory soften, and relations calmed by 1824. Four years later he retracted his earlier strictures.[147]

That year Old Hickory was on the presidential ballot but narrowly lost to John Quincy Adams when the election went into the House of Representatives. As the 1828 election approached, Jackson's new Democratic Party was at odds with the old Republicans, and there was political capital in turning on the Republican Monroe. The general and his supporters now blamed Monroe personally for the delay of the Pittsburgh guns, Jackson himself lying about the details, the message being that Old Hickory had saved New Orleans despite Monroe's negligence.[148] Opponents attacked his martial law, his conduct of the campaign, and his slanders of the legislature.[149] Supporters responded with equal venom and disregard for truth.[150] Jackson himself visited New Orleans for the January 8 anniversary to virtually co-opt the celebration as a campaign event.[151] He hardly needed to do so. He and the battle were inseparable. January 8 anniversary celebrations everywhere automatically celebrated Old Hickory as well.[152] In November 1828, Jackson rode the battle to the presidency. The "Age of Jackson" was at hand.

He carried every state west of the Appalachians, his ascendance moving in lockstep with the growing mythology about who won the battle, and how. It began with an immediate misconception of what scythed the redcoat harvest. Musketry lasted about forty minutes on January 8, but artillery hurled grape and canister at the enemy for ninety. One Kentuckian wrote soon afterward that, thanks to the big guns, "death now stalked triumphant o'er the field."[153] There is no scope to doubt that artillery was the reaper, as virtually everyone on the scene at the time, volunteer and professional alike, testified.[154] Proof lay in the high casualties among the 7th, the 43rd, the 93rd, and 1st West India. Although most of them never came under heavy rifle or musket fire, they actually suffered slightly more men killed and wounded than regiments that did. Only artillery could account for that. Plauché, Daquin, Lacoste, and many of the 44th fired their weapons little if at all, having no immediate targets.[155] Hundreds of Kentuckians and Tennesseans were not engaged, and what small-arms damage there was came mainly from muskets, since only Beale and parts of Coffee, Carroll, and Adair shouldered rifles.[156]

But a young nation's imagination wanted more than faceless, mechanistic crewmen serving belching cannons. It needed something more *American*, befitting its image of itself. Emotionally, it wanted the battle to be won by an individualistic weapon, a rifle, made deadly accurate in the hands of modern "Minute Men," the peerless volunteers of the West.

The myth began innocently, fed by ignorance and romanticism, and captured the American imagination. Its focus on Tennesseans and Kentuckians actually predated the main battle. On January 6 a Natchez woman repeated a garbled account of the January 1 engagement to say that "brave Tennesseans Kentuckians & Mississippians met them with the bayonet as fast as they mounted the wall."[157] There was no such fighting. Yankee rifles and muskets scarcely fired, and redcoats never neared the earthwork, but already westerners were the heroes.

On January 9 a Louisiana dragoon became midwife to the legend, writing that Kentucky "riflemen" did great execution, for "scarcely a rifle was discharged by them which did not bring down one or more of the enemy."[158] After that the outpouring never stopped. The two states' "Riflemen" tore the enemy to shreds, and British prisoners marveled at a people who could produce such marksmen.[159] Three days later a whole subliterature began celebrating William Withers's accuracy for killing Rennie at virtually point-blank range, making his name momentarily household even in the East.[160] Gabriel Winter dismissed rockets and shells as mere "Pomp of war," on January 12, while musketry was "the thing for execution."[161] In two weeks Coffee praised "the carnage of our Rifles," although he saw little of the battle from his line.[162]

Publication of this and more in the nation's press nourished the story of deadly marksmen of the West. Wounded redcoats and even the dead lent support. Lambert attributed most of his casualties to buck and ball, since grapeshot wounds could look like bullet holes.[163] Even Cochrane advanced the myth on January 20 by complaining that if officers exposed themselves recklessly, they would be cut down by "the American Rifle men."[164] In Bermuda the press described Yankees as "riflemen and excellent sharp-shooters," and Cobbett lectured Liverpool that Congreves were nothing against a backwoodsman and his Kentucky rifle.[165]

Multiple currents fed the rifleman myth and its connection to Kentuckians in particular. The narrative so masked memory of their performance under Morgan that less than a week after the battle an anonymous account credited the victory to the "expert riflemen" of Kentucky and the western country.[166] In a month they were bringing down "one or more of the enemy" with every round.[167] Almost overnight they went from panicked flight to killing two redcoats with a single bullet. Nor were Tennesseans left out: Captain James Kempe of Mississippi credited them with saving the nation.[168] By the end of February, people at home boasted that "the sons of the West, and *particularly from Tenn* have acquired more glory for themselves and country than ever was obtained by the same number of men in any country." They had amazed the world.[169]

Suddenly these Western men were cast in warlike raiment they never shed. The late war gave them the taste for arms, said a city visitor, and when word of the victory reached the East, readers found a taste for western marksmen.[170] "The bravery of the Kentuckians, the Tennesseans, &c shall be handed down to the latest posterity," editors exulted. They were fighters without peer who mowed the foe like grass.[171] Americans fought better than any other nation, and Jefferson himself hailed the "deadly aim" of rural militiamen.[172] Livingston's brother proclaimed that the British would never again challenge "a country that has such men."[173]

In an age when people expected their heroes big and unfettered by modesty, there were many ways to shape public perceptions. Stories swelled column inches in the press. Plans of the battle appeared as early as March, and the first crude illustrations appeared, with more than half a dozen following by 1817.[174] Starting in 1815 the battle was depicted on cotton handkerchiefs and linens, even a French snuff box, and commemorative china spilled from New England kilns, much featuring Jackson.[175] In May the New Museum of Wax-Work in Hartford, Connecticut, displayed effigies of Jackson, "the Hero of New-Orleans," and the mortally wounded Pakenham at twenty-five cents a view.[176] It all marketed the triumph of American republicanism.

Forgettable poetry and song celebrated the theme of incredible victory, but some stood out.[177] What gripped the country's imagination was a lyric set to an old tune about a maid who hanged herself in her garters after being seduced by a sea captain.[178] In 1819 a comic actor commissioned a new song to debut "in the character and dress of a Kentucky Rifleman." He died before he could perform it onstage, and the author later published it simply titled "New-Orleans."[179] Heavily influenced by the growing literature on Kentuckians and New Orleans, it opened declaring "we are a hardy freeborn race," and became even more specific to the theme:

> I 'spose you've read it in the prints, / how Packenham attempted
> To make old Hickory Jackson wince, / but soon his scheme repented,
> For we, with rifles ready cock'd, / thought such occasion lucky,
> And soon around the general flock'd / The hunters of Kentucky.

All the tropes were there in subsequent verses. The enemy came for New Orleans's "girls and cotton bags," but "*lead* was all their *booty*" when Jackson relied on "what aim we take, / With our Kentucky rifles." Every man was "half a horse, / And half an alligator," and Kentuckians' rifles won the battle and, by inference, the war. Cannon were not mentioned once.

It got limited notice even when retitled "The Hunters of Kentucky."[180] Alluded to in passing in 1824, when a candidate was referred to as a "hunter of Kentucky," the song played no role in that year's presidential race, although it spoke to the Jacksonian ideal of reliance on militia.[181] As the 1828 election approached, however, it came into its own, performed at battle anniversary celebrations that became Jackson rallies, and breathed a spirit of admiration for the men who saved New Orleans, and the man who led them.[182] Promoting Jackson and the marksman myth, it implied that only Kentuckians won the battle.[183] Days after the election, the song debuted in London and began shaping the English image of America and Americans.[184]

By then something else happened to set the mood for a backwoods rifleman. In 1826, James Fenimore Cooper published his most popular novel, *The Last of the Mohicans*, a story of "Hawkeye," his very name showing his deadly skill with a rifle. In fact, he bore two sobriquets, the other *"La Longue Carabine,"* which virtually forged man and rifle into one. Cooper had featured him in two previous books, but neither captured the imagination like his latest. It made this backwoods individualist, defender of the right, steadfast friend, merciless foe, and dispenser of certain death with his rifle one of the most enduring characters in American culture.

Hawkeye reflected a literature that emerged within months of the January 8 battle. In 1815, Joseph Dorris and Jesse Denson published their fictionalized *Chronicles of Andrew,* featuring redcoats who declared the backwoodsmen victors to be "all sharp-shooters and strangers to fear."[185] Its message was that freemen fought better than subjects, and American Westerners were natural fighters and crack shots. When more conventional histories began to appear, they played the same chord, extolling the Western volunteer and reshaping the battle narrative to reinforce current political and cultural values.[186] Although the Baratarians often appeared, absent were regulars, artillerymen, sailors, free blacks who fought, and slaves who built defenses. The growing myth gave Westerners a new sense of pride, poising the West to be a new powerhouse for American destiny.[187] Even Jackson's enemies embraced the Rifleman.[188]

Old Hickory naturally became the subject of books. The general would not write his own autobiography, finding the thought of it "insipid & disagreeable," but Livingston contemplated one and Jackson encouraged him. Major Reid also started a history with his cooperation and by April 1815 completed a sketch of Jackson's life and an account of the Louisiana campaign based on a partial account by Jackson himself. Reid died before the book's completion, and another of Jackson's protégés, Major John Eaton, finished it in 1817.[189] Hagiography at its best, it was essentially the first

campaign document of Old Hickory's inevitable run for the presidency. The
New Orleans campaign got a "biography" when Latour wrote a book destined to be a landmark in American military literature. His *Historical
Memoir of the War in West Florida and Louisiana in 1814–15* appeared in
1816, making Jackson the hero of the piece.[190]

The battle took the stage as well. Several plays followed Daudat's *Le
Camp de Jackson*, and then in 1819 *The Battle of New Orleans, or the Glorious 8th of January* introduced a "rifleman."[191] Among the first plays written
by Americans for their own stage, most promoted Jackson and the marksman myth.[192] Thereafter, few battle anniversaries passed without a new
drama.[193] *The Battle of New-Orleans, or—the Female Spy* in January 1828
portrayed the Bluegrass marksman firing through cotton embrasures and
shooting Pakenham, and concluded with a "Kentucky Rifleman" singing
"The Hunters of Kentucky."[194]

Two months later Andrew Jackson took office. The Battle of New Orleans, and how Americans reshaped it, had made him president.

"Who Would Not Be an American?"

THE NATION OBSERVED only two holidays prior to 1815—February 22 and July 4. At first some used Independence Day as an occasion to commemorate Jackson's victory as well. On July 4, 1815, a Virginian wrote his brother that he and his friends in Richmond would "commence *eating & drinking*" in commemoration of the battle and expected before evening to be walking "in a *curvilineal* direction."[1] Starting in 1816, and for the next half century, January 8 joined the other two holidays, tying New Orleans in Americans' minds to 1776 and making it, symbolically, the true "last battle" of the struggle with Britain, a new birth of liberty.

The first celebration actually honored the December 23 fight. A few companies of regulars and volunteers paraded in New Orleans, and *Louisiana* fired a salute on the morning of December 24, 1815. Ships on the levee flew flags, and a theater that evening presented a play about the battle that a viewer thought pitiful, not least because an actor made a burlesque of portraying Old Hickory.[2] On January 3 the rest of the celebration began, culminating on January 8. A British visitor who spoke intemperately of Jackson's army became arguably the battle's last casualty when he was challenged to a duel and mortally wounded.[3]

The celebrations quickly took on a political cast. Republicans effectively exploited the victory to cement the party's hold on national power as the Federalists dissolved. In 1819, Louisiana officially made it a day of thanksgiving, and thereafter public orators repeated and reshaped the story to fit their times. By 1820 it rivaled July 4 as a national holiday, soon becoming the most powerful weapon in the arsenal of Jackson's Democrats for more than a generation, and they wisely promoted it as a *national* victory.[4] Over time they found evidence of divine favor in January 8 being St. Victoria's Day. Only it was not. That was December 23; January 8 had no saint's day, but in 1828, as Jackson sought the presidency, Livingston linked him with the Almighty by claiming that it was the day for prayers to St. Victoria.[5] Davezac later asserted that on the morning of the battle, the book of daily prayers at the city's convent opened itself to the prayer of St. Victoria and that Old Hickory confessed premonitions of triumph. "I knew that God would not give me previsions of disasters, but signs of victory," he supposedly told Davezac, and that morning the Almighty promised him that "this ditch can never be passed."[6]

With God and Jackson on their side, no wonder these men believed in American exceptionalism. Foreigners noted that January 8 was "a constant theme of bragging in that country."[7] After Jackson left the presidency, the celebration remained linked to Democratic politics, but by the 1850s it waned as a national commemoration, especially as sectional controversy over slavery fragmented even holidays north and south.[8] By 1860 the anniversary became a celebration of the Union in the North and independence in the South. Interest in its celebration waned after 1865, making it one more casualty of the Civil War.

The battlefield itself remained a reminder of the victory, its few landmarks eloquent illustrations of the battle's stature in Americans' evolving self-image. Peace was barely weeks old before people began touring the Chalmette plain. Locals turned guides for friends, and when *Vesuvius* took a party in mid-April 1815 to view the battlefield, battle veterans aboard pointed out places of interest. They saw the holes in the McCarty house and a cannonball still lodged in the wall above Jackson's bed. A big mortar still sat on the far right of the earthwork near the river. Line Jackson was plain to see, and so was Line Dupré. Burned and blasted plantation buildings dotted the plain, and scorched spots in the clover marked redcoat campfires. Most eloquent was the ditch in front of the main earthwork. A large bloody stain still covered the ground, and with it an extremely offensive smell. Across the plain, the British mass graves were painfully evident, some bodies only half covered with earth, and there again that smell.[9] A few weeks later visitors saw putrefying, mold-covered corpses poking from the ground.[10]

With passing years Line Jackson eroded to an elevated bank, but Lieutenant Ross's bastion was still visible. Returning to the scene, Benjamin Latrobe heard many anecdotes circulating that were worth recording, and feared that in a few years they would be lost, as indeed they were.[11] A decade later visitors still saw evidence of the British officers' graves, and twenty years after the battle, novelist Joseph Holt Ingraham found much of the earthwork worn down to a grassy embankment about four feet high and six feet wide, and in places almost level with the surrounding ground. The Rodriguez canal or ditch remained, but so filled in that the British could walk over it now. Even after two decades, locals clung to certain moments, and one more than any other. When Ingraham's guide stepped a few paces up the embankment near the river, he tapped his foot on a mound to say, "*Here fell Renie.*"[12]

On the battlefield, visitors heard the story of a Tennessee marksman who five times leapt atop the breastwork to aim and bring down a redcoat at every shot, and another calling to an enemy officer: "Surrender, stranger—or, I may perforate ye!"[13] It was a garbled retelling of the capture of Major Ross of the 21st Fusiliers, which first appeared in a letter on January 13, 1815.[14] After Ingraham published the story, it appeared with variations into the next century.[15]

No one seemed to notice, or care, that as early as August 1852 the New Orleans press denounced the whole Tennessee-Kentucky marksman tale as a fiction.[16] Rather, the stories just proliferated, as when Davezac told of the day after the January 8 battle when a Kentucky sharpshooter bagged a dozen robins, each shot through the head, to put on Jackson's breakfast table.[17] The Rifleman's grip on American imagination was too firm to shake. He had become America's second great defining folk hero after the Minuteman of the Revolution, and he would continue to epitomize how Americans chose to think of themselves for more than half a century before giving way to his legitimate offspring, the Cowboy. Indeed, by 1876, with the Cowboy in his infancy, the Rifleman was so ingrained in the American mind that, with the centennial celebration in the offing, a humorist lampooned him by suggesting that Louisiana's contribution to exhibits should be "the squint made by the Kentucky rifleman in aiming at Gen. Pakenham."[18]

Former secretary of war Eustis declared in January 1815 that if Old Hickory and his men prevailed, "he & they will deserve immortality."[19] They prevailed. A few got their immortality, and men on both sides went on to live lives touched indelibly by their experience.

Vincent Gray profited little from his effort to be an American patriot. When *Plantagenet* landed at Havana early in February, Thornton and others gave him the particulars of their misfortunes, one experienced senior officer telling him that he had "never seen any thing to be compared with the affair at New Orleans."[20] Gray died bankrupt in 1831, his only compensation for his warnings being Jackson's intercession to get his son Andrew a commission in the navy.[21]

Those men of questionable loyalty, Workman and Kerr, took differing paths. Workman moved to Philadelphia after the war, sharing lodgings with onetime followers of Napoleon who hoped to create a new French colony in west Louisiana or Spanish Texas. Only after consulting Livingston as to his safety did he return to New Orleans in May 1817 to open a law partnership with notary Michel DeArmas.[22] Kerr went to the Bahamas to practice law, served in its colonial assembly, and later became solicitor and attorney general. He died on a visit to Philadelphia in 1834, his dreams of empire gone to dust. A year earlier he told Livingston, "I am one of those unhappy pill-garlics, that in spite of fate and fortune, are born never to be worth a groat."[23]

Other Orleanians fared better. Thomas Beale died five years after the battle, worth $124,000.[24] William Withers served as alderman and prospered from his mill, eventually owning a score of slaves before his death in 1829. Nathaniel Cox got involved with Livingston, Duncan, and others in financing Mexican filibusters after the war.[25] Beverly Chew resumed collecting debts and selling land to close his former business, but remained in the city.[26] In 1817 he became collector of the port, putting him at odds with the Laffites, and later became president of the city's branch of the Bank of the United States and vice consul to Russia.[27]

Major Carmick, the gallant marine, never recovered from his wounds, dying less than two years after the battles.[28] Captain Hudry tried unsuccessfully for years to secure repayment of what he spent for the defense of New Orleans. He was found dead in a Washington hotel on January 21, 1835, so covered in blood that it was believed he cut his own throat in despair over his rejected claim.[29] Actor Pierre Monier was back onstage by October 1815, performing recitations and songs about the late war.[30] While walking down New York's Broadway thirty years after the battle, planter Maunsel White passed a limping stranger who suddenly grabbed his hand. "Is not this Captain White, of Plauché's battalion?" asked a British accent. "It is," White replied, whereupon the other said, "I am Ensign Graves." They renewed their friendship until death.[31]

Among the city's civilians, Abraham Ellery, businessman, scholar, multilingual attorney, skilled mapmaker, nephew of a signer of the Declaration, and onetime aide to General Alexander Hamilton, died in the 1820 yellow fever epidemic.[32] Louis Louaillier remained several years in the legislature, ever resentful of Jackson. In 1827 he proposed an ironic toast to "General A. Jackson and the 8th of January," appending to it another to "Judge Dominique A. Hall and the Independence of our Courts of Justice!"[33] Judah Touro became one of the city's great philanthropists, founding a hospital and synagogue, helping to open Mount Sinai Hospital in New York City, and leaving half a million dollars to charities. The war done, merchant Vincent Nolte and Ensign Shields resumed their feud and finally met in a duel that left Nolte limping for life.[34]

Edward Livingston's fortunes entwined with Jackson's after New Orleans, not least because he relentlessly boosted Old Hickory's reputation.[35] He served Louisiana in Congress and the Senate until 1831 when President Jackson made him secretary of state before sending him to France as minister in 1833. Livingston died three years later in New York. In his last letter to Jackson he spoke of "my attachment to your person, and my desire to promote your public reputation, always identified in my mind with the glory of our country."[36]

Major Latour borrowed $3,000 to support himself while preparing his book and contracted with Livingston to secure subscribers to pay for the published work.[37] By the summer of 1816 he submitted excerpts to the Washington *Daily National Intelligencer* for publication, hoping that glowing reviews would stimulate subscriptions.[38] Initial reactions were mixed. Workman thought it did him great credit, but errors testified to its hurried composition. The *North American Review* gave it expansive favorable notice, but another reviewer dismissed it as dull and "insipid."[39] Only 350 copies were printed, and the book did not sell well. By that time Latour was back in the Southwest on a secret mission for Spain to survey American inroads, Indian sentiment, and the potential for filibusters to take root in the Arkansas country.[40] He soon moved to Havana, then France, where he died in 1837.

With him in Arkansas was another of Jackson's colorful civilians, Jean Laffite. Old Hickory honored his promise to support pardons for the brothers. "The Lafites are men of Enterprise, Courage," Livingston wrote in his name on February 2, 1815, "and in all the business in which I have employed them (frequently on hazardous service) of great Fidelity."[41] Madison did offer pardons for past crimes, but most Baratarians never applied for them, the Laffites and Dominique included.[42] The brothers returned to smuggling, and before long conflict with authorities forced them to leave Louisiana. They settled on uninhabited Galveston Island and flourished until 1820, when the United States forced them to abandon the Gulf Coast. Like many of their brethren, they met bad ends. By 1822, Pierre was privateering off Cancún when he fled pursuing Spaniards for the Yucatán Coast, where he died of fever on or about November 9, 1821. Jean eventually became a legitimate privateer for a change, commanding the *General Santander* for Simón Bolívar's insurrectionary Colombia. On February 4,

1823, in the Gulf of Honduras, a Spaniard bested him in a sea battle. Desperately wounded, he died before the next morning.[43]

Joseph Savary got kind words from Jackson, but little else. With peace, the fear of free armed Negroes reawakened. By 1825 the old black militia dwindled, and nine years later it was abolished.[44] Long before then, Savary and fourteen others joined the Laffites in Galveston, although he later returned to New Orleans when the legislature voted him a pension for his services.[45] Old Hickory gave promise of freedom to some slaves but eventually did nothing, arguing that martial law allowed him to supersede civil law but not to seize and free planters' property.[46] He was also tardy in honoring pledges to free blacks, although the two free battalions did get pay equal with that of white volunteers, and in time the legislature provided pensions to the wounded and to widows and orphans of the dead. Land bounties promised them for volunteering were not forthcoming until 1850, by which time most were gone.

In 1840, when Jackson made his last visit to the city, he shook hands with a few of the *creoles*, like music teacher Louis Desforges, and specifically asked to see some of the black veterans as well.[47] Eleven years later, on January 8, 1851, about ninety of them were at last allowed to walk in the annual celebration parade, the first public acknowledgment of their part in defending the city. An almost embarrassed *Daily Picayune* acknowledged that until that day "their good deeds have been consecrated only in their memories."[48]

No one tried to consecrate the actions of the Choctaw who joined Jackson. Theirs was a cruel irony. By contributing to victory, they helped preserve the region for the very people who would later expel them from it when Jackson's Indian Removal Act of 1830 virtually banished them west of the Mississippi. Captain Pierre Jugeat signed the 1830 removal treaty and led a group of Choctaw to the southeastern area of the Indian Territory that later became Choctaw County, Oklahoma, where he died in 1841.[49]

Claiborne got no thanks from Old Hickory. When his term as governor expired in 1816, the legislature elected him to succeed Brown in the Senate, but he never took his seat. He was ready to leave for Washington, when a recurring liver problem confined him to a bed that he left only on his death on the evening of November 23, 1817. "His private history is without a blemish," said an obituary. "With all the hostility which he has encountered, his integrity was always above suspicion."[50] Perversely, the eulogy said nothing of his efforts during the British threat. The memory of "all the hostility" was too fresh.

Patterson's wife tended Thomas ap Catesby Jones in his recuperation. A bullet stayed in his left shoulder for the rest of his life, gradually disabling the arm. By 1825 he could no longer dress himself; in another few years he could not lift his arm from his side.[51] He struggled for years to get a pension for his disability and, untrammeled by modesty, never ceased maintaining that, had he not delayed Cochrane on the lake, the redcoats might have been in the city by December 13 or 14. "I *fought* the enemy," he declared. "His was the victory, ours the gain—the gain of *time, all-important time.*"[52] He died in 1858, the last American casualty of the Battle of Lake Borgne.

Jones's friend Commodore Daniel Patterson received the Thanks of Congress for his part and promotion to captain in February. Immediately after the war, he resumed efforts to contain smuggling on the Gulf Coast and later helped push the Laffites out of the Gulf, though not before engaging in some questionable financial affairs with privateers. He went on to captain the USS *Constitution*, and in 1832 rose to command of the Mediterranean Squadron. Four years later he took over the Washington Navy Yard until his death in 1839.[53]

Nathaniel Pryor left the 44th Infantry in July 1815 to begin a career as a trader among the Osage. Taken prisoner twice and later reported killed by Cherokee, he was appointed government agent to the Osage with the endorsement of his friend Sam Houston, who told Old Hickory that "a 'braver' man never fought under the wings of your Eagle." He died a month into his new job, his final act a treaty among the Osage, Creek, and Cherokee, days before his death.[54]

Reuben Kemper took pride in his adopted state after the war, telling Livingston in 1818 that "Louisiana is begining [*sic*] to be thought an object among men of interprise [*sic*]."[55] A year later he moved to Alexandria, Louisiana, and spent the rest of his life trying to settle the debt for the arms that wound up being used at New Orleans, even appealing to his "Illustros [*sic*] friend General Jackson."[56] James Bowie, who reached New Orleans too late for the battle, later claimed to have purchased the arms debt and tried to use it to lever Reuben's potent influence in Arkansas on behalf of his anticipated run for Congress. Bowie soon became involved in one of the most legendary frontier brawls, the so-called Sandbar Fight near Natchez, and later met his fate at the Alamo. Kemper also went to Natchez, where he died on January 29, 1827. A friend at his bedside declared that when he passed, "the race of the old Romans would be extinct."[57]

Not quite, perhaps. His final mission for Old Hickory done, "Big Sam" Dale set off for home on the Alabama River.[58] He served in the state legislature, became a brigadier general in its militia, and in 1824 saw a county named for him. Dale cohosted the Marquis de Lafayette's visit to Alabama that same year, the Revolutionary War hero toasting him as "*the American*

Hercules, who *fought and slew* the seven headed monster" in the legendary Canoe Fight. Later he moved to Mississippi, where he died in 1841 in a town with his name.[59]

Captain Charles Wollstonecraft won brevet to major on March 15, 1815, but he was disillusioned with the army. He told Livingston he felt out of place in "a strange world" as a British-born soldier in the American army, married to a Louisiana woman, and brother of a notorious feminist non-conformist.[60] Visitors to New Orleans after the battle thought him unlikely to enhance the celebrity of his family name, and on September 28, 1817, aged just forty-seven, he died.[61] Nine months earlier his niece Mary Wollstonecraft married her lover, poet Percy Bysshe Shelley. The previous summer she had conceived the plot of her first book, and a year after her uncle's death it came off press as *Frankenstein; or, The Modern Prometheus*.

General Villeré would become the state's first native-born governor, but the other militia general, David B. Morgan, salvaged scant glory.[62] He defended himself in the press but was no better with ink than gunpowder, and almost precipitated a duel as a result.[63] Virtually everyone blamed the west bank defeat on his obstinacy and want of military talent. Time has not disagreed.[64] Perhaps because he had no political ambitions, Coffee remained close to Old Hickory until his death in 1831. He worked as a surveyor after the war, moved to Alabama, and became President Jackson's agent to secure the treaty with the Choctaw that relocated them west of the Mississippi. General William Carroll did have ambitions. He served twelve years as Tennessee's governor, a tenure still unmatched, and broke with Jackson over politics. Their friendship had not recovered by the time of Carroll's death in 1844. Adair supported Jackson's presidential bids in 1824 and 1828 and, after a term as governor, served one term in Congress, where he spoke only once, and then so inaudibly that no one then or later knew what he said.[65] He died in 1840, still honored at anniversary celebrations, where toasts sometimes recalled that his birthday was January 8.[66]

Their adversaries went home to diverse fortunes. Codrington took seashells for his daughter Emma. During the voyage he and Cochrane barely spoke, a breach Codrington regretted, but it did relieve him of having to deal with his commander's set of sycophants.[67] Even then he could not release his resentment. Cochrane embraced "the society of the tag rag & bobtail of every place he goes to," Codrington grumbled, delivering the devastating judgment that "he lessens the rank he holds."[68]

The remnant of Lambert's army boarded their transports on March 22, Ensign Gerard being one of the last men to leave Dauphin. They reached Havana on April 9 and eight days later set sail for home.[69] Wherever their squadrons stopped, even Wellington's seasoned veterans spoke of an intensity of fighting at New Orleans that surpassed anything they had known. They had fought hard battles in France and Spain, but never met "such play" as the Yankees gave them.[70] They left the remnants of the hapless West India regiments at Jamaica, where a planter found them worn-out and decayed, virtually abandoned without provisions.[71] One of the runaway slaves who enlisted in their ranks supposedly composed a doggerel about his experience:

> *Admiral now get mad, call "Yankee, son-a-bitch-e"*
> *Yankee man no care, he make one big ditch-e.*
> >*But when British man*
> >>*He go up to storm-e,*
> >*How de Yankees shoot!—*
> >>*O Lord ea'marcy on me!!!*[72]

The returning soldiers found England shocked by their experience. The court-martials of Mullins and others served notice of the war ministries' displeasure with the conduct of the American conflict. Perhaps only Pakenham's death saved him from an inquiry as well, for one critic charged that he had sacrificed himself and his men out of pride rather than retreat. Everyone underestimated the Americans, he added: "They have been held too cheap."[73]

When Pakenham's eviscerated body reached Portsmouth, it was removed from the rum cask and placed in a lead-lined coffin to be taken to London for official ceremonies.[74] From there he went home to Ireland and burial in the family vault at Killnean.[75] General Gibbs's remains came with him as far as Portsmouth, for interment on March 18 in the chapel at the Royal Garrison Church at Southsea. He never knew he had been made a Knight of the Bath on January 2. Public subscription sought to mask humiliation at defeat by placing a marble monument to both generals in St. Paul's Cathedral.

By May 1815, Cochrane was back in England, where Rear Admiral William Johnstone Hope congratulated him for "having given *Jonathan* as much uneasyness as could well be done with the means you had," a pale compliment at best.[76] Nor would there be further glory in a career that had all but run its course. Promoted full admiral in 1819, Cochrane became commander-in-chief, Plymouth, in 1821, served for three years, and died in 1832. Rear Admiral Pulteney Malcolm commanded a squadron off France during the spring campaign to contain Napoleon, spent two years watching the seas around the emperor's final prison on St. Helena, and later commanded the Mediterranean fleet. Made Admiral of the Blue in 1837, he died a year later. Codrington was knighted in 1815 for his New Orleans service, commanded the Mediterranean fleet in 1826, eventually rose to full admiral in 1837, and was commander-in-chief, Portsmouth, before his death in 1851. He blamed official laxity for the security breaches that gave away Cochrane's plans, confiding to Jane that "there have to be changes in the Admiralty."[77]

It was no wonder that fellow officers looked on peg-legged Captain Gordon as "one of the fine fellows of the Navy."[78] He continued commanding frigates until 1821, then took over the naval hospital at Plymouth and later the Chatham Dockyard. On June 26, 1830, as he walked past Westminster after attending King William IV's coronation, a group of rowdies confronted him. One yelled out, "By God! That's Jem Gordon. He flogged me in the *Active*, and now, mates, let's settle him." Putting his back to a wall, Gordon stared down his approaching assailant. "I don't remember you," he said, "but if I flogged you in the *Active*, you d——d rascal, you deserved it. Come on!" The gang cheered his bravery and restrained their companion. Gordon made rear admiral in 1837, vice in 1848, eventually to be admiral of the fleet in 1868. He died a year later, a eulogy praising him as "the Last of Nelson's Captains."[79]

Major Nicolls never got the promotion Cochrane promised. In 1817, after twenty-three years as an officer, having taken 107 wounds in nearly a hundred fights, he had nothing to show for it but a broken left leg, a wounded right leg that confined him to a bed for months, bullet holes in his right arm and body, a saber cut on his head, a bayonet scar on his chest, and a missing right eye.[80] He retired a lieutenant colonel and by 1854 held honorary rank as lieutenant general.[81] In 1815, Bathurst had observed that he was spirited and active "but a very wild fellow."[82]

Tylden was delighted to return to Havana and by early April he was on his way home, still reeling from the realization that they had been beaten by "a new-raised half-wild militia."[83] He survived the Louisiana campaign by more than half a century, dying in 1866. Artilleryman Dickson's career suffered little by the Louisiana defeat. He reached Waterloo in time to serve on the staff of the army's artillery commander and eventually rose to major general and fellow of the Royal Geographical Society. Lambert and his brigade, their losses in officers at New Orleans not yet replaced, joined Wellington's army by forced march just as the Battle of Waterloo opened.[84] Promoted lieutenant general in 1835 and full general six years later, he lived out his days until 1847 in a modest house on the village green at Thames Ditton, in Surrey, pursuing his lifelong passion for cricket. John Keane, who may have owed his life to his underwear, rose to lieutenant general, served as commander-in-chief in the West Indies and governor of St. Lucia and Jamaica, then in the 1830s commanded British forces in the Afghan War. In recognition, he was made Baron Keane of Ghuznee on December 23, 1839, the twenty-fifth anniversary of the night battle that kept him from marching into New Orleans.

There were no honors for Thomas Mullins. He dropped out of sight until July 11, when a court-martial charged him with disobedience, cowardice, and defeatism.[85] He conducted his own defense as befit his personality, defiantly and obtusely, trying to blame the defeat on others.[86] The court exonerated him of two charges but found him guilty of disobedience and cashiered him from the service.[87] Forgotten until his death on January 25, 1823, he was remembered only as the man who cost Pakenham victory.[88] One of Wellington's officers thought he should have hanged, "for shooting would have been far too honourable a death."[89]

Lieutenant Peddie got his promotion, little though he enjoyed it, dying three years after the battle.[90] Ensign Gerard won a lieutenancy and was soon on his way to a wound at Waterloo.[91] The unfortunate Ensign D'Arcy survived amputation by artillery to be awarded two pensions, one for each lost leg.[92] Ensign Benson Hill soon left the artillery to become an actor.[93] The American lieutenant Hamilton who refused to fight fellow Americans was allowed to resign his commission. Sergeant Reid of the 21st Royal Scots Fusiliers kept its colors wrapped around his body while a prisoner of war and turned them over to Captain Pringle when he rejoined the regiment.[94] One other flag went back to England, the colors of the 1st Louisiana militia, the only trophy of the expedition to be displayed at Whitehall. Despite the bravery of thousands of soldiers and sailors, only 227 men received something to pin to their chests. More than thirty years later, 227 survivors of the December 14, 1814, Battle of Lake Borgne received the Naval General Service medal with a clasp reading simply "December 14, 1814 Boat Service."[95]

Ensign Gleig soon returned home.[96] When his ship anchored off Spithead on May 9, 1815, he went ashore and kissed the ground.[97] Leaving the army, he completed studies for the ministry in 1820 but had already begun work on a memoir of his experiences in America. It appeared in 1821 to instant success, and after the passage of two centuries is still the most influential memoir by a British soldier of the War of 1812.[98] Six years later he published another memoir telling more of his somewhat fictionalized experiences, and although he did it anonymously, many suspected his authorship. It, too, became one of the essential memoirs of the war. While Gleig later spent thirty years as chaplain general of the British army, he never stopped writing, authoring almost fifty books of fiction, religion, history, and biography, to become one of Britain's most successful writers of the century.

Jasper Graham never got over being ignored by Cochrane. If only the admiral and Thornton had engaged him as guide and advisor, His Majesty's forces would be occupying New Orleans, he told the War Office that fall. For seven years he sought compensation that never came, so in 1822 he left Jamaica and moved to the country he had tried to betray, settling first in New York and later Rocky Hill, Connecticut, where locals honored him as Captain Graham until his death in 1841.[99]

Journalist William Cobbett declared, "This battle of New Orleans broke the heart of European despotism."[100] Certainly, everything Britain tried on the American coast had failed ultimately. They had done their worst against their infant enemy, and it had shown "a *giant's* power," wrote a London columnist. The rising greatness of this distant empire would make Europe relieved at its distance and astonish the nations.[101] Victory had given Americans a confidence in themselves that neither time nor changing circumstances were likely to diminish, and they were likely only to grow stronger.[102] New Orleans securely in hand, the United States was on the road to expanding farther across the continent and dominating New World trade, "and thus of laying the foundations of an immense empire."[103] Lurking in all that were hints of a fear that Britain herself might one day become subordinate to the irrepressible Yankees.

Inevitably, the same questions occupied men on both sides of the Atlantic then and afterward. What if the British had won the battle and taken New Orleans? Would they be bound by the treaty and hand it back, or keep the prize? While the negotiations were under way and success seemed certain, a Scottish editor asked if a treaty ought even to be concluded before the outcome in Louisiana was known. Surely the government would not make a hasty peace when taking New Orleans would empower Britain to dictate whatever it wanted.[104]

Many Britons expected more than temporary conquest and an opportunity to regain dominance over Gulf trade.[105] It still came down to a question of title. France never legitimately owned Louisiana, which invalidated the sale to Jefferson. The region still lawfully belonged to Spain, and if Mr. Madison could not substantiate his claim, then not an acre should be ceded back to him. Britain keeping New Orleans would teach the Yankees to extinguish their "arrogant pretensions" and discourage them from ever risking another war with John Bull.[106]

Officers on the spot were among the first to voice their views. Colonel Thornton and Captain Roberts told Consul Gray a month after the battle that Britain would ransom New Orleans back to Madison for millions of dollars or hold it indefinitely to discourage future adventuring in Canada.[107] Of course, their opinions did not signify, nor did Cochrane's or Pakenham's, for none had a voice in Whitehall councils. Wellington spoke with an authority backed by victories, however, and for all his skepticism about the expedition, he favored taking New Orleans to make it the object of a separate treaty.[108] It had value England could turn to mercantile and geopolitical advantage.[109] That largely echoed Lord Bathurst, the secretary of state for war, who had proposed back in September 1814 that Cochrane and the army "occupy some important and valuable possession, by the restoration of which we may improve the conditions of peace."[110] That hardly suggested an intent to hold such territory for a long period of time, but then he went on to add that holding such a place "may entitle us to exact its cession as the price of peace." Circumstances changed dramatically between September 1814 and February 1815, of course, but it is evident that Bathurst envisioned at least the possibility of keeping all or part of Louisiana indefinitely.

What the prime minister Lord Liverpool would have done is a mystery. The only hint is his expectation that Pakenham's army would be in the Chesapeake by early March to persuade Madison to ratify, or else approach the Hartford Convention about a separate peace. Both eventualities had the same goal, implementation of the Treaty of Ghent, including the *status quo ante bellum* provision. Furthermore, expecting Pakenham to be in the east after taking New Orleans implicitly argued against his leaving an occupying force to hold either the city or Louisiana.[111]

Since the treaty did not take effect until both sides ratified, the prince regent, anticipating early news of a victory at New Orleans, could have refused to ratify and then demanded a separate negotiation, as Wellington suggested. As of December 24, when Britain's commissioners signed the accord, the latest news from Cochrane dated from mid-November. If British envoys counted on victory in Louisiana, they could not expect it before mid-December at the earliest—as Keane's December 23 fight attests—nor could they hope to learn of it before the end of January. To take advantage of that, the prince regent would have to delay his signature fully a month, whereas in fact he signed on December 27, a dozen days before the main battle.

On the other hand, should his war leaders violate the treaty and try to keep a captured New Orleans, they risked undercutting the moral high ground they hoped to take in reshaping Europe, compromising the honor of the ministries and the prince regent and recasting Britain's war aims into a land grab not far removed from "beauty and booty."[112] Moreover, instructions to keep New Orleans could not reach Cochrane before late March, while news of Madison's ratification would arrive at least a week earlier from Havana, if not Jackson. In short, Britain likely would have yielded a captive New Orleans before any contrary order came.[113] Even if Jackson did not deny the city to them, early nineteenth-century communications would.

But was it that simple? Whitehall repeatedly emphasized that the United States had no lawful title to Louisiana. It explicitly told Cochrane and Pakenham they could encourage Louisianans to seek independence from the United States or a return to Spanish dominion so long as they did not promise British assistance or alliance. Pakenham was actually told that New Orleans would probably be handed over to Spain, and Spaniards shared that expectation.[114]

In fact, Britain's existing alliances with Spain and the Indian tribes complicated adherence to Ghent's territorial provisions. Spain wanted a friendly buffer state between an expansionist United States and its colonial possessions in Texas, Mexico, East Florida, and that part of West Florida east of the Pearl River. A British, French, or even independent Louisiana would provide that. Britain also wanted to contain the Americans and intended the treaty's demand for the return of Indian lands to accomplish that. Returning New Orleans or any part of Louisiana defeated both goals and left the Americans poised to spread west across the Mississippi, and east to Spanish East Florida's doorstep. That could only complicate British relations with its Spaniard allies. It came down to the value Whitehall put on those alliances.[115]

Moreover, the Americans were themselves already in violation of the treaty. When France ceded Louisiana to Spain in 1762, it made no claim on Florida, which the Spaniards had already settled. When Spain gave its territory east of the Mississippi to Britain in 1763, it included Florida, which the British divided into East and West at the Apalachicola. Another treaty in 1783 restored Louisiana and both Floridas to Spain as separate colonial entities, but when Napoleon took and sold it to Jefferson, the treaty language was deliberately vague. With no specific mention of the Floridas, it could be interpreted to include them. Jefferson and Madison certainly so read it, but they made no effort to occupy the Floridas, content to claim title while leaving Spain to govern them for the moment. When the 1810 West Florida rebels seized control of the western districts and claimed authority extending to the Apalachicola, they never managed to exercise it, and even after Madison asserted the American claim and soldiers occupied the West Florida Republic, he left all of the territory between the Pearl River and the

Atlantic under Spain's governance, including Mobile and Pensacola. On May 14, 1812, five weeks before declaring war on Britain, Congress annexed the "Mobile District," a strip of the Gulf Coast from the Pearl to the Perdido, yet how can a nation annex *territory it already owns*? Madison's act implicitly acknowledged that he had no surety that the district was really part of Jefferson's Purchase.

He then left Mobile in the Spaniards' hands, making annexation just a gesture until General Wilkinson seized the port in April 1813 to establish American control. But if the United States could not demonstrate that it had clear title to it, then the Ghent terms required Madison to return it to Spain. Of course he did not, a fair violation of the treaty and a pretext for Britain to keep New Orleans if taken and return it to Spain. The chains of title for both were murky, raising the question of what Cochrane would do had he taken New Orleans before learning of ratification. If the Americans did not return Mobile to Spain, would he give up any of Louisiana without receipt of instructions from Whitehall, which would take months to receive?

Even if his contemporaries misjudged Cochrane's appetite for prize money, New Orleans offered a fortune. Forced to abandon the city, Jackson likely would have destroyed its warehouses of cotton and sugar and taken off the slaves and other movable valuables, but that still left whatever personal valuables the citizenry could not evacuate, not to mention the yield from the rest of Louisiana. Would he forfeit all that without embracing a rationalization to hold the city even for a few months to realize some personal gain? In 1802 he had allegedly manufactured evidence to justify taking Spanish treasure ships, helping propel Spain to ally briefly with France against Britain. Two years later he conspired to discredit a fellow admiral standing in the way of his own ambitions. Given his circumstances and character, would Sir Alexander scruple at refusing to yield New Orleans even if it threatened renewed war, especially considering his frayed but lingering beliefs that New England was ready to revolt, legions of native warriors would rise against the Yankees, and thousands in Louisiana wanted freedom from the Americans?

Napoleon might preoccupy Whitehall until Waterloo in June, but the glacial speed of transatlantic communications could have delayed a diplomatic resolution of New Orleans into the fall, when Britain was free to focus on the Gulf again. With its treasury depleted by years of conflict, the ministries could retire millions of the war debt from Louisiana's riches. Granted, Britain was weary of war. So were the Yankees. With neither anxious for more conflict, negotiations might yield multiple shades of peace beyond absolute and perpetual sovereignty.

Those questions remain forever unanswerable. That they can be asked steals wind from the canvas of arguments then and later that, regardless of victor, the battle for New Orleans was unimportant so far as the war was concerned.[116] It had no influence on the outcome of a conflict already over, but had Britain won the day, there was enormous potential to complicate the ensuing peace. That depended not on a document signed in Belgium nor on ratifications in London or Washington. It rested in the motives, foibles, and ambitions of men on the scene whose actions could render impotent the most honorable intentions in faraway capitals.

"The affair at Orleans is a glorious one," wrote an Indian agent 250 miles northwest of the city, "but it is indebted to so many accidents for its glory, that it may almost be considered a miracle."[117] Indeed, chance authored much of the triumph's narrative, but it did not matter. The victory shot adrenaline into Americans' confidence in themselves, framing the foundation of a growing set of myths that undergirded these republicans' views of themselves and their world.[118] Major John Henry Eaton saw that early in 1817 when he completed Major Reid's hagiography of Jackson. "When we shall be told we have gained nothing by the war," he wrote, "we will point to our union, which it has more strongly and indissolubly cemented, as of greater importance than any thing that has happened, since the all-glorious hour our Independence was declared."[119]

Unity could be fragile, as the aftermath demonstrated, but for a few weeks Frenchmen, Spaniards, Portuguese, Germans, Italians, Anglos, Indians, and blacks, free and enslaved, overrode their social, ethnic, and political divisions to craft with outsiders from Tennessee, Kentucky, and Mississippi their infant nation's greatest victory. With it came the nascent sense that they were all Americans and had proven it on the plain at Chalmette.[120] Before the first guns ever fired, a new mythology already began to bind them simply because they were *there*.

If the Yankees' confidence in success fluttered, it never left them. In later years they adopted a myth of impossible victory against incredible odds, a narrative that became almost a religious precept, the cornerstone of their chosen view of themselves. It was only a short step from the Almighty and the Rifleman standing side by side at New Orleans to divine ordination that Americans push west to Pryor's Pacific Ocean to realize what a later writer called their "manifest destiny to overspread the continent allotted by Providence."[121]

New Orleans found its destiny in the aftermath of victory. The people of the West were destined to command the trade of the Mississippi.[122] Thanks to geography, Louisiana itself would be a vital link in a chain binding

Atlantic and Pacific.[123] By 1818, Orleanians boasted of being a new Gibraltar laughing defiance at the most powerful invaders. In future days the city would become to the United States what Paris was to France, "the emporium of its commerce, its wealth, its population and its political greatness."[124]

A market revolution was coming, much of it powered by command of the Mississippi cemented on January 8. In a few years cotton created fortunes, made cargoes to multiply 1815's steamboats by hundreds, and demanded labor that inflated the enslaved population of the Mississippi Valley sixfold by 1860. New Orleans alone did not build that stair, but every step rose on a conviction of American exceptionalism and destiny fathered by Jackson's victory.[125]

Driving it all was the attention focused on New Orleans by the press to satiate a hunger for news. It focused the nation's gaze on the Southwest. It was not the first time. Newspapers had fixed on Louisiana at the 1803 Purchase, during the Burr plot of 1806–1807, and in 1810 with West Florida's rebellion, but national attention from August 1814 to March 1815 eclipsed all else. Columns devoted to New Orleans trebled all that had appeared since the Purchase, and it attracted more than three times the press from August 1814 to March 1815 than it had since the outbreak of war.

The aftermath of the battle and its multiple intertwined myths gave a new face to a new breed of American. Shortly before the Revolution, the Frenchman Michel-Guillaume-Saint-Jean de Crèvecoeur asked in his *Letters from an American Farmer*, "What then is the American, this new man?" The man he discovered was "Yankee Doodle" and "Brother Jonathan," British nicknames for Americans, but by the War of 1812 those archetypes receded increasingly to New England. In their place came now another "new man," a man with no name, but everyone knew him: "Marksman," "Rifleman," "Hunter of Kentucky," the "Western" man. French observer Alexis de Tocqueville met him in 1831 on his visit to America. This man trusted his own ability to overcome any obstacle. He had ambition and he was in a hurry, for "before him lies a boundless continent, and he urges onward as if time pressed, and he was afraid of finding no room for his urges." Aware of the past, curious about the future, ever ready to argue over the present, he was "a highly civilized being, who consents, for a time, to inhabit the backwoods, and who penetrates into the wilds of the New World with the Bible, an axe, and a file of newspapers." He was a man who could do great things.[126]

He was Andrew Jackson. De Tocqueville thought Old Hickory "a man of a violent temper and mediocre talents," with nothing qualifying him to govern a free people. Yet twice the Americans made him their president, and the Frenchman believed they did it "solely by the recollection of a

victory which he gained twenty years ago under the walls of New Orleans."[127] The "new man" in Old Hickory's mold would be the preferred
American ideal for half a century until the Civil War. Elements of him,
good and bad, adhered tenaciously for the next 150 years. If not necessarily
what Americans were, he was what they wanted to be, and the rest of the
world gradually fell in love with the *idea* of him. Victory at New Orleans
showed that he would suffer no slights, that he demanded to be taken seriously, that his was a nation of common men who fought uncommonly well,
and that he would win his battles the American way.[128]

When first reports of the victory reached Baltimore, publisher Hezekiah
Niles rushed into print with the latest issue of his popular *Weekly Register*.
He could not restrain his joy as he announced the conclusion of the Ghent
treaty and the victory at New Orleans in the same issue. "Peace is signed in
the arms of victory!" he crowed.

"Who would not be an American?"[129]

ACKNOWLEDGMENTS

I am delighted to offer thanks to a number of friends and associates whose valuable advice or assistance has made writing this book both easier and more pleasant. Don Hickey, dean of War of 1812 scholars, gave valuable pointers at the outset. Curtis Manning at Nunez Community College in New Orleans repeatedly helped with references and providing material from the series of distinguished symposia he has organized in recent years. Gary Gallagher of the University of Virginia and Joseph Glatthaar at the University of North Carolina generously helped with obtaining copies of documents from their institutions' special collections. My dear friend Christina Vella of New Orleans, who left us far too soon, was always an enthusiastic supporter and critic.

Several able scholars have very generously taken the time to read and offer thoughts and corrections on the manuscript, including: Samantha Cavell of Southeastern Louisiana University at Hammond, herself a distinguished historian of the British Navy of the time; Pamela Keyes of Miami, Oklahoma, longtime student of the New Orleans operations and Baratarian smugglers; Dale Phillips, former superintendent of the Jean Lafitte National Historical Park and Preserve; Gene A. Smith of Texas Christian University in Fort Worth, distinguished historian of the Gulf region; and especially Jason Wiese, associate director of the Williams Research Center at the Historic New Orleans Collection.

As has ever been the case, archivists have been lifesavers, none more so than those at several of New Orleans's fine research institutions. Robert Ticknor, Heather Szafran, and Rebecca Smith, at the Historic New Orleans

Collection, were wonderfully patient during my two weeks of research there. Sean Benjamin and Lee Miller at the Jones Library at Tulane University in New Orleans were equally helpful, as was Erin Kinchen at the Louisiana History Center. Sally Reeves of the New Orleans Notarial Archives went out of her way as always. Old friend Leah Wood Jewett at Louisiana State University in Baton Rouge never failed to be of aid when called on. At Princeton University, Annalee Pauls was invaluable in helping me navigate the massive Livingston Papers. James Holmberg and Heather J. Potter at the Filson Historical Society in Louisville very kindly took time to open their collections to me, and Christine Schmid Engels at the Cincinnati Museum Center, and Anne B. Shepherd of the Cincinnati History Library and Archives located at the Center, graciously took time to provide access to manuscripts there despite the confusion of major renovation. Amy Herman was very helpful in securing the miniature of Andrew Jackson at Bard College's Montgomery Place Campus, Annandale on Hudson, New York. In the United Kingdom, Kevin W. Chambers and John McCavitt, both working on their own study of the campaign, were very helpful with queries.

A number of friends and freelance researchers helped in obtaining copies of documents from faraway archives. Cheryl Owen and Paul Hedges of Edinburgh, spent several days at the National Library of Scotland running down the George Gleig Papers. Tony Hall of Esher in Surrey, England, did the same for some materials at the National Archives in Kew. In the United States, Rachel Donovan was equally helpful in copying materials at the University of Texas in Austin, while Vonnie Zullo did the same in Washington, Avi Mowshewitz visited New York City archives, Brian Neumann located items for me at the University of Virginia, and Fernando Rodriguez made follow-up visits to places in Louisiana that I could not revisit. Kathleen McDermott gave a gracious favor at Harvard, and Bailey Filkoski of Blacksburg, Virginia, and Lane Bogar of Austin, Texas, provided invaluable assistance with translations of some of the documents in French. A special debt of gratitude is due to Max Miller of the National Park Service's Denver Service Center for his kindness in locating and making available modern scans of the wonderful maps produced in 1985 for Jerome Greene's *Jean Lafitte National Historical Park and Preserve: Chalmette Unit Historic Resource Study.*

Hardly least, I owe great gratitude to my agent, Jim Donovan, for sticking with a book that was too long and too tardy, and my editor, Brent Howard of Penguin Random House, for his wonderful patience with a book that ran months past deadline.

And no one has more practice at being patient with me than Sandra Davis.

Primary Sources

MANUSCRIPTS
Chicago History Museum
Charles Gunther Collection
Jackson, Andrew. Papers

Cincinnati History Library and Archives
Berns, James. Letter
Follett, Oran. Papers
Particulars in Relation to Battle of New Orleans furnished me by a French gentleman in
    1828—Summer
"Veritas," The Battle of New Orleans, January 8, 1855
Wallace, D. C. Letters

Connecticut State Library, Hartford
Connecticut Church Records, State Library Index, Killingworth First Congregational
    Church, 1735–1893

Duke University, Durham, NC
Campbell Family Papers

Filson Historical Society, Louisville, KY
Adair-Hemphill Family Papers
"Hunters of Kentucky. Or Half Horse and Half Alligator," broadsides ca. 1819
Joyes Family Papers
Weller Family Papers

Harvard University, Houghton Library, Cambridge, MA
Palfrey Family Papers

Historic New Orleans Collection (HNOC), New Orleans, LA
Aitchison, Robert. Memoir, ca. 1857
Carroll, William. Letters
Cobb, Robert L. Letters Concerning the Battle of New Orleans
Coffee, Eliza Croom. Sketch of the Life of Gen. John Coffee, 1897
Cook, William C. War of 1812 in the South Collection
Darby, William. Letter
Depositions concerning slaves liberated by British forces after the Battle of New Orleans
Early Louisiana Documents: Major Jean-Baptiste Plauché Report, December 26, 1814
Florian, Laura Eugenie. Letter
Hicks, Captain C. R. Letter, December 30, 1814
Hynes, Andrew. Papers
Jackson, Andrew. Collection
Latour, Arsène Lacarrière. Archive
Michell, Maj. John, Royal Artillery. Letter
Monroe, James. Letter to unknown, April 11, 1827
Morgan, David B. Report from Camp Morgan, February 14, 1815
Note Announcing Peace Treaty in Ghent
Ross, George and James M. Letters
Shaumburg, Bartholomew. Letter, January 25, 1815
Stirling, James. Memorandum, 1813
Tousard, Louis de. Letter
United States Army Morning Reports
Villeré, Jacques Philippe. Papers

Historical Society of Pennsylvania, Philadelphia
Parker, Daniel. Papers
Shaler Family Papers
Smith, Uselma Clarke. Collection
    Jones, William. Papers
Society Collection
    Lieutenant Carter, "Relative to the Vulnerable Points, and Means of Defense at
        Orleans," January 26, 1813
    Plan of Attack on New Orleans circa 1770

Library of Congress (LC), Washington, DC
Jackson, Andrew. Papers
Miscellaneous Manuscripts Collection
    [Story, Benjamin] Battle of New Orleans descriptive account, 1814–1815
    Volontaires d'Orléans muster roll, 1814–1815. Louisiana. Militia. Uniformed
        Battalion of Orleans Volunteers.
Monroe, James. Papers

Morgan, David Bannister. Papers
Naval Historical Foundation Papers
Patterson, Daniel Todd. Papers
Scacki, Francisco. "A Correct View of the Battle Near the City of New Orleans," print
Shaw, John. Papers

Lilly Library, Indiana University, Bloomington
War of 1812 Mss.

Louisiana Historical Center, New Orleans
Chotard, Henry. Collection
Cusachs, Gaspar. Estate Gift Collection
Johnson, W. Letter, December 31, 1814
List of Subscribers Who Gave Money or Hulled Rice to Purchase Garments for those
     Serving Under Andrew Jackson, December 29, 1814
Miscellaneous Collection
Morgan, David Bannister. Commission, September 10, 1812
Morgan, David Bannister. Papers
Nixon, John. "An Account of the Battle of New Orleans by John Nixon, Adjutant of the
     First Regiment of La. Militia"
Order Book, Louisiana Militia
Raynaud, L. M. [adjutant of the battalion of volunteers]. "Part Taken by the Battalion of
     Volunteers of Orleans, During the Invasion of Louisiana by the British Army"

**Louisiana State University (LSU), Louisiana and Lower Mississippi Valley
Collection, Baton Rouge**
Avery, Dudley. Letters, 1815
Claiborne, William C. C. Letters, February 18, 1814, October 30, 1815
Cutts, Richard. Letters
Hardin, J. Fair. Collection, 1718–1939
Hicky, Philip, and Family. Papers, 1778–1859
Johnson, Rachel. Letter, January 6–19, 1815
Kenner, William. Papers, 1774–1824
Lopez, Manuel. Papers
Miscellaneous Collection
Morgan, David Bannister. Papers
New Orleans Municipal Records, Series II Legal Papers, 1767–1898, Subseries 1
     Resolutions and Ordinances, 1767–1846.
Peire, Henry D. Report, February 17, 1815
Stirling, Lewis, and Family. Papers
Wagner, Peter K. Letter, 1815
Willis, William, and John B. Willis. Family Papers

Middle Tennessee State University, Gore Research Center, Murfreesboro
King, James Moore. Collection

Mississippi Department of Archives and History, Jackson
Trimble, Michael W. "Trimble's Account of the Battle of New Orleans"

Missouri Historical Society, St. Louis
Jefferson, Thomas. Papers

James Monroe Museum and Memorial Library, Fredericksburg, VA
Monroe, James. Collection

National Archives (Kew), Kew, UK
Admiralty Office Records
    ADM 50/122: Alexander F. I. Cochrane Journal
    ADM 1/505: Letters from Commanders-in-Chief, North America: 1814, nos. 1–140
    ADM 1/506: Letters from Commanders-in-Chief, North America: 1814, nos. 141–268
    ADM 1/508: Letters from Commanders-in-Chief, North America: 1815, nos. 1–126
    ADM 1/4360: Secret Letters
Colonial Office Records
    Office of Registry of Colonial Slaves and Slave Compensation Commission
    Return of Slaves in the Parish of Trelawney in the possession of Mark Trumbull as
        Attorney to Jasper McCalden Graham, 1817
Foreign Office Records
    General Correspondence, 1814–1815
    FO 5/105: Anthony St. John Baker, December 1814–November 1815
    FO 5/106: Anthony St. John Baker, February 1815–June 1815
War Office Records
    WO 1/141: Expedition to the Southern Coasts of the United States. Dispatches, July
        1814–March 1815
    WO 1/142: Expedition to the Southern Coasts of the United States. Papers, 1814
    WO 1/143: Expedition to the Southern Coasts of the United States. Papers, 1815
    WO 1/144: Expedition to the Southern Coasts of the United States. Papers, 1815–1817
    WO 6/2: Out-letters of the War Office, America (North) 1814
    WO 12/11538: Infantry Abroad Quarterly Pay Lists for the 5th West India Regiment
        of Foot
    WO 17/1218: Returns of Regiments Serving in the Chesapeake and New Orleans,
        1814–1815
    WO 92: Judge Advocate General's Office, General Courts Martial Register 1
    WO 92/1: General Courts Martial: Register 1806–1838, Piece 001
    War Department In-Letters and Papers, 1814–1815
    War Department In-Letters and Papers, 1815–1817

National Archives (NA), Washington, DC
Record Group 15
    War of 1812 Pension and Bounty Land Warrant Application Files
        de Marans, Louis Francis
        Desforges, Louis

Joly, Victor

Jones, Thomas ap Catesby

Maire, Lorenzo/Laurent

Record Group 24 Compiled Service Records

Record Group 59

Dispatches from the U.S. Consul in Havana, Cuba, 1783–1906. M899

Record Group 80

Navy Casualty Reports, 1776–1941, Men Who Died on Station 1812–1815

Naval Station New Orleans

Record Group 94

Index to Compiled Service Records of Volunteer Soldiers Who Served During the
War of 1812

Bouyee [Bowie], James

Letters Received by the Office of the Adjutant General, 1805–1821. M566

Monier/Monnier, Peter/Pierre

Records of Men Enlisted in the U.S. Army Prior to the Peace Establishment, May 17,
1815, No. 697

Registers of Enlistments in the United States Army, 1798–1914

Record Group 260

Letters Received by the Secretary of the Navy from Captains ("Captains' Letters")
1805–1861

National Archives, Southwest Region, Fort Worth, TX

Record Group 21, Records of District Courts of the United States, 1685–1993

Entry 21, United States District Court for the Eastern Region of Louisiana, New
Orleans, General Case Files, 1806–1932, Case #0734, Entry 21: Patterson and
Ross vs. Certain Goods Seized at Barataria

National Library of Scotland, Edinburgh

Blackwood Papers

Cochrane, Alexander F. I. Papers and Correspondence

Gleig, George R. Papers

National Maritime Museum, Caird Library, Greenwich, London, UK

Codrington, Edward. Papers, COD/6/1, 2, 4, COD 7/1–5

Malcolm, Charles. Papers, MAL/2

Malcolm, Pultney. Papers, MAL/104

Warren, Sir John Borlase. Papers, WAR/53

New Jersey Historical Society, Newark

Chew Family Papers

New Orleans Notarial Archives, New Orleans, LA

Broutin, Narcisse. Volumes 31, 32

De Armas, Michele. Volumes 8, 9

Dejean, Claude. Volume 1
Lafitte, Marc. Volumes 4, 5, 7
Lynd, John. Volumes 11, 12
Pedesclaux, Pierre. Volume 69

New Orleans Public Library (NOPL), New Orleans, LA
New Orleans City Archives: Orleans Parish
    Index to Slave Emancipation Petitions, 1814–1843
    Succession and Probate Records, Orleans Parish
        Beale, Thomas, Sr.
        Commyns, George
        Lawson, Columbus
        Parmlee, Oliver
    Wills and Probate Records, Jefferson Parish, 1756–1984
        George Commyns

New-York Historical Society (NYHS), New York, NY
Brooke, Peter. Journals, 1804–1832
Cochrane, Alexander F. I. Collection, 1807–1815

New York Public Library (NYPL), New York, NY
Ellery, Abraham Redwood. Account of the Battle of New Orleans
Macdonald, Gordon Gallie. Memoir, 1831
Tylden, John Maxwell. Journal, 1814–1815

New York University, Fales Library and Special Collections, Elmer Holmes Bobst Library, New York, NY
Manor, Sylvester. Archive

Princeton University Library, Princeton, NJ
de Coppet, André. Collection
Livingston, Edward. Papers
Simpson, Stephen. Letters

Tennessee Historical Society, Nashville
Dyas, Robert. Collection of John Coffee Papers
Winchester, James. Papers

Tennessee State Library and Archives, Nashville
Jackson, Andrew. Materials, Additions
RG 60 Legislative Records
    "British plan of carrying the American breastwork near New Orleans, Jan 8th, 1815"

Tulane University, Louisiana Research Collection, New Orleans, LA
Bowman Family Papers

De La Vergne Family Papers
Favrot, Pierre-Joseph. Letters
Favrot, Pierre-Joseph. Memorandum Concerning Louisiana Defenses,
    November 19, 1814
Hynes, Andrew. Papers
Kuntz, Rosamonde E. and Emile. Collection
Morgan, David Bannister. Papers
Rees, David. Papers
War of 1812 Collection, 1813–1965

United States Naval Academy (USNA), Nimitz Library, Annapolis, MD
Gerard, Arthur. "Campaigns of A British Officer in Europe & America Giving a
    particular account of the British Operations in the United States In
    1814 & 1815"

University of Michigan, William L. Clements Library, Ann Arbor
Malcolm, Pultney. Papers
Peddie, John. Letter and Enclosures
War of 1812 Collection

University of New Orleans, New Orleans, LA
Jean Lafitte National Historical Park Collection (JELAC), 1774–1982

**University of North Carolina, Southern Historical Collection (SHC, UNC),
Chapel Hill**
Coffee, John. Papers
Foscue Family Papers
Kempe, James. Letter, 1815
Mordecai, Samuel. Family Papers and Diary

University of Tennessee, Special Collections, Knoxville
Burford, David. Papers
Tennessee Historical Society Miscellaneous Files

University of Texas Library (UT), Briscoe Collection, Austin
Parsons, Edward A. Collection

University of Virginia (UVA), Charlottesville
Cutts, Richard. Papers
Jefferson Papers
Jefferson, Thomas. Letter to Henry Dearborn, February 1815

Virginia Museum of History and Culture (VHS), Richmond
Booker, John. Letter, February 26, 1815
Gould, Eliza Williams Chotard. Memoir, 1798–1825

Graham Family Papers
Hungerford, John R. Letter, January 15, 1815

COURT CASES
United States District Court, Eastern District of Louisiana,
United States v. Workman, 28 F. Cas. 771 (D. Orleans Terr. 1807)

UNITED STATES CENSUS
Hancock County, MS, 1820
Orleans Parish, LA, 1810

BOOKS
*A Compendious Account of the Most Important Battles of the Late War, to Which Is
    Added, the Curious Adventures of Corporal Samuel Stubbs (A Kentuckian of 65 Years
    of Age).* Boston: William Walter, 1817.
Appeal of L. Louaillier, Sen. Against the Charge of High Treason. N.p., 1827.
"Aristides" (William Peter Van Ness). *A Concise Narrative of Gen. Jackson's First
    Invasion of Florida, and of His Immortal Defence of New-Orleans: With Remarks.*
    Albany, NY: Albany *Argus*, 1828.
Arrest and Trial of E. Louis Louaillier. House of Representatives Document 69,
    37th Congress, 3d Session. Washington, DC: Government Printing Office,
    1843.
Barker, Eugene C., ed. *The Austin Papers. Annual Report of the American Historical
    Association for the Year 1919, Part 1.* 2 vols. Washington, DC: Government Printing
    Office, 1924.
Barrett, C. R. B., ed. *The 85th King's Light Infantry (Now 2nd Battalion, the King's
    Shropshire Light Infantry) by "One of Them."* London: Spottiswoode, 1913.
Bassett, John Spencer, ed. *The Correspondence of Andrew Jackson.* 7 vols. Washington,
    DC: Carnegie Institution, 1926–1935.
———, ed. *Major Howell Tatum's Journal.* Northampton, MA: Department of History
    of Smith College, 1922.
Binns, John. *Recollections of the Life of John Binns: Twenty-Nine Years in Europe and
    Fifty-Three in the United States.* Philadelphia: Parry and MacMillan, 1854.
Blair, William. *Sketch of the Life and Military Services of General John Adair, Written
    Principally in 1820 by Judge William Blair, and Continued to the Present Time by A
    Friend.* Harrodsburg, KY: *Harrodsburg American*, 1831.
Bourchier, Jane, ed. *Memoir of the Life of Admiral Sir Edward Codrington. With
    Selections from His Public and Private Correspondence.* 2 vols. London: Longmans,
    Green, and Co., 1873.
Bowden, Mary Weatherspoon, comp. *Private Letters from Before, During and After the
    Battle of New Orleans as Printed in the Newspapers of the Time.* N.p.: privately
    published, 2014.
Bowlby, Peter. *Walcheren, Spain, America and Waterloo: The Memoir of Captain Peter
    Bowlby 4th Foot (1791–1877),* ed. Gareth Glover. Godmanchester, UK: Ken Trotman,
    2016.

Brackenridge, H. M. *History of the Late War Between the United States and Great Britain: Comprising a Minute Account of the Various Military and Naval Operations.* Philadelphia: Hayes & Zell, 1854. Originally published 1839.

Bradley, Jared William. *Interim Appointment: W. C. C. Claiborne Letter Book, 1804–1805.* Baton Rouge: Louisiana State University Press, 2002.

Brannan, John, comp. *Official Letters of the Military and Naval Officers of the United States, During the War with Great Britain in the Years 1812, 13, 14, & 15.* Washington: Way and Gideon, 1823.

Brenton, Edward Pelham. *The Naval History of Great Britain, from the Year MDCCLXXXIII to MDCCCXXII.* 5 vols. London: C. Rice, 1825.

British and Foreign State Papers 1818–1819. 6 vols. London: James Ridgway, 1835.

Brown, David. *Diary of a Soldier, 1805–1827.* Ardrossan, Scotland: Arthur Guthrie, 1934.

Brown, Samuel. *To the Public.* Natchez, MS: Natchez *Ariel*, 1816–1817.

Burgoyne, Roderick Hamilton. *Historical Records of the 93rd Sutherland Highlanders.* London: Richard Bentley and Son, 1883.

Cannon, Richard, comp. *Historical Record of the Fourteenth, or the King's Regiment of Light Dragoons.* London: Parker, Furnivall, & Parker, 1847.

———, comp. *Historical Record of The Fourth, or The King's Own Regiment of Foot.* London: William Clowes & Sons, 1839.

———, comp. *Historical Record of the Seventh Regiment, or The Royal Fusiliers: Containing an Account of the Formation of the Regiment in 1685, and of Its Subsequent Services to 1846.* London: Parker, Furnivall, & Parker, 1847.

Carter, Clarence Edwin, ed. *The Territorial Papers of the United States.* Vol. 9, *The Territory of Orleans 1803–1812.* Washington, DC: Government Printing Office, 1940.

Chesterton, George Laval. *Peace, War, and Adventure: An Autobiographical Memoir of George Laval Chesterton.* 2 vols. London: Longman, Brown, Green, and Longmans, 1853.

Claiborne, J. F. H. *Life and Times of Gen. Sam. Dale, the Mississippi Partisan.* New York: Harper and Brothers, 1860.

———. *Mississippi, as a Province, Territory, and State, with Biographical Notices of Eminent Citizens.* Jackson, MS: Power and Barksdale, 1880.

Claiborne, Nathaniel Herbert. *Notes on the War in the South; with Biographical Sketches of the Lives of Montgomery, Jackson, Sevier, the Late Gov. Claiborne, and Others.* Richmond, VA: William Ramsay, 1819.

Clement, Samuel. *Truth Is No Slander: Therefore Read, Enquire, Reflect.* Natchez, MS: Natchez *Ariel*, 1824.

Cobbett, William. *Letters on the Late War Between the United States and Great Britain: Together with Other Miscellaneous Writings, on the Same Subject.* New York: J. Belden, 1815.

Cooke, John Henry. *A Narrative of Events in the South of France, and of the Attack on New Orleans, in 1814 and 1815.* London: T. & W. Boone, 1835.

Cooper, John Spencer. *Rough Notes of Seven Campaigns in Portugal, Spain, France and America During the Years 1809–1815.* Staplehurst, UK: Spellmount, 1996.

Coxe, Daniel. *A Description of the English Province of Carolana. By the Spaniards Call'd Florida, and by the French, La Louisiane.* London: Olive Payne, 1741.

Davison, Gideon M. *Sketches of the War, Between the United States and the British Isles: Intended as a Faithful History of All the Material Events from the Time of the Declaration in 1812, to and including the Treaty of Peace in 1815.* 2 vols. Rutland, VT: Fay and Davison, 1815.

Denson, Joseph Dorris, and Jesse Denson. *The Chronicles of Andrew; Containing an Accurate and Brief Account of General Jackson's Victories in the South, over the Creeks, Also His Victories over the British at Orleans, with A Biographical Sketch of His Life.* Lexington, KY: published by authors, 1815.

Eaton, John Henry, and Jerome Van Crowninshield. *The Complete Memoirs of Andrew Jackson, Seventh President of the United States.* New York: Hurst, 1885.

Eisenach, Bernhard, Duke of Saxe-Weimar. *Travels Through North America, During the Years 1825 and 1826.* 2 vols. Philadelphia: Carey, Lea & Carey, 1828.

Emerson, Edward Waldo, and Waldo Emerson Forbes, eds. *The Journals of Ralph Waldo Emerson.* 10 vols. Boston: Houghton Mifflin, 1909–1914.

Faithful Picture of the Political Situation of New Orleans, at the Close of the Last and the Beginning of the Present Year, 1807. Boston: privately published, 1808.

Forrest, Charles Ramus. *The Battle of New Orleans: A British View; The Journal of Major C. R. Forrest, Asst. QM General, 34th Regiment of Foot.* New Orleans: Hauser Press, 1961.

Francis Larche. House of Representatives Report 170. Washington, DC: 19th Congress, 1st Session, April 20, 1826.

Gayarré, Charles. *History of Louisiana: The American Domination.* 4 vols. New York: Redfield, 1854.

General and Biographical History of the British Royal Navy. Vol. 32. London: J. Gold, 1814.

General Court Martial, Held at the Royal Barracks, Dublin, for the Trial of Brevet Lieutenant-Colonel Hon. Thomas Mullins. Dublin, IR: William Espy, 1815.

Gleig, George Robert. *A Narrative of the Campaigns of the British Army at Washington and New Orleans, Under Generals Ross, Pakenham, and Lambert, in the Years 1814 and 1815.* London: John Murray, 1821.

———. *A Subaltern in America; Comprising His Narrative of the Campaigns of the British Army, at Baltimore, Washington, &c. &c. During the Late War.* Philadelphia: Carey and Hart, 1833.

Gordon, Elizabeth, Adelaide, and Sophia, comps. *Letters and Records of Admiral Sir J. A. Gordon G.C.B., 1782–1869.* London: privately printed, 1890.

Gurwood, John, ed. *The Dispatches of Field Marshal the Duke of Wellington.* 12 vols. London: John Murray, 1837–1838.

Hamilton, James A. *Reminiscences of James A. Hamilton; or, Men and Events, at Home and Abroad, During Three Quarters of a Century.* New York: Charles Scribner, 1869.

Hill, Benson Earle. *Recollections of an Artillery Officer: Including Scenes and Adventures in Ireland, America, Flanders and France.* 2 vols. London: Richard Bentley, 1836.

Hudry, John. *Petition of John Hudry, of Louisiana, Praying Remuneration for Services and Advances Made for the Defence of New Orleans in 1814, '15.* Washington, DC: John Hudry, 1834.

Hunt, Charles Havens. *Life of Edward Livingston*. New York: D. Appleton, 1864.

Hunt, Gilbert J. *The Late War, Between the United States and Great Britain, from June 1812, to February 1815. Written in the Ancient Historical Style*. New York: David Longworth, 1816.

Hunt, Louise Livingston. *Memoir of Mrs. Edward Livingston with Letters Hitherto Unpublished*. New York: Harper and Brothers, 1886.

Ingraham, Joseph Holt. *The South-West. By a Yankee*. 2 vols. New York: Harper & Brothers, 1835.

James, William. *A Full and Correct Account of the Military Occurrences of the Late War Between Great Britain and the United States of America*. 2 vols. London: published by author, 1818.

———. *A Full and Correct Account of the Chief Naval Occurrences of the Late War Between Great Britain and the United States of America*. London: T. Egerton, 1817.

Jones, Thomas ap Catesby. *Memorial . . . asking relief from the injustice visited on him by a certain board of navy officers, in which is embodied a letter from the memorialist to the Secretary of the Navy, giving a brief sketch of his long and varied services in the Navy of the United States*. Washington, DC: Gideon, [1856].

———. *Memorial of Thomas ap Catesby Jones to Samuel L. Southard, Richard Rush, and James Barbour, February 14, 1828*. Washington, DC: printed letter, no publisher, 1828.

Kreider, Angela, J. C. A. Stagg, Jeanne Kerr Cross, Anne Mandeville Colony, Mary Parke Johnson, and Wendy Ellen Perry, eds. *The Papers of James Madison, Presidential Series*, vol. 6, *8 February–24 October 1813*. Charlottesville: University of Virginia Press, 2008.

———, eds. *The Papers of James Madison. Presidential Series*, vol. 8, *July 1814–February 1815*. Charlottesville: University of Virginia Press, 2015.

Latour, Arsène Lacarrière. *Historical Memoir of the War in West Florida and Louisiana in 1814–15*. Philadelphia: John Conrad and Co., 1816. New edition edited by Gene A. Smith. New Orleans: Historic New Orleans Collection, 1999.

Latrobe, Benjamin Henry Boneval. *Impressions Respecting New Orleans: Diary and Sketches, 1818–1820*. New York: Columbia University Press, 1951.

Letters of Gen. Adair and Gen. Jackson Relative to the Charge of Cowardice Made by the Latter Against the Kentucky Troops at New Orleans. Lexington, KY: Thomas Smith, 1824.

Livingston, Edward. *An Answer to Mr. Jefferson's Justification of His Conduct in the Case of the New Orleans Batture*. Philadelphia: William Fry, 1813.

Looney, J. Jefferson, ed. *The Papers of Thomas Jefferson, Retirement Series*. Vol. 1, *4 March 1809 to 15 November 1809*. Princeton, NJ: Princeton University Press, 2004.

———, ed. *The Papers of Thomas Jefferson: Retirement Series*. Vol. 8, *1 October 1814 to 31 August 1815*. Princeton, NJ: Princeton University Press, 2011.

Lowrie, Walter, and Walter S. Franklin, eds. *American State Papers. Documents, Legislative and Executive, of the Congress of the United States, from the First Session of the First to the Second Session of the Seventeenth, Inclusive: Commencing March 4, 1789, and Ending March 3, 1823. Class IX: Claims*. Washington, DC: Gales and Seaton, 1834.

Marigny, Bernard de. *Reflections on General Andrew Jackson's Campaign in Louisiana in 1814 and 1815*. New Orleans: J. L. Sollée, 1848.

Martin, Francis Xavier. *The History of Louisiana, from the Earliest Period*. 2 vols. New Orleans: Lyman & Beardslee, 1827–1829.

McAfee, Robert Breckinridge. *History of the Late War in the Western Country*. Lexington, KY: Worsley & Smith, 1816.

McCarty, William. *History of the American War of 1812, from the Commencement, Until the Final Termination Thereof, on the Memorable Eighth of January, 1815, at New Orleans*. Philadelphia: McCarty & Davis, 1817.

Memorial of Beverly Chew and Others, Survivors of Beale's Rifle Company. Washington, DC: Gales and Seaton, 1835.

Memorial of Calvin J. Keith, February 5, 1846, Senate Document 116. Public Documents Printed by Order of the Senate of the United States. Vol. 4, 29th Congress, 1st Session. Washington, DC: Ritchie and Heiss, 1846.

Moser, Harold D., David R. Hoth, Sharon Macpherson, and John H. Reinbold, eds. *The Papers of Andrew Jackson*. Vol. 3, *1814–1815*. Knoxville: University of Tennessee Press, 1991.

Napier, W. C. E., ed. *Passages in the Early Military Life of General Sir George T. Napier, K.C.B. Written by Himself*. London: John Murray, 1884.

Nolte, Vincent. *The Memoirs of Vincent Nolte: Fifty Years in Both Hemispheres or, Reminiscences of the Life of a Former Merchant*. New York: G. Howard Watt, 1934.

O'Byrne, William Richard. *A Naval Biographical Dictionary: Comprising the Life and Services of Every Living Officer in Her Majesty's Navy*. London: John Murray, 1849.

O'Connor, Thomas. *An Impartial and Correct History of the War Between the United States of America and Great Britain*. New York: John Low, 1815.

Pakenham, Thomas, ed. *The Pakenham Letters 1800–1815*. London: John and Edward Bumpus, 1914.

Petition of John Hudry, of Louisiana, Praying Remuneration for Services and Advances Made for the Defence of New Orleans in 1814, '15. Washington, DC: 23d Congress, 1st Session, 1834.

Pringle, Norman. *Letters of Major Norman Pringle, Late of the 21st Royal Scots Fusiliers, Vindicating the Character of the British Army, Employed in North America in the Years 1814–15, from Aspersions Cast Upon It in Stuart's "Three Years in North America."* Edinburgh, UK: Evening Courant, 1834.

Reid, John, and John Henry Eaton. *The Life of Andrew Jackson*. Philadelphia: M. Carey and Son, 1817.

Report of the Committee of Claims on the Petition of Jacob Purkill: House of Representatives Report 32. Washington, DC: House of Representatives, January 6, 1820.

Roberts, James. *The Narrative of James Roberts, a Soldier Under Gen. Washington in the Revolutionary War, and Under Gen. Jackson at the Battle of New Orleans, in the War of 1812: "A Battle Which Cost Me a Limb, Some Blood and Almost My Life."* Chicago: printed for author, 1858.

Rowland, Dunbar, ed. *Official Letter Books of W. C. C. Claiborne 1801–1816*. 6 vols. Jackson, MS: Department of Archives and History, 1917.

Smith, G. C. Moore, ed. *The Autobiography of Lieutenant-General Sir Harry Smith, Baronet of Aliwal on the Sutlej G.C.B.* 2 vols. London: John Murray, 1901.

Smith, Gene A., ed. *A British Eyewitness at the Battle of New Orleans: The Memoir of Royal Navy Admiral Robert Aitchison, 1808–1827.* New Orleans: Historic New Orleans Collection, 2004.

Smith, Zachary F. *The Battle of New Orleans Including the Previous Engagements Between the Americans and the British, the Indians, and the Spanish which Led to the Final Conflict of the 8th of January, 1815.* Louisville, KY: John P. Morton, 1904.

Sparks, William Henry. *The Memories of Fifty Years.* Philadelphia: Claxon, Remsen and Haffelfinger, 1870.

State Papers and Correspondence Bearing Upon the Purchase of the Territory of Louisiana. Washington, DC: Government Printing Office, 1903.

Summary Statement of Facts, &c, by Thomas Ap C. Jones. Washington, DC: no publisher, November 2, 1832.

Surtees, William. *Twenty-Five Years in the Rifle Brigade.* London: Greenhill, 1996.

Tocqueville, Alexis de. *Democracy in America.* 2 vols. New York: D. Appleton, 1899.

The Trials of the Honb. James Workman, and Col. Lewis Kerr, Before the United States Court, for the Orleans District, on a Charge of High Misdemeanor. New Orleans: Bradford & Anderson, 1807.

Waldo, S. Putnam, and Andrew Jackson. *Memoirs of Andrew Jackson, Major-General in the Army of the United States, and Commander in Chief of the Division of the South.* Hartford, CT: Andrus, 1818.

Walker, Alexander. *Jackson and New Orleans: An Authentic Narrative of the Memorable Achievements of the American Army, Under Andrew Jackson, Before New Orleans, in the Winter of 1814, '15.* New York: J. C. Derby, 1856.

Wellington, Arthur Richard Wellesley, 2nd Duke of, ed. *Supplementary Despatches, Correspondence, and Memoranda of Field Marshal Arthur Duke of Wellington, K.G.* 15 vols. London: John Murray, 1858–1872.

Whitney, Thomas H. *Whitney's New-Orleans Directory, and Louisiana & Mississippi Almanac for the Year 1811.* New Orleans: printed by author, 1810.

Wilkinson, James. *Memoirs of My Own Times.* 3 vols. Philadelphia: Abraham Small, 1816.

Wrottesley, George. *Life and Correspondence of Field Marshal Sir John Burgoyne, Bart.* 2 vols. London: Richard Bentley and Son, 1873.

ARTICLES

"Annexation." *United States Magazine and Democratic Review* 17, no. 85 (July–August, 1845): 5–10.

"Battle of New Orleans Number." *Louisiana Historical Quarterly* 9, no. 1 (January 1926): 5–110.

"The Battle-Grounds of America. No. V.—New Orleans. From the MS of an Eye-Witness." *Graham's American Monthly Magazine of Literature and Art* 27, no. 1 (July 1845): 39–42.

Boyd, Mark F. "Events at Prospect Bluff on the Apalachicola River, 1808–1818: An Introduction to Twelve Letters of Edmund Doyle, Trader." *Florida Historical Quarterly* 14, no. 2 (October 1937): 55–96.

Brown, Everett S., ed. "Letters from Louisiana, 1813–1814." *Mississippi Valley Historical Review* 11, no. 4 (March 1925): 570–79.

"Correspondence." *The Naval Chronicle, for 1815: Containing a General and Biographical History of the Royal Navy of the United Kingdom.* Vol. 33 (January–June). London: Joyce Gold, 1815.

"Correspondence." *The Naval Chronicle, for 1815: Containing a General and Biographical History of the Royal Navy of the United Kingdom.* Vol. 34 (July–December). London: Joyce Gold, 1815.

"Deaths." *Gentleman's Magazine* 85 (March 1815): 278.

"Deaths." *Gentleman's Magazine* 85 (April 1815): 372.

DeWitt, John H., ed. "Letters of General John Coffee to His Wife, 1813–1815." *Tennessee Historical Magazine* 2, no. 4 (December 1916): 264–95.

Dickson, Alexander. "Journal of Operations in Louisiana, 1814 and 1815." *Louisiana Historical Quarterly* 44, no. 3–4 (July–October 1961): 1–110.

Forrest, Charles R. "Journal of the Operations Against New Orleans in 1814 and 1815." *Louisiana Historical Quarterly* 44, no. 3–4 (January–April 1961): 111–26.

Gatell, Frank Otto, ed. "Boston Boy in 'Mr. Madison's War.'" *Louisiana Historical Quarterly* 44, no. 3–4 (July–October 1961): 148–59.

Gayarré, Charles. "A Louisiana Sugar Plantation of the Old Régime." *Harper's New Monthly Magazine* 74, no. 442 (March 1887): 606–21.

"General David B. Morgan's Defense of the Conduct of the Louisiana Militia in the Battle on the Left Side of the River." *Louisiana Historical Quarterly* 9, no. 1 (January 1926): 16–29.

[Gleig, George Robert]. "A Subaltern in America." *Blackwood's Edinburgh Magazine* 21, no. 122 (March 1827): 243–59; no. 124 (April 1827): 417–33; no. 125 (May 1827): 531–49; no. 126 (June 1827): 709–26. 22, no. 127 (July 1827): 74–83; no. 128 (September 1827): 316–28.

Holmes, Jack D. L. "Robert Ross's Plan for Invasion of Louisiana." *Louisiana History* 5, no. 1 (Winter 1964): 161–77.

"The Journal of Capt. Thomas Joyes: From Louisville to the Battle of New Orleans." *Ohio Valley History* 8, no. 3 (Fall 2008): 19–39.

"Lafitte." *DeBow's Southern and Western Review* 13, no. 2 (August 1852): 204–5.

Leslie, J. H., ed. "Artillery Services in North America in 1814 and 1815, Being Extracts from the Journal of Colonel Sir Alexander Dickson." *Journal of the Society for Army Historical Research* 8, no. 32 (April 1929): 79–85; no. 33 (July 1929): 147–78; no. 34 (October 1929): 213–27.

"Letter from 'A West India Proprietor,' April 10, 1815." *Gentleman's Magazine* 85 (April 1815): 295–96.

"Letter of the Duke of Wellington (May 22, 1815) on the Battle of New Orleans." *Louisiana Historical Quarterly* 9, no. 1 (January 1926): 5–10.

"Lieutenant McKenzie's Reconnaissance on Mobile Bay, January 5–14, 1815." *Tennessee Historical Magazine* 1, no. 1 (March 1915): 66–69.

Lossing, Benson. "Scenes in the War of 1812: XII—Defense of New Orleans. *Harper's New Monthly Magazine* 30, no. 176 (January 1865): 168–86.

"Major Davezac." *United States Magazine and Democratic Review* 16, no. 80 (February 1845): 109–10.

Mayhew, Thaddeus. "A Massachusetts Volunteer at the Battle of New Orleans." *Louisiana Historical Quarterly* 9, no. 1 (January 1926): 30–31.

Michell, John. "Diary of Major J. Michell." *Louisiana Historical Quarterly* 44, no. 3–4 (July–October 1961): 127–30.

Murdoch, Richard K. "A British Report on West Florida and Louisiana, November, 1812." *Florida Historical Quarterly* 43, no. 1 (July 1964): 42–51.

"Obituary; with Anecdotes of Remarkable Persons." *Gentleman's Magazine* 85 (May 1815): 476.

"Political Portraits with Pen and Pencil—Henry Miller Shreve." *United States Magazine, and Democratic Review* 22, no. 116 (February 1848): 166–67.

"Recollections of the Expedition to the Chesapeake, and Against New Orleans, in the Years 1814–15. No. III. By an Old Sub." *United Service Journal and Naval and Military Magazine* 33, no. 139 (June 1840, Part 3): 183–95; no. 140 (July 1840, Part 4): 337–52.

"Report of the Committee of Inquiry on the Military Measures Executed Against the Legislature." *Louisiana Historical Quarterly* 9, no. 2 (April 1926): 223–80.

"Review of *Historical Memoir of the War in West Florida and Louisiana in 1814–15*, by Arsène Latour." *North-American Review and Miscellaneous Journal* 3, no. 8 (July 1816): 232–66.

"Review of *The Subaltern in America, and Man of War's Man*." *The Naval and Military Magazine* 2, no. 4 (December 1827): 479–80.

S[impson], R[obert]. "Battle of New Orleans, 8th January, 1815." *Blackwood's Edinburgh Magazine* 24, no. 143 (September 1828): 354–57.

Walcutt, William. "Recollections of the Last War. No II. Incidents in the Battle of New-Orleans." *Republic* 3, no. 1 (January 1852): 21–22.

Woodworth, Samuel. "New-Orleans." *Ladies' Literary Cabinet* 3, no. 14 (February 10, 1821), 112.

Autograph Catalogs

Neil Auction Company, Louisiana Purchase Auction, December 2, 2016.

Raab Collection Online Catalog, July 2016.

Schuyler J. Rumsey Philatelic Auction No. 68, June 1, 2016.

Stampauctionnetwork.com. Robert L. Cobb to John Cobb, February 3, 1815, listing.

Databases

Dolley Madison Digital Edition. University of Virginia, Charlottesville, 2004–2019.

Newspapers

United States

Albany, NY, *Albany Gazette*, 1815

Albany, NY, *Albany Argus*, 1815

Albany, NY, *Centinel*, 1799

Albany, NY, *Register*, 1815

Alexandria, VA, *Alexandria Gazette*, 1814, 1815, 1822, 1851

Alexandria, VA, *Alexandria Herald*, 1822

Augusta, GA, *Augusta Chronicle and Georgia Advertiser*, 1829

Augusta, GA, *Augusta Herald*, 1815

Baltimore, MD, *American, and Commercial Daily Advertiser*, 1814, 1815, 1816, 1821, 1842

Baltimore, MD, *Baltimore Patriot & Evening Advertiser*, 1814, 1815, 1816

Baltimore, MD, *Baltimore Telegraph*, 1815

Baltimore, MD, *Federal Gazette*, 1815

Baltimore, MD, *Niles' Weekly Register*, 1815

Bardstown, KY, *Bardstown Repository*, 1815

Bardstown, KY, *Western American*, 1815

Baton Rouge, LA, *Weekly Advocate*, 1847

Bennington, VT, *Bennington News-Letter*, 1815

Bennington, VT, *Green-Mountain Farmer*, 1815

Bloomsburg, PA, *Columbian*, 1898

Boston, MA, *Boston Commercial Gazette*, 1811, 1812, 1814, 1815

Boston, MA, *Boston Daily Advertiser*, 1814, 1815, 1818, 1819

Boston, MA, *Boston Patriot*, 1815

Boston, MA, *Boston Patriot & Daily Chronicle*, 1829

Boston, MA, *Boston Statesman*, 1832

Boston, MA, *Boston Weekly Messenger*, 1815

Boston, MA, *Columbian Centinel*, 1814, 1815, 1821

Boston, MA, *Independent Chronicle*, 1815

Boston, MA, *Intelligencer and Evening Gazette*, 1827

Boston, MA, *Massachusetts Spy*, 1815

Boston, MA, *New-England Palladium*, 1814, 1815

Boston, MA, *Repertory*, 1814, 1815

Boston, MA, *Whig*, 1815

Boston, MA, *Yankee*, 1815.

Bridgeport, CT, *Connecticut Courier*, 1815

Bridgeport, CT, *Republican Farmer*, 1815

Brownsville, PA, *American Telegraph*, 1815

Burlington, VT, *Burlington Gazette*, 1815

Burlington, VT, *Vermont Centinel*, 1815.

Camden, SC, *Camden Journal*, 1841

Carlisle, PA, *Gazette*, 1811

Carlisle, PA, *Journal*, 1814

Carthage, TN, *Carthage Gazette*, 1815

Cazenovia, NY, *Pilot*, 1815

Charles Town, VA, *Farmer's Repository*, 1815

Charleston, SC, *Charleston Courier*, 1815

Charleston, SC, *City Gazette and Commercial Daily Advertiser*, 1812, 1814, 1815

Charleston, SC, *Southern Patriot*, 1819

Chillicothe, OH, *Supporter*, 1815

Chillicothe, OH, *Weekly Recorder*, 1815

Cincinnati, OH, *Spirit of the West*, 1815

Cincinnati, OH, *Western Spy and Hamilton Gazette*, 1802

Clarksburg, VA, *Cooper's Clarksburg Register*, 1852

Clinton, OH, *Ohio Register*, 1815

Concord, NH, *New Hampshire Patriot and State Gazette*, 1814, 1815, 1818

Cooperstown, NY, *Otsego Herald*, 1807

Council Bluffs, IA, *Council Bluffs Nonpareil*, 1860

Danville, VT, *North Star*, 1830

Dayton, OH, *Ohio Republican*, 1815

Dedham, MA, *Dedham Gazette*, 1815

Dixon, IL, *Dixon Sun*, 1876

Dover, NH, *Sun*, 1815

Easton, MD, *Republican Star*, 1815, 1816

Elizabethtown, NJ, *New-Jersey Gazette*, 1815

Fayette, MS, *Fayette Chronicle*, 1889

Frankfort, KY, *Argus of Western America*, 1815, 1824

Georgetown, DC, *Federal Republican for the Country*, 1814, 1815

Georgetown, DC, *Metropolitan*, 1820

Goshen, NY, *Orange Farmer*, 1822

Hallowell, ME, *American Advocate*, 1815

Hallowell, ME, *Hallowell Gazette*, 1815

Hanover, NH, *Dartmouth Gazette*, 1815

Hartford, CT, *Connecticut Courant*, 1815, 1841

Hartford, CT, *Connecticut Herald*, 1814

Houston, TX, *Houston Chronicle*, 1935

Hudson, NY, *Bee*, 1815

Hudson, NY, *Northern Whig*, 1815

Keene, NH, *New-Hampshire Sentinel*, 1844

Kennebunk, ME, *Weekly Visitor*, 1815

Kingston, NY, *Ulster Gazette*, 1815

Lebanon, OH, *Western Star*, 1817

Leesburg, VA, *Genius of Liberty*, 1818

Lexington, KY, *Reporter*, 1815

Lexington, KY, *Western Monitor*, 1814, 1815

Little Rock, AR, *Weekly Arkansas Gazette*, 1822

Louisville, KY, *Courier-Journal*, 1888

Louisville, KY, *Louisville Correspondent*, 1815

Louisville, KY, *Louisville Daily Democrat*, 1846

Louisville, KY, *Western Courier*, 1815

Macon, GA, *Weekly Telegraph*, 1831

Manchester, NH, *Manchester Daily Union*, 1852

Marietta, OH, *American Friend*, 1815

Middletown, CT, *Connecticut Spectator*, 1814, 1815

Milledgeville, GA, *Georgia Journal*, 1815

Morristown, NJ, *Palladium of Liberty*, 1814

Nashville, TN, *Clarion*, 1814

Nashville, TN, *Daily Gazette*, 1858

Nashville, TN, *Nashville Examiner*, 1815

Nashville, TN, *Nashville Whig*, 1815

Natchez, MS, *Ariel*, 1828

Natchez, MS, *Mississippi Free Trader*, 1815

Natchez, MS, *Mississippi Messenger*, 1804

Natchez, MS, *Mississippi Republican*, 1814, 1815

New Bedford, MA, *New-Bedford Mercury*, 1815

New Haven, CT, *Columbian Register*, 1814, 1816

New Haven, CT, *Connecticut Herald*, 1815, 1828

New Haven, CT, *Connecticut Journal*, 1805, 1815

New London, CT, *Connecticut Gazette*, 1815

New Orleans, LA, *Daily Delta*, 1852, 1854

New Orleans, LA, *Daily Picayune*, 1851, 1852

New Orleans, LA, *L'Ami des Lois*, 1815

New Orleans, LA, *Louisiana Advertiser*, 1820, 1827

New Orleans, LA, *Louisiana Courier*, 1811, 1814, 1815

New Orleans, LA, *Louisiana Gazette and New Orleans Daily Advertiser*, 1814

New Orleans, LA, *Louisiana Gazette for the Country*, 1811, 1815

New Orleans, LA, *Louisiana State Gazette*, 1811, 1815

New Orleans, LA, *Orleans Gazette & Commercial Advertiser*, 1806, 1814, 1817, 1819, 1820

New Orleans, LA, *New Orleans Republican*, 1875

New Orleans, LA, *Orleans Gazette, for the Country*, 1805, 1806, 1812, 1814, 1815, 1817, 1819, 1820

New Orleans, LA, *Times-Democrat*, 1893, 1901

New Orleans, LA, *Times-Picayune*, 1950

New Orleans, LA, *Trumpeter*, 1812

New Orleans, LA, *Union*, 1804

New York, NY, *Columbian*, 1814, 1815

New York, NY, *Morning Herald*, 1837

New York, NY, *National Advocate*, 1815, 1819, 1828

New York, NY, *New-York American for the Country*, 1825

New York, NY, *New-York Commercial Advertiser*, 1813, 1814, 1815, 1833

New York, NY, *New-York Evening Post*, 1814, 1815, 1841

New York, NY, *New-York Gazette & General Advertiser*, 1814, 1815

New York, NY, *New-York Herald*, 1815

New York, NY, *New-York Mercantile Advertiser*, 1815

New York, NY, *New-York Spectator*, 1814, 1815, 1816

Newark, NJ, *Centinel of Freedom*, 1815

Newburyport, MA, *Newburyport Herald*, 1815

Newport, RI, *Newport Mercury*, 1815, 1835

Newport, RI, *Rhode-Island Republican*, 1814, 1815

Norfolk, VA, *American Beacon*, 1815

Norfolk, VA, *Norfolk Gazette & Publick Ledger*, 1815

Northampton, MA, *Hampshire Gazette*, 1815

Norwich, CT, *Courier*, 1815

Paris, KY, *Western Citizen*, 1814, 1815

Paris, KY, *Western Monitor*, 1815

Pensacola, FL, *Pensacola Gazette*, 1855

Peoria, IL, *Peoria Democratic Press*, 1842

Petersburg, VA, *Petersburg Daily Courier*, 1815

Philadelphia, PA, *Democratic Press*, 1813, 1814

Philadelphia, PA, *Freeman's Journal*, 1815

Philadelphia, PA, *National Gazette and Literary Messenger*, 1831, 1834

Philadelphia, PA, *Poulson's American Daily Advertiser*, 1804, 1815, 1819, 1829

Philadelphia, PA, *Relf's Philadelphia Gazette, and Daily Advertiser*, 1815, 1817

Philadelphia, PA, *True American*, 1815

Philadelphia, PA, *Weekly Aurora*, 1815

Pittsburgh, PA, *Pittsburgh Weekly Gazette*, 1815

Pittsfield, MA, *Sun*, 1815

Plattsburgh, NY, *Plattsburgh Republican*, 1815

Pomeroy, OH, *Pomeroy Weekly Telegraph*, 1861

Port Townsend, WA, *Puget Sound Weekly Argus*, 1875

Portland, ME, *Eastern Argus*, 1815

Poughkeepsie, NY, *Poughkeepsie Journal*, 1815

Providence, RI, *Gazette and American*, 1815

Providence, RI, *Providence Gazette and Country Journal*, 1815

Providence, RI, *Providence Patriot*, 1821

Providence, RI, *Rhode-Island American, and General Advertiser*, 1815

Raleigh, NC, *Star*, 1815

Richmond, VA, *Richmond Enquirer*, 1815

Richmond, VA, *Virginia Patriot*, 1815

Richmond, VA, *Whig and Public Advertiser*, 1833

Rockford, IL, *Rock River Democrat*, 1852

Rutland, VT, *Rutland Herald*, 1815

Salem, MA, *Essex Register*, 1815

Salem, MA, *Salem Gazette*, 1815

Saratoga Springs, NY, *Saratoga Sentinel*, 1828

Savannah, GA, *Columbian Museum & Savannah Advertiser*, 1819

Savannah, GA, *Georgian*, 1819

Savannah, GA, *Republican; and Savannah Evening Ledger*, 1812, 1815

Schenectady, NY, *Cabinet*, 1815

St. Francisville, LA, *Time-Piece*, 1814

St. Louis, MO, *Missouri Gazette*, 1815

Staunton, VA, *Staunton Eagle*, 1808

Troy, NY, *Farmer's Register*, 1815

Uniontown, MD, *Engine of Liberty, and Uniontown Advertiser*, 1815

Utica, NY, *Columbian Gazette*, 1815
Utica, NY, *Patrol*, 1815
Walpole, NH, *Political Observatory*, 1807, 1808
Warren, RI, *Telescope*, 1815
Washington, DC, *Daily National Intelligencer*, 1813, 1814, 1815, 1816, 1825, 1832, 1835
Washington, DC, *Monitor*, 1808
Washington, DC, *National Intelligencer*, 1804, 1810, 1815, 1817
Washington, DC, *Spirit of 'Seventy-Six*, 1810
Washington, DC, *Telegraph*, 1815
Washington, DC, *United States' Telegraph*, 1826, 1827, 1828, 1833
Washington, KY, *Union*, 1815
Washington, Mississippi Territory, *Washington Republican*, 1814, 1815
Washington, PA, *Washington Reporter*, 1814, 1815, 1821
White Cloud, KS, *White Cloud Kansas Chief*, 1872
Wilkes-Barre, PA, *Gleaner*, 1815
Wilkes-Barre, PA, *Susquehanna Democrat*, 1815
Williamsburgh, OH, *Western American*, 1815
Wilmington, DE, *American Watchman*, 1815, 1825, 1827
Wilmington, DE, *Delaware Gazette and State Journal*, 1815
Wilmington, NC, *Wilmington Gazette*, 1810, 1815
Winchester, KY, *Winchester Advertiser*, 1815
Windsor, VT, *Vermont Republican*, 1815, 1816
Windsor, VT, *Washingtonian*, 1815
Worcester, MA, *Massachusetts Spy, and Worcester County Advertiser*, 1827
Worcester, MA, *Massachusetts Weekly Spy*, 1875
Worcester, MA, *National Aegis*, 1815

United Kingdom and the British Colonies
Aberdeen, UK, *Press and Journal*, 1814
Adelaide, Australia, *South Australian Register*, 1869
Brighton, UK, *Brighton Gazette*, 1828
Brighton, UK, *Sussex Weekly Advertiser; or, Lewes Journal*, 1812
Cambridge, UK, *Cambridge Chronicle and Journal and Huntingdonshire Gazette*, 1813,
    1814
Canterbury, UK, *Kentish Gazette*, 1814
Dublin, IR, *Dublin Observer*, 1834
Dublin, IR, *Saunders's News-Letter, and Daily Advertiser*, 1809, 1815
Dublin, IR, *Weekly Nation*, 1859
Durham, UK, *Durham County Advertiser, and Commercial, and Agricultural, and
    Literary Journal*, 1815
Edinburgh, UK, *Caledonian Mercury*, 1812, 1813, 1815
Edinburgh, UK, *Scots Magazine, and Edinburgh Literary Miscellany*, 1814
Gloucester, UK, *Gloucester Journal*, 1814
Hereford, UK, *Hereford Journal*, 1809, 1814, 1815

Hull, UK, *Hull Advertiser and Exchange Gazette*, 1813

Ipswich, UK, *Suffolk Chronicle; Or, Weekly General Advertiser, & County Express*, 1812, 1814

Kingston, Jamaica, *Royal Gazette*, 1815

Kingston, Jamaica, *Weekly Jamaica Courant*, 1814

Lancaster, UK, *Gazette; and General Advertiser*, 1813

Leicester, UK, *Leicester Journal, and Midland Counties General Advertiser*, 1815

London, UK, *Bell's Weekly Messenger*, 1815

London, UK, *Cobbett's Weekly Political Register*, 1811, 1814, 1815

London, UK, *Correspondent and Public Cause*, 1815

London, UK, *Courier, and Evening Gazette*, 1814, 1815

London, UK, *Globe*, 1815

London, UK, *Military Register*, 1815

London, UK, *Morning Advertiser*, 1839

London, UK, *Morning Chronicle*, 1811, 1812, 1814, 1815, 1823

London, UK, *Morning Post*, 1812, 1814, 1815, 1828

London, UK, *National Register*, 1815

London, UK, *Pilot*, 1815

London, UK, *Public Ledger and Daily Advertiser*, 1809, 1810, 1812, 1813, 1814, 1815

London, UK, *Star*, 1814

London, UK, *Times*, 1814, 1815

Londonderry, IR, *Londonderry Sentinel and North-West Advertiser*, 1834

Manchester, UK, *Manchester Mercury, and Harrop's General Advertiser*, 1813, 1814, 1815

Montreal, Canada, *Montreal Herald*, 1815

Montrose, UK, *Montrose, Arbroath, & Brechkin Review, and Forfar and Kincardineshire Advertiser*, 1852

Newcastle, UK, *Newcastle Courant*, 1732

Nottingham, UK, *Nottingham Gazette, and Political, Literary, Agricultural & Commercial Register for the Midland Counties*, 1815

Oxford, UK, *Oxford University and City Herald, and Midland County Chronicle*, 1813, 1815

Perth, UK, *Courier*, 1814

Port Royal, Jamaica, *Gazette*, 1814

Portsmouth, UK, *Hampshire Telegraph and Sussex Chronicle*, 1815

St. George's, Bermuda, *Bermuda Gazette, and Weekly Advertiser*, 1815

Stamford, UK, *Lincoln, Rutland, and Stamford Mercury*, 1815

Whitehaven, UK, *Cumberland Pacquet and Ware's Whitehaven Advertiser*, 1815

Winchester, UK, *Hampshire Chronicle, and Weekly Advertiser*, 1810

Winchester, UK, *Hampshire Chronicle; or, South and West of England Pilot*

Europe
Ghent, Belgium, *Journal*, 1815

Secondary Sources

Books

A Century of Population Growth from the First Census of the United States to the Twelfth 1790–1900. Washington, DC: Government Printing Office, 1909.

Albright, Harry. *New Orleans: Battle of the Bayous*. New York: Hippocrene, 1990.

Arthur, Stanley Clisby. *The Story of the Battle of New Orleans*. New Orleans: Louisiana Historical Society, 1915.

Bassett, John Spencer. *The Life of Andrew Jackson*. New York: Doubleday, 1911. 2 vols.

Birkedal, Ted, ed. *Historical and Archaeological Investigations at the Chalmette Battlefield, Jean Lafitte National Historical Park and Preserve*. New Orleans: National Park Service, 2009. 3 vols.

Blair, Francis Preston. *The Life and Public Services of Gen. William O. Butler*. Baltimore: N. Hickman, 1848.

Brooks, Charles B. *Siege of New Orleans*. Seattle: University of Washington Press, 1961.

Brown, Wilburt S. *The Amphibious Campaign for West Florida and Louisiana, 1814–1815*. Tuscaloosa: University of Alabama Press, 1969.

Bruce, William Cabell. *John Randolph of Roanoke 1773–1833*. New York: Putnam's, 1922. 2 vols.

Buchan, John. *The History of the Royal Scots Fusiliers (1678–1918)*. London: Thomas Nelson, 1925.

Buell, Augustus C. *History of Andrew Jackson: Pioneer, Patriot, Soldier, Politician, President*. New York: Charles Scribner's Sons, 1904. 2 vols.

Bunn, Mike, and Clay Williams. *Battle for the Southern Frontier: The Creek War and the War of 1812*. Charleston, SC: History Press, 2008.

Carter, Samuel, III. *Blaze of Glory: The Fight for New Orleans, 1814–1815*. New York: St. Martin's, 1971.

Casey, Powell A. *Louisiana at the Battle of New Orleans*. New Orleans: Battle of New Orleans 150th Anniversary Committee of Louisiana, 1965.

————. *Louisiana in the War of 1812*. Baton Rouge: Battle of New Orleans 150th Anniversary Committee of Louisiana, 1963.

Cavendish, A. E. *The 93rd Sutherland Highlanders, 1799–1927*. N.p.: privately published,1928.

Chambers, Stephen. *No God but Gain: The Untold Story of Cuban Slavery, the Monroe Doctrine & the Making of the United States*. London: Verso, 2015.

Chapman, Ron. *The Battle of New Orleans: "But for a Piece of Wood."* New Orleans: Pelican Publishing, 2013.

Christian, Marcus Bruce. *Negro Soldiers in the Battle of New Orleans*. New Orleans: Battle of New Orleans 150th Anniversary Committee of Louisiana, 1965.

Clark, James. *Historical Record and Regimental Memoir of the Royal Scots Fusiliers, Formerly Known as the 21st Royal North British Fusiliers*. Edinburgh: Banks & Co., 1885.

Clayton, Lawrence A. *The Hispanic Experience in North America: Sources for Study in the United States*. Columbus: Ohio State University Press, 1992.

Clement, William Edwards. *Plantation Life on the Mississippi*. New Orleans: Pelican Publishing, 1952.

Cobbett, William. *Life of Andrew Jackson, President of the United States of America.* London: Mills, Jewett, and Mills, 1834, 67–68.

Coker, William S. *The Last Battle of the War of 1812: New Orleans. No, Fort Bowyer!* Pensacola, FL: Perdido Bay Press, 1981.

Collins, Richard H. *History of Kentucky.* Covington, KY: Collins and Co., 1874.

Cope, William H. *The History of the Rifle Brigade (The Prince Consort's Own) Formerly the 95th.* London: Chatto & Windus, 1877.

Cornelison, John E., Jr., and Tammy D. Cooper. *An Archaeological Survey of the Chalmette Battlefield at Jean Lafitte National Historical Park and Preserve.* Tallahassee, FL: National Park Service, 2002.

Cox, Isaac Joslyn. *The West Florida Controversy, 1798–1813: A Study in American Diplomacy.* Baltimore: Johns Hopkins University Press, 1918.

Dalton, Charles. *The Waterloo Roll Call, with Biographical Notes and Anecdotes.* London: Eyre and Spottiswoode, 1904.

Davis, William C. *A Way Through the Wilderness: The Natchez Trace and the Civilization of the Southern Frontier.* New York: HarperCollins, 1995.

———. *The Pirates Laffite: The Treacherous World of the Corsairs of the Gulf.* New York: Harcourt, 2005.

———. *The Rogue Republic: How Would-Be Patriots Waged the Shortest Revolution in American History.* New York: Houghton Mifflin Harcourt, 2011.

De Grummond, Jane Lucas. *Renato Beluche: Smuggler, Privateer, and Patriot, 1780–1860.* Baton Rouge: Louisiana State University Press, 1983.

———. *The Baratarians and the Battle of New Orleans.* Baton Rouge: Louisiana State University Press, 1961.

Dixon, Richard Remy. *The Battle on the West Bank.* New Orleans: Battle of New Orleans 150th Anniversary Committee of Louisiana, 1965.

Drez, Ronald J. *The War of 1812: Conflict and Deception.* Baton Rouge: Louisiana State University Press, 2014.

Ellis, A. B. *The History of the First West India Regiment.* London: Chapman and Hall, 1885.

Flint, Wayne. *Dixie's Forgotten People: The South's Poor Whites.* Bloomington: Indiana State University Press, 1979.

Fortescue, J. W. *A History of the British Army.* London: Macmillan, 1906. 10 vols.

French, Isabelle Marshall. *They Lived at Chalmette.* New Orleans: Hope Publications, 1978.

Gallagher, Winifred. *How the Post Office Created America: A History.* New York: Penguin, 2016.

Garrigoux, Jean. *A Visionary Adventurer: Arsène Lacarrière Latour, 1778–1837: The Unusual Travels of a Frenchman in the Americas.* Translated by Gordon S. Brown. Lafayette: University of Louisiana at Lafayette Press, 2017.

Gayarré, Charles. *History of Louisiana: The American Domination.* New York: Redfield, 1854. 4 vols.

Greene, Jerome A. *Jean Lafitte National Historical Park and Preserve: Chalmette Unit Historic Resource Study.* Denver, CO: National Park Service, 1985.

Groom, Winston. *Patriotic Fire: Andrew Jackson and Jean Lafitte at the Battle of New Orleans.* New York: Knopf, 2006.

Hamilton, William Baskerville. *Anglo-American Law on the Frontier: Thomas Rodney and His Territorial Cases*. Durham, NC: Duke University Press, 1953.

Hatcher, William B. *Edward Livingston: Jeffersonian Republican and Jacksonian Democrat*. Baton Rouge: Louisiana State University Press, 1940.

Heidler, David S., and Jean T. Heidler. *Encyclopedia of the War of 1812*. Santa Barbara, CA: ABC-CLIO, 1997.

Heitman, Francis B., comp. *Historical Register and Dictionary of the United States Army, from its Organization, September 29, 1789, to March 2, 1903*. Washington, DC: Government Printing Office, 1903. 2 vols.

Hickey, Donald R. *Don't Give Up the Ship!* Urbana: University of Illinois Press, 2006.

———. *Glorious Victory: Andrew Jackson and the Battle of New Orleans*. Baltimore: Johns Hopkins University Press, 2015.

———. *The War of 1812: A Forgotten Conflict*. Urbana: University of Illinois Press, 1989.

Hoffman, Paul E. *Florida's Frontiers*. Bloomington: Indiana University Press, 2002.

Horton, James Oliver, and Lois E. Horton, *Slavery and the Making of America*. New York: Oxford University Press, 2005.

Hyde, William, and Howard L. Conard, eds. *Encyclopedia of the History of St. Louis*. New York: Southern History Company, 1899. 4 vols.

Jumonville, Florence M., comp. *Louisiana History: An Annotated Bibliography*. Westport, CT: Greenwood Press, 2002.

Kanon, Tom. *Tennesseans at War 1812–1815: Andrew Jackson, the Creek War, and the Battle of New Orleans*. Tuscaloosa: University of Alabama Press, 2014.

Kilmeade, Brian, and Don Yaeger. *Andrew Jackson and the Miracle of New Orleans*. New York: Sentinel, 2017.

La Violette, Paul Estronza. *Sink or Be Sunk!: The Naval Battle in the Mississippi Sound That Preceded the Battle of New Orleans*. Waveland, MS: Annabelle, 2002.

Landry, Stuart O. *Side Lights on the Battle of New Orleans*. New Orleans: Pelican Publishing, 1965.

Linklater, Andro. *An Artist in Treason: The Extraordinary Double Life of General James Wilkinson*. New York: Walker, 2009.

Loomis, Rosemarie Fay. *Negro Soldiers, Free Men of Color in the Battle of New Orleans, War of 1812*. New Orleans: Aux Quatres Vents, 1991.

McConnell, Roland C. *Negro Troops of Antebellum Louisiana: A History of the Battalion of Free Men of Color*. Baton Rouge: Louisiana State University Press, 1968.

McElroy, Robert M. *Kentucky in the Nation's History*. New York: Moffatt, Yard and Co., 1909.

McLemore, Laura Lyons, ed. *The Battle of New Orleans in History and Memory*. Baton Rouge: Louisiana State University Press, 2016.

Meuse, William A. *The Weapons of the Battle of New Orleans*. New Orleans: Battle of New Orleans 150th Anniversary Committee of Louisiana, 1965.

Obadele-Starks, Ernest. *Freebooters and Smugglers: The Foreign Slave Trade in the United States After 1808*. Fayetteville: University of Arkansas Press, 2007.

Owsley, Frank Lawrence, Jr. *Struggle for the Gulf Borderlands*. Gainesville: University Presses of Florida, 1981.

Parton, James. *A Life of Andrew Jackson*. New York: Mason Brothers, 1860. 3 vols.

Perrett, Brian. *The Real Hornblower: The Life & Times of Admiral Sir James Gordon.* Annapolis, MD: Naval Institute Press, 1998.

Pierson, Marion John Bennett. *Louisiana Soldiers in the War of 1812.* Baton Rouge: Louisiana Genealogical and Historical Society, 1963.

Quisenberry, Anderson Chenault. *Kentucky in the War of 1812.* Frankfort: Kentucky Historical Society, 1915.

Rasmussen, Daniel. *American Uprising: The Untold Story of America's Largest Slave Revolt.* New York: Harper, 2011.

Reilly, Robin. *The British at the Gates.* New York: Putnam, 1974.

Remini, Robert V. *The Battle of New Orleans: Andrew Jackson and America's First Military Victory.* New York: Viking, 1999.

———. *Henry Clay: Statesman for the Union.* New York: W. W. Norton, 1991.

Rowland, Dunbar. *Andrew Jackson's Campaign Against the British, or the Mississippi Territory in the War of 1812.* New York: Macmillan, 1926.

Sanjek, Russell. *American Popular Music and Its Business: The First Four Hundred Years.* Vol. 2. *From 1790 to 1909.* New York: Oxford University Press, 1988.

Sawyer, Charles Winthrop. *Our Rifles.* Boston: Cornhill, 1920.

Scheele, Carl H. *A Short History of the Mail Service.* Washington, DC: Smithsonian Institution Press, 1970.

Scott, Valerie McNair, Lady Pakenham. *The Battle of New Orleans: Major-General Sir Edward M. Pakenham.* New Orleans: Battle of New Orleans 150th Anniversary Committee of Louisiana, 1965.

Smith, Gene A. *The Slaves' Gamble: Choosing Sides in the War of 1812.* New York: Palgrave Macmillan, 2013.

———. *Thomas ap Catesby Jones: Commodore of Manifest Destiny.* Annapolis, MD: Naval Institute Press, 2000.

Smythies, R. H. Raymond. *Historical Records of the 40th (Second Somersetshire) Regiment.* Devonport, UK: A. H. Swiss, 1894.

The Terrible and the Brave: The Battles for New Orleans, 1814–1815. Exhibition catalog. New Orleans: Historic New Orleans Collection, 2005.

Toledano, Roulhac and Mary Louise Christovich. *New Orleans Architecture: Faubourg Tremé and the Bayou Road.* New Orleans: Pelican Publishing, 2003.

Tregle, Joseph G., Jr. *Louisiana in the Age of Jackson: A Clash of Cultures and Personalities.* Baton Rouge: Louisiana State University Press, 1999.

Villeré, Sidney Louis. *Jacques Philippe Villeré: First Native-Born Governor of Louisiana 1816–1830.* New Orleans: Historic New Orleans Collection, 1981.

Ward, John William. *Andrew Jackson: Symbol for an Age.* New York: Oxford University Press, 1955.

Watson, Elbert L. *Tennessee at the Battle of New Orleans.* New Orleans: Battle of New Orleans 150th Anniversary Committee of Louisiana, 1965.

Watson, Thomas E. *The Life and Times of Andrew Jackson.* Thomson, GA: Jeffersonian Publishing Co., 1912.

Weir, Howard T., III. *A Paradise of Blood: The Creek War of 1813–1814.* Yardley, PA: Westholme, 2016.

Wilson, Samuel. *Plantation Houses on the Battlefield of New Orleans.* New Orleans: Battle of New Orleans 150th Anniversary Committee of Louisiana, 1965.

Wood, Bryce. *Peaceful Change and the Colonial Problem.* Studies in History, Economics and Public Law. New York: Columbia University Press, 1940.

ARTICLES

Bienvenu, Willie Z. "The Bienvenu Family of St. Martinville." *Attakapas Gazette* 15, no. 1 (Spring 1980): 2–12.

Billings, W. M. "A Neglected Treatise: Lewis Kerr's Exposition and the Making of Criminal Law in Louisiana." *Louisiana History* 38, no. 3 (Summer 1997): 261–86.

"Captain Nathaniel Pryor." *American Historical Review* 24, no. 2 (January 1919): 253–65.

Carr, James A. "The Battle of New Orleans and the Treaty of Ghent." *Diplomatic History* 3, no. 3 (July 1979): 273–82.

Cavell, Samantha A. "Cochrane's Grand Southern Strategy." In *The Battle of New Orleans Reconsidered*, edited by Curtis Manning, 35–54. New Orleans: Louisiana Institute of Higher Education, 2014.

Chambers, Stephen. "No country but their counting-houses." In *Slavery's Capitalism: A New History of American Economic Development*, edited by Sven Beckert and Seth Rockman, 195–208. Philadelphia: University of Pennsylvania Press, 2016.

Cheatham, Mark R. "'I Owe to Britain a Debt of Retaliatory Vengeance': Assessing Andrew Jackson's Hatred of the British." In *The Battle of New Orleans in History and Memory*, edited by Laura Lyons McLemore, 28–55. Baton Rouge: Louisiana State University Press, 2016.

Coker, William S. "How General Andrew Jackson Learned of the British Plans Before the Battle of New Orleans." *Gulf Coast Historical Review* 3, no. 1 (Fall 1987): 84–95.

———. "Indian Traders of the Southwestern Spanish Borderlands." In *The Hispanic Experience in North America: Sources for Study in the United States*, edited by Lawrence A. Clayton, 107–15. Columbus: Ohio State University Press, 1992.

Colvin, Alex. "Tennesseans at War, 1812–1815: Andrew Jackson, the Creek War, and the Battle of New Orleans." *Alabama Review* 69, no. 4 (October 2016): 338–42.

Cook, William C. "The Early Iconography of the Battle of New Orleans, 1815–1819." *Tennessee Historical Quarterly* 48, no. 4 (Winter 1989): 218–37.

De Grummond, Jane Lucas. "Platter of Glory." *Louisiana History* 3, no. 4 (Fall 1962): 316–59.

Deutsch, Eberhard. "The United States Versus Major General Andrew Jackson." *American Bar Association Journal* 46, no. 9 (September 1960): 966–72.

Dixon, Richard W. "The 1815 Battle of New Orleans: A Physical Geographical Analysis." In *Studies in Military Geography and Geology*, edited by Douglas R. Caldwell, Judy Ehlen, and Russell H. Harmon, 147–54. Dordrecht, Netherlands: Kluwer Academic, 2004.

Donlan, Seán Patrick. "Entangled Up in Red, White, and Blue: Spanish West Florida and the American Territory of Orleans, 1803–1810." In *Entanglements in Legal History: Conceptual Approaches,* Global Perspectives on Legal History, edited by Thomas Duve, 213–52. Frankfurt am Main, Germany: Max Planck Institute for European Legal History, 2014.

Dudley, William S. "The Pinchpenny Flotilla." *Naval History* 29, no. 1 (February 2015): 38–45.

Dunnavent, Blake. "Lessons Learned from the War of 1812 for the U.S. Military in the Twenty-First Century." In *The Battle of New Orleans in History and Memory*, edited by Laura Lyons McLemore, 116–28. Baton Rouge: Louisiana State University Press, 2016.

Gelpi, Paul. "In Defense of Liberty: The Battalion d'Orleans and Its Battle for New Orleans." In *The Battle of New Orleans in History and Memory*, edited by Laura Lyons McLemore, 100–15. Baton Rouge: Louisiana State University Press, 2016.

Graham, George R. *The Battle-Grounds of America. No. V.—New Orleans.* Philadelphia: George R. Graham, 1845.

Hamilton, Milton W. "Augustus C. Buell: Fraudulent Historian." *Pennsylvania Magazine of History and Biography* 80, no. 4 (October 1956): 478–92.

Haynes, Robert V. "The Southwest and the War of 1812." *Louisiana History* 5, no. 1 (Winter 1964): 41–51.

"The Hon. Sir Robert Cavendish Spencer." *The Annual Biography and Obituary: 1832.* Vol. 16. London: Longman, Rees, Orme, Brown, Green, & Longman, 1832: 3–4.

Keyes, Pamela. "How Lafitte Became the Real-Life Byronic Hero." *Laffite Chronicles* 13, no. 1 (February 2007): 19–22.

LeBreton, Dagmar Renshaw. "The Man Who Won the Battle of New Orleans." *Louisiana Historical Quarterly* 38, no. 3 (July 1955): 20–34.

Mahon, John K. "British Command Decisions Relative to the Battle of New Orleans." *Louisiana History* 6, no. 1 (Winter 1965): 53–76.

Melhorn, Donald F., Jr. "The Battle of New Orleans: What If the British Had Won?" *Northwest Ohio History* 81, no. 1 (Fall 2013): 60–70.

Morse, Edward C. "Captain Ogden's Troop of Horse in the Battle of New Orleans." *Louisiana Historical Quarterly* 10, no. 3 (July 1927): 381–82.

"Officers and Soldiers of the War 1814–1815." *Southern Historical Society Papers* 36 (January–December 1908): 133–40.

Padgett, James A., ed. "The Difficulties of Andrew Jackson in New Orleans, Including His Later Dispute with Fulwar Skipwith." *Louisiana Historical Quarterly* 21, no. 2 (April 1938): 367–419.

Pfaff, Caroline S. "Henry Miller Shreve." *Louisiana Historical Quarterly* 10, no. 2 (April 1927): 192–240.

Pratt, Julius W. "Western War Aims in the War of 1812." *Mississippi Valley Historical Review* 12, no. 1 (June 1925): 36–50.

Quisenberry, Anderson Chenault. "The Battle of New Orleans." *Register of the Kentucky State Historical Society* 13, no. 37 (January 1915): 9–28.

Ritchie, Carson I. A. "The Louisiana Campaign." *Louisiana Historical Quarterly* 44, no. 1–2 (January–April 1961): 13–103.

———, ed. "British Documents on the Louisiana Campaign, 1814–15." *Louisiana Historical Quarterly* 44, no. 1–2 (January–April 1961): 104–21; no. 3–4 (July–October 1961): 1–147.

Stoltz, Joseph F., III. "'It Taught our Enemies a Lesson': The Battle of New Orleans and the Republican Destruction of the Federalist Party." *Tennessee Historical Quarterly* 71, no. 2 (July 2012): 112–27.

Tregle, Joseph G., Jr. "British Spy Along the Mississippi: Thomas Hutchins and the Defenses of New Orleans, 1773." *Louisiana History* 8, no. 4 (Autumn 1967): 318–27.

Warshauer, Matthew S. "The Battle of New Orleans Reconsidered: Andrew Jackson and Martial Law." *Louisiana History* 39, no. 3 (Summer 1998): 261–91.

Wilkinson, Norman B., ed. "The Assaults on New Orleans, 1814–1815." *Louisiana History* 3, no. 1 (Winter 1962): 43–53.

ARTICLES ON WEBSITES

Keyes, Pamela. "Beverly Chew, the Man Behind the Curtain in Early New Orleans." http://www.historiaobscura.com/beverly-chew-the-man-behind-the-curtain-in-early-new-orleans/

———. "The Case of the Spanish Prize Ship at Dauphin Island." http://www.historiaobscura.com/the-case-of-the-spanish-prize-ship-at-dauphin-island/

———. "The Saga of Melita and the Patterson-Ross Raid at Barataria." http://www.historiaobscura.com/the-saga-of-melita-and-the-patterson-ross-raid-at-barataria/

———. "Eyewitness Report of Jean Laffite at Chalmette Battlefield." http://www.historiaobscura.com/eyewitness-report-of-jean-laffite-at-chalmette-battlefield/

———. "The Spy Who Led the British to the Back Door of New Orleans." http://www.historiaobscura.com/the-spy-who-led-the-british-to-the-back-door-of-new-orleans-in-1814/

———. "Nathaniel Pryor, the Unsung Veteran of the Battle of New Orleans."http://www.historiaobscura.com/nathaniel-pryor-the-unsung-veteran-of-the-battle-of-new-orleans/

Stewart, E. K. "William Carr Withers." ancestry.com

THESES AND DISSERTATIONS

Buckley, Roger N. "The Early History of the West India Regiments 1795–1815: A Study in British Colonial Military History." PhD dissertation, McGill University, Montreal, Quebec, Canada, 1975.

Cotton, Dustin W. "The Performance of the Louisiana Militia During the Battle of New Orleans,1814–1815." MA thesis, Southeastern Louisiana University, Hammond, 2007.

Dill, William A. "Growth of Newspapers in the United States." MA Thesis, University of Oregon, Eugene, 1908.

Edwards, Michael J. "A 'Melancholy Experience': William C. C. Claiborne and the Louisiana Militia, 1811–1815." MA thesis, University of New Orleans, New Orleans, LA, 2011.

Hatfield, Joseph Tennis. "The Public Career of William C. C. Claiborne." PhD dissertation, Emory University, Atlanta, GA, 1962.

Jesko, Howard. "Louisiana's Unique Conditions and Andrew Jackson's Martial Law Declaration, 1814–1815." MA thesis, Youngstown State University, Youngstown, OH, 2015.

Stoltz, Joseph F, III. "'A Victory as Never Crowned the Wars of the World': The Battle of New Orleans in American Historical Memory." PhD dissertation, Texas Christian University, Dallas, 2013.

Van Divier, Jesse D. "A Politically Selective Memory: The Battle for Memory in the Wake of War, 1812–1845." Honors thesis, University of Colorado, Boulder, 2016.

Vaughan, W. A. "The Black Militia in the Battle of New Orleans." MA thesis, University of Southern Mississippi, Hattiesburg, 1993.

NOTES

PREFACE

1. The 1811 comet was first sighted March 25, 1811, and was visible longer than any comet on record until the Hale-Bopp in 1997. It was last seen August 12, 1812. The four great quakes commonly called the New Madrid earthquakes began on December 7, 1811, and ended February 7, 1812, but large and small tremors continued frequently through 1815.
2. "Review of *Historical Memoir of the War in West Florida and Louisiana in 1814–15*, by Arsène Latour," *North-American Review and Miscellaneous Journal* 3, no. 8 (July 1816): 238n.

CHAPTER ONE: A SPOT ON THE GLOBE

1. Samuel Mordecai Diary, April 23, 1815, Mordecai Family Papers, Southern Historical Collection, University of North Carolina, Chapel Hill.
2. Windship to Plummer, April 2, 1814, Everett S. Brown, ed., "Letters from Louisiana, 1813–1814," *Mississippi Valley Historical Review* 11 (March 1925): 575.
3. Joseph G. Tregle Jr., *Louisiana in the Age of Jackson: A Clash of Cultures and Personalities* (Baton Rouge: Louisiana State University Press, 1999), 30–31; Vincent Nolte, *The Memoirs of Vincent Nolte: Fifty Years in Both Hemispheres or, Reminiscences of the Life of a Former Merchant* (G. Howard Watt, 1934), 198; Simpson to Mary Simpson, December 9, 1814, Stephen Simpson Letters, Princeton.
4. Paul Gelpi, "In Defense of Liberty: The Battalion d'Orleans and Its Battle for New Orleans," in *The Battle of New Orleans in History and Memory*, ed. Laura Lyons McLemore (Baton Rouge: Louisiana State University Press, 2016), 100–101.
5. *State Papers and Correspondence Bearing Upon the Purchase of the Territory of Louisiana* (Washington, DC: Government Printing Office, 1903), 87.
6. Donald F. Melhorn Jr., "The Battle of New Orleans: What If the British Had Won?" *Northwest Ohio History* 81, no. 1 (Fall 2013): 63; William S. Dudley, "The Pinchpenny Flotilla," *Naval History* 29 (February 2015): 39; James Wilkinson, *Memoirs of My Own Times* (Philadelphia: Abraham Small, 1816), 1:524; Abraham Redwood Ellery, Account of the Battle of New Orleans, New York Public Library, New York, NY.
7. Melhorn, "What If the British Had Won?" 63.
8. Plan of attack on New Orleans circa 1770, Society Collection, Historical Society of Pennsylvania, Philadelphia.
9. Joseph G. Tregle, Jr., "British Spy Along the Mississippi: Thomas Hutchins and the Defenses of New Orleans, 1773," *Louisiana History* 8, no. 4 (Autumn 1967): 318–27; Jack D. L. Holmes,

"Robert Ross's Plan for Invasion of Louisiana," *Louisiana History* 5, no. 1 (Spring 1964): 161–64, 169, 171–73, 176.

10. H. M. Brackenridge, *History of the Late War Between the United States and Great Britain: Comprising a Minute Account of the Various Military and Naval Operations* (Philadelphia: Hayes & Zell, 1854; originally published 1839), 287–88.

11. Jared William Bradley, *Interim Appointment: W. C. C. Claiborne Letter Book, 1804–1805* (Baton Rouge: Louisiana State University Press, 2002), 415–18; Essay signed Peter Squibb, Cincinnati, OH, *Western Spy and Hamilton Gazette*, May 8, 1802.

12. Cincinnati, OH, *Western Spy and Hamilton Gazette*, March 6, May 1, 8, July 24, 1802; Bradley, *Interim Appointment*, 419; Washington, DC, *National Intelligencer*, June 22, 1804; Natchez, MS, *Mississippi Messenger*, October 12, 1804; William Baskerville Hamilton, *Anglo-American Law on the Frontier: Thomas Rodney and His Territorial Cases* (Durham, NC: Duke University Press, 1953), 403–4.

13. There is continuing argument over the year of his birth, placing it from 1773 to 1775. The latter seems the best supported.

14. Carter, *Papers*, Clarence Edwin Carter, ed., *The Territorial Papers of the United States*, vol. 9, *The Territory of Orleans 1803–1812* (Washington, DC: Government Printing Office, 1940), 270, 286, 393–94, 632; Philadelphia, PA, *Poulson's American Daily Advertiser*, June 30, 1804.

15. Letter from New Orleans to Augusta, GA, February 25, 1805; New Haven, CT, *Connecticut Journal*, May 7, 1805; New Orleans, LA, *Union*, March 12, 1804; Natchez, MS, *Mississippi Messenger*, November 30, 1804; "Communication," Washington, DC, *Spirit of 'Seventy-Six*, November 23, 1810; New Orleans, LA, *Orleans Gazette and Commercial Advertiser*, October 16, 1806; Seán Patrick Donlan, "Entangled Up in Red, White, and Blue: Spanish West Florida and the American Territory of Orleans, 1803–1810," in *Entanglements in Legal History: Conceptual Approaches*, Global Perspectives on Legal History, ed. Thomas Duve (Frankfurt am Main, Germany: Max Planck Institute for European Legal History, 2014), 229. Kerr's *An Exposition of the Criminal Laws of the Territory of Orleans* became a basic primer for Louisiana's criminal courts for half a century.

16. *The Trials of the Honb. James Workman, and Col. Lewis Kerr, Before the United States Court, for the Orleans District, on a Charge of High Misdemeanor* (New Orleans: Bradford & Anderson, 1807), 12–14, 23–25.

17. See William C. Davis, *The Rogue Republic: How Would-Be Patriots Waged the Shortest Revolution in American History* (New York: Houghton Mifflin Harcourt, 2011), 71ff, 114–15.

18. James Workman to Thomas Jefferson, November 15, 1801, Thomas Jefferson Papers, Missouri Historical Society, St. Louis.

19. See W. M. Billings, "A Neglected Treatise: Lewis Kerr's Exposition and the Making of Criminal Law in Louisiana," *Louisiana History* 38, no. 3 (Summer 1997), 261–86.

20. "Communication," Washington, DC, *Spirit of 'Seventy-Six*, November 23, 1810; Bradley, *Interim Appointment*, 391; *Trials of Workman, and Kerr*, 29–30, 40–42, 73.

21. Deposition of Reuben Kemper, August 8, 1807, Carlisle, PA, *Gazette*, May 31, 1811.

22. William Henry Sparks, *The Memories of Fifty Years* (Philadelphia: Claxon, Remsen and Haffelfinger, 1870), 449–51.

23. Andro Linklater, *An Artist in Treason: The Extraordinary Double Life of General James Wilkinson* (New York: Walker, 2009), 257–63; *Faithful Picture of the Political Situation of New Orleans, at the Close of the Last and the Beginning of the Present Year, 1807* (Boston: privately published, 1808), 48.

24. See *United States v. Workman*, United States District Court, Eastern District of Louisiana, 28 F. Cas. 771 (D. Orleans Terr. 1807); Washington, DC, *Monitor*, June 16, 1808; *Trials of Workman, and Kerr*, 97, 101–2, 103, 108, 121, 123–24, 164, 174, 178–79; Cooperstown, NY, *Otsego Herald*, May 7, 1807; Bradley, *Interim Appointment*, 391; Staunton, VA, *Staunton Eagle*, February 26, 1808.

25. Claiborne to Henry Dearborn, April 21, 1808, Carter, *Territorial Papers*, 784; Eligius Fromentin letter, January 28, 1815, Philadelphia, PA, *Relf's Philadelphia Gazette, and Daily Advertiser*, February 1, 1815.

26. Workman to Livingston, May 20, 1812, Livingston Papers, Princeton University Library, Princeton, NJ. Subsequent letters from Workman to Livingston place him in Havana as late as 1813.

27. Charleston, SC, *City Gazette*, May 22, 1812; Bradley, *Interim Appointment*, 424–33.

28. Lewis Kerr to Livingston, February 4, 1833, Livingston Papers, Princeton.

29. Walpole, NH, *Political Observatory*, March 14, 1808; Isaac Joslyn Cox, *The West Florida Controversy, 1798–1813: A Study in American Diplomacy* (Baltimore: Johns Hopkins University Press, 1918), 211. On August 3, 1833, an article appeared in the New York, NY, *New-York Commercial Advertiser* that mistakenly dated Moreau's visit to 1810, and then presented a story claiming that he rode south of the city to the site of the future 1815 battle, in company with Edward Livingston and a "French engineer" probably meant to be Arsène Latour or Henry Latrobe. As they came to the Rodriguez Canal, Moreau pointed to it and supposedly said: "There, should your city ever be threatened by invasion—there is the proper place for the line of defense." The story went on to say that in 1814 the engineer showed General Jackson the position Moreau had endorsed, and there Old Hickory established his defensive line. The article was presented entirely without source or authority, and is surely apocryphal. Bernard Marigny absorbed the story into his 1848 memoir, as did Vincent Nolte in 1854, again with no authority, and both almost certainly just reiterated the 1833 newspaper anecdote and local lore (Bernard de Marigny, *Reflections on General Andrew Jackson's Campaign in Louisiana in 1814 and 1815* [New Orleans: J. L. Sollée, 1848], 12; Nolte, *Memoirs*, 213). That there was prior local lore about Moreau seems probable from the fact that the earliest appearance of the basic story was in 1815 in "Naval Officer" to unknown recipient, January 30, 1815, *The Naval Chronicle, for 1815: Containing a General and Biographical History of the Royal Navy*, Vol. 33 (May), 388, and also in the St. George's, Bermuda, *Bermuda Gazette, and Weekly Advertiser*, April 15, 1815.

30. London, UK, *Public Ledger and Daily Advertiser*, February 6, 1809; Dublin, IR, *Saunders's News-Letter, and Daily Advertiser*, February 9, 1809.

31. Hereford, UK, *Hereford Journal*, February 15, 1809; Linklater, *An Artist in Treason*, 284–88.

32. See, for instance, James Monroe to Augustus John Foster, July 8, 1811, London, UK, *Cobbett's Weekly Political Register*, December 28, 1811.

33. London, UK, *Public Ledger and Daily Advertiser*, January 15, September 26, 1810.

34. London, UK, *Morning Chronicle*, January 25, 1811; Washington, DC, *National Intelligencer*, December 1, 1810.

35. Daniel Rasmussen, *American Uprising: The Untold Story of America's Largest Slave Revolt* (New York: Harper, 2011), 172.

36. London, UK, *Morning Post*, November 5, 1812.

37. W. A. Vaughan, "The Black Militia in the Battle of New Orleans" (MA thesis, University of Southern Mississippi, Hattiesburg, 1993), 1–4, 20, 27, 46, 48.

38. New Orleans, LA, *Louisiana Courier*, July 5, 1811; Rasmussen, *American Uprising*, 181.

39. Letter from New Orleans, August 4, 1812, London, UK, *Public Ledger and Daily Advertiser*, October 20, 1812.

40. Cochrane to Melville, April 27–28, 1812, Alexander F. I. Cochrane Papers and Correspondence, National Library of Scotland, Edinburgh.

41. London, UK, *Morning Chronicle*, September 5, 1812.

42. Warren to Viscount Melville, November 18, 1812, Warren draft of letter to the Lords of the Admiralty, February 21, 1813, Admiral Sir John Borlase Warren Papers, WAR/53, Caird Library, National Maritime Museum, Greenwich, London, UK.

43. Captain Sir James Lucas Yeo to Robert Saunders Dundas, Viscount Melville, First Lord of the Admiralty, "Observations Relative to New Orleans," February 19, 1813, Edward A. Parsons Collection, Briscoe Collection, University of Texas, Austin.

44. Richard K. Murdoch, "A British Report on West Florida and Louisiana, November, 1812," *Florida Historical Quarterly* 43, no. 1 (July 1964): 42–51.

45. Captain James Stirling Memorandum to Lord Viscount Melville, March 17, 1813, Historic New Orleans Collection, New Orleans, LA; Oxford, UK, *Oxford University and City Herald, and Midland County Chronicle*, March 27, 1813.

46. Robert Saunders Dundas, Viscount Melville, to Admiral Sir John Borlase Warren, March 23, 1813, War of 1812 Mss., Lilly Library, Indiana University, Bloomington. Robin Reilly, *The British at the Gates* (New York: Putnam, 1974), 161–62, maintains that the plan to invade New Orleans originated with Warren's November 1812 proposal. Frank Lawrence Owsley Jr., *Struggle for the Gulf Borderlands* (Gainesville, FL: University Presses of Florida, 1981), 96n, agrees that Cochrane must have been familiar with Warren's proposal, but unconvincingly suggests

without evidence that Bahamian governor Charles Cameron first conceived the scheme adopted by Cochrane.

47. London, UK, *Public Ledger and Daily Advertiser*, June 8, 1813.

48. Edinburgh, UK, *Caledonian Mercury*, March 22, 1813.

49. Albany, NY, *Albany Gazette*, March 13, 1815.

50. Fromentin to Livingston, August 4, 1814, James Brown to Livingston, October 3, 1814, January 9, 1815, Livingston Papers, Princeton.

51. Fromentin to Livingston, May 5, 1812, Livingston Papers, Princeton.

52. "Thoughts, Military and Political, Concerning the Ultramontane States and Territories, and the Importance of the Mississippi River, March 28, 1812," Wilkinson, *Memoirs*, 1:472–88.

53. William Darby to Wilkinson, April 28, 1816, Wilkinson, *Memoirs*, 1:505–7, 526–27.

54. Claiborne to Jackson, March 15, 1813, Dunbar Rowland, ed., *Official Letter Books of W. C. C. Claiborne 1801–1816* (Jackson, MS: Department of Archives and History, 1917): 214.

55. Ibid.

56. Ipswich, UK, *Suffolk Chronicle; or Weekly General Advertiser, and County Express*, 1812; London, UK, *Public Ledger and Daily Advertiser*, October 9, 1812.

57. Lieutenant Carter, "Relative to the Vulnerable Points, and Means of Defense at Orleans," January 26, 1813, William Jones Papers, Uselma Clarke Smith Collection, Historical Society of Pennsylvania, Philadelphia (HSP).

58. William James, *A Full and Correct Account of the Military Occurrences of the Late War Between Great Britain and the United States of America* (London: published by author, 1818), 2:341–42; Linklater, *An Artist in Treason*, 299–300; Donald R. Hickey, *Glorious Victory: Andrew Jackson and the Battle of New Orleans* (Baltimore: Johns Hopkins University Press, 2015), 85.

59. Claiborne to Louisiana senators, June 10, 1813, Rowland, Letter Books, 6:220–21, Claiborne to Fromentin, July 15, 1813, 241; Joseph Tennis Hatfield, "The Public Career of William C. C. Claiborne" (PhD dissertation, Emory University, Atlanta, GA, 1962), 397–99.

60. Thomas Flournoy to Claiborne, June 14, 1813, Rowland, *Letter Books*, 6:225.

61. Claiborne to Philemon Thomas, September 10, 1813, Ibid., 6:267.

62. Flournoy to Madison, October 6, 1813, Angela Kreider, J. C. A. Stagg, Jeanne Kerr Cross, Anne Mandeville Colony, Mary Parke Johnson, and Wendy Ellen Perry, eds., *The Papers of James Madison, Presidential Series*, vol. 6, *8 February–24 October 1813* (Charlottesville: University of Virginia Press, 2008), 676–680.

63. Claiborne to Shaumburg, October 1, 1815, Rowland, *Letter Books*, 6:369–70; David B. Morgan to William Shaler, January 14, 1814, Despatches from U. S. Consuls in Havana, Cuba, 1783–1906, M899, General Records of the Department of State, Record Group 59, National Archives, Washington, DC (NA).

64. Flournoy to Secretary of War Armstrong, January 31, 1814, Owsley, *Borderlands*, 128.

65. Claiborne to Jackson, August 8, 1814, John Reid and John Henry Eaton, *The Life of Andrew Jackson* (Philadelphia: M. Carey and Son, 1817), 411–12.

66. Dudley, "Pinchpenny Flotilla," 41.

67. John Shaw to Daniel T. Patterson, December 21, 1813, Henry Wood, "Memoir of Commodore John Shaw of the United States Navy," John Shaw Papers, Naval Historical Foundation Collection, Library of Congress, Washington, DC (LC).

68. Dudley, "Pinchpenny Flotilla," 41.

69. Daniel T. Patterson to Livingston, September 27, 1813, Edward Livingston Papers, Princeton.

70. London, UK, *Public Ledger and Daily Advertiser*, February 21, 1814; Flournoy to Claiborne, December 6, 1813, Rowland, *Letter Books*, 6:281; Mary Weatherspoon Bowden, comp., *Private Letters from Before, During and After the Battle of New Orleans as Printed in the Newspapers of the Time* (N.p.: privately published, 2014), 2.

71. Dudley, "Pinchpenny Flotilla," 41–42

72. Patterson to William Jones, July 8, 1814, Letters Received by the Secretary of the Navy from Captains ("Captains' Letters," 1805–1861, Record Group 260, NA.

73. Jackson to Claiborne, July 21, 1814, Harold D. Moser, David R. Hoth, Sharon Macpherson, and John H. Reinbold, eds., *The Papers of Andrew Jackson*, vol. 3, 1814–1815 (Knoxville: University of Tennessee Press, 1991), 91.

74. London, UK, *Courier, and Evening Gazette*, May 21, 1814; Hereford, UK, *Hereford Journal*, June 1, 1814; London, UK, *Public Ledger and Daily Advertiser*, June 14, 1813.

75. Baltimore, MD, *Niles' Weekly Register*, February 18, 1815. A more conservative statement said there were 100,000 bales worth $1 million in Louisiana and up to $4 million in Europe. Boston, MA, *New-England Palladium*, January 24, 1815. In 1855, forty-one years later, Richard Call maintained that speculators at Liverpool coveted the cotton stuck in New Orleans due to blockade, and that this was the impetus for Cochrane's expedition. No evidence supports that claim, but it is certainly possible that Cochrane or even the Admiralty had contact with one or more mercantile houses in Liverpool and hoped to profit by their buying what cotton Cochrane might capture (Pensacola, FL, *Pensacola Gazette*, February 24, 1855).

76. James A. Carr, "New Orleans and the Treaty of Ghent," *Diplomatic History* 3, no. 3 (July 1979), 278–79, develops this theme somewhat convincingly.

77. John K. Mahon, "British Command Decisions Relative to the Battle of New Orleans." *Louisiana History* 6, no. 1 (Winter 1965): 54–55.

78. In the British Navy of the time, the senior officer was designated Admiral of the Fleet, a fleet being composed of three squadrons. The front squadron was commanded by an Admiral of the Red, the center by an Admiral of the White, and the rear by an Admiral of the Blue.

79. Wellington to Charles Penrose, March 21, 1814, John Gurwood, ed., *The Dispatches of Field Marshal the Duke of Wellington* (London: John Murray, 1837–1838), 11:995, and Wellington to R. Hill, May 5, 1814, 12:2; Wellington to Earl of Longford [brother of Pakenham], May 22, 1815, "Letter of the Duke of Wellington (May 22, 1815) on the Battle of New Orleans," *Louisiana Historical Quarterly* 9, no. 1 (January 1926): 5–10.

80. Declaration of King George, n.d., WO 6/2, Kew.

81. John Henry Cooke, *A Narrative of Events in the South of France, and of the Attack on New Orleans, in 1814 and 1815* (London: T. & W. Boone, 1835), 178; J. W. Fortescue, A History of the British Army (London: Macmillan, 1906), 10:151, would maintain that Cochrane's motive was prize money, while John Buchan, *The History of the Royal Scots Fusiliers (1678–1918)* (London: Thomas Nelson, 1925), 174, said that "prize-money had for nearly two centuries been the motive for all amphibious operations recommended by the navy, and this of New Orleans was no exception." Both are eloquent on the subject, yet they wrote decades after the fact, offering no authority for their statements, and scarcely concealing their army officers' bias.

82. Cochrane to Pigot, March 27, 1814, Cochrane Papers, NLS; Owsley, *Borderlands*, 96.

83. Pigot to Cochrane, June 8, 1814, ADM 1/506, Cochrane to Croker, June 20, 1814, WO 1/142, Kew.

84. Robert V. Remini, *The Battle of New Orleans: Andrew Jackson and America's First Military Victory* (New York: Viking, 1999), 202 n17, suggests Cochrane adopted his plan based on Warren's and suggestions by Governor Charles Cameron of Nassau. Owsley, *Borderlands*, 96n, says this, too. Reilly, *British at the Gates*, 161–62, says Cochrane's plan to invade New Orleans originated with the Warren plan, November 1812. None of these authors provides contemporary documentation to establish these suppositions. And Cochrane clearly had New Orleans in mind since at least April 1812.

85. Cochrane to Croker, June 20, 1814, ADM 1/506, Kew.

86. Cochrane to Croker, September 2, 1814, WO 1/141, Bathurst to Lambert, March 30, 1815, WO 6/2, Kew.

87. George Laval Chesterton, *Peace, War, and Adventure: An Autobiographical Memoir of George Laval Chesterton* (London: Longman, Brown, Green, and Longmans, 1853), 2:213; Memorial of Edward Nicolls, May 1817, WO 1/144, Kew.

88. Cochrane to Nicolls, July 4, 1814, ADM 1/506, Memorial of Edward Nicolls to Lord Melville, n.d. [1817], 1/144, Kew.

89. Proclamation, July 1, 1814, WO 1/143, Kew.

90. Cochrane to Bathurst, July 14, 1814, ADM 1/506, Cochrane to Croker, July 14, 1814, WO 1/141, Kew.

91. Robert Saunders Dundas, Viscount Melville, to Cochrane, July 29, 1814, War of 1812 Mss., Lilly Library.

92. J. W. Croker Admiralty office to Cochrane, August 10, 1814, WO 1/141, Kew.

93. Wellington to Longford, May 22, 1815, "Letter of the Duke of Wellington," 5–10; Croker to Cochrane, "Secret & Confid'l," August 10, 1814, WO 6/2, Kew.

94. Pay List of the 5th West India Regiment of Foot, December 1814–March 1815, Infantry Abroad Quarterly Pay Lists for the 5th West India Regiment of Foot, WO 12/11538, Kew.

95. Bathurst to Ross, August 10, 1814, WO 6/2, Kew.
96. Cochrane to Dundas, September 17, 1814, War of 1812 Mss., Lilly Library.
97. Edward Pelham Brenton, *The Naval History of Great Britain, from the Year MDCCLXXXIII to MDCCCXXII* (London: C. Rice, 1825), 5:186, states that Cochrane originally wanted Bermuda or Barbados. Wilburt S. Brown, *The Amphibious Campaign for West Florida and Louisiana, 1814–1815* (Tuscaloosa: University of Alabama Press, 1969), 23, says Brenton knew Cochrane and other officers involved and got this information from them, making Brenton virtually a "primary source." On January 20, 1815, after the defeat at New Orleans, Cochrane wrote Melville that Bermuda or Barbados would have been the better rendezvous, or any of the Leeward Islands. Negril suggested an operation to its west. Moreover, going ashore at Port Royal, trying to get shallow-draft landing boats, also gave away their destination. This, of course, was perhaps a case of 20/20 hindsight. Cochrane to Robert Saunders Dundas, January 20, 1815, War of 1812 Mss., Lilly Library.
98. Brenton, *Naval History*, 2:530.
99. Edward Nicolls to Cochrane, July 27, 1814, Cochrane Papers, NLS. The Canterbury, UK, *Kentish Gazette*, October 28, 1814, ran a notice that "it is reported, also, that a disposition has been shewn by the people occupying the city and district of New Orleans, to favour our enterprises, in conjunction with our Allies the Spaniards in that quarter." Given the time it took news from America to reach the British press, the origin of this item had to date to late August, raising the possibility that it and stories like it could have come from Kerr's assurances that Nicolls passed to Cochrane.
100. Durham, UK, *Durham County Advertiser, and Commercial, and Agricultural, and Literary Journal*, October 29, 1814.
101. Letter from Havana, August 6, 1814, London, UK, *Courier, and Evening Gazette*, September 26, 1814; Nicolls to Cochrane, August 4, 1814, Cochrane Papers, NLS; Anonymous [Vincent Gray] to Jackson, August 13, 1814, Jackson Papers, LC.
102. The several letters by Vincent Gray cited hereafter vary as to when Nicolls departed Havana, one saying August 13 and another August 9, while another letter writer—perhaps also Gray—gave August 6. Letter from Havana, August 6, 1814, London, UK, *Courier, and Evening Gazette*, September 26, 1814.
103. Stephen Chambers, "No Country but Their Counting-Houses," in *Slavery's Capitalism: A New History of American Economic Development*, eds. Sven Beckert and Seth Rockman (Philadelphia: University of Pennsylvania Press, 2016), 195–208; Stephen Chambers, *No God but Gain: The Untold Story of Cuban Slavery, the Monroe Doctrine & the Making of the United States* (London: Verso, 2015), 74–75.
104. Anonymous [Vincent Gray] to unknown Louisiana recipient, August 8, 1814, Arsène Lacarrière Latour, *Historical Memoir of the War in West Florida and Louisiana in 1814–15* (Philadelphia: John Conrad and Co., 1816; new edition edited by Gene A. Smith, New Orleans: Historic New Orleans Collection, 1999), 184–85. The letter's assumption that the recipient is in a position to rouse the people of Louisiana and has the duty and authority to "save the state" points to Claiborne as the addressee.
105. Vincent Gray to Livingston, February 12, 1828, with enclosures of various dates, August–September 1814, Livingston Papers, Princeton; Vincent Gray to William Shaler, October 31, 1814, Shaler Family Papers, HSP; William S. Coker, "How General Andrew Jackson Learned of the British Plans Before the Battle of New Orleans," *Gulf Coast Historical Review* 3, no. 1 (Fall 1987): 89–91.
106. Woodbine to Cochrane, July 25, August 9, 1814, Cochrane Papers, NLS; William Percy to Cochrane, September 9, 1814, ADM 1/505, Kew.
107. Percy to Cochrane, September 9, 1814, ADM 1/505, Kew; Nicolls Proclamation, August 29, 1814, Reid and Eaton, *Jackson*, 401–3.

Chapter Two: "Bloody Noses There Will Be"

1. Cambridge, UK, *Cambridge Chronicle and Journal and Huntingdonshire Gazette*, November 5, 1813. As evidence of continuing interest in the Laffite operation, this same article appeared again six months later in the London, UK, *Courier, and Evening Gazette* of May 21, 1814.
2. Nolte, *Memoirs*, 207.

3. Deposition of Edward Williams, December 3, 1814, Patterson and Ross vs. Certain Goods Seized at Barataria, Case #0734, Entry 21, United States District Court for the Eastern Region of Louisiana, New Orleans, General Case Files, 1806–1932, Record Group 21, Records of District Courts of the United States, 1685–1993, National Archives, Southwest Region, Fort Worth, TX.

4. Nolte, *Memoirs*, 207.

5. Dublin, IR, Saunders's News-Letter, April 22, 1814. For more on this see Pam Keyes, "How Laffite Became the Real-Life Byronic Hero," *Laffite Society Chronicles* 13, no. 1 (February 2007), 19–22. Keyes states that the charitable incident in the poem "actually is about a little known incident that Byron read about," which unfortunately misinterprets Byron's explanation, in which he clearly stated: "That the point of honour which is represented in one instance of Conrad's character has not been carried beyond the bounds of probability may perhaps be in some degree confirmed by the following anecdote of a Brother Buccaneer in the present year 1814." In other words, the Laffite anecdote is an *example* of a pirate showing the kind of humanity shown by Byron's fictional Conrad, not the basis for it.

6. Boston, MA, *Boston Commercial Gazette*, April 25, 1814. The original New Orleans paper has not been found, but since this was published in Boston in April, allowing for the month it took for mail to reach the Northeast from Louisiana, it had to have appeared in March, and probably in the *Louisiana Gazette for the Country*.

7. New Orleans, *Louisiana Gazette for the Country*, August 18, 1814, in Schenectady, NY, *Cabinet*, November 23, 1814. The "dead men tell no tales" proverb had been in common use referring to pirates and criminals since at least 1732, and probably many years earlier (Newcastle, UK, *Newcastle Courant*, April 1, 1732). Archer Taylor, *The Proverb* (Cambridge, MA: Harvard University Press, 1931), 9, says without citing a source that it dates to Elizabethan times.

8. Edward Nicolls to Cochrane, July 27, 1814, Cochrane Papers, NLS.

9. Percy to Cochrane, September 9, 1814, ADM 1/505, Kew.

10. The wonderful phrase "played a deep game" comes from James, *Military Occurrences*, 341, which deserves the credit for it.

11. Jean Laffite to Claiborne, September 10, 1814, Parsons Collection, Texas.

12. For a fuller account of this episode, see William C. Davis, *The Pirates Laffite: The Treacherous World of the Corsairs of the Gulf* (New York: Harcourt, 2005), 165–80.

13. New Orleans, LA, *Louisiana Gazette*, June 29, 1814, in Georgetown, DC, *Federal Republican for the Country*, August 16, 1814.

14. Jackson to Claiborne, July 21, 1814, Moser et al., *Papers*, 91; Marietta, OH, *American Friend*, September 3, 1814; London, UK, *Courier, and Evening Gazette*, October 17, 1814.

15. Claiborne to Jackson, August 12, 1814, in Reid and Eaton, *Jackson*, 412–13; Vaughan, "Black Militia," 50.

16. Jackson to Claiborne, August 30, 1814, Moser et al., *Papers*, 126; Matthew S. Warshauer, "The Battle of New Orleans Reconsidered: Andrew Jackson and Martial Law," *Louisiana History* 39, no. 3 (Summer 1998): 263; Tom Kanon, *Tennesseans at War 1812–1815: Andrew Jackson, the Creek War, and the Battle of New Orleans* (Tuscaloosa: University of Alabama Press, 2014), 140.

17. Claiborne to Bartholomew Shaumburg, October 1, 1815, Rowland, *Letter Books*, 6:369; Jackson to Claiborne, July 21, 1814, Moser et al., *Papers*, 91; New Orleans, LA, *Louisiana Courier*, August 8, 24, 1814; Jacques Philippe Villeré to?, August 12, 1814, Jacques Philippe Villeré Papers, HNOC.

18. Hatfield, *Claiborne*, 408–9; Henry Palfrey to Gorham Palfrey, July 15, 1814, Frank Otto Gatell, ed., "Boston Boy in 'Mr. Madison's War,'" *Louisiana Historical Quarterly* 44, no. 3–4 (July–October 1961), 154.

19. Letter from New Orleans, August 19, 1814, New York, *New-York Gazette & General Advertiser*, September 13, 1814.

20. *A Century of Population Growth from the First Census of the United States to the Twelfth 1790–1900* (Washington, DC: Government Printing Office, 1909), 32; Hull, UK, *Advertiser and Exchange Gazette*, August 28, 1813. The 1810 census reported 359 newspapers published in the United States, and it is assumed that new ones began publication in the ensuing two years.

21. Winifred Gallagher, *How the Post Office Created America: A History* (New York: Penguin, 2016), 53, 56, 63–64.

22. Henry Palfrey to Gorham Palfrey, July 15, 1814: [154], Gatell, "Boston Boy in 'Mr. Madison's War,'" 154.

23. Reuben Beasley to Monroe, May 9, 1814, Bryce Wood, *Peaceful Change and the Colonial Problem*, Studies in History, Economics and Public Law (New York: Columbia University Press, 1940), 503.

24. Carr, "New Orleans and the Treaty of Ghent," 274; Melhorn, "What If the British Had Won?" 65.

25. Gallatin to Monroe, August 20, 1814, quoted in Kanon, *Tennesseans at War*, 139.

26. Jackson to Monroe, February 13, 1815, Daniel Parker Papers, HSP; Brown, *Amphibious Campaign*, 49–50, 195 n24; George T. Ross to Jackson, August 15, 1814, John Spencer Bassett, ed., *The Correspondence of Andrew Jackson* (Washington, DC: Carnegie Institution, 1926–35), 2:26–27.

27. General Orders, February 20, 1815, Order Book, Louisiana Militia, RG 107, Louisiana Historical Center, New Orleans.

28. Vaughan, "Black Militia," 54–55; Jackson to Rachel Jackson, August 23, 1814, Moser et al., *Papers*, 117.

29. Jackson to John Armstrong, August 27, 1814, Moser et al., *Papers*, 122–23.

30. Alexander Walker, *Jackson and New Orleans: An Authentic Narrative of the Memorable Achievements of the American Army, Under Andrew Jackson, Before New Orleans, in the Winter of 1814, '15* (New York: J. C. Derby, 1856), 45.

31. Francis Xavier Martin, *The History of Louisiana, from the Earliest Period* (New Orleans: Lyman & Beardslee, 1827–1829), 2:239.

32. Cross-examination of John Oliver, December 8, 1814, Case #0734, National Archives, Fort Worth.

33. Patterson to Robert Spedden, September 15, 1814, Cochrane Papers, NLS.

34. Patterson to W. Jones, Secretary of the Navy, October 10, 1814, New York, NY, *New-York Evening Post*, November 16, 1814; General Orders, February 20, 1815, Order Book, Louisiana Militia, RG 107, Louisiana Historical Center, New Orleans.

35. See Davis, *Pirates Laffite*, 190–93 for a more detailed account of the Patterson raid.

36. Jackson to Rachel Jackson, August 5, 1814, Moser et al., *Papers*, 105.

37. For good background on antebellum poor whites—who were not yet called that—which frames something of a word portrait of Jackson himself, though he was in many ways atypical—see Wayne Flint, *Dixie's Forgotten People: The South's Poor Whites* (Bloomington: Indiana State University Press, 1979), 15–32, 67.

38. Howard Jesko, "Louisiana's Unique Conditions and Andrew Jackson's Martial Law Declaration, 1814–1815" (MA thesis, Youngstown State University, Youngstown, OH, 2015), 46.

39. Mark R. Cheatham, "'I Owe to Britain a Debt of Retaliatory Vengeance': Assessing Andrew Jackson's Hatred of the British," in *The Battle of New Orleans in History and Memory*, ed. Laura Lyons McLemore (Baton Rouge: Louisiana State University Press, 2016), 50–51.

40. Jackson to Rachel Jackson, August 5, 1814, Moser et al., *Papers*, 105.

41. Jackson to Rachel Jackson, August 23, 1814, ibid., 117; Jackson to John Armstrong, August 25, 1814, ibid., 122.

42. Pensacola, FL, *Pensacola Gazette*, February 24, 1855, in Coker, "How General Andrew Jackson Learned," 92–93. Gray to Jackson, December 30, 1826 and February 14, 1827, identifies him as the letters' author, Jackson Papers, LC.

43. Jackson to John Reid, August 27, 1814, Moser et al., *Papers*, 124–25.

44. Jackson to Armstrong, August 27, 1814, ibid., 12324; Jackson to John Reid, August 27, 1814, Ibid., 125.

45. Jackson to Claiborne, August 30, 1814, ibid., 125–26; Warshauer, "Jackson and Martial Law," 263.

46. William Percy to Cochrane, September 9, 1814, ADM 1/505, Memorial of Edward Nicolls to Lord Melville, n.d. [1817], WO 1/144, Kew.

47. Nicolls to Cochrane, n.d. [Spring–Summer 1817], Cochrane Papers, NLS. This document appears identified as "Nicolls to Cochrane, Report, Aug. 12 to Nov. 17, 1814" in Owsley, *Borderlands*, but this is a misdating. The letter appears in Cochrane's letterbook following a letter dated March 13, 1816, and it mentions the April 1815 public controversy involving Cockburn taking runaway American slaves to Bermuda, and the arrest of Woodbine at New Providence, which occurred in the spring of 1817. A better date would be May 1817 or later. See also William Ellis's journal, which was taken from him September 22–23. Ellis was interviewed by Nicolls on September 19, arrested, and sent aboard a British ship on September 22 or 23, when his papers

and journal were taken from him. William Ellis Journal, September 19, 22–23, 1814, Baltimore, MD, *Baltimore Patriot & Evening Advertiser*, January 3, 1815.

48. Lord Melville to William Domett, July 23, 1814, Domett to Melville, July 26, 1814, WO 1/142, Kew.

49. Bathurst to Ross, July 30, August 10, 1814, WO 6/2, Croker to Cochrane, August 10, 1814, WO 1/141, Kew; Melville to Cochrane, July 29, 1814, War of 1812 Mss., Lilly Library.

50. Croker to Cochrane, August 10, 1814, Secret Letters, ADM 1/4360, Bathurst to Ross, September 6, 1814, WO 6/2, Kew.

51. Bathurst to Ross, September 10, 13, 1814, WO 6/2, J. C. Searle to George Barren, September 7, 1814, WO 1/142, Kew.

52. Croker to Cochrane, September 14, 1814, Secret Letters, ADM 1/4360, Kew.

53. Hereford, UK, *Hereford Journal*, June 1, 1814; London, UK, *Morning Chronicle*, September 26, 1814; London, UK, *Courier, and Evening Gazette*, September 26, 1814; Baltimore, MD, *American, and Commercial Daily Advertiser*, February 6, 1815. The details of the Castlereagh statement in the last cited newspaper are not entirely consistent with fact. It states that he said this to a French official while in Paris after learning of the fall of Washington. Castlereagh was in Paris only on August 27–28 while on his way to the opening of the Council of Vienna (Oxford, UK, *Oxford University and City Herald, and Midland County Chronicle*, September 3, 1814). News of the burning of Washington did not reach London until about September 24, a full month after Castlereagh's departure for the continent. Consequently, if he did in fact say this or something like it, he could not have done so earlier than about the end of September, by which time the news could have reached him in Vienna. The quotation appears in a careless variant in Walker, *Jackson and New Orleans*, 58, which is the version usually cited.

54. Elizabeth, Adelaide, and Sophia Gordon, comps., *Letters and Records of Admiral Sir J. Gordon G.C.B. 1782–1869* (London: privately printed, 1890), 43–44, 50–51, 50–58; Walker, *Jackson and New Orleans*, 91.

55. Brian Perrett, *The Real Hornblower: The Life & Times of Admiral Sir James Gordon* (Annapolis, MD: Naval Institute Press, 1998), 10–17, makes a good circumstantial case that Gordon served as the model for C. S. Forester's fictional character Captain Horatio Hornblower.

56. James Gordon to Lydia Gordon, August 12, 1814, Gordon, *Letters and Records*, 177–78.

57. Gordon to Lydia Gordon, September 16, 1814, Gordon, *Letters and Records*, 180, September 19, 1814, 181n.

58. Secret Memo to Capt. Gordon, n.d., Cochrane Papers, NLS. Gordon's mention of these instructions in his September 19, 1814, letter to his wife places an approximate date of September 17 or 18 on this document, since he did not mention them in his September 16 letter. Gordon, *Letters and Records*, 180–81 and n.

59. Gordon to Lydia Gordon, September 19, 1814, Gordon, *Letters and Records*, 181n.

60. Ibid., 183; Gordon Journal, September 30, 1814, 186, Gordon to Lydia Gordon, October 4, 1814, 190, October 23, 1814, 193.

61. Cambridge, UK, *Cambridge Chronicle and Journal and Huntingdonshire Gazette*, November 25, 1814; Alexander Dickson Journal, March 23, 1815, cited in Carson I. A. Ritchie, "The Louisiana Campaign," *Louisiana Historical Quarterly* 44, no. 1–2 (January–April 1961): 100–101.

62. Gordon to Lydia Gordon, November 14, 1814, Gordon, *Letters and Records*, 194.

63. Robert Butler to John Coffee, September 10, 1814, John Coffee Order Book, John Coffee Papers, SHC, UNC.

64. Coffee to Robert Dyer, September 11, 1814, Butler to Coffee, September 13, September 19, 1814, Coffee to Deputy QM at Nashville, September 17, 1814, Coffee Order Book, Coffee Papers, SHC, UNC.

65. Gordon to Lydia Gordon, November 14, 19, 1814, Gordon, *Letters and Records*, 194, 196.

66. Gordon Journal, November 30, 1814, Ibid., 213.

67. Cochrane to Malcolm, September 19, 1814, Cochrane to Cockburn, September 23, 1814, Cochrane to William Brown, September 19, 1814, Cochrane Papers, NLS.

68. Cochrane to George Cockburn, September 23, 1814, Cochrane Papers, NLS; Liverpool to Wellington, September 27, 1814, Arthur Richard Wellesley, 2nd Duke of Wellington, ed., *Supplementary Despatches, Correspondence, and Memoranda of Field Marshal Arthur Duke of Wellington* (London: John Murray, 1862): 9:290.

69. Owsley, *Borderlands*, 176, says that William Hambly provided information to the Americans but provides no source for the claim. Jackson (Jackson to Edmund Gaines, September 30, 1814,

Moser et al., *Papers*, 386) said that Hambly was in fact inciting Indians against the United States a year later, but by 1819 he would be described as "a renegade Englishman, who was himself the agent of Nicolls, a turncoat, a traitor to his own country" (Boston, MA, *Boston Daily Advertiser*, January 9, 1819). In December 1818 some Creek chiefs accused Hambly of being "the instrumental cause" of the fort at Prospect Bluff being destroyed (Boston, MA, *Boston Daily Advertiser*, December 11, 1818), and Jackson himself in 1819 called Hambly a man of "attachment to the American cause" (Savannah, GA, *Georgian*, January 6, 1819). The preponderance of evidence suggests that Hambly was, indeed, working against Nicolls and for the Americans.

70. Ellery, New Orleans, NYPL. While the authorship of this unsigned manuscript is open to interpretation, multiple points in it suggest Ellery himself. It states that it is "By a member of the Mississippi Society, K. R." The meaning of the "K. R." is unknown. The Mississippi Society for the Acquirement and Dissemination of Useful Knowledge was a club founded October 1803 in Natchez. The maps in "Notes" are annotated in the same hand as the "Notes" themselves, a hand that closely matches that on a map that Ellery unquestionably produced in 1803 for Alexander Hamilton during the Louisiana Purchase negotiations. (http://raremaps.com/gal lery/detail/45359/A_Sketch_of_the_River_Mississippi_from_New_Orleans_up_to_Natchez _copied/McGrudar-Ellery-Hamilton.html). Ellery, born May 22, 1773, in Newport, Rhode Island, had come to the territory at Hamilton's behest, and settled first at Natchez in the summer of 1803, a few months before the formation of the Mississippi Society. He remained until 1804, when he moved to New Orleans, where he practiced law for several years before moving to Bay St. Louis, in Hancock County, Mississippi, where he died of yellow fever November 1, 1820 (United States Census, Hancock County, Mississippi, 1820). The author of "Notes" also teasingly refers to Ellery's literary and critical skills, calling him the "Yankee Bard," and states that he would "only make use of the song as a convenient vehicle for our own notes." Finally, "Notes" includes two verses of the song that do not appear in any of the published versions, suggesting that "Notes" includes the original author's version before newspaper editors made conscious or inadvertent changes. All of these reasons combined strongly argue that Ellery was himself the author.

The date of composition of the "Notes" can be settled with some precision. While the writer says Ellery's song was first published January 19, 1815, its earliest known extant printing is in the New-York *Herald*, March 25, 1815, which states that it was copied from the "*New-Orleans Gazette.*" This must mean the New Orleans, LA, *Louisiana Gazette for the Country*. However, the *Louisiana Gazette* of February 2, 1815, as quoted in Philadelphia, PA, *Poulson's American Daily Advertiser*, March 8, 1815, says that it did not recommence publication until February 2, hence it was not in operation on January 19. Ellery died on November 1, 1820, and the writer spoke of him as living, so this was written no later than October 1820. This is further refined by the author's mention of William Garrow as "the present" British attorney-general. Garrow left that office on May 6, 1817. The author of "Notes" also quotes a Kingston, Jamaica, *Royal Gazette* article that was first published in the United States on March 23, 1815. Thus, the possible timespan for composition of "Notes" is established at March 1815–May 1817.

71. Owsley, *Borderlands*, 176.

72. Talcott and Bowers to?, September 5, 1814, Kanon, *Tennesseans at War*, 140.

73. Claiborne to Nicholas Girod, September 8, 1814, Parsons Collection, Texas.

74. Claiborne to Jackson, September 8, 1814, Reid and Eaton, *Jackson*, 413; Claiborne to Isaac Shelby, September 8, 1814, War of 1812 Mss., Lilly Library.

75. Resolution, September 14, 1814, New Orleans Municipal Records, Series II Legal Papers, 1767–1898, Subseries 1, Resolutions and Ordinances, 1767–1846, LSU.

76. General Orders to militia, September 8, 1814, James A. Padgett, ed., "The Difficulties of Andrew Jackson in New Orleans, Including His Later Dispute with Fulwar Skipwith," *Louisiana Historical Quarterly* 21, no. 2 (April 1938): 372–74; David Burford to John Armstrong, September 8, 1814, David Burford Papers, University of Tennessee Special Collections, Knoxville; St. Francisville, LA, *Time-Piece*, September 8, 15, 1814; Letter from St. Francisville, September 22, 1814, Boston, MA, *New-England Palladium*, November 8, 1814.

77. William Kenner to Stephen Minor, September 9, 10, 1814, William Kenner Papers, Louisiana and Lower Mississippi Valley Collection, Louisiana State University, Baton Rouge.

78. Letter from commercial house in New Orleans to Philadelphia, September 15, 1814, Philadelphia, PA, *Democratic Press*, October 14, 1814.

79. Sparks, *The Memories of Fifty Years*, 453–55.

80. William Cabell Bruce, *John Randolph of Roanoke, 1773–1833* (New York: Putnam's, 1922), 2:197. This is the earliest known form of the saying, which in later years evolved into: "He is a man of splendid abilities, but utterly corrupt. He shines and stinks like rotten mackerel by moonlight." Robert V. Remini, *Henry Clay: Statesman for the Union* (New York: W. W. Norton, 1991), 83 and note, deals with the resilient myth that Randolph said this about Clay. He actually said it about Livingston in 1832, and at that Remini suggests that the story may be apocryphal. Its earliest known appearance in print was in the Richmond, VA, *Whig and Public Advertiser* in March 1833, which did not say where or when Randolph made the witticism, or at whom it was directed, but stated positively that it was not Clay (Washington, DC, *United States' Telegraph*, April 1, 1833). Within a few months, however, the press began linking the saying with Clay.

81. Benjamin Henry Boneval Latrobe, *Impressions Respecting New Orleans: Diary and Sketches, 1818–1820* (New York: Columbia University Press, 1951), 25.

82. New Orleans, LA, *Louisiana Gazette and New Orleans Daily Advertiser*, September 20, 24, 1814.

83. Subscription list, Livingston, Destrehan, Foucher, Delacroix, B. Morgan, W. Montgomery, William Nott, Bouligny, n.d. [1814], Livingston Papers, Princeton.

84. Committee of Safety to Jackson, September 18, 1814, Bassett, *Correspondence*, 2:51–54; Sidney Louis Villeré, Jacques Philippe Villeré, First Native-Born Governor of Louisiana 1816–1830 (New Orleans: Historic New Orleans Collection, 1981), 4143.

85. Villeré to Philippon, Toutant and Allard, September 20, 1814, Toutant to Villeré, September 21, 1814, Villeré Papers, HNOC; Claiborne to Alexander Declouet, September 19, 1814, David Rees Papers, Tulane; Claiborne to Villeré, September 19, 1814, De La Vergne Family Papers, Tulane.

86. Public Security Measures adopted by the Inhabitants of the 1st Senatorial District, September 23, 1814, Allard to Villeré, September 22, 1814, Villeré Papers, HNOC.

87. J. Henry Lüdeling to Livingston, December 4, 1814, Livingston Papers, Princeton.

88. Statement, n.d. [September 1814], Villeré Papers, HNOC.

89. Claiborne to Madison, September 22, 1814, Kreider et al., *Papers of James Madison*, 8:234–35; Claiborne to Jackson, September 19, 1814, Reid and Eaton, *Jackson*, 414.

90. Stephen A. Hopkins to Villeré, August 15, 1814, Villeré Papers, HNOC.

91. Jackson to Monroe, February 13, 1815, Parker Papers, HSP; Gene A. Smith, *The Slaves' Gamble: Choosing Sides in the War of 1812* (New York: Palgrave Macmillan, 2013), 161.

92. Letter from New Orleans, October 3, 1814, New Haven, CT, *Columbian Register*, November 15, 1814; Michael J. Edwards, "A 'Melancholy Experience': William C. C. Claiborne and the Louisiana Militia, 1811–1815" (MA thesis, University of New Orleans, 2011), 30–31, 86–87; Claiborne to Shaumburg, October 1, 1815, Rowland, *Letter Books*, 6:370.

93. Walker, *Jackson and New Orleans*, 72–73.

94. James Parton, *A Life of Andrew Jackson* (New York: Mason Brothers, 1860), 2:22.

95. Monroe to Jackson, September 7, 1814, Moser et al., *Papers*, 128; Coker, "How General Andrew Jackson Learned," 90–91.

96. Jackson to Rachel Jackson, October 10, 1814, Moser et al., *Papers*, 465.

97. Pierre L. Duplessis to Jackson, October 17, 1814, Moser et al., *Papers*, 467.

98. Shaumburg to Claiborne, October 30, 1815, Rowland, *Letter Books*, 6:375; Jackson to Monroe, October 10, 1814, Moser et al., *Papers*, 155. Context suggests that Shaumburg saw Jackson on or about October 10.

99. New York, NY, *Columbian*, November 28, 1814; Anderson Chenault Quisenberry, *Kentucky in the War of 1812* (Frankfort: Kentucky Historical Society, 1915), 135.

100. Letters Received by the Adjutant General's Office During the Period 1805–1821, RG 94, NA; London, UK, *Morning Advertiser*, November 7, 1839.

101. Jefferson to Isham Lewis, May 1, 1809, J. Jefferson Looney, ed., *The Papers of Thomas Jefferson, Retirement Series, Vol. 1, 4 March 1809 to 15 November 1809* (Princeton, NJ: Princeton University Press, 2004), 181–82.

102. George Romford to Monroe, February 4, 1815, Washington, DC, *National Intelligencer*, February 16, 1815.

103. Charles Wollstonecraft to?, August 5, 1814, Jackson Papers, LC.

104. Baltimore, MD, *American, and Commercial Daily Advertiser*, December 19, 1814.

105. Claiborne to Jackson, October 17, 1814, Bassett, *Correspondence*, 2:76; New Orleans, LA, *Louisiana Gazette and New Orleans Daily Advertiser*, October 18, 1814.

106. Andrew Jackson, Proclamation, September 21, 1814, Latour, *Historical Memoir*, 204–5.

107. New Orleans, LA, *Louisiana Gazette and New Orleans Daily Advertiser*, October 20, 1814.

108. Jean Laffite to Livingston, October 4, 1814, Livingston Papers, Princeton.

109. Livingston to Madison, October 24, 1814, Kreider et al., *Papers of James Madison*, 8:321.

110. Manchester, UK, *Manchester Mercury, and Harrop's General Advertiser*, October 18, 1814.

111. Villeré to Eligius Fromentin, October 19, 1814, Villeré Papers, HNOC.

112. Villeré to Thomas B. Robertson, October 19, 1814, Villeré Papers, HNOC; Robertson to Villeré, November 19, 1814, De La Vergne Family Papers, Tulane.

113. Nolte, *Memoirs*, 199–201. Nolte, as always, is to be taken advisedly, but his account seems credible.

114. Kenner to Stephen Minor, October 21, 1814, Kenner Papers, LSU.

115. October 22, 1814. Receipt, October 22, 1814, New Orleans Municipal Records, LSU.

116. Claiborne to Fromentin, October 24, 1814, Rowland, *Letter Books*, 6:285–86, Claiborne to Monroe, October 25, 1814, 290.

117. Claiborne to Jackson, October 17, 1814, Bassett, *Correspondence*, 2:76.

118. Proclamation, September 21, 1814, Latour, *Historical Memoir*, 205–6.

119. Jackson to Monroe, February 13, 1815, Parker Papers, HSP.

120. Gelpi, "In Defense of Liberty," 101–2; Walker, *Jackson and New Orleans*, 74–75.

121. Claiborne to Jackson, October 28, 1814, Rowland, *Letter Books*, 6:297–98.

122. Monroe to Jackson, September 27, 1814, Moser et al., *Papers*, 149.

123. Jackson to Monroe, October 23, 1814, Moser et al., *Papers*, 173.

124. Harry Toulmin to Willie Blount, October 25, 1814, Alexandria, VA, *Alexandria Gazette*, December 17, 1814.

125. The information in Jackson's subsequently cited letters is virtually identical to that contained in the reports that Monroe received on October 8, and must have come from the same source, though who sent it to him is unknown. In a letter to William Carroll of October 31, Jackson referred to having received "news from abroad." Moser et al., *Papers*, 175.

126. Jackson to Peter Early, October 31, 1814, War of 1812 Mss., Lilly Library.

127. Jackson to William Carroll, October 31, 1814, Moser et al., *Papers*, 175.

128. Letters dated October 31, 1814, in Bassett, *Correspondence*, 2:85–88, and Jackson Papers, LC.

129. Claiborne to Jackson, November 4, 1814, Moser et al., *Papers*, 177. Claiborne did not identify the source of his news, but he referred to it as a "paper," and in a letter that same day to William McRae he referred to it as "the News of the Morning." Rowland, *Letter Books*, 6:309. The Eastern press was full of letters and articles about the British terms from early October on, and he could have seen any of a number of them that arrived in that day's mail.

130. Claiborne to McRae, November 4, 1814, Rowland, *Letter Books*, 6:309, Claiborne to Jackson, November 5, 1814, 6:310–11.

131. *Petition of John Hudry, of Louisiana, Praying Remuneration for Services and Advances Made for the Defence of New Orleans in 1814, '15* (Washington, DC: 23rd Congress, 1st Session, 1834), 1.

132. Claiborne to Jackson, November 4, 1814, Rowland, *Letter Books*, 6:308.

133. Concord, NH, *New Hampshire Patriot and State Gazette*, December 20, 1814.

134. Claiborne to Jackson, November 4, 1814, Moser et al., *Papers*, 177.

135. Receipt, November 15, 1814, New Orleans Municipal Records, LSU.

136. Letter from St. Francisville to Baltimore, November 20, 1814, Baltimore, MD, *American, and Commercial Daily Advertiser*, January 4, 1815; Claiborne to Charles Tessier, October 30, 1815, Miscellaneous Collection, LSU.

137. Claiborne to Jackson, November 17, 1814, Rowland, *Letter Books*, 6:314–15, Claiborne to Blount, Nov. 18, 1814, 6:316.

138. Pierre-Joseph Favrot, Memorandum Concerning Louisiana Defenses, November 19, 1814, Tulane.

139. Parton, *Jackson*, 2:22.

140. Walker, *Jackson and New Orleans*, 72–73.

141. Kenner to Minor, November 4, 11, 18, 1814, Kenner Papers, LSU; Statement, n.d. [1818 or later], Villeré Papers, HNOC.

142. Jackson to Claiborne, October 31, 1814, Rowland, *Letter Books*, 6:312.

143. Jackson to Blount, November 14, 1814, Windsor, VT, *Vermont Republican*, January 9, 1815.

144. Jackson to Monroe, November 14, 1814, Bassett, *Correspondence*, 2:96–99; Jackson to Blount, November 14, 1814, Moser et al., *Papers*, 184–85, Jackson to Rachel Jackson, November 15, 1814, 186–87, November 17, 1815, 190.

145. Bartholomew Shaumburg to James Wilkinson, January 25, 1815, HNOC.

146. Jackson to Monroe, November 20, 1814, Moser et al., *Papers*, 192.

147. Jackson to Rachel Jackson, November 21, 1814, ibid., 195.

148. Coffee to Contractor's Agent, Fort Montgomery Boat Yard, November 11, 18, 1814, Coffee Order Book, SHC, UNC.

149. Howard T. Weir, III, *A Paradise of Blood: The Creek War of 1813–1814* (Yardley, PA: Westholme, 2016), 282–83, 494–95n; Augusta, GA, *Augusta Chronicle and Georgia Advertiser*, July 8, 1829; Danville, VT, *North Star*, June 22, 1830.

150. William McIntosh to Early, December 12, 1814, Poughkeepsie, NY, *Poughkeepsie Journal*, January 4, 1815; D. O. Dunham to Francis LeBaron, December 2, 1814, Albany, NY, *Albany Gazette*, January 9, 1815. Dunham's letter appears to be in response to Jackson's November 16 letter to McIntosh, Jackson Papers, LC.

151. "Sketch of a Tour of Service in Louisiana and of the Battle of New Orleans, by One of the 'Hunters of Kentucky,'" Louisville, KY, *Louisville Daily Democrat*, March 18, 1846; Lexington, KY, *Western Monitor*, November 25, 1814; Quisenberry, Kentucky in the War of 1812, 134–35; William Blair, *Sketch of the Life and Military Services of General John Adair, Written Principally in 1820 by Judge William Blair, and Continued to the Present Time by A Friend* (Harrodsburg, KY: *Harrodsburg American*, 1831), 12–13.

152. Carroll to?, October 21, 1814, MSS 211, William Carroll Letters, HNOC; Nashville, TN, *Clarion*, November 1, 1814; Broadside from the Nashville, TN, *Nashville Examiner*, November 2, 1814, extra, Andrew Jackson Materials, Additions, Tennessee State Library and Archives, Nashville; Andrew Hynes to Carroll, November 24, 1814, Hynes Papers, Tulane; William Priestley to Latour, March 4, 1816, Arsène Lacarrière Latour Archive, HNOC. In April 1815 Latour wrote to Carroll asking for his recollection of the New Orleans campaign. This document is Priestley's answer, which he titled "A Sketch of the part Major General William Carroll and Division bore in the late Expedition to New Orleans 1814–15."

153. Romford to Monroe, February 4, 1815, Washington, DC, *National Intelligencer*, February 16, 1815; Monroe to George Graham, January 12, February 5, 1827, Graham Family Papers, VHS; Washington, DC, *United States' Telegraph*, December 5, 1826.

154. Letter from New Orleans to Richmond, VA, November 26, 1814, Petersburg, VA, *Petersburg Daily Courier*, January 3, 1815; Letter from New Orleans, November 28, 1814, New Haven, CT, *Connecticut Journal*, January 10, 1815; Letter from New Orleans, November 30, 1814, Richmond, VA, *Richmond Enquirer*, January 3, 1815.

155. Letter from New Orleans, November 25, 1814, New York, NY, *New-York Mercantile Advertiser*, January 7, 1815.

156. See, for instance, Paris, KY, *Western Citizen*, November 11, 12, 26, 1814, Lexington, KY, *Western Monitor*, November 25, December 2, 1814, and Hartford, CT, *Connecticut Herald*, September 25, 1814.

157. Washington, DC, *Reporter*, October 17, 1814.

158. Carr, "New Orleans and the Treaty of Ghent," 274.

159. Jackson to Monroe, February 13, 1815, Parker Papers, HSP; John Spencer Bassett, ed., *Major Howell Tatum's Journal* (Northampton, MA: Department of History of Smith College, 1922), November 24–29, 1814, 91–95. Here as elsewhere some of Tatum's account is done from memory, probably based on semi-daily notes.

160. Bassett, *Tatum's Journal*, November 30, 1814, 96.

CHAPTER THREE: "BY THE GODS I THINK YOU WILL HAVE WARM WORK"

1. Port Royal, Jamaica, *Gazette*, November 5, 1814.

2. Robert Aitchison Memoir, ca. 1857, MSS 186, 59–60, HNOC. This has been published, edited by Gene A. Smith, as *A British Eyewitness at the Battle of New Orleans: The Memoir of Royal Navy Admiral Robert Aitchison, 1808–1827* (New Orleans: Historic New Orleans Collection, 2004). The original manuscript has been cited and quoted here to use Aitchison's original style.

3. Jane Bourchier, ed., *Memoir of the Life of Admiral Sir Edward Codrington, With Selections from His Public and Private Correspondence* (London: Longmans, Green, and Co., 1873), 1:1; Walker, *Jackson and New Orleans*, 91; Codrington to Jane Codrington, October 14–November 4, 1814, Edward Codrington Papers, COD/6/2, Caird.

4. Codrington to Jane Codrington, October 14–November 4, 1814, Edward Codrington Papers, COD/6/2, Caird.

5. Cochrane to Commanders of H. M. Ships & Vessels, November 3, 1814, Cochrane to James Leith, November 3, 1814, Cochrane Papers, NLS; Cochrane to Dundas, November 10, 1814, War of 1812 Mss., Lilly Library; Alexander F. I. Cochrane Journal, November 4, 1814, ADM 50/122, Kew.

6. Codrington to Jane Codrington, October 14–November 4, 1814, Codrington Papers, COD/6/2, Caird.

7. Ipswich, UK, *Suffolk Chronicle; Or, Weekly General Advertiser, and County Express*, November 12, 1814; Cochrane to Croker, December 7, 1814, ADM 1/508, Kew. Langford's name was sometimes spelled Laingford.

8. Cochrane Journal, November 11, 1814, ADM 50/122, Kew.

9. Wellington to Liverpool, November 9, 1814, Gurwood, *Dispatches of Field Marshal the Duke of Wellington*, 9:406.

10. Cochrane Journal, November 18, 19, 22, 1814, ADM 50/122, Kew.

11. Cochrane to William Brown, September 19, 1814, Cochrane Papers, NLS.

12. William Fothergill to James Bremer, October 8, 1814, ibid.

13. St. George's, Bermuda, *Bermuda Gazette, and Weekly Advertiser*, April 15, 1815; Port Royal, Jamaica, *Gazette*, November 5, 1814.

14. Samantha A. Cavell, "Cochrane's Grand Southern Strategy," in *The Battle of New Orleans Reconsidered*, ed. Curtis Manning (New Orleans: Louisiana Institute of Higher Education, 2014), 261 n72; United States Census, Orleans Parish, Louisiana, 1810; New Orleans, LA, *Louisiana State Gazette*, May 30, 1815; Paul E. Hoffman, *Florida's Frontiers* (Bloomington: Indiana University Press, 2002), 234; Thomas H. Whitney, *Whitney's New-Orleans Directory, and Louisiana & Mississippi Almanac for the Year 1811* (New Orleans: printed by author, 1810), 27; Cochrane to John Croker, December 7, 1814, ADM 1/508; St. George's, Bermuda, *Bermuda Gazette, and Weekly Advertiser*, April 15, 1815. A month after Cochrane learned of the leak, he believed John that Hudson got his news to Jackson "a few days" after Jackson captured Pensacola on November 7. He did not explain how he learned this, and it has to be considered hearsay that he picked up after anchoring off Pensacola on December 5. Still, in outline it seems possible, even probable. Since Hudson left Kingston prior to Cochrane's November 18 arrival, the admiral had no way of knowing firsthand Hudson's immediate destination. Allowing a generous three weeks for passage from the Chesapeake, Cochrane's dispatches surely reached Jamaica no later than the second week of October. If only one day passed from their arrival until Hudson's departure, then he left Kingston October 9 or 10, which should have put him on the Gulf Coast before November 1, when Jackson was camped about forty miles northwest of Pensacola, preparing to march against it. Cochrane's report can be read to say that Hudson landed first at Spanish-held Pensacola and then sailed to New Orleans, from which he sent his news via messenger to Jackson. Since any message took about ten days to travel overland from New Orleans to Pensacola—news of its November 7 fall did not reach New Orleans until November 17—anything Hudson sent Jackson would have arrived after he occupied the town (Claiborne to Jackson, November 18, 1814, Rowland, *Letter Books*, 6:316). Thus, it is evident that this "leak" had no impact or influence except in Cochrane's imagination and perhaps as an excuse, though as of December 7 he had no need yet for excuses. Jackson already knew enough from other sources what Cochrane intended to do (Jackson to Monroe, October 10, 1814, Moser et al., *Papers*, 155).

15. "Naval Officer" to unknown recipient, January 30, 1815, *Naval Chronicle, for 1815*, vol. 33 (June 1815), 388; Kingston, Jamaica, *Royal Gazette*, February 3, 9, 1815; Cochrane to Dundas, January 20, 1815, War of 1812 Mss., Lilly Library. Seventy years later A. B. Ellis of the 1st West India Regiment, obviously not a contemporary or eyewitness to the event, wrote: "The treachery of an official in the garrison office at Jamaica enabled them [Jackson] to receive positive information as to the aim and destination of the expedition. This official communicated the intelligence to an American trader residing in Kingston, and the latter at once sailed in a coasting schooner for Pensacola." A. B. Ellis, *The History of the First West India Regiment* (London: Chapman and Hall, 1885), 142.

16. Gleig to Mary Gleig Sutton, November 4, 1814, George R. Gleig Papers, NLS.
17. Benson Earle Hill, *Recollections of an Artillery Officer: Including Scenes and Adventures in Ireland, America, Flanders and France* (London: Richard Bentley, 1836), 1:295.
18. Cochrane Journal, November 19, 1814, ADM 50/122, Kew.
19. Cochrane Journal, November 19–23, 1814, ADM 50/122, Kew.
20. Return of Slaves in the Parish of Trelawney in the possession of Mark Trumbull as Attorney to Jasper McCalden Graham, 1817, Office of Registry of Colonial Slaves and Slave Compensation Commission, Kew; Goshen, NY, *Orange Farmer*, May 13, 1822; Hartford, CT, *Connecticut Courant*, March 20, 1841; New York, NY, *Morning Herald*, October 27, 1837.
21. Jasper Graham to Arthur Brooke, November 21, December 10, 1814, Graham to Cochrane and John Keane, November 25, December 10, 1814, Graham to Bathurst, April 20, 1815, WO 1/143, Kew.
22. Graham to Brooke, November 17, 18, 1814, ibid.; Moser et al., *Papers*, 127–28, 155. A comparison of Graham's November 18, 1814, report of artillery and an official War Department statement (George Romford to Monroe, February 4, 1815, Washington, DC, *National Intelligencer*, February 16, 1815) dated October 1, 1814, shows a considerable disparity:

Fort	Graham	War Department
St. Philip	58 42-pdrs	28 24-pdrs, 2 howitzers, 1 13-inch mortar
Petite Coquilles	20 various	9 18- and 24-pdrs
St. John	15–20 small caliber	4 9-pdrs
New Orleans	—	55 of varying size

23. Jasper Graham, "Observations Naval and Military for the Benefit of the Commanders of His Britannic Majesty's Forces Destined for the Reduction of Louisiana," November 18, 1814, WO 1/143, Kew. The actual armament of the forts appears in Romford to Monroe, February 4, 1815, Washington, DC, *National Intelligencer*, February 16, 1815.
24. Graham was apparently guessing in his exaggerated statements of armament in the forts protecting the city, but his description of the forts themselves and of the country suggests a fair degree of firsthand observation.
25. Notation on Graham to Brooke, November 18, 1814, WO 1/143, Kew.
26. Cochrane Journal, November 23, 25, 1814, ADM 50/122, Kew; Codrington to Jane Codrington, November 23–December 31, 1814, Codrington Papers, COD/6/2, Caird.
27. Edinburgh, UK, *Caledonian Mercury*, January 5, 1815.
28. Arthur Gerard, "Campaigns of A British Officer in Europe & America Giving a particular account of the British Operations in the United States In 1814 & 1815," 2, Nimitz Library, United States Naval Academy, Annapolis, MD.
29. London, UK, *Courier, and Evening Gazette*, March 7, 1815; R. Gubbins to unknown addressee, August 31, 1814, C. R. B. Barrett, *The 85th King's Light Infantry (Now 2nd Battalion, the King's Shropshire Light Infantry)* by "One of Them" (London: Spottiswoode, 1913), 152.
30. London, UK, *Times*, September 28, October 18, 1814; London, UK, *Morning Chronicle*, February 4, 1823.
31. London, UK, *Morning Chronicle*, September 28, 1814.
32. London, UK, *Public Ledger and Daily Advertiser*, October 18, 1814.
33. *General and Biographical History of the British Royal Navy*, vol. 32 (London: J. Gold, 1814), August 24, 1814; James Clark, *Historical Record and Regimental Memoir of the Royal Scots Fusiliers, Formerly Known as the 21st Royal North British Fusiliers* (Edinburgh: Banks & Co., 1885), 39, 114. This history of his own unit reported him killed at Bladensburg despite his celebrated death at New Orleans months later.
34. On November 18, during the voyage, Malcolm shifted his flag to white. Memorandum Book, Pultney Malcolm Papers, MAL/104, Caird.
35. Charles Dalton, *The Waterloo Roll Call, with Biographical Notes and Anecdotes* (London: Eyre and Spottiswoode, 1904), 19–20.
36. Barrett, *85th King's Light Infantry*, 113.
37. Gleig to Margaret Gleig, October 22, 1814, Gleig Papers, NLS.
38. George Robert Gleig, *A Narrative of the Campaigns of the British Army at Washington and New Orleans, Under Generals Ross, Pakenham, and Lambert, in the Years 1814 and 1815* (London: John Murray, 1821), 217–19.
39. Walker, *Jackson and New Orleans*, 94.

40. Buchan, *Royal Scots Fusiliers*, 174.

41. Ibid., 227–28.

42. Chesterton, *Peace, War, and Adventure*, 1:176; Gerard, Campaigns 2, USNA; Gleig, *Narrative*, 226; Gleig to Hamilton Gleig, November 10, 1814, Gleig Papers, NLS. Ensign Gerard served in the 4th Foot. While his "memoir" includes what are clearly diary entries, internal evidence establishes that the complete document was compiled no earlier than 1821.

43. "Recollections of the Expedition to the Chesapeake, and Against New Orleans, in the Years 1814–15. No. III. By an Old Sub," *United Service Journal and Naval and Military Magazine* 33, no. 139 (June 1840): 183–84. The author, who was clearly a junior officer in the 4th, 44th, or 85th, cannot be identified. After the passage of twenty-six years, his memory of dates was faulty, but in other respects quite precise.

44. George R. Gleig Diary, November 14–16, 1814, Barrett, *85th King's Light Infantry*, 192–93; Gerard, Campaigns 2, USNA. No diary of Gleig's is to be found in his papers at the National Library of Scotland, and its existence is established only by the several extracts that Barrett includes. Gleig's son Colonel A. C. Gleig loaned the diary to Barrett in the early 1900's as he prepared his book, and apparently it disappeared thereafter.

45. Gleig Diary, November 19, 1814, Barrett, *85th King's Light Infantry*, 193; Gerard, Campaigns 2, USNA.

46. Gleig Diary, November 22, 1814, Barrett, *85th King's Light Infantry*, 193–94.

47. Hill, *Recollections*, 1:295–97.

48. Lord Hill to John Burgoyne, August 9, 1814, George Wrottesley, *Life and Correspondence of Field Marshal Sir John Burgoyne, Bart.* (London: Richard Bentley and Son, 1873), 1:298.

49. Bunbery to Cochrane, August 14, 17, 1814, WO 6/2, Kew.

50. Return of Clothing and Equipments, September 1, 1814, WO 1/142, Kew.

51. Abstract of Brass Ordnance, Small Arms, Ammunition, Rockets and Swords shipped at Portsmouth . . . for a particular service, September 2, 1814, WO 1/142, Kew.

52. Roderick Hamilton Burgoyne, *Historical Records of the 93rd Sutherland Highlanders* (London: Richard Bentley & Son, 1883), 25.

53. Walker, *Jackson and New Orleans*, 78–79; Londonderry, IR, *Londonderry Sentinel and North-West Advertiser*, June 21, 1834.

54. Charles Ramus Forrest, *The Battle of New Orleans: A British View; The Journal of Major C. R. Forrest, Asst. QM General, 34th Regiment of Foot* (New Orleans: Hauser Press, 1961), November 25, 1814, 24.

55. H. S. Bunbery to Keane, September 12, 1814, WO 6/2, Kew.

56. Ibid.

57. Lords of the Admiralty to James Walker, September 14, 1814, ADM 1/4360; William Surtees, *Twenty-Five Years in the Rifle Brigade* (London: Greenhill, 1996), 331.

58. Burgoyne, *93rd Sutherland Highlanders*, 26; Letter from Barbados, November 7, 1814, Lexington, KY, *Reporter*, February 13, 1815.

59. Letter from Barbados, November 7, 1814, Lexington, KY, *Reporter*, February 13, 1815; Letter from Barbados, November 7, 1814, Norfolk, VA, *Norfolk Gazette & Publick Ledger*, January 14, 1815; Unnamed Barbados newspaper, November 9, 1814, in Pittsfield, MA, *Sun*, February 9, 1815; Letter from Barbados, November 9, 1814, London, UK, *Morning Post*, January 6, 1815.

60. Letter from St. Bart's to Baltimore, November 12, 1814, Dayton, OH, *Ohio Republican*, January 2, 1815.

61. Letter from Barbados, November 9, 1814, London, UK, *Morning Post*, January 6, 1815.

62. Forrest, *Battle of New Orleans*, November 25, 1814, 23. Forrest was Assistant Quartermaster General of the expeditionary army. There are many variant copies of the narrative, including Charles Ramus Forrest, "Journal of the movements of the Army acting on the Southern part of the North American Coast," Memorandum Book, 1814–1815, Pultney Malcolm Papers, MAL/104, Caird; two copies in the Alexander Cochrane Collection, 1807–1815, New-York Historical Society; and another in the John Peddie Letter and Enclosures, William L. Clements Library, University of Michigan, Ann Arbor. It has also been published as cited above, and as Charles R. Forrest, "Journal of the Operations Against New Orleans in 1814 and 1815," *Louisiana Historical Quarterly* 44 (January–April 1961). Unless otherwise cited, all references are taken from the published book edition.

63. Forrest, *Journal*, November 25, 1814, 24.

64. General Monthly Return of the Serjeants, Trumpeters, Drummers, and Rank and File belonging to the several Regiments Composing the Army employed on a Particular Service under the Command of Major General John Keane, November 25, 1814, WO 17/1218, Kew.

65. John James Knox to unknown addressee, November 23 [25], 1814, Barrett, *85th King's Light Infantry*, 153. This letter is headed "Jamaica" and dated November 23, but the 85th had been at sea since November 19. Moreover, Knox is listed with the officers present with his regiment at Negril in Description of Service of the Men belonging to the several Regiments employed upon a Particular Service & exclusive of those sent or left at Home, November 25, 1814, WO 17/1218, War Department In-Letters and Papers 1815–1817, War Office Records, National Archives, Kew. Consequently, either Knox erred when he wrote his letter, or Barrett transcribed it incorrectly.

66. Owsley, *Borderlands*, 136, suggests that Cochrane abandoned the Pontchartrain route on arriving at Negril, in part due to finding no landing boats, and also because of the security breach at Kingston.

67. Memorandum Book, November 26–27, 1814, Pultney Malcolm Papers, MAL/104, Caird; Cochrane Journal, November 26, 1814, ADM 50/122, Kew; Chesterton, *Peace, War, and Adventure*, 1:173.

68. Cochrane Journal, November 25, 1814, ADM 50/122, Kew.

69. Gleig, *Narrative*, 248–49.

70. Gleig Diary, November 2930, 1814, ibid., 195.

71. Alexander McLeary to Bunbury, October 1, 1814, WO 1/142, Kew.

72. Croker to James Chapman, October 7, 1814, McLeary to Bunbury, October 1, 1814, Abstract of ordnance ammunition and stores on board the undermentioned Transports for Foreign service, September 30, 1814, Abstract of provisions, October 9, 1814, WO 1/142, Kew.

73. General Monthly Return of the Serjeants, Trumpeters, Drummers, and Rank and File of the several Corps serving under the Command of Major General John Lambert, October 25, 1814, Description of Service of the Men belonging to the Corps, October 25, 1814, WO 17/1218, Kew.

74. Major Sir John Maxwell Tylden Journal, October 2, 11, 1814, New-York Public Library, New York, NY.

75. Tylden Journal, October 28, 1814, NYPL.

76. Cooke, *Narrative*, 100–101.

77. Tylden Journal, November 1, 1814, NYPL.

78. Ibid., November 19, 1814.

79. Bathurst to Ross, September 28, 1814, Bathurst to Lambert, October 5, 18, 1814, WO 6/2, Kew.

80. Valerie McNair Scott, Lady Pakenham, *The Battle of New Orleans: Major-General Sir Edward M. Pakenham* (New Orleans: Battle of New Orleans 150th Anniversary Committee of Louisiana, 1965), 6ff, quote 35.

81. W. C. E. Napier, ed., *Passages in the Early Military Life of General Sir George T. Napier, K. C. B. Written by Himself* (London: John Murray, 1884), 237–38.

82. Wellington to Robert Torrens, September 7, 1812, Gurwood, *Dispatches of Field Marshal the Duke of Wellington*, 9:395.

83. R. Hercules Pakenham to Lord Longford, December 20, 1814, Thomas Pakenham, ed., *The Pakenham Letters 1800–1815* (London: John and Edward Bumpus, 1914), 251.

84. Pakenham to Lady Longford, October 23, 1814, ibid., 250.

85. Journal of John Burgoyne, October 25, 1814, Wrottesley, *Life and Correspondence of Field Marshal Sir John Burgoyne*, 1:298–99. Bathurst told Pakenham that he thought it "not improbable" that "a general disposition may exist, peaceably to acquiesce in our Possession of the country during the war" (Bathurst to Pakenham, October 24, 1814, WO 6/2, Kew). Ronald J. Drez, *The War of 1812, Conflict and Deception* (Baton Rouge: Louisiana State University Press, 2014), 223, interprets Bathurst's meaning as an intent to permanently remove Louisiana and New Orleans from American control, saying "the key word was *possession* not *occupation*." This overlooks Bathurst's critical qualifier "during the War." Possession of territory for a limited period of time is, by definition, an occupation, not a possession, and implied return of custody postwar.

86. Bathurst to Pakenham, October 24, 26, 1814, WO 6/2, Christopher Robinson to Bathurst, October 26, 1814, WO 1/142, Kew.

87. Bathurst to Pakenham, October 24, 1814, WO 6/2, Kew; Brown, *Amphibious Campaign*, 205 n. 3. Drez, *War of 1812*, 223, here again misreads Bathurst's instructions as revealing intent to occupy New Orleans permanently.

88. London, UK, *Morning Post*, October 31, 1814; London, UK, *Star*, October 31, 1814.
89. "Return of Camp Equippage & Field Equipments . . . to rendezvous at Portsmouth," October 6, 1814, WO 1/142, List of Transports laden for the West Indies, October 14, 1814, WO 1/141, Kew.
90. G. C. Moore Smith, ed., *The Autobiography of Lieutenant-General Sir Harry Smith, Baronet of Aliwal on the Sutlej G. C. B.* (London: John Murray, 1903), 227; Napier, *Passages in the Early Military Life*, 239–40.
91. Journal of John Burgoyne, November 1, 1814, Wrottesley, *Life and Correspondence of Field Marshal Sir John Burgoyne*, 1:299–300.
92. Ibid.
93. Burgoyne to Sister, December 3, 1814, Burgoyne Journal, December 13, 1814, ibid., 299–300.
94. Tylden Journal, December 11, 13–14, 1814, NYPL; Cooke, *Narrative*, 100.
95. James Armstrong to Winchester, December 5, 1814, James Winchester Papers, Tennessee Historical Society.
96. Codrington to Jane Codrington, November 23–December 31, 1814, Codrington Papers, COD/6/2, Codrington to Jane Codrington, December 1, 1814, COD/7/1, Caird.
97. [Frederick] Stovin to Mrs. Stovin, December 5, 1814, MSS 557, William C. Cook Collection, HNOC.
98. Gordon to Lydia Gordon, December 3, 1814, Gordon, *Letters and Records*, 215.
99. St. George's, Bermuda, *Gazette and Weekly Advertiser*, April 15, 1815.
100. "To the Great and Illustrious Chiefs of the Creek and Other Indian Nations," December 5, 1814, WO 1/141, Cochrane Journal, December 3–5, 1814, ADM 50/122, Kew.
101. Cochrane Journal, December 7–10, 1814, ADM 50/122, Kew; Forrest, *Journal*, 24–25; Cochrane to Croker, December 16, 1814, *Naval Chronicle, for 1815*, vol. 33, 337.
102. Codrington to Jane Codrington, December 16, 1814, Codrington Papers, COD/6/2, Caird; Aitchison Memoir, 63, HNOC.
103. Surtees, *Rifle Brigade*, 334–35.
104. Cochrane to Croker, December 7, 1814, ADM 1/508, Caird. Cochrane's chronology is off in his letter, which clearly contains some assumptions that he could not know with certainty. The opened dispatches certainly reached Jamaica no later than the first or second week of October. If only four days really passed from their arrival to Hudson's departure, then fully three weeks subsequently passed unaccountably before Hudson got the news to Jackson. Cochrane went on to state that Hudson actually sailed to New Orleans, from where he conveyed his news to Jackson, who had taken Pensacola a few days earlier. Jackson actually captured Pensacola on November 7, so Hudson would have to have departed Kingston several days earlier for him to be getting his news to Jackson after Pensacola's fall. Owsley, *Borderlands*, 124, suggests that Cochrane decided to shift his attack to a direct one on New Orleans when he arrived at Negril, heard that Hudson had spread the news of his plans, and that Jackson was then marching to New Orleans. In fact, Jackson did not leave for New Orleans until four days before Cochrane left Negril, and the news of Jackson's march could not possibly have reached Cuba in that short time.
105. Bathurst to Ross, September 6, 1814, WO 6/2, Kew.
106. Cochrane to Admiralty, December 7, 1814, ADM 1/508, Kew.
107. Hickey, *Glorious Victory*, 94.
108. Gideon M. Davison, *Sketches of the War, Between the United States and the British Isles: Intended as a Faithful History of All the Material Events from the Time of the Declaration in 1812, to and Including the Treaty of Peace in 1815* (Rutland, VT: Fay and Davison, 1815), 2:466–67; Walker, *Jackson and New Orleans*, 11.
109. Charles Gayarré, *History of Louisiana: The American Domination* (New York: Redfield, 1854), 4:416.
110. Cochrane to Croker, December 16, 1814, *Naval Chronicle, for 1815*, vol. 33, 337.
111. This conclusion is based on the fact that as of December 16, Codrington still believed that Lake Pontchartrain was their intermediate objective. Codrington to Jane Codrington, November 23–December 31, 1814, Codrington Papers, COD/6/2, Caird.
112. Gleig Diary, December 912, 1814, Barrett, *85th King's Light Infantry*, 196–97; Gerard, Campaigns of a British Officer, USNA.
113. Chesterton, *Peace, War, and Adventure*, 175–76; Robert Aitchison Memoir, 62, HNOC.
114. Cochrane to Croker, December 16, 1814, London, UK, *Morning Post*, March 10, 1815.

115. Codrington to Jane Codrington, November 23–December 31, 1814, Codrington Papers, COD/6/2, Caird.
116. Cochrane to Croker, December 16, 1814, London, UK, *Morning Post*, March 10, 1815.

CHAPTER FOUR: "ONE OF THE MOST BRILLIANT THINGS ON RECORD"

1. Marigny, *Reflections*, n.p.
2. Kanon, *Tennesseans at War*, 143.
3. Letter from New Orleans, December 2, 1814, Plattsburgh, NY, *Plattsburgh Republican*, January 14, 1815; Simpson to Mary Simpson, December 9, 1814, Stephen Simpson Letters, Princeton.
4. Reid and Eaton, *Jackson*, 242.
5. Kenner to Minor, December 2, 1814, Kenner Papers, LSU; Jackson to Monroe, February 13, 1815, Parker Papers, HSP.
6. Benson Lossing, "Scenes in the War of 1812: XII—Defense of New Orleans," *Harper's New Monthly Magazine* 30, no. 176 (January 1865): 170; Skipwith to Jackson, May 13, 1827, Padgett, "Andrew Jackson in New Orleans," 406. The two authorities that cite a street number disagree on whether it was at 104 or 106, and in any case street numbers have changed more than once since that time.
7. Nolte, *Memoirs*, 203; Reid and Eaton, *Jackson*, 415.
8. "Major Davezac," *United States Magazine and Democratic Review* 16, no. 80 (February 1845): 109–10.
9. Bassett, *Tatum's Journal*, December 1, 1814, 96–97.
10. Shaumburg to Wilkinson, January 25, 1815, HNOC.
11. Nolte, *Memoirs*, 204.
12. Shaumburg to Wilkinson, January 25, 1815, HNOC; Livingston to Janet Montgomery, July 7, 1814, Jackson [M. P. Gales aide] to Livingston, September 30, 1814, Jackson to Livingston, October 23, 1814, Livingston to Timothy Pickering, April 21, 1828, J. L. Fernagus to Livingston, December 6, 1814, Livingston Papers, Princeton; Louise Livingston Hunt, *Memoir of Mrs. Edward Livingston with Letters Hitherto Unpublished* (New York: Harper and Brothers, 1886), 51; Edward Livingston, *An Answer to Mr. Jefferson's Justification of His Conduct in the Case of the New Orleans Batture* (Philadelphia: William Fry, 1813). Jackson may also have had a manuscript copy of William Darby's map, which was not published until 1816.
13. Tregle, *Louisiana in the Age of Jackson*, 132.
14. Charles Havens Hunt, *Life of Edward Livingston* (New York: D. Appleton, 1864), 196–98.
15. Shaumburg to Wilkinson, January 25, 1815, HNOC.
16. Shaumburg to Claiborne, October 30, 1815, Rowland, *Letter Books*, 6:377.
17. Claiborne to Monroe, December 9, 1814, ibid., 321–22.
18. Claiborne to Shaumburg, October 1, 1815, Rowland, *Letter Books*, 6:371, Shaumburg to Claiborne, October 30, 1815, 378.
19. Warshauer, "Jackson and Martial Law," 267–68.
20. Hunt, *Memoir of Mrs. Edward Livingston*, 51; Jackson to Monroe, December 2, 1814, Moser et al., *Papers*, 199–200; Jackson to James Brown, February 4, 1815, War of 1812 Mss., Lilly Library.
21. Morning Report of the 7th Infantry, December 14, 1814, MSS 213, United States Army Morning Reports, HNOC; Ross to Jackson, August 15, 1814, Bassett, *Correspondence*, 2:26–27.
22. Walpole, NH, *Political Observatory*, May 29, 1807; Nathaniel Pryor to William Clarke, October 16, 1807, New York, NY, *New-York Evening Post*, November 23, 1807; "Captain Nathaniel Pryor," *American Historical Review* 24, no. 2 (January 1919): 253–65; Pryor to John Armstrong, November 13, 1813, Letters Received by the Office of the Adjutant General, 1805–1821, RG 94, M566, NA; Francis B. Heitman, comp., *Historical Register and Dictionary of the United States Army, from its Organization, September 29, 1789, to March 2, 1903* (Washington: Government Printing Office, 1903), 1:808.
23. Jackson to Monroe, December 2, 1814, Moser et al., Papers, 199. In this letter it is implicit from Jackson's statement that the enemy could not invade "by land at any point East of Lake Ponchartrain [sic]," that he regarded that lake itself as the first point that a landing could be made. The only way into the lake was via Lake Borgne and the Rigolets. The fact that Jackson went on to say he was going to inspect Fort St. Philip suggests that as the only other avenue of invasion he felt concern for.

24. The Choctaw leader's name appears in myriad forms—Jugeat, Jugeant, Juzan, Dusong, and more. It is shown as Jugeat here and hereafter since that seems to be the usage prevailing in his family.

25. Villeré, *Villeré*, 48–49.

26. Letter from New Orleans, December 2, 1814, Plattsburgh, NY, *Plattsburgh Republican*, January 14, 1815.

27. Hunt, *Memoir of Mrs. Edward Livingston*, 52–53.

28. Letter from New Orleans, December 3, 1814, Philadelphia, PA, *American Daily Advertiser*, January 3, 1815; Letter from St. Francisville, December 4, 1814, Wilmington, DE, *Delaware Gazette and State Journal*, January 3, 1815; Letter from New Orleans, January 9, 1815, Wilkes-Barre, PA, *Susquehanna Democrat*, February 17, 1815.

29. Statement of David B. Morgan, March 28, 1815, Carthage, TN, *Carthage Gazette*, May 26, 1815.

30. Ibid.; Claiborne to Fromentin, December 9, 1814, Rowland, *Letter Books*, 6:320–21.

31. John Henry Eaton and Jerome Van Crowninshield, *The Complete Memoirs of Andrew Jackson, Seventh President of the United States* (New York: Hurst, 1885), 204.

32. Wollstonecraft to Livingston, January, February 27, 28, March 13, 1815, Livingston Papers, Princeton; Thomas G. Murray to Jackson, October 17, 1814, Wollstonecraft to?, August 5, 1814, Jackson Papers, LC; Records of Men Enlisted in the U.S. Army Prior to the Peace Establishment, May 17, 1815, No. 697, Registers of Enlistments in the United States Army, Compiled 1798–1914, RG 94, NA.

33. Jonathan J. Rees to David Rees, December 11, 1814, Rees Papers, Tulane.

34. Jackson to Claiborne, December 10, 1814, Moser et al., *Papers*, 202.

35. Bassett, *Tatum's Journal*, December 4, 1814, 97–100; Reid and Eaton, *Jackson*, 252–53.

36. Jackson to Monroe, February 13, 1815, Parker Papers, HSP.

37. Reid and Eaton, *Jackson*, 252.

38. Ibid., 252–53; Bassett, *Tatum's Journal*, December 9, 1814, 100; Jackson to Claiborne, December 10, 1814, Moser et al., *Papers*, 202.

39. Reid and Eaton, Jackson, 253.

40. Jackson to Coffee, December 11, 1814, Orderly Book of Brigadier General John Coffee, Cook Collection, MSS 557, HNOC.

41. Letter from New Orleans, December 9, 1814, New Haven, CT, *Connecticut Journal*, January 10, 1815; Letter from New Orleans, December 9, 1814, Boston, MA, *Boston Commercial Gazette*, January 5, 1815; Letter from New Orleans, December 9, 1814, Baltimore, MD, *Baltimore Patriot & Evening Advertiser*, January 6, 1815; Letter from New Orleans, December 9, 1814, Dedham, MA, *Gazette*, January 6, 1815.

42. Letter from New Orleans, December 9, 1814, Plattsburgh, NY, *Plattsburgh Republican*, January 14, 1815.

43. Claiborne to Fromentin, December 9, 1814, Rowland, *Letter Books*, 6:320.

44. Letter from New Orleans, December 9, 1814, New Haven, CT, *Connecticut Journal*, January 9, 1815; Letter from New Orleans, December 12, 1814, New York, NY, *New-York Mercantile Advertiser*, January 17, 1815; Claiborne to Fromentin, December 9, 1814, Rowland, *Letter Books*, 6:320.

45. Boston, MA, *New-England Palladium*, January 20, 1815; Baltimore, MD, *Federal Gazette*, January 10, 1815, in Philadelphia, PA, *Relf's Philadelphia Gazette, and Daily Advertiser*, January 13, 1815.

46. Boston, MA, *New-England Palladium*, January 20, 1815.

47. James, *Military Occurrences*, 347; Lossing, "Scenes in the War of 1812," 170.

48. Bassett, *Tatum's Journal*, December 11, 1814, 100–1.

49. Shaumburg to Wilkinson, January 25, 1815, MSS 21, HNOC.

50. Jackson to James Brown, February 4, 1815, War of 1812 Mss., Lilly Library.

51. Ibid.

52. Jackson to Monroe, February 13, 1815, Parker Papers, HSP.

53. Henry Chotard to Alexander A. White, December 11, 1814, Moser et al., *Papers*, 222, 481, Jackson to Robert Hays, December 26, 1814, 221.

54. Bassett, *Tatum's Journal*, December 15, 1815, 101–2. Tatum's special concern over Villeré and Bayou Bienvenue may be written from hindsight. No one yet knew what sort of craft the British

would have, though they did have abundant intelligence that Cochrane had been collecting shallow draft boats that could make Bienvenue a likely prospect.

55. Louisiana General Assembly Resolution, February 1, 1815, Baltimore, MD, *Baltimore Telegraph*, March 16, 1815; Rasmussen, *American Uprising*, 179–80.

56. Bassett, *Tatum's Journal*, December 15, 1815, 10–12.

57. Jackson to Monroe, February 13, 1815, Parker Papers, HSP.

58. Cochrane to Croker, December 16, 1814, London, UK, *Morning Post*, March 10, 1815; Cochrane Journal, December 11, 1814, ADM 50/122, Kew.

59. Memorandum, December 12-13, 1814, Codrington Papers, COD/6/4, Memorandum Book, December 12, 1814, Pultney Malcolm Papers, MAL/104, Caird.

60. Nicholas Lockyer to Cochrane, December 16, 1814, *Naval Chronicle, for 1815*, vol. 33, 338; Hill, *Recollections*, 1:300.

61. Forrest, Journal, December 11-13, 1814, 25; Cochrane to Croker, December 16, 1814, *Naval Chronicle, for 1815*, vol. 33, 337; Gleig Diary, December 13–15, 1814, Barrett, *85th King's Light Infantry*, 197.

62. Ellery, "Notes," NYPL.

63. Gene A. Smith, *Thomas ap Catesby Jones: Commodore of Manifest Destiny* (Annapolis, MD: Naval Institute Press, 2000), 19, 21–23, 31.

64. Jones to Patterson, December 11, 1814, quoted in Jane Lucas De Grummond, *Renato Beluche: Smuggler, Privateer, and Patriot, 1780–1860* (Baton Rouge: Louisiana State University Press, 1983), 97; Surtees, *Rifle Brigade*, 335.

65. Jones to Patterson, March 12, 1815, Captains' Letters, RG 260, NA; Thomas Urquhart to Fromentin, December 16, 1814, Boston, MA, *New-England Palladium*, January 17, 1815.

66. Owsley edition of Reid and Eaton, *Jackson*, xxxviii, note 132. John Reid and John Henry Eaton, *The Life of Andrew Jackson*, ed. Frank L. Owsley Jr. (Tuscaloosa: University of Alabama Press, 2007).

67. Paul Estronza La Violette, *Sink or Be Sunk!: The Naval Battle in the Mississippi Sound That Preceded the Battle of New Orleans* (Blairsville, PA: Annabelle Books, 2002), 45–47.

68. Statement of effective force of a Division of United States Gun Boats under the command of Lieut Comdr Thomas ap Catesby Jones, n.d., Captains' Letters, RG 260, NA.

69. London, UK, *Courier, and Evening Gazette*, March 10, 1815. This statement of armament from Lockyer's report was made after the gunboats' capture and shows all of them having more guns and men than Jones's report of armament, but offers details on the size of the guns not otherwise available.

70. Statement of the British Forces which were engaged in the capture of the late United States Gun Boats, n.d., Captains' Letters, RG 260, NA.

71. Laura Eugenie Florian to Lydia Latrobe Roosevelt, January 9, 1815, MS645, HNOC; New York, NY, *New-York Spectator*, July 20, 1816. Some legend has grown around this episode, to the point that Isabella herself fired a cannon when everyone else just stood helplessly watching. See, for instance, La Violette, *Sink or Be Sunk!*, 125. It is clear from her letter that Laura Florian knew Isabella at Natchez, and that she had been at Bay St. Louis for her health, and apparently saw her while there, judging from her physical description. Written just twenty-seven days after the event, this seems an authentic account no doubt received from one or more of the several people who came into New Orleans from Bay St. Louis immediately after the fight, and possibly from William Johnson himself.

72. Jones to Patterson, March 12, 1815, Captains' Letters, RG 260, NA; Urquhart to Fromentin, December 16, 1814, Boston, MA, *New-England Palladium*, January 17, 1815.

73. Jones to Patterson, March 12, 1815, Captains' Letters, RG 260, NA.

74. *Summary Statement of Facts, &c, by Thomas Ap C. Jones* (Washington, DC: no publisher, November 2, 1832), 11–12; Memorial of Thomas ap Catesby Jones to Samuel L. Southard, Richard Rush, and James Barbour, February 14, 1828 (printed letter: n.p., 1828), [1], Jones Pension File, RG 15, NA.

75. Jones to Patterson, March 12, 1815, Captains' Letters, RG 260, NA.

76. *Summary Statement of Facts, &c, by Thomas Ap C. Jones*, 11–12.

77. Codrington to Jane Codrington, November 23–December 31, 1814, Codrington Papers, COD/6/2, Caird.

78. Jones to Patterson, March 12, 1815, Captains' Letters, RG 260, NA; Lockyer to Cochrane, December 16, 1814, *Naval Chronicle, for 1815*, vol. 33, 338–39.

79. Codrington to Jane Codrington, November 23–December 31, 1814, Codrington Papers, COD/6/2, Caird; Hill, *Recollections*, 1:301.

80. Robert Aitchison Memoir, 65, MSS 186, HNOC.

81. Jones to Patterson, March 12, 1815, Captains' Letters, RG 260, NA.

82. Letter from Kingston, Jamaica, January 27, 1815, Richmond, VA, *Virginia Patriot*, March 25, 1815; London, UK, *Courier, and Evening Gazette*, March 10, 1815; "Deaths," *Gentleman's Magazine* 85 (April 1815): 372; Gordon to Lydia Gordon, January 9, 1815, Gordon, *Letters and Records*, 216.

83. Smith, *Catesby Jones*, 28–29; Memorial of Thomas ap Catesby Jones to Samuel L. Southard, [1], Jones Pension File, RG 15, NA.

84. Jones to Patterson, March 12, 1815, Captains' Letters, RG 260, NA.

85. Lockyer to Cochrane, December 16, 1814, *Naval Chronicle, for 1815*, vol. 33, 338–39.

86. William Johnson report, December 16, 1814, Louisville, KY, *Western Courier*, January 12, 1815; Letter to Editor, December 14, 1814, Washington, KY, *Union*, January 14, 1815; Letter from "an enlightened gentleman of high standing," December 16, 1814, Hallowell, ME, *American Advocate*, February 4, 1815.

87. Cochrane to Croker, December 16, 1814, London, UK, *Morning Post*, March 10, 1815; Cochrane Journal, December 13, 1814, ADM 50/122, Kew; Memorandum Book, December 13, 1814, Pultney Malcolm Papers, MAL/104, Caird.

88. Chesterton, *Peace, War, and Adventure*, 179.

89. Gordon to Lydia Gordon, December 15, 1814, Gordon, *Letters and Records*, 215.

90. Codrington to Jane Codrington, November 23–December 31, 1814, Codrington Papers, COD/6/2, Caird.

91. Ibid.

92. Dublin, IR, *Saunders's News-Letter, and Daily Advertiser*, March 17, 1815. This comes from a statement by Codrington attached to Cochrane's January 18, 1815, report. Its own figures conflict within the document, so the figures must be considered approximate, however close.

93. Gordon Gallie MacDonald Memoir, 1831, NYPL.

94. Codrington to Captain Walker on *Bedford*, December 15, 1814, Codrington Papers, COD/6/4, Caird; Smith, Catesby Jones, 29–30.

95. Jonathan D. Ferris to Cochrane, January 26, 1815, Cochrane Papers, NLS.

96. Codrington to officers and seamen employed in capture of the gun vessels, January 1815, Codrington Papers, COD/6/4, Caird.

97. "*Tonnant* Surveys &c," Passages Ordered, COD/6/2, Codrington to Captain Lloyd, January 23, 1815, Codrington Papers, COD/6/4, Caird.

98. Gordon Gallie MacDonald Memoir, 1831, NYPL.

99. Cochrane Journal, December 15, 1814, ADM 50/122, Kew.

100. Codrington to Jane Codrington, November 23–December 31, 1814, Codrington Papers, COD/6/2, Caird.

101. Order of Disembarkation Delivered to Divisional Captains by Rear Admiral Malcolm, December 1814, Distribution for Landing the Troops, December 12, 1814, Return of Boats on Board His Majesty's Ships and Vessels Attached to the Expedition, December 21, 1814, Disposition of Men, n.d. [December 1814], Disposition of Boats to Land, n.d. [December 1814], Charles R. Forrest Memorandum, December 13, 1814, Memorandum Book, Pultney Malcolm Papers, MAL/104, Caird.

102. Codrington to Jane Codrington, November 23–December 31, 1814, Codrington Papers, COD/6/2, Caird.

Chapter Five: "The American States Are Doomed"

1. Bassett, *Tatum's Journal*, December 15, 1814, 102.

2. Officer in the army to Governor Brown, December 15, 1814, Frankfort, KY, *Argus of Western America*, January 16, 1815; Francis Newman to William McRae, December 14 [15], 1814, copy in Jean Lafitte National Historical Park Collection, 1774–1982, University of New Orleans. The

original may be in the Charles Gunther Collection, Chicago History Museum. Another account written this same day said that the news of the capture of the fleet was sent from Bay St. Louis and arrived at two p.m. A morning arrival seems more probable. Letter to Editor, December 14, 1814, Washington, KY, *Union*, January 14, 1815.

3. Letter by an officer in the Navy, December 15, 1814, Boston, MA, *Boston Commercial Gazette*, January 16, 1815.

4. Butler to Coffee, December 15, 1814, Orderly Book of Brigadier General John Coffee, MSS 557, Cook Collection, HNOC.

5. Eaton and Van Crowninshield, *Memoirs of Andrew Jackson*, 212–13; Reid and Eaton, *Jackson*, 262, 265; Jackson to Coffee, December 16, 1814, Orderly Book of Brigadier General John Coffee, MSS 557, Cook Collection, Shaumburg to Wilkinson, January 25, 1815, HNOC; Owsley, *Borderlands*, 140.

6. Officer in the army to Governor Brown, December 15, 1814, Frankfort, KY, *Argus of Western America*, January 16, 1815; Kenner to Minor, December 17, 1814, Kenner Papers, LSU.

7. See, for instance, Letter from New Orleans, December 16, 1814, Chillicothe, OH, *Supporter*, January 7, 1815; Letter from New Orleans, December 22, 1814, Charleston, SC, *City Gazette*, January 21, 1814; Florian to Roosevelt, January 9, 1815, HNOC; Letter from New Orleans, December 16, 1814, Williamsburg, OH, *Western American*, January 21, 1815.

8. Letter from officer in the navy, December 15, 1814, Boston, MA, *Boston Commercial Gazette*, January 16, 1815; Urquhart to Fromentin, December 16, 1814, Boston, MA, *New-England Palladium*, January 17, 1815; Letter from "an enlightened gentleman of high standing," December 16, 1814, Hallowell, ME, *American Advocate*, February 4, 1815; Samuel Clement, *Truth Is No Slander: Therefore Read, Enquire, Reflect* (Natchez, MS: Natchez *Ariel*, 1824), 4–6; Letter by "intelligent officer in the Army," December 16, 1814, Baltimore, MD, *American and Daily Commercial Advertiser*, January 11, 1815; Letter written from the Guard Room, December 16, 1814, Hallowell, ME, *American Advocate*, January 21, 1815.

9. Letters from New Orleans, December 14–16, 1814, Washington, KY, *Union*, January 14, 1815; Letter to Editor, December 15, 1814, Washington, KY, *Union*, January 14, 1815; Clement, *Truth Is No Slander*, 4; Kenner to Minor, December 17, 1814, Kenner Papers, LSU.

10. Letter from New Orleans, December 16, 1814, Paris, KY, *Western Citizen*, January 14, 1815; Letter by "intelligent officer in the Army," December 16, 1814, Baltimore, MD, *American, and Daily Commercial Advertiser*, January 11, 1815; Simpson to Mary Simpson, December 16, 1814, Stephen Simpson Letters, Princeton; Letter from New Orleans, December 16, 1814, Lexington, KY, *Western Monitor*, January 6, 1815; Letter of December 16, 1814, Chillicothe, OH, *Supporter*, January 7, 1815; Letter of December 16, 1814, Georgetown, DC, *Federal Republican for the Country*, January 10, 1815; Mr. Winter to [Elisha] Winter, December 16, 1814, New York, NY, *New-York Evening Post*, January 11, 1815.

11. Jackson to Coffee, December 16, 1814, Orderly Book of Brigadier General John Coffee, Cook Collection, MSS 557, HNOC; Letter from "an enlightened gentleman of high standing," December 16, 1814, Hallowell, ME, *American Advocate*, February 4, 1815; Baltimore, MD, *American, and Commercial Daily Advertiser*, January 16, 1815; Eliza Williams Chotard Gould Memoir, 1798–1825, VHS; Jackson to Monroe, February 13, 1815, Parker Papers, HSP; Thomas L. Butler to Citizens of New Orleans, December 15, 1814, Broadside, Hynes Papers, HNOC.

In her memoir, Eliza Williams Chotard Gould gives a dramatic portrayal of Jackson getting the news at a ball when a messenger interrupted the dancing with word of the disaster. The dancing immediately ended and many began to take hats and coats to leave for their homes, but the general reassured them that only he and his staff needed to leave, there was no immediate danger, and he wanted them to continue the ball. Some tried to regain the evening's spirit after Jackson left, but soon virtually all left for their homes. Given that this memoir was written in 1868 when she was seventy years old, some fifty-three years after the fact, and that no dancing or ball was likely being held in the morning when Johnson certainly arrived in town, the story must be considered highly embellished. The substance of her statement that Jackson tried to calm the people, however, is consistent with his other efforts and pronouncements at the time.

12. Warshauer, "Jackson and Martial Law," 264; Appeal of L. Louaillier, Sen., Against the Charge of High Treason (n.p., 1827), 16–17; the legislature was just "rotten."

13. Reid and Eaton, *Jackson*, 276.

14. Anonymous to William Flakner, n.d. [December 1814], M. Guise to Cochrane, January 21, 1815, Cochrane Papers, NLS.

15. S. Putnam Waldo, *Memoirs of Andrew Jackson, Major-General in the Army of the United States; and Commander in Chief of the Division of the South* (Hartford, CT: Andrus, 1818; 4th edition), 182–83.

16. Jackson to L. F. Linn, March 1842, Baltimore, MD, *American and Commercial Daily Appeal*, May 27, 1842.

17. Bassett, *Tatum's Journal*, December 15, 1814, 102–3.

18. Warshauer, "Jackson and Martial Law," 266; Jesko, "Jackson's Martial Law Declaration," 41, 45, 109.

19. Latour, *Historical Memoir*, 287.

20. General Orders, December 16, 1814, David Bannister Morgan Papers, LC. The time of day on December 16 that the decree was made public is uncertain. Some writers do not mention it at all, while others seem to imply that they learned of it in the afternoon. Letter written from the Guard Room, December 16, 1814, Hallowell, ME, *American Advocate*, January 21, 1815, says it occurred that evening, but Lewis Livingston to Janet Montgomery, December 16, 1814, Hunt, *Life of Edward Livingston*, 198, clearly states that "the martial law was published this morning, and is now in execution."

21. Jackson to L. F. Linn, March 1842, Baltimore, MD, *American and Commercial Daily Appeal*, May 27, 1842.

22. Nathaniel Herbert Claiborne, *Notes on the War in the South; with Biographical Sketches of the Lives of Montgomery, Jackson, Sevier, The Late Gov. Claiborne, and Others* (Richmond, VA: William Ramsay, 1819), 55.

23. Jesko, "Jackson's Martial Law Declaration," 109.

24. Livingston to Timothy Pickering, April 21, 1828, Livingston Papers, Princeton.

25. Letter from New Orleans, December 16, 1814, Bennington, VT, *Bennington News-Letter*, January 23, 1815; Letter to Editor, December 16, 1814, Washington, KY, *Union*, January 14, 1815; Letter written from the Guard Room, December 16, 1814, Hallowell, ME, *American Advocate*, January 21, 1815.

26. George H. Nixon to Jackson, December 17, 1814, Jean Lafitte National Historical Park Collection, 1774–1982, University of New Orleans (hereinafter cited as JELAC). The man arrested was Pierre Charles Chavenet, who eight years hence was living in New Orleans and teaching school. No record of the nature of the charges against him has been found, but the fact he was sent from Pearl River shortly after the gunboat battle suggests that he was suspected of having some dealings with the enemy in that vicinity.

27. Sterret to Fromentin, December 16, 1814, Albany, NY, *Albany Register*, January 17, 1815.

28. Bassett, *Tatum's Journal*, December 18, 1814, 104.

29. Eaton and Van Crowninshield, *Memoirs of Andrew Jackson*, 214.

30. Letter from New Orleans, December 19, 1814, Bowden, *Private Letters*, 54; Ellery, "Notes," NYPL.

31. Chotard to Ross, December 16, 1814, Moser et al., *Papers*, 222, 483; Jackson to Monroe, December 27, 1814, Baltimore, MD, *Baltimore Telegraph*, January 31, 1815.

32. Bassett, *Tatum's Journal*, December 16, 1814, 103–4; Jackson to Coffee, December 16, 1814, Moser et al., *Papers*, 205; Jackson to Coffee, December 16, 1814, Orderly Book of Brigadier General John Coffee, Cook Collection, MSS 557, HNOC; Jackson to Monroe, February 13, 1815, Parker Papers, HSP.

33. Militia Gen. Orders, December 13, 1814, Louisville, KY, *Western Courier*, January 19, 1815; Letter from New Orleans, December 15, 1814, Washington, KY, *Union*, and January 14, 1815.

34. H. Chotard to Morgan, December 16, 1815, Thomas Piatt to Morgan, December 16, 1814, Morgan Papers, LC.

35. Extract of a letter from New Orleans to a member of Congress, December 22, 1814, Boston, MA, *Boston Weekly Messenger*, January 27, 1815.

36. Grymes to Jackson, February 15, 1843, Jackson Papers, LC.

37. Act of December 15, 1814, Michel De Armas, 8, January–December 1814, 296–97, New Orleans Notarial Archives.

38. Nolte, *Memoirs*, 205–6; Latour, *Historical Memoir*, 78–79.

39. Louisiana General Assembly Resolution, February 1, 1815, Baltimore, MD, *Baltimore Telegraph*, March 16, 1815; Smith, *Slaves' Gamble*, 162–64; Latour, *Historical Memoir*, 53–54.

40. New Orleans, *Orleans Gazette & Commercial Advertiser*, April 22, 1814; Nolte, *Memoirs*, 206, 212.

41. New Orleans, *Louisiana Gazette for the Country*, February 2, 1815, in Washington, DC, *Daily National Intelligencer*, March 6, 1815.

42. George Commens Service Record, Captain Beale's Company, Riflemen, Louisiana Militia, War of 1812 Service Record Index, RG 94, NA; Estate of the Late George Commyns, Louisiana, Wills and Probate Records, 1756–1984, New Orleans City Archives: Orleans Parish, New Orleans Public Library, New Orleans, LA; Whitney, *Whitney's New-Orleans Directory*, 25.

43. Connecticut Church Records, State Library Index, Killingworth First Congregational Church, 1735–1893, 2, 56, 100, Connecticut State Library, Hartford.

44. Wilmington, NC, *Wilmington Gazette*, January 2, 1810; Boston, MA, *Boston Commercial Gazette*, September 2, 1811, March 16, 1812.

45. Estate of the Late Oliver Parmlee, probated May 4, 1815, Succession and Probate Records, Jefferson Parish, New Orleans City Archives, NOPL.

46. Nolte, *Memoirs*, 206.

47. United States Census, New Orleans, Orleans Parish, Louisiana, 1810.

48. E. K. Stewart, "William Carr Withers," ancestry.com.

49. Letter from Greenville, Mississippi Territory, January 31, 1815, Wilmington, DE, *American Watchman*, March 4, 1815.

50. Beverly Chew Memoir, New Jersey Historical Society, Newark.

51. W. Johnson to father, December 31, 1814, Miscellaneous Collection, RG 68, Louisiana Historical Center, New Orleans. No service record for a Johnson can be found for Beale's Riflemen, yet the writer's statement that Judah Touro was in his company definitely places him with Beale.

52. Letter from New Orleans, December 16, 1814, Williamsburg, OH, *Western American*, January 21, 1815; Letter written from the Guard Room, December 16, 1814, Hallowell, ME, *American Advocate*, January 21, 1815.

53. Edward Palfrey to John Palfrey, December 16, 1814, Gatell, "Boston Boy in 'Mr. Madison's War,'" 154–55; Letter to Editor, December 16, 1814, Washington, KY, *Union*, January 14, 1815.

54. Letter to Editor, December 16, 1814, Washington, KY, *Union*, January 14, 1815; Letters from New Orleans, December 1416, 1814, Washington, KY, *Union*, January 14, 1815; John R. Hungerford to Richard T. Brown or Daniel Carmichael, January 15, 1815, VHS.

55. Reid and Eaton, *Jackson*, 262.

56. Letter from an "intelligent officer in the Army," December 16, 1814, Baltimore, MD, *American, and Daily Commercial Advertiser*, January 11, 1815. The writer was probably Lieutenant Colonel George H. Nixon, commanding a regiment of Mississippi militia. On December 16 from the mouth of the Pearl River he saw what he estimated to be thirty enemy vessels near Ship Island, some under sail, though he could not tell their destination. George H. Nixon to Jackson, December 17, 1814, JELAC.

57. Louisville, KY, *Western Courier*, January 12, 1815.

58. Letter from officer in the Navy, December 17, 1814, Boston, MA, *Boston Commercial Gazette*, January 16, 1815.

59. Caroline S. Pfaff, "Henry Miller Shreve," *Louisiana Historical Quarterly* 10, no. 2 (April 1927): 199; Reid and Eaton, *Jackson*, 270.

60. Peter V. Ogden to Livingston, October 13, 1812, Livingston Papers, Princeton; Bassett, *Tatum's Journal*, December 18, 1814, 104–5.

61. Jackson to James Winchester, December 16, 1814, Moser et al., *Papers*, 208.

62. Reid and Eaton, *Jackson*, 270.

63. Sterret to Fromentin, December 16, 1814, Albany, NY, *Albany Register*, January 17, 1815; Letter from New Orleans, December 16, 1814, Washington, DC, *Daily National Intelligencer*, January 14, 1815; Letter from New Orleans, December 16, 1814, Philadelphia, PA, *Relf's Philadelphia Gazette, and Daily Advertiser*, February 6, 1815.

64. Thomas Johnston to Fromentin, December 17, 1814, Washington, DC, *Daily National Intelligencer*, January 10, 1815; Letter from New Orleans, December 17, 1814, New York, NY, *National Advocate*, January 12, 1815.

65. Elizabeth Clement to Jacob Wood, January 11, 1815, William Edwards Clement, *Plantation Life on the Mississippi* (New Orleans: Pelican, 1952), 127.

66. Militia Gen. Orders, December 13, 1814, Louisville, KY, *Western Courier*, January 19, 1815; Marigny, *Reflections*, n.p.; Gaspard M. Debuys to Claiborne, January 3, 1815, Jackson Papers, LC.

67. Skipwith to Jackson, May 13, 1827, Padgett, "Andrew Jackson in New Orleans," 406.

68. Smith, *Slaves' Gamble*, 162–64; Claiborne to Thomas, December 17, 1814, Rowland, *Letter Books*, 6:323.

69. *Report of the Committee of Claims on the Petition of Jacob Purkill: House of Representatives Report 32* (Washington, DC: House of Representatives, January 6, 1820), 12.

70. Reid and Eaton, *Jackson*, 265–66; Latour, *Historical Memoir*, 216–17.

71. Butler to Plauché, December 18, 1814, Plauché to Butler, December 18, 1814, Extracts of the Order Book of Plauché's Battalion, December 18, 1814–March 14, 1815, Parsons Collection, Texas.

72. Letter from New Orleans, December 19, 1814, Bowden, *Private Letters*, 54.

73. Jean Laffite to Livingston, October 4, 1814, Livingston Papers, Princeton; Livingston to Madison, October 24, 1814, William B. Hatcher, *Edward Livingston: Jeffersonian Republican and Jacksonian Democrat* (Baton Rouge: Louisiana State University Press, 1940), 203n.

74. Morristown, NJ, *Palladium of Liberty*, November 3, 1814; Boston, MA, *New-England Palladium*, November 22, 1814; Boston, MA, *Boston Daily Advertiser*, November 28, 1814; Boston, MA, *Boston Commercial Gazette*, November 28, December 1, 1814; Boston, MA, *Repertory*, November 28, 1814.

75. Davis, *Pirates Laffite*, 209–10.

76. Ibid, 203; Marigny, *Reflections*, n.p.

77. Resolution of the Louisiana Legislature Concerning the Baratarians, December 14, 1814, Bassett, *Correspondence*, 2:114; Baton Rouge, LA, *Weekly Advocate*, October 20, 1847; Claiborne to the Barratarriors [sic], December 17, 1814, Rowland, *Letter Books*, 6:324.

78. Jackson note on Monroe to Jackson, December 10, 1814, Bassett, *Correspondence*, 2:110, Jackson to Monroe, February 18, 1815, 174.

79. Davis, *Pirates Laffite*, 208–9; Baton Rouge, LA, *Weekly Advocate*, October 20, 1847. Owsley, *Borderlands*, 131, mistakenly says the Laffites brought Jackson 7,500 pistols. They brought only flints, though Hallowell, ME, *Hallowell Gazette*, March 1, 1815, said they brought 800 muskets, which is highly unlikely given that they lost virtually everything at Barataria to Patterson. Brown, *Amphibious Campaign*, 192 n1, completely accepts the spurious Journal of Jean Laffite for fictitious details of their entrance into service at New Orleans.

80. Latour, *Historical Memoir*, 58; *Appeal of L. Louaillier*, 18.

81. Letter from New Orleans, December 19, 1814, Bowden, *Private Letters*, 53.

82. Tousard to John Stocker, January 6, 1815, Norman B. Wilkinson, ed., "The Assaults on New Orleans, 1814–1815," *Louisiana History* 3, no. 1 (Winter 1962): 48; Unknown writer to his mother in France, March 21, 1815, War of 1812 Collection, Tulane.

83. Patterson to Cochrane, December 15, 1814, Captains' Letters, RG 260, NA.

84. Smith, *Catesby Jones*, 29–30; George Marshall to Patterson, December 17, 1814, New York, NY, *New-York Gazette & General Advertiser*, February 1, 1815; Jackson to Blount, December 17, 1814, New York, NY, *Columbian*, January 23, 1815.

85. Unsigned note, December 18, 1814, Villeré Papers, HNOC.

86. "Labat" [probably Jean Baptiste Labatut] to his sister [probably Luisa Delphina Beauvais], December 16, 1814, Walker, *Jackson and New Orleans*, 138–139n.

87. Letter from New Orleans, December 19, 1814, Bowden, *Private Letters*, 54; Letter from New Orleans, December 19, 1814, Nashville, TN, *Examiner*, January 3, 1815.

88. Letter from New Orleans, December 19, 1814, in Bowden, *Private Letters*, 52.

89. Tench Coxe to Madison, January 25, 1815, Kreider et al., *Papers of James Madison*, 8:526.

90. Cambridge, UK, *Cambridge Chronicle and Journal and Huntingdonshire Gazette*, December 16, 1814.

CHAPTER SIX: TREACHERY OPENS A WAY

1. Distribution for landing the troops, December 12, 1814, Charles Forest Memorandum, December 13, 1814, Memorandum Book, Pultney Malcolm Papers, MAL/104, Caird.

2. Codrington to Jane Codrington, November 23–December 31, 1814, Codrington Papers, COD/6/2, Caird; Cochrane to Croker, January 18, 1815, London, UK, *Courier, and Evening Gazette*, March 10, 1815; Forrest, *Journal*, 26; Memorandum Book, December 16, 1814, Pultney Malcolm Papers, MAL/104, Caird; Tylden Journal, December 17, 1814, NYPL. This place is today Pearl River Island.

3. Codrington to Jane Codrington, November 27–December 31, 1814, Codrington Papers, COD/6/2, Caird. The manakin is a tropical bird now confined to Central and South America. The Spanish fishermen who habituated the island in 1814 may have been using the term loosely to mean "birds," or as the British so understood them.

4. Surtees, *Rifle Brigade*, 339; St. George's, Bermuda, *Bermuda Gazette and Weekly, Advertiser,* April 15, 1815; Tylden Journal, January 5, 1815, NYPL. Surtees believed it was from these men that Cochrane learned about Bayou Catalan and Bienvenue. While it cannot be stated with absolute certainty, it is demonstrable that prior to December 16 when Cochrane landed on the island, he and Codrington both spoke only of Lakes Borgne and Pontchartrain as the antici-pated line of advance. Neither made any mention of a route via the bayous until immedi-ately after they landed on the island, making the conclusion that they first learned of it here inescapable.

5. Forrest, *Journal*, December 14, 1814, 25; Codrington to Jane Codrington, November 23–December 31, 1814, Codrington Papers, COD/6/2, Caird.

6. Codrington to Jane Codrington, November 23–December 31, 1814, Codrington Papers, COD/6/2, Caird; Cochrane to Croker, January 18, 1815, London, UK, *Courier, and Evening Gazette,* March 10, 1815.

7. Report of Major General John Keane to Pakenham, December 26, 1814, London, UK, *Morning Post,* March 10, 1815. Walker, *Jackson and New Orleans,* while often cited almost as a primary source, says Cochrane only learned this on December 20, but by then Spencer and Peddie had been to the Mississippi and back (113–14).

8. "The Hon. Sir Robert Cavendish Spencer," *The Annual Biography and Obituary: 1832* (London: Longman, Rees, Orme, Brown, Green, & Longman, 1832), 16:3–4.

9. John Peddie to William Henry Clinton, January 24, 1815, War of 1812 Collection, University of Michigan, Ann Arbor; Forrest, *Journal*, December 14, 1814, 25–26; Hill, *Recollections,* 1:302; "Naval Officer" to unknown recipient, January 30, 1815, *Naval Chronicle, for 1815,* vol. 33, 386. The writer of this letter is described only as "a young but intelligent Naval Officer."

10. Wilkinson, *Memoirs*, 1:536.

11. This guide or guides was in later years often referred to as a smuggler, and while that was likely the case, there is no contemporary evidence of the fact. See, for instance, "Recollections of the Expedition," Part 3, 188, and James, *Military Occurrences,* 2:358.

12. Latour, *Historical Memoir,* 65. Half a century later Benson Lossing would state that the village was "inhabited by Spanish and Portuguese, who were spies and traitors." He was probably only repeating earlier accounts and did not back up the statement with any evidence. Lossing, "Scenes in the War of 1812," 172.

13. Report of Major General John Keane to Pakenham, December 26, 1814, London, UK, *Morning Post,* March 10, 1815.

14. "Recollections of the Expedition," Part 3, 187–88.

15. Claiborne to Fromentin, December 30, 1814, Baltimore, MD, *American, and Commercial Daily Advertiser,* January 31, 1815.

16. Nolte, *Memoirs,* 210.

17. Cochrane to Croker, January 18, 1815, London, UK, *Courier, and Evening Gazette,* March 10, 1815; Forrest, *Journal,* 26; Report of Major General John Keane to Pakenham, December 26, 1814, London, UK, *Morning Post,* March 10, 1815; Cochrane to Croker, January 18, 1815, *Naval Chronicle, for 1815,* vol. 33, 341–43.

18. "Naval Officer" to unknown recipient, January 30, 1815, *Naval Chronicle, for 1815,* vol. 33, 386.

19. Cochrane Journal, December 18, 1814, ADM 50/122, Kew.

20. Gleig Diary, December 19, 1814, Barrett, *85th King's Light Infantry,* 197; Letter from the HMS *Ramillies,* January 5, 1814, Kingston, Jamaica, *Courant,* January 27, 1814; Surtees, *Rifle Brigade,* 336.

21. Gleig Diary, December 18, 1814, Barrett, *85th King's Light Infantry,* 197; Memorandum Book, December 18, 1814, Pultney Malcolm Papers, MAL/104, Caird.

22. Codrington to Jane Codrington, November 23–December 31, 1814, Codrington Papers, COD/6/2, Caird.

23. Aitchison Memoir, 67, HNOC; Gordon to Lydia Gordon, January 9, 1815, Gordon, *Letters and Records,* 216–17; Codrington to Jane Codrington, November 23–December 31, 1814, Codrington Papers, COD/6/2, Caird.

24. Order, December 15, 1814, Codrington Papers, COD/6/4, Caird; Eaton and Van Crownin-shield, *Memoirs of Andrew Jackson*, 221.

25. Gleig, *Narrative*, 265–66; Forrest, *Journal*, 26.

26. Ellis, *First West India Regiment*, 145; Letter from the HMS *Ramillies*, January 5, 1815, Washington, DC, *Daily National Intelligencer*, March 23, 1815.

27. Gordon to Lydia Gordon, January 9, 1815, Gordon, *Letters and Records*, 216–17; Surtees, *Rifle Brigade*, 336; Gleig Diary, December 20, 1814, Barrett, *85th King's Light Infantry*, 197.

28. Disembarkation Return of the Advance Guard, December 21, 1814, Memorandum Book, Pultney Malcolm Papers, MAL/104, Caird.

29. Gleig, *Narrative*, 266, said in 1821 that several Americans had already deserted to them and told them of the alarm in New Orleans after Jones's defeat, saying that Jackson had barely 5,000 men and the inhabitants were leaving in droves, while those remaining would join the British. The deserters also spoke of the wealth of the town and all the plunder there would be. Six years later in his "A Subaltern in America" articles for *Blackwood's Edinburgh Magazine*, Gleig said that the two American officer deserters were also taken along to act as guides. No one else seems to have mentioned them (see George Robert Gleig, *A Subaltern in America; Comprising His Narrative of the Campaigns of the British Army, at Baltimore, Washington, &c. &c. During the Late War* [Philadelphia: Carey and Hart, 1833], 207).

Debate has long swirled around the authorship of "A Subaltern in America," which appeared first in *Blackwood's Edinburgh Magazine* 21–22, in March–September 1827. Many suspected Gleig was the author (see, for instance, "Subaltern in America, and Man of War's Man," *Naval and Military Magazine* 2, no. 4 (December 1828): 479. Historians have gone back and forth, though most accept his authorship (see, for instance, Remini, *New Orleans*, 206 n.17; Brown, *Amphibious Campaign*, 198 n.2, 202 n.7). The most modern student, Hickey, concluded that Gleig authored the articles. In March–September 1825 *Blackwood's* had serialized a memoir of his service in Europe during the late war, listing the author only as "Subaltern"; but it was soon common knowledge that Gleig was the author, and he admitted it. That same year Blackwood brought it out in book format. The next year a second edition of his *Narrative* appeared from its publisher, John Murray, capitalizing on the popularity of the Blackwood book by stating that it was "By the Author of the 'Subaltern'." The appearance at the same time of a second edition of the European memoir evidenced the marketability of the sobriquet.

In January 1827 Gleig wrote to magazine publisher William Blackwood that he had ample material for another memoir. A new series of articles in *Blackwood's* might be the answer, but he feared to offend Murray, the publisher of his 1821 *Narrative*. Consequently, he wrote the articles listing himself only as "Subaltern." After the first installment of "A Subaltern in America" appeared in *Blackwood's* in March 1827, there was immediate speculation about his authorship. "I would not on any account have the secret [revealed]," he told Blackwood. A year later, he sought Blackwood's permission to compile the installments into a book. Blackwood must have balked at that, for it never appeared in book form in England, but installments published in America appeared as a book in Philadelphia in 1833 (Gleig to Blackwood, January 6, March 9, 1827, December 25, 1828, Blackwood Papers, NLS).

30. Disembarkation Return of the Advance Guard Under the Command of Colonel William Thornton, December 21, 1814, Memorandum Book, Pultney Malcolm Papers, MAL/104, Caird.

31. Charles R. Forrest Memorandum, December 20, 1814, Alexander Skene Memorandum, December 21, 1814, Memorandum Book, Pultney Malcolm Papers, MAL/104, Caird.

32. Forrest Memorandum, December 20, 1814, Alexander Skene Memorandum, December 21, 1814, Memorandum Book, December 22, 1814, Pultney Malcolm Papers, MAL/104, Caird; Memo, December 21, 1814, Forrest, *Journal*, 27–28.

33. Gleig Diary, December 21, 1814, Barrett, *85th King's Light Infantry*, 197–98. Nothing more is to be found on these supposed deserters. Gleig also mentioned them in *Subaltern*, 207. Surtees, *Rifle Brigade*, 339–40, stated that half a dozen "French Americans" appeared that same day with much the same story that Jackson had "scarcely any troops in the district," and if the British were to land on the west bank of the Mississippi, they could "march right on to the town," where the local population would welcome them without resistance. He may have been recollecting this same group or it could have been another. They might also have been the "former Spanish residents of New Orleans" referred to fifty years later by Lossing, who portrayed them as onetime city officials and as the informants who alerted Cochrane to Bayou Bienvenue and

represented Jackson as "an ignorant tyrant, detested by the people, and void of any efficient means for defending the city." This is more likely a garbled recollection of some earlier stories. Lossing, "Scenes in the War of 1812," 171.

34. Letter from New Orleans to Washington, December 30, 1814, Georgetown, DC, *Federal Republican for the Country*, January 31, 1815; Surtees, *Rifle Brigade*, 339–40. Surtees wrote his account sometime prior to his death in 1830, so it is at least a dozen years after the fact. Gleig wrote his diary the same day of course, and his *Narrative* account in 1821, and his *Subaltern* version in 1827. It is important to acknowledge that neither Surtees nor Gleig would ordinarily have been in a position to know firsthand the content of any information provided by Americans, *creoles*, or Spaniards, though Gleig did state in his diary that he spoke with them at the time. Still, what he and Surtees have to say about the episode could be nothing more than hearsay. William Surtees suspected the visitors of being Jackson's spies sent to feed Keane false information, which seems unlikely given that Old Hickory did not yet know that the British were on Pine Island. Jane De Grummond speculated that Baratarians and planters told the British where to land to lure them into a trap, but virtually nothing supports that theory (De Grummond, *Beluche*, 96).

35. Reid and Eaton, *Jackson*, 255.

36. Cochrane to Croker, January 18, 1815, London, UK, *Courier, and Evening Gazette*, March 10, 1815; Letter from the HMS *Ramillies*, January 5, 1814, Kingston, Jamaica, *Courant*, January 27, 1814; Gleig, *Narrative*, 274–76; Cochrane Journal, December 22–23, 1814, ADM 50/122, Kew.

37. Walker, *Jackson and New Orleans*, 119.

38. Forrest, *Journal*, 28–29.

39. *Naval Chronicle, for 1815*, vol. 33, 485.

40. Gleig Diary, December 22, 1814, Barrett, *85th King's Light Infantry*, 199; Surtees, *Rifle Brigade*, 340; Codrington to Jane Codrington, November 23–December 31, 1814, Codrington Papers, COD/6/2, Caird.

41. Gordon to Lydia Gordon, January 9, 1815, Gordon, *Letters and Records*, 217.

42. Gleig Diary, December 22, 1814, Barrett, *85th King's Light Infantry*, 199; Forrest, *Journal*, 28–29; Cooke, *Narrative*, 183.

43. "Historical Incidents Before the Battle of New Orleans," New Orleans, *Daily Picayune*, November 14, 1852. The full version of the event as given in this article is rather a fanciful account, yet has elements that appear to agree with the few more contemporary sources. This source says the guards were in a tent, but contemporary sources refer to it as a hut or huts.

44. Gleig Diary, December 22, 1814, Barrett, *85th King's Light Infantry*, 198–99.

45. Ibid.

46. "Historical Incidents before the Battle of New Orleans," New Orleans, *Daily Picayune*, November 14, 1852.

47. Surtees, *Rifle Brigade*, 341.

48. Gleig Diary, January 22, 1815, Barrett, *85th King's Light Infantry*, 231.

49. Codrington to Jane Codrington, November 23–December 31, 1814, Codrington Papers, COD/6/2, Caird.

50. Gordon to Lydia Gordon, January 9, 1815, Gordon, *Letters and Records*, 217; Cochrane to Croker, January 18, 1815, London, UK, *Courier, and Evening Gazette*, March 10, 1815.

51. "Naval Officer" to unknown recipient, January 30, 1815, *Naval Chronicle, for 1815*, vol. 33, 386–88. The writer of this letter is described only as "a young but intelligent Naval Officer."

52. Chesterton, *Peace, War, and Adventure*, 180.

53. Report of Major General John Keane to Pakenham, December 26, 1814, London, UK, *Morning Post*, March 10, 1815; Letter from the HMS *Ramillies*, January 5, 1815, Washington, DC, *Daily National Intelligencer*, March 23, 1815.

54. Letter from the HMS *Ramillies*, January 5, 1815, Washington, DC, *Daily National Intelligencer*, March 23, 1815.

55. Letter from an officer aboard the British fleet off Louisiana coast, January 30, 1815, *Naval Chronicle, for 1815*, vol. 33, 385–88.

56. Surtees, *Rifle Brigade*, 340.

57. Forrest, *Journal*, 29.

58. "Recollections of the Expedition," Part 3, 189–90; Report of Major General John Keane to Pakenham, December 26, 1814, London, UK, *Morning Post*, March 10, 1815. Judging from context,

the anonymous author of "Recollections" was with either the 4th or 85th Regiment. Gordon, who was not with this contingent, was surely repeating what some who were told him about thinking they heard the enemy felling trees to block the path. No Americans were anywhere in the vicinity. Gordon to Lydia Gordon, January 9, 1815, Gordon, *Letters and Records*, 217.

59. Chesterton, *Peace, War, and Adventure,* 182–83.

60. "Recollections of the Expedition," Part 3, 187–88.

61. William H. Cope, *The History of the Rifle Brigade (The Prince Consort's Own) Formerly the 95th* (London: Chatto & Windus, 1877), 182–83; Hill, *Recollections*, 1:305.

62. Burgoyne, *93rd Sutherland Highlanders*, 27.

63. Cope, *Rifle Brigade*, 183.

64. Thomas Johnston to friend in Lexington, KY, January 6, 1815, Lexington, KY, *Western Monitor*, January 27, 1815.

65. Elizabeth Clement to Jacob Wood, January 11, 1815, Clement, *Plantation Life*, 127; Report of the Managers of the Louisiana Bible Society, New Orleans, *Louisiana Gazette*, April 25, 1815, in Utica, NY, *Patrol*, June 22, 1815.

66. L. Leresne to Girod, October 28, 1815, Girod to Charles Louis Blache, December 5, 1814, New Orleans Municipal Records, LSU.

67. Notary John Lynd, Volume 11 January–December 1814, 474–81, 487–90, 492–94, 846–67, Notary Claude Dejean, Volume 1 April 1813 to December 1814, 178–82, Notary Michel DeArmas, Volume 8 1814, 292–96, 521, 525, 529–36, Notary Marc Lafitte, Volume 4 1814, 393, Volume 7 Protests Jan–Dec 1811–1815, Notary Narcisse Broutin, Volume 31 1814, 606, 610–11, 613–15, 621–22, Notary Pierre Pedescleaux, Volume 69 July 9, 1814–March 9, 1815, 185–202, 204, New Orleans Notarial Archives; P. Pedescleaux, Plauché's Battalion, Index to Compiled Service Records of Volunteer Soldiers Who Served During the War of 1812, RG 94, NA. Roulhac Toledano and Mary Louise Christovich, *New Orleans Architecture: Faubourg Tremé and the Bayou Road* (New Orleans: Pelican Publishing, 2003), 93. Lafitte's Volume 7 is not paginated, but the pertinent acts are on dates December 14 and 17, 1814.

68. Claiborne to Louisiana Senators and Congressmen, December 20, 1814, Rowland, *Letter Books*, 6:325; Daniel Rodman to Livingston, February 13, 1815, Livingston Papers, Princeton; John Forsythe to R. H. Wilde, January 8, 1815, Parsons Collection, Texas.

69. Claiborne to Jackson, December 20, 1814, ibid., 211.

70. Claiborne to Jackson, December 22, 1814, ibid., 214–15.

71. Jackson to Villeré, December 19, 1814, Moser et al., *Papers*, 210, 222n.

72. Manuscript Concerning the Army Under General Morgan at English Turn, Arsène Lacarrière Latour Archive, HNOC.

73. Jackson to Morgan, December 22, 1814, Morgan Papers, LC.

74. Ibid.

75. David Morgan to Villeré, December 20, 21, 1814, Villeré Papers, HNOC; James Rinker, Index to Compiled Service Records of Volunteer Soldiers Who Served During the War of 1812, RG 94, NA.

76. Bassett, *Tatum's Journal*, December 22, 1814, 106.

77. Hicky to John Keisen, December 22, 1814, David Fluker to Hicky, December 22, 1814, Philip Hicky and Family Papers, LSU.

78. Butler to Ogden, December 22, 1814, Moser et al., *Papers*, 487.

79. Jackson to Philemon Thomas, December 22, 1814, Moser et al., *Papers*, 214.

80. Jackson to Villeré, December 22, 1814, ibid., 486.

81. *Appeal of L. Louaillier*, 18; Latour, *Historical Memoir*, 71–72.

82. Reynolds to Morgan, January 29, 1815, Parsons Collection, Texas.

83. Reynolds to Jackson, December 24, 1814, Moser et al., *Papers*, 487.

84. Extract of a letter from New Orleans to a member of Congress, December 22, 1814, Boston, MA, *Boston Weekly Messenger*, January 27, 1815; Bassett, *Tatum's Journal*, December 22, 1814, 106.

85. Letter from an officer in Jackson's Army, December 22, 1814, Charleston, SC, *City Gazette*, January 21, 1814.

86. Simpson to Mary Simpson, December 19, 1814, Stephen Simpson Letters, Princeton.

87. Thomas Shields and Robert Morrell to Cochrane, January 3, 1815, Cochrane Papers, NLS.

88. Patterson to Cochrane, January 23, 1815, Cochrane Papers, NLS. Certainly, other British officers saw the Shields-Morrell mission as an effort to gain intelligence. "Recollections of the Expedition," part 3, 187.

89. Shields and Morrell to Patterson, January 14, 1814, Shields and Morrell to B. B. Bowden, December 26, 1814, Bowden to Shields and Morrell, December 26, 1814, Captains' Letters, RG 260, NA.

90. Eaton and Van Crowninshield, *Memoirs of Andrew Jackson*, 229–30; Reid and Eaton, *Jackson*, 285.

91. Letter from an officer in Jackson's Army, December 22, 1814, Charleston, SC, *City Gazette*, January 21, 1814.

92. Reid and Eaton, *Jackson*, 268–69.

93. Letter from St. Francisville, December 16, 1814, Paris, KY, *Western Citizen*, January 14, 1815; Jackson to Coffee, December 16, 1814, Robert Butler to Coffee, December 15, 1814, Orderly Book of Brigadier General John Coffee, Cook Collection, MSS 557, HNOC; Coffee to Mary Donelson Coffee, December 15, 1814, John H. DeWitt, ed., "Letters of General John Coffee to His Wife, 1813–1815," *Tennessee Historical Magazine* 2, no. 4 (December 1916): 289.

94. Eaton and Van Crowninshield, *Memoirs of Andrew Jackson*, 218.

95. Coffee to Jackson, December 17, 1814, Moser et al., *Papers*, 209.

96. Jackson to Coffee December 17, 1814, Orderly Book of Brigadier General John Coffee, Cook Collection, MSS 557, HNOC.

97. Reid and Eaton, *Jackson*, 268–69; Concord, NH, *New Hampshire Patriot and State Gazette*, October 13, 1818.

98. Andrew Hynes to Samuel Carswell, January 6, 1815, Hynes Papers, Tulane; Urquhart to Fromentin, December 16, 1814, Boston, MA, *New-England Palladium*, January 17, 1815.

99. Reid and Eaton, *Jackson*, 248–49.

100. Nashville, TN, *Nashville Daily Gazette*, November 10, 1858.

101. Monroe to Graham, February 5, 1827, Graham Family Papers, VHS.

102. William Carroll to Jackson, December 14, 1814, Moser et al., *Papers*, 203.

103. Letter from Carroll's division to citizen in Paris, KY, December 29, 1814, Alexandria, VA, *Alexandria Gazette*, January 31, 1815.

104. Moser et al., *Papers*, 204n.

105. Letter from New Orleans, December 21, 1814, Utica, NY, *Columbian Gazette*, January 24, 1815.

106. Letter from New Orleans to Robertson, December 22, 1814, Boston, MA, *Boston Weekly Messenger*, January 27, 1815.

107. Letter from New Orleans, December 21, 1814, Utica, NY, *Columbian Gazette*, January 24, 1815.

108. Bassett, *Tatum's Journal*, December 22, 1814, 105–6.

109. Monroe to Graham, February 5, 1827, Graham Family Papers, VHS.

110. Brigade Order, December 21, 1814, Orderly Book of Brigadier General John Coffee, Cook Collection, MSS 557, HNOC.

111. Jackson to Monroe, February 13, 1815, Parker Papers, HSP.

112. Davis, *Rogue Republic*, 231, 288–89.

113. Romford to Monroe, February 4, 1815, Washington, DC, *National Intelligencer*, February 16, 1815.

114. Washington, DC, *Daily National Intelligencer*, February 16, 1815.

115. Boston, MA, *Boston Commercial Gazette*, April 6, 1815.

116. Louisiana General Assembly Resolution, February 1, 1815, Baltimore, MD, *Baltimore Telegraph*, March 16, 1815.

117. Brown to Livingston, November 2, 1814, Livingston Papers, Princeton; Robertson to Villeré, November 19, 1814, De La Vergne Family Papers, Tulane.

118. Melhorn, "What If the British Had Won?" 65–69.

119. Ellis, First West India Regiment, 145–46; Cooke, *Narrative*, 188.

CHAPTER SEVEN: "BY THE ETERNAL! I'LL FIGHT THEM TONIGHT"

1. Florian to Roosevelt, New Orleans, January 9, 1815, HNOC. The earliest known account crediting Gabriel Villeré with bringing the alarm to New Orleans is in Letter from New Orleans, December 24, 1814, Albany, NY, *Register*, January 27, 1815. The account is skimpy, saying only that the British entered General Villeré's home unobserved and encountered "Mr. Villaret's [*sic*] son who however, effected his escape came to town, and informed us of the enemy's approach." Burlington, VT, *Gazette*, February 3, 1815, paraphrases what may or may not be

the same letter, dating it to the morning of December 24, saying that an unnamed son of Villeré's was captured but "escaped to the city and gave the alarm."

This/these December 24 letter[s] is/are the earliest actual circumstantial account of Gabriel Villeré's capture and escape that refers to him by name. It is supported by a later letter written from New Orleans that referred to Villeré's warning Jackson by saying "a young creole, whom they had made prisoner escaped and told the General." Letter from New Orleans, January 9, 1815, Wilkes-Barre, PA, *Susquehanna Democrat*, February 17, 1815.

2. "Historical Incidents Before the Battle of New Orleans," New Orleans, *Daily Picayune*, November 14, 1852. The author of this account has not been identified. It differs substantially from the account by Bernard de Marigny written four months earlier for the New Orleans, LA, *Daily Delta*, July 8, 1852. Given that it was written thirty-eight years after the fact, it cannot be regarded as definitively accurate on all counts.

3. General Orders, March 3, 1815, Court Martial of Major René Gabriel Villeré, Order Book, Louisiana Militia, RG 107, Louisiana Historical Center, New Orleans. Thomas Joyes identified the man as Jesus, which is close enough to Hishoche phonetically to suggest that the common Spanish given name is correct. Joyes Journal, February 28, 1815, Joyes Papers, Filson.

4. Cope, *Rifle Brigade*, 183; Surtees, *Rifle Brigade*, 342–43.

5. Isabelle Marshall French, *They Lived at Chalmette* (New Orleans: Hope Publications, 1978), 14; Samuel Wilson, *Plantation Houses on the Battlefield of New Orleans* (New Orleans: Battle of New Orleans, 150th Anniversary Committee of Louisiana, 1965), 87–90.

6. Forrest, *Journal*, 31.

7. Ibid., 30; Surtees, *Rifle Brigade*, 340, 342–43.

8. "Recollections of the Expedition," part 3, 189–90; "Naval Officer" to unknown recipient, January 30, 1815, *Naval Chronicle, for 1815*, vol. 33, 386, 388; Report of Major General John Keane to Pakenham, December 26, 1814, London, UK, *Morning Post*, March 10, 1815.

9. Cope, *Rifle Brigade*, 183; Surtees, *Rifle Brigade*, 340; Forrest, *Journal*, 30–31.

10. Bernard de Marigny obituary of Jacques Villeré, New Orleans, LA, *Daily Delta*, July 8, 1852; "Historical Incidents Before the Battle of New Orleans," New Orleans, LA, *Daily Picayune*, November 14, 1852; Dusuau de la Croix to the Editor, July 19, 1852, New Orleans, LA, *Daily Delta*, July 25, 1852; Villeré, *Villeré*, 50–51. Given the number of references made in letters of December 23–25 to Villeré being the first source of information on the landing, there seems no reasonable doubt that his news predated that of anyone else. The narrative here presented, including the story of the unfortunate dog, is clearly the story as Villeré told it repeatedly through the years.

11. Latour, *Historical Memoir*, 54; Walker, *Jackson and New Orleans*, 150. Walker claimed that Villeré arrived at 1:30.

12. Jackson was wildly imprecise as to when he got this information. Forty-eight hours afterward he said he was not informed of the enemy landing "until evening." A day later he said he learned of it at "12 M," meaning midday or noon. Jackson to David Holmes, December 25, 1814, Moser et al., *Papers*, 219, Jackson to Robert Hays, December 26, 1814, 221.

13. John H. Johnson to St. Francisville, LA, *Time-Piece*, December 30, 1814, Washington, DC, *National Intelligencer*, February 4, 1815.

14. James H. Gordon to Joseph Dubuclet, December 23, 1814, Gaspar Cusachs Estate Gift Collection RG 112, Louisiana Historical Center, New Orleans.

15. Latour, *Historical Memoir*, 68; Eaton and Van Crowninshield, *Memoirs of Andrew Jackson*, 230–31.

16. De la Croix to the Editor, July 19, 1852, New Orleans, LA, *Daily Delta*, July 25, 1852.

17. "Historical Incidents Before the Battle of New Orleans," New Orleans, LA, *Daily Picayune*, November 14, 1852; New Orleans, LA, *Daily Delta*, July 8, 1852.

18. Edward Palfrey to John Palfrey, December 30, 1814, Palfrey Family Papers, MS Am 1704.7 (73), Houghton Library, Harvard University, Cambridge, MA.

19. Jackson to Monroe, February 13, 1815, Parker Papers, HSP.

20. This theme is well developed in Blake Dunnavent, "Lessons Learned from the War of 1812 for the U. S. Military in the Twenty-First Century," in McLemore, *History and Memory*, 126ff. In modern parlance, it comes down to the fruity aphorism, "When life gives you lemons, make lemonade."

21. Jackson to Hays, December 23, 1814, Moser et al., *Papers*, 217.

22. Letter from a member of Adams's troop of cavalry to a friend in Natchez, December 30, 1814, Natchez, MS, *Mississippi Republican*, January 4, 1814, in New York, NY, *New-York Evening Post*, February 1, 1815; Reid and Eaton, *Jackson*, 299.

23. Ellery, "Notes," NYPL.

24. Bassett, *Tatum's Journal*, December 23, 1814, 107.

25. Shaumburg to Wilkinson, January 25, 1815, HNOC; Unknown writer to his mother in France, March 21, 1815, War of 1812 Collection, Tulane.

26. See, for instance, letter from New Orleans to New York, December 30, 1814, Boston, MA, *Boston Daily Advertiser*, February 4, 1815, and letter from New Orleans to a merchant in Baltimore, January 1, 1815, Baltimore, MD, *American, and Commercial Daily Advertiser*, February 3, 1815; Letter from an officer in Jackson's army to Nashville, January 5, 1815, Washington, DC, *National Intelligencer*, February 4, 1815.

27. Florian to Roosevelt, New Orleans, January 9, 1815, HNOC; Letter to friend in New York, n.d., New York, NY, *New-York Spectator*, February 1, 1815; Ellery, "Notes," NYPL; Fromentin to unknown, January 28, 1815, Philadelphia, PA, *Relf's Philadelphia Gazette, and Daily Advertiser*, February 1, 1815; Eaton and Van Crowninshield, *Memoirs of Andrew Jackson*, 230; Ritchie, "Louisiana Campaign," 41; Dustin W. Cotton, "The Performance of the Louisiana Militia During the Battle of New Orleans, 1814–1815" (MA thesis, Southeastern Louisiana University, Hammond, LA, 2007), 33; Martin, *Louisiana*, 2:239.

28. Edward Palfrey to John Palfrey, December 30, 1814, Palfrey Family Papers, Harvard.

29. Letter from New Orleans, December 23, 1814, Rutland, VT, *Rutland Herald*, February 1, 1815. Most immediately contemporaneous sources put the sounding of the alarm at or close to two p.m.

30. Unknown writer to his mother in France, March 21, 1815, War of 1812 Collection, Tulane.

31. Ellery, "Notes," NYPL.

32. Elizabeth Clement to Jacob Wood, January 11, 1815, Clement, *Plantation Life*, 127; Florian to Roosevelt, January 9, 1815, HNOC.

33. Letter from Greenville, Mississippi Territory, to Philadelphia, January 31, 1815, Wilmington, DE, *American Watchman*, March 4, 1815.

34. New Orleans, LA, *L'Ami des Lois*, January 16, 1815, Bowden, Private Letters, 245.

35. Walker, *Jackson and New Orleans*, 161; Michael W. Trimble, "Trimble's Account of the Battle of New Orleans," Mississippi Department of Archives and History, Jackson, MS. See also J. F. H. Claiborne, Mississippi, as a Province, Territory and State, with Biographical Notices of Eminent Citizens (Jackson, MS: Power and Barksdale, 1880), 342.

36. Shaumburg to Wilkinson, January 25, 1815, HNOC.

37. Reid and Eaton, *Jackson*, 287; Nolte, *Memoirs*, 209; Eaton and Van Crowninshield, *Memoirs of Andrew Jackson*, 234.

38. Letter from New Orleans, December 23, 1814, Rutland, VT, *Rutland Herald*, February 1, 1815.

39. Letter from New Orleans, December 26, 1814, Richmond, VA, *Richmond Enquirer*, January 28, 1815.

40. Latour, *Historical Memoir*, 214.

41. Richard K. Call to William Tanner, April 3, 1844, Francis Preston Blair, *The Life and Public Services of Gen. William O. Butler* (Baltimore: N. Hickman, 1848), 11–12.

42. Letter from New Orleans, December 30, 1814, Boston, MA, *Columbian Centinel*, February 4, 1815.

43. Forrest, *Journal*, December 23, 1814, 30–31; Letter from New Orleans, December 26, 1814, Natchez, MS, *Mississippi Republican*, December 31, 1814, in New York, NY, *New-York Evening Post*, February 1, 1815; Walker, *Jackson and New Orleans*, 166.

44. Letter from a Tennessee volunteer, December 29, 1814, Richmond, VA, *Richmond Enquirer*, February 1, 1815.

45. John Coffee to Mary Coffee, January 20, 1815, Robert Dyas Collection of John Coffee Papers, Tennessee State Library and Archives, Nashville; Letter from Carroll's division to citizen in Paris, KY, December 29, 1814, Alexandria, VA, Alexandria *Gazette*, January 31, 1815.

46. Letter from New Orleans, January 2, 1815, New York, NY, *New-York Evening Post*, February 8, 1815.

47. Robert Cobb to John Cobb, February 3, 1815, Robert L. Cobb Letters Concerning the Battle of New Orleans, HNOC.

48. Letter from an officer in Coffee's command army to friend in Charleston, January 5, 1815, Charleston, SC, *City Gazette*, February 4, 1815; Trimble, "Trimble's Account," MDAH.

49. Shaumburg to Wilkinson, January 25, 1815, HNOC; General Return of the Militia of the State of Louisiana, December 25 or 28, 1814, Arsène Lacarrière Latour Archive, HNOC.

50. Claiborne to Labatut, September 22, 1815, Rowland, *Letter Book*, 6:367, Michael Fortier to Claiborne, November 11, 1815, 386.

51. Jean-Baptiste Plauché Report, December 26, 1814, Early Louisiana Documents, HNOC; Nolte, *Memoirs*, 210.

52. Plauché Report, December 26, 1814, Early Louisiana Documents, HNOC; Louisiana General Assembly Resolution, February 1, 1815, Baltimore, MD, *Baltimore Telegraph*, March 16, 1815; Latour, *Historical Memoir*, 78–79.

53. Account of the Battle of New Orleans, 1815, Jackson Papers, LC; Latour, *Historical Memoir*, 78–79.

54. Walker, *Jackson and New Orleans*, 157; Parton, *Jackson* 2:73n. Neither of these sources offers any authority for their statements.

55. Jackson to McLean, March 22, 1824, *Appeal of L. Louaillier*, 20–21n; Elizabeth Clement to Wood, January 11, 1815, Clement, *Plantation Life*, 127.

56. Gould Memoir, VHS.

57. Morning Report of the 7th Infantry, December 14, 1814, United States Army Morning Reports, HNOC; Latour, *Historical Memoir*, 78–79.

58. Numbers are always uncertain in these situations. New Orleans, LA, *Louisiana Gazette for the Country*, April 29, June 10, 1815, reports him as having 2,325 on December 23. Latour, *Historical Memoir*, 78–79, made it 2,131. See also Jackson to Hays, December 26, 1814, Moser et al., *Papers*, 221.

59. Account of the Battle of New Orleans, 1815, Jackson Papers, LC.

60. Ibid.

61. Letter from New Orleans, December 23, 1814, Lexington, KY, *Reporter*, January 13, 1815.

62. Letter from New Orleans to the Philadelphia, PA, *Gazette*, December 24, 1814, New York, NY, *New-York Gazette & General Advertiser*, January 26, 1815; Letter from Fort St. John to Editor, [December 30, 1814], Washington, KY, *Union*, January 27, 1815; Chew to Maria Chew, December 23, 1814, Norfolk, VA, *Norfolk Gazette & Publick Ledger*, January 25, 1815.

63. Plauché Report, December 26, 1814, Early Louisiana Documents, HNOC.

64. Letter from Fort St. John to Editor, [December 30, 1814], Washington, KY, *Union*, January 27, 1815.

65. William Priestley to Latour, March 4, 1816, Latour Archive, HNOC; Jackson to Hays, December 26, 1814, War of 1812 Mss., Lilly Library; Bassett, *Tatum's Journal*, December 23, 1814, 111.

66. Louisiana General Assembly Resolution, February 1, 1815, Baltimore, MD, *Baltimore Telegraph*, March 16, 1815.

67. Shaumburg to Wilkinson, January 25, 1815, HNOC.

68. Account of the Battle of New Orleans, 1815, Jackson Papers, LC; Jackson to Claiborne, December 23, 1814, Moser et al., *Papers*, 218.

69. Claiborne to Shaumburg, October 1, 1815, Rowland, *Letter Books*, 6:371–72.

70. Shaumburg to Claiborne, October 30, 1815, ibid., 378.

71. Forrest, *Journal*, 43.

72. John Michell, "Diary of Major J. Michell," *Louisiana Historical Quarterly* 44, nos. 3–4 (July–October 1961), December 23, 1814, 127; Surtees, *Rifle Brigade*, 344.

73. Cope, *Rifle Brigade*, 184.

74. Surtees, *Rifle Brigade*, 344–45; Cooke, *Narrative*, 189.

75. Gleig Diary, December 23, 1814, Barrett, *85th King's Light Infantry*, 199.

76. Tregle, *Louisiana in the Age of Jackson*, 2–3; Hill, *Recollections*, 1:305.

77. Gordon to Lydia Gordon, January 9, 1815, Gordon, *Letters and Records*, 217.

78. Walker, *Jackson and New Orleans*, 132–33, 136.

79. Gerard, Campaigns 2, USNA.

80. Martin, Louisiana, 2:374.

CHAPTER EIGHT: "FURY AND CONFUSION"

1. Account of the Battle of New Orleans, 1815, Jackson Papers, LC.
2. John Coffee statement, n.d., Parsons Collection, Texas; Davis, *Pirates Laffite*, 214–15.
3. Henry Palfrey to John Palfrey, January 20, 1815, Gatell, "Boston Boy in 'Mr. Madison's War,'" 159.
4. List of Military Volunteers Who Participated in the Battle of New Orleans, L. M. Raynaud, "Part Taken by the Battalion of Volunteers of Orleans, During the Invasion of Louisiana by the British Army, In 1814 and 1815," Miscellaneous Collection, RG 68, Louisiana Historical Center.
5. Plauché Report, December 26, 1814, Early Louisiana Documents, HNOC.
6. Account of the Battle of New Orleans, 1815, Jackson Papers, LC.
7. Ibid.
8. Unknown writer to his mother in France, March 21, 1815, War of 1812 Collection, Tulane; New Orleans, LA, *Louisiana Gazette for the Country*, February 2, 1815, in Washington, DC, *Daily National Intelligencer*, March 6, 1815; Jackson to Monroe, December 27, 1814, Baltimore, MD, *Baltimore Telegraph*, January 31, 1815.
9. Eaton and Van Crowninshield, *Memoirs of Andrew Jackson*, 245; Trimble, "Trimble's Account," MDAH.
10. A few sources then and later maintained that *Carolina* had two gunboats with her, but such was not the case. Ritchie, "Louisiana Campaign," 35; Keane to Pakenham, December 26, 1814, WO/141, Kew.
11. William Murphy to his mother, December 27, 1814, Charleston, SC, *City Gazette*, January 28, 1815; Washington, DC, *Daily National Intelligencer*, June 7, August 17, 1813.
12. The moon for that date was waxing gibbous, 79 percent of it visible, and it began to rise at 3:32 that afternoon. https://predicalendar.com/moon/phases/1814/December.
13. Account of the Battle of New Orleans, 1815, Jackson Papers, LC.
14. As usual with such events, times are approximate. Some sources say the action started at eight o'clock, others much earlier or later.
15. Forrest, *Journal*, 32.
16. Cope, *Rifle Brigade*, 183–84; Surtees, *Rifle Brigade*, 344–45; Hill, *Recollections*, 1:307.
17. Gleig Diary, December 23, 1814, Barrett, *85th King's Light Infantry*, 198–99.
18. William Graves to Maunsel White, n.d., [1845–53], New Orleans, LA, *Daily Delta*, January 8, 1854.
19. Letter from an officer aboard the British fleet off Louisiana coast, January 30, 1815, *Naval Chronicle, for 1815*, vol. 33, 388.
20. Ellery, "Notes," NYPL.
21. Cope, *Rifle Brigade*, 184.
22. Surtees, *Rifle Brigade*, 353.
23. Codrington to Jane Codrington, November 23–December 31, 1814, Codrington Papers, COD/6/2, Caird.
24. Reid and Eaton, *Jackson*, 289.
25. Gleig Diary, December 23, 1814, Barrett, *85th King's Light Infantry*, 199; Cooke, *Narrative*, 190–91.
26. Chesterton, *Peace, War, and Adventure*, 1:186.
27. Clement, *Truth Is No Slander*, 9. Clement states that Henley later told him this episode.
28. Surtees, *Rifle Brigade*, 345.
29. Murphy to his mother, December 27, 1814, Charleston, SC, *City Gazette*, January 28, 1815.
30. Graves to White, n.d. [1845–53], New Orleans, LA, *Daily Delta*, January 8, 1854.
31. Cooke, *Narrative*, 190–91; Gleig Diary, December 23, 1814, Barrett, *85th King's Light Infantry*, 199.
32. Peter Bowlby, *Walcheren, Spain, America and Waterloo: The Memoir of Captain Peter Bowlby 4th Foot (1791–1877)*, ed. Gareth Glover (Godmanchester, UK: Ken Trotman, 2016), 53.
33. Bassett, *Tatum's Journal*, December 23, 1814, 108; Clement, *Truth Is No Slander*, 9; Keane to Pakenham, December 26, 1814, WO/141, Kew; Forrest, *Journal*, 32.
34. Richard Cannon, comp., *Historical Record of The Fourth, or The King's Own Regiment of Foot* (London: William Clowes & Sons, 1839), 125.
35. Forrest, *Journal*, 32.

36. "Recollections of the Expedition," part 3, 190.
37. Clipping from undated issue of the New Orleans, LA, *Bulletin*, Henry Chotard Collection, RG 229, Louisiana Historical Center, New Orleans.
38. Bassett, *Tatum's Journal*, December 23, 1814, 107–8; Latour, *Historical Memoir*, 70.
39. Letter from Fort St. John to Editor, [December 30, 1814], Washington, KY, *Union*, January 27, 1815.
40. Eaton and Van Crowninshield, *Memoirs of Andrew Jackson*, 238–39.
41. Plauché Report, December 26, 1814, Early Louisiana Documents, HNOC.
42. Clement, *Truth Is No Slander*, 11; Shaumburg to Wilkinson, January 25, 1815, HNOC. A hyperbolic account that suffers from being secondhand, fourteen years after the fact, confused, probably not by an eyewitness or participant, and translated from French to English, maintains that if Plauché had obeyed Ross, the whole American line would have been captured. Nevertheless, it does reinforce other sources, particularly Plauché's report, that indicate Colonel Ross was performing erratically. Content suggests that the author was John Hudry. Particulars in relation to Battle of New Orleans furnished me by a French gentleman in 1828—Summer, Oran Follett Papers, Cincinnati Museum Center, Cincinnati History Library and Archives.
43. Nolte, *Memoirs*, 211.
44. Particulars in relation to Battle of New Orleans furnished me by a French gentleman in 1828—Summer, Follett Papers, Cincinnati History Library and Archives.
45. Claiborne, *Notes on the War*, 60.
46. "In Pakenham's Camp: War Diary, Hitherto Unpublished, of Mr. Benjamin Story, Orleans Rifle Company, Prisoner of War, From Dec. 23, 1814, to Jan. 18, 1815," New Orleans, LA, *Times-Democrat*, June 18, 1893. A typescript of this, identified only as "Battle of New Orleans descriptive account", 1814–1815, is in the Miscellaneous Manuscripts Collection, LC.
47. New Orleans, LA, *Louisiana Gazette for the Country*, February 2, 1815, in Washington, DC, *Daily National Intelligencer*, March 6, 1815.
48. Nolte, *Memoirs*, 211.
49. Plauché Report, December 26, 1814, Early Louisiana Documents, HNOC.
50. Edward Palfrey to John Palfrey, December 30, 1814, Palfrey Family Papers, Harvard; Plauché Report, December 26, 1814, Early Louisiana Documents, HNOC.
51. Ellery, "Notes," NYPL.
52. Ibid.
53. William A. Meuse, *The Weapons of the Battle of New Orleans* (New Orleans: Battle of New Orleans 150th Anniversary Committee of Louisiana, 1965), 4–5, 10–12.
54. Cope, *Rifle Brigade*, 184.
55. Surtees, *Rifle Brigade*, 345.
56. Ibid., xvii, 347–48.
57. Gleig Diary, December 23, 1814, Barrett, *85th King's Light Infantry*, 199–200. In his diary Gleig makes it clear that he is writing of his own personal experience, but seven years later in his *Narrative*, 291–94, he presented this experience as being related to him by "a friend of mine," probably from modesty.
58. Surtees, *Rifle Brigade*, 348–49.
59. R. Gubbins to unknown addressee, January 10, 1815, Barrett, *85th King's Light Infantry*, 228.
60. Ibid.; Report of Major General John Keane to Pakenham, December 26, 1814, WO/141, Kew; "Recollections of the Expedition," part 3, 190–91; Cannon, *The King's Own Regiment*, 126.
61. Tousard to John Stocker, January 6, 1815, Wilkinson, "Assaults on New Orleans," 50.
62. Rôle du Bataillon des Volontaires d'Orléans, Miscellaneous Manuscripts Collection, LC; Samuel Prince Winter to Elisha Winter, December 30, 1814, Washington, DC, *Daily National Intelligencer*, January 28, 1815.
63. Walker, *Jackson and New Orleans*, 190.
64. Cope, *Rifle Brigade*, 185.
65. Ibid., 184.
66. Surtees, *Rifle Brigade*, 349.
67. Gleig Diary, December 23, 1814, Barrett, *85th King's Light Infantry*, 200.
68. Particulars in relation to Battle of New Orleans furnished me by a French gentleman in 1828—Summer, Follett Papers, Cincinnati History Library and Archives; Letter by British naval officer, January 30, 1815, Lexington, KY, *Reporter*, August 2, 1815.

69. Cooke, *Narrative*, 190–91; Surtees, *Rifle Brigade*, 348. Cooke was in the 43rd Regiment and not yet landed, but had many friends in the 85th who he says told him of the engagement.

70. Ellery, "Notes," NYPL.

71. Account of the Battle of New Orleans, 1815, Jackson Papers, LC.

72. Bassett, *Tatum's Journal*, December 23, 1814, 108–9; Reid and Eaton, *Jackson*, 294.

73. Ellery, "Notes," NYPL; Reid and Eaton, *Jackson*, 294; Eaton and Van Crowninshield, *Memoirs of Andrew Jackson*, 241; Account of the Battle of New Orleans, 1815, Jackson Papers, LC.

74. General Orders, January 21, 1815, New Orleans, LA, *Louisiana Courier*, January 25, 1815.

75. Reid and Eaton, *Jackson*, 295.

76. Particulars in relation to Battle of New Orleans furnished me by a French gentleman in 1828—Summer, Follett Papers, Cincinnati History Library and Archives; Coffee to Donelson, January 25, 1815, Tennessee Historical Society Miscellaneous Files, University of Tennessee.

77. Bassett, *Tatum's Journal*, December 23, 1814, 107–8.

78. Ellery, "Notes," NYPL.

79. *Memorial of Beverly Chew and Others, Survivors of Beale's Rifle Company* (Washington, DC: Gales and Seaton, 1835), 1; John Coffee statement, n.d., Parsons Collection, Texas.

80. Robert Cobb to John Cobb, February 3, 1815, Robert L. Cobb Letters Concerning the Battle of New Orleans, HNOC.

81. James Moore King to James Moore, March [April] 15, 1815, James Moore King Collection, Gore Research Center, Middle Tennessee State University, Murfreesboro.

82. Walker, *Jackson and New Orleans*, 175–76.

83. Coffee to Donelson, January 25, 1815, Tennessee Historical Society Miscellaneous Files, University of Tennessee.

84. Robert Cobb to John Cobb, February 3, 1815, Robert L. Cobb Letters Concerning the Battle of New Orleans, HNOC.

85. William B. Fort to Abraham Fort, February 24, 1815, Cook Collection, HNOC.

86. Bassett, *Tatum's Journal*, December 23, 1814, 107–8; Reid and Eaton, *Jackson*, 299.

87. Jackson to Monroe, December 27, 1814, morning, Baltimore, MD, *Baltimore Telegraph*, January 31, 1815.

88. Letter from an officer in Coffee's command to a friend in Charleston, January 5, 1815, Charleston, SC, *City Gazette*, February 4, 1815.

89. Robert Cobb to John Cobb, February 3, 1815, Robert L. Cobb Letters Concerning the Battle of New Orleans, HNOC.

90. Letter from an officer in Coffee's command to a friend in Charleston, January 5, 1815, Charleston, SC, *City Gazette*, February 4, 1815.

91. William B. Fort to Abraham Fort, February 24, 1815, Cook Collection, HNOC. The expression is an American variant of the English expression "pull devil, pull baker," meaning essentially "every man for himself."

92. Reid and Eaton, *Jackson*, 297–98.

93. Trimble, "Trimble's Account," MDAH.

94. Kanon, *Tennesseans at War*, 154.

95. James Moore King to James Moore, March [April] 15, 1815, King Collection, Middle Tennessee State University, Murfreesboro. Cornet was the lowest commissioned rank, immediately below a lieutenant.

96. John Donelson, Jr. to John Donelson, January 27, 1815, Tennessee Historical Society Miscellaneous Files, 1688–1951, University of Tennessee, Knoxville.

97. Letter from New Orleans, January 2, 1815, New York, NY, *New-York Evening Post*, February 8, 1815.

98. "War Diary, Hitherto Unpublished, of Mr. Benjamin Story," New Orleans, *Times-Democrat*, June 18, 1893.

99. Letter from New Orleans, December 24, 1814, Baltimore, MD, *Baltimore Patriot & Evening Advertiser*, January 25, 1815. Chew to John Chew, January 6, 1815, Norfolk, VA, *Norfolk Gazette & Publick Ledger*, February 1, 1815; Edward Palfrey to John Palfrey, December 30, 1814, Palfrey Family Papers, Harvard. Chew's memoir in the New Jersey Historical Society makes no mention of his activities in the battle.

100. Letter from New Orleans to Chillicothe, January 6, 1815, Clinton, OH, *Ohio Register*, January 31, 1815.

101. Thomas Beale statement, October 1815, Commyns Estate, Succession and Probate Records, Orleans Parish, NOPL.
102. Boston, MA, *Columbian Centinel*, February 4, 1815.
103. Letter from a member of Beale's New Orleans Riflemen to?, December 30, 1814, Hanover, NH, *Dartmouth Gazette*, February 15, 1815.
104. Clement, *Truth Is No Slander*, 10; Elizabeth Clement to Wood, January 11, 1815, Clement, *Plantation Life*, 127.
105. Elizabeth Clement to Wood, January 11, 1815, Clement, *Plantation Life*, 128; New Orleans, LA, *Times-Picayune*, January 8, 1901.
106. Lewis to Robertson, December 23, 1814, Philadelphia, PA, *Relf's Philadelphia Gazette, and Daily Advertiser*, January 23, 1815.
107. Report of Major General John Keane to Pakenham, December 26, 1814, WO/141, Kew; Burgoyne, *93rd Sutherland Highlanders*, 39; Letter from New Orleans to Richmond, December 29, 1814, Augusta, GA, *Augusta Herald*, February 9, 1815; "Recollections of the Expedition," part 3, 190.
108. Pultney Malcolm to Cochrane, December 24, 1815, Charles Malcolm Papers, MAL/2, Caird.
109. Hill, *Recollections*, 1:307.
110. Clark, *Royal Scots Fusiliers*, [31].
111. Gordon to Lydia Gordon, January 9, 1815, Gordon, *Letters and Records*, 217.
112. Ellis, *First West India Regiment*, 146–47.
113. Roger N. Buckley, "The Early History of the West India Regiments 1795–1815: A Study in British Colonial Military History" (PhD dissertation, McGill University, Montreal, Quebec, Canada, 1975), 341.
114. Letter from Kingston, Jamaica, January 27, 1815, Richmond, VA, *Virginia Patriot*, March 25, 1815.
115. Report of Major General John Keane to Pakenham, December 26, 1814, WO/141, Kew; "Recollections of the Expedition," part 3, 190.
116. Forrest, *Journal*, 32.
117. Hill, *Recollections*, 1:308–9.
118. "Recollections of the Expedition," part 3, 190; Michell, "Diary of Major J. Michell," December 23, 1814, 127.
119. Letter from New Orleans, January 2, 1815, New York, NY, *New-York Evening Post*, February 8, 1815.
120. Livingston to Janet Montgomery, January 6, 1815, Livingston Papers, Princeton.
121. Rachel Johnson to William Johnson, January 6, 1815, Miscellaneous Collection, LSU; Reid and Eaton, *Jackson*, 304–5. The Rachel Johnson letter says that when asked their unit the British replied "the 155th." There was no such unit in Keane's army. Johnson was writing from Woodville, Mississippi Territory, two weeks after the fight, but the editor of the St. Francisville *Time-Piece* knew the story just one week after the fact (John H. Johnson to St. Francisville *Time-Piece*, December 30, 1814, Washington, DC, *National Intelligencer*, February 4, 1815). It almost certainly had to come from Kemper himself or one of the few men of Hinds's dragoons with him, but still could have gone through one or two intermediaries, affording opportunity for misstatement of the prisoners' regiment.
122. Particulars in relation to Battle of New Orleans furnished me by a French gentleman in 1828—Summer, Follett Papers, Cincinnati History Library and Archives.
123. Ellery, "Notes," NYPL.
124. Account of the Battle of New Orleans, 1815, Jackson Papers, LC.
125. Eaton and Van Crowninshield, *Memoirs of Andrew Jackson*, 245.
126. Jackson to Monroe, December 26, 1814, Baltimore, MD, *Baltimore Telegraph*, January 31, 1815; Bassett, *Tatum's Journal*, December 23, 1814, 111.
127. Call to Tanner, April 3, 1844, Blair, *Gen. William O. Butler*, 12.
128. Eaton and Van Crowninshield, *Memoirs of Andrew Jackson*, 245–46.
129. Surtees, *Rifle Brigade*, 352.
130. Account of the Battle of New Orleans, 1815, Jackson Papers, LC; Statement of G. Mre. Guichard, January 28, 1815, "Report of the Committee of Inquiry on the Military Measures Executed Against the Legislature," *Louisiana Historical Quarterly* 9, no. 2 (April 1926): 275.
131. Jonathan J. Rees to Rees, February 11, 1815, Rees Papers, Tulane.

132. Manuscript concerning the Army under General Morgan at English Turn, Latour Archive, HNOC. This document is unsigned and undated. Since Latour used it almost verbatim in *Historical Memoir*, 76, it clearly was written 1815–1816. It is docketed "Thomas," and the only man of that name with Declouet's regiment was his adjutant Lieutenant John Thomas.

133. Ellery, "Notes," NYPL.

134. Surtees, *Rifle Brigade*, 352.

135. Jackson to Monroe, February 13, 1815, Parker Papers, HSP; Livingston to Janet Montgomery, January 6, 1815, Livingston Papers, Princeton.

136. Jackson to Monroe, December 27, 1814, Baltimore, MD, *Baltimore Telegraph*, January 31, 1815.

137. Reid and Eaton, *Jackson*, 296; Bassett, *Tatum's Journal*, December 23, 1814, 109–11.

138. Account of the Battle of New Orleans, 1815, Jackson Papers, LC; Eaton and Van Crowninshield, *Memoirs of Andrew Jackson*, 240–42.

139. Account of the Battle of New Orleans, 1815, Jackson Papers, LC; Trimble, "Trimble's Account," MDAH; Jackson to Monroe, December 27, 1814, Baltimore, MD, *Baltimore Telegraph*, January 31, 1815; Bassett, *Tatum's Journal*, December 23, 1814, 109.

140. Coffee to Mary Coffee, January 20, 1815, Dyas Collection, Tennessee State Library and Archives, Nashville; Account of the Battle of New Orleans, 1815, Jackson Papers, LC.

141. Letter from New Orleans to the Editor, February 14, 1815, Washington, KY, *Union*, March 10, 1815.

CHAPTER NINE: "THE *BEST* FOUGHT ACTION IN THE ANNALS OF MILITARY WARFARE"

1. Letter from New Orleans to Richmond, December 29, 1814, Augusta, GA, *Augusta Herald*, February 9, 1815.

2. Gerard, Campaigns 2, USNA; Codrington to Jane Codrington, November 23–December 31, 1814, Codrington Papers, COD/6/2, Caird; Letter by British naval officer, January 30, 1815, Lexington, KY, *Reporter*, August 2, 1815.

3. Arguably, not for another half century, until June 1864 and Ulysses S. Grant's stunning crossing of the James River, would the continent see another such case of a major portion of an army appearing entirely unsuspected in its enemy's rear at a time when the opposing forces were not yet actually engaged.

4. "War Diary, Hitherto Unpublished, of Mr. Benjamin Story," New Orleans, LA, *Times-Democrat*, June 18, 1893.

5. Hill, *Recollections*, 1:312–13.

6. St. George's, Bermuda, *Gazette and Weekly Advertiser*, April 8, 1815. This account, which appeared earlier in an unknown issue of the Kingston, Jamaica, *Royal Gazette*, stated only that the note was found on the body of "an American Colonel" lying among the slain. The only American colonels killed in the New Orleans operations were James Lauderdale on December 23 and James Henderson on December 28. Of the two, context makes Lauderdale seem the more likely, since Jackson abandoned the field after the December 23 fight and the bodies of Lauderdale and others were thus available through the night for redcoats to examine and pilfer from. Henderson's body was recovered within hours of the close of action on December 28 and from a part of the field that was never open to the British after fighting there ceased.

7. Bassett, *Tatum's Journal*, December 28, 1814, 118; The General Monthly Return of the Serjeants, Trumpeters, Drummers, and Rank and File of the several Corps serving in the Army under the Command of Major General the Honble Sir E. M. Pakenham KB, December 25, 1814, WO 17/1218, Kew, shows no desertions from any British unit between November 25 and December 25. Since it also lists no deaths but only men taken prisoner or missing, it is apparent that it is incomplete. Thus, there could have been deserters among those listed as missing.

8. Return of Casualties in the Army Under the Command of Major General Keane in Action with the Enemy near New Orleans on the 23rd December 1814, WO 17/1218, Kew; Ellis, *First West India Regiment*, 148.

9. Codrington to Jane Codrington, November 23–December 31, 1814, Codrington Papers, COD/6/2, Caird.

10. Letter from the HMS *Ramillies*, January 5, 1815, Kingston, Jamaica, *Royal Gazette*, January 27, 1815; Letter from soldier of the 85th or 95th at New Orleans to the Editor, January 2, 1815, Kingston, Jamaica, *Courant*, January 27, 1814.

11. Gleig Diary, December 2324, 1814, Barrett, *85th King's Light Infantry*, 200–201; Gleig, *Narrative*, 298.

12. Gerard, Campaigns 2, USNA.

13. "War Diary, Hitherto Unpublished, of Mr. Benjamin Story," New Orleans, LA, *Times-Democrat*, June 18, 1893.

14. Surtees, *Rifle Brigade*, 354; Cope, *Rifle Brigade*, 184; "War Diary, Hitherto Unpublished, of Mr. Benjamin Story," New Orleans, LA, *Times-Democrat*, June 18, 1893.

15. Codrington to Jane Codrington, November 23–December 31, 1814, Codrington Papers, COD/6/2, Caird; Chesterton, *Peace, War, and Adventure*, 190. There are some discrepancies in these two accounts. Codrington's, being the earlier by almost forty years, is preferred.

16. Gleig Diary, December 24, 1814, Barrett, *85th King's Light Infantry*, 201; Forrest, *Journal*, 33.

17. Gerard, Campaigns 2, USNA; "Naval Officer" to unknown recipient, January 30, 1815, *Naval Chronicle, for 1815*, vol. 33, 386.

18. Gerard, Campaigns 2, USNA.

19. Michell, "Diary of Major J. Michell," December 23–24, 1814, 127.

20. Codrington to Jane Codrington, November 23–December 31, 1814, Codrington Papers, COD/6/2, Caird.

21. Codrington to the Respective Captains, December 24, 1814, Codrington Papers, COD/6/4, Caird.

22. Aitchison Memoir, 68–70, HNOC.

23. Reilly, *British at the Gates*, 233, faults Jackson for not placing forward pickets in advance of Major Villeré's small company.

24. John Donelson, Jr. to John Donelson, January 27, 1815, Tennessee Historical Society Miscellaneous Files, 1688–1951, University of Tennessee, Knoxville.

25. Ellery, "Notes," NYPL.

26. Letter from New Orleans, December 30, 1814, Boston, MA, *Columbian Centinel*, February 4, 1815.

27. Letter from St. Francisville to Baltimore, January 1, 1815, Baltimore, MD, *American, and Commercial Daily Advertiser*, January 30, 1815.

28. Robert Butler to Morgan, December 25, 1814, Morgan Papers, LC.

29. Letter from New Orleans, December 24, 1814, four a.m., Baltimore, MD, *Baltimore Patriot & Evening Advertiser*, January 25, 1815; Letter from New Orleans, December 23, 1814, Rutland, VT, *Rutland Herald*, February 1, 1815; Jackson to Monroe, December 27, 1814, Baltimore, MD, *Baltimore Telegraph*, January 31, 1815.

30. Jackson to Brown, February 4, 1815, War of 1812 Mss., Lilly Library.

31. Edmund P. Gaines to J. F. H. Claiborne, December 23, 1845, J. F. H. Claiborne, *Life and Times of Gen. Sam. Dale, the Mississippi Partisan* (New York: Harper and Brothers, 1860), 159n; Account of the Battle of New Orleans, 1815, Jackson Papers, LC.

32. Letter from a Tennessee volunteer, December 29, 1814, Richmond, VA, *Richmond Enquirer*, February 1, 1815; Letter from Carroll's division to citizen in Paris, KY, December 29, 1814, Alexandria, VA, *Alexandria Gazette*, January 31, 1815.

33. Letter from New Orleans, December 24, 1814 four a.m., Baltimore, MD, *Baltimore Patriot & Evening Advertiser*, January 25, 1815.

34. Trimble, "Trimble's Account," MDAH.

35. Jackson to Robert Hays, December 26, 1814, War of 1812 Mss., Lilly Library; Account of the Battle of New Orleans, 1815, Jackson Papers, LC; Bassett, *Tatum's Journal*, December 24, 1814, 111. In a long preamble to this entry, Tatum also stated that Jackson's decision was influenced by his anxiety to protect the wealth of New Orleans and the property in its warehouses, since booty was a principal goal of the enemy. This was probably written sometime after the actual journal entry for that day, and after the multiple stories accusing Cochrane of promising his men "beauty and booty" became common.

36. John H. Johnson to St. Francisville *Time-Piece*, December 30, 1814, Washington, DC, *National Intelligencer*, February 4, 1815.

37. This is the line that Napoleon's old companion General Moreau supposedly identified during his 1808 visit to New Orleans as the ideal place from which to defend the city, a story that first appeared in the New York, NY, *New-York Commercial Advertiser*, August 3, 1833. Nolte accepted it, as years later did Jane De Grummond. As stated earlier, the story is wholly apocryphal. Walker, often a willing victim of such stories, in this instance branded it "an absurd

fiction." (Nolte, *Memoirs*, 213; Jane Lucas De Grummond, "Platter of Glory," *Louisiana History* 3, no. 4 [Fall 1962]: 326; Walker, *Jackson and New Orleans*.) Interestingly, an earlier suggestion that Jackson was not responsible for spotting the utility of the position came from steamboatman Samuel Clement, who in 1824 stated that he heard the position was suggested to Jackson by local militia privates. Clement, being an outspoken opponent of Jackson's in the 1824 election, was hardly likely to award Old Hickory credit for anything (Clement, *Truth Is No Slander*, 11). That this was not an isolated local story is evident from the fact that in 1826, Bernhard Eisenach, Duke of Saxe-Weimar, was told essentially the same thing and that on the morning of December 24 some young militiamen began throwing up a little breastwork on the canal, which gave Jackson the idea (*Travels Through North America During the Years 1825 and 1826* [Philadelphia: Carey, Lea & Carey, 1828], 2:65). Twenty-four years later Marigny stated that the position was suggested to Jackson by a Captain St. James commanding a company in Plauché's Battalion d'Orleans (Marigny, *Reflections*, n.p.). No such captain has been identified, and none of these stories seems credible.

38. Wilson, *Plantation Houses*, 33–35; Jerome A. Greene, *Jean Lafitte National Historical Park and Preserve: Chalmette Unit Historic Resource Study* (Denver, CO: National Park Service, 1985), 172–73, 177.

39. Account of the Battle of New Orleans, 1815, Jackson Papers, LC.

40. Wilson, *Plantation Houses*, 39; Priestley to Latour, March 4, 1816, Latour Archive, HNOC; Letter from an officer in Coffee's command to a friend in Charleston, January 5, 1815, Charleston, SC, *City Gazette*, February 4, 1815.

41. Bassett, *Tatum's Journal*, December 24, 1814, 112; Coffee to John Donelson, January 25, 1815, Tennessee Historical Society Miscellaneous Files, University of Tennessee; Officer Lee to Mr. Robinson in Washington, December 30, 1814, Cazenovia, NY, *Pilot*, February 8, 1815; Mr. Lee to Thomas B. Robertson, December 30, 1814, New York, NY, *New-York Mercantile Advertiser*, February 1, 1815.

42. Wilson, *Plantation Houses*, 19, 22, 26; Walker, *Jackson and New Orleans*, 134–35; Latrobe, *Impressions*, 43, 45. Joseph Holt Ingraham, *The South-West. By a Yankee* (New York: Harper & Brothers, 1835), 1:198, describes the house in 1835 as a single story, which is clearly mistaken.

43. Greene, *Chalmette Unit Historic Resource Study*, 66–68.

44. Letter from correspondent of the *Philadelphia Gazette*, December 24, 1814, New York, NY, *New-York Gazette & General Advertiser*, January 26, 1815.

45. Letter from New Orleans to man in Marietta, OH, December 24, 1814, Marietta, OH, *American Friend*, January 28, 1815; Lewis to Robertson, December 23, 1814, one a.m., Philadelphia, PA, *Relf's Philadelphia Gazette, and Daily Advertiser*, January 23, 1815; Letter to the Postmaster General in DC, December 23 [midnight], 1814, Washington, DC, *Daily National Intelligencer*, January 21, 1815.

46. Gould Memoir, VHS.

47. Letter from New Orleans, December 24, 1814 four a.m., Baltimore, MD, *Baltimore Patriot & Evening Advertiser*, January 25, 1815.

48. Letter from New Orleans, December 25, 1814, Boston, MA, *Whig*, January 4, 1815.

49. Letter from New Orleans, December 24, 1814, Lexington, KY, *Western Monitor*, January 13, 1815; Letter from New Orleans, December 23, 1814, Lexington, KY, *Reporter*, January 13, 1815; Jean-Nicholas de Maciot to John Pierre Cabanne, December 24, 1814, Bowden, *Private Letters*, 67.

50. Letter from New Orleans, December 23, 1814, Lexington, KY, *Reporter*, January 13, 1815.

51. Letter from New Orleans, January 6, 1815, Louisville, KY, *Louisville Correspondent*, January 27, 1815.

52. Walker, *Jackson and New Orleans*, 161.

53. Ellery, "Notes," NYPL. Ellery's pre-1820 brief mention is the earliest reference to Mrs. Bienvenu, whose story in time became fixed and exaggerated in the lore of the siege. The number of her sons in service and other details became clouded, but it appears to be six divided between two companies. Houston, TX, *Houston Chronicle*, March 31, 1935; Willie Z. Bienvenu, "The Bienvenu Family of St. Martinville," *Attakapas Gazette* 15, no. 1 (Spring 1980): 89.

54. Gabriel Winter to William Willis, January 12, 1815, William and John B. Willis Family Papers, LSU; Letter from New Orleans, December 24, 1814, Albany, NY, *Register*, January 27, 1815.

55. Letter from New Orleans to New York, December 30, 1814, New York, NY, *New-York Spectator*, February 1, 1815.

56. Letter from New Orleans, December 23, 1814, Rutland, VT, *Rutland Herald*, February 1, 1815; Letter from New Orleans, December 24, 1814, Baltimore, MD, *Baltimore Patriot & Evening Advertiser*, January 25, 1815.

57. Memorial of Beverly Chew and Others, 1; Chew, Memoir, New Jersey Historical Society, Newark; Letter from New Orleans, December 24, 1814, Baltimore, MD, *Baltimore Patriot & Evening Advertiser*, January 25, 1815; Lewis to Robertson, December 23, 1814, Washington, DC, *Daily National Intelligencer*, January 21, 1815; Gould Memoir, VHS.

58. Trimble, "Trimble's Account," MDAH.

59. Lee to Mr. Robinson, December 30, 1814, Cazenovia, NY, *Pilot*, February 8, 1815; Jackson to Robert Hays, December 26, 1814, War of 1812 Mss., Lilly Library.

60. Jackson to Monroe, December 27, 1814, Baltimore, MD, *Baltimore Telegraph*, January 31, 1815.

61. Coffee to Donelson, January 25, 1815, Tennessee Historical Society Miscellaneous Files, University of Tennessee.

62. "Report of the Killed, wounded and missing of the army under the command of Maj. Gen. Andrew Jackson, in the actions of the 23rd and 28th December 1814 and 1st and 8th January 1815," Jackson Papers, LC, Wilmington, DE, *American Watchman*, February 18, 1815.

63. Fromentin to?, January 28, 1815, Philadelphia, PA, *Relf's Philadelphia Gazette, and Daily Advertiser*, February 1, 1815; "Historical Incidents Before the Battle of New Orleans," New Orleans, *Daily Picayune*, November 14, 1852.

64. W. Johnson, a member of Beale's company, wrote to his father on December 31, 1814, and said the company had 63 men at the beginning of the action and 22 were left (Miscellaneous Collection, RG 68, Louisiana Historical Center, New Orleans). That same day John Brandegee wrote that of 64 engaged, 38 were killed, wounded, or missing (John Brandegee to?, December 31, 1814, Miscellaneous Collection, RG 68, Louisiana Historical Center, New Orleans). An unidentified officer of the company told his brother on January 2 that the unit lost 30 of 60 engaged (Letter from New Orleans to Richmond, January 2, 1815, Charleston, SC, *City Gazette*, February 3, 1815). Edward Palfrey, who was not in the unit, wrote to John Palfrey on December 30, 1814, to say Beale started with 64 and ended with 26 (Palfrey Family Papers, Harvard). Johnson's number has been used here. See also New Orleans, LA, *Louisiana Gazette for the Country*, February 2, 1815, in Washington, DC, *Daily National Intelligencer*, March 6, 1815; Baltimore, MD, *Baltimore Telegraph*, February 14, 1815. As always, numbers vary depending on reports, but this is one of the earliest statements.

65. Beverly Chew Memoir, New Jersey Historical Society, Newark; "Officers and Soldiers of the War 1814–1815," *Southern Historical Society Papers* 36 (January–December, 1908): 135.

66. New Orleans, LA, *Louisiana Gazette for the Country*, February 3, 1815, in Philadelphia, PA, *Relf's Philadelphia Gazette, and Daily Advertiser*, March 7, 1815.

67. Letter from New Orleans, January 3, 1815, New York, NY, *New-York Herald*, February 4, 1815.

68. Letter from New Orleans to Chillicothe, January 6, 1815, Clinton, OH, *Ohio Register*, January 31, 1815.

69. W. & J. Montgomery to R. Bowen, December 30, 1814, Washington, PA, *Washington Reporter*, January 30, 1815; John Brandegee to?, December 31, 1814, Miscellaneous Collection, RG 68, Louisiana Historical Center, New Orleans.

70. Estate of the Late George Commyns, Louisiana, Wills and Probate Records, NOPL.

71. John Brandegee to?, December 31, 1814, Miscellaneous Collection, RG 68, Louisiana Historical Center, New Orleans; Letter from New Orleans, January 27, 1815, New York, NY, *New-York Gazette & General Advertiser*, February 24, 1815. See also extract of a letter from a friend in New Orleans, December 30, 1814, Boston, MA, *Boston Daily Advertiser*, February 4, 1815.

72. Walker, *Jackson and New Orleans*, 181, 183.

73. Ellery, "Notes," NYPL.

74. Eliza Croom Coffee, Sketch of the Life of Gen. John Coffee, 1897, HNOC. Hubbard later went into Alabama politics to win a seat in Congress. On the hustings he self-promoted himself to major at New Orleans, and often told this story, so it may be exaggerated.

75. Account of the Battle of New Orleans, 1815, Jackson Papers, LC; Jackson to Robert Hays, December 26, 1814, War of 1812 Mss., Lilly Library.

76. Letter from New Orleans to Robertson, January 13, 1815, Baltimore, MD, *Baltimore Telegraph*, February 8, 1815.

77. Coffee to Donelson, January 25, 1815, Tennessee Historical Society Miscellaneous Files, University of Tennessee.

78. Ensign J. Brown, Jr. to a friend in Paris, KY, December 30, 1814, Clinton, OH, *Ohio Register*, January 31, 1815.

79. Lewis to Robertson, December 23, 1814, one a.m., Washington, DC, *Daily National Intelligencer*, January 21, 1815; Letter to the Postmaster General in DC, December 23, 1814, Washington, DC, *Daily National Intelligencer*, January 21, 1815.

80. Letter from Correspondent of the *Philadelphia Gazette*, December 24, 1814, New York, NY, *New-York Gazette & General Advertiser*, January 26, 1815.

81. Codrington to Jane Codrington, November 23–December 31, 1814, Codrington Papers, COD/6/2, Caird.

82. Florian to Roosevelt, January 9, 1815, HNOC.

83. Edinburgh, UK, *Caledonian Mercury*, August 20, 1812.

84. The story of the killing of Captain William Conran of the 21st first appeared in print in Surtees, *Rifle Brigade*, 348–49, in 1833, then in Clark, *Royal Scots Fusiliers*, 31, in 1885. Buchan, *Royal Scots Fusiliers*, 175, repeated the story in 1925 basically taken from Clark. The earliest known account comes from an American source, however, the Thomas Joyes Journal entry for January 24, 1815, Joyes Papers, Filson, and that is the version recounted here. Joyes said he was told the story on January 24 by a British soldier captured on January 8. No actual contemporary British accounts have been found. When Surtees told the story nineteen years later in 1833, he described the captured American as an officer, his weapon a dirk, and said he was shot instead of bayonetted. In 1885, now seventy years after the fact, Clark, *Royal Scots Fusiliers*, 31, 36, stated that one of the last surviving members of the men of the 21st present told him that the captive was an officer, and that Conran invited him to come warm himself at a fire, when the American pulled a dagger and stabbed him. In Buchan, *Royal Scots Fusiliers*, the American's weapon evolved into a carving knife.

85. Letter to the Postmaster General in DC, December 23, 1814, Washington, DC, *Daily National Intelligencer*, January 21, 1815; James H. Gordon to Debuclet, December 23, 1814, Cusachs Estate Gift Collection; Gordon to Debuclet, December 24, 1814, Parsons Collection, Texas.

86. Bassett, *Tatum's Journal*, December 24, 1814, 112; Account of the Battle of New Orleans, 1815, Jackson Papers, LC.

87. Bassett, *Tatum's Journal*, December 24, 1814, 112; Ellery, "Notes," NYPL; Account of the Battle of New Orleans, 1815, Jackson Papers, LC.

88. "Losses Occasioned by Acts of the Enemy During the Late War with Great Britain," House Document 293, 14th Congress, 1st Session, February 14, 1816, Walter Lowrie and Walter S. Franklin, eds., *American State Papers. Documents, Legislative and Executive, of the Congress of the United States, from the First Session of the First to the Second Session of the Seventeenth, Inclusive: Commencing March 4, 1789, and Ending March 3, 1823, Class IX: Claims* (Washington, DC: Gales and Seaton, 1834), 461–62.

89. Reid and Eaton, *Jackson*, 310.

90. Reynolds to Jackson, eight a.m., December 24, 1814, Jackson Papers, LC.

91. Washington, DC, *Daily National Intelligencer*, February 16, 1815; Jackson to Samuel Southard, March 6, 1827, Bassett, *Correspondence*, 3:347. There is no documentation to establish just when the Laffites turned over the flints, but this timing would seem about right.

92. Natchez, MS, *Mississippi Republican*, December 25, 1814; Alexandria, VA, *Alexandria Gazette*, January 21, 1815.

93. Ellery, "Notes," NYPL; General Orders, December 24, 1814, Morgan Papers, LC.

94. Jackson to Lacoste, December 24, 1814, Reid and Eaton, *Jackson*, 308–9.

95. General Order, December 24, 1814, Cusachs Collection, Neil Auction Company, Louisiana Purchase Auction, December 2, 2016, #91, #109.

96. Warshauer, "Jackson and Martial Law," 272–73.

97. Account of the Battle of New Orleans, 1815, Jackson Papers, LC.

98. Ellery, "Notes," NYPL.

99. Account of the Battle of New Orleans, 1815, Jackson Papers, LC.

100. Claiborne, *Mississippi*, 344; General Orders, January 21, 1815, New Orleans, LA, *Louisiana Courier*, January 25, 1815.

101. Account of the Battle of New Orleans, 1815, Jackson Papers, LC.

102. John Donelson, Jr. to John Donelson, January 27, 1815, Tennessee Historical Society Miscellaneous Files, 1688–1951, University of Tennessee, Knoxville.

103. Trimble, "Trimble's Account," MDAH. While Trimble began writing his recollections in January 1860, his War of 1812 account must have been written sometime after January 1863 when his fellow soldier Levi C. Harris died. Trimble refers to him in this episode as "the late Levi C. Harris."

104. Livingston to Jackson, December 25, 1814, Moser et al., *Papers*, 220.

105. Bassett, *Tatum's Journal*, December 25, 1814, 112; Priestley to Latour, March 4, 1816, Latour Archive, HNOC.

106. Account of the Battle of New Orleans, 1815, Jackson Papers, LC; James Moore King to James Moore, March [April] 15, 1815, King Collection, Middle Tennessee State University, Murfreesboro; Jackson to Major Ricks, December 25, 1814, André de Coppet Collection, Princeton.

107. Butler to Morgan, December 25, 1814, Morgan Papers, LC.

108. Livingston to Morgan, December 25, 1814, Parsons Collection, Texas.

109. Butler to Morgan, December 25, 1814, Morgan Papers, LC.

110. Robert Sprigg to D. C. Wallace, December 25, 1814, D. C. Wallace Letters, Cincinnati History Library and Archives.

111. Jackson to David Holmes, December 25, 1814, Moser et al., *Papers*, 219.

112. Letter from an officer aboard the British fleet off Louisiana coast, January 30, 1815, *Naval Chronicle, for 1815*, vol. 33, 386; Windsor, VT, *Washingtonian*, March 27, 1815; Edinburgh, UK, *Caledonian Review*, February 23, 1815.

113. Letter from the HMS *Ramillies*, January 5, 1815, Washington, DC, *Daily National Intelligencer*, March 23, 1815.

114. Cochrane Journal, December 23, 1814, ADM 50/122, Kew, states that HMS *Statira* arrived a day earlier, but is mistaken.

115. Alexander Dickson, "Journal of Operations in Louisiana, 1814 and 1815," *Louisiana Historical Quarterly* 44, no. 3–4 (July–October 1961), December 24, 1814: 1–5.

116. Codrington to Jane Codrington, November 23–December 31, 1814, Codrington Papers, COD/6/2, Caird; Cochrane Journal, December 24, 1814, ADM 50/122, Kew.

117. Dickson, "Journal," December 25, 1814, 5–7; Hill, *Recollections*, 1:316.

118. Hill, *Recollections*, 1:317.

119. General Monthly Return of the Serjeants, Trumpeters, Drummers, and Rank and File of the several Corps serving under the Command of Major General John Lambert, January 25, 1815, WO 17/1218, Kew.

120. Wylly to Duke of Wellington, March 4, 1815, Pakenham, *Pakenham Letters*, 259.

121. Ibid., 253–55.

122. Smith, *Autobiography of Lieutenant-General Sir Harry Smith*, 228.

123. Wylly to Duke of Wellington, March 4, 1815, Pakenham, *Pakenham Letters*, 259.

124. Cooke, *Narrative*, 203, is the only British source that speaks of the general voicing displeasure, and Cooke was not with the army yet, nor as a mere subaltern would he be in Pakenham's confidence. Anything he says on this point was hearsay, which does not mean it was entirely inaccurate. Walker, *Jackson and New Orleans*, 211–13, presents a dramatic account, supposedly leaked out by subordinate officers present, of Pakenham meeting with his officers to express displeasure with the situation, saying he wanted to pull them out and find a better position, while Cochrane blustered that if the army would not attack then and there, the navy would, and that shamed Pakenham into remaining. The account is probably fictitious or years-after-the-fact rumor, and no source for it has been found.

125. Codrington to Jane Codrington, November 23–December 31, 1814, Codrington Papers, COD/6/2, Caird.

126. Dickson, "Journal," December 26, 1814, 13–14.

127. Chesterton, *Peace, War, and Adventure*, 192–93.

128. Michell, "Diary of Major J. Michell," December 25, 1814, 127.

129. Order, n.d., Codrington Papers, COD/6/4, Caird.

130. Dickson, "Journal," December 25, 1814, 8–10; Forrest, *Journal*, 33.

131. Dickson, "Journal," December 25, 1814, 10; Michell, "Diary of Major J. Michell," December 25, 1814, 127.

132. Coffee to John Donelson, January 25, 1815, Tennessee Historical Society Miscellaneous Files, University of Tennessee.

133. Gleig Diary, December 25, 1814, Barrett, *85th King's Light Infantry*, 216; List of deaths which have taken place among the officers during the preceding month, January 25, 1815, WO 17/1218, Kew; Ellis, *First West India Regiment*, 148.

134. Gerard, Campaigns 2, USNA.

135. Gleig Diary, December 25, 1814, Barrett, *85th King's Light Infantry*, 216.

136. London, UK, *Cobbett's Weekly Political Register*, December 24, 1814.

137. London, UK, *Times*, January 31, 1815.

CHAPTER TEN: "CANNON AND BATTERIES ARE ITS PROPER DEFENCE"

1. Letter from New Orleans, January 13, 1815, Wilmington, DE, *American Watchman*, February 11, 1815.

2. New Orleans, LA, *Louisiana Gazette for the Country*, February 2, 1815, in Washington, DC, *Daily National Intelligencer*, March 6, 1815; Letter from Greenville, Mississippi Territory, to Philadelphia, January 31, 1815, Wilmington, DE, *American Watchman*, March 4, 1815. An article in an unidentified issue of the Milledgeville, GA, *Georgia Journal* dated ca. April 1, 1815, told of a British officer coming to Jackson's lines under a white flag to convey a message. While waiting for the response he spoke with a corporal about the likely outcome of the campaign, stating that the British had great leaders like Pakenham, Picton, Cochrane, Keane, and others on their side. The corporal supposedly replied, "On our side we have the Lord God, Almighty, the Lord Jesus Christ, and the Hero Andrew Jackson, and I'll be d—— if we dont whip you." Of course, General Thomas Picton was not on that continent, and there is no evidence of any communications between the armies by truce flag prior to January 8. It should be noted that the article as published said that this episode was "said to have occurred." It is quite certainly apocryphal, and a good example of the early development of anecdotal myths about the battle. Charleston, SC, *City Gazette*, April 6, 1815.

3. *Francis Larche: House of Representatives Report 170* (Washington, DC: 19th Congress, 1st Session, April 20, 1826), 5; Henry Palfrey to John Palfrey, January 20, 1815, Gatell, "Boston Boy in 'Mr. Madison's War,'" 159.

4. Zachary F. Smith, *The Battle of New Orleans Including the Previous Engagements Between the Americans and the British, the Indians, and the Spanish Which Led to the Final Conflict of the 8th of January, 1815* (Louisville, KY: John P. Morton, 1904), 70–71.

5. Clement, *Truth Is No Slander*, 12.

6. Stewart, "Withers"; Hunt, *Life of Edward Livingston*, 200–201n; Warshauer, "Jackson and Martial Law," 268–69; Letter from New Orleans, January 20, 1815, Raleigh, NC, *Star*, February 17, 1815; William Flood request for reimbursement, March 27, 1815, Cook Collection, HNOC; Cooke, *Narrative*, 210.

7. Bassett, *Tatum's Journal*, December 24, 1814, 112.

8. Letter from New Orleans to New York, December 30, 1814, New Bedford, MA, *New-Bedford Mercury*, February 10, 1815.

9. Brown to Jackson, January 3, 1815, Moser et al., *Papers*, 229; Jackson to Brown, February 4, 1815, War of 1812 Mss., Lilly Library.

10. General Orders, January 21, 1815, New Orleans, LA, *Louisiana Courier*, January 25, 1815.

11. Coffee to John Donelson, January 25, 1815, Tennessee Historical Society Miscellaneous Files, University of Tennessee; Jackson to Monroe, February 13, 1815, Parker Papers, HSP.

12. Greene, *Chalmette Unit Historic Resource Study*, 185; John E. Cornelison, Jr., and Tammy D. Cooper, *An Archaeological Survey of the Chalmette Battlefield at Jean Lafitte National Historical Park and Preserve* (Tallahassee, FL: National Park Service, 2002), 12, 15, 17.

13. Walker, *Jackson and New Orleans*, 134–35; French, *They Lived at Chalmette*, 23, 24; Wilson, *Plantation Houses*, 44–46, 55–56, 68–69.

14. Ted Birkedal, ed., *Historical and Archaeological Investigations at the Chalmette Battlefield, Jean Lafitte National Historical Park and Preserve* (New Orleans: National Park Service, 2009), 1:13, offers a more detailed account of the flora and topography of the battlefield.

15. Jackson to Robert Hays, December 26, 1814, War of 1812 Mss., Lilly Library.

16. Reid and Eaton, *Jackson*, 313.

17. John D. Henley to Patterson, December 28, 1814, Richmond, VA, *Virginia Patriot*, February 22, 1815.

18. Samuel —— to R. Trudeau, December 26, 1814, Villeré Papers, HNOC.

19. Jackson to Morgan, December 26, 1814, Morgan Papers, LC.

20. Jackson to Monroe, December 26, 1814, Baltimore, MD, *Baltimore Telegraph*, January 31, 1815.

21. Joseph Stillwell Winter to Elisha Winter, December 30, 1814, Washington, DC, *Daily National Intelligencer*, January 28, 1815; Marigny, *Reflections*, n.p.

22. Louisiana General Assembly Resolution, February 1, 1815, Baltimore, MD, *Baltimore Telegraph*, March 16, 1815.

23. James Berns letter to Andrew Jackson, February 8, 1815, Cincinnati History Library and Archives.

24. *Appeal of L. Louaillier*, 19.

25. James A. Gordon order, December 26, 1814, Parsons Collection, Texas.

26. Letter from New Orleans, December 26, 1814, Charleston, SC, *City Gazette*, January 28, 1815.

27. Bowlby, *Memoir*, 53.

28. Gerard, Campaigns 2, USNA; Dickson, "Journal," December 26, 1814, 12–14.

29. Dickson, "Journal," December 26, 1814, 14–15.

30. Gerard, Campaigns 2, USNA.

31. John Michell to Jane Michell, January 22, 1815, HNOC.

32. Aitchison Memoir, 70, HNOC; Hill, *Recollections*, 1:326.

33. Peter Brooke Journals, New-York Historical Society.

34. Aitchison Memoir, ca. 1857, 70, MSS 186, HNOC.

35. Hill, *Recollections*, 1:323.

36. Codrington to Jane Codrington, December 27, 1814, Codrington Papers, COD/7/1, Caird.

37. "War Diary, Hitherto Unpublished, of Mr. Benjamin Story," New Orleans, LA, *Times-Democrat*, June 18, 1893.

38. Graves to White, n.d. [1845–53], New Orleans, LA, *Daily Delta*, January 8, 1854.

39. Dickson, "Journal," December 26, 1814, 13, 15; Chesterton, *Peace, War, and Adventure*, 210; John Michell to Jane Michell, January 22, 1815, HNOC.

40. Hill, *Recollections*, 1:322.

41. Surtees, *Rifle Brigade*, 355.

42. Henley to Patterson, December 28, 1814, Richmond, VA, *Virginia Patriot*, February 22, 1815.

43. Surtees, *Rifle Brigade*, 355; Dickson, "Journal," December 27, 1814, 16; Gerard, Campaigns 2, USNA.

44. Dickson, "Journal," December 27, 1814, 16.

45. Henley to Patterson, December 28, 1814, Richmond, VA, *Virginia Patriot*, February 22, 1815.

46. Dickson, "Journal," December 27, 1814, 16.

47. Murphy to his mother, December 27, 1814, Charleston, SC, *City Gazette*, January 28, 1815.

48. Henley to Patterson, December 28, 1814, Richmond, VA, *Virginia Patriot*, February 22, 1815; Navy Casualty Reports, 1776–1941, Men Who Died on Station 1812–1815, Naval Station New Orleans, Department of the Navy, RG 80, NA, stated that two crewmen of *Carolina* were killed.

49. W. Johnson to his father, December 31, 1814, Miscellaneous Collection, RG 68, Louisiana Historical Center, New Orleans; Letter from New Orleans to a brother who is editor of the *Philadelphia Gazette*, December 30, 1814, Elizabethtown, NJ, *New-Jersey Gazette*, February 7, 1815.

50. Walker, *Jackson and New Orleans*, 216.

51. Dickson, "Journal," December 27, 1814, 17. Dickson says she exploded at 10:30. Forrest, *Journal*, 33, says it was at nine a.m., and both are firsthand eyewitness accounts. As always, times are almost impossible to reconcile.

52. Surtees, Rifle Brigade, 355; Letter by British naval officer, January 30, 1815, Lexington, KY, *Reporter*, August 2, 1815; Codrington to Jane Codrington, November 23–December 31, 1814, Codrington Papers, COD/6/2, Caird.

53. Codrington to Jane Codrington, November 23–December 31, 1814, Codrington Papers, COD/6/2, Caird.

54. Dickson, "Journal," December 27, 1814, 18.

55. Ibid., 17; Gerard, Campaigns 2, USNA.

56. Dickson, "Journal," December 27, 1814, 19–20.

57. Michell, "Diary of Major J. Michell," December 27, 1814, 128; Dickson, "Journal," December 27, 1814, 18–19.

58. Norman Pringle to Editor, January 25, 1834, James Sinclair to Norman Pringle, January 27, 1834, Norman Pringle, *Letters of Major Norman Pringle, Late of the 21st Royal Scots Fusiliers, Vindicating the Character of the British Army, Employed in North America in the Years 1814–15, from Aspersions Cast Upon It in Stuart's "Three Years in North America"* (Edinburgh, UK: *Evening Courant*, 1834), 12–13.

59. Memorandum, December 27, 1814, Codrington Papers, COD/6/4, Caird.

60. Codrington to Jane Codrington, November 23–December 31, 1814, Codrington Papers, COD/6/2, Caird.

61. Gleig Diary, December 26 [27], 1814, Barrett, *85th King's Light Infantry*, 216. Walker, *Jackson and New Orleans*, 219, described an evening advance of the British army preceded by a rocket signal, with Hinds's dragoons rushing in and out to fire volleys at them. No such advance occurred, and there is no evidence of a rocket being fired for that purpose. Pakenham's brigades did take position for their advance the next day, December 28.

62. Letter from New Orleans to Robertson, December 27, 1814, Windsor, VT, *Washingtonian*, January 30, 1815.

63. Letter from New Orleans to Augusta, GA, December 27, 1814, Augusta, GA, *Augusta Herald*, February 2, 1815.

64. Letter from St. Francisville to Baltimore, January 1, 1815, Philadelphia, PA, *Poulson's American Daily Advertiser*, February 1, 1815.

65. Letter from Natchez, December 27, 1814, Louisville, KY, *Western Courier*, January 19, 1815.

66. J. Henry Lüdeling to Livingston, December 4, 1814, Brown to Livingston, October 26, 1814, Livingston Papers, Princeton.

67. Utica, NY, *Columbian Gazette*, January 24, 1815; Letter from Natchez, December 28, 1814, Washington, PA, *Washington Reporter*, January 23, 1815.

68. Lexington, KY, *Reporter*, January 13, 1815.

69. Letter from Warrenton, NC, January 20, 1815, Philadelphia, PA, *Freeman's Journal*, January 28, 1815, in New Haven, CT, *Connecticut Herald*, January 31, 1815.

70. Letter from St. Francisville to Baltimore, January 1, 1815, Philadelphia, PA, *Poulson's American Daily Advertiser*, February 1, 1815; Whitehaven, UK, *Cumberland Pacquet and Ware's Whitehaven Advertiser*, February 28, 1815; St. George's, Bermuda, *Bermuda Gazette, and Weekly Advertiser*, April 15, 1815.

71. Account of the Battle of New Orleans, 1815, Jackson Papers, LC.

72. Bassett, *Tatum's Journal*, December 27, 1814, 113. Fromentin told a correspondent a month later that Captain Henley actually got the guns ashore before he abandoned ship, but that seems highly unlikely. Fromentin to unknown, January 28, 1815, Philadelphia, PA, *Relf's Philadelphia Gazette, and Daily Advertiser*, February 1, 1815.

73. Walker, *Jackson and New Orleans*, 216.

74. John H. Johnson to St. Francisville *Time-Piece*, December 30, 1814, Washington, DC, *National Intelligencer*, February 4, 1815; Murphy to his mother, December 27, 1814, Charleston, SC, *City Gazette*, January 28, 1815.

75. Letter from New Orleans to Petersburg, January 5, 1815, Petersburg, VA, *Petersburg Daily Courier*, February 1, 1815.

76. Account of the Battle of New Orleans, 1815, Jackson Papers, LC.

77. Particulars in relation to Battle of New Orleans furnished me by a French gentleman in 1828—Summer, Follett Papers, Cincinnati History Library and Archives.

78. Clement, *Truth Is No Slander*, 16–17.

79. Fortier to Claiborne, November 11, 1815, Rowland, *Letter Books*, 6:386.

80. Bassett, *Tatum's Journal*, December 26, 1814, 113; Jackson to Claiborne, December 24, 1814, Bassett, *Correspondence* 2, 123–24.

81. Bassett, *Tatum's Journal*, December 27, 1814, 114.

82. Chotard to Reynolds, December 27, 1814, Jackson Papers, LC.

83. Letter from New Orleans to Augusta, GA, December 27, 1814, Augusta, GA, *Augusta Herald*, February 2, 1815.

84. General Return of the Militia of the State of Louisiana, December 25 or 28, 1814, Latour Archive, HNOC.

85. Claiborne to Shaumburg, October 1, 1815, Rowland, *Letter Books*, 6:372.

86. Alexander Declouet to Speaker of the House, January 7, 1815, "Report of the Committee of Inquiry," 227–28, 234, Statement of G. Mre. Guichard, January 28, 1815, 274–75. Declouet often contradicted himself in his statement, and is not entirely to be relied upon.
87. Account of the Battle of New Orleans, 1815, Jackson Papers, LC.
88. "Aristides" (William Peter Van Ness), *A Concise Narrative of Gen. Jackson's First Invasion of Florida, and of His Immortal Defence of New-Orleans: With Remarks* (Albany, NY: *Albany Argus*, 1828), 8.
89. New Haven, CT, *Connecticut Journal*, February 13, 1815.
90. London, UK, *Courier, and Evening Gazette*, December 27, 1814.
91. Bathurst to Pakenham, December 27, 1814, WO 6/2, Kew.

Chapter Eleven: "I Am Now on the Move"

1. "Nestor" to the Editor, June 10, 1815, *Naval Chronicle, for 1815*, vol. 34 (July 1815), 471.
2. "Recollections of the Expedition," part 3, 192.
3. Letter from New Orleans to man in Washington, December 30, 1814, New York, NY, *Columbian*, February 2, 1815; St. George's, Bermuda, *Bermuda Gazette, and Weekly Advertiser*, April 15, 1815.
4. Letter from the HMS *Ramillies*, January 5, 1815, Washington, DC, *Daily National Intelligencer*, March 23, 1815; Pakenham, *Pakenham Letters*, 259.
5. Fromentin letter, January 28, 1815, Philadelphia, PA, *Relf's Philadelphia Gazette, and Daily Advertiser*, February 1, 1815.
6. Eaton and Van Crowninshield, *Memoirs of Andrew Jackson*, 267–68.
7. Pakenham, *Pakenham Letters*, 259.
8. Wrottesley, *Life and Correspondence of Field Marshal Sir John Burgoyne*, 305; Smith, *Autobiography of Lieutenant-General Sir Harry Smith*, 229–30.
9. Pay List of the 5th West India Regiment of Foot, December 1809–March 1810, Infantry Abroad Quarterly Pay Lists for the 5th West India Regiment of Foot, WO 12/11538, National Archives, Kew. This interesting episode is not dated in the published account that first appeared in March 1815. However, the December 28 engagement was the first in which the 5th West India participated, and since the nature of Lieutenant Hamilton's gesture implicitly suggests that he did it prior to his first probable action against the Americans, December 28 is a likely date. It cannot have been prior to December 25 since as of that date he was listed as an officer on active service with the regiment in good standing. Hence his act had to have taken place on one of the three following days ("List of Officers Present Serving in the Army Employed on a Particular Service," December 25, 1814, WO 17/1218, Kew; John McCavitt to the author, April 22, 2018).
    The earliest statement of the Hamilton story appears to have been in a March 1815 issue of the Kingston, Jamaica, *Royal Gazette* that Jane De Grummond quoted without full citation in her 1962 article "Platter of Glory." It was republished from the *Royal Gazette* in the St. George's, Bermuda, *Bermuda Gazette, and Weekly Advertiser* for April 8, 1815. It did not begin to appear in the American press until the Baltimore, MD, *Baltimore Patriot & Evening Advertiser*, on May 10, 1815, and all subsequent publications of it appear to trace to that. The article suggests that Hamilton was from New York originally, but John McCavitt and Kevin Chambers generously provided the further information that Lieutenant Hamilton was from Boston and was subsequently allowed to resign.
10. Letter from a member of the Adams troop of cavalry to Natchez, December 30, 1814, Natchez, MS, *Mississippi Republican*, January 4, 1814, in New York, NY, *New-York Evening Post*, February 1, 1815.
11. Gleig, *Narrative*, 309–11. Thanks to Stanley Clisby Arthur, *The Story of the Battle of New Orleans* (New Orleans: Louisiana Historical Society, 1915), 60, the story gained currency that Jugeat's Choctaws terrorized the British in this fashion, and in particular one Indian of mixed blood known as Poindexter, who killed five British pickets over the space of three nights. "They patrolled the edge of the swamp, leaping unperceived from one log to another . . . and shot every redcoat who came within rifle range," said Arthur. "Not less than fifty British soldiers were killed and many more severely wounded by this method of assassination." Unfortunately, Arthur took this from the fictitious narrative of David Ogilvie forged by Augustus C. Buell, as detailed elsewhere.

12. Ellery, "Notes," NYPL.

13. Patterson to Secretary of the Navy, December 29, 1814, Richmond, VA, *Virginia Patriot*, February 22, 1815; Ellery, "Notes," NYPL.

14. Ellery, "Notes," NYPL; Account of the Battle of New Orleans, 1815, Jackson Papers, LC; Walker, *Jackson and New Orleans*, 222, 227; Pakenham, *Pakenham Letters*, n.p.; Burgoyne, *93rd Sutherland Highlanders*, 27; Dickson, "Journal," 20.

15. Walker, *Jackson and New Orleans*, 227; French, *They Lived at Chalmette*, 5.

16. Reid and Eaton, *Jackson*, 314.

17. Gerard, Campaigns 2, USNA.

18. Burgoyne, *93rd Sutherland Highlanders*, 27; St. George's, Bermuda, *Bermuda Gazette, and Weekly Advertiser*, April 8, 1815.

19. Cope, *Rifle Brigade*, 186–87; Gleig Diary, December 27 [28], 1814, Barrett, *85th King's Light Infantry*, 217–18; Gleig, *Narrative*, 170; Gleig to Janet Gleig, January 11, 1815, Gleig Papers, NLS.

20. Letter from an officer in Coffee's command army to friend in Charleston, January 5, 1815, Charleston, SC, *City Gazette*, February 4, 1815.

21. Bassett, *Tatum's Journal*, December 28, 1814, 116; Dickson, "Journal," December 28, 1814, 20.

22. Ellery, "Notes," NYPL; Letter from New Orleans, January 7, 1815, New York, NY, *New-York Evening Post*, February 8, 1815.

23. Letter from New Orleans to Richmond, December 29, 1814, Augusta, GA, *Augusta Herald*, February 9, 1815.

24. Dickson, "Journal," 20; Surtees, *Rifle Brigade*, 359.

25. Burgoyne, *93rd Sutherland Highlanders*, 27.

26. Gleig to Janet Gleig, January 11, 1815, Gleig Papers, NLS.

27. Bassett, *Tatum's Journal*, December 28, 1814, 116.

28. Dickson, "Journal," 20–21.

29. Bassett, *Tatum's Journal*, December 28, 1814, 119.

30. Priestley to Latour, March 4, 1816, Latour Archive, HNOC; Return of Adjutant General, December 28, 1814, Georgetown, DC, *Federal Republican for the Country*, April 4, 1815. A December 28 statement showed Carroll with 1,312, Coffee with 834, and a combined total of 658 regulars, giving Old Hickory just over 2,800 rifles and muskets on the line, and the other volunteer companies increased his total force to 3,282, but that did not include all elements of his command. New Orleans, LA, *Louisiana Gazette for the Country*, April 29, June 10, 1815.

31. Ellery, "Notes," NYPL. Bassett, *Tatum's Journal*, December 24, 1814, 112, states that the flooding from the opened levee continued to let water onto the ground below Jackson for almost a week, down to about January 1, which gainsays the charge in Ritchie, "Louisiana Campaign," 39, that Latour failed in his mission to cut the levee, though he did not flood the British camps.

32. Bassett, *Tatum's Journal*, December 28, 1814, 114.

33. Reid and Eaton, *Jackson*, 315.

34. Meuse, *Weapons*, 28.

35. Petition of John Hudry [2]; Dagmar Renshaw LeBreton, "The Man Who Won the Battle of New Orleans," *Louisiana Historical Quarterly* 38, no. 3 (July 1955): 20–34.

36. According to Latour in 1816, some days after Jackson accepted the Laffites' offer of service, "a certain number of them formed a corps under the command of captains Dominique and Beluche," and served two 24-pounders in Batteries 3 and 4, while some Baratarians enlisted in other companies of mariners sent to Petites Coquilles, Fort St. Philip, and Fort St. John. Latour's statement seems to establish that Jean Laffite, whose whereabouts are murky through January 8, was not with the battery. If he had been, Latour surely would have said so, and likely he would have commanded in that case rather than Beluche or Dominique (Latour, *Historical Memoir*, 58).

37. Bassett, *Tatum's Journal*, December 28, 1814, 119; Meuse, *Weapons*, 28–30; Ritchie, "Louisiana Campaign," 44, 46; William James, *A Full and Correct Account of the Naval Occurrences of the Late War Between Great Britain and the United States of America* (London: T. Egerton, 1817), 45.

38. [Gabriel Winter] to Elisha Winter, December 30, 1814, Washington, DC, *Daily National Intelligencer*, January 28, 1815.

39. Bassett, *Tatum's Journal*, December 28, 1814, 118–19.

40. Statement of G. Mre. Guichard, January 28, 1815, "Report of the Committee of Inquiry," 274, 276–77.

41. Duncan Deposition, January 14, 1815, "Report of the Committee of Inquiry," 234–36.

42. Letter from New Orleans to merchant in Baltimore, January 1, 1815, New York, *New-York Herald*, February 15, 1815.

43. Tregle, "Andrew Jackson and the Continuing Battle of New Orleans," 6, JELAC.

44. Statement of Abner Duncan, January 16, 1815, "Report of the Committee of Inquiry," 267.

45. Abner Duncan deposition, January 14, 1815, "Report of the Committee of Inquiry," 236, 242.

46. Jackson to Louisiana General Assembly, December 31, 1814, Moser et al., *Papers*, 226; Padgett, "Andrew Jackson in New Orleans," 414; "Report of the Committee of Inquiry," 245. No holographic copy of Jackson's order survives, making it uncertain what he actually wrote.

47. Owsley edition, Reid and Eaton, *Jackson*, lxviii-lxix.

48. Padgett, "Andrew Jackson in New Orleans," 415.

49. Duncan Deposition, January 14, 1815, "Report of the Committee of Inquiry," 234–35, 244.

50. Fortier Deposition, January 6, 1815, "Report of the Committee of Inquiry," 254–55.

51. Smith, *New Orleans*, 138.

52. Claiborne to Committee, January 4, 1815, "Report of the Committee of Inquiry," 252–53, Statement of General Labatut, January 6, 1815, 255–56.

53. Surtees, *Rifle Brigade*, 359–60.

54. Forrest, *Journal*, 34.

55. Dickson, "Journal," 21.

56. Gerard, Campaigns 2, USNA.

57. Bassett, *Tatum's Journal*, December 28, 1814, 116; Gleig Diary, December 27 [28], 1814, Barrett, *85th King's Light Infantry*, 218; Cope, *Rifle Brigade*, 187.

58. Forrest, *Journal*, 34.

59. Dickson, "Journal," 21.

60. Smith, *Autobiography of Lieutenant-General Sir Harry Smith*, 228–29.

61. Dickson, "Journal," 21.

62. Gerard, Campaigns 2, USNA.

63. Sinclair to Pringle, January 27, 1834, Pringle, *Letters*, 12.

64. Letter from New Orleans, December 29, 1814, Augusta, GA, *Augusta Herald*, February 9, 1815.

65. Letter from member of Adams troop to friend in Natchez, December 30, 1814, Natchez, MS, *Mississippi Republican*, January 4, 1815, in New York, NY, *New-York Evening Post*, February 1, 1815; Letter from New Orleans, December 29, 1814, Augusta, GA, *Augusta Herald*, February 9, 1815.

66. John H. Johnson to St. Francisville *Time-Piece*, December 30, 1814, Washington, DC, *National Intelligencer*, February 4, 1815; Gabriel Winter to Elijah Winter, December 30, 1814, Washington, DC, *Daily National Intelligencer*, January 28, 1815.

67. Gabriel Winter to Elijah Winter, December 30, 1814, Washington, DC, *Daily National Intelligencer*, January 28, 1815.

68. Letter of a Tennessee Volunteer with Carroll from New Orleans, December 29, 1814, Richmond, VA, *Richmond Enquirer*, February 1, 1815; Gabriel Winter to William Willis, January 12, 1815, Willis Family Papers, LSU.

69. Letter from New Orleans, December 30, 1814, Richmond, VA, *Virginia Patriot*, January 28, 1815; Robert L. Cobb to John Cobb, February 3, 1815, Cobb letters, HNOC.

70. Marine Corps lore has it that his refusal to give up the recently abandoned uniform leather neck stock somehow credited him with fathering the Corps sobriquet "leathernecks," but this cannot be verified. Bradley, *Interim Appointment*, 470.

71. There has been some confusion about the nature and cause of Carmick's wounds, which have gotten more than ordinary attention thanks to his importance in the early history of the Marine Corps. Bradley, *Interim Appointment*, 474, says that Carmick was hit while riding to the center of Jackson's line to deliver an order. He cites Charles B. Brooks, *Siege of New Orleans* (Seattle: University of Washington Press, 1961), 188, who in turn cited Nolte, *Memoirs*, 218. Nolte, however, said nothing about delivering an order and merely stated that Carmick was "struck by a Congreve rocket on the forehead, knocked off his horse, and both his arms injured." Nolte did not claim to have been an eyewitness to this. Report of the killed, wounded, and missing of the army under the command of Major General Andrew Jackson, in the actions of the 23d and 28th December 1814 and 1st and 8th January 1815 (Jackson Papers, LC), says that he was wounded in the arm and hand and mentioned no head wound.

A rocket was almost certainly the cause of Carmick's injuries. Only British rockets and exploding artillery shells were causing injuries behind the high earthwork. Musket fire that passed over the parapet would have fallen too far in the rear of the American line to cause damage to anyone on or immediately behind the main line, and since Carmick was mounted, he was not on the earthwork itself to be exposed to direct fire. The fact that Congreve rockets were packed with "case shot"—iron balls—would account for the multiple mentions of Carmick being hit by "balls." He definitely was not hit in the head by a rocket as later commonly represented.

The earliest known mention of his wounding is in Edward Palfrey to John Palfrey, December 30, 1814 (Palfrey Family Papers, Harvard), which states little more than that he was wounded by a rocket. An anonymous letter from New Orleans to Baltimore dated January 2, 1815 (Baltimore, MD, *American, and Commercial Daily Advertiser*, February 3, 1815), did not mention a rocket, but stated that a "ball" hit his right arm and a grape shot took off his thumb, and he received an undefined wound in the head, the mention of a ball and grape implying a rocket or artillery. Four weeks later on January 29, Fromentin sent to Baltimore a variant account that was obviously sent to him by a New Orleans correspondent, stating that three "balls" went through Carmick's hat, one just scratching his head, while only one hit his right arm, another broke but did not sever his right thumb, and a sixth killed his horse (Boston, MA, *New-England Palladium*, February 10, 1815). The New Orleans, LA, *Louisiana Gazette for the Country*, February 2, 1815 (in the Washington, DC, *Daily National Intelligencer*, March 6, 1815) stated that he lost his right thumb and "had other wounds."

The only known eyewitness claim to seeing Carmick wounded came from Captain Jean-Claude Hudry of the Compagnie des Francs in Plauché's Orleans Battalion. He stated in notes or a narrative written twenty years after the battle in 1832–34 that "Major Cornick [sic] was seriously wounded alongside of me, his horse was shot from under him, his thumb was shot off and his hat was pierced by seven bullets." This appeared in Francois Miquet, *Un Emigrant chablaisien, Jean-Claude Hudry (1774–1832)* (Annecy, FR: 1888), as quoted in LeBreton, "The Man Who Won the Battle of New Orleans," 21n, 29. Miquet stated that the account was assembled from "extracts" from Hudry's "manuscript diary." The content quoted in the pamphlet, however, is too confused, contradictory, and hyperbolic to have come from contemporary 1814 diary entries. It confuses the *Louisiana* with the *Carolina*, has the latter blowing up on December 28 instead of the 27th, and comments on British 18-pounder cannon being in the fight on the 28th when those guns did not arrive until that evening after the engagement. Moreover, Hudry claimed that, "had it not been for me, New Orleans would have been pillaged and burned," calling himself the city's "deliverer," and implying that he was, therefore, responsible for Jackson's election to the presidency (33–34). Consequently, the Hudry account is more likely notes or a narrative assembled by Hudry in 1832–34 to support his application to Congress for compensation for his expenditures in 1814, and at a time when he was approaching sixty years old, ill, destitute, depressed, and perhaps unbalanced, explaining his probable suicide on January 28, 1835.

By 1856, Walker, *Jackson and New Orleans*, 232, repeated common lore forty years after the fact, that Carmick "was struck by a rocket, which tore his horse to pieces and wounded the Major in the arm and head," a statement possibly drawn from Nolte's account.

72. Letter from New Orleans to Baltimore, January 2, 1815, Baltimore, MD, *American, and Commercial Daily Advertiser*, February 3, 1815.

73. St. George's, Bermuda, *Bermuda Gazette, and Weekly Advertiser*, April 8, 1815.

74. Dickson, "Journal," 21–22; Surtees, *Rifle Brigade*, 360.

75. Priestley to Latour, March 4, 1816, Latour Archive, HNOC; Account of the Battle of New Orleans, 1815, Jackson Papers, LC; Bassett, *Tatum's Journal*, 115; Sinclair to Pringle, January 27, 1834, Pringle, *Letters*, 12–13.

76. Letter from Natchez, January 3, 1815, Charleston, SC, *City Gazette*, January 28, 1815.

77. Priestley to Latour, March 4, 1816, Latour Archive, HNOC; Reid and Eaton, *Jackson*, 317–18; Bassett, *Tatum's Journal*, December 28, 1814, 116.

78. Account of the Battle of New Orleans, 1815, Jackson Papers, LC; Letter from Tennessee Volunteer with Carroll, December 29, 1814, Richmond, VA, *Richmond Enquirer*, February 1, 1815; Bassett, *Tatum's Journal*, December 28, 1814, 115, 117.

79. Patterson to Secretary of the Navy, December 29, 1814, Richmond, VA, *Virginia Patriot*, February 22, 1815.

80. Bassett, *Tatum's Journal*, December 28, 1814, 117; Letter from New Orleans, January 7, 1815, New York, NY, *New York Evening Post*, February 8, 1815.

81. Ellery, "Notes," NYPL.

82. Patterson to Secretary of the Navy, December 29, 1814, Richmond, VA, *Virginia Patriot*, February 22, 1815; [Gabriel Winter] to Elisha Winter, December 30, 1814, Washington, DC, *Daily National Intelligencer*, January 28, 1815.

83. "War Diary, Hitherto Unpublished, of Mr. Benjamin Story," New Orleans, *Times-Democrat*, June 18, 1893.

84. Bassett, *Tatum's Journal*, December 28, 1814, 117.

85. Gleig Diary, December 27 [28], 1814, Barrett, *85th King's Light Infantry*, 218; Cope, *Rifle Brigade*, 187.

86. Bassett, *Tatum's Journal*, December 28, 1814, 117.

87. Gleig Diary, December 27 [28], 1814, Barrett, *85th King's Light Infantry*, 218; Cope, *Rifle Brigade*, 187; Surtees, *Rifle Brigade*, 361; Burgoyne, *93rd Sutherland Highlanders*, 27.

88. Sinclair to Pringle, January 27, 1834, Pringle, *Letters*, 13; Dickson, "Journal," 21–22.

89. Burgoyne, *93rd Sutherland Highlanders*, 27; Forrest, *Journal*, 35; Gleig Diary, December 28–29, 1814, Barrett, *85th King's Light Infantry*, 218.

90. Gleig to Janet Gleig, January 11, 1815, Gleig Papers, NLS.

91. Graves to White, n.d. [1845–53], New Orleans, *Daily Delta*, January 8, 1854.

92. Gerard, Campaigns 2, USNA.

93. Surtees, *Rifle Brigade*, 361.

94. Return of Casualties in the Army under the Command of M. Genl. The Honb Sir Edwd Pakenham K B in Action with the Enemy near New Orleans between the 25th and 31st December 1814, WO 1/141, List of Deaths which have taken place among the Officers during the preceding Month, January 25, 1815, WO 17/1218, Kew.

95. Dickson, "Journal," 23.

96. Hayne to Jackson, January 10, 1815, Augusta, GA, *Augusta Herald*, February 23, 1815; Hynes to Blount, December 30, 1814, New York, NY, *New-York Gazette & General Advertiser*, February 1, 1815.

97. "Report of the Killed & wounded of Genl Jno Coffees Brigade, Report of the Killed, wounded and missing of the army under the command of Major General Andrew Jackson, in the actions of the 23d and 28th December 1814 and 1st and 8th January 1815," Jackson Papers, LC; Bassett, *Tatum's Journal*, December 28, 1814, 117; Baltimore, MD, *Baltimore Telegraph*, February 14, 1815.

98. Bassett, *Tatum's Journal*, December 28, 1814, 117.

99. Account of the Battle of New Orleans, 1815, Jackson Papers, LC.

100. Letter from New Orleans, December 29, 1814, Augusta, GA, *Augusta Herald*, February 9, 1815; Robert Butler to unknown, December 30, 1814, Baltimore, MD, *Baltimore Patriot & Evening Advertiser*, January 30, 1815; Philadelphia, PA, *Poulson's American Daily Advertiser*, January 31, 1815.

101. Bassett, *Tatum's Journal*, December 28, 1814, 118; Jackson to Monroe, December 29, 1814, Baltimore, MD, *Baltimore Telegraph*, January 31, 1815; Letter from a volunteer in Beale's company, December 28, 1814, New York, NY, *New-York Evening Post*, February 1, 1815; Letter from New Orleans to Philadelphia, December 30, 1814, Bennington, VT, *Bennington News-Letter*, February 6, 1815; Letter from a Tennessee Volunteer with Carroll from New Orleans, December 29, 1814, Richmond, VA, *Richmond Enquirer*, February 1, 1815.

102. Letter from New Orleans to Washington, December 30, 1814, Georgetown, DC, *Federal Republican for the Country*, January 31, 1815.

103. Letter from Tennessee Volunteer with Carroll from New Orleans, December 29, 1814, Richmond, VA, *Richmond Enquirer*, February 1, 1815; Gabriel Winter to Elijah Winter, December 30, 1814, Washington, DC, *Daily National Intelligencer*, January 28, 1815; W. Johnson to father, December 31, 1814, Miscellaneous Collection, RG 68, Louisiana Historical Center, New Orleans.

104. Charles K. Blanchard to Jackson, March 20, 1815, John Brannan, comp., *Official Letters of the Military and Naval Officers of the United States, During the War with Great Britain in the Years 1812, 13, 14, & 15* (Washington: Way and Gideon, 1823), 468–69. This letter first appeared in

print in the Carthage, TN, *Carthage Gazette*, May 26, 1815. Jackson would have received the letter on March 20 or 21 at the latest, since it was written from New Orleans. His attorneys used it in his defense before Judge Hall's court on March 27.

105. Pakenham to Cochrane, December 28, 1814, Cochrane Papers, NLS; Cochrane to Croker, January 18, 1815, London, UK, *Courier, and Evening Gazette*, March 10, 1815.

Chapter Twelve: "Giving Us the Whole Campaign"

1. Edward Palfrey to John Palfrey, December 30, 1814, Palfrey Family Papers, Harvard; John Donelson, Jr. to John Donelson, January 27, 1815, Tennessee Historical Society Miscellaneous Files, 1688–1951, University of Tennessee, Knoxville; Letter from a man in Beale's company, December 28, 1814, New York, NY, *New-York Evening Post*, February 1, 1815. Drez, *War of 1812*, 309, argues unconvincingly that Pakenham's December 28 reconnaissance and his January 1 attempt at bombardment were attacks. The British commander did not commit his forces in the first, and when he saw the strength of the American line he halted of his own accord, having learned some of what he set out to glean. The January 1 bombardment can hardly be called an attack, with the British infantry entirely uninvolved except as spectators.
2. Marigny, *Reflections*, n.p.; Letter from New Orleans to Richmond, VA, December 30, 1814, Richmond, VA, *Richmond Enquirer*, January 28, 1815.
3. Letter to friend in New York, [December 29–31, 1814], New York, NY, *New-York Spectator*, February 1, 1815; Ellery, "Notes," NYPL.
4. Jackson to Monroe, December 29, 1814, Moser et al., *Papers*, 224.
5. Auguste Davezac Deposition, January 23, 1815, "Report of the Committee of Inquiry," 238–39, Jackson to the Legislature, 251.
6. "Report of the Committee of Inquiry," 247–48, Statement of Levi Wells, January 6, 1815, 224–25, 254.
7. Claiborne to Committee, January 4, 1815, "Report of the Committee of Inquiry," 252–53, Statement of General Labatut, January 6, 1815, 255–56, Statement of Duncan, January 16, 1815, 266; *Appeal of L. Louaillier*, 20; *Arrest and Trial of E. Louis Louaillier*, House of Representatives Document 69, 37th Congress, 3d Session (Washington, DC: Government Printing Office, 1843), 11.
8. Martin, *Louisiana*, 2:376. Martin says this happened the evening of December 23, which is clearly mistaken. It had to have been December 28; Skipwith to Jackson, May 13, 1827, Padgett, "Andrew Jackson in New Orleans," 409–10. The date of this episode is not recorded but context suggests December 28. Skipwith stated further that the rumor came into town from some of the Kentuckians with Jackson, though they would not arrive for a week yet, clearly a lapse of Skipwith's memory.
9. Claiborne to Committee, January 4, 1815, "Report of the Committee of Inquiry," 252–53, Statement of General Labatut, January 6, 1815, 255–56.
10. Carr, "New Orleans and the Treaty of Ghent," 280.
11. Ellery, "Notes," NYPL.
12. Letter from Carroll's division to citizen in Paris, KY, December 29, 1814, Alexandria, VA, *Alexandria Gazette*, January 31, 1815.
13. Lee to Robertson, December 30, 1814, New York, NY, *New-York Mercantile Advertiser*, February 1, 1815.
14. Letter from New Orleans to Richmond, December 29, 1814, Augusta, GA, *Augusta Herald*, February 9, 1815; Patterson to Secretary of the Navy, December 29, 1814, Richmond, VA, *Virginia Patriot*, February 22, 1815; Patterson to Secretary of Navy, January 2, 1815, Captains' Letters, RG 26, NA.
15. Account of the Battle of New Orleans, 1815, Jackson Papers, LC.
16. Letter from member of Beale's Company, December 30, 1814, Hanover, NH, *Dartmouth Gazette*, February 15, 1815.
17. John H. Johnson to St. Francisville *Time-Piece*, December 30, 1814, Washington, DC, *National Intelligencer*, February 4, 1815.
18. Reid and Eaton, *Jackson*, 322–23.
19. Lee to Robertson, December 30, 1814, New York, NY, *New-York Mercantile Advertiser*, February 1, 1815.

20. Letter from New Orleans, January 2, 1815, Charleston, SC, *City Gazette*, February 3, 1815; Letter from member of Beale's company, December 30, 1814, Boston, MA, *Independent Chronicle*, February 6, 1815; General Orders, December 29, 1814, Hicky Papers, LSU.

21. "Officers and Soldiers of the War 1814–1815," *Southern Historical Society Papers* 36 (January–December 1908): 135.

22. Account of the Battle of New Orleans, 1815, Jackson Papers, LC.

23. Bassett, *Tatum's Journal*, December 28, 1814, 119; Account of the Battle of New Orleans, 1815, Jackson Papers, LC.

24. Peoria, IL, *Peoria Democratic Press*, March 16, 1842. This quotes a speech by Davezac in New York that year.

25. Bassett, *Tatum's Journal*, December 28, 1814, 119; Account of the Battle of New Orleans, 1815, Jackson Papers, LC.

26. Bassett, *Tatum's Journal*, December 28, 1814, 119.

27. Cochrane to Bathurst, December 31, 1814, WO 1/141, Kew.

28. Cockburn to Cochrane, January 26, 1815, Cochrane Papers, NLS.

29. Cochrane to Bathurst, December 31, 1814, WO 1/141, Kew.

30. Letter from the HMS *Ramillies*, January 5, 1815, Washington, DC, *Daily National Intelligencer*, March 23, 1815; St. George's, Bermuda, *Bermuda Gazette, and Weekly Advertiser*, April 8, 1815.

31. Graves to White, n.d. [1845–53], New Orleans, LA, *Daily Delta*, January 8, 1854.

32. No one in New Orleans was measuring temperatures during the campaign, though the modern thermometer had been developed in the 1700's. However, tree-ring analysis has determined that 1814–1815 was an El Niño winter, with colder than normal temperatures in Louisiana, and more than average precipitation. The year 2010 was a similar El Niño season, with late-December and early January nighttime temperatures in the twenties, and daytime highs in the forties. See Richard W. Dixon, "The 1815 Battle of New Orleans: A Physical Geographical Analysis," in Douglas R. Caldwell, Judy Ehlen, and Russell S. Harmon, eds., *Studies in Military Geography and Geology* (Dordrecht, Netherlands: Kluwer Academic, 2004), 152–53.

33. St. George's, Bermuda, *Bermuda Gazette, and Weekly Advertiser*, April 22, 1815.

34. Letter from the HMS *Ramillies*, January 5, 1815, Washington, DC, *Daily National Intelligencer*, March 23, 1815; Pay List of the 5th West India Regiment of Foot, December 1814–March 1815, Infantry Abroad Quarterly Pay Lists for the 5th West India Regiment of Foot, WO 12/11538, Kew.

35. Ellis, *First West India Regiment*, 151.

36. Hill, *Recollections*, 1:333; MacDonald *Memoir*, NYPL.

37. St. George's, Bermuda, *Bermuda Gazette, and Weekly Advertiser*, April 22, 1815.

38. Hill, *Recollections*, 1:334; Chesterton, *Peace, War, and Adventure*, 214–15.

39. Dickson, "Journal," December 29, 1814, 26–27.

40. Forrest, *Journal*, 35.

41. Gleig Diary, December 28–29, 1814, Barrett, *85th King's Light Infantry*, 218; Gerard, Campaigns 2, USNA.

42. Gerard, Campaigns 2, USNA.

43. Pakenham to Cochrane, December 28, 1814, Cochrane Papers, NLS; Cochrane to Croker, January 18, 1815, London, UK, *Courier, and Evening Gazette*, March 10, 1815.

44. Letter from Kingston, Jamaica, January 27, 1815, Richmond, VA, *Virginia Patriot*, March 25, 1815.

45. Ibid.

46. Ritchie, "Louisiana Campaign," 44–49.

47. Dickson, "Journal," 23.

48. Ibid. 23; Forrest, *Journal*, 35.

49. Michell, "Diary of Major J. Michell," December 28, 1814, 128.

50. Dickson, "Journal," December 29, 1814, 24–25.

51. Ibid.

52. Forrest, *Journal*, 35; John Michell to Jane Michell, January 22, 1815, HNOC.

53. Dickson, "Journal," December 29, 1814, 25.

54. Ibid., 25, 27; Forrest, *Journal*, 35.

55. Smith, *Autobiography of Lieutenant-General Sir Harry Smith*, 230–31.

56. Pakenham to Cochrane, December 28, 1814, Cochrane Papers, NLS. Owsley, *Borderlands*, 149, maintains that Pakenham "probably knew from prisoners that Jackson had first expected an attack through Lake Pontchartrain," an unwarranted conclusion given that the American prisoners taken thus far were virtually all private soldiers who had no access to what Jackson was thinking or speculation in his headquarters. The only officers in their hands were Jones's gunboat officers, who had tried their best to mislead the British as to Jackson's numbers. Owsley goes on to speculate (149n) that in making a diversion toward Chef Menteur via Lake Pontchartrain, Cochrane believed that thanks to the leak of information of his landing plans, Jackson would expect an attack there. However, the leaked October 8 correspondence from Fothergill mentioned only Lake Pontchartrain generally as the landing site, with no mention of Chef Menteur or any other spot.

57. Letter from New Orleans to Richmond, January 2, 1815, Charleston, SC, *City Gazette*, February 3, 1815.

58. Hill, *Recollections*, 1:335–37.

59. Walker, *Jackson and New Orleans*, 180.

60. Boston, MA, *New-England Palladium*, February 7, 1815.

61. Shields and Morrell to Bowden, December 28, 1814, Captains' Letters, RG 260, NA.

62. Letter from New Orleans, February 10, 1815, Boston, MA, *Boston Daily Advertiser*, February 10, 1815.

63. Letter from New Orleans to Washington DC, February 3, 1815, Burlington, VT, *Vermont Centinel*, March 24, 1815. Cochrane's expression is obscure, but in context seems to refer to grabbing a man's wig as an act deflating ego or conceit. In this case it was his acknowledgment that Laverty's pun had gotten the best of him.

64. Gleig Diary, December 30, 1814, Barrett, *85th King's Light Infantry*, 218.

65. Dickson, "Journal," December 30, 1814, 30, January 1, 1815, 38; Surtees, *Rifle Brigade*, 368. General Monthly Return of Officers belonging to the several Corps serving in the Army under the Command of Major General Lambert, January 25, 1815, WO 17/1218, Kew, lists Wright as "killed in action" January 1.

66. Letter from an officer on the HMS *Ramillies*, January 5, 1815, Washington, DC, *Daily National Intelligencer*, March 23, 1815.

67. Dickson, "Journal," December 30, 1814, 27–28.

68. [Gabriel] Winter to Elisha Winter, December 30, 1814, Washington, DC, *Daily National Intelligencer*, January 28, 1815; Edward Palfrey to John Palfrey, December 30, 1814, Palfrey Family Papers, Harvard; Letter to friend in New York, n.d. [December 30, 1814], New York, NY, *New-York Spectator*, February 1, 1815; Lee to Robertson, December 30, 1814, New York, NY, *New-York Mercantile Advertiser*, February 1, 1815; Claiborne to [Willie Blount], December 30, 1814, Rowland, Letter Books, 6:328.

69. Gabriel Winter to Elisha Winter, December 30, 1814, Washington, DC, *Daily National Intelligencer*, January 28, 1815; Johnston to Nashville postmaster, December 30, 1814, Clinton, OH, *Ohio Register*, January 31, 1815; Richard Relf to the Editor of the *Philadelphia Gazette*, December 30, 1814, Elizabethtown, NJ, *New-Jersey Gazette*, February 7, 1815; Letter from New Orleans to New York, December 30, 1814, New York, NY, *New-York Spectator*, February 1, 1815; Butler to?, December 30, 1814, New York, NY, *New-York Gazette & General Advertiser*, February 1, 1815; Lee to Robertson, December 30, 1814, New York, NY, *New-York Mercantile Advertiser*, February 1, 1815.

70. Letter from New Orleans to man in Washington, December 30, 1814, New York, NY, *Columbian*, February 2, 1815; Lee to Robertson, December 30, 1814, New York, NY, *New-York Mercantile Advertiser*, February 1, 1815.

71. Letter from member of Adams troop to friend in Natchez, December 30, 1814, Natchez, MS, *Mississippi Republican*, January 4, 1815, in New York, NY, *New-York Evening Post*, February 1, 1815.

72. Hynes to Blount, December 30, 1814, Marietta, OH, *American Friend*, January 28, 1815.

73. Letter from Fort St. John to Editor, [December 30, 1814], Washington, KY, *Union*, January 27, 1815.

74. Letter from member of Adams troop to friend in Natchez, December 30, 1814, Natchez, MS, *Mississippi Republican*, January 4, 1815, in New York, NY, *New-York Evening Post*,

February 1, 1815; Letter from New Orleans to Philadelphia, December 30, 1814, Bennington, VT, *Bennington News-Letter*, February 6, 1815; W. and J. Montgomery to Captain R. Bowen, December 30, 1814, Brownsville, PA, *American Telegraph*, February 8, 1815.

75. Edward Palfrey to John Palfrey, December 30, 1814, Palfrey Family Papers, Harvard.

76. Florian to Roosevelt, New Orleans, January 9, 1815, HNOC.

77. L. C. Hardy to William M. Reid, April 3, 1815. War of 1812 Collection, Tulane.

78. Gould Memoir, VHS.

79. Ellery, "Notes," NYPL.

80. Letter from Carroll's division to citizen in Paris, KY, December 29, 1814, Alexandria, VA, *Alexandria Gazette*, January 31, 1815; Letter from Fort St. John to Editor, [December 30, 1814], Washington, KY, *Union*, January 27, 1815.

81. List of Subscribers Who Gave Money or Hulled Rice to Purchase Garments for Those Serving Under Andrew Jackson December 29, 1814, Miscellaneous Collection, RG 68, Louisiana Historical Center, New Orleans.

82. Letter from New Orleans, December 30, 1814, Philadelphia, PA, *Relf's Philadelphia Gazette, and Daily Advertiser*, February 11, 1815; Letter from New Orleans to a merchant in Baltimore, January 1, 1815, New York, NY, *New-York Herald*, February 15, 1815.

83. "Report of the Committee of Inquiry," 266.

84. Letter from New Orleans, December 30, 1814, Philadelphia, PA, *Relf's Philadelphia Gazette, and Daily Advertiser*, February 11, 1815.

85. Reid and Eaton, *Jackson*, lxix; Jackson to McLean, March 22, 1824, *Appeal of L. Louaillier*, 20–21n. The account in Reid and Eaton would have been by Eaton, Reid having died before the book was finished. Jackson and Marigny each gave later accounts of the meeting that conflict at several points, and neither is wholly trustworthy.

86. Maunsel White, in New Orleans, LA, *Louisiana Advertiser*, in Washington, DC, *United States' Telegraph*, August 16, 1827.

87. Lee to Robertson, December 30, 1814, New York, NY, *New-York Mercantile Advertiser*, February 1, 1815.

88. Graves to White, n.d. [1845–53], New Orleans, *Daily Delta*, January 8, 1854.

89. Ensign J. Brown, Jr. to a friend in Paris, KY, December 30, 1814, Clinton, OH, *Ohio Register*, January 31, 1815; Letter from New Orleans, January 2, 1815, New York, NY, *New-York Evening Post*, February 8, 1815.

90. Edward Palfrey to John Palfrey, December 30, 1814, Palfrey Family Papers, Harvard.

91. Letter from Fort St. John to Editor, [December 30, 1814], Washington, KY, *Union*, January 27, 1815; Letter from member of Beale's Company, December 30, 1814, Hanover, NH, *Dartmouth Gazette*, February 15, 1815.

92. Gabriel Winter to Elisha Winter, December 30, 1814, Washington, DC, *Daily National Intelligencer*, January 28, 1815; Charles R. Hicks to Claiborne, December 30, 1814, MSS 716, HNOC.

93. Hicks to Claiborne, December 30, 1814, MSS 716, HNOC.

94. James H. Gordon to Morgan, December 30, 1814, Parsons Collection, Texas.

95. Letter from New Orleans, January 7, 1815, New York, NY, *New-York Evening Post*, February 8, 1815.

96. Gabriel Winter to Elisha Winter, December 30, 1814, Washington, DC, *Daily National Intelligencer*, January 28, 1815.

97. William Rice Johnson to William Martin Johnson, December 31, 1814, Miscellaneous Collection, RG 68, Louisiana History Center, New Orleans; Letter from New Orleans, January 1, 1815, Boston, MA, *New-England Palladium*, February 10, 1815.

98. Fayette, MS, *Chronicle*, June 28, 1889.

99. Trimble, "Trimble's Account," MDAH; Claiborne, *Notes on the War*, 69.

100. Letter from member of Adams troop to friend in Natchez, December 30, 1814, Natchez, MS, *Mississippi Republican*, January 4, 1815, in New York, NY, *New-York Evening Post*, February 1, 1815. According to Trimble's later memoir, Jackson also said, "You have this day been the admiration of one army, and the astonishment of the other." Fayette, MS, *Fayette Chronicle*, June 28, 1889.

101. Letter from member of Adams troop to friend in Natchez, December 30, 1814, Natchez, MS, *Mississippi Republican*, January 4, 1815, in New York, NY, *New-York Evening Post*, February 1, 1815; Letter from New Orleans to Washington, December 30, 1814, Georgetown, DC, *Federal Republican for the Country*, January 31, 1815; John H. Johnson to St. Francisville *Time-Piece*,

December 30, 1814, Washington, DC, *National Intelligencer*, February 4, 1815. Ascertaining just how many redcoats deserted is impossible. Letters by American writers at the time give the impression of a substantial number, but of course many writers repeated the same stories gleaned from just a few deserters. General Monthly Return of the Serjeants, Trumpeters, Drummers, and Rank and File of the several Corps serving in the Army under the Command of Major General the Honble Sir E. M. Pakenham KB, December 25, 1814, WO 17/1218, Kew, in fact lists no deserters from the army during the November 26–December 25 period. It also lists no deaths, however, even though several were killed in the night action December 23–24. Hence it seems probable that when the rolls were taken on December 25, it was too soon to determine who might just be missing in action, captured or dead on the field, and who had deserted, and that all who did not answer roll call were lumped together in the 215 reported as missing and prisoners of war. General Monthly Return of Officers belonging to the several Corps serving in the Army under the Command of Major General Lambert, January 25, 1815, WO 17/1218, Kew, shows a total of eight deserters for the period December 26, 1814, to January 25, 1815, which includes December 28–29 when several came to American lines. Of course, it also includes the period through January 25. Again, any number of men who deserted might have been listed as missing in action, so the figure of eight deserters should not be taken as conclusive.

102. Letter from Kingston, Jamaica, January 27, 1815, Richmond, VA, *Virginia Patriot*, March 25, 1815.
103. Letter by a British staff officer, January 16, 1815, Boston, MA, *Yankee*, May 19, 1815.
104. Letter from member of Adams troop to friend in Natchez, December 30, 1814, Natchez, MS, *Mississippi Republican*, January 4, 1815, in New York, NY, *New-York Evening Post*, February 1, 1815.
105. Letter from New Orleans, December 30, 1814, Baltimore, MD, *American, and Commercial Daily Advertiser*, January 31, 1815; Letter from New Orleans to Washington, December 30, 1814, Georgetown, DC, *Federal Republican for the Country*, January 31, 1815.
106. William Rice Johnson to William Martin Johnson, December 31, 1814, Miscellaneous Collection, RG 68, Louisiana History Center, New Orleans.
107. Tousard to John Stocker, January 6, 1815, Wilkinson, "Assaults on New Orleans," 49.
108. Theodore Tureaud to René Trudeau, January 8, 1815, Carlier d'Outremer to Villeré, n.d. [January 1815], Villeré Papers, HNOC.

CHAPTER THIRTEEN: "THUNDER, AND SMOKE, AND SLAUGHTER"

1. Tousard to John Stocker, January 6, 1815, Wilkinson, "Assaults on New Orleans," 49; Letter from New Orleans, January 7, 1815, New London, CT, *Connecticut Gazette*, February 8, 1815.
2. Edward Palfrey to John Palfrey, December 30, 1814, Palfrey Family Papers, Harvard.
3. Letter from New Orleans, January 1, 1815, Boston, MA, *New-England Palladium*, February 10, 1815.
4. Philemon Thomas to Hicky, December 30, 1814, Hicky Papers, LSU.
5. Elizabeth Clement to Wood, January 11, 1815, Clement, *Plantation Life*, 129.
6. Letter from Natchez, December 28, 1814, Washington, PA, *Washington Reporter*, January 23, 1815; Letter from New Orleans to Richmond, January 2, 1815, Charleston, SC, *City Gazette*, February 3, 1815; Letter from St. Francisville, LA, to Baltimore, MD, January 8, 1815, Baltimore, MD, *Baltimore Telegraph*, February 1, 1815.
7. John Brandegee to ?, December 31, 1814, Miscellaneous Collection, RG 68, Louisiana Historical Center, New Orleans; Letter to friend in New York, n.d., New York, NY, *New-York Spectator*, February 1, 1815.
8. Tousard to John Stocker, January 6, 1815, Wilkinson, "Assaults on New Orleans," 49; William Rice Johnson to William Martin Johnson, December 31, 1814, Miscellaneous Collection, RG 68, Louisiana History Center, New Orleans.
9. Gordon to Morgan, December 31, 1814, Parsons Collection, Texas.
10. Letter from New Orleans, December 30, 1814, New York, NY, *Columbian*, February 2, 1815.
11. Jackson to Louisiana Assembly, December 31, 1814, Moser et al., *Papers*, 226–27.
12. Letter from New Orleans, December 30, 1814, Philadelphia, PA, *Relf's Philadelphia Gazette, and Daily Advertiser*, February 11, 1815. No record of service for Marigny, Blanque, or

Rouffignac appears in the National Archives files. The four who served were General Garrigue Flaujac, Major Eziel, M. Bufort, and Sebastian Hiriart, though none seem to have been enlisted in any militia unit (Jane Lucas De Grummond, *The Baratarians and the Battle of New Orleans* [Baton Rouge: Louisiana State University Press, 1961], 110n).

13. Walter A. Overton to Lt. Flouer [*sic*], December 29, 1814 from Fort. St. Philip. Cusachs Collection RG 112, Louisiana Historical Center, New Orleans.
14. Gordon to Morgan, December 31, 1814, Parsons Collection, Texas.
15. Letter from New Orleans, December 31, 1814, Boston, MA, *Independent Chronicle*, February 6, 1815.
16. Tylden Journal, December 31, 1814, NYPL.
17. Brackenridge, *History of the Late War*, 294.
18. Memorandum, December 31, 1814, Forrest, *Journal*, 36–37.
19. Gerard, Campaigns, 2, USNA.
20. Dickson, "Journal," December 31, 1814, 29.
21. Ibid., 30–31.
22. Gerard, Campaigns, 2, USNA.
23. Dickson, "Journal," December 31, 1814, 31–33.
24. Gerard, Campaigns, 2, USNA.
25. Dickson, "Journal," December 31, 1814. 34–35; Gerard, Campaigns 2, USNA; Michell, "Diary of Major J. Michell," December 31, 1814, 128; Forrest, *Journal*, 35.
26. Gleig Diary, December 31, 1814, Barrett, *85th King's Light Infantry*, 218; Gleig to Janet Gleig, January 11, 1815, Gleig Papers, NLS.
27. Dickson, "Journal," December 31, 1814, 34–35.
28. Letter from the HMS *Ramillies*, January 5, 1815, Washington, DC, *Daily National Intelligencer*, March 23, 1815.
29. Stamford, UK, *Lincoln, Rutland, and Stamford Mercury*, February 24, 1815.
30. Kingston, Jamaica, *Royal Gazette*, quoted in De Grummond, "Platter of Glory," 331.
31. Tylden Journal, December 31, 1814, NYPL.
32. London, UK, *Morning Chronicle*, January 21, 1815.
33. Lt. R. Phelan testimony, *General Court Martial, Held at the Royal Barracks, Dublin, for the Trial of Brevet Lieutenant-Colonel Hon. Thomas Mullins* (Dublin, IR: William Espy, 1815), 51, Adjutant R. Barry testimony, 58.
34. Dickson, "Journal," January 1, 1815, 35.
35. Letter to the Editor of the Washington, KY, *Union*, February 14, 1815, Raleigh, NC, *Star*, April 14, 1815.
36. Gleig Diary, January 1, 1815, Barrett, *85th King's Light Infantry*, 218–19.
37. Dickson, "Journal," January 1, 1815, 35.
38. Reid and Eaton, *Jackson*, 326. This information about Jackson's headquarters may be an example of the information that Peddie later claimed came to the British from citizens in the city, but it could also be an example of Jackson's suspicions manufacturing facts since this appears in a biography by staff favorites informed chiefly by Jackson himself.
39. Patterson to Secretary of Navy, January 2, 1815, Captains' Letters, RG 26, NA, said that British artillery opened fire at four a.m. but is surely mistaken.
40. Bassett, *Tatum's Journal*, January 1, 1815, 121; Reid and Eaton, *Jackson*, 326.
41. Bassett, *Tatum's Journal*, January 1, 1815, 120–21.
42. Ibid.
43. Walker, *Jackson and New Orleans*, 256–57. Walker's account here, as elsewhere, is probably tinged with some imagination and the aged memories of his informants.
44. Reid and Eaton, *Jackson*, 326.
45. Dickson, "Journal," January 1, 1815, 35. According to Major Forrest, "Great confusion was apparent in that of the Enemy for some time." Forrest, *Journal*, January 1, 1815, 37–38. Writing four days later, an officer from the *Ramillies* who was present that morning not only claimed that they surprised the enemy with their heavy artillery fire but that they "almost completely silenced all their guns," a hyperbolic claim in that Jackson's gun had not yet fired. Letter from the HMS *Ramillies*, January 5, 1815, Washington, DC, *Daily National Intelligencer*, March 23, 1815.

46. Cope, *Rifle Brigade*, 188; Cooke, *Narrative*, 210–11. In his first memoir, published in 1821, Gleig told a bizarre story that was pure invention, his purpose unclear. On the fog lifting, he said, he could see Jackson's army. "The different regiments were upon parade; and being dressed in holiday suits, presented really a fine appearance." Bands played, mounted officers rode back and forth, colors were flying, and "all seemed jollity and gala." When the British batteries opened fire, the Yankee ranks broke and regiments dispersed, fleeing in all directions. "The utmost terror and disorder appeared to prevail," Gleig wrote. "Instead of nicely dressed lines, nothing but confused crowds could be observed" (*Narrative*, 320–21). This was all fiction. Not a single American source mentions anything about a parade that morning. Of a dozen or more letters written January 1 from Jackson's army, none speaks of a parade, and neither do any of the scores of letters later that week that summarize events from the 1st forward. John Coffee's Orderly Book (Cook Collection, HNOC) has general orders from army headquarters for that period, and none say anything of a parade. Moreover, the American works at this date were at least six feet high in most places, and higher in others. A man standing immediately in front of the works could not have seen over them without a ladder except perhaps through a gun embrasure, yet Gleig claimed that his view was made from 300 yards below Jackson's line. In fact, it was more like 650, but even at 300 yards it would have been plainly impossible to see over the American works. The common supposition among the British being that Jackson was taken by surprise by the opening of the British barrage, Gleig apparently invented the disrupted parade as a device to make that presumed surprise more dramatic. The only support for any of Gleig's statement comes from the journals of Dickson and Forrest cited below, who mention only enemy confusion at first.

47. Gerard, Campaigns, 2, USNA; Surtees, *Rifle Brigade*, 365.
48. Particulars in relation to Battle of New Orleans furnished me by a French gentleman in 1828— Summer, Follett Papers, Cincinnati History Library and Archives; Ellery, "Notes," NYPL.
49. Bassett, *Tatum's Journal*, January 1, 1815, 121; Letter from New Orleans to a printer of the Mississippi Republican, January 8, 1815, in New York, NY, *Columbian*, February 2, 1815; Letter from an officer in Coffee's command army to friend in Charleston, January 5, 1815, Charleston, SC, *City Gazette*, February 4, 1815.
50. Dudley Avery to Mary Ann Avery [in Baton Rouge], January 6, 1815, Dudley Avery Letters, LSU; Coffee to John Donelson, January 25, 1815, Tennessee Historical Society Miscellaneous Files, University of Tennessee; Hynes to Samuel Carswell, January 6, 1815, Andrew Hynes Papers, Tulane; Diary of the Siege of New Orleans, January 1, 1815, New York, NY, *New-York Mercantile Advertiser*, February 8, 1815.
51. A Hinds Dragoon to J. A. Browder, January 6, 1815, JELAC.
52. Burgoyne, *93rd Sutherland Highlanders*, 29.
53. Gleig to Janet Gleig, January 11, 1815, Gleig Papers, NLS.
54. Forrest, *Journal*, January 1, 1815, 37–38; Dickson, "Journal," January 1, 1815, 35.
55. Dickson, "Journal," January 1, 1815, 37–38; "War Diary, Hitherto Unpublished, of Mr. Benjamin Story," New Orleans, LA, *Times-Democrat*, June 18, 1893.
56. Codrington to Jane Codrington, January 4, 1815, Codrington Papers, COD/6/2, Caird.
57. Surtees, *Rifle Brigade*, 366.
58. Chesterton, *Peace, War, and Adventure*, 194.
59. Ibid.
60. Dickson, "Journal," January 1, 1815, 35; Surtees, *Rifle Brigade*, 365; Pakenham, *Pakenham Letters*, 257.
61. Chesterton, *Peace, War, and Adventure*, 193.
62. Ibid., 196–98; Perth, Scotland, *Courier*, March 30, 1815; Dickson, "Journal," 37; List of Deaths which have taken place among the Officers during the preceding Month, January 25, 1815, WO 17/1218, Kew.
63. Patterson to Secretary of Navy Crowninshield, January 2, 1815, Captains' Letters, RG 260, NA.
64. Bassett, *Tatum's Journal*, January 1, 1815, 122.
65. Fromentin to the Editors of the Baltimore *Telegraph*, January 29, 1815, Wilmington, DE, *Delaware Gazette and State Journal*, February 7, 1815.
66. Ibid.
67. Tousard to John Stocker, January 6, 1815, Wilkinson, "The Assaults on New Orleans," 49.

68. Particulars in relation to Battle of New Orleans furnished me by a French gentleman in 1828—Summer, Follett Papers, Cincinnati History Library and Archives. While this document does not reveal the name of the "French gentleman" informant, it is obviously John Hudry, whose *Petition of John Hudry*, 2, is virtually identical. Hudry claimed to have silenced Michell's battery, saying it had five guns, an error due to memory and failing health. Michell had seven guns and was not silenced.

69. Fredericktown *Gazette*, n.d., in Savannah, GA, *The Republican; and Savannah Evening Ledger*, April 4, 1815.

70. Gabriel Winter to William Willis, January 12, 1815, Willis Family Papers, LSU.

71. Fredericktown *Gazette*, n.d., in Savannah, GA, *The Republican; and Savannah Evening Ledger*, April 4, 1815; Le Blanc to?, January 9, 1815, Portland, ME, *Eastern Argus*, February 16, 1815; John H. Paschell, application, February 14, 1815, Cook Collection, HNOC.

72. Statement of John Labatut and J. E. Ker, August 15, 1843, Louis Desforges to Jackson, August 1843, Louis Desforges Pension file, RG 15, NA; Fromentin to the Editors of the Baltimore *Telegraph*, January 29, 1815, Wilmington, DE, *Delaware Gazette and State Journal*, February 7, 1815; Walker, *Jackson and New Orleans*, 267–69; Russell Sanjek, *American Popular Music and Its Business, the First Four Hundred Years: Volume II, from 1790 to 1909* (New York: Oxford University Press, 1988), 126.

73. Fromentin to the Editors of the Baltimore *Telegraph*, January 29, 1815, Wilmington, DE, *Delaware Gazette and State Journal*, February 7, 1815; Walker, *Jackson and New Orleans*, 267–69. Some sources state that a 12-pound ball hit Touro, but Pakenham had no 12-pounders, and the nature of the wound argues for shrapnel from a rocket or perhaps one of Michell's howitzers.

74. It seems probable that Pierre Laffite remained on the left of the line with Coffee during the period December 27–January 3, to watch movements in the direction of Bayou Bienvenue, but his presence at Battery No. 3 on January 1 is attested in a letter by an unidentified army officer, dated November 30, 1851, in Washington, DC, *Daily National Intelligencer*, December 9, 1851.

75. Nolte, *Memoirs*, 218; Walker, *Jackson and New Orleans*, 259.

76. Nolte, *Memoirs*, 218. The compiled service record for La Borde gives only his last name as Laborde. RG 24, NA.

77. Letter from New Orleans to a printer of the *Mississippi Republican*, January 8, 1815, in New York, NY, *Columbian*, February 2, 1815; A Hinds Dragoon to J. A. Browder, January 6, 1815, JELAC.

78. New Orleans, LA, *Louisiana Gazette for the Country*, February 2, 1815, in Washington, DC, *Daily National Intelligencer*, March 6, 1815; Columbus Lawson, Succession and Probate Records for Jefferson Parish, NOPL.

79. Letter from New Orleans to a printer of the *Mississippi Republican*, January 8, 1815, in New York, NY, *Columbian*, February 2, 1815; A Hinds Dragoon to J. A. Browder, January 6, 1815, JELAC.

80. Ellery, "Notes," NYPL; *Francis Larche*, 3–6.

81. Letter from camp New Orleans, January 6, 1815, Washington, DC, *Daily National Intelligencer*, January 31, 1815; Walker, *Jackson and New Orleans*, 259; Bassett, *Tatum's Journal*, January 1, 1815, 121; Ellery, "Notes," NYPL. Ellery also stated that a boat loaded with gunpowder was sunk as it approached Jackson's line. No other source mentions this and it was probably hearsay.

82. Dickson, "Journal," January 1, 1815, 35.

83. Surtees, *Rifle Brigade*, 365.

84. Michell, "Diary of Major J. Michell," January 1, 1815, 128.

85. Dickson, "Journal," January 1, 1815, 36–37.

86. Chew to John Chew, January 6, 1815, Charleston, SC, *City Gazette*, February 3, 1815; Bassett, *Tatum's Journal*, January 1, 1815, 121; Letter from New Orleans, January 7, 1815, New London, CT, *Connecticut Gazette*, February 8, 1815; Coffee to John Donelson, January 25, 1815, Tennessee Historical Society Miscellaneous Files, University of Tennessee; Letter from an officer in Coffee's command army to friend in Charleston, January 5, 1815, Charleston, SC, *City Gazette*, February 4, 1815; Letter from camp New Orleans, January 6, 1815, Uniontown, MD, *Engine of Liberty, and Uniontown Advertiser*, February 2, 1815; Letter from New Orleans to Richmond, January 2, 1815, Charleston, SC, *City Gazette*, February 3, 1815; Louisville, KY, *Western Courier*,

January 26, 1815. Patterson reported that British firing ceased at two p.m. (Patterson to Secretary of Navy, January 2, 1815, Captains' Letters, RG 26, NA).

87. Adjutant General's Report, January 1, 1815, Georgetown, MD, *Federal Republican for the Country,* April 4, 1815; New Orleans, LA, *Louisiana Gazette for the Country,* April 29, June 10, 1815.

88. Reid and Eaton, *Jackson,* 329.

89. Letter from New Orleans to a printer of the *Mississippi Republican,* January 8, 1815, in New York, NY, *Columbian,* February 2, 1815; Coffee to John Donelson, January 25, 1815, Tennessee Historical Society Miscellaneous Files, University of Tennessee; Bassett, *Tatum's Journal,* January 1, 1815, 121.

90. J. H. Leslie, ed., "Artillery Services in North America in 1814 and 1815, Being Extracts from the Journal of Colonel Sir Alexander Dickson," *Journal of the Society for Army Historical Research* 8, no. 33 (July 1929): 149.

91. Dickson, "Journal," January 1, 1815, 38.

92. Forrest, *Journal,* January 1, 1815, 37–38.

93. Dickson, "Journal," January 1, 1815, 37; Chesterton, *Peace, War, and Adventure,* 195; Cooke, *Narrative,* 212; "Recollections of the Expedition," part 3, 195. Cooke's statement about fiddle players and trumpeters is hearsay and cannot be eyewitness since he did not arrive with Pakenham's army until January 3.

94. Thomas Johnston to friend in Lexington, KY, January 6, 1815, Lexington, KY, *Western Monitor,* January 27, 1815.

95. Chesterton, *Peace, War, and Adventure,* 195.

96. Dickson, "Journal," January 1, 1815, 38; Gerard, Campaigns 2, USNA.

97. Aitchison Memoir, 73–74, HNOC.

98. Gleig Diary, January 1, 1815, Barrett, *85th King's Light Infantry,* 218–19; Gleig to Janet Gleig, January 11, 1815, Gleig Papers, NLS.

99. Dickson, "Journal," January 1, 1815, 41.

100. Ibid., 38–40; Smith, *Autobiography of Lieutenant-General Sir Harry Smith,* 232; Aitchison Memoir, 73–74, HNOC.

101. Testimony of Adjutant R. Barry, *General Court Martial . . . Trial of Brevet Lieutenant-Colonel Hon. Thomas Mullins,* 58.

102. Forrest, *Journal,* January 1, 1815, 37–38; Codrington to Jane Codrington, January 4, 1815, Codrington Papers, COD/6/2, Caird.

103. Aitchison Memoir, 73–74, HNOC.

104. Hill, *Recollections,* 2:6; Return of Casualties in the Army Under the Command of Major General The Honble Sir E. M. Pakenham K B in Action with the Enemy near New Orleans Between the 1st & 5th January 1815, WO 1/141, Kew.

105. Dickson, "Journal," January 3, 1815, 47.

106. Ibid., January 1, 1815, 40.

107. Thomas Johnston to friend in Lexington, KY, January 6, 1815, Lexington, KY, *Western Monitor,* January 27, 1815.

108. Report of the Killed, wounded and missing of the army under the command of Major General Andrew Jackson, in the actions of the 23d and 28th December 1814 and 1st and 8th January 1815, Jackson Papers, LC; Dickson, "Journal," January 3, 1815, 47.

109. Washington, DC, *National Intelligencer,* October 2, 1817. The source does not say when the anonymous author died but it had to be between January 1 and 7, since the opening line anticipates battle the next day. If Lawson wrote it, then it was written December 31, 1814, since he was dead by January 7, the night before the big battle. Moreover, it is also implied in a brief introductory note that the author lived for some period of time after being hit, and that it was during this time that his "dying wish" was for his poems not to be published. Lawson lived until January 5.

110. Letter from New Orleans, January 1–2, 1815, New York, NY, *New-York Mercantile Advertiser,* February 8, 1815.

111. Dickson, "Journal," January 1, 1815, 40; Bassett, *Tatum's Journal,* January 1, 1815, 122; Letter from camp New Orleans, January 6, 1815, Washington, DC, *Daily National Intelligencer,* January 31, 1815.

112. Florian to Roosevelt, January 9, 1815, HNOC.

113. Letter from New Orleans to Baltimore, January 1, 1815, New York, NY, *New-York Herald*, February 15, 1815.
114. Hynes to Samuel Carswell, January 6, 1815, Hynes Papers, Tulane; Fromentin to the Editors of the Baltimore *Telegraph*, January 29, 1815, Wilmington, DE, *Delaware Gazette and State Journal*, February 7, 1815. Fromentin had just received Claiborne's January 6 letter, and no doubt others from New Orleans that went out with the January 6 weekly mail.
115. Gould Memoir, VHS; Florian to Roosevelt, January 9, 1815, HNOC.
116. General Order, January 1, 1815, Orderly Book of Brigadier General John Coffee, Cook Collection, HNOC.
117. Letter from the HMS *Ramillies*, January 5, 1815, Washington, DC, *Daily National Intelligencer*, March 23, 1815.
118. Oxford, UK, *Oxford University and City Herald, and Midland County Chronicle*, February 25, 1815.

CHAPTER FOURTEEN: "THE NECESSITY OF DOING SOMETHING"

1. Codrington to Jane Codrington, January 4, 1815, Codrington Papers, COD/6/2, Caird.
2. Ibid.
3. Thomas Johnston to a friend in Lexington, KY, January 6, 1815, Lexington, KY, *Western Monitor*, January 27, 1815.
4. "Diary of the occurrences at and near New-Orleans, from the 1st to the 13th of January," Wilmington, DE, *American Watchman*, February 8, 1815; Claiborne to Shelby, January 4, 1815, Louisville, KY, *Western Courier*, January 26, 1815; Claiborne to Fromentin, n.d., Letter to the Editor of the New York, NY, *New-York Evening Post*, Kennebunk, ME, *Weekly Visitor*, February 11, 1815.
5. Cochrane Journal, January 1–2, 1815, ADM 50/122, Kew.
6. Codrington to Jane Codrington, January 4, 1815, Codrington Papers, COD/6/2, Caird.
7. Pakenham, *Pakenham Letters*, 257; Dickson, "Journal," January 1, 1815, 38–40.
8. "Naval Officer" to unknown recipient, January 30, 1815, *Naval Chronicle, for 1815*, vol. 33, 387. This officer is unidentified, but very well informed. Wrottesley, *Life and Correspondence of Field Marshal Sir John Burgoyne*, 1:305, also credits Cochrane with proposing widening the canal to use it to get the small boats and 85th across the river to take the batteries.
9. Cochrane Journal, January 1, 1815, ADM 50/122, Kew; Claiborne to Shelby, January 4, 1815, Louisville, KY, *Western Courier*, January 26, 1815; Claiborne to Fromentin, n.d., Letter to the Editor of the New York, NY, *New-York Evening Post*, Kennebunk, ME, *Weekly Visitor*, February 11, 1815.
10. Memorial of Edward Nicolls to Lord Melville, n.d. [1817], 1/144, Kew.
11. Cochrane Journal, January 6, 1815, ADM 50/122, Kew; Cooke, *Narrative*, 165.
12. Gleig Diary, January 2, 1815, Barrett, *85th King's Light Infantry*, 219.
13. Gerard, Campaigns 2, NYPL.
14. Letter from New Orleans, January 2, 1815, New York, NY, *New-York Evening Post*, February 8, 1815; James Moore King to James Moore, March [April] 15, 1815, King Collection, Middle Tennessee State University, Murfreesboro; Letter from New Orleans to Richmond, January 2, 1815, Charleston, SC, *City Gazette*, February 3, 1815; Letter from New Orleans to a printer of the *Mississippi Republican*, January 2, 1815, in New York, NY, *Columbian*, February 2, 1815.
15. Letter from New Orleans, January 1–2, 1815, New York, NY, *New-York Mercantile Advertiser*, February 8, 1815; Letter from New Orleans, January 3, 1815, New York, NY, *New-York Herald*, February 4, 1815; Diary of the siege of New Orleans, January 2, 1815, New York, NY, *New-York Mercantile Advertiser*, February 8, 1815; A Hinds Dragoon to J. A. Browder, January 6, 1815, JELAC.
16. Reid and Eaton, *Jackson*, 330.
17. Bassett, *Tatum's Journal*, January 1, 1815, 122; Letter from New Orleans to Editor of the *Philadelphia Gazette*, January 6, 1815, Wilkes-Barre, PA, *Gleaner*, February 10, 1815; Avery to Mary Ann Avery, January 6, 1815, Avery Letters, LSU.
18. Muster Report, January 3, 1815, Armament Report 1st Division, January 5, 1815, Villeré Papers, HNOC.
19. Fromentin to the Editor, January 29, 1815, Washington, DC, *Telegraph*, January 29, 1815.
20. Romford to Monroe, February 4, 1815, Washington, DC, *Daily National Intelligencer*, February 16, 1815; Fromentin to the Editors of the Baltimore *Telegraph*, January 29, 1815, Wilmington, DE, *Delaware Gazette and State Journal*, February 7, 1815.

21. Romford to Monroe, February 4, 1815, Washington, DC, *Daily National Intelligencer*, February 16, 1815.

22. General Order, November 15, 1814, Regimental Order November 15, 1814, Adair to Colonel Gray, November 18, 1814, General Order, November 20, 1814, Thomas Joyes Order Book, War of 1812, Joyes Family Papers, Filson.

23. Regimental Order, November 20, 1814, Joyes Order Book, Thomas Joyes Journal, November 21, 1814, ibid.

24. Joyes Journal, November 24–30, 1814, Thomas Joyes Papers.

25. General Orders, November 23, 27, 1814, Joyes Order Book, ibid.

26. General Orders, November 23, 27, 28, 1814, ibid.

27. General Orders, November 23, 27, 1814, ibid.

28. Special order, December 7, 1814, General Order, December 8, 1814, Joyes Order Book, Joyes Journal, December 6–10, 1814, ibid.

29. Joyes Journal, December 2, 6–10, 1814, ibid.

30. Joyes Journal, December 11–14, 1814, Account of ration drawn in Capt'n Thomas Joyes' Company of Infantry, Joyes Order Book, ibid.

31. General Orders, December 13, 1814, ibid.

32. Court of Inquiry, December 28, 1814, ibid.

33. Persons drafted in my company who are not Present, December 1, 1814, ibid.

34. Joyes Journal, December 14–15, 1814, ibid.

35. Joyes Journal, December 21, 1814, ibid.

36. "Sketch of A Tour of Service in Louisiana and of the Battle of New Orleans," part 1, Louisville, KY, *Louisville Daily Democrat*, March 18, 1846.

37. Joyes Journal, December 25, 1814, Joyes Family Papers, Filson.

38. Joyes Journal, December 25–29, 1814, ibid; David Weller to Samuel Weller, January 6, 1815, Weller Family Papers, Filson.

39. Washington, Mississippi Territory, *Washington Republican*, December 28, 1814.

40. "Sketch of A Tour of Service in Louisiana and of the Battle of New Orleans," part 1, Louisville, KY, *Louisville Daily Democrat*, March 18, 1846.

41. Mordecai Diary, May 2, 1815, Mordecai Family Papers, SHC, UNC.

42. Jackson to Monroe, January 3, 1815, Moser et al., *Papers*, 228.

43. Adair to Shelby, January 13, 1815, Louisville, KY, *Western Courier*, February 2, 1815; Blair, *Sketch of the Life*, 13; Claiborne, *Notes on the War*, 70–71; Coffee order of January 2, 1815, Jackson Papers, LC.

44. "Diary of the occurrences at and near New-Orleans, from the 1st to the 13th of January," Wilmington, DE, *American Watchman*, February 8, 1815; Letter from New Orleans, January 1–2, 1815, New York, NY, *New-York Mercantile Advertiser*, February 8, 1815.

45. Louisville, KY, *Louisville Correspondent*, January 11, 1815.

46. Joyes Journal, January 3–6, 1815, Joyes Papers, Filson.

47. Jackson to Monroe, January 3, 1815, Moser et al., *Papers*, 228; Jackson to Claiborne, January 3, 1813, 491; Debuys to Claiborne, January 3, 1815, Jackson Papers, LC; "Diary of the occurrences at and near New-Orleans, from the 1st to the 13th of January," Wilmington, DE, *American Watchman*, February 8, 1815.

48. Claiborne to Labatut, September 22, 1815, Rowland, *Letter Books*, 6:638; Marigny, *Reflections*, n.p.

49. Bassett, *Tatum's Journal*, January 1–7, 1815, 122–23; Fromentin to?, January 29, 1815, Boston, MA, *New-England Palladium*, February 10, 1815; Robert Breckinridge McAfee, *History of the Late War in the Western Country* (Lexington, KY: Worsley & Smith, 1816), 515; Marigny, *Reflections*, n.p. Marigny says that the legislature made the arms appeal, but that conflicts with Claiborne's statement.

50. Letter from Natchez to a merchant in New York, January 16, 1815, New York, NY, *New-York Evening Post*, February 6, 1815; Bassett, *Tatum's Journal*, January 1–7, 1815, 122–23; McAfee, *History of the Late War*, 516; John Thomas to Shelby, February 10, 1815, Frankfort, KY, *Argus of Western America*, March 3, 1815.

51. Letter from New Orleans to Editor of the *Philadelphia Gazette*, January 6, 1815, Wilkes-Barre, PA, *Gleaner*, February 10, 1815.

52. "Sketch of A Tour of Service," Louisville, KY, *Louisville Daily Democrat*, March 18, 1846.

53. New Orleans, LA, *Orleans Gazette & Commercial Advertiser*, in Savannah, GA, *The Republican; and Savannah Evening Ledger*, June 2, 1812.

54. Cox, *West Florida*, 458.

55. Letter from Kentucky volunteer to Frankfort, KY, January 6, 1815, Louisville, KY, *Louisville Correspondent*, January 27, 1815.

56. Reid and Eaton, *Jackson*, 332.

57. Claiborne to Monroe, January 4, 1815, Rowland, *Letter Books*, 6:330; Claiborne to Shelby, January 4, 1815, Louisville, KY, *Western Courier*, January 26, 1815; Claiborne to Fromentin, January 6, 1815, New York, NY, *New-York Evening Post*, February 3, 1815.

58. Letter from New Orleans to Richmond, January 2, 1815, Charleston, SC, *City Gazette*, February 3, 1815.

59. Natchez, MS, *Mississippi Republican*, January 4, 1815, in New York, NY, *New-York Evening Post*, February 1, 1815; "Diary of the occurrences at and near New-Orleans, from the 1st to the 13th of January," Wilmington, DE, *American Watchman*, February 8, 1815.

60. Fromentin to the Editors of the Baltimore *Telegraph*, January 29, 1815, Wilmington, DE, *Delaware Gazette and State Journal*, February 7, 1815; Muster report, January 5, 1815, Villeré Papers, HNOC; James Winchester to Jackson, January 3, 1815, Moser et al., *Papers*, 230.

61. Louisville, KY, *Western Courier*, January 4, 1815.

62. Jackson to Monroe, January 3, 1815, Moser et al., *Papers*, 228.

63. Letter from New Orleans, January 6, 1815, New York, NY, *New-York Spectator*, February 4, 1815.

64. Dickson, "Journal," January 1, 1815, 38. Owsley, *Borderlands*, 151, states that Dickson concluded that his artillery on January 1 was inadequate to the task assigned, and that this was his tacit admission that Pakenham was already defeated. He cites Dickson's January 1, 1815, journal entry as referenced in Reilly, *British at the Gates*, 281–82 (the actual citation should be pages 272–73) but does not note that this was Reilly's conclusion, not Dickson's.

65. Gleig, *Narrative*, 321–22.

66. Hill, *Recollections*, 2:6.

67. Gleig Diary, January 3, 1815, Barrett, *85th King's Light Infantry*, 219.

68. Edinburgh, Scotland, *Caledonian Review*, February 23, 1815.

69. Memorandum, January 3, 1815, Codrington Papers, COD/6/4, Caird.

70. Gleig to Janet Gleig, January 11, 1815, Gleig Papers, NLS.

71. List of Deaths which have taken place among the Officers during the preceding Month, January 25, 1815, WO 17/1218, Kew.

72. Gleig, *Narrative*, 321–23.

73. St. George's, Bermuda, *Bermuda Gazette, and Weekly Advertiser*, April 15, 1815.

74. The earliest mention of the Moreau story is in a January 30, 1815, letter written by a man identified in one instance as "a young and intelligent Naval Officer," and in another as "a young, but intelligent naval officer." It appeared in the London, UK, *Pilot*, May 6, 1815, and also in *Naval Chronicle, for 1815*, vol. 33, 385–88. The addressee is unknown, though it was probably a friend or fellow officer with the initials "D. S." who provided it to the *Naval Chronicle* for publication. Internal content shows that the author was in the navy, and commanded one of the four boats equipped with a small cannon in transporting the 85th Regiment across the Mississippi on January 8. That would match Captain James Money of the marines but is not a definitive attribution.

The earliest known mention of the Moreau story in print is in the St. George's, Bermuda, *Gazette and Weekly Advertiser*, April 15, 1815, in a summary of the New Orleans expedition dated March 16 at Barbados, and which was itself compiled from earlier private letters and Jamaican newspapers unavailable to the author for examination. Thus, there was possibly an appearance of the Moreau story in the Kingston press as early as January or February 1815. The account in the *Royal Gazette* states: "It is said they obtained the celebrated General Moreau's plan of defence of that city, which they had adopted." This is also the source for Pakenham's supposed declaration about the strength of Jackson's defenses.

75. Dickson, "Journal," January 3–4, 1815, 47; Gerard, Campaigns 2, USNA.

76. Hill, *Recollections*, 2:6.

77. Mullins defense statement, *General Court Martial . . . Trial of Brevet Lieutenant-Colonel Hon. Thomas Mullins*, 41, statement of A. M'Auley, 59, statement of R. Phelan, 52.

78. Statement of William Knight, ibid., 18.

79. Gerard, Campaigns 2, USNA.

80. M'Auley statement, *General Court Martial . . . Trial of Brevet Lieutenant-Colonel Hon. Thomas Mullins*, 62, J. E. Kipping statement, 62–63.

81. Dickson, "Journal," January 2, 1815, 40–41.

82. Cooke, *Narrative*, 157.

83. Tylden Journal, January 2, 1815, NYPL.

84. Ibid., January 5, 1815.

85. Croker to Gordon, January 3, 1815, Gordon, *Letters and Records*, 202; Perrett, *The Real Hornblower*, 126.

86. Dickson, "Journal," January 3, 1815, 47.

87. Cooke, *Narrative*, 162.

88. Dickson, "Journal," January 4, 1815, 47; John Spencer Cooper, *Rough Notes of Seven Campaigns in Portugal, Spain, France and America During the Years 1809–1815* (Staplehurst, UK: Spellmount, 1996), 127.

89. Cooke, *Narrative*, 163–64; Cooper, *Rough Notes*, 127.

90. Dickson, "Journal," January 4, 1815, 47; Forrest, *Journal*, January 5, 1815, 39; Pultney Malcolm Memorandum Book, January 5, 1815, Pultney Malcolm Papers, MAL/104, Caird.

91. Hill, *Recollections*, 2:9.

92. Gleig, *Narrative*, 324.

93. Codrington to Jane Codrington, January 4, 9, 1815, Codrington Papers, COD/6/2, Caird.

94. Lambert to Bathurst, January 10, 1815, London, UK, *Morning Chronicle*, March 10, 1815.

95. Lambert to Bathurst, January 29, 1815, WO 1/141, Kew.

96. Tylden Journal, January 5, 1815, NYPL.

97. Cooke, *Narrative*, 169.

98. Letter from New Orleans to Richmond, January 2, 1815, Charleston, SC, *City Gazette*, February 3, 1815.

99. Claiborne to Shelby, January 4, 1815, Louisville, KY, *Western Courier*, January 26, 1815; [Claiborne to Fromentin, January 6, 1815], New York NY, *New-York Evening Post*, February 3, 1815. Claiborne's letter to Fromentin cited above (which context suggests was written early January 6) was shown by Fromentin to a Washington correspondent of the *Evening Post* and summarized by him on January 30. He identified the deserter only as "a subaltern officer," which in the British army at the time could mean a junior grade lieutenant or an ensign. Casualty reports for Pakenham's army between December 23 and January 7 show only one subaltern missing, Ensign George Ashton of the 85th, and one lieutenant of the same regiment who might have been considered a subaltern, Lieutenant William Walker. Both were listed as missing on December 25, as casualties of the December 23 action, which suggests that neither had sufficient time between landing at Villeré's and capture to take a register of the army. Of course, not being a military man, Claiborne—or the editor who paraphrased him—could easily have confused the rank. Still, the deserter must have had access to headquarters to get the register that he brought with him. There were a few volunteer aides with the generals, and one of them might be the culprit. The statement that the register listed eight regiments dates its preparation prior to Lambert's arrival (when the number went up to ten regiments). Claiborne's actual letter to Fromentin has not been found, but on January 29, 1815, Fromentin wrote a lengthy letter to the editor of the Baltimore, MD, *Telegraph*, in which he repeated information in a letter he just received that internal context dates to being written late on January 6. In it he does not mention the "subaltern" deserter, but does refer to "a deserter who came in our camp on the 6th," and then attributes to that source virtually all of the information given by the *Evening Post* correspondent.

100. Thomas Johnston to friend in Lexington, KY, January 6, 1815, Lexington, KY, *Western Monitor*, January 27, 1815.

101. James H. Gordon to Morgan, January 1, 1815, Morgan Papers, Louisiana Historical Center; Neil Auction Catalog #89, Gaspar Cusachs Collection, December 2–4, 2016.

102. Dickson, "Journal," January 3, 1815, 47; Henri Chotard to Coffee, n.d., Jackson Papers, LC.

103. James A. Gordon to Morgan, January 2, 1815, Parsons Collection, Texas.

104. Gordon to Morgan, January 1, 1815, Morgan Papers, LC; Weekly Report, Consolidated of a Detachment of Drafted Militia under the Command of Capt. R. T. Sackett Stationed at Fort St. Leon, from the 1st day of Jany. 1815 to the 5th of Feb. 1815, Parsons Collection, Texas.

105. Gordon to Morgan, January 3, 1815, Parsons Collection, Texas.
106. Ibid.
107. Letter from New Orleans to Editor of the *Philadelphia Gazette*, January 6, 1815, Wilkes-Barre, PA, *Gleaner*, February 10, 1815.
108. Morgan to Gordon, January 2, 4, 1815, Parsons Collection, Texas.
109. Letter from New Orleans to Editor of the *Philadelphia Gazette*, January 6, 1815, Wilkes-Barre, PA, *Gleaner*, February 10, 1815.
110. W. H. Overton to Jackson, January 19, 1815, New York, NY, *New-York Evening Post*, March 22, 1815.
111. "Political Portraits with Pen and Pencil—Henry Miller Shreve," *United States Magazine, and Democratic Review* 22, no. 116 (February 1848): 166–67; Pfaff, "Shreve," 200–201.
112. Bassett, *Tatum's Journal*, January 1–7, 1814, 123.
113. Morgan to Gordon, January 2, 1815, Parsons Collection, Texas.
114. Bassett, *Tatum's Journal*, January 1–7, 1815, 122; Announcement, n.d. [January 1815], Villeré Papers, HNOC; Livingston to Morgan, January 3, 1815, Parsons Collection, Texas.
115. McAfee, *History of the Late War*, 515; Morgan to Gordon, January 2, 1815, Parsons Collection, Texas.
116. Patterson to Secretary of the Navy, January 13, 1815, Bridgeport, CT, *Republican Farmer*, February 22, 1815; Fromentin to the Editor, January 29, 1815, Washington, DC, *United States Telegraph*, January 29, 1815.
117. Patterson to Secretary of the Navy, January 13, 1815, Bridgeport, CT, *Republican Farmer*, February 22, 1815.
118. French, *They Lived at Chalmette*, 56.
119. Dickson, "Journal," January 4, 1815, 48, 50; Cooke, *Narrative*, 168.
120. Call to Tanner, April 3, 1844, Blair, *William O. Butler*, 11.
121. Louisiana General Assembly Resolution, February 1, 1815, Baltimore, MD, *Baltimore Telegraph*, March 16, 1815.
122. Ibid.
123. Letter from New Orleans, January 13, 1815, Philadelphia, PA, *Poulson's American Daily Advertiser*, February 6, 1815; Lowrie and Franklin, *American State Papers, Class IX: Claims*, 461, 521, 525, 531, 759–60, 835.

Chapter Fifteen: "Strike Our Foes with Fear"

1. Letter from Natchez, January 6, 1815, New York, NY, *New-York Evening Post*, February 1, 1815.
2. *Report of the Committee of Claims on the Petition of Jacob Purkill*, 1–5.
3. James Moore King to James Moore, March [April] 15, 1815, King Collection, Gore Research Center, Middle Tennessee State University, Murfreesboro.
4. Louaillier to Morgan, January 3, 1815, Morgan Papers, LC; Subscription statements, Dec. 29, 1814, January 1815, War of 1812 Collection, Tulane; New Orleans, LA, *L'Ami des Lois*, January 15, 1815; Latour, *Historical Memoir*, 141.
5. Louisiana General Assembly Resolution, February 1, 1815, Baltimore, MD, *Baltimore Telegraph*, March 16, 1815; Citizens and Soldiers to Jackson, January 3, 1815, Moser et al., Papers, 491; *Appeal of L. Louaillier*, 15–16n; Fromentin to the Editors of the *Baltimore Telegraph*, January 29, 1815, Wilmington, DE, *Delaware Gazette and State Journal*, February 7, 1815.
6. Shaumburg to Wilkinson, January 25, 1815, HNOC; Livingston to Mrs. Montgomery, January 6, 1815, Hunt, *Life of Edward Livingston*, 199; Hunt, *Memoir of Mrs. Edward Livingston*, 54.
7. Florian to Roosevelt, New Orleans, January 9, 1815, HNOC.
8. Hunt, *Memoir of Mrs. Edward Livingston*, 56–57.
9. Dickson, "Journal," January 3, 1815, 47, January 5, 1815, 50; Gerard, Campaigns 2, USNA.
10. Reid and Eaton, *Jackson*, 341; Latrobe, *Impressions*, 45; Claiborne, *Mississippi*, 343–44.
11. Letter from a Kentuckian to Frankfort, KY, January 5–6, 1815, Pittsburgh, PA, *Pittsburgh Weekly Gazette*, February 4, 1815.
12. Dickson, "Journal," January 4, 1815, 48, January 6, 1815, 52–53; Gerard, Campaigns, 2, USNA; Cooke, *Narrative*, 167.
13. Dickson, "Journal," January 3, 1815, 42, 45.

14. Ibid., 45–46, 48–49, January 6, 1815, 52–53; Gerard, Campaigns 2, USNA; Cooke, *Narrative*, 167.

15. Dickson, "Journal," January 2, 1815, 42, January 4, 1815, 47, 49, January 6, 1815, 51; Forrest, *Journal*, 38–39; Gerard, Campaigns 2, USNA.

16. Tylden Journal, January 6, 1815, NYPL.

17. Gerard, Campaigns, 2, USNA; Dickson, "Journal," January 4, 1815, 48.

18. Mordecai Diary, May 2, 1815, Mordecai Family Papers, SHC, UNC; James Bradford to?, January 6, 1815, Lexington, KY, *Western Monitor*, January 27, 1815.

19. Dickson, "Journal," January 6, 1815, 50–51.

20. Tylden Journal, January 6, 1815, NYPL; Dickson, "Journal," January 6, 1815, 50–51; Daniel Lawrence to Cochrane, January 7, 1815, Cochrane Papers, NLS; Latour, *Historical Memoir*, 98–100.

21. James Bradford to?, January 6, 1815, Lexington, KY, *Western Monitor*, January 27, 1815; Dickson, "Journal," January 5–6, 1815, 50–51.

22. Tylden Journal, January 6, 1815, NYPL.

23. Letter from New Orleans, January 6, 1815, New York, NY, *New-York Spectator*, February 4, 1815.

24. William Johnson to Patterson, January 7, 1815, Wilmington, DE, *Delaware Gazette and State Journal*, February 23, 1815; Letter from Fort St. John to Editor of the *Union*, January 9, 1815, Brownsville, PA, *American Telegraph*, February 22, 1815; Letter from New Orleans, January 1–2, 1815, New York, NY, *New-York Mercantile Advertiser*, February 8, 1815; Reid and Eaton, *Jackson*, 335.

25. Letter from New Orleans to Lexington, KY, January 13, 1815, Lexington, KY, *Western Monitor*, February 3, 1815; Thomas Johnston to friend in Lexington, KY, January 6, 1815, Lexington, KY, *Western Monitor*, January 27, 1815. Samuel Carter, III, *Blaze of Glory, the Fight for New Orleans, 1814–1815* (New York: St. Martin's, 1971), 239, states that the men Johnson captured told him Pakenham planned to attack Jackson on January 8. This is impossible given that the *Cyrus* had just arrived from Jamaica. Its crew could know nothing firsthand of events in the army, and certainly nothing at all of plans made at headquarters. Their only information as of that moment had to come from the boat crews who came from Bayou Bienvenue to pick up Lambert's men, and they could know nothing more recent than January 4 or very early January 5 at the latest.

26. Claiborne to Fromentin, January 6, 1815, New York, NY, *New-York Evening Post*, February 3, 1815.

27. Cochrane to Edward Griffith [Colpoys], January 5, 1815, Cochrane Papers, NLS.

28. Cochrane Journal, January 5, 1815, ADM 50/122, Kew.

29. Tylden Journal, January 6, 1815, NYPL; Gerard, Campaigns 2, USNA.

30. Tylden Journal, January 8, 11, 1815, NYPL.

31. Forrest, *Journal*, 39; Dickson, "Journal," January 6, 1815, 51.

32. Tylden Journal, January 5–6, 1815, NYPL.

33. Dickson, "Journal," January 6, 1815, 51; "Diary of the occurrences at and near New-Orleans, from the 1st to the 13th of January," Wilmington, DE, *American Watchman*, February 8, 1815.

34. Kingston, Jamaica, *Jamaica Courant*, January 27, 1814; Letter from Kingston, Jamaica, January 27, 1815, Richmond, VA, *Virginia Patriot*, March 25, 1815.

35. London, UK, *Times*, February 21, 1815.

36. Letter from the HMS *Ramillies*, January 5, 1815, Washington, DC, *Daily National Intelligencer*, March 23, 1815; Letter to the Editor, January 2, 1815, Kingston, Jamaica, *Courant*, January 27, 1814.

37. Letter from New Orleans to member of Congress, January 13, 1815, Washington, DC, *National Intelligencer*, February 7, 1815.

38. Isaac L. Baker to Stephen A. Austin, January 4, 1815, Eugene C. Barker, ed., *Annual Report of the American Historical Association for the Year 1919, Part 1 The Austin Papers*: (Washington, DC: Government Printing Office, 1924), 2:246.

39. General Order, January 5, 1815, Cusachs Collection, RG 112, Louisiana Historical Center, New Orleans.

40. Monroe to Jackson, January 5, 1814, Jackson Papers, LC.

41. Priestley to Latour, March 4, 1816, Latour Archive, HNOC.

42. John Reid to Abram Maury, January 7, 1815, Cook Collection, HNOC.

43. Letter from a Kentuckian in New Orleans to Frankfort, KY, January 5–6, 1815, Pittsburgh, PA, *Pittsburgh Weekly Gazette*, February 4, 1815.

44. Letter from Natchez to Mr. Ralston in Richmond, January 3, 1815, Richmond, VA, *Richmond Enquirer*, January 28, 1815.

45. Jackson to Monroe, January 3, 1815, Moser et al., *Papers*, 228.

46. Brown to Jackson, January 3, 1815, ibid., 229.

47. Claiborne to Fromentin, January 6, 1815, New York, NY, *New-York Evening Post*, February 3, 1815.

48. New Haven, CT, *Connecticut Journal*, February 13, 1815.

49. London, UK, *Times*, February 18, 1815.

50. New Orleans, LA, *L'Ami des Lois*, January 16, 1815.

51. Georgetown, DC, *Federal Republican for the Country*, February 3, 1815.

52. Baltimore, MD, *Baltimore Telegraph*, January 24, 1815.

53. Washington, DC, *Daily National Intelligencer*, January 9, 1815.

54. Nashville, TN, *Nashville Whig*, January 3, 1815; Washington, DC, *Daily National Intelligencer*, January 21, 1815.

55. London, UK, *Morning Post*, January 6, 1815.

56. New Bedford, MA, *New Bedford Mercury*, January 6, 1815.

57. Manchester, UK, *Manchester Mercury, and Harrop's General Advertiser*, March 7, 1815.

58. Livingston to Janet Montgomery, January 6, 1815, Livingston Papers, Princeton; John Reid to Abram Maury, January 7, 1815, Cook Collection, HNOC.

59. Letter from camp New Orleans, January 6, 1815, Uniontown, MD, *Engine of Liberty, and Uniontown Advertiser*, February 2, 1815.

60. Letter from New Orleans to the Editor of the *Philadelphia Gazette*, January 6, 1815, Boston, MA, *Boston Daily Advertiser*, February 6, 1815.

61. Chew to John Chew, January 6, 1815, Norfolk, VA, *Norfolk Gazette and Publick Ledger*, February 1, 1815.

62. Chew to John Chew, January 6, 1815, Norfolk, VA, *Norfolk Gazette and Publick Ledger*, February 1, 1815; Letter from New Orleans, January 6, 1815, Louisville, KY, *Western Courier*, January 26, 1815; David Weller to Samuel Weller, January 6, 1815, Weller Family Papers, Filson.

63. Letter from Camp M'Carty, January 6, 1815, Clinton, OH, *Ohio Register*, January 31, 1815.

64. Hector M. Organ to Samuel Mordecai, January 19, 1815, Mordecai Family Papers, SHC, UNC; Tousard to John Stocker, January 6, 1815, Wilkinson, "The Assaults on New Orleans," 46.

65. Avery to Mary Ann Avery, January 6, 1815, Avery Letters, LSU.

66. Adair-Hemphill Family Papers, Filson Historical Society, Louisville. This poem is identified only as "written just before the battle of New Orleans—and whilst we were in daily expectation of hearing of the attack made on that place by the British."

67. Tousard to Stocker, January 6, 1815, Wilkinson, "Assaults on New Orleans," 46.

68. David Weller to Samuel Weller, January 6, 1815, Weller Family Papers, Filson; Washington, DC, *Daily National Intelligencer*, January 31, 1815; John Reid to Abram Maury, January 7, 1815, Cook Collection, HNOC; Letter from officer in the Navy to Baltimore, January 6, 1815, Baltimore, MD, *Baltimore Telegraph*, February 1, 1815.

69. Hynes to Carswell, January 6, 1815, Hynes Papers, Tulane.

70. Letter from New Orleans to a mercantile house in New York, January 6, 1815, Albany, NY, *Albany Gazette*, February 6, 1815.

71. Claiborne to Jackson, January 6, 1815, Moser et al., *Papers*, 231, 492.

72. Jackson to Livingston, May 17, 1815, Livingston Papers.

73. Shaumburg to Wilkinson, January 25, 1815, HNOC; Marigny, *Reflections*, n.p. There may be a badly garbled echo of this incident in a story told years later in Nolte, *Memoirs*, 219. Nolte stated that in the January 1 action, Jackson's batteries No. 1 and 2 ran short of ammunition, and Old Hickory blamed Claiborne, sending a message to him in New Orleans stating, "By the Almighty God, if you do not send me balls and powder instantly, I shall chop off your head, and have it rammed into one of those field-pieces." Nolte said that Claiborne, who was in charge of munitions in the city, "was so frightened that he could scarcely speak." The story is nonsense, like much in Nolte's memoir. Claiborne never had charge of munitions at any time, and there is

no credible evidence that the governor was frightened, though the anecdote echoes a postwar accusation from one of Claiborne's enemies that during the January 8 fight he went into hiding.

74. Mordecai Diary, May 2, 1815, Mordecai Family Papers, SHC, UNC.

75. Natchez, MS, *Ariel*, June 7, 1828. James K. Cook, editor of the *Ariel*, rode down the river to New Orleans with the Kentuckians, and is likely the source for this story.

76. Nolte, *Memoirs*, 220, has another of his confused accounts of an actual event. He states that Colonel Denis De La Ronde calmly appeared at British headquarters at the Villeré house on the evening of January 6 and shared dinner with Pakenham, Gibbs, and Lambert, who believed him to be one of those *creoles* opposed to the Americans. Supposedly they discussed their plans for the January 8 attack in front of him, then allowed De La Ronde to leave, whereupon he crossed the river in a canoe the next morning and rushed up the right bank to cross again and bring what he had learned to Jackson. It is a badly garbled echo of De La Ronde's actual December 23 flight to bring Jackson word of the British appearance at Villeré's.

77. Jackson to Monroe, January 9, 1815, Augusta, GA, *Augusta Herald*, February 23, 1815.

78. Letter from New Orleans, January 6, 1815, Louisville, KY, *Western Courier*, January 26, 1815; Florian to Roosevelt, January 9, 1815, HNOC.

79. Letter from New Orleans to Natchez, January 6, 1815, Windsor, VT, *Washingtonian*, February 13, 1815; Bassett, *Tatum's Journal*, January 8, 1815, 129.

80. Priestley to Latour, March 4, 1816, Latour Archive, HNOC.

81. Claiborne, *Notes on the War*, 76.

82. Reid and Eaton, *Jackson*, 334; A. D. Tureaud to Sosthene Roman, January 6, 1815, Villeré Papers, HNOC; David Weller to Samuel Weller, January 6, 1815, Weller Family Papers, Filson.

83. Joyes Journal, January 7, 1815, Joyes Papers, Filson.

84. Hynes to Carswell, January 6, 1815, Hynes Papers, Tulane.

85. Tousard to Stocker, January 6, 1815, Wilkinson, "The Assaults on New Orleans," 50.

86. Reid and Eaton, *Jackson*, 334.

87. "Sketch of A Tour of Service," Louisville, KY, *Louisville Daily Democrat*, March 19, 1846.

88. Letter from New Orleans to Lexington, KY, January 13, 1815, Lexington, KY, *Western Monitor*, February 3, 1815.

89. Ellery, "Notes," NYPL.

90. Account of the Battle of New Orleans, 1815, Jackson Papers, LC; Bassett, *Tatum's Journal*, January 7, 1815, 124–25.

91. Walker, *Jackson and New Orleans*, 306–7. There is no earlier authority for Jackson making this statement and it could be apocryphal.

92. Florian to Roosevelt, January 9, 1815, HNOC; Gould Memoir, VHS.

93. Fromentin to the Editor, January 29, 1815, Washington, DC, *Telegraph*, January 29, 1815.

94. Fromentin letter to Baltimore, January 6, 1815, Boston, MA, *New-England Palladium*, February 10, 1815; War of 1812 Service Record, Peter/Pierre Monier/Monnier, RG 94, NA.

95. Estate of Columbus Lawson, Succession and Probate Records, Orleans Parish, NOPL.

96. Cochrane Journal, January 7, 1815, ADM 50/122, Kew.

97. Laurence to Cochrane, January 7, 1815, Cochrane Papers, NLS.

98. Walker, *Jackson and New Orleans*, 321. Letter from St. Francisville, LA, to Baltimore, January 8, 1815, Baltimore, MD, *Baltimore Telegraph*, February 1, 1815, says that prisoners taken after January 1 were carrying 1.4-pound rations of horsemeat in their knapsacks supposed to last them four days. It seems possible but unlikely, given that men did not go into action weighted down with their knapsacks, and not many horses were likely to get by Dickson's orders for artillery use. The more likely source of this is a deserter who exaggerated army conditions.

99. Joyes Journal, February 2, 1815, Joyes Papers, Filson.

CHAPTER SIXTEEN: "WE AWAIT OUR FATE"

1. Burgoyne, *93rd Sutherland Highlanders*, 28–31.

2. Cooke, *Narrative*, 216–17.

3. Surtees, *Rifle Brigade*, 369.

4. Dickson, "Journal," January 7, 1815, 53; "Naval Officer" to unknown recipient, January 30, 1815, *Naval Chronicle, for 1815*, vol. 33, 387.

5. Gleig, *Narrative*, 325–26.

6. Michell, "Diary of Major J. Michell," January 7, 1815, 128–29.

7. Pakenham, *Pakenham Letters*, 258.

8. "Naval Officer" to unknown recipient, January 30, 1815, *Naval Chronicle, for 1815*, vol. 33, 387; Account of January 8 in Tylden Journal, January 11, 1815, NYPL.

9. R[obert] S[impson], "Battle of New Orleans, 8th January, 1815, *Blackwood's Edinburgh Magazine* 24, no. 143 (September 1828): 354. The author of this brief first-person account stated that he passed by and saw the whole of the American defenses, "partly as conqueror, and partly as a wounded prisoner," (page 356n), and also that on January 8 he "remained the whole day in the American field hospital" (page 357n). For him to have spent all of January 8 in the American hospital could suggest that he was one of those wounded and captured in the fighting on the night of December 23, but no officer with those initials appears on the British casualty reports for that action, or on the reports of subsequent losses through January 5, 1815. The only British officer with the initials R. S. reported wounded and captured in the entire campaign was Captain Robert Simpson of the 43rd Regiment of Foot, a casualty of the January 8 main battle. He must be the man, particularly since the most circumstantial portion of this account is that covering the action on the far right of the American line where a company of the 43rd was engaged in the temporary capture of the riverside bastion. Indeed, his is the best surviving description of the redoubt.

10. Account of January 8 in Tylden Journal, January 11, 1815, NYPL.

11. "Naval Officer" to unknown recipient, January 30, 1815, *Naval Chronicle, for 1815*, vol. 33, 387.

12. David Weller to Samuel Weller, January 6, 1815, Weller Family Papers, Filson; Letter from New Orleans, January 7, 1815, New London, CT, *Connecticut Gazette*, February 8, 1815; John Reid to Abram Maury, January 7, 1815, Cook Collection, HNOC; Letter from New Orleans, January 7, 1815, New York, NY, *New-York Evening Post*, February 8, 1815.

13. Pfaff, "Shreve," 202.

14. General Orders, January 21, 1815, New Orleans, LA, *Louisiana Courier*, January 25, 1815.

15. General Orders, January 21, 1815, ibid., refers to a Battery No. 9, which is probably the guns in the redoubt.

16. Smith, *New Orleans*, 70–71; Latour, Memoirs, plate vii; Meuse, *Weapons*, 28–30.

17. H. J. Boneval Latrobe to Villeré, January 7, 1815, Villeré Papers, HNOC; Louisiana General Assembly Resolution, February 1, 1815, Baltimore, MD, *Baltimore Telegraph*, March 16, 1815.

18. Smith, *New Orleans*, 71–73; Adair to Shelby, April 10, 1815, Louisville, KY, *Western Courier*, May 11, 1815.

19. Bassett, *Tatum's Journal*, December 28, 1814, 119.

20. William Eustis to Richard Cutts, February 13, 1815, Richard Cutts Papers, UVA.

21. Letter from New Orleans, January 7, 1815, Georgetown, DC, *Federal Republican for the Country*, February 24, 1815; Boston, MA, *New-England Palladium*, February 7, 1815.

22. Letter from New Orleans. January 7, 1815, New London, CT, *Connecticut Gazette*, February 8, 1815.

23. David Weller to Samuel Weller, January 6, 1815, Weller Family Papers, Filson.

24. New York, NY, *New-York Evening Post*, January 8, 1841. Though anonymous, this account is presented as being by an "eye-witness." Content suggests it is by a member of Jackson's staff or someone who was in the McCarty house on January 7–8.

25. Letter from New Orleans to Lexington, KY, January 13, 1815, Lexington, KY, *Western Monitor*, February 3, 1815.

26. New Orleans, LA, *Orleans Gazette & Commercial Advertiser*, April 22, 1814; Morgan to Jackson, January 7, 1815, Moser et al., *Papers*, 234–35; Bassett, *Tatum's Journal*, January 7, 1815, 124.

27. Reid and Eaton, *Jackson*, 336.

28. Patterson to Secretary of the Navy, January 13, 1815, Bridgeport, CT, *Republican Farmer*, February 22, 1815.

29. Ritchie, "Louisiana Campaign," 69.

30. Patterson to Crowninshield, January 13, 1815, Bridgeport, CT, *Republican Farmer*, February 22, 1815.

31. Jackson to Morgan, January 7, 1815, Andrew Jackson Collection, HNOC.

32. Provision Returns for Captain Ross's Company, Captain Bill's company, Captain Nesom's company, 10th Louisiana Militia, January 7, 1815, Cook Collection, HNOC.

33. Robert Butler to Villeré, January 7, 1815, Villeré Papers, Muster Reports, January 3, 5, 1815, Statement of company captains, n.d., Armament Report 1st Division, January 5, 1815, Villeré Papers, Morning Report of Third Regiment of Infantry, January 8, 1815, Cook Collection, HNOC.

34. General Order of Bartholomew Shaumburg, January 7, 1815, Cook Collection, HNOC.

35. General Orders, January 7, 1815, Morgan Papers, LC.

36. Patterson to Secretary of the Navy, January 13, 1815, Bridgeport, CT, *Republican Farmer*, February 22, 1815; Bassett, *Tatum's Journal*, January 7, 1815, 124.

37. Adair to Jackson, March 20, 1815, Bardstown, KY, *Bardstown Repository*, May 18, 1815.

38. Joyes Journal, January 7, 1815, Joyes Papers, Filson.

39. Bassett, *Tatum's Journal*, January 7, 1815, 124; Adair to Jackson, March 20, 1815, Bardstown, KY, *Bardstown Repository*, May 18, 1815. Smith, *New Orleans*, 73–74, tells a story of Adair appealing to the mayor and Committee of Safety to lend him arms, and their agreement to lend 400 from the city armory, on condition that it be done secretly at night so as not to alarm the public, and that they be used to defend the city and protect against any slave insurrection. The weapons were taken to the Kentuckians' camp that night in boxes and handed over. The story is apocryphal, particularly since the city and state armories had already been depleted, and there seems to be no contemporary documentary support for it.

40. Joyes Journal, January 7, 1815, Joyes Papers, Filson.

41. Claiborne, *Mississippi*, 344.

42. Joyes Journal, January 7, 1815, Joyes Papers, Filson.

43. "Sketch of A Tour of Service," Louisville, KY, *Louisville Daily Democrat*, March 18, 1846; David Weller to Samuel Weller, January 13, 1815, Weller Family Papers, Filson.

44. "Sketch of A Tour of Service," Louisville, KY, *Louisville Daily Democrat*, March 18, 1846. The source remembers the moon appearing at midnight, but the moon was in the final days of its last quarter and did not appear in the sky until after dawn.

45. Letter from British officer in fleet, January 5, 1815, Providence, RI, *Providence Gazette and Country Journal*, April 1, 1815.

46. Lambert's original January 10, 1815, report in WO 1/141, Kew.

47. Gerard, Campaigns 2, USNA.

48. Ibid.

49. Dickson, "Journal," January 7, 1815, 56.

50. Edward Pakenham, Memorandum, January 7, 1815, Codrington Papers, COD/7/2, Caird.

51. Wrottesley, *Life and Correspondence of Field Marshal Sir John Burgoyne*, 305; "Naval Officer" to unknown recipient, January 30, 1815, *Naval Chronicle, for 1815*, vol. 33, 387.

52. Dickson, "Journal," January 7, 1815, 54.

53. Codrington to Jane Codrington, January 1–31, 1815, Codrington Papers, COD/6/2, Caird.

54. Reid and Eaton, *Jackson*, 351.

55. "Naval Officer" to unknown recipient, January 30, 1815, *Naval Chronicle, for 1815*, vol. 33, 387.

56. Lambert to Bathurst, January 29, 1815, WO 1/141, Kew.

57. Wylly to Duke of Wellington, March 4, 1815, Pakenham, *Pakenham Letters*, 254–55.

58. Lambert to Bathurst, January 10, 1815, London, UK, *Morning Chronicle*, March 10, 1815.

59. Account of January 8 in Tylden Journal, January 11, 1815, NYPL.

60. Reid and Eaton, *Jackson*, 351; "British plan of carrying the American breastwork near New Orleans, Jan 8th, 1815," Legislative Records, Record Group 60, Tennessee State Library and Archives, Nashville. This latter document covers only Rennie's assignment, strongly suggesting that it was drafted from the full original the night before the battle and carried by Rennie.

61. Haymes statement, *General Court Martial . . . Trial of Brevet Lieutenant-Colonel Hon. Thomas Mullins*, 1.

62. Mullins statement, ibid., 35–36.

63. Johnston statement, ibid., 29–30.

64. Johnston statement, Emmet statement, ibid, 31, Emmett statement, 11, 31, Tapp statement, 12.

65. Johnston statement, ibid., 31, Mullins statement, 36, Phelan statement, 51. The actual original note written by Gibbs was presented in court and published in Johnston statement, 30. It differs in minor respects from other versions of it introduced.

66. Mullins defense statement, ibid., 38. Johnston statement, 31.

67. Debbeigg statement, ibid., 33.

68. Johnston statement, ibid., 30.

69. Debbeigg statement, ibid., 2–3, 5.

70. Mullins defense statement, ibid., 47, Johnston statement, 33.

71. Mullins defense statement, ibid., 47, Debbeigg statement, 3.

72. Mullins defense statement, ibid., 38.

73. Knight statement, ibid., 33.

74. Knight statement, ibid., 14–15, 18, 19.

75. M'Auley statement, ibid., 61, Knight statement, 18.

76. Hill, *Recollections*, 2:9–10.

77. Dickson to Major Munro, January 7, 1815, Dickson, "Journal," January 7, 1815, 56.

78. Dickson, "Journal," January 7, 1815, 56.

79. Ibid., 57.

80. The earliest actual hint of "beauty and booty" comes in a January 9 letter by a member of the Adams Troop from Natchez who wrote that he and others heard British officers exhorting their troops as they approached the works, shouting "Well done my brave fellows, mount the works! take the city!—and you shall have money and women in plenty!!!" (Letter from man in the Adams Troop to a friend in Washington, Mississippi Territory, January 9, 1815, Washington, Mississippi Territory, *Washington Republican*, January 18, 1815).

81. Smith, *Autobiography of Lieutenant-General Sir Harry Smith*, 235. The revelation and subsequent controversy over the "beauty and booty" business will be discussed hereafter. What is salient here is that it seems virtually certain that prior to the January 8 engagement there was talk at some level or levels of seizing plunder, and an assumption on the part of some that it might be condoned or even encouraged by the high command once New Orleans was in British hands. Donald R. Hickey, *Don't Give Up the Ship!* (Urbana: University of Illinois Press, 2006), 278–81, provides an excellent summary of the controversy and finds no credible evidence of a high-level plan to sack the city. Like others, he accepts that the accusation of a "beauty and booty" plan on the part of the British traces to a January 20, 1815, letter by Mississippian George Poindexter, then a volunteer aide on Carroll's staff. However, Poindexter was only one of at least four men in New Orleans known to have raised the issue on that same day, and none of the others could have been repeating Poindexter since they all wrote on January 20. French consul Tousard wrote that prisoners said "the word was 'Beauty and Booty,' and all the prisoners unite in saying that they were promised the plunder of the city and complete license," some saying for three days and others for eight (Tousard to Stocker, January 20, 1815, Wilkinson, "Assaults on New Orleans," 52). An officer in the United States Army, thus likely a man from the 7th or 44th Infantry, wrote that "the watch word and countersign the night previous to the battle was, BEAUTY and BOOTY" (Officer of United States Army to a friend in Lexington, KY, January 20, 1815, Lexington, KY, *Reporter*, February 13, 1815). Finally, an unidentified man in New Orleans wrote to the editor of the Philadelphia, PA, *Relf's Philadelphia Gazette, and Daily Advertiser* to say it was "notorious that the watch word and countersign on the morning of the 8th inst. were 'BEAUTY AND BOOTY'" (Letter to the Editor, January 20, 1815, Philadelphia, PA, *Relf's Philadelphia Gazette, and Daily Advertiser*, February 15, 1815). Four separate statements written the same day (for the weekly January 20 mail) seem too many to put down to coincidence. Of course, the statements may have been on the streets for several days prior to that date, but not likely before January 13's mail or else letters going out in it would likely have mentioned it. So, while the rumor of British intent to rape and plunder originated about January 9, the alliterative "Beauty and Booty" version gained currency between January 13 and 20.

Furthermore, Benjamin Morgan, writing on January 27, told a friend that he had heard that the redcoats were promised "*three days of rapine and plunder* of our city as an encouragement to them to force our lines," a clear echo of the earlier statements minus only the "beauty and booty" expression. None of the January 20 letters had yet been published, so Morgan could not have been repeating what he read in the press. (Benjamin Morgan to friend in Philadelphia, January 27, 1815, Wilmington, DE, *American Watchman*, March 1, 1815). In 1818, arguing that the British had stopped using passwords, paroles, and countersigns during the Peninsula campaign, William James speculated quite reasonably of the "beauty and booty" matter that "the same sentiment, but expressed in less reined language, may, however, have been uttered by, or in the hearing of, some soldier or sailor, who afterwards deserted to the enemy" (James, *Military Occurrences*, 390–91). An unidentified officer, probably of the 4th, confirmed this in 1840, stating that "there was neither parole, countersign, nor anything of the sort, given out to our army before New Orleans," and that "that old-school custom was abolished in the army of the Peninsula, and it was not revived in America" ("Recollections of the Expedition" 33, no. 140 [July 1840]: 350). It is also worth noting that since the attack was to be made in daylight when uniforms could be recognized, signs or countersigns were hardly necessary or useful.

82. James H. Ficklin to Wingfield Bullock, January 13, 1815, Clinton, OH, *Ohio Register*, February 21, 1815.

83. New York, NY, *New-York Evening Post*, January 8, 1841.

84. Ibid.

85. Patterson to Secretary of the Navy, January 13, 1815, Bridgeport, CT, *Republican Farmer*, February 22, 1815.

86. Walker, *Jackson and New Orleans*, 318–19; Lossing, "Scenes in the War of 1812," 180–81. Both sources state that Jackson sent 500 Kentuckians to Morgan after getting Shepherd's news, but they have their chronology wrong. Lossing, writing in 1865, is probably based on Walker's 1856 work, and Walker very likely took his account from McAfee, *History of the Late War*, 516, which says nothing about reinforcements for Morgan, but does provide the basis for timing Shepherd's arrival at one a.m.

87. John Reid to Abram Maury, January 7, 1815, Cook Collection, HNOC.

88. Letter from New Orleans, January 7, 1815, New London, CT, *Connecticut Gazette*, February 8, 1815.

89. "Report of the Committee of Inquiry," 226–27.

90. Letter from Natchez, January 7, 1814, New York, NY, *New-York Gazette & General Advertiser*, February 1, 1815.

91. James Bouyee [Bowie] Compiled Military Service Record, RG 94, NA.

92. Hallowell, ME, *American Advocate*, January 7, 1815.

93. William Eustis to Cutts, February 13, 1815, Cutts Papers, UVA.

94. James Geddes to John Keen, January 7, 1815, Philadelphia, PA, *Poulson's American Daily Advertiser*, January 24, 1815.

95. Cooke, *Narrative*, 224–25.

96. John Reid to Myra Reid, ca. January 13, 1815, Augusta, GA, *Augusta Herald*, February 23, 1815.

97. Reid and Eaton, *Jackson*, 351; Cooke, *Narrative*, 169.

98. Cooke, *Narrative*, 227.

99. Cooper, *Rough Notes*, 129, 131.

100. Graves to White, n.d. [1845–53], New Orleans, LA, *Daily Delta*, January 8, 1854.

101. Walker, *Jackson and New Orleans*, 322–23.

102. Pringle to Editor, November 13, 1833, Pringle, *Letters*, 5.

103. Surtees, *Rifle Brigade*, 372.

104. Gleig Diary, January 7, 1815, Barrett, *85th King's Light Infantry*, 219; Dickson, "Journal," January 7, 1815, 56; Cooke, *Narrative*, 218.

105. Cooke, *Narrative*, 219–20, 222. The expression was in use in England since at least 1810, when it was defined as "a fashionable term when any gentleman reduces his establishment of cattle." That hardly fits the notion of something not going well—which is clearly Cooke's meaning—but in the cited reference, it was used humorously to describe a drunken revelry, and that closely fits Cooke's intent. At some time, it also referred to a broken-down horse, the "broken-down" also applicable to what Cooke described (Winchester, UK, *Hampshire Chronicle; and Weekly Advertiser*, July 16, 1810).

106. Smith, *Autobiography of Lieutenant-General Sir Harry Smith*, 235.

107. Account of January 8 in Tylden Journal, January 11, 1815, NYPL.

108. Ibid.; Forrest, *Journal*, January 7–8, 1815, 42; Codrington to Jane Codrington, January 1–31, 1815, Codrington Papers, COD/6/2, Caird.

109. "Recollections of the Expedition," (July), part 4, 338. While this is mostly an account drawn from earlier sources, the few apparent firsthand descriptions suggest that the author was a subaltern in the 85th Foot or possibly a member of Keene's staff.

110. Forrest, *Journal*, January 8, 1815, 39; "Naval Officer" to unknown recipient, January 30, 1815, *Naval Chronicle, for 1815*, vol. 33, 388. Malcolm said "about 50 boats" made it, and Codrington

agreed (Memorandum Book, January 7, 1815, Pultney Malcolm Papers, MAL/104, Codrington to Jane Codrington, January 1–31, 1815, Codrington Papers, COD/6/2, Caird). Dickson, *Journal*, January 7, 1815, 53, said the total was 42: 12 barges, 8 pinnaces, 17 cutters, and 5 gigs.

111. Account of January 8 in Tylden Journal, January 11, 1815, NYPL; Forrest, *Journal*, January 7–8, 1815, 39, 42; Pakenham, *Pakenham Letters*, 258; Codrington to Jane Codrington, January 1–31, 1815, Codrington Papers, COD/6/2, Caird; Gleig to Janet Gleig, January 11, 1815, Gleig Papers, NLS. Some years later, Gleig, *Narrative*, 327, gave the numbers as 250 from the 85th, and 50 each of marines and sailors, totaling 350. Codrington's figure has been accepted here. It is directly contemporary and he was better placed to know accurate figures.

112. "Naval Officer" to unknown recipient, January 30, 1815, *Naval Chronicle, for 1815*, vol. 33, 388.

113. Chesterton, *Peace, War, and Adventure*, 205.

114. Codrington to Jane Codrington, January 1–31, 1815, Codrington Papers, COD/6/2, Caird.

115. Account of January 8 in Tylden Journal, January 11, 1815, NYPL.

116. Cochrane Journal, January 7, 1815, ADM 50/122, Kew; Cooke, *Narrative*, 223.

117. Vincent Gray to Shaler, May 3, 1815, Shaler Family Papers, HSP.

118. "Naval Officer" to unknown recipient, January 30, 1815, *Naval Chronicle, for 1815*, vol. 33, 387; Gleig to Janet Gleig, January 11, 1815, Gleig Papers, NLS.

119. Natchez, MS, *Mississippi Republican*, March 1, 1815. The headline of the column with the Kingston prediction sarcastically read "Good Guessing!"

120. Brown to Livingston, January 9, 1815, Livingston Papers.

121. Cooke, *Narrative*, 227.

Chapter Seventeen: "We Shall Have a Warm Day"

1. Dickson, "Journal," January 8, 1815, 58; Account of January 8 in Tylden Journal, January 11, 1815, NYPL.

2. Cooke, *Narrative*, 225, 226, 228–29. The Highlanders are often depicted as wearing kilts in the battle, but they did not. See Hickey, *Don't Give Up the Ship!*, 285.

3. Debbeigg statement, *Trial of Brevet Lieutenant-Colonel Hon. Thomas Mullins*, 3, 7, Lambert statement, 29, Tapp statement, 24, Knight statement, 15, 18, 27, Pringle statement, 21, Johnston statement, 31. Mullins, in his defense statement, 36, said that he moved out shortly after three a.m., which conflicts with all other statements about time.

4. Johnston statement, ibid., 30, Tapp statement, 12, Mullins defense statement, 36, Johnston statement, 32, Mullins defense statement, 39–40, 72, Lambert statement, 28, M'Auley statement, 59.

5. Barry statement, ibid., 56, 58, Knight statement, 18, M'Auley statement, 60, 62.

6. Barry statement, ibid., 56, 58–59.

7. Knight statement, ibid., 15, Lambert statement, 28.

8. Smith, *Autobiography of Lieutenant-General Sir Harry Smith*, 232; Dickson, "Journal," January 8, 1815, 58–59.

9. Dickson, "Journal," January 8, 1815, 59.

10. Ibid., January 8, 1815, 60; Wylly to Wellington, March 4, 1815, Pakenham, *Pakenham Letters*, 259–60; Smith, *Autobiography of Lieutenant-General Sir Harry Smith*, 235–36. Smith seems to employ some excellent hindsight in his account, which may not be entirely reliable.

11. Tylden statement, General Court Martial . . . *Trial of Brevet Lieutenant-Colonel Hon. Thomas Mullins*, 10; Account of January 8 in Tylden Journal, January 11, 1815, NYPL; Dickson, "Journal," January 8, 1815, 60.

12. Letter of a British staff officer of the 7th Foot, January 16, 1815, Boston, MA, *Yankee*, May 19, 1815.

13. Account of January 8 in Tylden Journal, January 11, 1815, NYPL.

14. Dickson, "Journal," January 8, 1815, 64.

15. Mullins statement, *General Court Martial . . . Trial of Brevet Lieutenant-Colonel Hon. Thomas Mullins*, 36–37, Phelan statement, 50, Debbeigg statement, 3, Knight statement, 15–16, Barry statement, 57, Lambert statement, 27.

16. Dickson, "Journal," January 8, 1815, 63.

17. Account of January 8 in Tylden Journal, January 11, 1815, NYPL.

18. Mullins statement, *General Court Martial . . . Trial of Brevet Lieutenant-Colonel Hon. Thomas Mullins*, 36–37, Pringle statement, 19, Debbeigg statement, 4.

19. Lambert statement, ibid., 28–29.

20. Knight statement, ibid., 15–16.

21. Haymes statement, ibid., 1, Debbeigg statement, 4.

22. Knight statement, ibid., 15–16, Tapp statement, 12, 24–25, Pringle statement, 20.

23. Cooke, *Narrative*, 229–31.

24. Hill, *Recollections*, 2:10–11; Dickson, "Journal," January 8, 1815, 60.

25. Archaeological digging at Chalmette by the National Park Service has found that balls fired by British muskets stopped appearing at about 700 feet from Jackson's line. That could be a sign that officers managed to regain some control of the men who were firing without orders. It seems more likely that as they got closer and were better able to see Jackson's line, their aim became better. Also, the balls found may have been fired from the rear, well out of range of Jackson's line, and thus fell short. From 700 feet onward to the American line, what were found were unfired dropped American balls. These probably fell or were dropped accidentally by American pickets in the days before January 8, or else as soldiers went over the earthwork to pursue retreating redcoats on January 8. Cornelison and Cooper, *Chalmette*, 54–55.

26. Kipping statement, *General Court Martial . . . Trial of Brevet Lieutenant-Colonel Hon. Thomas Mullins*, 21–22.

27. Knight statement, ibid., 19, Debbeigg statement, 4, Pringle statement, 20.

28. Account of January 8 in Tylden Journal, January 11, 1815, NYPL; Tylden statement, *General Court Martial . . . Trial of Brevet Lieutenant-Colonel Hon. Thomas Mullins*, 10, Tapp statement, 12, M'Aulay statement, 60.

29. Debbeigg statement, ibid., 6, Mullins statement, 74–75; McAfee, *History of the Late War*, 517.

30. Debbeigg statement, *General Court Martial . . . Trial of Brevet Lieutenant-Colonel Hon. Thomas Mullins*, 5.

31. Bassett, *Tatum's Journal*, January 1, 1815, 122.

32. Cope, *Rifle Brigade*, 188.

33. Keating statement, *General Court Martial . . . Trial of Brevet Lieutenant-Colonel Hon. Thomas Mullins*, 64.

34. Dennison statement, ibid., 69, Johnston statement, 31–32.

35. Mullins defense statement, ibid., 37, Keating statement, 63–64, Debbeigg statement, 6, Haymes statement, 2, 50, Barry statement, 56–57, M'Aulay statement, 61, Phelan statement, 51.

36. Mullins defense statement, ibid., 50, Curwen statement, 14, William Dennison statement, 67–68.

37. Pringle to Editor, November 13, 1833, Pringle, *Letters*, 4.

38. Phelan statement, *General Court Martial . . . Trial of Brevet Lieutenant-Colonel Hon. Thomas Mullins*, 50; Reid and Eaton, *Jackson*, 339; Cochrane Journal, January 8, 1815, ADM 50/122, Kew.

39. Smith, *Autobiography of Lieutenant-General Sir Harry Smith*, 236.

40. Cooke, *Narrative*, 231.

41. Phelan statement, *General Court Martial . . . Trial of Brevet Lieutenant-Colonel Hon. Thomas Mullins*, 50.

42. MacDougall statement, ibid., 7–8.

43. Ibid.

44. Phelan statement, ibid., 51; Tylden account of January 8 in Journal, January 11, 181, NYPL.

45. Dickson, "Journal," January 8, 1815, 62.

46. "The Battle-Grounds of America. No. V.—New Orleans. From the MS of an Eye-Witness," *Graham's American Monthly Magazine of Literature and Art* 27 (July 1845): 41.

47. "Sketch of A Tour of Service," Louisville, KY, *Louisville Daily Democrat*, March 19, 1846.

48. Bassett, *Tatum's Journal*, January 8, 1815, 125; David Weller to Samuel Weller, January 13, 1815, Weller Family Papers, Filson; Letter from New Orleans, January 13, 1815, Wilmington, DE, *American Watchman*, February 11, 1815.

49. Return of British loss, Newport, RI, *Rhode-Island Republican*, February 15, 1815; Letter from New Orleans, January 13, 1815, Dover, NH, *Sun*, February 11, 1815. Myriad times were given in contemporary letters for the firing of the signal rocket and first guns, but 6:20 a.m. seems both the most common and the most likely.

50. Letter from New Orleans to Lexington, KY, January 13, 1815, Lexington, KY, *Western Monitor*, February 3, 1815; New York, NY, *New-York Evening Post*, January 8, 1841. The latter is demonstrably an eyewitness account, though written a quarter century after the fact.

51. New York, NY, *New-York Evening Post*, January 8, 1841; Jackson to Robert Hays, February 9, 1815, cited in Stuart O. Landry, *Side Lights on the Battle of New Orleans* (New Orleans: Pelican Publishing, 1965), 26.

52. New Haven, CT, *Connecticut Herald*, October 14, 1828. This story was told by the Reverend Selah Paine, a Methodist minister who may have been one of the chaplains involved as chaplain of Carroll's 5th East Tennessee Militia. The timing of the story, one month before the 1828 presidential election, was no coincidence. Opponents were accusing Jackson of godlessness for his February 21, 1815, execution of militia deserters.

53. Georgetown, DC, *Federal Republican for the Country*, April 4, 1815; New Orleans, LA, *Louisiana Gazette for the Country*, June 10, 1815; Boston, MA, *Boston Commercial Gazette*, April 6, 1815; *Letters of Gen. Adair and Gen. Jackson Relative to the Charge of Cowardice Made by the Latter Against the Kentucky Troops at New Orleans* (Lexington, KY: Thomas Smith, 1824), 9. The Adjutant General's Report, January 8, 1815, shows a total of 4,698 but omits some companies. Jackson later understated his force at no more than 3,200, with only 600 regulars rather than 735, but that was for the secretary of war's consumption. Jackson to Monroe, February 13, 1815, Parker Papers, HSP.

54. Smith, *New Orleans*, 75.

55. James Kempe to friend in Natchez, January 16, 1815, Wilmington, DE, *Delaware Gazette and State Journal*, February 7, 1815; Letter from New Orleans, January 13, 1815, Dover, NH, *Sun*, February 11, 1815; Claiborne, *Mississippi*, 344.

56. John A. Fort to brother, January 28, 1815, Parsons Collection, Texas.

57. Letter from New Orleans, January 13, 1815, Wilmington, DE, *American Watchman*, February 11, 1815.

58. Claiborne, *Mississippi*, 380 and n.; Samuel Brown, *To the Public* (Natchez, MS: Natchez *Ariel*, 1816–1817), 12; Priestley to Latour, March 4, 1816, Latour Archive, HNOC.

59. Thomas to Shelby, February 10, 1815, Frankfort, KY, *Argus of Western America*, March 3, 1815.

60. Blair, *Sketch of the Life and Military Services of General John Adair*, 13.

61. "Sketch of A Tour of Service," Louisville, KY, *Louisville Daily Democrat*, March 19, 1846.

62. Organ to Mordecai, January 19, 1815, Mordecai Family Papers, SHC, UNC; Letter from New Orleans, January 13, 1815, Newport, RI, *Newport Mercury*, February 11, 1815.

63. Walker, *Jackson and New Orleans*, 337.

64. S[impson], "New Orleans," 355. Burgoyne agrees that "R. S" is Captain Robert Simpson of the 43rd. Burgoyne, *93rd Sutherland Highlanders*, 31n.

65. Cooper, *Rough Notes*, 131.

66. Pringle to Editor, November 13, 1833, Pringle, *Letters*, 5. Three American letter writers in New Orleans stated that the calf of one of Rennie's legs was shot away during his advance, the earliest one writing the day after the battle and specifying that it was done by a cannonball (Letter from a man in the Adams Troop to a friend in Washington, M.T., January 9, 1815, Washington, Mississippi Territory, *Washington Republican*, January 18, 1815). Three days later merchant Joseph Winter wrote that Rennie's calf was shot away before he began climbing the slope of the bastion (Joseph S. Winter to Elisha I. Winter, New Orleans, January 12, 1814 [1815], War of 1812 Collection, Michigan). The day after that a correspondent of the *Philadelphia Gazette* spoke of Rennie losing his calf (Letter from New Orleans to the Editor, January 13, 1815, Philadelphia, PA, *Relf's Philadelphia Gazette, and Daily Advertiser*, February 8, 1815). They all could be repeating a story making the rounds immediately after the battle. However, since the Americans had possession of Rennie's body for some hours, certainly long enough for William Withers to empty its pockets, many eyewitnesses must have seen the body's appearance immediately after the fight ended, lending credulity to the reports of his missing calf. Given the difficulty of American artillery on the right bank training their guns on the moving column, it seems more likely that Rennie was hit by fire from Humphreys's Battery No. 1 before he crossed the levee. Other sources at the time stated that he was wounded but with no specifics.

67. S[impson], "New Orleans," 355; Reid and Eaton, *Jackson*, 341; New York, NY, *New-York Evening Post*, January 8, 1841. Though anonymous, this account is presented as being by an "eyewitness."

68. "An American Officer" to the Editor, Baltimore, MD, *American, and Commercial Daily Advertiser*, June 7, 1821. The writer was almost certainly an officer of the 7th United States Infantry.

69. Letter by member of Jackson's staff, January 13, 1815, New York, NY, *New-York Herald*, February 8, 1815; Letter from New Orleans to Lexington, KY, January 13, 1815, Lexington, KY, *Western Monitor*, February 3, 1815.

70. Auguste Davezac to Andrew Ross, February 6, 1822, Cook Collection, HNOC.

71. Letter from New Orleans city official to Boston, January 13, 1815, Boston, MA, *New-England Palladium*, February 10, 1815; D. Talcott to N. and D. Talcott, n.d. (ca. January 10, 1815), Boston, MA, *New-England Palladium*, February 10, 1815; Letter from New Orleans to New York, January 13, 1815, New York, NY, *New-York Gazette & General Advertiser*, February 9, 1815.

72. Noël Auguste Baron to A. D. Tureaud, January 13, 1815, ibid.; Gabriel Winter to William Willis, January 12, 1815, Willis Family Papers, LSU.

73. Letter from man in Beale's company, January 13, 1815, Newport, RI, *Newport Mercury*, February 11, 1815; Letter from Greenville, Mississippi Territory, to Philadelphia, January 31, 1815, Wilmington, DE, *American Watchman*, March 4, 1815.

74. Letter from man in the Adams Troop to a friend in Washington, M.T., January 9, 1815, Washington, Mississippi Territory, *Washington Republican*, January 18, 1815.

75. Walker, *Jackson and New Orleans*, 258; "Political Portraits with Pen and Pencil—Henry Miller Shreve," 167.

76. Cooke, *Narrative*, 231–33.

77. Letter from New Orleans to Middletown, CT, Middletown, CT, *Connecticut Spectator*, February 15, 1815. No evidence supports this notion of Jackson holding fire as a lure.

78. Claiborne, *Notes on the War*, 71; Letter from New Orleans, January 13, 1815, Boston, MA, *New-England Palladium*, February 10, 1815.

79. Pringle to Editor, November 13, 1833, Pringle, *Letters*, 5.

80. S[impson], "New Orleans," 355.

81. Ibid., 355–56; Cooke, *Narrative*, 254.

82. Bassett, *Tatum's Journal*, January 8, 1815, 126; Tylden account of January 8 in Journal, January 11, 1815, NYPL.

83. "An American Officer" to the Editor, Baltimore, MD, *American, and Commercial Daily Advertiser*, June 7, 1821.

84. Louis Francis de Marans, War of 1812 Pension Application File, RG 15, NA.

85. Two letter writers stated that Rennie killed two men with his pistols, the context suggesting that it was in taking the bastion. On January 12, Joseph Winter wrote his brother Elisha saying Rennie killed "a Sergeant & Corporal of our Regulars with his two pistols" (Joseph S. Winter to Elisha I. Winter, New Orleans, January 12, 1814 [1815], War of 1812 Collection, Michigan). An unidentified Frenchman wrote the next day that while Rennie was "holding onto our entrenchments," he "killed two men with his pistols" (Letter from unidentified Frenchman to Philadelphia, January 13, 1815, Philadelphia, PA, *Relf's Philadelphia Gazette, and Daily Advertiser*, February 8, 1815). Winter does not appear to have been a participant in the battle, and no French volunteers were in that immediate sector of the line, so neither writer was likely an eyewitness, but repeating camp gossip, though it could well have originated with someone from the 7th, 44th, or even Beale's riflemen, all of whom could have witnessed the incident. Winter's brother Gabriel was a captain in the 44th and could have been the source of his brother's statement. Adjutant Robert Butler's report of January 16, 1815, confirms that a sergeant and a corporal of the 7th were killed (Robert Butler report, January 16, 1815, Baltimore, MD, *Baltimore Telegraph*, February 14, 1815).

86. Davezac to Ross, February 6, 1822, Cook Collection, HNOC.

87. Letter from New Orleans, January 13, 1815, Bowden, *Private Letters*, 188; Hudson, NY, *Bee*, February 8, 1815; Broadside, War of 1812 Mss., Lilly Library.

88. S[impson], "New Orleans," 356. A New Orleans city official also stated that Rennie's party turned one of the bastion's 8-pounders on Jackson's line, though did not state if it fired, or if so, effectively. Letter from New Orleans city official to Boston, January 13, 1815, Boston, MA, *New-England Palladium*, February 10, 1815.

89. D. Talcott to N. and D. Talcott, n.d. [ca. January 10, 1815], Boston, MA, *New-England Palladium*, February 10, 1815. No evidence supports this rumor of Jackson ordering his right to cease firing.

90. Hudson, NY, *Bee*, February 8, 1815; Broadside, War of 1812 Mss., Lilly Library.

91. Eaton and Van Crowninshield, *Memoirs of Andrew Jackson*, 284; Reid and Eaton, *Jackson*, 342.

92. New York, NY, *New-York Evening Post*, January 8, 1841. Though anonymous, this account is presented as being by an "eye-witness."

93. Tylden statement, *General Court Martial . . . Trial of Brevet Lieutenant-Colonel Hon. Thomas Mullins*, 11, MacDougall statement, 9.

94. Pringle to Editor, November 13, 1833, Pringle, *Letters*, 5.

95. S[impson], "New Orleans," 355–56.

96. James M. Bradford to the St. Francisville *Time-Piece*, January 13, 1815, St. Francisville, LA, *Time-Piece*, January 17, 1815; Letter by member of Jackson's staff, January 13, 1815, New York, NY, *New-York Herald*, February 8, 1815.

97. Letter from New Orleans, January 20, 1815, Wilmington, DE, *American Watchman*, February 18, 1815.

98. S[impson], "New Orleans," 355n, 355–56; Letter from Greenville, Mississippi Territory, to Philadelphia, January 31, 1815, Wilmington, DE, *American Watchman*, March 4, 1815; Joseph S. Winter to Elisha I. Winter, New Orleans, January 12, 1814 [1815], War of 1812 Collection, Michigan; Letter from unidentified Frenchman to Philadelphia, January 13, 1815, Philadelphia, PA, *Relf's Philadelphia Gazette, and Daily Advertiser*, February 8, 1815. John William Ward, *Andrew Jackson, Symbol for an Age* (New York: Oxford University Press, 1955), 23, disputes the claim that Withers's marksmanship was such that he put a bullet through Rennie's eye, citing Simpson's statement that when he examined Rennie's body there were two wounds in his head without mentioning an eye. He concludes that Rennie was probably hit instead by a volley from several guns. That is certainly possible, but given that Withers would have been standing little more than a dozen feet from the embrasure at the back of a cannon, no marksmanship was necessary. Probably conclusive is Tatum's January 8 journal entry stating that a "Weathers" shot Rennie in the eye (Bassett, *Tatum's Journal*, January 8, 1815, 126).

99. Bassett, *Tatum's Journal*, January 8, 1815, 126.

100. Gabriel Winter to William Willis, January 12, 1815, Willis Family Papers, LSU.

101. Joseph S. Winter to Elisha I. Winter, New Orleans, January 12, 1814 [1815], War of 1812 Collection, Michigan.

102. Surtees, *Rifle Brigade*, 374–75. This claim is based on the statement of Lieutenant Alexander Steele of the 43rd who was in the bastion.

103. Letter from New Orleans, January 9, 1815, Boston, MA, *New-England Palladium*, February 10, 1815; Letter by a member of Hinds's Mississippi Dragoons to New York, January 13, 1815, Dover, NH, *Sun*, February 11, 1815; Le Blanc to?, January 9, 1815, Portland, ME, *Eastern Argus*, February 16, 1815; Alex C. Henderson to his father, January 9, 1815, Natchez, MS, *Mississippi Republican*, January 16, 1815, in Baltimore, MD, *American, and Commercial Daily Advertiser*, February 6, 1815.

104. Joseph S. Winter to Elisha I. Winter, January 9, 1815, War of 1812 Collection, Michigan.

105. Letter by a member of Hinds's Mississippi Dragoons to New York, January 13, 1815, Dover, NH, *Sun*, February 11, 1815.

106. Kempe to friend in Natchez, January 9, 1815, Natchez, MS, *Mississippi Republican*, January 16, 1815, in Baltimore, MD, *Baltimore Patriot & Evening Advertiser*, February 4, 1815.

107. S[impson], "New Orleans," 356.

108. "An American Officer" to the Editor, Baltimore, MD, *American, and Commercial Daily Advertiser*, June 7, 1821; Davezac to Ross, February 6, 1822, Cook Collection, HNOC; Bassett, *Tatum's Journal*, January 8, 1815, 126.

109. "An American Officer" to the Editor, Baltimore, MD, *American, and Commercial Daily Advertiser*, June 7, 1821. The writer was almost certainly an officer of the 7th United States Infantry and an eyewitness participant, perhaps Ross himself, and states that after the fight one of Jackson's adjutants ordered him to count the British dead and wounded personally.

110. Baron to Tureaud, January 13, 1815, Cook Collection, HNOC; Letter from New Orleans, January 9, 1815, Boston, MA, *New-England Palladium*, February 10, 1815; Kempe to friend in Natchez, January 9, 1815, Natchez, MS, *Mississippi Republican*, January 16, 1815, in Baltimore, MD, *Baltimore Patriot*, February 4, 1815; Letter from man in Beale's company, January 13, 1815, Newport, RI, *Newport Mercury*, February 11, 1815.

111. Bradford to the St. Francisville *Time-Piece*, January 13, 1815, St. Francisville, LA, *Time-Piece*, January 17, 1815.

112. Bassett, *Tatum's Journal*, January 8, 1815, 126.

113. S[impson], "New Orleans," 355n.

114. Kempe to friend in Natchez, January 9, 1815, Natchez, MS, *Mississippi Republican*, January 16, 1815, in Baltimore, MD, *Baltimore Patriot*, February 4, 1815. Kempe did not identify Simpson as his informant, but context suggests it was him.

115. *Memorial of Beverly Chew and Others*, 3.

116. Fort to brother, January 28, 1815, Parsons Collection, Texas; Ellery, "Notes," NYPL.

117. Letter from New Orleans, January 13, 1815, Boston, MA, *New-England Palladium*, February 10, 1815; General Orders, January 21, 1815, New Orleans, LA, *Louisiana Courier*, January 25, 1815. While the black units performed creditably, their service needs to be distinguished from the claims made in 1858 in a purported memoir so fanciful as to approach the bizarre, James Roberts, *The Narrative of James Roberts, a Soldier Under Gen. Washington in the Revolutionary War, and Under Gen. Jackson at the Battle of New Orleans, in the War of 1812: "A Battle Which Cost Me a Limb, Some Blood and Almost My Life"* (Chicago; printed for the author, 1858). It has been accepted as genuine by a number of historians, as for instance James Oliver Horton and Lois E. Horton, *Slavery and the Making of America* (New York: Oxford University Press, 2005), 81–83. However, other than the name of slaveowner Calvin Smith living in Adams County, Mississippi (whom Roberts erroneously placed in Louisiana), virtually nothing in the narrative can be corroborated. It appeared forty-three years after the fact and Roberts claimed to have been eighty when he wrote it, which alone would be enough for doubt. What Roberts wrote of actual events is almost hallucinatory, as in his beheading six British soldiers in the January 8 battle, or Jackson coming to Smith's plantation personally to select 500 slaves, including Roberts, to fight (13–19). Slaves did not participate as soldiers in the battle, only free blacks who volunteered. The fact that Roberts gave black soldiers credit for winning the Battle of New Orleans, and then made them the victims of satanic slaveowners embodied in the character of Smith, makes it probable that the book was a propaganda piece to promote the Republican anti-slavery cause in the 1858 senatorial contest between Abraham Lincoln and Stephen A. Douglas. Given what Roberts could have been doing at New Orleans, and where he could have been, this book should be regarded as little more than very colorful—and perhaps effective—propaganda, and nothing it says about the battle should be regarded as reliable.

118. "Captain Nathaniel Pryor," 253–65.

119. Joseph S. Winter to Elisha I. Winter, New Orleans, January 12, 1814 [1815], War of 1812 Collection, Michigan.

CHAPTER EIGHTEEN: "A SPECTACLE OF CARNAGE"

1. [Otto Norris] to a friend in Lexington, KY, January 20, 1815, Lexington, KY, *Reporter*, February 13, 1815; Letter from a Lieutenant in the Navy January 14, 1815, Newport, RI, *Rhode-Island Republican*, February 15, 1815.

2. Bassett, *Tatum's Journal*, January 8, 1815, 125.

3. Bradford to St. Francisville *Time-Piece*, January 13, 1815, St. Francisville, LA, *Time-Piece*, January 17, 1815; "An American Officer" to Baltimore *American*, n.d., Washington, PA, *Washington Reporter*, July 9, 1821.

4. Cornelison and Cooper, Chalmette, 53–54; Bradford to St. Francisville *Time-Piece*, January 13, 1815, St. Francisville, LA, *Time-Piece*, January 17, 1815.

5. Joseph S. Winter to Elisha I. Winter, New Orleans, January 12, 1814 [1815], War of 1812 Collection, Michigan; Coffee to John Donelson, January 25, 1815, Tennessee Historical Society Miscellaneous Files, University of Tennessee.

6. Letter from New Orleans, January 13, 1815, Washington, DC, *National Intelligencer*, February 7, 1815.

7. Joseph S. Winter to Elisha I. Winter, New Orleans, January 12, 1814 [1815], War of 1812 Collection, Michigan; C. R. Hicks to Claiborne, December 30, 1814, HNOC.

8. Letter from man in the Adams Troop to a friend in Washington, M.T., January 9, 1815, Washington, Mississippi Territory, *Washington Republican*, January 18, 1815.

9. James H. Ficklin to Wingfield Bullock, January 13, 1815, Clinton, OH, *Ohio Register*, February 21, 1815; Dudley Avery letter to Mary Avery, January 10, 1815, War of 1812 Collection, Tulane;

Letter from New Orleans, January 14, 1815, Baltimore, MD, *American, and Commercial Daily Advertiser*, February 6, 1815.

10. John Reid to his father, January 17, 1815, Richmond, VA, *Richmond Enquirer*, February 18, 1815.

11. Carroll to W. Tannahill, January 13, 1815, St. Louis, MO, *Missouri Gazette*, February 11, 1815. Gleig maintained in his *Narrative* (330) that Carroll's men, unable to see over the parapet, lifted their muskets above their heads and fired without aiming, thus not exposing their heads. However, he was not an eyewitness to this, being on the other side of the river with Thornton. This and other problems with some of Gleig's narrative license were discussed by "An American Officer" in a rejoinder to Gleig excerpted in Washington, DC, *Daily National Intelligencer*, September 26, 1821.

12. Claiborne, *Gen. Sam. Dale*, 148. Though Claiborne's narrative is highly colorful, he did base it on a memoir dictated by Dale prior to his death in 1841.

13. Ibid., 148–49.

14. Letter from New Orleans to member of Congress, January 13, 1815, Washington, DC, *National Intelligencer*, February 7, 1815; Bird S. Hurt to a friend in Columbia, TN, January 20, 1815, Augusta, GA, *Augusta Herald*, February 23, 1815.

15. Joseph S. Winter to Elisha I. Winter, January 9, 1815, War of 1812 Collection, Michigan.

16. Coffee to John Donelson, January 25, 1815, Tennessee Historical Society Miscellaneous Files, University of Tennessee; Adair to Shelby, January 13, 1813, Washington, KY, *Union*, February 3, 1815.

17. Ficklin to Wingfield Bullock, January 13, 1815, Clinton, OH, *Ohio Register*, February 21, 1815; Letter from New Orleans, January 13, 1815, Baltimore, MD, *American, and Commercial Daily Advertiser*, February 6, 1815; Reid to his father, January 17, 1815, Richmond, VA, *Richmond Enquirer*, February 18, 1815.

18. Letter from New Orleans, January 13, 1815, Washington, DC, *National Intelligencer*, February 7, 1815.

19. Knight statement, *General Court Martial . . . Trial of Brevet Lieutenant-Colonel Hon. Thomas Mullins*, 16–17, 19, 26–27, Fontelew statement, 22.

20. Pringle statement, ibid., 20.

21. Pringle to Editor, November 13, 1833, Pringle, *Letters*, 4.

22. Johnston statement, *General Court Martial . . . Trial of Brevet Lieutenant-Colonel Hon. Thomas Mullins*, 31–32.

23. Gowe statement, ibid., 53–54, Dennison statement, 68, Shea statement, 64–65, Browne statement, 66.

24. Shea statement, ibid., 65, Browne statement, 67, William Jeffry statement, 69, Choppin statement, 69.

25. Knight statement, ibid., 16–17, 19, 25–27, Debbeigg statement, 4, 6, Pringle statement, 20.

26. Tapp statement, ibid., 13, 23.

27. Phelan statement, ibid., 52.

28. Johnston statement, ibid., 31–32.

29. Gowe statement, ibid., 54.

30. Gowe statement, ibid., 54, Dennison, 52–53.

31. Tapp statement, ibid., 13.

32. Barry statement, ibid., i, 56. Sunrise occurred at 6:58 that day according to https://www.esrl.noaa.gov/gmd/grad/solcalc/sunrise.html calculator. Dickson placed it at 6:57, which was remarkably accurate (Leslie, "Artillery Services," 158).

33. Barry statement, *General Court Martial . . . Trial of Brevet Lieutenant-Colonel Hon. Thomas Mullins*, 56, 63.

34. "Obituary; with Anecdotes of Remarkable Persons," *Gentleman's Magazine* 85 (May 1815): 476.

35. Cooke, *Narrative*, 255.

36. S[impson], "New Orleans," 356n; London, UK, *Morning Post*, March 24, 1815; "Obituary; with Anecdotes of Remarkable Persons," 476.

37. As stated elsewhere, the assertion that Wilkinson was shot from his horse by a Kentucky marksman named Morgan Ballard, as detailed in the Bloomsburg, PA, *Columbian*, January 6, 1898, is an invention by Augustus C. Buell.

38. Dennison statement, *General Court Martial . . . Trial of Brevet Lieutenant-Colonel Hon. Thomas Mullins*, 53; Cooke, *Narrative*, 255. Being with the 43rd, Cooke would not have heard

Wilkinson's words himself, but they must have spread in the camps afterward. In 1846 the anonymous Kentucky author of "Sketch of A Tour of Service" told a story of a British officer jumping on the American works while calling for his men to "Come on boys, the day's our own," before Joseph Smith of the 15th Kentucky yelled back "You're not so sure of that," and shot him in the face. This could be a garbled version of Wilkinson's death. Louisville, KY, *Louisville Daily Democrat*, March 19, 1846.

39. Fonblanque statement, *General Court Martial . . . Trial of Brevet Lieutenant-Colonel Hon. Thomas Mullins*, 22–23.

40. Ibid.

41. Major Norman Pringle of the 21st Foot to Editor of Edinburgh, UK, *Evening Courant*, November 13, 1833, in Pringle, *Letters*, 3–4. Pringle confirms that men reached and crossed the ditch and went up and over the earthwork.

42. Letter from unidentified Frenchman, January 13, 1815, Philadelphia, PA, *Relf's Philadelphia Gazette, and Daily Advertiser*, February 8, 1815. The only British majors captured were George King of the 7th and Ross of the 21st. Since the 7th was in reserve and did not go into action against the breastwork, this story—if true—can only refer to Ross. It has the major calling for the "45th" to come up after him. There was no 45th Regiment in the action, of course, and the 44th must be who he called on, but the number got changed in the story's retelling (Letter from Greenville, M.T., January 30, 1815, Wilmington, DE, *American Watchman*, March 4, 1815). The anonymous Kentuckian who wrote "Sketch of A Tour of Service" in 1846 told a story of a British "major" who raised a white handkerchief on his sword on or in front of the earthwork, which he then climbed to surrender. A Tennessean nicknamed "Paleface" demanded the sword, and when the major hesitated, a Kentucky officer yelled "g-d d—m you! Give it up—give it up to him in a minute," whereupon the Englishman handed it over. This sounds like a memory-garbled version of Major Ross's surrender ("Sketch of A Tour of Service," Louisville, KY, *Louisville Daily Democrat*, March 20, 1846).

43. "Sketch of A Tour of Service," Louisville, KY, *Louisville Daily Democrat*, March 19, 1846.

44. John Coffee to his wife, January 30, 1815, Cook Collection, HNOC.

45. J. & D. Urquhart to J. and N. Heard Co., January 12, 1815, Boston, MA, *Boston Patriot*, February 11, 1815.

46. "An American Officer" to Baltimore *American*, n.d., Washington, PA, *Washington Reporter*, July 9, 1821.

47. Cooke, *Narrative*, 255–56, 260; Buchan, *Royal Scots Fusiliers*, 176.

48. Letter from New Orleans, January 13, 1815, Boston, MA, *New-England Palladium*, February 10, 1815.

49. Reid and Eaton, *Jackson*, 339; Organ to Mordecai, January 19, 1815, Mordecai Family Papers, SHC, UNC; Fort to his brother, January 28, 1815, Parsons Collection, Texas.

50. Letter from New Orleans, January 13, 1815, Newport, RI, *Newport Mercury*, February 11, 1815.

51. Letter from Greenville, M.T., January 30, 1815, Wilmington, DE, *American Watchman*, March 4, 1815; "A Friend to Truth" to Editor, n.d., Bardstown, KY, *Bardstown Repository*, March 23, 1815; Easton, MD, *Republican Star*, October 29, 1816.

52. "Sketch of A Tour of Service," Louisville, KY, *Louisville Daily Democrat*, March 19, 1846.

53. Fort to brother, January 28, 1815, Parsons Collection, Texas.

54. Letter from man in the Adams Troop to a friend in Washington, M.T., January 9, 1815, Washington, Mississippi Territory, *Washington Republican*, January 18, 1815. This may be the origin of the "Beauty and Booty" rumors that appeared subsequently.

55. Bassett, *Tatum's Journal*, January 8, 1815, 125. This entry was written about January 20.

56. Reid to his father, January 17, 1815, Richmond, VA, *Richmond Enquirer*, February 18, 1815.

57. Adair to Shelby, January 13, 1813, Washington, KY, *Union*, February 3, 1815; Alex C. Henderson to his father, January 9, 1815, Natchez, MS, *Mississippi Republican*, January 16, 1815, in Baltimore, MD, *American, and Commercial Daily Advertiser*, February 6, 1815.

58. Letter from New Orleans, January 13, 1815, Philadelphia, PA, *Poulson's American Daily Advertiser*, February 7, 1815.

59. "Recollections of the Expedition," (July) part 4, 347.

60. Bassett, *Tatum's Journal*, January 8, 1815, 125. Written about January 20.

61. Alney M'Lean to Robert Ewing, January 10, 1815, Washington, KY, *Union*, February 3, 1815; Letter from New Orleans to Middletown, CT, *Connecticut Spectator*, February 15, 1815.

62. Coffee to his wife, January 30, 1815, Cook Collection, HNOC.
63. Letter from Le Blanc, January 9, 1815, New York, NY, *New-York Gazette & General Advertiser*, February 7, 1815.
64. Letter from New Orleans to member of Congress, January 13, 1815, Washington, DC, *National Intelligencer*, February 7, 1815; "An American Officer" to Baltimore *American*, n.d., Washington, PA, *Washington Reporter*, July 9, 1821.
65. Joseph S. Winter to Elisha I. Winter, New Orleans, January 12, 1814 [1815], War of 1812 Collection, Michigan; M'Lean to Ewing, January 10, 1815, Washington, KY, *Union*, February 3, 1815.
66. Hynes to Carswell, January 13, 1815, New York, NY, *New-York Commercial Advertiser*, February 8, 1815; Hynes to Blount, February 3, 1815, Lexington, KY, *Reporter*, March 13, 1815.
67. Thomas Johnston to Dolley Madison, January 19, 1815, Dolley Madison Digital Edition.
68. General Orders, January 21, 1815, New Orleans, LA, *Louisiana Courier*, January 25, 1815.
69. David Weller to Samuel Weller, January 13, 1815, Weller Family Papers, Filson.
70. Clark, *Royal Scots Fusiliers*, 136. The sergeant is identified as one Reid. Eight sergeants of the 21st were among the missing, either killed or captured.
71. Tylden account of January 8 in Journal, January 11, 1815, NYPL; Gerard, Campaigns 2, USNA.
72. Bowlby, *Memoir*, 54.
73. Reilly, *British at the Gates*, 290.
74. Bassett, *Tatum's Journal*, January 8, 1815, 129–30.
75. Graves to White, n.d. [1845–53], New Orleans, *Daily Delta*, January 8, 1854. Reilly, *British at the Gates*, 291, cites this quotation in his text as coming from the diary of Lieutenant Charles Gordon of the 93rd, but in his notes attributes it to an account by Graves in the "Maunsel White Papers in the Louisiana Planters' Papers" at Tulane. Neither citation is correct. Tulane has no record of any such document or collection, and Charles Gordon had nothing to do with it.
76. Burgoyne, *93rd Sutherland Highlanders*, 29; Elizabeth Clement to Wood, January 11, 1815, Clement, *Plantation Life*, 130.
77. Burgoyne, *93rd Sutherland Highlanders*, 30n.
78. Londonderry, Ireland, *Londonderry Sentinel and North-West Advertiser*, June 21, 1834.
79. Codrington to Jane Codrington, January 1–31, 1815, Codrington Papers, COD/6/2, Caird.
80. Pringle to Editor, November 13, 1833, Pringle, *Letters*, 4–5; Surtees, *Rifle Brigade*, 374–75. The anonymous naval officer who wrote a letter on January 30, 1815, said that officers from the 93rd told him that when that regiment began falling back from the ditch, Keane yelled to them to "Remember Egypt," a peculiar thing to do since the regiment had not served in Egypt. Another Highlander regiment, the 42nd, had been at the 1801 Battle of Alexandria and fought with distinction, so perhaps Keane was appealing to Highlander pride in general. When the men kept falling back, Keane then supposedly yelled to them to "bayonet the rascals," meaning men of the 21st whose confused retreat from the ditch was disrupting the 93rd. Both attributed exclamations are possible, but being at least second- or thirdhand, they are probably of a piece with the many other rumored expressions attributed to the fallen generals ("Naval Officer" to unknown recipient, January 30, 1815, *Naval Chronicle, for 1815*, vol. 33, 388).
81. Pringle to Editor, November 13, 1833, Pringle, *Letters*, 5; Pringle to Editor, January 25, 1834, 14; Lambert to Bathurst, January 10, 1815, London, UK, *Morning Chronicle*, March 10, 1815; Codrington to Jane Codrington, January 1–31, 1815, Codrington Papers, COD/6/2, Caird; Hill, *Recollections*, 2: 17–18. One unidentified source soon claimed that Keane received five flesh wounds, St. George's, Bermuda, *Bermuda Gazette, and Weekly Advertiser*, April 15, 1815.
82. Dickson, "Journal," January 8, 1815, 61, 64; Hill, *Recollections*, 2:12.
83. It has sometimes been asserted that Pakenham confronted Mullins personally. There are two principal sources for such a meeting, both relating only rumor and neither by an eyewitness. "A young but intelligent naval officer" wrote a letter on January 30, 1815, that appeared in the London, UK, *Pilot* on May 6, 1815, and was republished in the May issue of *Naval Chronicle, for 1815*, vol. 33, 385–88, and in the United States in the Lexington, KY, *Reporter*, August 2, 1815. It is clear in the letter that the writer was with the small flotilla of boats commanded by Captain Roberts accompanying Thornton's operation on the right bank. He stated that he witnessed much of the battle from his boat but of course could know nothing firsthand regarding Pakenham's and Gibbs's last moments other than army rumor. He stated that just before being mortally wounded Pakenham said that if he survived "if possible he would hang [Mullins]." He also

stated that before his mortal wounding, Gibbs declared that "whoever should find the [colonel] of the [44th] ought to hang him to the first tree for cowardice."

A later variant appeared before this letter was published, representing a separate version of the same rumor, though it is always possible that both originated with the same anonymous naval officer. It first appeared in the Charleston, SC, *Courier*, March 22, 1815, no copy of which has been found, but was widely reprinted starting with the Baltimore, MD, *American, and Commercial Daily Advertiser*, March 30, 1815. The "interesting anecdote" is attributed to "a gentleman who conversed with an officer of the late British expedition." In it, after unsuccessfully sending two aides to order Mullins and the 44th to move to the front, Pakenham rode to the head of the regiment himself to rally it, at which time he was mortally wounded. When Mullins appeared, the dying general brandished his sword over his head, declaring "You cowardly villain, if I live till to-morrow, I will have you hanged." None of those present around Pakenham at that time mention any meeting with Mullins.

A further confirmation that this rumor was prevalent on one or more vessels in Cochrane's fleet is an entry in the Joyes Journal for February 2, 1815 (Joyes Papers, Filson). In it Joyes stated that on that date he spoke with Captain Peter Ogden, who had been captured on December 23 and was recently released. Ogden told Joyes that he had heard aboard ship that when Mullins and the 44th failed to get the ladders and fascines in place, Gibbs yelled "You damn rascal if I survive this I'll hang you."

84. Account of January 8 in Tylden Journal, January 11, 1815, NYPL (Tylden says substantially the same thing in his statement, *General Court Martial . . . Trial of Brevet Lieutenant-Colonel Hon. Thomas Mullins*, 10–11); Dickson, "Journal," January 8, 1815, 63. Reilly, *British at the Gates*, 292, dismisses the idea of Gibbs leaving his column to come to Pakenham, stating further that there is "no evidence to support it." In fact, he indirectly cited such evidence himself from John Spencer Bassett, *The Life of Andrew Jackson* (New York: Doubleday, 1911), 1:194, but in a note on the following page Bassett himself cited Tylden's testimony in the Mullins court martial. Reilly was clearly unaware of the existence of Tylden's manuscript journal, whose January 11, 1815, entry covering January 8 provided ample evidence of Gibbs's movement and statement.

85. Peter Brooke Journals, New-York Historical Society.

86. Account of January 8 in Tylden Journal, January 11, 1815, NYPL.

87. Wylly to Wellington, March 5, 1815, Pakenham, *Pakenham Letters*, 258.

88. Wylly to Wellington, March 4, 1815, ibid., 260–61.

89. Graves to White, n.d. [1845–53], New Orleans, *Daily Delta*, January 8, 1854.

90. Gray (unsigned) to John Graham, February 8, 1815, Dispatches from the U. S. Consul in Havana, Cuba, 1783–1906, M899, General Records of the Department of State, Record Group 59, NA; Account of January 8 in Tylden Journal, January 11, 1815, NYPL. Details are puzzlingly few for Gibbs's wounding, and these appear to be the only two contemporary accounts that specifically say where he was hit. Gray recounts a conversation at Havana with Colonel William Thornton less than a month after the battle and is more detailed than Tylden, who only suggests Gibbs was hit in the lower abdomen. Lambert and others said that Keane and Gibbs were hit at the same time, and others say that Pakenham and Gibbs were hit simultaneously. Thornton's account to Gray in fact says both Gibbs and Pakenham were hit by the same exploding shell, which could be the case, though since he was on the other side of the river at the time, he could only be repeating what he heard from others. The best evidence indicates that Pakenham's wounding came very quickly after Gibbs's fall. (Lambert to Bathurst, January 10, 1815, London, UK, *Morning Chronicle*, March 10, 1815). In 1831 G. G. MacDonald, a naval officer aboard the frigate *Nymph*, claimed that Pakenham and Gibbs were both killed by the same shot—which could mean shell explosion rather than a single bullet—while in the act of upbraiding Mullins, but MacDonald was not present on the field (MacDonald Memoir, NYPL).

91. Account of January 8 in Tylden Journal, January 11, 1815, NYPL; Dickson, "Journal," January 8, 1815, 63. The usual sequence given for Pakenham's injuries is that he was hit in the knee first and his horse killed at the same time, and that as he mounted another animal, he received his fatal wound. That is the story Duncan MacDougall related to Dickson that day, recorded by Dickson in his "Journal," January 8, 1815, 63. Tylden's account in his Journal, however, says the general's horse was killed first and Pakenham subsequently received both his wounds as he remounted (Account of January 8 in Tylden Journal, January 11, 1815, NYPL). Since Dickson's

version was secondhand, even though apparently written the same day, and Tylden's was that of an eyewitness written within three days, the latter has been taken as the authority. The London, UK, *Correspondent and Public Cause*, March 22, 1815, stated without citing authority that Pakenham was first hit in both knees, which cannot have been the case, since he was able to remount, meaning he must have had at least one good leg even with his aide's assistance. Non-eyewitness sources also say he was hit in one arm. The accounts of Tylden and MacDougall, the immediate eyewitnesses, say nothing of these additional wounds. Not surprisingly in all the confusion, solid details on Pakenham's death are few, and variations many. Five days after the battle one of Patterson's officers heard a rumor in the city that he was cut in half by a shot from Battery No. 4's 32-pounder, and that same day another writer gloated that "a Heaven-directed shot from one of our 32 pounders, laid him low" (Letter from an officer in the Navy to a friend in Boston, January 14, 1815, Boston, MA, *New-England Palladium*, February 10, 1815; Letter from New Orleans to editor of Frankfort *Palladium*, January 13, 1815, Lexington, KY, *Western Monitor*, February 3, 1815). Lambert, who could not have been witness from his position with the reserve, gave an account in his report that was clearly meant to burnish Pakenham's reputation to mollify the embarrassment of the humiliating defeat. He stated that Pakenham "ran at full gallop to the front of the line, to animate the men by his presence," and "was seen to wave his hat on the crest of the glacis, to encourage them." Quite certainly Pakenham did not reach or mount the enemy breastworks (Lambert to Bathurst, January 10, 1815, London, UK, *Military Register*, March 15, 1815). Ritchie maintained that Pakenham was hit by grapeshot from a 12-pounder, which is always possible, though the only 12-pounders on the field were the two in Humphrey's Battery No. 1 near the river, and entirely occupied with Rennie, and a single one in Spotts's Battery No. 6, which was dealing with Keane and the left of Gibbs's column. If Pakenham was hit by grapeshot, it most likely came from the 6- or 18-pounder in Flaujac's Battery No. 7 (Ritchie, "Louisiana Campaign," 73).

92. Hereford, UK, *Hereford Journal*, March 22, 1815; Wylly to Wellington, March 4, 1815, Pakenham, *Pakenham Letters*, 258. Pakenham's last words became a source of disagreement. Reilly, *British at the Gates*, 292, states that "it is said that his dying order was for Lambert to throw in the reserve brigade," but he cites two twentieth-century works, neither of which gives a source for their claims. Disparagements of Mullins were quickly attributed to both Pakenham and Gibbs as last words. This same set of rumors seems to be the origin of the accusation that Mullins ran away during the fight, which certainly he did not ("Naval Officer" to unknown recipient, January 30, 1815, *Naval Chronicle, for 1815*, vol. 33, 388). Ritchie speculates that Pakenham's unfinished final sentence "was no doubt a dying wish to be remembered to the duke, which the commander must have uttered as he was carried off the field" (Ritchie, "Louisiana Campaign," 44).

93. Bassett, *Tatum's Journal*, January 8, 1815, 126.

94. *Petition of John Hudry*, 5; Hudry to Bertel and J. D. Morenos, n.d., Particulars in relation to Battle of New Orleans furnished me by a French gentleman in 1828—Summer, Follett Papers, Cincinnati History Library and Archives.

95. Peoria, IL, *Peoria Democratic Press*, March 16, 1842. This is from a speech delivered to the New York state assembly by Davezac, who claimed that it was Pakenham's horse, which is possible. Far less possible is his claim that it leapt over the ditch and then jumped over the earthworks. Bassett, *Tatum's Journal*, January 8, 1815, 126, does confirm that after the battle, an American went out on the field and brought back the uninjured horse of a general believed to have been knocked from its saddle. The horse could have been Pakenham's, Gibbs's, or another officer's. Davezac said the animal was subsequently presented to Jackson.

96. Tylden statement, *General Court Martial . . . Trial of Brevet Lieutenant-Colonel Hon. Thomas Mullins*, 10–11.

97. National Park Service archaeological work revealed that as the rate of American balls found in the soil increased closer to Jackson's line, so did the ratio of dropped British balls, an indication of the heavy fire the British were under. Cornelison and Cooper, *Chalmette*, 52–53.

98. Lambert to Bathurst, January 10, 1815, London, UK, *Morning Chronicle*, March 10, 1815.

99. Dickson, "Journal," January 8, 1815, 61, 63; Hill, *Recollections*, 2:12–13.

100. Codrington to Jane Codrington, January 1–31, 1815, Codrington Papers, COD/6/2, Caird.

101. Letter by a member of Hinds's Mississippi Dragoons to New York, January 13, 1815, Dover, NH, *Sun*, February 11, 1815.

102. Surtees, *Rifle Brigade*, 376. Surtees's source was Lieutenant Alexander Steele of the 43rd, who was in the bastion.

103. Cooke, *Narrative*, 237.

104. Ibid., 252–53; *The Terrible and the Brave: The Battles for New Orleans, 1814–1815* (Exhibition catalog; New Orleans: Historic New Orleans Collection, 2005), 9.

105. Chesterton, *Peace, War, and Adventure*, 208.

106. Eaton and Van Crowninshield, *Memoirs of Andrew Jackson*, 285; Cooper, *Rough Notes*, 131–32; British staff officer of the 7th letter, January 16, 1815, Boston, MA, *Yankee*, May 19, 1815; Cooke, *Narrative*, 254.

107. Cooke, *Narrative*, 254; Bassett, *Tatum's Journal*, January 8, 1815, 126–27.

108. Cooke, *Narrative*, 254.

109. S[impson], "New Orleans," 356–57.

110. Charles Gayarré, "A Louisiana Sugar Plantation of the Old Régime," *Harper's New Monthly Magazine* 74, no. 442 (March 1887): 613.

111. Elizabeth Clement to Wood, January 11, 1815, Clement, *Plantation Life*, 127, 129–30.

112. D. Talcott to N. and D. Talcott, New Orleans, January 11, 1815, ten a.m., New York, NY, *New-York Spectator*, February 8, 1815.

113. New Orleans, LA, *L'Ami des Lois*, January 16, 1815, Bowden, *Private Letters*, 245.

114. Letter to Editor of *Philadelphia Gazette*, January 13, 1815, Philadelphia, PA, *Relf's Philadelphia Gazette, and Daily Advertiser*, February 6, 1815.

115. Louise Livingston to sister-in-law Mrs. Montgomery, January 12, 1815, Hunt, *Memoir of Mrs. Edward Livingston*, 61.

116. Letter from New Orleans, January 9, 1815, Wilkes-Barre, PA, *Susquehanna Democrat*, February 17, 1815.

117. Florian to Roosevelt, New Orleans, January 9, 1815, HNOC.

118. Gould Memoir, VHS.

119. Florian to Roosevelt, New Orleans, January 9, 1815, HNOC.

120. Joseph S. Winter to Elisha I. Winter, January 9, 1815, War of 1812 Collection, Michigan.

121. Letter from New Orleans, February 5, 1815, Bridgeport, CT, *Connecticut Courier*, March 22, 1815.

122. Blair, *Sketch of the Life*, 13.

123. Organ to Mordecai, January 19, 1815, Mordecai Family Papers, SHC, UNC.

124. Lewis Livingston to Villeré, January 9, 1815, Villeré Papers, HNOC.

125. Claiborne, *Mississippi*, 361.

126. *Letters of Gen. Adair and Gen. Jackson*, 26.

127. Brown, *To the Public*, 2.

128. Shaumburg to Claiborne, October 30, 1815, Rowland, *Letter Books*, 6: 379–80, Claiborne to Monroe, January 9, 1815, 332.

129. *Letters of Gen. Adair and Gen. Jackson*, 10, 25.

130. Jackson, Account of the Battle of New Orleans, 1815, Andrew Jackson Papers, LC.

131. Shaumberg to Claiborne, October 30, 1815, Rowland, *Letter Books*, 6: 380.

132. Claiborne to Labatut, September 22, 1815, ibid., 368, Shaumburg to Claiborne, October 30, 1815, 379–80.

133. Shaumberg to Claiborne, October 30, 1815, ibid., 381–82.

Chapter Nineteen: "The Greatest Fury"

1. Dickson, "Journal," January 8, 1815, 58; Cochrane to Croker, January 18, 1815, London, UK, *Courier, and Evening Gazette*, March 10, 1815.

2. Account of January 8 in Tylden Journal, January 11, 1815, NYPL.

3. Lambert to Bathurst, January 10, 1815, London, UK, *Morning Chronicle*, March 10, 1815; Wylly to Wellington, March 5, 1815, Pakenham, *Pakenham Letters*, 258; Account of January 8 in Tylden Journal, January 11, 1815, NYPL.

4. Letter by British naval officer, January 30, 1815, Lexington, KY, *Reporter*, August 2, 1815; Memorial of Edward Nicolls, May 1817, WO 1/144, Kew; Cochrane to Croker, January 18, 1815, *Naval Chronicle, for 1815*, vol. 33, 341; Aitchison Memoir, 77, HNOC; "William Hole," in

William Richard O'Byrne, *A Naval Biographical Dictionary: Comprising the Life and Services of Every Living Officer in Her Majesty's Navy* (London: John Murray, 1849), 529.

5. Cannon, *The King's Own Regiment*, 127; William Thornton to Pakenham, January 8, 1815, WO 1/141, Kew; Gleig Diary, January 7, 1815, Barrett, *85th King's Light Infantry*, 219.

6. Thornton to Pakenham, January 8, 1815, WO 1/141, Kew; Forrest, *Journal*, 42; Michell, "Diary of Major J. Michell," January 8, 1815, 129.

7. Louis Valentin Foelckel to Jackson, January 8, 1815, Moser et al., *Papers*, 237.

8. Bassett, *Tatum's Journal*, January 8, 1815, 129; Bradford to St. Francisville *Time-Piece*, January 13, 1815, St. Francisville, LA, *Time-Piece*, January 17, 1815; Fragment of a copy of Testimony by Several Participants in the Battle on the West Bank, January 8, 1815, Latour Archive, HNOC; Letter from New Orleans to Lexington, KY, January 13, 1815, Lexington, KY, *Western Monitor*, February 3, 1815.

9. "A Friend to Truth" to Editor, n.d., Bardstown, KY, *Bardstown Repository*, March 23, 1815; Fragment of a copy of Testimony by Several Participants in the Battle on the West Bank, January 8, 1815, Latour Archive, HNOC.

10. Patterson to Secretary of the Navy, January 13, 1815, Bridgeport, CT, *Republican Farmer*, February 22, 1815.

11. General David B. Morgan to the Editors of the *Reporter*, April 15, 181[7], "General David B. Morgan's Defense of the Conduct of the Louisiana Militia in the Battle on the Left Side of the River," *Louisiana Historical Quarterly* 9, no. 1 (January 1926): 24; Joyes Journal, January 7, 1815, Joyes Papers, Filson. Morgan said Davis brought 260 and Joyes said 240.

12. Adair to Jackson, March 20, 1815, Bardstown, KY, *Bardstown Repository*, May 18, 1815; Bradford to St. Francisville *Time-Piece*, January 13, 1815, St. Francisville, LA, *Time-Piece*, January 17, 1815; Foelckel to Jackson, January 8, 1815, Moser et al., *Papers*, 237.

13. Gleig to Janet Gleig, January 11, 1815, Gleig Papers, NLS.

14. Gleig, *Narrative*, 301.

15. General David B. Morgan to the Editors of the *Reporter*, April 15, 181[7], "General David B. Morgan's Defense," 18.

16. Adair to Jackson, March 20, 1815, Bardstown, KY, *Bardstown Repository*, May 18, 1815.

17. Letter from an officer [William Hole] aboard the British fleet off Louisiana coast, January 30, 1815, *Naval Chronicle, for 1815*, Vol. 33, 387–88.

18. Foelckel to Jackson, January 8, 1815, Moser et al., *Papers*, 237; Report of the Troops under the command of Brig. Genl. Morgan on the right Bank of Mississippi, January 12, 1815, Latour Archive, HNOC. As is usually the case, no authorities entirely agree on numbers. Foelckel was immediately on the scene, wrote within hours of the action, and seems entitled to credibility.

19. John Nixon statement, July 29, 1817, appended to "An Account of the Battle of New Orleans. By John Nixon, Adjutant of the First Regiment of La. Militia," January 9, 1815, Miscellaneous Collection, RG 68, Louisiana Historical Center, New Orleans.

20. General Orders, February 19, 1815, Bardstown, KY, *Bardstown Repository*, March 23, 1815.

21. John Nixon statement, July 29, 1817, Miscellaneous Collection, RG 68, Louisiana Historical Center; Lexington, KY, *Reporter*, March 13, 1815.

22. Nixon, "An Account of the Battle of New Orleans," January 9, 1815, Louisiana Historical Center; General David B. Morgan to the Editors of the *Reporter*, April 15, 181[7], "General David B, Morgan's Defense", 20–21.

23. Adair to Jackson, March 20, 1815, Bardstown, KY, *Bardstown Repository*, May 18, 1815.

24. Fragment of a copy of Testimony by Several Participants in the Battle on the West Bank, January 8, 1815, Latour Archive, HNOC.

25. Natchez, MS, *Ariel*, June 7, 1828.

26. Thornton report to Pakenham, January 8, 1815, WO 1/141, Kew; Gleig Diary, January 8, 1815, Barrett, *85th King's Light Infantry*, 219.

27. Fragment of a copy of Testimony by Several Participants in the Battle on the West Bank, January 8, 1815, Latour Archive, MSS 555, HNOC.

28. Patterson to Secretary of the Navy, January 13, 1815, Bridgeport, CT, *Republican Farmer*, February 22, 1815.

29. Nixon, "An Account of the Battle of New Orleans," Louisiana Historical Center.

30. *Letters of Gen. Adair and Gen. Jackson*, 10.

31. Morgan to the Editors of the *Reporter*, April 15, 181[7], "General David B. Morgan's Defense," 21; Foelckel to Jackson, January 8, 1815, Moser et al., *Papers*, 237.
32. Nixon, "An Account of the Battle of New Orleans," Louisiana Historical Center.
33. Fragment of a copy of Testimony by Several Participants in the Battle on the West Bank, January 8, 1815, Latour Archive, HNOC.
34. Adair to Jackson, March 20, 1815, Bardstown, KY, *Bardstown Repository*, May 18, 1815.
35. Gleig to Janet Gleig, January 11, 1815, Gleig Papers, NLS; Gleig, *Narrative*, 332–33; Foelckel to Jackson, January 8, 1815, Moser et al., *Papers*, 237.
36. Tully Robinson to Morgan, January 25, 1815, Parsons Collection, Texas; Fragment of a copy of Testimony by Several Participants in the Battle on the West Bank, January 8, 1815, Latour Archive, HNOC.
37. Joyes Journal, January 8, 1815, Joyes *Papers*, Filson.
38. "Historical Incidents Before the Battle of New Orleans," New Orleans, LA, *Daily Picayune*, November 14, 1852.
39. Foelckel to Jackson, January 8, 1815, Moser et al., *Papers*, 237; Bassett, *Tatum's Journal*, January 8, 1815, 129; Fragment of a copy of Testimony by Several Participants in the Battle on the West Bank, January 8, 1815, Latour Archive, HNOC. There was at the time and since some debate about whether or not Morgan and Patterson's artillerymen spiked their guns before abandoning them. Ritchie, "Louisiana Campaign," 77n, argues strenuously that Patterson did not spike his guns on the right bank as he claimed after the fact. Le Blanc to?, January 9, 1815, Portland, ME, *Eastern Argus*, February 16, 1815, stated that the guns were lost after being spiked. Seemingly conclusive, however, is the statement of the unknown author of a January 13, 1815, letter in the Boston, MA, *New-England Palladium* of February 10, 1815, that "we were compelled to retreat and spike our cannon." He added further that at the moment of writing he was engaged in cleaning the spiked guns and can certainly be assumed to have recognized what he saw before him.
40. Fragment of a copy of Testimony by Several Participants in the Battle on the West Bank, January 8, 1815, Latour Archive, HNOC.
41. Morgan to the Editors of the *Reporter*, April 15, 181[7], "General David B, Morgan's Defense," 21–25; Fragment of a copy of Testimony by Several Participants in the Battle on the West Bank, January 8, 1815, Latour Archive, HNOC.
42. Gabriel Winter to William Willis, January 12, 1815, Willis Family Papers, LSU.
43. "Historical Incidents Before the Battle of New Orleans," New Orleans, LA, *Daily Picayune*, November 14, 1852.
44. Baron to Tureaud, January 13, 1815, Cook Collection, HNOC; Bassett, *Tatum's Journal*, January 8, 1815, 128. Dustin Cotton agrees that the Louisiana militia did not perform well on the West Bank (Cotton, "Performance of the Louisiana Militia," 87–93).
45. Fragment of a copy of Testimony by Several Participants in the Battle on the West Bank, January 8, 1815, Latour Archive, HNOC.
46. Bassett, *Tatum's Journal*, January 8, 1815, 129; Patterson to Secretary of the Navy, January 13, 1815, Bridgeport, CT, *Republican Farmer*, February 22, 1815.
47. Gleig, *Narrative*, 333.
48. Cochrane to Dundas, January 20, 1815, War of 1812 Mss., Lilly Library.
49. Gleig, of course, is confirmed in his own letters as the author of *Subaltern*, yet in it he offers some "recollections" that are not identical to those in his 1821 *Narrative*. It seems possible that he incorporated experiences of fellow officers of his regiment as his own, and in having himself wounded so seriously on January 8 as to be unconscious for nine days, he may have unintentionally revealed one source. The 85th had only two officers wounded that day, Lieutenant Colonel Thornton and Lieutenant Beauchamp C. Urquhart, who was reported as wounded "seriously but not dangerously." Thus, Urquhart fits perfectly the only evidence that *Subaltern* provided for his identification. Return of Casualties in the Army Under the Command of Major General the Honble Sir Edward M. Pakenham KB in Action with the Enemy near New Orleans on the 8th January 1815, WO 1/141, Return of the General and Staff Officers at present serving in the Army under the Command of Major General the Hon'ble Sir E. M. Pakenham KB in Camp near New Orleans, December 25, 1814, War Department In-Letters and Papers 1815–1817, Returns of Regiments Serving in the Chesapeake and New Orleans, 1814–1815, WO 17/1218, Kew.
50. Hill, *Recollections*, 2:10.

51. Gray (unsigned) to Graham, February 8, 1815, RG 59, NA. Though unsigned, this letter is clearly in Gray's handwriting.

52. Thornton report to Pakenham, January 8, 1815, WO 1/141, Kew; Gleig Diary, January 8, 1815, Barrett, *85th King's Light Infantry*, 219–20.

53. S[impson], "New Orleans," 357n.

54. Gleig Diary, January 8, 1815, Barrett, *85th King's Light Infantry*, 220.

55. Gray to Shaler, May 3, 1815, Shaler Family Papers, HSP.

56. Letter from an officer [William Hole] aboard the British fleet off Louisiana coast, January 30, 1815, *Naval Chronicle, for 1815*, vol. 33, 385–88.

57. Patterson to Secretary of the Navy, January 13, 1815, Bridgeport, CT, *Republican Farmer*, February 22, 1815.

58. Letter from New Orleans to the Editor of the *Philadelphia Gazette*, January 13, 1815, Newport, RI, *Newport Mercury*, February 11, 1815; Letter from New Orleans, January 13, 1815, Boston, MA, *New-England Palladium*, February 10, 1815.

59. Patterson to Secretary of the Navy, January 13, 1815, Bridgeport, CT, *Republican Farmer*, February 22, 1815; Nixon, "An Account of the Battle of New Orleans," Louisiana Historical Center.

60. Claiborne, *Mississippi*, 345–46, 353; Wilkins to Adair, May 13, 1817, *Letters of Gen. Adair and Gen. Jackson*, 14; Morgan to the Editors of the *Reporter*, April 15, 181[7], "General David B. Morgan's Defense," 25–26. This whole letter by Morgan is an attack on Davis and Adair, largely in response to Kentuckian McAfee's aggressive defense of the two in his 1816 *History of the Late War*. Morgan's statements can hardly be assumed to be unbiased.

61. Foelckel to Jackson, January 8, 1815, Moser et al., *Papers*, 237.

62. Morgan to Jackson, January 8, 1815, Gunther Memorial Collection, Chicago History Museum. Film and fiction to the contrary, it is not possible to place Jean Laffite during the battle. His last known whereabouts were with Major Reynolds at the Temple, and that is probably where he remained, as he was useful to Jackson there. Surely *someone* would have mentioned seeing him had he been with the army at Chalmette on January 8, as he was arguably the biggest celebrity in the area next to Jackson. Contemporary eyewitness mentions of the Baratarians at their battery are numerous, and Captain Dominique was universally acknowledged to be their commander, but there is not a peep about Jean. Even Pierre was mentioned a couple of times, and he was not the celebrity his brother was.

    Researcher Pam Keyes has found depositions in the War of 1812 pension files in which statements supporting widows' applications attested that their husbands Lorenzo/Laurent Maire and Victor Joly served in "one of the artillery squads under Captain Lafitte, the pirate," or "in the company of artillery commanded by Capt. Lafitte . . . generally known and called by the natives 'Lafitte le Pirate.'" One added that both Laffite brothers were with the artillery on Line Jackson, each commanding a company of 10–15 gunners. The War Department noted with the applications that it had no record of Jean Laffite whatever, though it also had no record of Dominic You. If the Laffites, as acknowledged leaders of the Baratarians, were in the action with that battery, it seems hardly likely that everyone at the time would have failed to mention the fact, and instead credited You with the command. The depositions' references to "Captain Lafitte" reflect a generic usage by all Baratarians, who regarded themselves as Jean Laffite's men as his celebrity grew greater and rubbed off on them. Moreover, the statements in these files are respectively forty-two and sixty-six years after the fact, written long after fiction and romance had made a local hero of Jean. (Jacques Rouzan deposition, February 16, 1881, Barthelemy Populas and Jacques David St. Herman deposition, August 13, 1857, Pension Application Files of Lorenzo/Laurent Maire and Victor Stanislaus Joly, RG 15, NA.)

63. Thornton report to Pakenham, January 8, 1815, WO 1/141, Kew.

64. Letter by British naval officer [William Hole], January 30, 1815, Lexington, KY, *Reporter*, August 2, 1815.

65. Lambert to Bathurst, January 28, 1815, London, UK, *Morning Chronicle*, March 10, 1815; Dickson, "Journal," January 8, 1815, 65; Return of the Ordnance taken from the Enemy, January 8, 1815, WO 1/141, Kew; Gray to Shaler, May 3, 1815, Shaler Family Papers, HSP.

66. Carson I. A. Ritchie, ed., "British Documents on the Louisiana Campaign, 1814–15," *Louisiana Historical Quarterly* 44, no. 1–2 (January–April 1961): 113; "Diary of Major J. Michell," January 8, 1815, 129.

67. *General Court Martial . . . Trial of Brevet Lieutenant-Colonel Hon. Thomas Mullins*, 83.
68. Pringle to Editor, November 13, 1833, Pringle, *Letters*, 5.
69. Knight statement, *General Court Martial . . . Trial of Brevet Lieutenant-Colonel Hon. Thomas Mullins*, 16–17.
70. Pringle statement, ibid., 20.
71. Cooke, *Narrative*, 245, said that "the tribe of savages" accompanied Jones.
72. Pay List of the 5th West India Regiment of Foot, December 1814–March 1815, Infantry Abroad Quarterly Pay Lists for the 5th West India Regiment of Foot, WO 12/11538, Kew.
73. Sinclair to Pringle, January 27, 1834, Pringle, *Letters*, 12–13; Dickson, "Journal," January 8, 1815, 63; "Recollections of the Expedition," (July) part 4, 347.
74. Adjutant Barry estimated the distance at three-fourths of a mile, which was a wild exaggeration. Barry statement, *General Court Martial . . . Trial of Brevet Lieutenant-Colonel Hon. Thomas Mullins*, 57.
75. Knight statement, ibid., 16–17, 19, Keating statement, 64.
76. Thomas Dudley statement, ibid., 69–70, Henry Dwyer statement, 70, Thomas Wren statement, 67.
77. Gowe statement, ibid., 53, 63, Barry statement, 55, 63, Wren statement, 67.
78. Michael Dennison statement, ibid., 52, Knight statement, 16–17.
79. David Brown, *Diary of a Soldier, 1805–1827* (Ardrossan, Scotland: Arthur Guthrie, 1934), n.p.
80. Londonderry, Ireland, *Londonderry Sentinel and North-West Advertiser*, June 21, 1834.
81. Graves to White, n.d. [1845–53], New Orleans, LA, *Daily Delta*, January 8, 1854.
82. Cope, *Rifle Brigade*, 189–90.
83. British staff officer of the 7th letter, January 16, 1815, Boston, MA, *Yankee*, May 19, 1815.
84. Smith, *Autobiography of Lieutenant-General Sir Harry Smith*, 237; Tylden account of January 8 in Journal, January 11, 181, NYPL.
85. Cooke, *Narrative*, 233–34.
86. Ibid., 235.
87. Ibid., 235–36; Frederick Stovin Letter, January 24, 1815, Cook Collection, HNOC; Smith, *Autobiography of Lieutenant-General Sir Harry Smith*, 247.
88. Cooke, *Narrative*, 236–37.
89. Hill, *Recollections*, 2:11–12. The curiosity would seem to have been a variant of "acoustic shadow," perhaps caused by temperature, the fog, and the clouds of thick black powder smoke hanging over the field. Hill later concluded that "I leave the solution of the mystery to time and the curious."
90. Lambert to Lord Bathurst, January 10, 1815, London, UK, *Morning Chronicle*, March 10, 1815; Dickson, "Journal," January 8, 1815, 64.
91. Richard Cannon, comp., *Historical Record of the Seventh Regiment, or The Royal Fusiliers: Containing an Account of the Formation of the Regiment in 1685, and of Its Subsequent Services to 1846* (London: Parker, Furnivall, & Parker, 1847), 84, 86; British staff officer of the 7th letter, January 16, 1815, Boston, MA, *Yankee*, May 19, 1815.
92. Lambert to Bathurst, January 10, 1815, London, UK, *Morning Chronicle*, March 10, 1815; British staff officer of the 7th letter, January 16, 1815, Boston, MA, *Yankee*, May 19, 1815.
93. Letter from New Orleans, January 13, 1815, Boston, MA, *New-England Palladium*, February 10, 1815. The author was assigned to clean and repair the spiked guns taken on the west bank and was clearly an ordnance officer.
94. Gray to Shaler, May 3, 1815, Shaler Family Papers, HSP.
95. Gleig to Janet Gleig, January 11, 1815, Gleig Papers, NLS; Gleig Diary, January 19, 1815, Barrett, *85th King's Light Infantry*, 231.
96. Gleig Diary, January 8, 1815, Barrett, *85th King's Light Infantry*, 220; Gleig to Janet Gleig, January 11, 1815, Gleig Papers, NLS; Gleig, *Narrative*, 334–35.
97. Dickson, "Journal," January 8, 1815, 66–68.
98. Lambert to Bathurst, January 10, 1815, London, UK, *Morning Chronicle*, March 10, 1815; Hill, *Recollections*, 2:13–14; Wrottesley, *Life and Correspondence of Field Marshal Sir John Burgoyne*, 1:306.
99. Shaumburg to Claiborne, October 30, 1815, Rowland, *Letter Books*, 6:381–82.
100. Baron to Tureaud, January 13, 1815, Cook Collection, HNOC. Baron mistakenly wrote that Morgan's dispute was with General Stephen Hopkins, whereas it was certainly Humbert.

101. Claiborne to Labatut, September 22, 1815, Rowland, *Letter Books*, 6:368, Shaumburg to Claiborne, October 30, 1815, 379, Claiborne to Shaumberg, October 1, 1815, 372–73.

102. Claiborne to Shaumberg, October 1, 1815, ibid., 372–73, Shaumberg to Claiborne, October 30, 1815, 381–82.

103. Gabriel Winter to William Willis, January 12, 1815, Willis Family Papers, LSU.

104. Codrington to Jane Codrington, January 9, 1815, Codrington Papers, COD/6/2, Caird; Letter from an officer aboard the British fleet off Louisiana coast, January 30, 1815, *Naval Chronicle, for 1815*, vol. 33, 387–88; "Sketch of A Tour of Service," Louisville, KY, *Louisville Daily Democrat*, March 21, 1846; John Michell to Jane Michell, January 22, 1815, HNOC.

105. *General Court Martial . . . Trial of Brevet Lieutenant-Colonel Hon. Thomas Mullins*, 83; Hynes to Blount, February 3, 1815, Lexington, KY, *Reporter*, March 13, 1815.

106. Tylden account of January 8 in Journal, January 11, 181, NYPL. Surtees, *Rifle Brigade*, 389, seconded Tylden's belief that the 7th and 43rd ought to have spearheaded the attack.

107. London, UK, *National Register*, January 8, 1815.

108. Bassett, *Tatum's Journal*, January 8, 1815, 125. Written about January 20.

109. Ibid., 127; Reid to his father, January 17, 1815, Richmond, VA, *Richmond Enquirer*, February 18, 1815; Letter from New Orleans to Robertson, January 13, 1815, Washington, DC, *National Intelligencer*, February 7, 1815; Letter from New Orleans to New York, January 13, 1815, New York, NY, *New-York Gazette & General Advertiser*, February 9, 1815; Ficklin to Bullock, January 13, 1815, Clinton, OH, *Ohio Register*, February 21, 1815; Letter from New Orleans, January 13, 1815, Philadelphia, PA, *Poulson's American Daily Advertiser*, February 7, 1815; Carroll to Tannahill, January 13, 1815, St. Louis, MO, *Missouri Gazette*, February 11, 1815; Letter from New Orleans, January 9, 1815, Boston, MA, *New-England Palladium*, February 10, 1815; Letter from Le Blanc, January 9, 1815, New York, NY, *New-York Gazette & General Advertiser*, February 7, 1815; David Weller to Samuel Weller, January 13, 1815, Weller Family Papers, Filson.

110. Letter from New Orleans to Middletown, CT, Middletown, CT, *Connecticut Spectator*, February 15, 1815.

111. Henderson to his father, January 9, 1815, Natchez, MS, *Mississippi Republican*, January 16, 1815, in Baltimore, MD, *American, and Commercial Daily Advertiser*, February 6, 1815; Letter from New Orleans, January 13, 1815, Boston, MA, *New-England Palladium*, February 10, 1815.

112. David Weller to Samuel Weller, January 13, 1815, Weller Family Papers, Filson.

113. Letter from New Orleans, January 20, 1815, Wilmington, DE, *American Watchman*, February 18, 1815.

114. Letter from New Orleans, January 9, 1815, Boston, MA, *New-England Palladium*, February 10, 1815.

115. Letter from Le Blanc, seven p.m., January 9, 1815, New York, NY, *New-York Gazette and General Advertiser*, February 7, 1815.

CHAPTER TWENTY: "ALL FEAR IS AT AN END"

1. British staff officer of the 7th letter, January 16, 1815, Boston, MA, *Yankee*, May 19, 1815.

2. Codrington to Jane Codrington, January 1–31, 1815, Codrington Papers, COD/6/2, Caird; Lambert to Bathurst, January 29, 1815, WO 1/141, Kew; Smith, *Autobiography of Lieutenant-General Sir Harry Smith*, 238. Smith offers an unlikely exchange in which Codrington supposedly said "the troops must attack or the whole will be starved!" whereupon Smith "saucily" retorted that they should "Kill plenty more, Admiral; fewer rations will be required."

3. Tylden Journal, January 12, 1815, NYPL.

4. Dickson, "Journal," January 8, 1815, 69–70.

5. Lambert to Bathurst, January 28, 1815, WO 1/141, Kew; Codrington to Cockburn, January 11, 1815, HMS *Tonnant* Letter Book 1, Codrington Papers, COD/6/1, Caird.

6. Letter from New Orleans to Editor of Frankfort *Palladium*, January 13, 1815, Lexington, KY, *Western Monitor*, February 3, 1815.

7. Avery letter to his wife, January 10, 1815, War of 1812 Collection, Tulane.

8. Letter from New Orleans to Robertson, January 13, 1815, Washington, DC, *National Intelligencer*, February 7, 1815, says it was 368 bodies. In Jackson to Winchester, January 10, 1815, Moser et al., *Papers*, 242, Jackson said his men gathered "upwards of 300" dead, which seems understated.

9. Jackson to Winchester, January 10, 1815, Moser et al., *Papers*, 242.

10. Hunt, *Memoir of Mrs. Edward Livingston*, 54–55.

11. British staff officer of the 7th letter, January 16, 1815, Boston, MA, *Yankee*, May 19, 1815.

12. Gordon to Lydia Gordon, January 9, 1815, Gordon, *Letters and Records*, 218.

13. Letter from New Orleans ca. January 9, 1815, Boston, MA, *Boston Commercial Gazette*, February 9, 1815.

14. Winter to Willis, January 12, 1815, Willis Family Papers, LSU; Cooper, *Rough Notes*, 132–33; Powell A. Casey, *Louisiana at the Battle of New Orleans* (New Orleans: Battle of New Orleans 150th Anniversary Committee of Louisiana, 1965), 29.

15. S[impson], "New Orleans," 355n; Pringle to Editor, November 13, 1833, Pringle, *Letters*, 5. Extract from a Bulletin of Operations, January 9, 1815, Boston, MA, *Repertory*, February 11, 1815, implies that Rennie's body was carried back to the British camp on January 9, and it well could have been during the truce to collect bodies. It is impossible to tell, however, if this was an actual diary kept by an anonymous author, or an editorial compilation. The Norwich, CT, *Courier*, February 15, 1815, reprinted it from the Philadelphia, PA, *Weekly Aurora* of February 6, 1815, for which no issue is known to exist. The *Aurora*, it was stated, reprinted it from a diary kept at New Orleans. Walker, *Jackson and New Orleans*, 361, stated that "we believe" Rennie's body was returned to be taken to England. Yet Pringle stated that Jackson specifically said that Rennie had been given a burial by the Americans, and as Rennie's best friend he seems the best authority. Note also that Vincent Gray, in describing the arrival of the *Plantagenet* at Havana on February 8, mentioned the bodies of Pakenham and Gibbs being aboard but said nothing of any others (Gray to John Graham, February 8, 1815, Dispatches from the U. S. Consul in Havana, Cuba, RG 59, NA). Most conclusive is a letter by an "American Officer," probably from the 7th Infantry, to the Baltimore, MD, *American, and Daily Commercial Advertiser*, published on June 7, 1821. In it the writer stated that thirty-one redcoats were killed at the bastion, including Rennie, "whom we buried ourselves."

16. Surtees, *Rifle Brigade*, 381.

17. Hill, *Recollections*, 2:15; Cooper, *Rough Notes*, 132–33.

18. Cooke, *Narrative*, 236, 268.

19. List of Deaths which have taken place among the Officers during the preceding Month, January 25, 1815, WO 17/1218, Kew. On claims that Gibbs's last words were imprecations against Mullins, see, for instance, Letter from an officer [William Hole] aboard the British fleet off Louisiana coast, January 30, 1815, *Naval Chronicle, for 1815*, vol. 33, 385–88.

20. Letter from New Orleans, January 12, 1815, New London, CT, *Connecticut Gazette*, February 15, 1815.

21. Cannon, *The King's Own Regiment*, 128.

22. Burgoyne, *93rd Sutherland Highlanders*, 29.

23. Return of Casualties in the Army . . . on the 23rd December 1814, Return of Casualties in the Army . . . between the 25th and 31st December 1814, Return of Casualties in the Army . . . between the 1st & 7 Jany 1815, Return of Casualties in the Army . . . on the 8th January 1815, WO 1/141, General Monthly Returns of . . . the Army under the Command of Major General Lambert, January 25, 1815, WO 17/1218, Kew; Burgoyne, *93rd Sutherland Highlanders*, 29. Numbers and losses are always a problem, and there remains conjecture about Lambert's total casualties. His January 10, 1815, report, cited in Reilly, *British at the Gates*, 297, listed 285 killed, 1,186 wounded, and 484 taken prisoner, to which Reilly made adjustments rounding it up to 2,500. But Lambert had incomplete information as of January 10. Meanwhile, the Returns of Casualties covering dates December 23–24, 25–31, January 1–7, 8, and 9–26 (WO 1/141, Kew), done in the field, show campaign totals of 386 killed, 1,471 wounded, and 552 missing and presumed wounded and captured, for a total casualty figure of 2,409, which included all units, artillery, and staff. Further confusing matters, the January 9–26 casualty return does not include the loss of a net of about 73 prisoners taken by Shields January 19–24, nor does it include any losses among sailors and the marines. Meanwhile, the above-cited January 25 field return would have included all ambulatory wounded except the approximately 500 seriously wounded left behind at Villeré's, which further confuses the numbers. Taking all of this into account, the total casualties would have been about 2,000, and the number of dead would increase and the wounded decrease as the latter continued to die of their wounds for some time thereafter.

24. Gleig to Janet Gleig, January 11, 1815, Gleig Papers, NLS.

25. Florian to Roosevelt, January 9, 1815, HNOC.

26. Letter from New Orleans, January 13, 1815, Newport, RI, *Newport Mercury*, February 11, 1815.

27. Hunt, *Life of Edward Livingston*, 202; Account of the Battle of New Orleans, 1815, Jackson Papers, LC.

28. Shaumburg to Wilkinson, January 25, 1815, HNOC.

29. Dickson, "Journal," January 14, 1815, 74. This sortie is not mentioned elsewhere, and Dickson mistook it for a raid to retrieve slaves at Villeré's.

30. Priestley to Latour, March 4, 1816, Latour Archive, HNOC; Pierre Charbonnier to Livingston, February 15, 1828, Livingston Papers, Princeton.

31. "Sketch of A Tour of Service," Louisville, KY, *Louisville Daily Democrat*, March 23, 1846.

32. Gayarré, "Louisiana Sugar Plantation," 613.

33. Gould Memoir, VHS.

34. "Sketch of A Tour of Service," Louisville, KY, *Louisville Daily Democrat*, March 21, 1846.

35. Florian to Roosevelt, January 9, 1815, HNOC.

36. A. Spears to brother in Kentucky, January 9, 1815, Paris, KY, *Western Citizen*, February 4, 1815.

37. Florian to Roosevelt, January 9, 1815, HNOC.

38. Ibid.

39. Gould Memoir, VHS; Letter from New Orleans, n.d. [January 1815], to member of Congress, Bennington, VT, *Green-Mountain Farmer*, February 20, 1815.

40. Bond, February 7, 1815, Robert Sprigg statement, April 30, 1815, D. C. Wallace Letters, Cincinnati History Library and Archives.

41. D. Talcott to N. and D. Talcott, New Orleans, January 11, 1815, New York, NY, *New-York Spectator*, February 8, 1815.

42. Letter from one of Beale's Rifles, January 13, 1815, Boston, MA, *New-England Palladium*, February 10, 1815.

43. Florian to Roosevelt, New Orleans, January 9, 1815, HNOC.

44. Receipt for payment to Rose, March 3, 1815, Cook Collection, HNOC; Florian to Roosevelt, January 9, 1815, HNOC; New Orleans, LA, *Times-Picayune*, November 6, 1950. Lore states that she was honored and carried on soldiers' shoulders and publicly commended by Jackson, though there is no substantiation for the claim.

45. Florian to Roosevelt, New Orleans, January 9, 1815, HNOC.

46. S[impson], "New Orleans," 356n; Account of the Battle of New Orleans, Jackson Papers, LC; Letter to the Editor of the *Philadelphia Gazette*, January 13, 1815, Philadelphia, PA, *Relf's Philadelphia Gazette, and Daily Advertiser*, February 6, 1815.

47. Holland to mother, January 20, 1815, New York, NY, *New-York Mercantile Advertiser*, February 16, 1815; Letter from gentleman in New Orleans to his brother in Fredericksburg, VA, January 26, 1815, New Haven, CT, *Connecticut Journal*, March 13, 1815; Richmond, VA, *Richmond Enquirer*, March 18, 1815.

48. Report of the Managers of the Louisiana Bible Society, New Orleans, LA, *Louisiana Gazette for the Country*, April 25, 1815.

49. Graves to White, n.d. [1845–53], New Orleans, LA, *Daily Delta*, January 8, 1854; Louise Livingston to Jane Montgomery, January 12, 1815, Hunt, *Memoir of Mrs. Edward Livingston*, 60. There is some confusion in this matter. The *Daily Delta* editorial account preceding Graves's letter indicates that White took Graves to his own home, but Graves's letter says only that White found him on the battlefield. Hunt, *Memoir of Mrs. Edward Livingston*, 55–56, says that the Livingstons took in a "Major Graves," but also states that it was after the December 23 action. The January 12, 1815, letter quoted does not name Graves, saying only that "I have in the house one of their officers, badly wounded." Since there was no "Major Graves" with Pakenham and the only major captured on December 23 was Mitchell, who was unwounded, it seems evident that Hunt, writing in 1886, was careless or confused about the date of Graves's capture as well as his rank. Arthur, *New Orleans*, 216–18n, concludes that the officer at Livingston's was Graves. The British casualty lists show only a Lieutenant Graves of the 93rd wounded January 8 (Return of Casualties in the Army Under the Command of Major General the Honbl. Sir Edwd. M. Pakenham K.B. in Action with the Enemy near New Orleans on the 8th January 1815, WO 1/141, Kew).

50. This story appears in Walker, *Jackson and New Orleans*, 384. No independent corroboration has been found, and Kerr does not appear in the list of medical men with the army in "Return of the General and Staff Officers at present serving in the Army under the Command of Major General the Honble Sir E. Pakenham," December 1814, WO 17/1218, Kew, but that is not conclusive. The characters are quite genuine, as was their May 14, 1817, marriage in New Orleans. Since Kerr died in 1850 in living memory of many whom Walker would have consulted in writing his book, it seems safe to assume that he got the story right in broad terms.

51. Letter from one of Beale's Rifles, January 13, 1815, Boston, MA, *New-England Palladium*, February 10, 1815.

52. Tousard to Stocker, January 13, 1815, Parsons Collection, Texas.

53. Cheatham, "'I owe to Britain a Debt of Retaliatory Vengeance,'" 50–51.

54. Patterson to Cochrane, January 9, 1815, Captains' Letters, RG 260, NA.

55. S[impson], "New Orleans," 357n.

56. Letter from New Orleans, January 20, 1815, Wilmington, DE, *American Watchman*, February 18, 1815; Reid to Myra Reid, ca. January 13, 1815, Augusta. GA, *Augusta Herald*, February 23, 1815.

57. Tylden Journal, January 12, 1815, NYPL.

58. Letter from one of Beale's Rifles, January 13, 1815, Boston, MA, *New-England Palladium*, February 10, 1815.

59. D. Talcott to N. and D. Talcott, New Orleans, January 11, 1815, New York, NY, *New-York Spectator*, February 8, 1815; Letter from New Orleans, January 12, 1815, Boston, MA, *Boston Daily Advertiser*, February 9, 1815.

60. Holland to mother, January 20, 1815, Providence, RI, *Rhode-Island Republican*, February 22, 1815.

61. Reid to his father, January 17, 1815, Richmond, VA, *Richmond Enquirer*, February 18, 1815.

62. Reid to Myra Reid, ca. January 13, 1815, Augusta. GA, *Augusta Herald*, February 23, 1815. In 1817 Reid and Eaton (*Jackson*, 334, 357–58) told the story of an American who deserted on January 6 and informed the British that the weakest spot in Jackson's line was where Carroll's Tennesseans were posted, which is where Pakenham directed his main attack. After the battle and the bloody repulse of Gibbs, Lambert supposedly had the deserter hanged for misleading them. Reid and Eaton gave no source of any kind for the story, saying only that it was a "fact told, to which general credit seems to be attached"; in other words, a rumor. No other reference to such an incident has been found, and the fact that on-the-spot diarists, including Dickson, Tylden, Gleig, and others, make no mention of such an unusual event as an execution, strongly suggests that it was nothing but a postwar rumor. None of the score of later memoirs and recollections by British officers mentions it, either.

63. Kempe to friend in Natchez, January 9, 1815, Natchez, MS, *Mississippi Republican*, January 16, 1815, in Baltimore, MD, *Baltimore Patriot*, February 4, 1815.

64. Jackson to Lewis Heerman, January 27, 1815, Jackson Collection, HNOC; *Appeal of L. Louaillier*, 14.

65. Louaillier to Morgan, January 15, 1815, Morgan Papers, LC; Statement of subscriptions January 16, 1815, Rosamonde E. and Emile Kuntz Collection, Tulane; Morgan to Louaillier, January 23, 1815, Parsons Collection, Texas; Letter from New Orleans, n.d. [post January 9, 1815], to member of Congress, Bennington, VT, *Green-Mountain Farmer*, February 20, 1815; Florian to Roosevelt, January 9, 1815, HNOC; Circular, January 29, 1815, Order Book, Louisiana Militia, RG 107, Louisiana Historical Center, New Orleans; *Appeal of L. Louaillier*, 16. The last-cited source mentions a free man of color named "Dompierre" who lost his life, though it does not say where or when. No service record has been found for a soldier of that name.

66. Louise Livingston to Jane Montgomery, January 12, 1815, Hunt, *Memoir of Mrs. Edward Livingston*, 59–60.

67. Letter from Frenchman in New Orleans to a friend in Marietta, OH, January 20, 1815, Marietta, OH, *American Friend*, February 11, 1815.

68. Letter from New Orleans, January 20, 1815, Wilmington, DE, *American Watchman*, February 18, 1815.

69. Gould Memoir, VHS; L. C. Hardy to William M. Reid, April 3, 1815, War of 1812 Collection, 1813–1965, Tulane; Notary Pierre Pedesclaux, volume 69, 202–3, Notarial Archives, New Orleans.

70. Kenner to Minor, March 10, 24, July 17, August 18, 1815, Kenner Papers, LSU; Letter from New Orleans, March 13, 1815, Boston, MA, *Boston Patriot*, April 22, 1815; New Haven, CT, *Connecticut Journal*, April 17, 1815.

71. Letter from New Orleans, January 30, 1815, Brownsville, PA, *American Telegraph*, March 29, 1815.

72. Letter from a merchant in New Orleans, March 10, 1815, New Haven, CT, *Connecticut Journal*, April 17, 1815; Hardy to William M. Reid, April 3, 1815, War of 1812 Collection, Tulane; Letter from New Orleans, January 15, 1815, Easton, MD, *Republican Star*, February 14, 1815; Claiborne to Monroe, March 16, 1815, Rowland, *Letter Books*, 6:351.

73. Jacques Villeré statement, n.d. [1818 or later], Villeré Papers, HNOC.

74. Notary Broutin, volume 32, 1; Marc Lafitte, volume 5, 1, Michel De Armas, volume 9, 1, Pedesclaux, volume 69, 206–9, New Orleans Notarial Archives.

75. Orleans Parish Court, Index to Slave Emancipation Petitions, City Archives, NOPL.

76. Alexis Daudet to Jackson, March 8, 1815, Moser et al., *Papers*, 304–5n.

77. Randall Easting to Rees, March 26, Rees Papers, Tulane.

78. Watchwords January 26, 1815, Order Book, Louisiana Militia, RG 107, Louisiana Historical Center.

79. On February 11, 1815, *Niles, Weekly Register* paraphrased unspecified "letters from New Orleans" which stated "on the information of deserters and prisoners" that Pakenham was to be governor and had with him "a whole regiment of magistrates, custom-house officers, merchants and dealers!" (378). That this rumor originated among British soldiers is further evident from the fact that in its most complete form it reached Havana aboard the *Plantagenet* on February 8 and was "a matter of perfect notoriety" there by the time the ship left for England three days later. That vessel had left the inner anchorage with the bodies of Pakenham and Gibbs and many wounded on January 12, hence anyone aboard actually would have left British lines January 10 or 11, and had little if any opportunity to be influenced by any rumors coming out of New Orleans (Cochrane Journal, January 12, 1815, ADM 50/122, Kew; Tylden Journal, January 28, 1815, NYPL; Gray to Graham, February 8, 1815, Dispatches from the U. S. Consul in Havana, Cuba, RG 59, NA). Hence the story was fully developed by January 12. It was heard in Havana by a man who arrived in Philadelphia on or about February 20, and it appeared in the Philadelphia, PA, *Relf's Philadelphia Gazette, and Daily Advertiser* on February 22, 1815.

80. Boston, MA, *Bostan Commercial Gazette*, February 9, 1815; D. Talcott to N. and D. Talcott, New Orleans, January 11, 1815, New York, NY, *New-York Evening Post*, February 7, 1815; Letter from New Orleans to Robertson, January 13, 1815, Washington, DC, *National Intelligencer*, February 7, 1815; Letter from New Orleans, January 20, 1815, Raleigh, NC, *Star*, February 17, 1815; Letter from New Orleans, n.d. [January 13, 1815], to Robertson, Bennington, VT, *Green-Mountain Farmer*, February 20, 1815 (this last letter is extracted and undated, but the similarity to the letters cited above is clear, though this version is the only one found that mentions bringing household goods); Pierre-Joseph Favrot to Marie-Françoise Gerard Favrot, January 21, 1815, Pierre-Joseph Favrot Letters, Tulane.

81. Shields to Patterson, January 25, 1815, Worcester, MA, *National Aegis*, March 1, 1815; Patterson to Cochrane, February 3, 1815, Captains' Letters, RG 260, NA; Jackson to Monroe, January 25, 1815, Moser et al., *Papers*, 255. Jackson repeated this in a letter to Brown, February 4, 1815, War of 1812 Mss., Lilly Library.

82. Boston, MA, *Columbian Centinel*, February 11, 1815. In a column headed "Other Particulars," the *Centinel* gave extracts from several New Orleans letters dated January 13, and closed with the trenchant observation that "no mention has ever been made in the English papers of the embarkation of these civil officers, though they were very minute in naming the staff &c." Early histories of the battle repeated the stories from published letters in the press. See, for instance, McAfee, *History of the Late War*, 524, and William McCarty, *History of the American War of 1812, from the Commencement, until the Final Termination Thereof, on the Memorable Eighth of January, 1815, at New Orleans* (Philadelphia: McCarty & Davis, 1817), 234. James Parton repeated them in 1888 (*Jackson*, 2:40), adding that the man who was to be collector had brought with him his "five beautiful daughters," his source unstated. Some later historians have done likewise (see Drez, *War of 1812*, 309, and Owsley, *Borderlands*, 168). In 1904 the industrious Augustus C. Buell enhanced the story by inventing further details, including a man from Trinidad named Elwood being lieutenant governor, and a man from Barbados, collector for the

port. Buell also adopted Parton's unsupported assertion about five daughters and added that they were all blond and hoped to find rich husbands in New Orleans. He further mentioned offices of attorney general, admiralty court judge, and a secretary for the "colony" coming from Britain. There would even be a superintendent of Indian affairs from Canada, a man named Dockstader, the son of a notorious Colonel Dockstader who had been a Tory during the American Revolution. With typical brazenness, Buell stated that all of this additional material came from Cooke's *Narrative* and Gleig's *Subaltern*, whereas not a syllable of this appeared in either work (Buell, *Andrew Jackson*, 71–73).

83. Jackson to Winchester, January 10, 1815 Moser et al., *Papers*, 242; Latour, *Historical Memoir*, 243. Morgan also had nineteen missing but virtually all of them had been scattered in the rout and would return to their regiments.

84. A Detachment report of the Killed wounded and missing of the Kenty Militia, January 8, 1815, Report of the Killed & wounded of Genl Jno Coffees Brigade, Jackson Papers, Report of the Killed and wounded in the artillery, navy and volunteers, January 8, 1815, Report of the Killed, wounded and missing of the army under the command of Major General Andrew Jackson, in the actions of the 23d and 28th December 1814 and 1st and 8th January 1815, Jackson Papers, LC; Robert Butler report, January 16, 1815, Baltimore, MD, *Baltimore Telegraph*, February 14, 1815.

85. Jackson to Monroe, January 13, 1815, Augusta, GA, *Augusta Herald*, February 23, 1815.

86. Patterson to Crowninshield, January 13, 1815, Bridgeport, CT, *Republican Farmer*, February 22, 1815; Letter from New Orleans to Lexington, KY, January 13, 1815, Lexington, KY, *Western Monitor*, February 3, 1815.

87. Account of the Battle of New Orleans, 1815, Jackson Papers, LC; Letter "from a gentleman in the service," n.d. [January 13, 1815], Boston, MA, *New-England Palladium*, February 10, 1815.

88. General orders, January 9, 10, 14, 15, 1815, Orderly Book of Brigadier General John Coffee, Cook Collection, HNOC.

89. Letter from New Orleans, January 13, 1815, Newport, RI, *Newport Mercury*, February 11, 1815; Surtees, *Rifle Brigade*, 384; Cooke, *Narrative*, 268.

90. Cochrane to Croker, January 18, 1815, London, UK, *Courier, and Evening Gazette*, March 10, 1815.

91. W. H. Overton to Jackson, January 19, 1815, New York, NY, *New-York Evening Post*, March 22, 1815; Gordon to Morgan, January 9, 1815, Parsons Collection, Texas.

92. Consolidated Morning Report Fort St. Leon, January 13, 1815, Morgan Papers, LC; Caldwell to Morgan, January 17, 1815, Neil Auction Catalog, #114; Penne to Morgan, January 29, 1815, Morgan to Gordon, January 12, 1815, Parsons Collection, Texas.

93. Return of the Artillery now existing at Fort Leon, January 13, 1815, Morgan Papers, LC; Gordon to Morgan, January 10, 1815, DeCluny to Gordon, January 10, 1815, Parsons Collection, Texas.

94. Letter from one of Beale's Rifles, January 13, 1815, Boston, MA, *New-England Palladium*, February 10, 1815; Letter from New Orleans ca. January 9, 1815, Boston, MA, *Boston Commercial Gazette*, February 9, 1815; Baron to Tureaud, January 13, 1815, Cook Collection, HNOC; Avery to Mary Ann Avery, January 10, 1815, Avery Letters, LSU; Letter from an officer in New Orleans to Washington, January 13, 1815, Charles Town, VA, *Farmer's Repository*, February 9, 1815.

95. Overton to Jackson, January 19, 1815, New York, NY, *New-York Evening Post*, March 22, 1815; Bassett, *Tatum's Journal*, January 1–7, 1814, 123; Account of the Battle of New Orleans, 1815, Jackson Papers, LC; Jackson to Morgan, January 10, 1815, Moser et al., *Papers*, 241.

96. Letter from New Orleans to Philadelphia, January 13, 1815, New York, NY, *New-York Evening Post*, February 8, 1815.

97. M'Lean to Ewing, January 10, 1815, Washington, KY, *Union*, February 3, 1815.

98. Gleig Diary, January 9–17, 1815, Barrett, *85th King's Light Infantry*, 230.

99. Greene, *Chalmette Unit Historic Resource Study*, 185; Morgan to Jackson, January 10, 1815, Neil Auction Catalog, #91; Jackson to Morgan, January 10, 1815, Moser et al., *Papers*, 241.

100. "Sketch of A Tour of Service," Louisville, KY, *Louisville Daily Democrat*, March 23, 1846; Account of the Battle of New Orleans, 1815, Jackson Papers, LC; Dickson, "Journal," January 10, 1815, 71.

101. Gerard, Campaigns, 2, USNA; Tylden Journal, January 11, 1815, NYPL.

102. Surtees, *Rifle Brigade*, 383; Cooper, *Rough Notes*, 134–35; Cooke, *Narrative*, 268–69; Return of Casualties in the Army Under the Command of Major General Lambert between the 9th and 26th Jany near New Orleans, WO 1/141, Kew; Tylden Journal, January 17, 1815, NYPL; "Sketch of

A Tour of Service," Louisville, KY, *Louisville Daily Democrat*, March 23, 1846. "Sketch" is thirty-one years after the fact, of course, but generally reliable. Identification of the 43rd as the regiment hit by the shell is based on the fact that Report of Casualties in the Army . . . between the 9th and 26th Jany (WO 1/141, Kew) shows one man killed and four wounded in the 43rd. Subtracting Lieutenant D'Arcy would leave one man killed and three wounded, which circumstantially argues that they could all have been injured at the same time. There being no action for the 43rd during that period, the most likely source of the injuries is a single shell exploding in the midst of a group.

103. Gerard, Campaigns 2, USNA; Letter by a British staff officer, January 16, 1815, Boston, MA, *Yankee*, May 19, 1815; Tylden Journal, January 15, 1815, NYPL. Surtees, *Rifle Brigade*, 387, later agreed that "it is not an easy matter to reconcile this cautious and timid conduct with their furious onset on the night of the 23d."

104. Memorandum Book, January 9, 1815, Pultney Malcolm Papers, MAL/104, Codrington to Captain Delafons, January 11, 1815, HMS *Tonnant* Letter Book 1, Codrington Papers, COD/6/1, Caird; Dickson, "Journal," January 11–12, 1815, 72, 74; Tylden Journal, January 12, 1815, NYPL.

105. Tylden Journal, January 16, 1815, NYPL; Cooke, *Narrative*, 270; C. Langford to Cochrane, January 16, 1815, Cochrane Papers, NLS; Letter by a British staff officer, January 16, 1815, Boston, MA, *Yankee*, May 19, 1815.

106. R. H. Raymond Smythies, *Historical Records of the 40th (Second Somersetshire) Regiment* (Devonport, UK: A. H. Swiss, 1894), 173–74.

107. Surtees, *Rifle Brigade*, 402.

108. Hynes to Carswell, January 13, 1815, New York, NY, *New-York Commercial Advertiser*, February 8, 1815; Kempe to friend in Natchez, January 9, 1815, Natchez, MS, *Mississippi Republican*, January 16, 1815, in Baltimore, MD, *Baltimore Patriot & Evening Advertiser*, February 4, 1815.

109. Codrington to Jane Codrington, January 1–31, 1815, Codrington Papers, COD/6/2, Caird.

110. Letter from New Orleans, January 13, 1815, Boston, MA, *New-England Palladium*, February 14, 1815; Letter from a member of Beale's company, January 13, 1815, Newport, RI, *Newport Mercury*, February 11, 1815.

111. Reid to Maury, January 13, 1815, Cook Collection, HNOC; Bradford to St. Francisville *Time-Piece*, January 13, 1815, St. Francisville, LA, *Time-Piece*, January 17, 1815.

112. Dickson, "Journal," January 14–15, 1815, 74–75.

113. Tylden Journal, January 15, 1815, NYPL; Letter from New Orleans, January 13, 1815, Philadelphia, PA, *Poulson's American Daily Advertiser*, February 7, 1815.

114. "Lieutenant McKenzie's Reconnaissance on Mobile Bay, January 5–14, 1815," *Tennessee Historical Magazine* 1, no. 1 (March 1915): 69.

115. Gordon to Morgan, January 14, 1815, Parsons Collection, Texas.

116. Washington, DC, *Daily National Intelligencer*, February 16, 1815.

117. Mordecai Diary, April 10, 1815, Mordecai Family Papers, SHC, UNC.

118. Overton to Jackson, January 19, 1815, New York, NY, *New-York Evening Post*, March 22, 1815.

119. Wollstonecraft to Livingston, February 28, 1815, Livingston Papers, Princeton.

120. Tylden Journal, January 12, 1815, NYPL; Dickson, "Journal," January 11, 1815, 71.

121. Tylden Journal, January 15, 1815, NYPL; Dickson, "Journal," January 13, 1815, 72, 74.

122. Dickson, "Journal," January 12, 1815, 73.

123. Codrington to captains of the *Bucephalus* and *Fox*, January 11, 1815, Codrington to captain of the *Alceste*, January 11, 1815, Codrington Papers, COD/6/4, Caird; Cochrane to Croker, January 18, 1815, London, UK, *Courier, and Evening Gazette*, March 10, 1815.

124. Dickson, "Journal," January 16, 1815, 75–76; Michell, "Diary of Major J. Michell," January 12, 15–16, 1815, 129.

125. Gerard, Campaigns 2, USNA.

126. Letter from New Orleans, January 13, 1815, Philadelphia, PA, *Poulson's American Daily Advertiser*, February 7, 1815.

127. Claiborne to Jackson, January 13, 1815, Moser et al., *Papers*, 496.

128. Carroll to Tannahill, January 13, 1815, St. Louis, MO, *Missouri Gazette*, February 11, 1815; Letter from Tennessee officer to friend in Nashville, January 13, 1815, Clinton, OH, *Ohio Register*, February 21, 1815; David Weller to Samuel Weller, January 13, 1815, Weller Family Papers, Filson; Reid to Maury, January 13, 1815, Cook Collection, HNOC.

129. Reid to his father, January 17, 1815, Richmond, VA, *Richmond Enquirer*, February 18, 1815; Bassett, *Tatum's Journal*, January 8, 1815, 134.

130. Account of the Battle of New Orleans, 1815, Jackson Papers, LC; Chotard to Morgan, January 17, 1815, Cook Collection, HNOC; James Dunlap to Henry Chotard, January 17, 1815, Order, January 17, 1815, Cusachs Collection, RG 112, Louisiana Historical Center; Morgan to Alexander La Neuville, January 17, 1815, David Bannister Morgan Papers, Tulane.

131. General order No. 2, January 17, 1815, Order Book of Plauché's Battalion, Parsons Collection, Texas.

132. Gordon to Lydia Gordon, January 9, 1815, Gordon, *Letters and Records*, 218.

133. Ibid.

134. Ibid.; Cochrane to Croker, January 18, 1815, London, UK, *Courier, and Evening Gazette*, March 10, 1815.

135. Cochrane Journal, January 9, 1815, ADM 50/122, Kew; Patterson to Cochrane, January 9, 11, 12, 16, 1815, Captains' Letters, RG 260, NA.

136. Jackson to Lambert, January 11, 1815, Moser et al., *Papers*, 243.

137. Commanding officer of 43rd Foot to Livingston, January 9, 1815, Livingston Papers, Princeton. This communication is puzzling in that it also mentions sending the baggage of Lieutenant D'Arcy, who had not been captured, or if captured he somehow was back in the British camp the night of January 17 to be wounded by Yankee artillery.

138. Smith, *Autobiography of Lieutenant-General Sir Harry Smith*, 245.

139. Tylden Journal, January 17, 1815, NYPL; Provisional Articles, January 17, 1815, Cochrane Papers, NLS.

140. Dickson, "Journal," January 17, 1815, 76–79.

141. Ibid., 76.

142. Ibid., January 18, 1815, 80.

143. Craven P. Luckett to J. Gwathmey, January 20, 1815, Louisville, KY, *Western Courier*, February 9, 1815.

144. "Historical Incidents Before the Battle of New Orleans," New Orleans, LA, *Daily Picayune*, November 14, 1852.

145. Hill, *Recollections*, 2:20–21.

146. Smith, Autobiography of Lieutenant-General Sir Harry Smith, 245.

147. Dickson, "Journal," January 17, 1815, 79–80.

148. Ibid., January 18, 1815, 80–81; Tylden Journal, January 20, 1815, NYPL; Gleig Diary, January 18, 1815, Barrett, *85th King's Light Infantry*, 231. Cannon, *The Royal Fusiliers*, 84, 86, says the 7th stayed behind covering the withdrawal, but multiple journals say it left earlier.

149. Dickson, "Journal," January 18, 1815, 81.

150. Chesterton, *Peace, War, and Adventure*, 212; Patterson to Crowninshield, January 20, 1815, Boston, MA, *Boston Commercial Gazette*, February 27, 1815.

151. Dickson, "Journal," January 17, 1815, 76–79.

152. Ibid., January 18–19, 1815, 80–82; Gubbins to unknown addressee, January 25, 1815, Barrett, *85th King's Light Infantry*, 229.

153. Eisenach, *Travels Through North America*, 2:68.

154. Cooper, *Rough Notes*, 136; Cooke, *Narrative*, 271–72. Cooper suggests that the bugler was drowned but Report of Casualties in the army . . . between the 9th and 26th Jany 1815, WO 1/141, Kew, shows no losses of any kind for the 93rd during this period.

155. Dickson, "Journal," January 18, 1815, 80–82; Cooper, *Rough Notes*, 136–37; Gleig Diary, January 18, 1815, Barrett, *85th King's Light Infantry*, 231.

156. Cooke, *Narrative*, 271–72.

157. Hill, *Recollections*, 2:29–31; Gordon to Lydia Gordon, January 21, 1815, Gordon, *Letters and Records*, 220.

158. Hill, *Recollections*, 2:31–32.

159. Cooke, *Narrative*, 273.

160. Codrington to Jane Codrington, January 18, 22–28, 1815, Codrington Papers, COD/6/2, Caird.

161. Cochrane to Dundas, January 20, 1815, War of 1812 Mss., Lilly Library.

162. Ibid; Cochrane Journal, January 17, 18, 1815, ADM 50/122, Kew.

163. Codrington to Captain Langford, January 25, 1815, HMS *Tonnant* Letter Book 1, Codrington Papers, COD/6/1, Caird.

164. Overton to Morgan, January 17, 1815, Gordon to Morgan, January 18, 1815, Parsons Collection, Texas.

165. Overton to Jackson, January 19, 1815, New York, NY, *New-York Evening Post*, March 22, 1815.
166. Cochrane to Croker, January 18, 1815, London, UK, *Courier, and Evening Gazette*, March 10, 1815.
167. Overton to Jackson, January 19, 1815, New York, *New-York Evening Post*, March 22, 1815. The captain of the bomb ship *Volcano* confirmed that the flotilla had fired 1,000 shells or more at the fort. Dickson, "Journal," January 27, 1815, 83. Butler to Hayes, January 19, 1815, Washington, KY, *Union*, February 17, 1815.
168. W. H. Overton to Jackson, January 19, 1815, New York, NY, *New-York Evening Post*, March 22, 1815.
169. Officer of US army to a friend in Lexington, KY, January 20, 1815, Lexington, NY, *Reporter*, February 13, 1815.

CHAPTER TWENTY-ONE: "THE FINGER OF HEAVEN WAS IN THIS THING"

1. Cochrane to Croker, January 18, 1815, London, UK, *Courier, and Evening Gazette*, March 10, 1815.
2. Letter from New Orleans, January 20, 1815, Wilmington, DE, *American Watchman*, February 18, 1815; Bassett, *Tatum's Journal*, January 8, 1815, 134–35; Joyes Journal, January 19, 1815, Joyes Papers, Filson. The unknown author of "Sketch of A Tour of Service," Louisville, KY, *Louisville Daily Democrat*, March 23, 1846, said that an Irish deserter came to the American camp that morning with the first word of the evacuation. Walker, *Jackson and New Orleans*, 382, wrote in 1856 that Jackson surveyed the enemy camps through his telescope from McCarty's that morning but could not feel certain the British had gone until Humbert took a look and saw a crow flying near one of the visible soldiers. Concluding that no bird would get that close to a living man, Humbert declared that it was a stuffed dummy and that Lambert had departed. Like many of the stories in Walker, this one must be regarded with skepticism, though Cooke, *Narrative*, 271, in 1835 told of British efforts to disguise some artillery under piles of straw to conceal preparations for departure. As with the Walker story, this cannot be corroborated.
3. Robert Butler to Hayes, January 19, 1815, Washington, KY, *Union*, February 17, 1815; Letter from New Orleans, January 20, 1815, Raleigh, NC, *Star*, February 17, 1815.
4. Letter from United States Army officer to a friend in New York, January 20, 1815, New York, NY, *National Advocate*, February 15, 1815.
5. Letter from a woman in New Orleans, February 3, 1815, New London, CT, *Connecticut Gazette*, May 31, 1815.
6. Patterson to Crowninshield, January 20, 1815, Boston, MA, *Boston Commercial Gazette*, February 27, 1815.
7. Jackson to Monroe, January 19, 1815, War of 1812 Collection, Tulane.
8. Jackson to Brown, January 26, 1815, War of 1812 Mss., Lilly Library; Jackson to Winchester, January 19, 1815, Moser et al., *Papers*, 252.
9. Shaumburg to Wilkinson, January 25, 1815, HNOC.
10. Letter from New Orleans to Robertson, January 13, 1815, Washington, DC, *National Intelligencer*, February 7, 1815.
11. Joseph S. Winter to Elisha I. Winter, New Orleans, January 12, 1814 [1815], War of 1812 Collection, Michigan; Holland to his mother, January 20, 1815, New York, NY, *New-York Mercantile Advertiser*, February 16, 1815.
12. Reid to Maury, January 13, 1815, Coffee to Mary Coffee, January 30, 1815, Cook Collection, HNOC; Organ to Mordecai, January 19, 1815, Mordecai Family Papers, SHC, UNC.
13. Duke W. Sumner to Joseph Philips, January 19, 1815, Cook Collection, HNOC.
14. Letter from New Orleans, January 14, 1815, Concord, NH, *New Hampshire Patriot and State Gazette*, February 28, 1815.
15. Letter from Frankfort, KY, February 28, 1815, Richmond, VA, *Virginia Patriot*, March 15, 1815; Letter from New Orleans to a friend in Baltimore, January 21, 1815, Baltimore, MD, *American, and Commercial Daily Advertiser*, February 16, 1815; Letter from New Orleans, January 20, 1815, Raleigh, NC, *Star*, February 17, 1815.
16. Baron to Tureaud, January 13, 1815, Cook Collection, HNOC.
17. Coffee to Mary Coffee, January 20, 1815, Dyas Collection, Tennessee State Library and Archives; Benjamin Morgan to a man in Philadelphia, January 27, 1815, Philadelphia, PA, *True American*, February 25, 1815; Chew to his wife, January 20, 1815, Raleigh, NC, *Star*, February 17, 1815.

18. Jeremiah Lambert to Lambert, January 20, 1815, War of 1812 Mss., Lilly Library.

19. Jackson to Priest at cathedral, January 19, 1815, War of 1812 Collection, Tulane.

20. Unknown writer to his mother in France, March 21, 1815, War of 1812 Collection, Tulane.

21. Richmond, VA, *Richmond Enquirer*, February 15, 1815.

22. Tousard to Stocker, January 9, 1815, HNOC.

23. Letter by a Beale rifleman, January 16, 1815, Boston, MA, *Boston Daily Advertiser*, February 9, 1815; Letter from New Orleans to Robertson, January 13, 1815, Washington, DC, *National Intelligencer*, February 7, 1815; Favrot to Marie-Françoise Favrot, January 21, 1815, Favrot Letters, Tulane; Shaumburg to Wilkinson, January 25, 1815, HNOC.

24. Livingston to Timothy Pickering, April 21, 1828, Livingston Papers, Princeton.

25. New York, NY, *New-York Commercial Advertiser*, March 3, 1815.

26. Chew to his wife, January 20, 1815, Raleigh, NC, *Star*, February 17, 1815; William Rodes to David Thomas, January 20, 1815, Chillicothe, OH, *Weekly Recorder*, February 16, 1815.

27. See, for instance, Letter from New Orleans to Robertson, January 19, 1815, New York, NY, *National Advocate*, February 15, 1815; Robert L. Cobb to John Cobb, February 3, 1815, listing on stamp auctionnetwork.com; Letter from New Orleans to Salem, MA, January 20, 1815, Salem, MA, *Salem Gazette*, February 17, 1815; Thomas to Shelby, February 10, 1815, Frankfort, KY, *Argus of Western America*, March 3, 1815; Letter from New Orleans to a friend in Baltimore, January 21, 1815, Baltimore, MD, *American, and Commercial Daily Advertiser*, February 16, 1815.

28. Coffee to Mary Coffee, January 20, 1815, Dyas Collection of John Coffee Papers, Tennessee State Library and Archives, Nashville.

29. Thomas Hinds to Jackson, January 25, 1815, Moser et al., *Papers*, 256; Account of the Battle of New Orleans, 1815, Jackson Papers, LC.

30. Jackson to Blount, January 27, 1815, New Haven, CT, *Connecticut Herald*, March 21, 1815.

31. General Order, January 20, 1815, Orderly Book of Brigadier General John Coffee, Cook Collection, HNOC; Priestley to Latour, March 4, 1816, Latour Archive, HNOC; Address, January 20, 1815, Lexington, KY, *Reporter*, February 20, 1815; Drafts of "Address to Soldiers," January 21, 1815, Livingston Papers, Princeton; Shaumburg to Wilkinson, January 25, 1815, HNOC.

32. Jackson to Beale, January 20, 1815, Beverly Chew Memoir, New Jersey Historical Society, Newark; Letter from New Orleans, January 20, 1815, Newark, NJ, *Centinel of Freedom*, February 21, 1815.

33. Tylden Journal, January 20, 1815, NYPL; Peddie to William Henry Clinton, January 24, 1815, War of 1812 Collection, Michigan.

34. Lambert to Jackson, January 20, 1815, Moser et al., *Papers*, 253; Thomas Butler to Villeré, January 21, 1815, Villeré Papers, HNOC.

35. Hill, *Recollections*, 2:19–20; Codrington to Captain Langford, January 23, 1815, Codrington to Lockyer, January 24, 1815, Codrington Papers, COD/6/4, Caird.

36. Cooke, *Narrative*, 273–75; Surtees, *Rifle Brigade*, 393; Hill, *Recollections* 2, 32; Gleig Diary, January 19–20, 1815, Barrett, *85th King's Light Infantry*, 231.

37. Dickson, "Journal," January 20, 1815, 83; Gleig Diary, January 20, 1815, Barrett, *85th King's Light Infantry*, 231; Tylden Journal, January 20, 1815, NYPL; Peddie to William Henry Clinton, January 24, 1815, War of 1812 Collection, Michigan.

38. Benjamin Morgan to a man in Philadelphia, January 27, 1815, Philadelphia, PA, *True American*, February 25, 1815; Letter from New Orleans to Editor of the *Philadelphia Gazette*, January 27, 1815, Wilmington, DE, *American Watchman*, February 25, 1815; Letter from one of Beale's riflemen to New York, January 27, 1815, Boston, MA, *Boston Commercial Gazette*, February 27, 1815.

39. Tylden Journal, January 22–23, 1815, NYPL.

40. Ibid., January 24–25, 1815, NYPL.

41. Ibid., January 23, 1815, NYPL.

42. Chesterton, *Peace, War, and Adventure*, 217.

43. Surtees, *Rifle Brigade*, 393.

44. Hill, *Recollections*, 2:39–40.

45. Dickson, "Journal," January 27, 1815, 83; Malcolm to Cochrane, January 28, 1815, Malcolm Papers, MAL/2, Caird.

46. Tylden Journal, January 26, 1815, NYPL.

47. Joyes Journal, January 21, 1815, Joyes Papers, Filson.

48. Bassett, *Tatum's Journal*, January 20, 1815, 135–36; Letter from New Orleans to Wilmington, DE, January 28, 1815, Hallowell, ME, *American Advocate*, March 4, 1815.

49. Letter from gentleman in New Orleans to his brother in Fredericksburg, VA, January 26, 1815, New Haven, CT, *Connecticut Journal*, March 13, 1815; Tylden Journal, January 23, 1815, NYPL.

50. Bassett, *Tatum's Journal*, January 8, 1815, 133; Shields and Morrell to Patterson, January 14, 1814, Captains' Letters, RG 260, NA.

51. Bassett, *Tatum's Journal*, January 8, 1815, 133–34.

52. Patterson to Crowninshield, January 27, 1815, Worcester, MA, *National Aegis*, March 1, 1815.

53. Shields to Editor of Baltimore *Register*, January 17, 1815, Richmond, VA, *Richmond Enquirer*, March 1, 1815.

54. Richard Cannon, comp., *Historical Record of the Fourteenth, or the King's Regiment of Light Dragoons* (London: Parker, Furnivall, & Parker, 1847), 52; List of Prisoners captured by U.S. Naval Forces on 19th Jany 1815, Cochrane Papers, NLS; Surtees, *Rifle Brigade*, 395; Gerard, Campaigns 2, USNA; Lambert to Bathurst, January 29, 1815, WO 1/141, Kew; Bowlby, *Memoir*, 55.

55. Claiborne to Jackson, January 20, 1815, Moser et al., *Papers*, 500.

56. Shields to Patterson, January 25, 1815, Worcester, MA, *National Aegis*, March 1, 1815; William V. Morris to brother [probably James Morris], January 28, 1815, Washington, KY, *Union*, March 3, 1815. Hill (*Recollections*, 2:48–51) told a garbled version of this episode in which some of his prisoners surprised Shields and threw him overboard while overpowering his crew, then hauled him back aboard and tied him and his crew back-to-back.

57. Patterson to Cochrane, January 23, 25, 29, 1815, Richard Tankersley to Cochrane, February 22, 1815, Captains' Letters, RG 260, NA; Cochrane Journal, January 25–26, 29, 1815, ADM 50/122, Kew; Joyes Journal, February 27, 1815, Joyes Papers, Filson.

58. Receipt for 57 Prisoners of War Discharged from His Majesty's Ship *Tonnant*, January 30, 1815, Cochrane Papers, NLS; Patterson to Benjamin Crowninshield, March 3, 1815, Captains' Letters, RG 260, NA.

59. Gray to Graham, February 8, 1815, Dispatches from the U. S. Consul in Havana, RG 59, NA.

60. Joyes Journal, March 7, 1815, Joyes Papers, Filson; Cochrane to Patterson, January 30, 1815, Captains' Letters, RG 260, NA; Wollstonecraft to Jackson, February 20, 1815, Jackson Papers, LC.

61. Jonathan D. Ferris to Cochrane, January 26, 1815, Cochrane Papers, NLS; Codrington to Respective officers and seamen employed at the Capture of the Gun Vessels, January 18, 1815, Codrington Papers, COD/6/4, Caird.

62. Codrington to Jane Codrington, January 1–31, 1815, Codrington Papers, COD/6/2, Caird.

63. Jackson to Hays, February 4, 1815, Moser et al., *Papers*, 269, Keane to Jackson, February 8, 1815, 256; Jackson to Keane, February 4, 1815, Bassett, *Correspondence*, 2:447; Peoria, IL, *Peoria Democratic Press*, March 16, 1842.

64. Rodes to Thomson, January 20, 1815, Winchester, KY, *Winchester Advertiser*, February 11, 1815.

65. Robert Butler to Colonel Hays, January 19, 1815, Williamsburg, OH, *Western American*, February 25, 1815; Jackson to Winchester, January 19, 1815, Moser et al. *Papers*, 252; Letter from New Orleans, January 26, 1815, Richmond, VA, *Richmond Enquirer*, March 1, 1815; Letter from gentleman in New Orleans to his brother in Fredericksburg, VA, January 26, 1815, New Haven, CT, *Connecticut Journal*, March 13, 1815; Jackson to Winchester, January 31, 1815, Moser et al., *Papers*, 261–62.

66. Cochrane to Dundas, January 20, 1815, War of 1812 Mss., Lilly Library.

67. New York, NY, *Columbian*, June 19, 1815.

68. Codrington to Jane Codrington, January 22–28, 1815, Codrington Papers, COD/6/2, Caird.

69. "*Tonnant* Surveys &c," Passages Ordered, January 24, 29, 1815, COD/6/2, Caird.

70. John R. Mascall to Messrs. Cox & Son, January 27, 1815, lot 12 in New York 2016 catalog of Schuyler J. Rumsey Public Auction No. 68, June 1, 2016, (San Francisco: Schuyler J. Rumsey, 2016), 14.

71. Gubbins to unknown addressee, January 25, 1815, Barrett, *85th King's Light Infantry*, 228.

72. "*Tonnant* Surveys &c," Passages Ordered, Codrington Papers, COD/6/2, Codrington to Captain Lloyd, January 23, 1815, Codrington Papers, COD/6/4, Caird.

73. Memorandum Book, January 27–28, 1815 Pultney Malcolm Papers, MAL/104, Caird; Tylden Journal, January 28, 30, 1815, NYPL.

74. Gordon to Lydia Gordon, January 25, 1815, Gordon, *Letters and Records*, 220.

75. Hill, *Recollections*, 2:43.

76. Gerard, Campaigns 2, USNA.

77. Gleig Diary, January 27–31, 1815, Barrett, *85th King's Light Infantry*, 232.

78. John Michell to Jane Michell, January 22, 1815, HNOC.

79. Cooper, *Rough Notes*, 136.

80. Cannon, *The Royal Fusiliers*, 84; Letter from New Orleans, February 15, 1815, Portland, ME, *Eastern Argus*, March 23, 1815. No confirmation of this has been found. It may be worthy of note that Return of Casualties in the Army Under the Command of Major General Lambert between the 9th and 26th of Jany, WO1/141, Kew, shows no casualties of any kind for the 7th, and no missing at all. However, this report may be incomplete.

81. Gould Memoir, VHS.

82. The complete poem or song appears in Ellery's hand in Abraham Redwood Ellery Account of the Battle of New Orleans, NYPL. The earliest extant complete printing of Ellery's poem is in the New York, NY, *New-York Herald*, March 25, 1815, which said it was copied from the "*New-Orleans Gazette.*" It appeared in garbled versions in several other papers thereafter, including Troy, NY, *Farmer's Register*, April 4, 1815, and Easton, MD, *Republican Star*, April 4, 1815.

83. Simpson to Mary Simpson, January 30, 1815, Simpson Letters, Princeton.

84. Letter from New Orleans to Versailles, KY, January 27, 1815, Lexington, KY, *Reporter*, February 20, 1815; Letter from a woman in New Orleans, February 3, 1815, New London, CT, *Connecticut Gazette*, May 31, 1815; Marietta, OH, *American Friend*, March 10, 1815; Letter from New Orleans to Wilmington, DE, January 28, 1815, Hallowell, ME, *American Advocate*, March 4, 1815.

85. Simpson to Mary Simpson, January 30, 1815, Simpson Letters, Princeton; Joyes Journal, January 24, 1815, Joyes Papers, Filson.

86. Lewis Livingston to Mrs. Montgomery, February 2, 1815, Hunt, *Life of Edward Livingston*, 201.

87. Letter from New Orleans to Editor of the *Philadelphia Gazette*, January 27, 1815, Wilmington, DE, *American Watchman*, February 25, 1815.

88. Shaumburg to Wilkinson, January 25, 1815, HNOC.

89. Florian to Roosevelt, January 9, 1815, HNOC.

90. Jackson to Girod, January 27, 1815, Jackson Collection, HNOC.

91. Josiah Johnston to Morgan, January 27, 1815, Parsons Collection, Texas.

92. Jackson to Brown, January 26, 1815, War of 1812 Mss., Lilly Library; Jackson to Blount, January 27, 1815, New Haven, CT, *Connecticut Herald*, March 21, 1815.

93. Smith, Corsey & Co. of New Orleans to Smith, Corsey & Co. of Boston, February 4, 1815, Boston, MA, *Boston Weekly Messenger*, March 10, 1815; Letter from New Orleans, February 3, 1815, Petersburg, VA, *Petersburg Daily Courier*, March 7, 1815; Letter from New Orleans, February 14, 1815, Washington, KY, *Union*, March 10, 1815.

94. Sumner to Philips, January 19, 1815, Cook Collection, HNOC; Tousard to Stocker, January 20, 1815, Wilkinson, "Assaults on New Orleans," 51; John Palfrey to Edward Palfrey, January 19, 1815, Gatell, "Boston Boy in 'Mr. Madison's War,'" 157.

95. Jackson to Hayne, January 25, 1815, Richmond, VA, *Virginia Patriot*, March 18, 1815; Jackson to Monroe, January 25, 1815, Moser et al., *Papers*, 255; Greene, *Chalmette Unit Historic Resource Study*, 136; Reynolds to Morgan, January 30, 1815, Parsons Collection, Texas; Reid to Tatum and Latour, January 27, 1815, Jackson Papers, LC.

96. Morgan to Captain Perrie, January 25, 1815, Parsons Collection, Texas; General Orders, February 1, 1815, Order Book, Louisiana Militia, RG 107, Louisiana Historical Center; General Orders, February 10, 1815, Coffee Order Book, SHC, UNC.

97. Jackson address to review of army, February 2, 1815, Lexington, KY, *Reporter*, March 17, 1815; New Orleans Rifleman to friend in Washington, February 3, 1815, Washington, DC, *Daily National Intelligencer*, March 2, 1815; Letter from New Orleans to Washington, February 3, 1815, Burlington, VT, *Vermont Centinel*, March 24, 1815; Boston, MA, *Boston Patriot*, March 18, 1815; Robert L. Cobb to John Cobb, February 3, 1815, Cobb Letters, HNOC; Joyes Journal, February 2, 1815, Joyes Papers, Filson.

98. Jackson to Brown, February 4, 1815, War of 1812 Mss., Lilly Library; Jackson to Monroe, February 13, 1815, Daniel Parker Papers, HSP.

99. General Order, February 15, 1815, Orderly Book of Brigadier General John Coffee, Cook Collection, HNOC; Hopkins to Villeré, February 3, 1815, Villeré Papers, HNOC; Butler to Morgan, General Order, February 13, 1815, Neil Louisiana Purchase Auction, # 120; General Order No. 10, February 13, 1815, Order Book of Plauché's Battalion, Parsons Collection, Texas.

100. Jackson to Monroe, February 13, 1815, Parker Papers, HSP.

101. Robert Hays to Jackson, December 20, 1814, Moser et al., *Papers*, 213.

102. James Jackson to Jackson, January 13, 1815, ibid., 245, January 26, 1815, 260.

103. Jackson to Hays, February 17, 1815, ibid., 281; Nolte, *Memoirs*, 238.

104. Jackson to Livingston, May 17, 1815, Livingston Papers, Princeton; Nolte, *Memoirs*, 238–39; Wollstonecraft to Rachel Jackson, May 5, 1815, Jackson Papers, LC; Gould Memoir, VHS.

105. Wollstonecraft to Livingston, January, February 27, 1815, Livingston Papers.

106. Letter from New Orleans, January 9, 1815, Wilkes-Barre, PA, *Susquehanna Democrat*, February 17, 1815.

107. Shields to Editor of *Baltimore Weekly Register*, January 17, 1815, Richmond, VA, *Richmond Enquirer*, March 1, 1815.

108. Johnston to Madison, January 19, 1815, Dolley Madison Digital Edition.

109. Tousard to Stocker, January 20, 1815, Wilkinson, "Assaults on New Orleans," 52.

110. Letter from New Orleans, January 20, 1815, Wilmington, DE, *American Watchman*, February 18, 1815; Officer of United States Army to a friend in Lexington, KY, January 20, 1815, Lexington, KY, *Reporter*, February 13, 1815.

111. Letter to the Editor, January 20, 1815, Philadelphia, PA, *Relf's Philadelphia Gazette, and Daily Advertiser*, February 15, 1815.

112. Poindexter to Editors Isler and M'Curdy of the Natchez, MS, *Mississippi Republican*, January 20, 1815, in Nashville, TN, *Nashville Whig*, January 31, 1815. This is the earliest extant version of the Poindexter letter, which would later be edited in other papers. Perhaps because it reached the eastern press first, Poindexter's January 20 letter got the most circulation. Federalist papers denounced it as a fabrication designed to boost popularity for Madison's administration for saving Louisiana's ladies. Far from falsifying anything—excepting perhaps his field service with Hinds—he merely repeated what others said before him. In 1870, William Henry Sparks stated, citing no authority, that either a negro or a soldier found a note with the countersign "Beauty and booty" on a note on the battlefield and took it to Poindexter. Poindexter said nothing himself of such a detail. Sparks, *Memories of Fifty Years*, 339.

113. Letter from New Orleans to a friend in Baltimore, January 21, 1815, Baltimore, MD, *American, and Commercial Daily Advertiser*, February 16, 1815.

114. Benjamin Morgan to friend in Philadelphia, January 27, 1815, Wilmington, DE, *American Watchman*, March 1, 1815.

115. London, UK, *Cobbett's Weekly Political Register*, September 23, 1815; William Cobbett, *Life of Andrew Jackson, President of the United States of America* (London: Mills, Jewett, and Mills, 1834), 67–68.

116. Address, January 20, 1815, Lexington, KY, *Reporter*, February 20, 1815.

117. Claiborne to Jackson, February 6, 1815, Order Book, Louisiana Militia, RG 107, Louisiana Historical Center. Claiborne was speaking specifically of plunder in slaves.

118. Account of Military Operations Terminating with the Battle of New Orleans, ca. 1815, Livingston Papers, Princeton.

119. New Haven, CT, *Connecticut Herald*, May 2, 1815.

120. Statement of Lambert, Keane, Thornton, Blakeney, and Dickson, 1833, Hallowell, ME, *Hallowell Gazette*, March 29, 1815.

121. Keene, NH, *New-Hampshire Sentinel*, September 18, 1844; "Recollections of the Expedition," (July) part 4, 350.

122. Lexington, KY, *Reporter*, April 5, 1815. Latour would repeat the "Beauty and Booty" claims in his 1816 *Historical Memoir*, as would Reid and Eaton in their 1817 biography of Jackson, and Eaton again in his 1824 revision.

123. Cochrane Journal, January 17, 1815, ADM 50/122, Kew.

124. Thomas Cochrane to Pigot, February 12, 1815, Philadelphia, PA, *Relf's Philadelphia Gazette, and Daily Advertiser*, March 30, 1815.

125. Mr. Swainson to Lieutenant Douglass, February 9, 1815, ibid., March 30, 1815, J. Gallon to J. O'Reilly, February 9, 1815, J. R. Glover to Captain Westfall, February 1, 1815.

126. Cockburn to Captain Evans, February 11, 1815, ibid., March 30, 1815.

127. London, UK, *Correspondent and Public Cause*, March 22, 1815.

128. Dickson, "Journal," January 28, 1815, 83.

129. Lambert to Bathurst, January 29, February 14, 1815, WO 1/141, Kew.

130. Gray to Graham, February 8, 1815, Dispatches from the U. S. Consul in Havana, RG 59, NA; Lambert to Bathurst, January 29, 1815, aboard *Tonnant*, WO 1/141, Kew.

131. Jackson to Winchester, January 10, 1815, Moser et al., *Papers*, 242.

132. Tylden Journal, February 1, 1815, NYPL.

133. Cochrane to Lambert, February 3, 1815, WO 1/143, Kew.

134. Codrington to Jane Codrington, February 2–10, 1815, Codrington Papers, COD/6/2, Caird.

135. Ibid.

136. Tylden Journal, February 5, 1815, NYPL.

137. Francis Newman to the commander of the British Cartel Vessel, February 1, 1815, Cook Collection, HNOC.

Chapter Twenty-Two: "Rescued Is *Orleans* from the English wolves"

1. New York, NY, *New-York Commercial Advertiser*, January 16, 25, 1815; Boston, MA, *Repertory*, February 2, 1815.

2. Baltimore, MD, *Federal Gazette*, January 24, 1815; Frances Smith to Mary Campbell, February 8, 1815, Campbell Family Papers, Duke University, Durham, NC.

3. Providence, RI, *Rhode-Island American, and General Advertiser*, January 20, 1815.

4. Washington, Mississippi Territory, *Washington Republican*, January 25, 1815. No copy of the *Mississippi Republican* extra seems to have survived, but it is referenced frequently on its receipt in other newspapers, and the republication of the Kempe and Henderson letters and nothing else virtually guarantees that nothing more than those two letters appeared in the Natchez extra.

5. Fort Jackson stood near modern Wetumpka, Alabama, Fort Decatur near Milstead, Alabama, and Fort Hawkins at modern Macon, Georgia.

6. Claiborne, *Gen. Sam. Dale*, 151–52, 154.

7. A. B. Fannin to Early, January 29, 1815, Charleston, SC, *City Gazette*, February 8, 1815.

8. Claiborne, *Gen. Sam. Dale*, 156, 162–65; Adam G. Saffold to a friend in Augusta, January 27, 1815, Augusta, GA, *Augusta Herald*, February 9, 1815.

9. Richmond, VA, *Richmond Enquirer* extra, January 28, 1815; John Campbell to David Campbell, January 21, 1815, Campbell Family Papers, Duke.

10. Romford to Monroe, February 4, 1815, Washington, DC, *National Intelligencer*, February 16, 1815.

11. Blount to Hynes, February 6, 1815, Hynes Papers, HNOC; Unsigned to David Porter, February 7, 1815, Parsons Collection, Texas.

12. D. B. Lyles to James Cox, February 13, 1815, Cook Collection, HNOC.

13. New York, NY, *New-York Gazette & General Advertiser*, February 9, 1815; Philadelphia, PA, *Relf's Philadelphia Gazette, and Daily Advertiser*, February 17, 1815.

14. Binns, *Recollections*, 243; Baltimore, MD, *Niles' Weekly Register*, February 11, 1815.

15. Florian to Roosevelt, January 9, 1815, HNOC.

16. Monroe to Jackson, February 5, 1815, Jackson Papers, LC.

17. Mary H. Campbell to?, January 20, 1815, Campbell Family Papers, Duke.

18. Stokely to Jackson, February 13, 1815, Moser et al., *Papers*, 277–78.

19. Winchester, UK, *Hampshire Chronicle; or, South and West of England Pilot*, February 27, 1815; London, UK, *Public Ledger and Daily Advertiser*, February 21, 1815; Kingston, *Jamaica, Royal Gazette*, quoted in De Grummond, "Platter of Glory," 333, with no date; Edinburgh, UK, *Caledonian Mercury*, February 23, 1815; Dublin, IR, *Saunders's News-Letter, and Daily Advertiser*, March 4, 1815; Leicester, UK, *Leicester Journal, and Midland Counties General Advertiser*, February 24, 1815.

20. Montreal, Canada, *Montreal Herald*, February 21, 1815.

21. Nottingham, UK, *Nottingham Gazette, and Political, Literary, Agricultural & Commercial Register for the Midland Counties*, March 10, 1815.

22. Lexington, KY, *Reporter*, May 17, 1815.

23. "Expedition Against New Orleans," WO 1/142, Kew.

24. London, UK, *Morning Chronicle*, March 3, 9, 1815; London, UK, *Bell's Weekly Messenger*, March 12, 1815.

25. Wellington to Earl of Longford, May 22, 1815, "Letter of the Duke of Wellington (May 22, 1815) on the Battle of New Orleans," 5–10.

26. Catherine Sara Dorothea, Duchess of Wellington, to unknown recipient, January 30, 1815, second letter undated [February 1815], Cook Collection, HNOC.

27. William Cobbett to Earl of Liverpool, March 20, 1815, William Cobbett, *Letters on the Late War Between the United States and Great Britain: Together with Other Miscellaneous Writings, on the Same Subject* (New York: J. Belden, 1815), 400.

28. London, UK, *Bell's Weekly Messenger*, January 22, 1815.

29. Bowden lists 317 dating from Jackson's arrival to take command, and there are many more in the press that she did not find, not to mention the files of many newspapers that have disappeared completely since 1815.

30. William A. Dill, "Growth of Newspapers in the United States," (master's thesis, University of Oregon, Eugene, 1908), 11, 24.

31. St. George's, *Bermuda, Bermuda Gazette, and Weekly Advertiser*, April 15, 22, 1815.

32. Cochrane Journal, February 6, 1815, ADM 50/122, Kew; Tylden Journal, February 7, 1815, NYPL.

33. Gleig, *Narrative*, 356–57; Gerard, Campaigns 2, USNA.

34. Return of the American Garrison in Fort Bowyer, February 17, 1815, WO 1/141, Kew; Gerard, Campaigns 2, USNA.

35. Jackson to Winchester, January 19, 1815, Moser et al., *Papers*, 252.

36. Gerard, Campaigns 2, USNA.

37. Lambert to Bathurst February 25, 1815, WO 1/141, Cochrane to Lambert, February 3, 1815, WO 1/143, Kew.

38. Codrington to Jane Codrington, February 2–10, 1815, Codrington Papers, COD/6/2, Caird.

39. Cochrane to Lambert, February 17, 1815, WO 1/143, Kew.

40. Tylden Journal, February 13, 1815, NYPL; Smith, *Autobiography of Lieutenant-General Sir Harry Smith*, 251.

41. Codrington to Jane Codrington, February 11–15, 1815, Codrington Papers, COD/6/2, Caird.

42. Malcolm Journal, MAL 104, Caird; Cochrane to Pultney Malcolm, February 17, 1815, WO 1/143, Kew; Malcolm to Cochrane, March 13, 1815, Cochrane Papers, NLS.

43. Deposition of Colonel Maunsel White, November 26, 1824, Depositions concerning slaves liberated by British forces after the Battle of New Orleans, HNOC; Livingston to Cochrane, February 9, 1815, Cochrane Papers, NLS; Livingston to Cochrane, February 9, 1815, Cochrane to Livingston, February 9, 1815, Livingston Papers, Princeton.

44. Speech by Davezac, Peoria, IL, *Peoria Democratic Press*, March 16, 1842; Statement of Bartholomew McCaferty, May 19, 1821, Depositions concerning slaves liberated by British forces after the Battle of New Orleans, HNOC.

45. Letter from New Orleans, February 28, 1815, Warren, RI, *Telescope*, March 25, 1815; Deposition of Colonel Maunsel White, November 26, 1824, Depositions concerning slaves liberated by British forces after the Battle of New Orleans, HNOC.

46. Lambert to Jackson, February 27, 1815, Moser et al., *Papers*, 290.

47. Cochrane to Pultney Malcolm, February 17, 1815, WO 1/143, Kew.

48. Ritchie, "Louisiana Campaign," 91.

49. Letter from New Orleans, April 4, 1815, Louisville, KY, *Western Courier*, June 1, 1815; John Power to Claiborne, March 30, 1815, Rowland, *Letter Books*, 6:353–54. Twenty New Orleans planters lost at least 160 slaves valued at more than $170,000, Villeré alone missing 57 worth $52,800 (Assorted statements by planters in Depositions concerning slaves liberated by British forces after the Battle of New Orleans, HNOC).

50. Ritchie, "Louisiana Campaign," 91.

51. Note Announcing Peace Treaty in Ghent, February 19, 1815, HNOC; Joyes Journal, February 19, 1815, Joyes Papers, Filson.

52. Jackson to soldiers and citizens, February 19, 1815, Lexington, KY, *Reporter*, March 17, 1815; Joyes Journal, February 21, 1815, Joyes Papers, Filson; John Reed [sic] to Godwin B. Cotton, February 21, 1815, New York, NY, *New-York Spectator*, March 29, 1815.

53. William B. Fort to Abraham Fort, February 24, 1815, Cook Collection, HNOC; Jackson to Philemon Thomas, March 4, 1815, Moser et al., *Papers*, 297.

54. Washington, DC, *United States' Telegraph*, December 5, 1826.

55. Kenner to Minor, March 10, 1815, Kenner Papers, LSU; Warshauer, "Jackson and Martial Law," 282.

56. Philip Barton Key to Livingston, February 15, 1815, Livingston Papers, Princeton.

57. Thomas Jefferson to William H. Crawford, February 14–26, 1815, Raab Collection Online Catalog, July 2016; Jefferson to Henry Dearborn, March 17, 1815, J. Jefferson Looney, ed., *The Papers of Thomas Jefferson: Retirement Series, vol. 8, 1 October 1814 to 31 August 1815* (Princeton, NJ: Princeton University Press, 2011), 357–58; Jefferson to Charles Clay, February 21, 1815, Jefferson Papers, Special Collections, University of Virginia, Charlottesville.

58. William Gaston to Editor of the Newbern, NC, *Federal Republican*, February 19, 1815, Burlington, VT, *Burlington Gazette*, March 31, 1815.

59. George Hay to Monroe, February 15, 1815, Monroe Papers, LC.

60. Bathurst to Baker, March 21, 1815, FO 5/106, Kew.

61. Joyes Journal, March 13, 1815, Joyes Papers, Filson; General Orders, March 13, 1815, Order Book, Louisiana Militia, RG 107, Louisiana Historical Center.

62. Receipts, February—, February 28, March 10, 1815, Quartermaster return, January 1815, Receipt for 8 muskets, January 28, 1815, Lewis Stirling and Family Papers, LSU; Coffee to Col. W. Piatt, February 22, 1815, Brigade Order, February 26, 1815, General Orders, February 27, 1815, Coffee Order Book, SHC, UNC; Division Orders, February 14, 1815, Joyes Order Book, Joyes Family Papers, Filson.

63. Abraham Spears to brother in Kentucky, January 9, 1815, Paris, KY, *Western Citizen*, February 4, 1815.

64. Report of the Managers of the Louisiana Bible Society, New Orleans, LA, *Louisiana Gazette for the Country*, April 25, 1815.

65. James Moore King to Jeanette Moore King, March 16, 1815, King Papers, Middle Tennessee State University, Murfreesboro.

66. Hopkins to Villeré, January 29, 1815, Villeré Papers, HNOC; George Foster to Editor, Lexington *Reporter*, February 3, 1815, Lexington, KY, *Reporter*, March 13, 1815.

67. Hynes to Blount, February 3, 1815, Lexington, KY, *Reporter*, March 13, 1815; Robert Cobb to John Cobb, February 3, 1815, Cobb Letters concerning the Battle of New Orleans, HNOC.

68. Thomas to Shelby, February 10, 1815, Frankfort, KY, *Argus of Western America*, March 3, 1815; Boston, MA, *New-England Palladium*, March 21, 1815.

69. Receipts February 3, 28, March 6, 1815, Lewis Stirling and Family Papers, LSU.

70. John McHugh to "Dear Partner," February 12, 1815, Miscellaneous Collection, RG 68, Louisiana Historical Center.

71. Priestley to Latour, March 4, 1816, Latour Archive, HNOC.

72. Nashville, TN, *Nashville Whig*, April 18, 1815. The general field hospital had mass graves with the dead from both New Orleans volunteers and the regulars. Since Hurricane Katrina severely eroded the ground in 2005, New Orleans–made uniform buttons from several regiments have been found on the site, which in 1834 became Jackson Barracks.

73. New Orleans, LA, *Daily Delta*, July 8, 1852; Joyes Journal, February 28, 1815, Joyes Papers, Filson; A. Chotard to Claiborne, February 17, 1815, General Orders, March 3, 1815, Order Book, Louisiana Militia, RG 107, Louisiana Historical Center; Decision of the Court Martial in the Case of Major Villeré, March 13, 1815, Philadelphia, PA, *Weekly Aurora*, May 2, 1815.

74. Jackson to troops stationed on the right bank of the Mississippi, January 18, 1815, War of 1812 Mss., Lilly Library; Baron to Tureaud, January 13, 1815, Cook Collection, HNOC; Gabriel Winter to William Willis, January 12, 1815, Willis Family Papers, LSU; Nixon, "An Account of the Battle of New Orleans," Miscellaneous Collection, RG 68, Louisiana Historical Center.

75. Tully Robinson to Morgan, January 14, 1815, General Order No. 7, February 4, 1815, General Order No. 12, February 19, 1815, Order Book of Plauché's Battalion, Morgan to Jackson, January 21, 26, 1815, Parsons Collection, Texas; General Orders, February 4, 1815, Coffee Order Book, SHC, UNC; Morgan to Arnaud, January 14, 1815, Cusachs Collection RG 112, Louisiana Historical Center; Claiborne to Jackson, February 8, 1815, Moser, *Papers*, 274. General Orders, February 19, 1815, Joyes Order Book, Joyes Family Papers, Filson; Quisenberry, *Kentucky in the War of 1812*, 147.

76. Shaumburg to Wilkinson, January 25, 1815, HNOC; General Order No 3, January 19, 1815, General Order No. 5, January 22, 1815, Order Book of Plauché's Battalion, Parsons Collection, Texas;

Henry D. Peire Report, February 17, 1815, Miscellaneous Collection, LSU; Davezac to Ross, February 6, 1822, Cook Collection, Orderly Book of Brigadier General John Coffee, HNOC.

77. Jackson to troops stationed on the right bank of the Mississippi, January 18, 1815, War of 1812 Mss., Lilly Library; Warshauer, "Jackson and Martial Law," 276; Morgan to Captain F. Penne, January 30, 1815, Morgan Papers, LC; William Knox to Morgan, January 25, 1815, Parsons Collection, Texas; John Thompson to Rees, January 28, 1815, Rees Papers, Tulane; Butler to Villeré, January 20, 1815, Villeré Papers, HNOC.

78. Jackson to John Thomas, February 10, 1815, Moser et al., *Papers*, 275; Butler to Morgan, January 11, 1815, unknown to Morgan, January 13, 1815, Morgan Papers, LC; Morgan to Jackson, January 13, 1815, Parsons Collection, Texas; Account of the Battle of New Orleans, 1815, Jackson Papers, LC.

79. Robert McCausland to Jackson, February 24 [25], 1815, Moser et al., *Papers*, 287, John Wright to Jackson, March 3, 1815, 295; *Arrest and Trial of E. Louis Louaillier*, 11–12.

80. Warshauer, "Jackson and Martial Law," 276–77; General Orders No. 7, February 26, 1815, Order Book of Plauché's Battalion, Parsons Collection, Texas; Citizens of Louisiana to Jackson, February 27, 1815, Moser et al., *Papers*, 291.

81. Jackson to Winchester, January 31, 1815, Winchester Papers, Tennessee Historical Society; Jackson to Monroe, February 13, 1815, Parker Papers, HSP; Letter from officer on the *Enterprise* to its owners, January 20, 1815, Brownsville, PA, *American Telegraph*, February 22, 1815; Monroe to Jackson, February 5, 1815, Jackson Papers, Chotard to Morgan, February 8, 1815, Morgan Papers, LC; Jackson to Holmes, January 18, 1815, Moser et al., *Papers*, 250.

82. Jackson to Monroe, February 13, 1815, Parker Papers, HSP.

83. James A. Hamilton, *Reminiscences of James A. Hamilton; or, Men and Events, at Home and Abroad, During Three Quarters of a Century* (New York: Charles Scribner, 1869), 69. The statement certainly has the ring of Jackson about it, but it must be remembered that Hamilton's was a 40-year-old recollection.

84. *Appeal of L. Louaillier*, 5–6; Charbonnier to Jackson, January 22, 1815, Jackson Papers, LC; Pierre Charbonnier to Livingston, January 25, 1815, Livingston Papers, Princeton.

85. Roland C. McConnell, *Negro Troops of Antebellum Louisiana: A History of the Battalion of Free Men of Color* (Baton Rouge: Louisiana State University Press, 1968), 90; Joshua Baker to Jackson, February 2, 1815, Moser et al., *Papers*, 264; Lewis Livingston to Villeré, January 9, 1815, Villeré Papers, HNOC; Order Book, Louisiana Militia, RG 107, Louisiana Historical Center; Morgan to Captain F. Penne, January 30, 1815, Morgan Papers, LC.

86. Morgan to Livingston, January 16, 1815, David Bannister Morgan Papers, LSU; Louisiana General Assembly Resolution, February 1, 1815, Baltimore, MD, *Baltimore Telegraph*, March 16, 1815; Joseph Savary et al. to Jackson, March 16, 1815, Moser et al., *Papers*, 315; Claiborne to Jackson, February 16, 1815, Order Book, Louisiana Militia, RG 107, Louisiana Historical Center.

87. Jackson to Claiborne, January 17, 1815, Moser, *Papers*, 246–47.

88. Claiborne to Shaumburg, October 1, 1815, Rowland, *Letter Books*, 6:373.

89. Morgan to Claiborne, January 14, 1815, Robert Butler to Morgan, January 18, 1815, Morgan Papers, Tulane; Morgan to Jackson, January 14, 1815, Moser et al., *Papers*, 246.

90. Jackson to Claiborne, January 18, 1815, Moser et al., *Papers*, 248.

91. Favrot to Marie-Françoise Gerard Favrot, January 21, 1815, Favrot Letters, Tulane.

92. Jackson to Unknown, March 31, 1815, Moser et al., *Papers*, 338; Account of the Battle of New Orleans, 1815, Jackson Papers, LC; Hatfield, *Claiborne*, 419–21; Bassett, Correspondence 2, 202–3; Jackson to Claiborne, January 18, 1815, Moser et al., *Papers*, 248, Private Journal, 249.

93. John McHugh to "Dear Partner," February 12, 1815, Miscellaneous Collection, RG 68, Louisiana Historical Center; Division Orders, February 21, 1815, Joyes Order Book, Joyes Family Papers, Filson; Claiborne to Jackson, January 31, 1815, Moser et al., *Papers*, 263, February 24, 1815, 286; Tregle, "Andrew Jackson and the Continuing Battle of New Orleans," 6, JELAC.

94. Claiborne to Jackson, February 3, 1815, Moser et al., *Papers*, 267.

95. Claiborne to Stephen Marerceau, February 24, 1815, Rowland, *Letter Books*, 6:338–39, Circular, February 1815, 347, Claiborne to Monroe, March 2, 1815, 349.

96. Diego Morphy to Jackson, February 17, 1815, Moser et al., *Papers*, 282.

97. Warshauer, "Jackson and Martial Law," 277–78; General Orders, February 28, 1815, Order Book, Louisiana Militia, RG 107, Louisiana Historical Center.

98. Letter from New Orleans March 10, 1815, New Haven, CT, *Connecticut Journal*, April 17, 1815; *Appeal of L. Louaillier*, 10. Though the parish court did reopen, Judge Hall's federal court remained in recess until February 20. John Randolph Grymes to Jackson, February 15, 1843, Jackson Papers, LC.

99. New Orleans, LA, *L'Ami des Lois*, April 4, 1815; *Appeal of L. Louaillier*, 7–13.

100. Letter from New Orleans, March 10, 1815, New Haven, CT, *Connecticut Journal*, April 17, 1815.

101. Ibid.; Warshauer, "Jackson and Martial Law," 273–74; Padgett, "Andrew Jackson in New Orleans," 370.

102. Citizens of Louisiana to Jackson, February 27, 1815, Moser et al., *Papers*, 291; Warshauer, "Jackson and Martial Law," 272–73; Charbonnier to Livingston, February 15, 1828, Livingston Papers, Princeton; Letter from New Orleans, January 20, 1815, Raleigh, NC, *Star*, February 17, 1815.

103. *Arrest and Trial of E. Louis Louaillier*, 3–12; Warshauer, "Jackson and Martial Law," 278–79; Reid and Eaton, *Jackson*, 417.

104. General Order, February 18, 1815, Joyes Order Book, Joyes Family Papers, Filson.

105. New Orleans, LA, *Louisiana Gazette for the Country*, February 23, 1815, in Schenectady, NY, *Cabinet*, April 5, 1815.

106. David Weller to Samuel Weller, March 3, 1815, Weller Family Papers, Filson; Letter from officer in the 7th or 44th Infantry, January 12, 1815, Easton, MD, *Republican Star*, February 14, 1815.

107. Report from Camp Morgan, February 14, 1815, HNOC.

108. Bird S. Hurt to a friend in Columbia, TN, January 20, 1815, Augusta, GA, *Augusta Herald*, February 23, 1815.

109. Simpson to Mary Simpson, January 30, 1815, Simpson Letters, Princeton.

110. Letter from officer on the *Enterprise* to its owners, January 20, 1815, Brownsville, PA, *American Telegraph*, February 22, 1815.

111. Letter from New Orleans, March 6, 1815, Bardstown, KY, *Western American*, April 22, 1815; Martin, *Louisiana*, 2:399; Letter from New Orleans, March 10, 1815, New Haven, CT, *Connecticut Journal*, April 17, 1815.

112. Padgett, "Andrew Jackson in New Orleans," 387.

113. Jackson to Thomas Beale, March 6, 1815, Moser et al., *Papers*, 301.

114. Tregle, "Andrew Jackson and the Continuing Battle of New Orleans," 6, JELAC.

115. Tylden Journal, February 17, 1815, NYPL.

116. Hill, *Recollections*, 2:58.

117. Gerard, Campaigns 2, USNA; Cooke, *Narrative*, 304–6; Hill, *Recollections*, 2:62–64; Cooper, *Rough Notes*, 138; Chesterton, *Peace, War, and Adventure*, 232–34.

118. Letter from an officer in Jackson's army, February 24, 1815, Paris, KY, *Western Citizen*, March 25, 1815; Jackson to Monroe, February 24, 1815, Baltimore, MD, *American, and Commercial Daily Advertiser*, March 21, 1815; Memorandum Book, February 27–28, 1815, Pultney Malcolm Papers, MAL/104, Caird.

119. Jackson to Hays, February 17, 1815, Moser et al., *Papers*, 281–82, Winchester to Jackson, March 7, 1815, 526; Cope, *Rifle Brigade*, 193–94; Surtees, *Rifle Brigade*, 396–97.

120. Letter from an officer at New Orleans to a friend in Charleston, SC, March 24, 1815, Boston, MA, *Boston Patriot*, May 17, 1815.

121. Gleig Diary, March 16, 1815, Barrett, *85th King's Light Infantry*, 235; Malcolm to Cochrane, March 16, 1815, Cochrane Papers, NLS; Memorandum Book, March 16, 1815, Pultney Malcolm Papers, MAL/104, Caird; Lambert to Jackson, March 18, 1815, Moser et al., *Papers*, 316.

122. Tylden Journal, February 23, 1815, NYPL.

123. Lambert to Livingston, March 10, 1815, Livingston Papers, Princeton.

124. Chesterton, *Peace, War, and Adventure*, 238; Cooper, *Rough Notes*, 138.

125. Mordecai Diary, May 2, 1815, Mordecai Family Papers, SHC, UNC.

126. Proclamation of Peace, March 13, 1815, Moser et al., *Papers*, 310; General Orders, March 1, 1815, Order Book, Louisiana Militia, RG 107, Louisiana Historical Center.

127. Jackson to Jean Baptiste Plauché et al., March 16, 1815, Moser, *Papers*, 313.

128. John Leclerc Invoice, April 5, 1815, Cook Collection, HNOC. Buell, *Andrew Jackson*, 2:80, offers a story of Captain Henry Garland of Coffee's command speaking at a banquet held by Louisiana officers for the officers from Coffee's, Carroll's, Adair's, and Hinds's militias before

they left for home. In his speech, Garland argued that Britain never admitted Napoleon's right to sell Louisiana, and thus "did not mean to include the Louisiana Purchase in the territorial *status quo ante bellum!*" The victory at New Orleans "taught all the princes and kings and emperors on the face of the earth that they must let our young Republic alone!" There was no Captain Garland in the Tennessee volunteers, and Buell's inclusion of his fictitious ancestor David Buell at the dinner further defines the episode as one of his inventions.

129. Coffee to Mr. Brent, March 15, 1815, Coffee to Piatt, February 27, 1815, Coffee Order Book, SHC, UNC; Nashville, TN, *Nashville Whig*, April 18, 1815; Priestley to Latour, March 4, 1816, Latour Archive, MSS 555, HNOC.
130. Joyes Journal, March 18, April 6, 1815, Joyes Papers, Filson; Nashville, TN, *Nashville Whig*, April 18, 1815; David Weller to Samuel Weller, March 3, 1815, Weller Family Papers, Filson.
131. Report of the Managers of the Louisiana Bible Society, New Orleans, LA, *Louisiana Gazette for the Country*, April 25, 1815.
132. Warshauer, "Jackson and Martial Law," 284–91; Eberhard Deutsch, "The United States Versus Major General Andrew Jackson," *American Bar Association Journal* 46, no. 9 (September 1960): 966–72.
133. Address to Citizens and Soldiers of New Orleans, March 31, 1815, Moser et al., *Papers*, 337.
134. Jackson to Unknown, March 31, 1815, ibid., 337–38.
135. Randall Easting to Rees, March 26, Rees Papers, Tulane.
136. De La Vergne to a Friend, April 24, 1815, De La Vergne Family Papers, Tulane.
137. Jackson to Coffee, April 24, 1815, Moser, *Papers*, 348; De La Vergne to a Friend, April 24, 1815, De La Vergne Family Papers, Tulane.
138. Jackson to Pierre Laffite, n.d. [March 1815], Parsons Collection, Texas. A story later current said that Jean Laffite was talking with Surgeon Cobb of Tennessee at one of these dinners, when Coffee approached and Cobb made introductions. The general seemed unable to place Laffite. Irritated at what seemed a rebuff, Laffite advanced aggressively a step or two toward Coffee and said loudly that he was "Lafitte the pirate!" Coffee recognized him at that and cordially extended a hand. As was often the case with the Laffites, Jean was made the protagonist in this anecdote, but Pierre is more likely, since Coffee certainly had met him, and likely never met Jean. More probable still, the whole story is mythical. Coffee left New Orleans on March 17, and these congratulatory dinners for Jackson came more than a week later after his March 24 court appearance. W. H. K. to the editor, May 20, 1852, "Lafitte," *DeBow's Southern and Western Review* 13 (August 1852): 204–5.
139. Joyes Journal, April 4, 1815, Joyes Papers, Filson; William Darby to Levin Wailes, April 7, 1815, HNOC; New Orleans Volunteer Rifle Company Address, March 31, 1815, Newport, RI, *Rhode-Island Republican*, May 31, 1815.
140. Wollstonecraft to Rachel Jackson, May 5, 1815, Jackson Papers, LC.
141. Letter from Boston, March 28, 1815, London, UK, *Cobbett's Weekly Political Register*, June 3, 1815.
142. Joseph I. Tregle, "Andrew Jackson and the Continuing Battle of New Orleans," 7, JELAC.
143. Livingston to Jackson, April 28, 1815, Moser et al., *Papers*, 352, Jackson to Livingston, May 17, 1815, 357.
144. Jackson to Monroe, April 27, 1815, ibid., 350.
145. Adair to Shelby, April 10, 1815, Louisville, KY, *Western Courier*, May 11, 1815; Account of the Battle of New Orleans, 1815, Jackson Papers, LC.
146. Jackson to Adair, April 2, 1815, Bardstown, KY, *Bardstown Repository*, May 18, 1815; Jackson to Adair, July 23, 1817, *Letters of Gen. Adair and Gen. Jackson*, 6–7, Adair to Jackson, October 21, 1816, 18–24, Butler to Jackson, July 23, 1817, 15–16, Gabriel Slaughter to Adair, October 2, 1817, 28–29, McLean to Adair, August 13, 1817, 30–31; Quisenberry, *Kentucky in the War of 1812*, 147; Worley & Smith to Jackson, March 22, 1817, War of 1812 Mss., Lilly Library.
147. Quisenberry, *Kentucky in the War of 1812*, 147.
148. Washington, DC, *United States' Telegraph*, December 5, 1826. Jackson quite certainly received communications from Monroe dated October 19, 21, December 7, 31, 1814, and January 5, February 4 and 5, 1815, prior to the arrival of the packet missing the treaty notification on March 6. There may have been others that have not survived.

A few weeks later Monroe was surprised to hear himself being charged with such neglect, and first considered publishing the correspondence he had on the subject, but demurred. Still, he had his defenders. At a dinner in Washington in January 1827, Secretary of the Navy Samuel Southard denounced the charge, and declared that Monroe really deserved credit for the victory, for Jackson dallied at Mobile until Monroe ordered him to go to New Orleans, a charge as untrue as Adair's. Monroe did send Jackson a veiled order to go to New Orleans on December 7, but Jackson had already arrived in the city six days earlier. Monroe refused to get into a public controversy in the matter, though he did ask the War Department if it had Jackson's responses to his letters as evidence that he did communicate with the general. Word of Southard's accusation reached Jackson, and threatened to produce a public controversy that Monroe himself thought would be a "political manoeuvre to produce an effect on the approaching election" that would be harmful to the Republican Party. Hence, he refused to see anything published in the matter. James Monroe to George Graham, January 12, February 5, 1827, Graham Family Papers, VHS; Samuel Southard to Monroe, February 11, 1827, Monroe Collection, James Monroe Museum, Fredericksburg, VA; Monroe to unknown addressee, April 11, 1827, HNOC.

149. Tregle, "Andrew Jackson and the Continuing Battle of New Orleans," 1–2, JELAC; Hudry to Bertel and Morenos, Particulars in relation to Battle of New Orleans furnished me by a French gentleman in 1828—Summer, Follett Papers, Cincinnati History Library and Archives. Jackson would be defending martial law years after he left the presidency, arguing that without it the enemy would have taken the city. Martial law would not be imposed again in the United States until 1862 when the states were disunited, and ironically it came again in a then-Confederate New Orleans. Joseph F. Stoltz, III, "'A Victory as Never Crowned the Wars of the World': The Battle of New Orleans in American Historical Memory" (PhD dissertation, Texas Christian University, Dallas, 2013), 90; Jackson to L. F. Linn, March 1842, Baltimore, MD, *American and Commercial Daily Appeal*, May 27, 1842.

150. Skipwith to Jackson, May 13, 1827, Padgett, "Andrew Jackson in New Orleans," 407; *Appeal of L. Louaillier*, 14–15n; "Aristides" (William Peter Van Ness), *A Concise Narrative*, 4.

151. Tregle, "Andrew Jackson and the Continuing Battle of New Orleans," 21ff, JELAC.

152. Stoltz, "The Battle of New Orleans in American Historical Memory," 81.

153. Hudson, NY, *Bee*, February 8, 1815; Broadside, War of 1812 Mss., Lilly Library; Letter from New Orleans to Editor of Frankfort *Palladium*, January 13, 1815, Lexington, KY, *Western Monitor*, February 3, 1815.

154. See, for instance, Tousard to Stocker, January 9, 1815, HNOC; Letter from New Orleans, January 13, 1815, Concord, NH, *New Hampshire Patriot and State Gazette*, February 14, 1815; Letter from an officer in the Navy to a friend in Boston, January 14, 1815, Boston, MA, *New-England Palladium*, February 10, 1815; "Veritas," The Battle of New Orleans, January 8, 1855, Follett Papers, Cincinnati History Library and Archives.

155. Powell A. Casey, "Artillery in the Battle of New Orleans," 36, J. Fair Hardin Collection, LSU; Latour, *Historical Memoir*, 315.

156. Owsley, *Borderlands*, 163–64n.

157. Rachel Johnson to William Johnson, January 6, 1815, Miscellaneous Collection, LSU.

158. John A. Fort to unknown addressee, January 9, 1815, Boston, MA, *New-England Palladium*, February 10, 1815.

159. Joseph S. Winter to Elisha I. Winter, January 9, 1815, War of 1812 Collection, Michigan; M'Lean to Ewing, January 10, 1815, Washington, KY, *Union*, February 3, 1815.

160. Joseph S. Winter to Elisha I. Winter, New Orleans, January 12, 1814 [1815], War of 1812 Collection, Michigan; Letter from unidentified Frenchman to Philadelphia, January 13, 1815, Philadelphia, PA, *Relf's Philadelphia Gazette, and Daily Advertiser*, February 8, 1815; Letter from Greenville, Mississippi Territory, to Philadelphia, January 31, 1815, Wilmington, DE, *American Watchman*, March 4, 1815. Ward, *Andrew Jackson, Symbol for an Age*, 23, suggests that the rifleman myth began with the early publicity given William Withers's killing of Rennie in a newspaper article titled "Sharp Shooting," but that hardly stands scrutiny today. The earliest traceable incarnation of the Withers story came from Natchez on January 13, and appeared in the Augusta, GA, *Augusta Herald*, February 23, 1815 (see also Petersburg, VA, *Petersburg Daily Courier*, March 3, 1815). For a start, since Withers could have been standing no more than twenty feet from Rennie when he shot him, it was hardly a feat of marksmanship. More to the point, the comments about sharpshooting at New Orleans were already numerous well before Withers's story made print, though it certainly supported the growing myth.

161. Gabriel Winter to William Willis, January 12, 1815, Willis Family Papers, LSU.
162. Coffee to John Donelson, January 25, 1815, Tennessee Historical Society Miscellaneous Files, University of Tennessee.
163. Lambert to Bathurst, January 29, 1815, WO 1/141, Kew.
164. Cochrane to Dundas, January 20, 1815, War of 1812 Mss., Lilly Library.
165. St. George's, Bermuda, *Bermuda Gazette, and Weekly Advertiser*, April 15, 1815; William Cobbett to the Earl of Liverpool, n.d., Windsor, VT, *Vermont Republican*, June 24, 1816.
166. Letter from New Orleans, January 14, 1815, Concord, NH, *New Hampshire Patriot and State Gazette*, February 28, 1815.
167. Boston, MA, *Boston Commercial Gazette*, February 9, 1815.
168. Kemp to friend in Natchez, January 16, 1815, Wilmington, DE, *Delaware Gazette and State Journal*, February 7, 1815.
169. Fletcher to Hynes, February 28, 1815, William P. Duval to Hynes, February 1815, Hynes Papers, Tulane; King to James Moore, March [April] 15, 1815, King Collection, Middle Tennessee State University, Murfreesboro.
170. Mordecai Diary, April 23, 1815, Mordecai Family Papers, SHC, UNC.
171. Salem, MA, *Essex Register*, February 11, 1815; Hudson, NY, *Bee*, February 8, 1815, Broadside, War of 1812 Mss., Lilly Library.
172. Claiborne, *Notes on the War*, 60; Jefferson to Henry Dearborn, March 17, 1815, Looney, *Papers of Thomas Jefferson*, vol. 8, 357–58.
173. John R. Livingston to Livingston, February 24, 1815, Livingston Papers, Princeton.
174. William C. Cook, "The Early Iconography of the Battle of New Orleans, 1815–1819," *Tennessee Historical Quarterly* 48, no. 4 (Winter 1989): 219–20, 235–36; Thomas O'Connor, *An Impartial and Correct History of the War Between the United States of America and Great Britain* (New York: John Low, 1815); Stoltz, "The Battle of New Orleans in American Historical Memory," 42–44; Stoltz, "'It Taught Our Enemies a Lesson,'" 115, 117.
175. Cook, "Iconography," 233, 236; Stoltz, "'It Taught Our Enemies a Lesson,'" 114.
176. Hartford, CT, *Connecticut Courant*, May 10, 1815.
177. Stoltz, "The Battle of New Orleans in American Historical Memory," 42–44; Lebanon, OH, *Western Star*, March 26, 1817.
178. The tune was "The Unfortunate Miss Bailey."
179. The actor was Hopkins Robertson and the writer Samuel Woodworth. Philadelphia, PA, *Poulson's American Daily Advertiser*, November 26, 1819; Samuel Woodworth, "New-Orleans," *Ladies' Literary Cabinet* 3, no. 14 (February 10, 1821): 112; Providence, RI, *Providence Patriot*, March 10, 1821; New York, NY, *National Advocate*, November 15, 1819. It has been asserted that the song was written in 1815 and first published in Boston. There is no authority for this other than a broadside in the Filson Club titled *Hunter's of Kentucky, Or Half Horse and Half Alligator*, printed in Boston by L. Deming, which carries no date printed, but has been tentatively dated by the collection as ca. 1815. This runs counter to the statement of Woodworth, who said he wrote it for Robertson, who died November 13, 1819, before he could perform it. That suggests a composition date much later than 1815, and more likely mid–late in 1819 close to the time of Robertson's death. No copy or version of it datable prior to February 1821 has been located, and Woodworth's own statement seems conclusive that it had not been published until he gave it to the *Ladies' Literary Cabinet*.
180. Alexandria, VA, *Alexandria Herald*, December 13, 1822.
181. Frankfort, KY, *Argus of Western America*, June 9, 1824; Wilmington, DE, *American Watchman*, March 1, 1825; New York, NY, *New-York American for the Country*, July 6, 1825. Stoltz, "The Battle of New Orleans in American Historical Memory," 42–44, suggests that the song was used politically in the 1824 election, but one looks in vain in the press for 1824 for any connection between the song and the Jackson campaign. The song was issued over the years in broadsides in numerous versions under slight variants in the title. Copies are at the Library of Congress, the Filson Club, and elsewhere, variously printed at Boston, Providence, RI, and elsewhere.
182. Stoltz, "The Battle of New Orleans in American Historical Memory," 83; Washington, DC, *United States' Telegraph*, January 9, 1828; Saratoga Springs, NY, *Saratoga Sentinel*, October 21, 1828.
183. Stoltz, "'It Taught Our Enemies a Lesson,'" 114.
184. London, UK, *Morning Post*, November 18, 1828.

185. Joseph Dorris and Jesse Denson, *The Chronicles of Andrew; Containing an Accurate and Brief Account of General Jackson's Victories in the South, Over the Creeks. Also His Victories over the British at Orleans, with a Biographical Sketch of His Life* (Lexington, KY: published by author, 1815), n.p.

186. See, for instance, Gideon M. Davison's two-volume *Sketches of the War, Between the United States and the British Isles*; O'Connor's *An Impartial and Correct History of the War Between the United States of America and Great Britain*; and McCarty's *History of the American War of 1812, from the Commencement, Until the Final Termination Thereof, on the Memorable Eighth of January, 1815, at New Orleans*, which made New Orleans a part of its full title; and Gilbert J. Hunt's *The Late War, Between the United States and Great Britain, from June, 1812, to February, 1815: Written in the Ancient Historical Style* (New York: David Longworth, 1816). Some did not scruple at gross fictionalization, no better example appearing than *A Compendious Account of the Most Important Battles of the Late War, to Which Is Added, the Curious Adventures of Corporal Samuel Stubbs (A Kentuckian of 65 Years of Age)* (Boston: William Walter, 1817), a work populated with fictitious soldiers and regiments that were nowhere near New Orleans.

187. Stoltz, "'It Taught Our Enemies a Lesson,'" 118–22.

188. The most notable example was his fellow Tennessean David "Davy" Crockett, whose 1834 memoir, a bestseller mixing anti-Jackson politics with the backwoods marksman ideal, pointedly ignored New Orleans, since Crockett had left Coffee's command during the Creek campaign. The myth virtually imprisoned Crockett, forcing him again and again to set aside his broadcloth for buckskins to give audiences what they wanted, despite his aspirations to be accepted as a gentleman.

189. Jackson to Livingston, May 17, 1815, Moser et al., *Papers*, 357; John Reid to Livingston, April 22, 1815, Jackson to Livingston, June 12, July 5, September 5, 1815, Livingston Papers, Princeton.

190. Peter S. Du Ponceau to Latour, June 17, 1816, Latour Archive, HNOC.

191. Baltimore, MD, *American, and Commercial Daily Advertiser*, January 4, 1816; Washington, DC, *Daily National Intelligencer*, February 21, 1816; Savannah, GA, *Columbian Museum & Savannah Advertiser*, January 7, 1819. William Dunlap wrote the three-act drama.

192. Stoltz, "'It Taught Our Enemies a Lesson,'" 114.

193. On January 8, 1828 in New York City, three productions vied for ticket sales: *The Eighth of January, The Battle of New Orleans*, and *Battle of New-Orleans, or—The Female Spy*. New York, NY, *National Advocate*, January 8, 1828.

194. Boston, MA, *Boston Patriot and Daily Chronicle*, January 8, 1829. Two other plays debuting at this same time were *Glorious 8th, or Hero of New Orleans*, at the Walnut Street Theatre on January 8, 1829, while the Chestnut Street Theatre staged *The Eighth of January*. Philadelphia, PA, *Poulson's American Daily Advertiser*, January 8, 1829; Boston, MA, *Bostan Patriot and Daily Chronicle*, January 15, 1829.

EPILOGUE: "WHO WOULD NOT BE AN AMERICAN?"

1. John Campbell to David Campbell, July 4, 1815, Campbell Family Papers, Duke.

2. John Hoffman to Maurice Hoffman, Dec 24, 1815, Bowman Family Papers, Tulane.

3. New Haven, CT, *Columbian Register*, February 24, 1816.

4. Stoltz, "'It Taught Our Enemies a Lesson,'" 117–18.

5. Ward, *Andrew Jackson, Symbol for an Age*, 131–32.

6. Edward Waldo Emerson and Waldo Emerson Forbes, eds., *The Journals of Ralph Waldo Emerson* (Boston: Houghton, Mifflin, 1909–1914), 7:351–52.

7. Dublin, IR, *Dublin Observer*, January 25, 1834.

8. Stoltz, "The Battle of New Orleans in American Historical Memory," 72–73, 91, 93–94; Ibid., 2, 4.

9. Mordecai Diary, April 22, 24, 1815, Mordecai Family Papers, SHC, UNC.

10. Letter from New Orleans, June 4, 1815, Boston, MA, *Massachusetts Spy*, July 19, 1815.

11. Latrobe, *Impressions*, 43, 73–74.

12. Eisenach, *Travels Through North America*, 2:68; Ingraham, *The South-West*, 1:201–3.

13. Ingraham, *The South-West*, 202–3.

14. Philadelphia, PA, *Gazette and Daily Advertiser*, February 8, 1815.

15. Altered, amended, and reshaped, the most popular version of the story was published by William Walcutt in January 1852, titled "Incidents in the Battle of New-Orleans" (William Walcutt,

"Recollections of the Last War. No II. Incidents in the Battle of New-Orleans," *Republic* 3, no. 1 [January 1852]: 21–22. This article has been carelessly cited in places as being by Walter Walcott and appearing in 1832 rather than 1852, and in a newspaper, the *Boston Republican*, rather than the magazine *The Republic*. Historian Z. F. Smith supposedly claimed that the story first appeared in Gleig's *Narrative* but in fact it does not appear in either of Gleig's books). In August of that year this version began reappearing in newspapers and did so until at least 1872, eventually retitled "The Fatal Marksman" (Clarksburg, VA, *Cooper's Clarksburg Register*, August 25, 1852; Council Bluffs, IA, *Council Bluffs Nonpareil*, January 21, 1860; Pomeroy, OH, *Pomeroy Weekly Telegraph*, August 9, 1861; White Cloud, KS, *White Cloud Kansas Chief*, May 23, 1872). Presented as a "recollection" by a British officer, its marksman was a Kentuckian, a "western hunter," and it concluded with a breast-beating assertion of American invincibility—"so long as thousands and thousands of rifles remain in the hands of the people," and the nation had marksmen like the lone Kentuckian (See, for instance, Manchester, NH, *Manchester Daily Union*, August 20, 1852; Rockford, IL, *Rock River Democrat*, November 2, 1852; Montrose, UK, *Montrose, Arbroath, & Brechin Review, and Forfar and Kincardineshire Advertiser*, November 5, 1852; Dublin, IR, *Weekly Nation*, September 3, 1859). A few years later in 1856, Alexander Walker, author of the most complete history of the battle then to date, promoted the accuracy of the militia with their small arms, and assertively claimed that Jackson's artillery did not do as much damage as once supposed (Walker, *Jackson and New Orleans*, 328).

The story resurfaced from time to time and then a coincidental juxtaposition recast it. Richard H. Collins in his 1874 *History of Kentucky* stated that Ensign Ephraim M. Brank of the 14th Kentucky Militia, "while the battle was raging hottest, mounted the breastworks to repel the British" (Richard H. Collins, *History of Kentucky* [Covington, KY: Collins and Co., 1874], 641). On August 5, 1875, Brank died aged eighty-three at Greenville, Kentucky, and a St. Louis newspaper conflated Collins's comment with the Walcutt article and published it, affirming that Brank was the anonymous hero of the piece, though there is no evidence that he ever made such a claim himself. Soon retitled "A Dead Shot" and "A Kentucky Rifleman," the rehash of Ingraham's original tale saw new life (New Orleans, LA, *New Orleans Republican*, September 3, 1875; Worcester, MA, *Massachusetts Weekly Spy*, September 10, 1875; Port Townsend, WA, *Puget Sound Weekly*, September 18, 1875). Just who connected Brank with the fictitious marksman is uncertain, though it does appear that Kentucky antiquarian Reuben T. Durrett made a manuscript copy of the article and on it identified Brank as the hero (Robert M. McElroy, *Kentucky in the Nation's History* [New York: Moffatt, Yard and Co., 1909], 365). By 1899 claims were made that marksman Brank fired the shot that killed Pakenham (William Hyde and Howard L. Conard, eds., *Encyclopedia of the History of St. Louis* [New York: Southern History Company, 1899], 1:216). Thus are myths born out of accident, carelessness, and coincidence.

Some myths are manufactured by intent, and no one more assiduously invented material to cement the "western hunter" marksmanship myth at New Orleans than the industrious Augustus C. Buell, who actively created forgeries from the 1890s or earlier until his death in 1904. He is chiefly known for his biographies of Andrew Jackson and John Paul Jones, both of which he laced with invented quotations and episodes based on nonexistent sources. His posthumously published two-volume biography *History of Andrew Jackson: Pioneer, Patriot, Soldier, Politician, President* (New York: Charles Scribner's Sons, 1904) has numerous instances for several parts of Jackson's life, but most particularly the Battle of New Orleans, for which Buell was particularly anxious to bolster the prevailing myth that deadly American rifle marksmanship by Kentuckians and Tennesseans won the battle.

Buell began laying the groundwork for his deception at least six years earlier with an unsigned article in the Bloomsburg, PA, *Columbian*, January 6, 1898, that has his unmistakable stamp upon it. He drew material on the battle from a fictitious 1828 pamphlet titled *The Kentucky Volunteer* by Richard Oglesby, a Presbyterian minister serving with the Kentucky volunteers. Among other things it described a miraculous deadly long shot by a rifleman named Morgan Ballard who supposedly brought down Major "Wilky" Wilkinson from his horse. In addition to Ballard, "extracts" from the pamphlet named several other Kentucky volunteers, for none of whom any record survives, including Oglesby himself (Buell, *Jackson*, 1:407–9, 425; 2:8, 15–18, 43–44, 86–88, 179). There was no such Oglesby and no such pamphlet.

Further to his end, Buell invented an 1874 interview with William O. Butler in which Butler supposedly told him that the British were "literally melted down by our rifle-fire." Buell also cited fictitious material supposedly drawn from an article by E. N. Burroughs in an 1818 issue of the *British Military Journal*, Burroughs being an agent or official of the British quartermaster department. In it, Burroughs corroborated Oglesby's description of Morgan Ballard's long-distance shot (Buell, *Jackson*, 1:373–74, 2:19–22). In fact, there was no such article, no quartermaster Burroughs, and no such publication as the *British Military Journal*. In addition, Buell invented a return from the medical director of Pakenham's army stating that 3,000 of the 3,326 redcoat casualties were caused by small bullets used by American sharpshooters and that 400 of them were bull's-eye hits in the head (Buell, *Jackson*, 2:41–42). Buell even invented a letter from Jackson to Secretary of War James Monroe in which he described a rifleman bringing down Pakenham himself, Jackson adding that he believed the marksman was a free man of color (Arthur, *New Orleans*, 196). Brown, *Amphibious Campaign*, 208 n21, quotes this, citing Thomas E. Watson, *The Life and Times of Andrew Jackson* (Thomson, GA: Jeffersonian Publishing Co., 1912), 217. Watson cited no source, however. In his "Introductory" essay he did say that he "consulted original authorities, official documents, and other sources of information which had never been used," but quite obviously his only source was Buell's fictitious article (1).

Buell's most explicit effort to embed the idea of brilliant American marksmanship came with his invention of an 1836 exchange between General Malcolm Mitchell Forbes, a lieutenant in the 93rd Highlanders in the battle, and a Colonel Dupin, "one of the greatest of French military writers." Buell has Dupin speaking of the Americans in Jackson's line and of how "they killed everybody who came within the range of their rifles." From that he went on to conclude that Dupin "unconsciously offers irrefragable evidence that the men who won the battle of New Orleans and saved the Louisiana Purchase—next to Yorktown the most momentous single fact in our warlike history—were not the motley crews who stood behind Jackson's old smoothbore cannon, but the Tennessee and Kentucky riflemen" (Buell, *Jackson*, 2:42–43). It should hardly be necessary to say that there was no lieutenant named Forbes in the 93rd regiment, nor in Pakenham's army, and there has never been a general Malcolm Mitchell Forbes in the British army. Colonel Dupin equally defies corroboration. There was a Colonel Charles-Louis Du Pin in the French army, but he was just eleven days old on the date of the battle, and just twenty-two years old and not even a lieutenant in 1836 when Buell made him a distinguished colonel.

Buell's forgeries as presented in his Jackson biography were unfortunately accepted at face value by some subsequent historians. Stanley C. Arthur, admittedly not a trained historian but a fine commentator and preserver of New Orleans history, used much of Buell's fiction in his *New Orleans*, inadvertently muddying the business further by carelessness. He changed Richard Oglesby to John R. Ogilvy and the title of the fictitious pamphlet from *The Kentucky Volunteer* to *Kentucky at New Orleans*, and added that Zachary Smith quoted from it in his 1904 work *The Battle of New Orleans*. In fact, Buell's creation is nowhere mentioned in Smith's book (Arthur, *The Story of the Battle of New Orleans*, 160).

More recently, Carter's *Blaze of Glory* borrowed considerably, and carelessly, from Buell's inventions, tampering with quotations and changing Burroughs's fictitious article in the nonexistent 1818 issue of the *British Military Journal* to an 1816 issue of the *Royal Military Chronicle*, though all of the content traced in fact back to Buell's article in the Bloomsburg *Columbian* and the Jackson biography. As for the famous pamphlet, Carter presented the author as John Richard Ogilvy in one instance, and Richard Ogilvy in another (Carter, *Blaze of Glory*, 236, 253–54).

Given that Buell was born in 1847, he cannot be suspected of authorship of the 1852 Walcutt article, and it seems highly unlikely that he wrote under the pseudonym of E. M. Brant in 1875, since Brant was a genuine person, and Buell did not commence his known forgeries relating to American marksmanship until twenty-three years later. He might very well have seen the Walcutt/Brant articles, however, and based his fictional account on them. Suffice it to say that nothing Buell wrote can be taken on its own as either reliable or honest. For more on him and his forgeries, see Milton W. Hamilton, "Augustus C. Buell: Fraudulent Historian," *Pennsylvania Magazine of History and Biography* 80, no. 4 (October 1956): 490–92.

The invention of material promoting the marksmanship legend continued into the twentieth century. Noted firearms collector Charles Winthrop Sawyer, in his 1920 work *Our Rifles* (Boston: Cornhill, 1920), referred to "the famous rifle battle of the 1812 war, the Battle of New Orleans," and wrote a fictional story that has been taken as factual about a rifleman named John Metcalf. "Such as he composed the raw militia who, under a leader with ability to control him, won the extraordinary Battle of New Orleans," claimed Sawyer. "It was the first large battle between the smooth bore and the rifle," he went on to say. "Jackson's riflemen did the shooting that counted," he said, making no mention of artillery at all, saying rather that "regardless of all side influences, the astonishing casualties were the result of accurate shooting" (10, 30–38, 91–102, 216).

16. New Orleans, LA, *Daily Picayune*, August 27, 1852; New Orleans, LA, *Daily Delta*, August 29, 1852.

17. Alexandria, VA, *Alexandria Gazette*, May 23, 1851.

18. Dixon, IL, *Dixon Sun*, May 17, 1876.

19. Eustis to Cutts, January 28, 1815, Cutts Papers, UVA.

20. Gray to Graham, February 8, 1815, Dispatches from the U. S. Consul in Havana, RG 59, NA; Gray to Shaler, May 3, 1815, Shaler Family Papers, HSP.

21. Shaler to David Brent, November 9, 1831, ibid.

22. New Orleans, LA, *Orleans Gazette & Commercial Advertiser*, July 5, 1817, February 24, 1819; Workman to Livingston, June 3, 1816, Livingston Papers.

23. Brighton, UK, *Brighton Gazette*, May 8, 1828; Philadelphia, PA, *National Gazette and Literary Messenger*, October 11, 1834; Lewis Kerr to Livingston, February 4, 1833, Livingston Papers, Princeton.

24. New Orleans, LA, *Louisiana Advertiser*, January 26, 1827; Petition of Celeste Beale, April 27, 1830, Succession and Probate Records, Thomas Beale Sr., Orleans Parish, New Orleans.

25. Memorial of Calvin J. Keith, February 5, 1846, Senate Document 116, Public Documents Printed by Order of the Senate of the United States 29th Congress, 1st Session (Washington, DC: Ritchie and Heiss, 1846), 4:1–3.

26. Beverly Chew Memoir, New Jersey Historical Society, Newark.

27. *Memorial of Beverly Chew and Others*, 1–3.

28. Ibid., December 9, 1816.

29. Washington, DC, *Daily National Intelligencer*, January 26, 1835; Newport, RI, *Newport Mercury*, January 31, 1835.

30. Norfolk, VA, *American Beacon*, November 24, 1815; New Orleans, LA, *Orleans Gazette and Commercial Advertiser*, January 20, 1820.

31. Graves to White, n.d. [1845–53], New Orleans, LA, *Daily Delta*, January 8, 1854.

32. New Orleans, LA, *Louisiana Advertiser*, November 18, 1820; Albany, NY, *Albany Centinel*, August 2, 1799; Boston, MA, *Columbian Centinel*, January 6, 1821.

33. Worcester, MA, *Massachusetts Spy, and Worcester County Advertiser*, November 7, 1827; Wilmington, DE, *American Watchman*, July 6, 1827.

34. Nolte, *Memoirs*, 241–45.

35. Particulars in relation to Battle of New Orleans furnished me by a French gentleman in 1828— Summer, Follett Papers, Cincinnati History Library and Archives.

36. Livingston to Jackson, January 11, 1836, Hunt, *Life of Edward Livingston*, 428.

37. Obligation, D. C. Williams to Arsene Latour, notary John Lynd 1815, 13, #345, Protest, Williams vs Amory Callender & Co., Lynd, 16, 626–27, New Orleans Notarial Archives; Promissory note, August 2, 1815, Livingston Papers.

38. Washington, DC, *Daily National Intelligencer*, December 2, 1816.

39. Workman to Livingston, June 3, 1816, Livingston Papers; Review, *The North American Review and Miscellaneous Journal* 3, no. 8 (1816): 265; Baltimore, MA, *Baltimore Patriot and Evening Advertiser*, August 1, October 9, 1816.

40. Latour to Livingston November 1, 1816, Livingston Papers.

41. Draft of Letter for Jackson to?, February 2, 1815, Livingston Papers, Princeton.

42. Petition of Vincent Gamby, July 12, 1815, Parsons Collection, Texas.

43. Davis, *Pirates Laffite*, 453–54, 461–63.

44. Vaughan, "Black Militia," 92–93.

45. Davis, *Pirates Laffite*, 340; Smith, *Slaves' Gamble*, 206.

46. Smith, *Slaves' Gamble*, 164–65.

47. Desforges to Jackson, August 1843, Jackson to J. M. Porter, October 3, 1843, Louis Desforges Pension file, RG 15, NA.

48. Smith, *Slaves' Gamble*, 173, 205–7; Vaughan, "Black Militia," 94, 95; New Orleans, LA, *Daily Picayune*, January 9, 1851.

49. This information on Pierre Jugeat/Juzan was kindly provided by his descendant Kathy Hawkins of Joplin, MO.

50. Philadelphia, PA, *Relf's Philadelphia Gazette, and Daily Advertiser,* December 22, 1817; Washington, DC, *National Intelligencer,* December 25, 1817. Claiborne has sometimes been said to have died of yellow fever, but November was not the fever season.
51. Smith, *Catesby Jones,* 30–31; Jones to secretary of the Navy Smith Thompson, January 26, 1819, Thomas ap Catesby Jones Pension File, RG 15, NA; *Summary Statement of Facts, &c, by Thomas Ap C. Jones,* 12.
52. Memorial of Thomas ap Catesby Jones to Samuel L. Southard, Richard Rush, and James Barbour, February 14, 1828, [1]; Jones Pension File, RG 15, NA; Summary Statement of Facts, &c, by Thomas Ap C. Jones, 12.
53. Davis, *Pirates Laffite,* 309–11.
54. Alexandria, VA, *Alexandria Gazette,* February 6, 1822; Little Rock, AR, *Weekly Arkansas Gazette,* March 19, 1822; Philadelphia, PA, *National Gazette and Literary Messsenger,* July 19, 1831; Macon, GA, *Weekly Telegraph,* June 25, 1831; "Captain Nathaniel Pryor," 253–65; Pamela Keyes, "Nathaniel Pryor, the Unsung Veteran of the Battle of New Orleans," http://www.histo riaobscura.com/nathaniel-pryor-the-unsung-veteran-of-the-battle-of-new-orleans/
55. Kemper to Livingston, August 13, 1818, Livingston Papers, Princeton.
56. Ibid., January 8, 23, 1824.
57. Davis, *Rogue Republic,* 284–91.
58. Adam G. Saffold to a "friend" in Augusta, GA, January 27, 1815, Augusta, GA, *Augusta Herald,* February 9, 1815. This same issue carries an excerpt from the Milledgeville, GA, *Journal*'s January 30 extra stating: "Major Dale arrived here this Evening as an Express from New Orleans, with Despatches for the General Government and for Governor Early."
59. Augusta, GA, *Augusta Chronicle and Georgia Advertiser,* July 8, 1829; Washington, DC, *Daily National Intelligencer,* March 10, 1825; Camden, SC, *Camden Journal,* September 29, 1841.
60. Registers of Enlistments in the United States Army, 1798–1914, RG 94, NA; Wollstonecraft to Livingston, February 28, 1815, Livingston Papers.
61. Mordecai Diary, April 10, 1815, Mordecai Family Papers, SHC, UNC; Registers of Enlistments in the United States Army, 1798–1914, RG 94, NA.
62. Eisenach, *Travels Through North America,* 2:67; Villeré, *Villeré,* 55–56.
63. Letter to Peter K. Wagner, 1815, Miscellaneous Collection, LSU.
64. Natchez, MS, *Ariel,* June 7, 1828.
65. Washington, DC, *Daily National Intelligencer,* June 11, 1832.
66. Boston, MA, *Boston Statesman,* January 28, 1832.
67. Codrington to Jane Codrington, February 17–25, 1815, Codrington Papers, COD/6/2, Caird.
68. Codrington to Jane Codrington, March 2, 1815, ibid.
69. Gerard, Campaigns 2, USNA.
70. St. George's, Bermuda, *Bermuda Gazette, and Weekly Advertiser,* April 1, 1815; Letter from the fleet, January 19, 1815, in Kingston, Jamaica, *Royal Gazette,* quoted in De Grummond, "Platter of Glory," 337; Lexington, KY, *Reporter,* March 13, 1815; Letter from an officer at New Orleans to a friend in Charleston, SC, March 24, 1815, Northampton, MA, *Hampshire Gazette,* May 24, 1815.
71. Letter from "A West India Proprietor," April 10, 1815, *Gentleman's Magazine* 85 (April 1815): 295–96.
72. Bardstown, KY, *Bardstown Repository,* April 27, 1815.
73. "Albion" to the Editor, August 12, 1815, *Naval Chronicle, for 1815,* vol. 34, 226.
74. London, UK, *Correspondent and Public Cause,* March 22, 1815.
75. "Letter of the Duke of Wellington (May 22, 1815) on the Battle of New Orleans," 5–10.
76. William Johnstone Hope to Cochrane, May 18, 1815, Cochrane Papers, NLS.
77. Codrington to Jane Codrington, January 22–28, 1815, Codrington Papers, COD/6/2, Caird.
78. Bowlby, *Memoir,* 55.
79. Adelaide, AU, *South Australian Register,* June 3, 1869.
80. Memorial of Edward Nicolls to Lord Melville, n.d. [1817], Nicolls to Bathurst, May 5, 1817, WO 1/144, Kew.
81. Memorial of Edward Nicolls to Lord Melville, n.d. [1817], WO 1/144, Kew.
82. Owsley, *Borderlands,* 182n; John Quincy Adams to Monroe, September 19, 1815, *British and Foreign State Papers 1818–1819* (London: James Ridgway, 1835), 6:368.

83. Tylden Journal, April 3, 5, 1815, NYPL.

84. Dalton, *Waterloo Roll Call*, 22, 122.

85. St. George's, Bermuda, *Bermuda Gazette, and Weekly Advertiser*, April 29, 1815.

86. Defense statement 46, *General Courts Martial . . . Trial of Brevet Lieutenant-Colonel Hon. Thomas Mullins.*

87. Piece 001: General Courts Martial: Register 1806–1838, WO 92/1 Judge Advocate General's Office, General Courts Martial Register 1, WO 92, Kew.

88. London, UK, *Morning Chronicle*, February 4, 1823.

89. Napier, *Passages in the Early Military Life*, 239–41.

90. Peddie to Clinton, January 24, 1815, War of 1812 Collection, Michigan.

91. Gerard, Campaigns 2, USNA; Dalton, *Waterloo Roll Call*, 120.

92. Surtees, *Rifle Brigade*, 383.

93. Chesterton, *Peace, War, and Adventure*, 238.

94. *Clark, Royal Scots Fusiliers*, 136; Buchan, *Royal Scots Fusiliers*, 178.

95. One of the medals, presented to James Trill, is in the Cook Collection, HNOC.

96. Gleig to George Gleig, March 26, 1815, Gleig Papers, NLS.

97. Gleig Diary, May 9, 1815, Barrett, *85th King's Light Infantry*, 245.

98. Gleig, *Narrative*.

99. Graham to Henry Goulburn, 1815, WO 1/143, Kew; Goshen, NY, *Orange Farmer*, May 13, 1822; New York, NY, *Morning Herald*, October 27, 1837; Hartford, CT, *Connecticut Courant*, March 20, 1841.

100. Quoted in Anderson Chenault Quisenberry, "The Battle of New Orleans," *Register of the Kentucky State Historical Society* 13, no. 37 (January 1915): 23.

101. "Albion" to the Editor, March 12, 1815, *Naval Chronicle, for 1815*, vol. 33, 295–96.

102. Colonel Malcolm to Pultney Malcolm, February 5, 1815, Philadelphia, PA, *Relf's Philadelphia Gazette, and Daily Advertiser*, March 30, 1815; St. George's, Bermuda, *Bermuda Gazette, and Weekly* Advertiser, April 15, 1815.

103. London, UK, *Morning Chronicle*, November 5, 1815.

104. Edinburgh, UK, *Scots Magazine, and Edinburgh Literary Miscellany*, December 1, 1814.

105. Edinburgh, UK, *Caledonian Mercury*, January 5, 1815; London, UK, *Morning Chronicle*, November 4, 1815.

106. Letter from Crooked Island, Jamaica, January 23, 1815, London, UK, *Public Ledger and Daily Advertiser*, February 21, 1815.

107. Gray to Livingston, February 12, 1828, Livingston Papers.

108. Wellington to Liverpool, November 9, 1814, Carr, "New Orleans and the Treaty of Ghent," 278–79.

109. Liverpool to George Canning, December 28, 1814, Wellington, *Supplementary Despatches*, 9, 513.

110. Bathurst to Ross, September 6, 1814, WO 1/142, Kew.

111. Carr, "New Orleans and the Treaty of Ghent," 277–78. Owsley, *Borderlands*, 178, argues that Louisiana was not covered by the *status ante bellum* terms of the treaty because Britain denied the legality of the Louisiana Purchase. In short, Louisiana was never legitimately American territory. He further argues that "considerable evidence" supports the conclusion that Britain intended to reopen new treaty negotiations when notified that New Orleans had been captured. He cites none of that evidence.

112. For more, see Carr, "New Orleans and the Treaty of Ghent," 276.

113. Hickey maintains that the British would not have tried to hold on to New Orleans if taken, citing their desire for peace and the risk of renewed war if they tried to keep the city. For all that negotiators at Ghent had challenged the legitimacy of the Louisiana Purchase, their motive seemed to be more to make a point about American imperialism. Hickey, *Don't Give Up the Ship!*, 286.

114. Owsley, *Borderlands*, 178–79, strongly questions the idea that Britain would have returned New Orleans to the Americans, arguing that there is "compelling reason to doubt that this would have been the case." Robert Remini, distinguished biographer of Jackson, maintained equally emphatically that "it is certain that had the British won the Battle of New Orleans the treaty would have been repudiated or drastically altered to take such a victory into account" (Remini, *New Orleans*, 214–15 n23). Not surprisingly, the indefatigable faker Buell invented something about this subject, too. He created an 1836 conversation between Jackson and Congressman William Allen from Arkansas, which Allen supposedly related to Buell himself in 1875. In it, Old

Hickory claimed that if New Orleans had been lost, the whole Louisiana territory would have been lost as well, and that the British commissioners at Ghent had declared that they did not intend the treaty to apply to Louisiana. Indeed, according to Jackson, Lord Liverpool, Secretary of State Castlereagh, former prime ministers William Pitt the Younger, Lord Spencer Perceval, and Lord William Grenville, among others, all denied Napoleon's lawful right to sell Louisiana to the United States. Instead, they had determined that after its conquest, Britain would make a claim for the territory entirely separate from the treaty provisions. As usual with otherwise unsupported statements by Buell, it is complete invention, marred not least by the fact that Pitt and Perceval were both dead before the war even began. Smith, *New Orleans*, 151–53.

115. Melhorn, "What If the British Had Won?" 67–68, argues that had Britain captured New Orleans, any effort to hold it, or to use it to extort fisheries concessions in the Northeast or navigation rights on the Mississippi would have risked renewed conflict.

116. See, for instance, Hickey, *Don't Give Up the Ship!*, 287. Jackson's critics during his presidency tried to diminish the battle's importance, and thereby Old Hickory, by pointing out that the treaty made it pointless (Stoltz, "The Battle of New Orleans in American Historical Memory," 89).

117. Thomas M. Linnard to Shaler, May 28, 1815, Shaler Family Papers, HSP; Washington, DC, *Daily National Intelligencer*, April 119, 1813.

118. Hickey, *Don't Give Up the Ship!*, 287.

119. Reid and Eaton, *Jackson*, 399.

120. Remini, *New Orleans*, 189–90.

121. "Annexation," *United States Magazine and Democratic Review* 17, no. 85 (July–August 1845): 5.

122. Letter from Frankfort, KY, February 28, 1815, Richmond, VA, *Virginia Patriot*, March 15, 1815.

123. Letter from New Orleans to Washington DC, February 3, 1815, Burlington, VT, *Vermont Centinel*, March 24, 1815.

124. Letter from New Orleans, March 10, 1818, Leesburg, VA, *Genius of Liberty*, May 19, 1818.

125. Remini, *New Orleans*, 198, has some discussion of this, though unsupported.

126. Alexis de Tocqueville, *Democracy in America* (New York: D. Appleton, 1899), 2:316, 342.

127. Ibid., 310.

128. Stoltz, "The Battle of New Orleans in American Historical Memory," 99.

129. Baltimore, MD, *Niles' Weekly Register*, February 18, 1815.

INDEX

ABOUT THE AUTHOR

William C. Davis is author or editor of over fifty books on the Civil War and early Southern history. Following a career in book and magazine publishing and marketing, he spent thirteen years as a professor of history at Virginia Tech, and lives in Blacksburg. He is the only four-time winner of the Jefferson Davis Award of the American Civil War Museum, given for book-length works on the Civil War and the Confederacy.